Professional Stage

Module F

Financial Reporting Environment

ACCA Textbook

2303/J00

British Library Cataloguing-in-Publication Data

A catalogue record for this book is available from the British Library.

Published by Foulks Lynch Ltd
Number 4
The Griffin Centre
Staines Road
Feltham
Middlesex
TW14 0HS

ISBN 0 7483 4230 3

Printed in Great Britain by Ashford Colour Press Ltd

Acknowledgements

We are grateful to the Association of Chartered Certified Accountants, the Chartered Institute of Management Accountants and the Institute of Chartered Accountants in England and Wales for permission to reproduce past examination questions. The answers have been prepared by Foulks Lynch Ltd.

CONTENTS

		Page
Preface & format of the examination		iv
The syllabus		vi
The official ACCA teaching guide		ix
Accounting standards and other examinable documents		xviii

The accountant as a professional

Chapter 1	The financial reporting environment	1
Chapter 2	International issues	35
Chapter 3	Tangible fixed assets	52
Chapter 4	Intangible fixed assets	94
Chapter 5	Stocks and long-term contracts	115
Chapter 6	Tax in company accounts	130
Chapter 7	Accounting for pension costs	169
Chapter 8	Reporting the substance of transactions	189
Chapter 9	Leasing contracts	213
Chapter 10	Reporting financial performance	240

Preparing financial statements and reports

Chapter 11	Realised and legally distributable profit	274
Chapter 12	Accounting for the effects of changing prices	286
Chapter 13	Consolidated accounts - simple groups	320
Chapter 14	Consolidated accounts - more complex groups	335
Chapter 15	Consolidated accounts - changes in a group	350
Chapter 16	Consolidated accounts - mergers and acquisitions	371
Chapter 17	Associated companies	393
Chapter 18	Overseas transactions	415
Chapter 19	Cash flow statements	450
Chapter 20	The preparation of additional reports	489
Chapter 21	Share valuation	526

Accounting for reconstructions, mergers and combinations

Chapter 22	Changes in organisational structure	542
Chapter 23	Reconstructions, mergers and takeovers	571

Analysing and appraising financial and related information

Chapter 24	Financial analysis - ratio analysis	589
Chapter 25	Financial analysis - additional statements	616
Chapter 26	Corporate failure prediction	642
Chapter 27	Limitations of ratio analysis	655
Chapter 28	Financial instruments	672

Current issues and controversies

Chapter 29	Current issues and controversies	698
Appendix	Auditing Standards and Guidelines	722
Index		743

PREFACE

This Textbook is the ACCA's official text for paper 13, Financial Reporting Environment, and is part of the ACCA's official series produced for students taking the ACCA examinations. It has been produced with direct guidance from the examiner specifically for paper 13, and covers the syllabus and teaching guide in great detail giving appropriate weighting to the various topics.

This Textbook is, however, very different from a reference book or a more traditional style textbook. It is targeted very closely on the examinations and is written in a way that will help you assimilate the information easily and give you plenty of practice at the various techniques involved. Particular attention has been paid to producing an interactive text that will maintain your interest with a series of carefully designed features.

- **Introduction with learning objectives**. We put the chapter into context and set out clearly the learning objectives that will be achieved by the reader.

- **Definitions**. The text clearly defines key words or concepts. The purpose of including these definitions is **not** that you should learn them - rote learning is not required and is positively harmful. The definitions are included to focus your attention on the point being covered.

- **Brick-building style**. We build up techniques slowly, with simpler ideas leading to exam standard questions. This is a key feature and it is the natural way to learn.

- **Activities**. The text involves you in the learning process with a series of activities designed to arrest your attention and make you concentrate and respond.

- **Conclusions**. Where helpful, the text includes conclusions that summarise important points as you read through the chapter rather than leaving the conclusion to the chapter end. The purpose of this is to summarise concisely the key material that has just been covered so that you can constantly monitor your understanding of the material as you read it.

- **Self test questions**. At the end of each chapter there is a series of self test questions. The purpose of these is to help you revise some of the key elements of the chapter. The answer to each is a paragraph reference, encouraging you to go back and re-read and revise that point.

- **End of chapter questions**. At the end of each chapter we include examination style questions. These will give you a very good idea of the sort of thing the examiner will ask and will test your understanding of what has been covered.

Complementary Revision Series and Lynchpins

Revision Series - The ACCA Revision Series contains all the relevant current syllabus exam questions from June 1994 to December 1999 with the examiner's own official answers, all updated in January 2000.

What better way to revise for your exams than to read and study the examiner's own answers!

Lynchpins - The ACCA Lynchpins, pocket-sized revision aids which can be used throughout your course, contain revision notes of all main syllabus topics, all fully indexed, plus numerous examples and diagrams. They provide invaluable focus and assistance in keeping key topics in the front of your mind.

FORMAT OF THE EXAMINATION

The format of the examination will be:

	Number of marks
Section A 1 compulsory accounting question	30
Section B 2 (out of 3) accounting questions of 25 marks	50
Section C 1 (out of 2) auditing questions	20
	100

Time allowed: 3 hours

Section A will be based on more technical topics whereas Sections B and C will be based on recent pronouncements, articles from the current accounting and auditing issues and areas not examined in detail in earlier papers.

SYLLABUS

Professional stage - Module F Paper 13: FINANCIAL REPORTING ENVIRONMENT

Introduction

This Paper builds upon the financial accounting knowledge gained in the Papers 1, 6 and 10. Coverage of the topics will make reference to their audit implications.

			Chapter reference
(1)	**THE ACCOUNTANT AS A PROFESSIONAL**		
	(a)	Interpretation and application of all extant SSAPs and FRSs.	Various
	(b)	Critically appraising, evaluating proposed changes and promoting changes in	
		(i) accounting theories and principles	
		(ii) concepts	
		(iii) Accounting Standards	
		(iv) Financial Reporting Standards	Various
		(v) Financial Reporting Exposure Drafts	
		(vi) Discussion Drafts	
		(vii) guidelines	
		(viii) major pronouncements of the Urgent Issues Task Force and the Review Panel	
		(ix) accounting aspects of company law.	
	(c)	Monitoring and evaluating	
		(i) international issues	2
		(ii) ethical issues.	29
(2)	**PREPARING FINANCIAL STATEMENTS AND REPORTS**		
	(a)	Preparation of financial statements and reports under conditions of stable or changing prices.	Various
	(b)	Groups of companies	
		(i) explaining statutory and professional requirements relating to the preparation for publication of consolidated accounts for groups and the audit thereof	13

Chapter reference

	(ii)	accounting for the following organisational situations	
		• foreign subsidiary undertaking	18
		• mixed and vertical groups.	14
(c)		The preparation of reports for a variety of users including	
	(i)	shareholders relating to offers for sale, rights issues, profit forecasts	20
	(ii)	lenders to assist in decisions relating to company loan obligations	20
	(iii)	employees	20
	(iv)	assessing the valuation of shares in unquoted companies for balance sheet purposes	21
	(v)	calculating and appraising the impact on profit reporting and balance sheet of the available methods of valuation.	21

(3) ACCOUNTING FOR RECONSTRUCTIONS, MERGERS AND COMBINATIONS

(a)		Accounting for changes in organisational structures	
	(i)	single companies	
		• reconstruction	
		• capital reorganisations	
		• amalgamations and absorptions	22
	(ii)	groups	
		• changes of parent company interest.	15
(b)		Explaining the major features of reconstructions, mergers and take-overs, their principal aspects and the legal and audit consequences in relation to	
	(i)	control of mergers and the public interest	
	(ii)	regulation of take-overs; statutory procedures	23
	(iii)	obligations on directors	
	(iv)	minority rights.	
(c)		Explaining the major features of dissolution, its principal aspects and the legal consequences in relation to	
	(i)	administrative receivership	
	(ii)	voluntary winding up	23
	(iii)	compulsory winding up.	

Chapter reference

(4) ANALYSING AND APPRAISING FINANCIAL AND RELATED INFORMATION

The analysis and appraisal of implications of financial and related information for accounting purposes and for the auditor's analytical review to include

(a) Evaluating internal consistency and validity of the information collected/produced for the accounts. 27

(b) Identifying matters for further interpretation in the information produced (eg, by comparing it to other information such as prior years, budgets/targets, industry norms, state of the economy). 27

(c) Interpreting and analysing accounts and statements (eg, by ratio analysis) for indications of aspects of business performance (such as value for money, quality, long-term solvency and stability, short-term solvency and liquidity, profitability, efficiency, growth, failure prediction using, for example

(i) inter-temporal analysis
(ii) intra and inter-firm comparisons
(iii) multi-variate analysis 24, 25, 26, 27
(iv) trend analysis.

(d) Assessing the impact of price level changes on the analysis. 27

(e) Assessing informational weaknesses/limitations of statements and analyses. 27

(f) Presenting financial and related information and analysis in reports taking account of

(i) sources of information for the purpose of comparisons, such as financial statements for previous periods, industry norms

(ii) background to the organisation (eg, market, sales, profits, capital investment, management structure, employees and industrial relations)

(iii) future trends affecting the organisation (national and international)

(iv) types and relevance of different ratios and trends

(v) levels of ratios expected for the organisation/sector. 24, 25, 26, 27

(5) CURRENT ISSUES AND CONTROVERSIES

(a) The evaluation of current issues and controversies relating to auditing, including audit expectations, the regulation of audits. 29

(b) The monitoring and evaluation of international issues affecting auditing including EC developments. 29

(c) Monitoring developments in auditing theories and their implications for the profession. 29

THE OFFICIAL ACCA TEACHING GUIDE

Paper 13 - Financial Reporting Environment

	Syllabus Reference	*Chapter Reference*
Session 1 ***The Financial Reporting Environment***		
♦ critically evaluate the role of each of the following bodies in relation to the development of a UK regulatory framework; Company Legislation, the Stock Exchange, ASB, Review Panel, Urgent Issues Task Force, EU Directives and the IASC.	1a, b	1
♦ examine the relative importance of each of the above sources on UK regulation and the effectiveness of this regulation		
♦ discuss the effect of SORPs on financial reporting		
♦ discuss and apply UITFs		4, 26
♦ describe the benefits to standard setters and users a conceptual framework would bring		
♦ discuss the stated intentions of the ASB regarding the role and development of a conceptual framework		
♦ discuss the effect of the ASB Statement of Principles on the formulation of financial reporting standards		
♦ discuss the effect of developments in corporate governance on financial reporting		
♦ discuss recent pronouncements of the ASB regarding Statement of Principles for Financial Reporting		
Session 2 ***International Issues***		
♦ identify the barriers to international harmonisation	1c	2
♦ describe advantages of closer harmonisation		
♦ assess progress on harmonisation		
♦ identify major differences from overseas accounts		
♦ restate overseas accounts in line with UK accounting policies		
♦ discuss in outline the work in the USA of the Financial Accounting Standards Board (FASB) on the development of a conceptual framework		
♦ assess the success or failure of the FASB's work		
♦ compare the IASC/ASB's view of a conceptual framework with that of the FASB		
♦ assess the impact of IASs on UK accounting practices		
Session 3 ***Tangible Fixed Assets***		
♦ explain and critically discuss alternative definitions of assets	1a, b	3
♦ describe and apply accounting standards on impairment and measurement (FRS 11, 15)		
♦ appraise the conceptual validity of current standards and discuss anomalies they create		
Self Study		
♦ describe the requirements of SSAP 19 and the Companies Act		
♦ comment on the conflict between SSAP 19 and the Companies Act		
♦ identify the weaknesses in SSAP 19		
♦ discuss significant changes in regulations that come into effect as the status of an investment changes		
♦ describe current proposals relating to accounting for investments and comment on their usefulness		
♦ discuss and apply relevant UITFs		
♦ describe and apply Companies Act provisions to specific situations		

Session 4 ***Intangible Fixed Assets***

- discuss critically the requirements of FRS 10 — 1a, b — 4
- evaluate the effect of alternatives on performance ratios
- discuss the main elements of FRS 10 'Goodwill and Intangible Assets'
- assess problems of defining, recognising, valuing and depreciating intangibles
- describe the Companies Act requirements relating to intangible fixed assets
- critically discuss the conceptual validity of current practice of treating R & D expenditure

Self Study ***Stocks and Long Term Contracts***

- describe, apply and evaluate the requirements of SSAP 9 and the Companies Act to the disclosure and valuation of stock — 1a, b — 5
- illustrate the problem areas that have not been resolved in relation to long-term contracts

Session 5 ***Tax in Company Accounts***

- discuss the relative merits of accounting for deferred tax on full provision, nil provision and partial provision basis — 1a, b — 6
- describe the requirements of SSAP 15 and the main reasons why it has been criticised
- describe and discuss recent ASB proposals for Accounting for tax set out in FRED 19
- discuss and apply relevant UITFs
- discuss and apply the arguments for charging deferred tax on revalued assets, fair value adjustments, post retirement benefits and discounting deferred tax

Self Study

- revise SSAP 15

Session 6 ***Accounting for Pension Costs***

- discuss the conceptual nature of pension rights and pension costs — 1a, b — 7
- describe the regulations relating to the treatment and disclosure of pension costs
- describe and apply the accounting treatment for over and under funded schemes
- describe and discuss recent ASB proposals for Pension costs
- discuss how future regulation of pension costs and funds might avoid recent scandals
- discuss and apply relevant UITFs

Self Study

- prepare financial statements in accordance with SSAP 24

Session 7 ***Reporting the Substance of Transactions***

- explain the perceived benefits company managers believe result from schemes of off balance sheet finance — 1a, b — 8
- describe the concept of substance over form and explain how the concept is intended to prevent off balance sheet finance
- identify common forms of off balance sheet finance
- assess how the current regulations and pronouncements would treat these
- apply FRS 5 to complex business situations

- the recognition, measurement and disclosure of provisions - current standard Provisions and Contingencies (FRS 12)
- offsetting and future operating losses
- contingencies and restructuring provisions

Session 8	***Leasing Contracts***		
	♦ describe the requirements of SSAP 21 in the lessee's accounts ♦ apply the requirements to given situations to classify leases as finance or operating ♦ describe the requirements of SSAP 21 in the lessor's accounts ♦ apply the requirements to given situations to classify leases as finance or operating ♦ summarise the effect on the financial statements of treating a lease as a finance or operating lease ♦ critically examine the usefulness of SSAP 21 ♦ discuss and apply relevant UITFs ♦ describe the amendment to SSAP 21 'Tax free grants' *Self Study* ♦ apply the requirements of SSAP 21 to the preparation of lessee's and lessor's financial statements to incorporate leases and hire purchase agreements	1a, b	9
Session 9	***Reporting Financial Performance***		
	♦ explain what is meant by reserve accounting and illustrate its abuse ♦ apply the current regulations in this area to given situations ♦ evaluate the regulations for dealing with reserve accounting and compare with international treatment ♦ critically examine why SSAP 3 was replaced ♦ describe the existing circumstances that will cause a company's future EPS to be diluted, and why it is important to report a fully diluted EPS ♦ describe and apply FRS 14 'Earnings per share' ♦ critically evaluate the requirements of FRS 3 ♦ assess the likelihood of FRS 3's requirements enhancing the value of reported information *Self Study* ♦ describe and apply the accounting and disclosure requirements of FRS 3 ♦ quantify the effect that all types of share issues have on the reported EPS	1a, b	10
Session 10	***Realised and Legally Distributable Profit***		
	♦ define realised profits in accordance with the Companies Act and UK GAAP ♦ identify which, and to what extent, SSAPs/FRSs contribute to the definition of realised profits ♦ define and explain distributable profits in accordance with the Companies Act ♦ discuss why distributable profits need to be defined and how effectively the current regulations achieve this	1b	11
Session 11	***Accounting for the Effects of Changing Prices***		
	♦ analyse reported historic cost profits into their different types of gains/losses ♦ explain the deficiencies of a historic cost balance sheet ♦ discuss the ways in which historic cost accounts can be misleading for decision making purposes	2a	12

- explain why, despite their limitations, modified historic cost accounts still prevail
- distinguish between general and specific price changes
- calculate and explain the nature of gains or losses caused by the impact of general inflation on a company's net monetary position
- explain and illustrate the process of restating a historic cost profit and loss account for the movement in the retail price index
- explain and illustrate how balance sheet items, including shareholders' funds, are restated in current purchasing power adjusted accounts
- discuss the strengths and weaknesses of the CPP model
- explain and apply the concepts of deprival value and operating capital maintenance
- explain and calculate the four main current cost adjustments
- discuss the strengths and criticisms of the current cost deprival value model
- discuss and apply relevant UITFs

Self Study

- prepare CPP adjusted financial statements
- prepare current cost accounts

Session 12 Consolidated Accounts - Accounting for Groups

- describe FRS 2's regulations in relation to acquisition accounting — 2b — 13, 14
- apply the regulations to given situations
- appraise the usefulness and problems of the current requirements
- describe the different possible structures of a group
- describe the effect on the group financial statements of using the direct and indirect methods to consolidate sub-subsidiaries
- prepare the group financial statements using acquisition accounting involving sub-subsidiaries

Self Study

Consolidated Accounts - Legal Requirements — 2b

- compare the definitions of subsidiaries internationally
- describe the current ASB accounting and disclosure requirements and Companies Act requirements that apply to subsidiary undertakings that have not been consolidated
- apply the above regulations in given situations
- evaluate the validity of the arguments that advocate the non-consolidation of certain subsidiary undertakings

Session 13/14 Consolidated Accounts - changes in the Composition of a Group

- identify the problems caused by piecemeal acquisitions — 3a (ii) — 15
- explain the effects of a subsequent bonus issue or a capital reduction of a subsidiary company
- identify the principal treatment of profits (or losses) and the related taxation that arises on a partial disposal of shares held in a subsidiary in both the holding company's own accounts and the group accounts
- discuss the treatment of a subsidiary's goodwill on disposal, and how it can affect the reported profit
- describe FRS 2's accounting and disclosure requirements relating to the disposal of shares in a subsidiary
- critically examine the conceptual validity of FRS 2's requirements relating to group disposals
- identify the reasons why groups change their internal structures
- assess the effects on consolidated accounts and the individual company accounts of changes in the direct ownership of subsidiaries

- explain why a company may demerge some of its subsidiaries and prepare financial statements after a demerger
- discuss and apply relevant UITFs
- prepare consolidated financial statements incorporating piecemeal acquisitions
- prepare group financial statements incorporating a partial disposal of shares in a remaining subsidiary
- prepare group accounts following a disposal of shares resulting in an associate, a fixed or current asset investment, a total disposal

Session 15 ***Consolidated Accounts - the Merger Method and Problems arising under Acquisition Accounting***

- distinguish conceptually between an acquisition and a merger — 2b, 3b — 16
- describe the requirements of the Companies Act and FRS 6 relating to merger accounting including merger relief with a numerical example
- apply FRS 6 in given situations
- compare consolidated financial accounts prepared under merger accounting and acquisition accounting
- identify the abuses and criticisms of 'Business Combinations' (Discussion Paper)
- describe and appraise the latest ASB pronouncements on merger accounting
- describe the requirements of FRS 7
- define the fair values of purchase consideration, assets and liabilities generally
- apply FRS 7 in given situations
- discuss the problems of more contentious items

Self Study

- prepare consolidated accounts using merger accounting

Session 16 ***Associated Companies***

- describe and compare the equity method of accounting with proportional consolidation — 2b — 17
- identify situations where current regulations require the use of equity accounting or proportional consolidation
- describe the Companies Act and ASB requirements relating to associated undertakings
- discuss the benefits and weaknesses of using equity accounting for both associates and subsidiaries
- describe and evaluate FRS 9 'Associates and Joint Ventures'

Self Study

- prepare group financial statements incorporating associated undertakings

Session 17 ***Overseas Transactions***

- describe the temporal and closing rate methods of translating assets and liabilities denominated in a foreign currency — 2b — 18
- examine the arguments for and against the temporal and closing rate methods of translation
- translate the trial balance of an overseas branch using the temporal or closing rate method, and, after year end adjustments, incorporate this into the company's financial statements
- describe the requirements of SSAP 20 as they relate to individual companies

- discuss the conflict between SSAP 20 and the Companies Act requirements in relation to the treatment of foreign exchange gains and losses
- evaluate the adequacy of the current regulations governing the treatment of foreign exchange losses
- discuss the net investment concept, indicating when it should be applied, and the factors that determine its appropriateness
- describe SSAP 20's accounting and disclosure requirements relating to the consolidation of foreign subsidiaries
- discuss the limitations and criticisms of SSAP 20, and group financial statements prepared under its requirements
- apply relevant UITFs to overseas operations

Self Study
- prepare the financial statements of individual companies that engage in foreign currency transactions
- prepare consolidated financial statements incorporating a foreign subsidiary translated using the closing rate or temporal method

Session 18 Cash Flow Statements

- define and distinguish cash flows and funds flows 1a, b 19
- describe and evaluate the requirements of FRS 1 (revised)
- examine the utility of the direct and indirect methods of presentation
- describe FRS 1 (revised) as it relates to consolidated cash flows
- evaluate the provisions of FRS 1 (revised)

Self Study
- apply FRS 1 (revised) to the preparation of consolidated cash flows
- identify the problems of the treatment of foreign exchange gains and losses in cash flow statements
- prepare consolidated cash flow statements involving a foreign subsidiary

Session 19 The Preparation of Additional Reports

- describe the disclosure requirements of SSAP 25 and the Companies Act in relation to segmental reporting 2c 20
- identify areas in which SSAP 25 is too vague and flexible, and discuss the criticism that it does not go far enough
- describe and discuss recent ASB proposals relating to segmental reporting
- identify the alternative user groups and their information needs
- discuss the 'managerial' and 'risk and return' approaches to segmental reporting
- discuss recent ASB statements regarding interim reports
- prepare reports directed towards satisfying the specific groups and their requirements
- discuss the ASB's current proposals on preliminary announcements

Self Study
- prepare a report offering advice and guidance to investors in respect of prospectuses, offers for sale, rights issues, conversion rights
- prepare a report offering advice and guidance to lenders in respect of advisability of loans/overdrafts, creditworthiness, when to call in receiver/administrator
- prepare a report offering advice and guidance to employees in respect of profit sharing schemes, pay negotiations, redundancies

Note: This Session is useful preparation for Sessions 20 - 26

Session 20	***Share Valuation***		
♦	calculate a range of acceptable values for shares in an unquoted company based on different valuation methods	2c(iv), (v)	21
♦	advise a prospective buyer/seller on the appropriate share valuation method in given circumstances		
♦	discuss why recent legislation allowing companies to purchase their own shares may make unquoted shares more attractive investments than in the past		
♦	discuss the 'Financial Reporting Standard for Smaller Entities'		
Session 21	***Changes in Organisational Structure - Single Companies***		
♦	describe the Companies Act regulations relating to capital reductions and reorganisations	3a (i)	22
♦	describe how a capital reduction scheme can be effected using S110 of the Insolvency Act 1986 and compare this to the above Companies Act regulations		
♦	illustrate how a company can achieve some of the objectives of a capital reduction by using the Companies Act regulations relating to the redemption and purchase of its own shares		
♦	calculate the proceeds interested parties would receive if a company is liquidated		
♦	describe the circumstances where a scheme of capital reduction or reorganisation is normally recommended		
♦	explain the advantages of business combinations		
♦	calculate and allocate the purchase consideration		
	Self Study		
♦	prepare financial statements in accordance with a given scheme of capital reduction or reorganisation and evaluate its merits for each interested party		
♦	prepare the financial statements of companies after carrying out a scheme of amalgamation or absorption		
	Note: Students will NOT be required to design a reconstruction scheme		
Session 22	***Dissolution of Companies***		
♦	explain the major features and the legal processes by which a company may be wound up under the Insolvency Act 1986 covering administrative receivership, voluntary and compulsory liquidation	3c	23
	The Major Features of Reconstructions, Mergers and Takeovers		
♦	explain the role of the Stock Exchange, the Competition Commission and the EC in relation to the control and regulation of takeovers and mergers in the public interest	3b	23
♦	discuss the obligations on directors during takeover bids		
♦	identify the ways in which the rights of the minority are protected		
Session 23	***Financial Analysis***		
♦	discuss the demand for financial analysis and the sources of information	4f	24
♦	assess the role of accounting theory		
♦	identify the social and political considerations affecting corporate regulation and reporting		

- briefly describe the problems that multi-national companies face in complying with different countries' legislation and accounting policies
- describe the role that the Stock Exchange plays in the operation of the efficient market hypothesis and the economy in general
- explain the nature of insider information
- describe the Stock Exchange regulations and their effectiveness to prevent the above, and the penalties that can be imposed
- describe the other regulations relating to membership of the Stock Exchange
- revise definition, variations in definition and calculation of important ratios
- explain the aspects of financial performance that each ratio is intended to assess
- explain the acceptable range of values that a healthy company should achieve for those ratios
- explain the relationship between the market price of a share and its EPS
- evaluate the results of companies to advise potential investors
- identify the likely causes of changes in profitability by calculating its component parts
- discuss the problem of defining profit and net assets
- describe the importance of maintaining a healthy liquid position
- identify the component cause of changes in liquidity
- recommend corrective action where weaknesses are identified
- describe the implications of high or low gearing
- identify ways in which the application of GAAP affects the gearing of an individual company
- discuss the difficulty in assessing the gearing of a group

Self Study

- calculate ratios relevant to potential investors
- calculate ratios to determine the return on capital employed
- calculate relevant ratios and assess short term and current liquidity position of companies allowing for the nature of the business
- calculate and explain importance of a company's cash cycle
- use of financial analysis for post audit review, assessing going concern, identifying and locating cut-off errors, reporting on profit forecasts and measuring audit risk

Session 24 Trend Analysis

- calculate and interpret ratios based on current cost and current purchasing power accounts 4b, c, d 25
- critically examine a company's financial performance based on current value accounts and how this may differ from the position implied by historic cost accounts
- discuss the quality and value, to alternative users, of current value financial statements as a source of information
- discuss the ways in which a company's cash flow statement can aid the interpretation of financial performance
- explain why cash flow information may be superior to that of the profit and loss account and balance sheet, and also where it is lacking
- discuss the nature and value of information obtained from financial statements
- discuss the nature and value of information obtained from other internal reports including value added statements, employee reports, prospectuses and profit statements
- discuss the nature and value of information obtained from national and international external sources including stockbrokers' circulars, reports from credit rating agencies and press comment

Session 25	***Corporate Failure Prediction***		
♦	explain the importance of corporate failure prediction	4c	26
♦	identify the major causes of insolvency		
♦	discuss the technique and usefulness of multi-variate analysis to predict corporate failure		
♦	advise and critically comment on the information provided in a given statement of affairs produced under the Insolvency Act 1986		
Session 26	***Limitations of Ratio Analysis***		
♦	discuss the impact and distortion inflation causes to trend analysis	4a, e	27
♦	adjust selected trends for the effects of inflation to allow valid comparisons over time		
♦	discuss the arbitrary nature of profit and how easily different accounting policies can manipulate profits		
♦	assess the impact that seasonal trading can have on calculated ratios		
♦	explain and give examples of window dressing		
♦	explain the distortion that related party transactions can cause to financial statements		
♦	discuss whether the Companies Act and Stock Exchange requirements concerning related party transactions prevent distortions		
♦	describe the current ASB requirements for dealing with related party transactions (FRS 8)		
♦	evaluate the effectiveness of the existing requirements		
♦	identify related parties in given situations		
Session 27	***Financial Instruments***		
♦	describe and evaluate the main provisions of FRS 4 and FRS 13	1a, b	28
♦	apply the provisions of FRS 4 to complex business transactions		
♦	discuss the problems of accounting for derivatives and financial instruments		
♦	describe current ASB proposals for dealing with derivatives and financial instruments		
♦	apply relevant UITFs and discuss their implications		
Session 28	***Current Issues and Controversies***		
♦	the financial reporting standard for smaller entities	General	29
♦	the legal liability problem for auditors		
♦	limited liability and the audit profession		
♦	current ethical issues		
♦	international issues of harmonisation and standardisation		
♦	the increasing importance of IASC and IFAC		
♦	current issues and controversies in audit and accounting		
♦	interim reporting - principles, proposals and practice		
♦	the problem of independence and the business approach to audit risk		
♦	the way ahead for the 'Statement of Principles'		

ACCOUNTING STANDARDS

	Title	*Issue date*	*Page*
	Foreword to accounting standards	June 1993	2, 47

Statements of Standard Accounting Practice (SSAPs)

No	*Title*	*Issue date*	*Page*
2	Disclosure of accounting policies	Jan 1972	26
4	Accounting for government grants (revised)	July 1990	85
5	Accounting for value added tax	Jan 1974	130
9	Stocks and long-term contracts (revised)	Sept 1988	115
13	Accounting for research and development (revised)	Jan 1989	107
15	Accounting for deferred tax (revised)	Dec 1992	146, 179
17	Accounting for post balance sheet events	Sept 1980	624
19	Accounting for investment properties (revised)	July 1994	71
20	Foreign currency translation (including aspects on consolidated financial statements)	April 1983	415
21	Accounting for leases and hire purchase contracts	July 1984	189, 213
	(amended for tax free grants)	March 1997	232
24	Accounting for pension costs	May 1988	155, 172, 177
25	Segmental reporting	July 1990	489

Financial Reporting Standards (FRSs)

No	*Title*	*Issue date*	*Page*
FRS 1	Cash flow statements (revised) (including group cash flow statements)	Oct 1996	450
FRS 2	Accounting for subsidiary undertakings	July 1992	320, 351
FRS 3	Reporting financial performance	Oct 1992	240
FRS 4	Capital instruments	Dec 1993	672
FRS 5	Reporting the substance of transactions	April 1994	190
FRS 6	Acquisitions and mergers	Sept 1994	106, 371
FRS 7	Fair values in acquisition accounting	Sept 1994	155, 382
FRS 8	Related party disclosures	Oct 1995	663
FRS 9	Associates and joint ventures	Nov 1997	396
FRS 10	Goodwill and intangible assets	Dec 1997	94, 101
FRS 11	Impairment of fixed assets and goodwill	July 1998	74, 103
FRS 12	Provisions, contingent liabilities and contingent assets	Sept 1998	199, 277
FRS 13	Derivatives and other financial instruments: disclosures	Sept 1998	683
FRS 14	Earnings per share	Oct 1998	256
FRS 15	Tangible fixed assets	Feb 1999	53
FRS 16	Current tax	Dec 1999	133
	Financial Reporting Standard for Smaller Entities	Dec 1999	698

Urgent Issues Task Force (UITF) Abstracts

No	*Title*	*Issue date*	*Page*
	Foreword to UITF Abstracts	Feb 1994	6
UITF Abstract 4	Presentation of long-term debtors in current assets	July 1992	7
UITF Abstract 5	Transfers from current assets to fixed assets	July 1992	88
UITF Abstract 6	Accounting for post-retirement benefits other than pensions	Nov 1992	179
UITF Abstract 7	True and fair view override disclosures	Dec 1992	74
UITF Abstract 9	Accounting for operations in hyper-inflationary economies	June 1993	437
UITF Abstract 10	Disclosure of directors' share options	Sept 1994	630
UITF Abstract 11	Capital instruments: issuer call options	Sept 1994	676
UITF Abstract 12	Lessee accounting for reverse premiums and similar incentives	Dec 1994	232
UITF Abstract 13	Accounting for ESOP trusts	June 1995	193
UITF Abstract 14	Disclosure of changes in accounting policy	Nov 1995	247
UITF Abstract 15	Disclosure of substantial acquisitions	Feb 1999	379
UITF Abstract 16	Income and expenses subject to non-standard rates of tax	Feb 1997	
UITF Abstract 17	Employee share schemes	May 1997	208, 263
UITF Abstract 18	Pension costs following the 1997 tax changes in respect of dividend income	Dec 1997	179
UITF Abstract 19	Tax on gains and losses on foreign currency borrowings that hedge an investment in a foreign enterprise	Feb 1998	438
UITF Abstract 20	Year 2000 issues: accounting and disclosures	Mar 1998	630
UITF Abstract 21	Accounting issues arising from the proposed introduction of the euro	Mar 1998	631
	Appendix	Aug 1998	
UITF Abstract 22	The acquisition of a Lloyd's business	June 1998	631

Other documents

Title	*Issue date*	*Page*
The Cadbury Report	Dec 1992	702
The Hampel Report	Jan 1998	708
Operating and Financial Review	July 1993	629
Interim Reports	Sept 1997	515, 716
Preliminary Announcements	July 1998	516
Statement of Principles for financial reporting	Dec 1999	10

Financial Reporting Exposure Drafts (FREDs) (issued by ASB)

Title		*Issue date*	*Page*
FRED 19	Deferred tax	Aug 1999	156
FRED 20	Retirement benefits	Nov 1999	181
FRED 21	Accounting policies	Dec 1999	26

Discussion Drafts (DDs)

Title	*Issue date*	*Page*
Derivatives and other financial instruments	July 1996	691
Business combinations	Dec 1998	380
Reporting financial performance: proposals for change	June 1999	250
Leases: implementation of a new approach	Dec 1999	232
Year end financial reports: improving communication	Feb 2000	517

AUDITING STANDARDS AND GUIDELINES

Statements of Auditing Standards (SASs) (issued by APB)

No		*Title*	*Issue date*	*Page*
Series	001/099	**Introductory matters**		
	010	The scope and authority of APB pronouncements	May 1993	722
	011	The auditor's code	Feb 1996	722
Series	100/199	**Responsibility**		
	100	Objective and general principles governing an audit of financial statements	March 1995	722
	110	Fraud and error	Jan 1995	723
	120	Consideration of law and regulations	Jan 1995	723
	130	The going concern basis in financial statements	Nov 1994	274
	140	Engagement letters	March 1995	725
	150	Subsequent events	March 1995	725
	160	Other information in documents containing audited financial statements	Oct 1999	726
Series	200/299	**Planning, controlling and recording**		
	200	Planning	March 1995	727
	210	Knowledge of the business	March 1995	727
	220	Materiality and the audit	March 1995	727
	230	Working papers	March 1995	728
	240	Quality control for audit work	March 1995	728
Series	300/399	**Accounting systems and internal control**		
	300	Accounting and internal control systems and audit risk assessments	March 1995	729
Series	400/499	**Evidence**		
	400	Audit evidence	March 1995	730
	410	Analytical procedures	March 1995	731
	420	Audit of accounting estimates	March 1995	731
	430	Audit sampling	March 1995	732
	440	Management representations	March 1995	733
	450	Opening balances and comparatives	March 1995	733
	460	Related parties	Nov 1995	734
	470	Overall review of financial statements	March 1995	736
	480	Service organisations	Jan 1999	736
Series	500/599	**Using the work of others**		
	500	Considering the work of internal audit	March 1995	737
	510	The relationship between principal auditors and other auditors	March 1995	738
	520	Using the work of an expert	March 1995	738
Series	600/699	**Reporting**		
	600	Auditors' reports on financial statements	May 1993	738
	601	Imposed limitation of audit scope	March 1999	740
	610	Reports to directors or management	March 1995	740
	620	The auditors' right and duty to report to regulators in the financial sector	March 1994	740

Statements of standards for reporting accountants (issued by APB)

	Title	*Issue date*	*Page*
	Audit exemption reports	Oct 1994	741

Statements of investment circular reporting standards (issued by APB)

No	*Title*	*Issue date*	*Page*
100	Investment circulars and reporting accountants	Dec 1997	741
200	Accountants' reports on historical financial information in investment circulars	Dec 1997	741

Auditing guidelines (issued by APC)

No	*Title*	*Issue date*	*Page*
308	Guidance for internal auditors	June 1990	741
405	Attendance at stocktaking	Oct 1983	742

Exposure drafts (issued by APB)

	Title	*Issue date*	*Page*
Proposed SAS 240 (revised)	Quality control for audit work	Jan 2000	728

Discussion papers (issued by APB)

Title	*Issue date*	*Page*
Internal financial control effectiveness	April 1995	706
The audit agenda - next steps	Feb 1996	711
The audit of small businesses	March 1996	714

The auditing section of the paper will comprise two questions which will concentrate on current professional and ethical issues, and the professional conduct of the auditor. Each paper will comprise one question on current professional issues and one question on ethical and professional conduct or based on a case study. The auditing standards will not be examined in detail but students should have a knowledge of the principles of the auditing standards. Students should read accounting publications in order to gain knowledge of current auditing issues and have knowledge of the rules of professional conduct.

Examples of the types of topics are as follows:

(i) The move to the provision of business assurance services by auditors.

(ii) Changes in audit regulation/liability.

(iii) The impact of international developments on auditors.

(iv) The role of the auditors in corporate governance.

(v) Professional relationships between the auditor and clients and related problems.

(vi) Ethical dilemmas.

(vii) Case study based on current audit practice.

1 THE FINANCIAL REPORTING ENVIRONMENT

INTRODUCTION & LEARNING OBJECTIVES

This chapter reviews the work of the bodies involved in the standard setting process and should largely be revision to you.

Much of the detail of this chapter is however concerned with the ASB's Statement of Principles. You may find reading this heavy going at first. It is better for you not to spend a lot of time on the contents for now but to return to the chapter from time to time as various theoretical concepts are covered in later chapters.

When you have studied this chapter you should be able to do the following:

- Discuss the aims and operating process of the bodies involved in the standard setting process.
- Describe the role and features of the Statement of Principles.
- Appreciate the role of SORPs.

1 THE ROLE OF THE BODIES INVOLVED IN THE UK REGULATORY FRAMEWORK

1.1 Company legislation

The regulatory framework of accounting is affected by company law in a number of areas.

(a) Financial statements of companies must show a 'true and fair view'.

(b) Accounting standards issued by the ASB are given legal authority as recognised accounting standards.

(c) Prescribed formats for the profit and loss account and balance sheet are required.

(d) Detailed disclosures of information are required.

(e) A company is limited in the amounts of profits it can distribute to its shareholders.

(f) Various provisions have to be satisfied if a company wishes to increase or reduce its share capital.

Arguably the most important way in which company legislation influences financial reporting is the requirement for accounts to show a 'true and fair view'. This requirement overrides all other regulatory requirements, including those of accounting standards. There is no absolute definition of 'true and fair', which is a legal concept. In extreme cases, its meaning may be decided by the courts. It is now widely accepted that the meaning of 'true and fair' evolves over time and in accordance with changes in generally accepted accounting practice.

The prescribed formats for the profit and loss account and balance sheet and the disclosure requirements have contributed greatly to the comparability of financial information published in the UK. Another important effect of legislation is that it gives the fundamental accounting principles and certain basic principles (eg, depreciation of fixed assets) the force of law.

However, the Companies Acts are largely based on legislation which was originally enacted almost twenty years ago. During that time, business practice has become very much more sophisticated and complex and accounting treatments have had to evolve in response to this. There have always been a small number of occasions on which the requirements of accounting standards have been in conflict with those of the Companies Acts (the 'true and fair view override' applies), though the standard setters try to minimise the number of areas where this is the case.

1.2 The Stock Exchange

The Stock Exchange is a market place for trading in the securities of companies. The purpose of **The Listing Rules** publication (known as the 'Yellow Book') is to set out and explain the requirements which apply to applicants for 'listing' (ie, admission to the Official List of the Stock Exchange), the manner in which any proposed marketing of securities is to be conducted and the continuing obligations of issuers.

A most important condition for listing is acceptance of the *continuing obligations* which will apply following admission. These obligations form the basis of the relationship between an issuer and the Stock Exchange, governing the disclosure of information necessary to protect investors and maintain an orderly market.

The Stock Exchange has the power to withdraw a company's listing if it fails to comply with the Listing Rules. It is therefore in a position to have considerable influence on the financial statements of listed companies.

The Stock Exchange requirements in some areas are more extensive than the Companies Acts requirements. In addition, the Stock Exchange has responded to the recent public concerns about corporate governance and ethical standards in business by requiring listed companies to state whether they have complied with the Combined Code which incorporates the Cadbury Committee's Code of Best Practice. Some commentators have argued that this does not go far enough and that the Stock Exchange should exert more influence over listed companies.

1.3 The ASB

The aims of the Accounting Standards Board (ASB) are to establish and improve standards of financial accounting and reporting, for the benefit of users, preparers, and auditors of financial information.

The ASB works to achieve its aims by:

(a) developing principles to guide it in establishing standards and to provide a framework within which others can exercise judgement in resolving accounting issues;

(b) issuing new accounting standards, or amending existing ones, in response to evolving business practices, new economic developments and deficiencies being identified in current practice;

(c) addressing urgent issues promptly.

In June 1993 the ASB issued a **Foreword to accounting standards** in which the scope and application of accounting standards was made clear, and the procedures for issuing standards were laid down. Accounting standards are applicable to all financial statements intended to give a true and fair view, but need not be applied to immaterial items.

To date, the ASB has issued sixteen numbered Financial Reporting Standards (FRSs) as well as the FRSSE (Financial Reporting Standard for Smaller Entities).

The current standard setting process was introduced in 1990 at a time when public confidence in the accounting profession was low and UK financial reporting lacked credibility. In its first few years of existence the ASB concentrated on preventing abuses and reducing the scope for 'creative accounting'.

The need for international harmonisation of accounting standards has now become an important influence on the ASB's work and this is discussed in the next chapter.

Arguably, one of the ASB's most significant recent achievements has been the issue of FRS 10 *Goodwill and intangible assets*. Accounting for goodwill has been a contentious issue for several years, but it appears that the ASB has managed to produce a workable standard which has gained the support of most users and preparers of accounts.

Some of the ASB's recent proposals have been very radical (for example, the use of fair value to account for derivatives, which is discussed in a later chapter).

1.4 Has the ASB been a success?

There is general agreement that the ASB has been very much more effective than its predecessor, the ASC. One of the reasons for this is that the ASB is able to issue accounting standards on its own authority rather than relying on each of the professional bodies to approve and enforce them. It is therefore less susceptible to pressure from particular interest groups.

The ASB consults all interested parties and encourages comment. However, the ultimate content of an FRS is determined by the Board's own judgement, based on research, public consultation and careful deliberation about the benefits and costs of providing the resulting information.

The ASB's approach has been underpinned by the development of its Statement of Principles for Financial Reporting, which forms a conceptual framework for UK financial reporting practice. (The Statement of Principles will be discussed later in this chapter.) Most commentators support the idea of a conceptual framework and the ASB's 'principles based' approach has contributed to its credibility.

Critics of the ASB have attacked it for producing accounting standards which are long, difficult to understand and impractical to apply. They argue that this leads to financial statements which meet the information needs of investors and analysts at the expense of less sophisticated users. A few commentators disagree strongly with particular concepts and principles supported by the ASB (discussed later in this chapter).

1.5 The FRC

The Financial Reporting Council (FRC) guides the standard setting process and ensures that the ASB's work is properly funded. It is ultimately responsible for the enforcement of standards, and achieves the enforcement by the use of the Review Panel.

It is the 'political' front to the bodies involved in the standard setting process and produces an annual review which summarises recent events and likely action by the ASB, the Review Panel and the UITF.

The FRC's main contribution to the regulatory framework has been the support and authority that it has given to the ASB and the Urgent Issues Task Force through the Financial Reporting Review Panel.

1.6 The Financial Reporting Review Panel

The Financial Reporting Review Panel (FRRP) examines apparent departures from the accounting requirements of the Companies Acts and relevant accounting standards. It normally deals with public and large private companies; the Department of Trade and Industry deals with other cases.

The FRRP has the power to seek a court order to remedy defective accounts. Wherever possible, it attempts to persuade directors to revise defective accounts voluntarily and to date no court orders have been sought.

The FRRP does not actively monitor company accounts for possible defects, but investigates matters which are brought to its attention. Individuals and corporate bodies may lodge complaints with the FRRP, but approximately 60% of investigations result from a qualified audit report or from press comment.

The FRRP issues reports on the accounts of companies brought to its attention and quite early in its life there were a number of highly publicised cases (notably concerning Trafalgar House plc). More recently there have been fewer cases, but companies are still occasionally asked to revise their accounts.

(a) **Trafalgar House plc**

There were a number of issues relating to the accounts for the year ended 30 September 1991. The main issue was the decision to revalue and transfer a number of commercial properties from developments for sale (included in current assets) to tangible fixed assets. The other issues related to the amount of ACT carried forward in the balance sheet, disclosure of an associated undertaking and the format of the profit and loss account.

The revaluation resulted in a total reduction in value of £102.7 million which was written off against a revaluation reserve of only £84 million. The properties were previously valued at the lower of cost and net realisable value, which is the required treatment for current assets. If the properties had remained in current assets, the write down would have reduced pre-tax profits of £122.4 million to £19.7 million. UITF Abstract 5 *Transfers from current assets to fixed assets* was issued in July 1992, in order to prevent companies from avoiding a charge to the profit and loss account by transferring unsold trading assets to fixed assets. Technically, Trafalgar House was not in breach of UITF Abstract 5 as it had not yet come into force, but the FRRP took the view that the accounts breached the true and fair spirit of the Companies Act.

Initially, the directors refused to revise the accounts. After several months of negotiation, the FRRP finally threatened to apply for a court order. At the last minute, the directors agreed to make the appropriate changes to their 1992 accounts, including restating the comparative figures for 1991. This resulted in a charge of £102.7 million to the profit and loss account and an increase of £20 million to the tax charge.

(b) **Foreign and Colonial Investment Trust plc**

Foreign and Colonial Investment Trust plc has twice been the subject of an FRRP report.

In 1992 the company was referred to the FRRP for inadequate disclosure of directors' remuneration and non-consolidation of a subsidiary (on the grounds that it was not material). The accounts for the following year included additional information on directors' remuneration and consolidated the subsidiary (with comparative figures in both cases).

The 1994 accounts were referred to the FRRP because the company had departed from SSAP 1 *Accounting for associated companies* on the grounds that the accounting method used presented a more true and fair view. A fuller explanation of the accounting treatment adopted was provided in the 1995 accounts.

(c) **Reckitt and Colman plc**

Reckitt and Colman plc was forced to alter its 1995 accounts because of inadequate disclosure.

In 1994 the company acquired L&F, a US company. It was only able to make a provisional asset valuation in its 1994 accounts, with the result that an £81 million adjustment to the accounts was necessary in 1995. The FRRP held that Reckitt and Colman did not explain this adjustment adequately and was therefore in breach of FRS 6 *Acquisitions and mergers* and FRS 7 *Fair values in acquisition accounting*.

The FRRP maintained that it regarded the disclosure requirements as an important part of FRS 6 because they gave key information to users of the accounts.

(d) **Burn Stewart**

Burn Stewart, a whisky producer, was forced to increase the disclosures in its 1996 accounts. The FRRP ruled that the company had not complied with FRS 5 *Reporting the substance of transactions*.

Burn Stewart had not included a sale of whisky to a customer in its accounts on the grounds that the transaction had not been fully completed and receipt of the balance outstanding on the invoice was conditional on the customer selling the whisky. The FRRP agreed with this accounting treatment. However, the figures involved were very significant. Had the transaction been included in the financial statements, its profit for the year would have been three times higher. The FRRP ruled that Burn Stewart had not complied with FRS 5, and stated that 'sufficient disclosure of the transaction should have been given to enable an understanding of its commercial effect and the consequences of its exclusion from the accounts'.

(e) **RMC plc**

RMC suffered a fine of £5 million that was imposed by the Restrictive Trade Practices Court. It disclosed the fine as a contingent liability in its 1994 group accounts and disclosed the sum in the 1995 accounts of the relevant subsidiaries, but not in the group accounts. The FRRP ruled that the amount was material because of the nature and circumstances of the fines and should therefore be disclosed. The 1995 accounts were restated.

This decision was controversial, because the amount would not normally have been material on grounds of quantity. The basis for the decision was an ICAEW technical release which says 'in some cases, the nature and circumstances of an item can be of such importance to users that a size threshold is of little practical significance in determining materiality'.

(f) **Reuters**

Reuters was forced to restate its 1997 accounts. Reuters had adopted FRS 10 *Goodwill and intangible assets* early, but incorrectly. Instead of showing the company's goodwill amortisation charge in operating costs Reuters disclosed the charge separately below operating profit. This enhanced its results.

(g) **AIM Group plc**

AIM Group had to revise its 1998 accounts after the FRRP ruled that it had failed to comply with FRS 7 *Fair values in acquisition accounting.* A provision of £951,000 in respect of the future costs of closing a factory was included in the net assets of an acquired entity and invoked the 'true and fair view override'. This was necessary because FRS 7 requires that the net assets of the acquired entity included in the goodwill calculation must be those of the acquired entity at the date of acquisition.

The FRRP ruled that the closure decision was a post-acquisition event, because the decision was taken by AIM and not the acquired company.

It can be seen from the cases discussed above that referrals to the FRRP occur for a number of reasons. Normally they arise from breach of an accounting standard, but there have been a few instances where companies have been asked to correct errors in the cash flow statement. The case of Trafalgar House plc shows that accounts can be referred where it is believed that they do not give a true and fair view, even if no regulations have been breached. Many cases involve inadequate disclosure, rather than actual adjustments. One commentator has pointed out that many of the cases concern the implementation of new accounting standards or changes in accounting policy.

In the early months of the FRRP's life there was some concern that companies were being required to restate their accounts for immaterial amounts. More recently, the published reports have tended to be concerned with significant matters.

The existence of the FRRP is critical to the success of the ASB. The possibility of investigation by the FRRP and the attendant adverse publicity acts as a deterrent to directors who might otherwise be tempted to breach accounting standards.

One possible weakness of the FRRP is that it can only take action where there has been an apparent breach of legislation or of an accounting standard. It cannot deal with cases of creative accounting as such.

1.7 Consensus pronouncements of the UITF

In 1991 the UITF issued its first pronouncement together with a statement explaining the function of its **consensus pronouncements**. This statement has subsequently been incorporated into a 'Foreword to UITF Abstracts'.

The main points in the foreword are summarised below. An example of an abstract is shown after the explanatory statement. As at 1 June 2000 there were twenty-two Abstracts issued; some of these have now been incorporated in FRSs.

Summary of Foreword

(a) **Introduction**

The Urgent Issues Task Force (UITF) is a committee of the ASB comprising a number of people of major standing in the field of financial reporting. Its purpose is to enlist the experience and influence of its members to assist the ASB in the maintenance and development of good accounting standards and best practice in financial reporting.

The UITF's main role is to assist the ASB in areas where an accounting standard or a Companies Act provision exists, but where unsatisfactory or conflicting interpretations have developed or seem likely to develop. In such circumstances it operates by seeking a voluntary consensus as to the accounting treatment that should be adopted. Such a consensus is reached against the background of the ASB's declared aim of relying on principles rather than detailed prescription. Thus within its remit the UITF is only concerned with serious divergences of current practice or with major developments likely to create serious divergences in the future.

Nothing in the abstracts issued by the UITF is to be construed as amending or overriding the accounting standards or other statements issued by the ASB.

(b) **Scope and application**

Consensus pronouncements are applicable to financial statements of a reporting entity that are intended to give a true and fair view of its state of affairs at the balance sheet date and of its profit and loss (or income and expenditure) for the financial period ending on that date. Consensus pronouncements need not be applied to immaterial items.

(c) **Compliance with consensus pronouncements**

Consensus pronouncements should be considered to be part of the corpus of practices forming the basis for determining what constitutes a true and fair view. Such pronouncements consequently may be taken into consideration by the Financial Reporting Review Panel in deciding whether financial statements call for review.

(d) **Dissemination**

Consensus pronouncements are disseminated by means of published abstracts. These include a discussion of the matter, the accounting issues identified, reference sources, and a summary of the UITF's deliberations, and clearly indicate what conclusion has been reached.

A consensus will have been attained where not more than two UITF members have voted against the proposed accounting treatment in question.

1.8 Example of UITF Abstract

UITF - Abstract 4. Presentation of long-term debtors in current assets, 22 July 1992

(a) **The issue**

Both for liabilities and for debtors the *Companies Act* requires a distinction to be drawn between the amounts payable or receivable within one year and those due to be settled or received after more than one year. Although the distinction is disclosed in the notes for each of the items forming part of debtors, unlike in the case of liabilities it is not required to be carried through to the total of current assets nor to the significant Format 1 sub-total of net current assets (liabilities).

In consequence, there is a certain imbalance between the items that the formats require to be classified under current assets or current liabilities. Examples of long-term debtor items include much of the trade debtors of lessors and pension fund surpluses recognised as a prepayment.

(b) **UITF consensus**

There will be some instances where the amount is so material in the context of the total net current assets that in the absence of disclosure of debtors due after more than one year on the face of the balance sheet, readers may misinterpret the accounts. In such circumstances the amount should be disclosed on the face of the balance sheet.

1.9 Impact of UITF Abstracts

The FRRP has indicated that it may take the requirements of UITF Abstracts into account in its investigations into company accounts. Indeed it has done so in practice, with the result that M & W Mack was forced to restate its 1996 accounts to comply with UITF Abstract 13.

It has also become clear that the courts are likely to treat UITF Abstracts as of considerable standing. This means that compliance with UITF Abstracts may be necessary in order for accounts to show a true and fair view.

Companies have been urged to consult the UITF on the treatment of potentially contentious items in cases where a precedent may be set. However, the UITF has been relatively cautious in its output, pronouncing on relatively few matters. With very few exceptions (eg, UITF Abstract 13 on ESOP trusts), its Abstracts have been uncontroversial. Nevertheless the UITF has made a significant impact in specific areas such as accounting for goodwill on disposal of a subsidiary.

1.10 EU Directives

It is the aim of the European Union (EU) that its member states will eventually become parts of a single economic entity. To achieve this goal businesses must operate under the same legal and accounting requirements.

The **Fourth Directive** resulted in accounts formats and detailed disclosure requirements being contained in *Sch 4 CA85*. Other EU members have passed similar legislation.

The **Seventh Directive** on group accounts was passed by the EU council in June 1983. The provisions are contained in *CA89*.

EU Directives have contributed to comparability of financial statements within the UK and to international harmonisation. Unlike International Accounting Standards, their requirements are mandatory since their provisions must be enacted in the law of each member state of the EU.

1.11 The IASC

The International Accounting Standards Committee (IASC) came into existence in 1973 as a result of an agreement by the leading accountancy bodies of several countries.

The objectives of the IASC are to 'formulate and publish, in the public interest, standards to be observed in the presentation of audited financial statements and to promote their world-wide acceptance and observance.'

It is important to achieve harmonisation because:

(a) it enables comparisons to be made on an international basis: this is particularly useful for overseas investors, suppliers and customers;

(b) it can help to resolve practical problems with overseas subsidiaries (this may result in cost savings for multinationals);

(c) it is useful for companies whose shares are traded internationally as it ensures that information on overseas competitors is available on a comparable basis; thus their results and position may be fairly assessed;

(d) securities exchanges in some countries require foreign registered companies to reconcile their financial statements to the accounting and disclosure requirements of that country; this is a burden to the companies and an obstacle to international trading; and

(e) if UK standards follow International Standards then this enhances their credibility.

The influence of the IASC upon UK accounting practice is discussed in the next chapter.

2 APPRAISAL OF INFLUENCES

2.1 Bodies involved in the regulation of UK accounts

The key body in the UK standard setting process is clearly the ASB. The ASB believes that it must be forceful in its approach so that preparers of accounting information follow its requirements. Many support the strong approach taken to reduce the incidence of creative accounting. It however remains to be seen whether the more recent standards such as *Goodwill and intangible assets* run into problems.

The other bodies are in a supporting but necessary role to the ASB. The ultimate force of company law which requires the revision of defective accounts gives clear authority to the ASB via the FRC and the Review Panel to take a strong stand. The UITF should allow immediate problems to be resolved before they affect the general standard setting process.

The Stock Exchange is generally happy with the increased power of the ASB and therefore also supports its enforcement abilities due to the 'continuing obligations' imposed on listed companies.

2.2 Activity

What criticisms do you think can be made of the ASB's role?

2.3 Activity solution

Criticisms of the ASB include the following.

(a) Standards need to be set by legislation.

The ASB despite its strong approach may not be powerful enough to issue and get enforced, certain required standards.

(b) Standards should be set by non-accountants.

It is the users of accounting information who should set the framework and requirements as the information is being produced for their needs.

(c) The ASB is too strict.

There are supporters of the more liberal regime that used to exist on the grounds that no one accounting treatment is necessarily relevant to all situations. The enforcement of rigid rules may be at the expense of the true and fair principle.

3 A CONCEPTUAL FRAMEWORK

3.1 Definition

A conceptual framework is a coherent system of inter-related objectives and fundamentals that can lead to consistent standards and that prescribes the nature, function and limits of financial accounting and financial statements.

3.2 Activity

The basic objective and need for a conceptual framework is to enable accounting standards to be developed which are less likely to be attacked as they would fit within the agreed principles of a conceptual framework.

Why have the ASB adopted this conceptual approach?

3.3 Activity solution

Reasons for adopting a conceptual approach

(a) The ASC was often criticised for its 'fire fighting' approach, whereby accounting standards were developed in a piecemeal way in response to specific problems or abuses. This led to inconsistencies between different accounting standards and between accounting standards and the Companies Act. (For example, SSAP 12 and SSAP 19 were inconsistent with each other in that SSAP 12 required depreciation of all fixed assets with a finite useful life and SSAP 19 does not.)

(b) Some accounting standards (eg, SSAP 13) permit a choice of accounting treatment. Others (eg, SSAP 21) require the exercise of judgement. Existing accounting standards are open to abuse for these reasons.

(c) Lack of a framework means that certain critical issues are not addressed. For example, there is no accounting standard which deals with the general problem of revenue recognition. Until recently there was no definition of basic terms such as 'asset' or 'liability' in any accounting standard.

(d) Transactions are becoming more complex and businesses are becoming more sophisticated. A conceptual framework will help preparers and auditors of accounts to deal with transactions which are not the subject of an accounting standard.

(e) The alternative to a conceptual framework is a prescriptive 'cookbook' approach. This approach is thought to be undesirable because a detailed set of rules can be circumvented. In the 1980's 'creative accounting' practices were developed which manipulated the view given by the financial statements without actually breaching any regulations. Accounting standards based on principles would be harder to circumvent.

(f) A conceptual framework would strengthen the credibility of UK financial reporting and the accounting profession.

(g) A conceptual approach would make it harder for the standard setting process to be influenced by 'vested interests'.

3.4 The intentions of the ASB regarding the role of a conceptual framework

The Statement of Principles is an attempt to formulate a conceptual framework within which accounting standards can be issued.

In detail the intended role of the Statement is to:

(a) assist the ASB in the development of future accounting standards and in its review of existing accounting standards;

(b) assist the ASB by providing a basis for reducing the number of alternative accounting treatments permitted by law and accounting standards;

(c) assist preparers of financial statements in applying accounting standards and in dealing with topics that do not form the subject of an accounting standard;

(d) assist auditors in forming an opinion whether financial statements conform with accounting standards;

(e) assist users of financial statements in interpreting the information contained in financial statements prepared in conformity with accounting standards; and

(f) provide those who are interested in the work of the ASB with information about its approach to the formulation of accounting standards.

3.5 Topics to be covered

The following topics are covered in the various chapters of the Statement of Principles:

1 The objective of financial statements
2 The reporting entity
3 The qualitative characteristics of financial information
4 The elements of financial statements
5 Recognition in financial statements
6 Measurement in financial statements
7 Presentation of financial information
8 Accounting for interests in other entities

The chapters were initially issued as Exposure Drafts and Discussion Drafts. The entire Statement of Principles was then revised and re-issued in 1995 as a complete Exposure Draft. A revised version of the Exposure Draft was issued in March 1999. The final version of the Statement was published in December 1999.

3.6 International work

Much work has been published on the principles underlying accounting and financial reporting – notably in the USA by the Financial Accounting Standards Board (FASB), which carried out the pioneering work on a conceptual framework in the late 1970s and early 1980s. More recently the International Accounting Standards Committee (IASC) published its **Framework for the Preparation and Presentation of Financial Statements** which sets out the principles of accounting in an international context.

3.7 Status and scope

The Statement of Principles is not an accounting standard nor does it have a status that is equivalent to an accounting standard.

It is intended to be relevant to the financial statements of profit-oriented entities, including public sector profit-oriented entities, regardless of their size. The Statement is also relevant to not-for-profit entities, but some of the principles would need to be re-expressed and others would need changes of emphasis before they could be applied to that sector.

3.8 True and fair

The Introduction to the Statement of Principles states that it is not intended to be a definition or an explanation of the meaning of true and fair. Detailed legal requirements, accounting standards and other evidence of generally accepted accounting practice normally determine the content of financial statements intended to give a true and fair view.

However, the Introduction acknowledges that the concept of a true and fair view lies at the heart of financial reporting in the UK. Although the Statement of Principles does not discuss the true and fair view, that does not mean that the concept has been abandoned.

3.9 Standard setting and the ASB's objectives

There is widespread support for a conceptual framework. However, several aspects of the 1995 version of the draft Statement were controversial and the ASB was heavily criticised.

Before revising the Statement the ASB issued a progress paper *Statement of Principles - The Way Ahead* which attempted to reply to specific concerns. Parts of this paper remain relevant as they clarify the ASB's intentions.

The standard setting process

The Statement of Principles is expected to play an important role in the ASB's development of standards. However, in setting standards the ASB will also take into account legal requirements, cost-benefit considerations, industry-specific issues, the desirability of evolutionary change and implementation issues.

The ASB's objectives

Many traditional accounting principles were originally devised for manufacturing companies with an emphasis on accounting for stocks and fixed assets. They are not adequate to cope with issues such as accounting for intangibles and complex financial instruments.

The ASB has set itself five principal objectives:

(i) Exclude from the balance sheet items that are neither assets nor liabilities.

(ii) Make 'off balance sheet' assets and liabilities more visible by putting them on the balance sheet wherever possible.

(iii) Ensure that all gains and losses are reported prominently so that nothing can be overlooked.

(iv) Reverse the 'bottom line' mentality by focusing performance reporting on the components of income.

(v) Use up-to-date measures, where appropriate, if other measures such as historical cost are ineffective.

The ASB believes that implementing principles based on these objectives will result in evolutionary change in financial reporting, rather than revolutionary change.

4 CHAPTERS 1 TO 3

4.1 Introduction

The conceptual statements issued by the FASB and IASC have started by considering the objective of financial statements and the qualitative characteristics of financial information. On these topics the various statements show a large measure of agreement. Any differences tend to be limited to matters of emphasis and drafting rather than matters of substance.

For these initial chapters, therefore, the ASB has mainly used the IASC text.

4.2 Chapter 1 – The objective of financial statements

Definition The objective of financial statements is to provide information about the reporting entity's financial performance and financial position, that is useful to a wide range of users for assessing the stewardship of the entity's management and for making economic decisions.

This objective can usually be met by focusing exclusively on the information needs of present and potential investors, the defining class of user.

4.3 Users and their needs

Investors (providers of risk capital) are interested in information that:

- helps them to assess how effectively management has fulfilled its stewardship role (ie, the safekeeping of the entity's resources and their proper, efficient and profitable use); and
- is useful in taking decisions about their investment or potential investment in the entity.

They are, as a result, concerned with the risk inherent in, and return provided by, their investments and need information on the entity's **financial performance and financial position** that helps them to assess its **cash generation abilities** and its **financial adaptability**.

Other users of financial statements, and their information needs, include the following:

(a) **Lenders** are interested in information that enables them to determine whether their loans will be repaid, and the interest attaching to them paid, when due. Potential lenders are interested in information that helps them to decide whether to lend to the entity and on what terms.

(b) **Suppliers and other trade creditors** are interested in information that enables them to decide whether to sell to the entity and to assess the likelihood that amounts owing to them will be paid when due.

(c) **Employees** are interested in information about the stability and profitability of their employers. They are also interested in information that enables them to assess the ability of their employer to provide remuneration, employment opportunities and retirement benefits.

(d) **Customers** are interested in information about the entity's continued existence. This is especially so when they are dependent on the entity (eg, if product warranties are involved or if specialised replacement parts may be needed).

(e) **Governments and their agencies** are interested in the allocation of resources and, therefore, the activities of entities. They also require information in order to regulate the activities of entities, assess taxation and provide a basis for national statistics.

(f) **The public** may be interested in information about the trends and recent developments in the prosperity of the entity and the range of its activities (for example, an entity may make a substantial contribution to a local economy by providing employment and using local suppliers).

4.4 Limitations of financial statements

The inherent limitations of financial statements are as follows:

(a) They involve a substantial degree of classification and aggregation and the allocation of the effects of continuous operations to discrete reporting periods.

(b) They focus on the financial effects of transactions and other events and do not focus to any significant extent on their non-financial effects or on non-financial information in general.

(c) They provide information that is largely historical. They do not reflect future events or transactions, nor do they anticipate the impact of changes in the economic or potential environment.

4.5 Information required by investors

Investors (and other users of the financial statements) require information that focuses on four key areas.

(a) The **financial performance** of an entity comprises the return it obtains on the resources it controls, the components of that return and the characteristics of those components.

(b) The **financial position** of an entity encompasses:

(i) the economic resources it controls;
(ii) its financial structure;
(iii) its liquidity and solvency; and
(iv) its capacity to adapt to changes in the environment in which it operates.

(c) Information about the ways in which an entity **generates and uses cash** in its operations, its investment activities and its financing activities provides an additional perspective on its financial performance - one that is largely free from allocation and valuation issues.

(d) An entity's **financial adaptability** is its ability to take effective action to alter the amount and timing of its cash flows so that it can respond to unexpected needs or opportunities.

It may come from the ability to:

(a) raise new capital at short notice;
(b) repay capital or debt at short notice;
(c) obtain cash by selling assets without disrupting continuing operations; and
(d) achieve a rapid improvement in the net cash inflows generated by operations.

4.6 Chapter 2 - The reporting entity

An entity should prepare and publish financial statements if there is a legitimate demand for the information that its financial statements would provide and it is a cohesive economic unit.

The boundary of the reporting entity is determined by the scope of its control. For this purpose, first direct control and, secondly, direct plus indirect control are taken into account.

FRS 2 *Accounting for subsidiary undertakings* uses the concept of the reporting entity described in this chapter.

4.7 Control

Definition **Control** has two aspects:

- the ability to deploy the economic resources involved; and
- the ability to benefit (or to suffer) from their deployment.

To have control, an entity must have both these abilities.

An entity will have control of a second entity if it has the ability to direct that entity's operating and financial policies with a view to gaining economic benefit from its activities. Control will be evidenced in a variety of ways depending on its basis (for example ownership or other rights) and the way in which it is exercised (interventionist or not). Control does not necessarily involve share ownership or voting rights.

Evidence that will help to determine whether control exists can be obtained by considering:

(a) the respective rights held;
(b) the inflows and outflows of benefit; and
(c) exposure to risk – how and to what extent the investor suffers or gains from variability in outcome.

4.8 Chapter 3 - The qualitative characteristics of financial information

Definition Qualitative characteristics are the characteristics that make the information provided in the financial statements useful to users for assessing the financial position, performance and financial adaptability of an enterprise.

The relationship between these characteristics is shown in the diagram below.

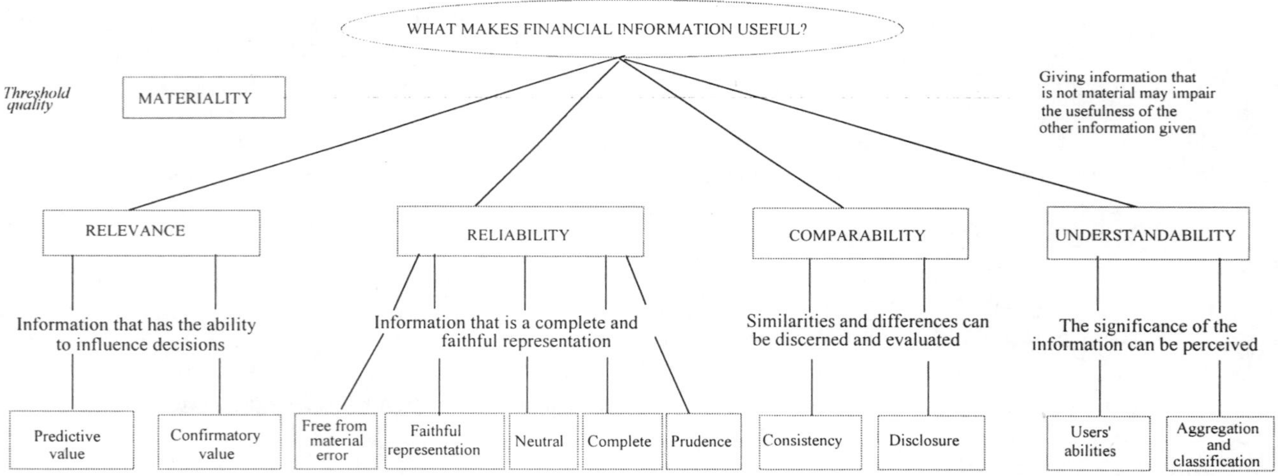

4.9 Relevance

Definition Information is relevant if it has the ability to influence the economic decisions of users and is provided in time to influence those decisions.

Information provided by the financial statements needs to be relevant. Where choices have to be made between mutually exclusive options, the option selected should be the one that results in the relevance of the information being maximised - in other words, the one that would be of most use in taking economic decisions.

Information that is relevant has predictive value or confirmatory value. It has predictive value if it enables users to evaluate or assess past, present or future events. It will have confirmatory value if it helps users to confirm or correct their past evaluations and assessments. Information may have both predictive and confirmatory value. For example, information about the current level and structure of asset holdings helps users to assess the entity's ability to exploit opportunities and react to adverse situations. The same information helps to confirm past assessments about the structure of the entity and the outcome of operations.

To have predictive value, information need not be in the form of an explicit forecast. The ability to make predictions from financial statements is enhanced, however, by the manner in which information concerning past transactions and events is displayed. For example, the predictive value of the income statement is enhanced if unusual, abnormal and infrequent items of income or expense are separately disclosed.

4.10 Reliability

Information provided by the financial statements must be reliable.

Definition Information is reliable when:

(a) it can be depended upon by users to represent faithfully what it either purports to represent or could reasonably be expected to represent;

(b) it is free from deliberate or systematic bias (ie, it is neutral);

(c) it is free from material error;

(d) it is complete within the bounds of materiality; and

(e) in conditions of uncertainty, a degree of caution (ie, prudence) has been applied in exercising judgement and making the necessary estimates.

(a) **Faithful representation**

If information is to represent faithfully the transactions and other events that it purports to represent, it is necessary that they are accounted for and presented in accordance with their substance and economic reality and not merely their legal form.

(b) **Neutrality**

Information must be neutral, that is free from bias. Financial statements are not neutral if, by the selection or presentation of information, they influence the making of a decision or judgement in order to achieve a predetermined result or outcome.

(c) **Completeness**

The information must be complete and free from error within the bounds of materiality. A material error or an omission can cause the financial statements to be false or misleading and thus unreliable and deficient in terms of their relevance.

(d) **Prudence**

Uncertainty surrounds many of the events and circumstances that are reported on in the financial statements and it is dealt with in those statements by disclosing the nature and extent of the uncertainty involved and by exercising prudence.

Prudence is the inclusion of a degree of caution in the exercise of the judgements needed in making the estimates required under conditions of uncertainty, such that gains and losses are not overstated and losses and liabilities are not understated. More confirmatory evidence is required about the existence of, and greater reliability of measurement for assets and gains than is required for liabilities and losses.

It is not necessary to exercise prudence where there is no uncertainty. Nor is it appropriate to use prudence as a reason for, for example, creating hidden reserves or excessive provisions, deliberately understating assets or gains, or deliberately overstating liabilities or losses. That would mean that the financial statements are not neutral and, therefore, not reliable.

4.11 Comparability

Users must be able to compare the financial statements of an entity over time to identify trends in its financial position and performance. Users must also be able to compare the financial statements of different entities to evaluate their relative financial position, performance and financial adaptability. **Consistency** and **disclosure** are therefore required.

Consistency

Consistency is not an end in itself nor should it be allowed to become an impediment to the introduction of improved accounting practices. Consistency can be useful in enhancing comparability between entities, but it should not be confused with a need for absolute uniformity.

Disclosure

Users need to be able to identify differences between:

(a) the accounting policies adopted from period to period;
(b) the accounting policies adopted to account for like transactions and other events; and
(c) the accounting policies adopted by different entities.

Disclosure of the accounting policies adopted, and any changes to them therefore enhances the usefulness of financial statements.

4.12 Understandability

Information needs to be understandable; users need to be able to perceive its significance.

Understandability depends on:

(a) the way in which the effects of transactions and other events are characterised, aggregated and classified;
(b) the way in which information is presented; and
(c) the capabilities of users.

It is assumed that users have a reasonable knowledge of business and economic activities and are willing to study the information provided with reasonable diligence.

4.13 Materiality

Materiality is a threshold quality that is demanded of all information given in the financial statements.

Information that is material needs to be given in the financial statements and information that is not material need not be given.

Definition Information is **material** to the financial statements if its misstatement or omission might reasonably be expected to influence the economic decisions of users.

Whether information is material will depend upon the size and nature of the item in question judged in the particular circumstances of the case.

4.14 Constraints on the qualitative characteristics

Conflicts may arise between the key qualitative characteristics. In these circumstances a trade off needs to be found that still enables the objective of the financial statements to be met.

(a) **Relevance and reliability**

Where there is a conflict, it is usually appropriate to use the information that is the most relevant of whichever information is available.

Conflicts may arise over timeliness. A delay in providing information can make it out of date and less relevant, but reporting on transactions and other events before all the uncertainties are resolved may make information less reliable. Financial information should not be provided until it is sufficiently reliable.

(b) **Neutrality and prudence**

Neutrality involves freedom from bias. Prudence is potentially biased because it seeks to ensure that gains and assets are not overstated and losses or liabilities are not understated in conditions of uncertainty. It is necessary to find a balance that ensures that deliberate understatement of assets or gains and overstatement of liabilities or losses does not occur.

(c) **Understandability**

Information that is relevant and reliable should not be excluded from the financial statements simply because it is too difficult for some users to understand.

4.15 Analysis

Although the Statement of Principles has only recently been published in its final form, many of the ideas in the first three Chapters have already influenced the development of accounting standards.

Examples:

(a) Information may be relevant because it has predictive value. FRS 1 *Cash flow statements* and FRS 3 *Reporting financial performance* both increase the predictive value of financial information. FRS 3 requires reporting entities to analyse results between continuing operations, acquisitions and discontinued operations and to disclose details of unusual and infrequent items of income and expenditure.

(b) Information is reliable if it reports the substance of transactions rather than their strict legal form. FRS 5 *Reporting the substance of transactions* now requires all reporting entities to do this.

(c) One of the more controversial parts of the Statement of Principles has been its attitude to prudence. Some commentators express fears that the ASB's approach will require a radical re-appraisal of the way in which the prudence concept is applied. Time will show whether these fears are well founded.

Hidden reserves and excessive provisions are problems that the ASB has already addressed in FRS 3 and in FRS 7 *Fair values in acquisition accounting*. FRS 3 requires extensive disclosure of reserve movements and restricts provisions for losses on discontinued operations. FRS 7 prohibits provisions for re-organisation costs and future losses when a subsidiary is acquired. FRS 12 *Provisions, contingent liabilities and contingent assets*, which is discussed in a later chapter, is also based on ideas in the Statement of Principles and has introduced further restrictions on the scope that reporting entities currently have to manipulate earnings through the exercise of 'prudence'.

5 CHAPTERS 4 AND 5

5.1 Introduction

Chapters 4 and 5 are described by the ASB as forming the core of the Statement of Principles. FRS 5 *Reporting the substance of transactions* is very closely based on the ideas in these two chapters.

5.2 Chapter 4: The elements of financial statements

Seven elements of financial statements are identified, all of which are seen to be interrelated. In order for an item to be included in financial statements it must fall within one of the definitions of elements, but it must also meet the recognition criteria of Chapter 5. The definitions of assets and liabilities are the same as those used in FRS 5.

(a) **Assets**

Definition Assets are rights or other access to future economic benefits controlled by an entity as a result of past transactions or events.

(i) **'Rights or other access'**

For example property is only an asset because of the rights (shared or sole) deriving from ownership or the other rights of occupation and use.

(ii) **'Future economic benefits'**

These are evidenced by the prospective receipt of cash. This could be cash itself, a debt receivable or any item which may be sold. Although, for example, a factory may not be sold (on a going concern basis) it houses the manufacture of goods. When these goods are sold the economic benefit resulting from the use of the factory is realised as cash.

There does not need to be certainty that the economic benefits will arise. Therefore items that represent the right to exchange property on terms that will or may be favourable are also assets.

(iii) **'Controlled by an entity'**

Control is the ability to obtain the economic benefits and to restrict the access of others (eg, by a company being the sole user of its plant and machinery, or by selling surplus plant and machinery).

(iv) **'Past transactions or events'**

The transaction or event must be 'past' before an asset can arise.

(b) **Liabilities**

Definition Liabilities are obligations of an entity to transfer economic benefits as a result of past transactions or events.

(i) **'Obligations'**

These may be legal or not. For example an entity may have no realistic alternative to refunding the price of goods that fail to meet the expectations of customers, even though there is no legal requirement to do so.

Obligation implies that the outflow of resources is **unavoidable**. Costs to be incurred in the future do not represent liabilities as long as the entity can choose to avoid the expenditure. For example, decisions of the board of directors cannot, in themselves, create a liability, because the board of directors has the power to rescind its own decisions.

(ii) **'Transfer of economic benefits'**

This could be a transfer of cash, or other property, the provision of a service, or the refraining from activities which would otherwise be profitable.

(iii) **'Past transactions or events'**

Similar points are made here to those under assets.

(c) **Ownership interest**

Definition Ownership interest is the residual amount found by deducting all of the entity's liabilities from all of the entity's assets.

Owners invest in an entity in the hope of a return (for example, the payment of dividends). Unlike creditors, owners cannot insist that a transfer is made to them regardless of the circumstances. Their interest is in the assets of the entity after all the liabilities have been deducted.

(d) **Gains and losses**

These are counted as two of the seven elements.

Definition Gains are increases in ownership interest, not resulting from contributions from owners.

Definition Losses are decreases in ownership interest, not resulting from distributions to owners.

(e) **Contributions from owners**

Definition Contributions from owners are increases in ownership interest resulting from transfers from owners in their capacity as owners.

Owners contribute to entities by transferring assets, performing services or accepting ownership interest in satisfaction of liabilities. Rights in the ownership interest are usually granted in return for a contribution from owners. For example, owners may provide cash (additional capital) to an entity in return for additional shares.

(f) **Distributions to owners**

Definition Distributions to owners are decreases in ownership interest resulting from transfers to owners in their capacity as owners.

Distributions to owners include the payment of dividends and the return of capital. For example, when a company purchases its own shares, this is reflected by reducing the amount of ownership interest.

5.3 Chapter 5: Recognition in Financial Statements

Recognition involves depicting an item in words (with additional disclosure if necessary) and by a monetary amount within the financial statements.

The recognition process has the following stages:

(a) initial recognition, which is where an item is depicted in the primary financial statements for the first time (eg, the purchase of an asset);

(b) subsequent remeasurement, which involves changing the amount at which an already recognised asset or liability is stated in the primary financial statements (eg, revaluation); and

(c) derecognition, which is where an item that was until then recognised ceases to be recognised (eg, the sale of an asset).

All events that may have an effect on elements of the financial statements should be, as far as possible, identified and reflected in an appropriate manner in the financial statements.

Transactions are the most common form of such events. Other events that may result in recognition are:

(a) discovery, growth, extraction, processing or innovation that results in new assets;
(b) the imposition of a penalty by a court that may create a new liability;
(c) events that damage assets (eg, fire); and
(d) lapse of time that results in an obligation expiring.

5.4 Recognition and derecognition

If a transaction or other event has created a new asset or liability or added to an existing asset or liability, that effect is recognised if:

(a) sufficient evidence exists that the new asset or liability has been created or that there has been an addition to an existing asset or liability; and

(b) the new asset or liability or the addition to the existing asset or liability can be measured at a monetary amount with sufficient reliability.

An asset or liability is wholly or partly derecognised if:

(a) sufficient evidence exists that a transaction or other past event has eliminated all or part of a previously recognised asset or liability; or

(b) although an item continues to be an asset or liability, the criteria for recognition are no longer met.

5.5 Sufficient evidence

What constitutes sufficient evidence is a matter of judgement in the particular circumstances of each case. The main source of evidence is experience, including:

(a) evidence provided by the event that has given rise to the item;
(b) past experience with similar items;
(c) current information directly relating to the item;
(d) evidence provided by transactions of other entities in similar items.

5.6 Measurement

Items that are recognised must be capable of being measured at a monetary amount. This involves two steps: selecting a suitable measurement basis (eg, historical cost or current value) for the item and determining for the basis chosen an appropriate monetary amount.

5.7 Revenue recognition

The starting point for the recognition process is always the effect that the transaction or other event involved has had on the reporting entity's assets and liabilities. Assuming that no contribution from owners or transfer to owners is involved:

(a) if net assets increase, a gain is recognised; and

(b) a loss is recognised if, and to the extent that, previously recognised assets are reduced or eliminated.

However, applying the matching (accruals) concept will often help in identifying these effects.

When goods or services are sold, the recognition criteria are met on the occurrence of the critical event in the operating cycle involved. (This is usually, but not always, the delivery of the goods.)

5.8 Analysis

There are several important things to note in relation to the ideas in this part of the Statement.

(a) The principles of FRS 5 (and to some extent FRS 4 *Capital instruments*) are based on the recognition criteria set out above. More recently, FRS 12 *Provisions, contingent liabilities and contingent assets* has also used the definition of a liability and the principles for recognising liabilities.

(b) Two important points are made which are likely to have implications for future accounting standards. These are:

- Costs to be incurred in the future do not represent liabilities.
- The event which triggers recognition of an asset or a liability must be a past event.

For example, the ASB's current proposal that deferred tax should be calculated on a full provision basis is partly based on the idea that partial provision is inadequate because it provides for tax arising on **future** events. (FRED 19 *Deferred tax* is covered in a later chapter of this text).

These two points are also at the heart of FRS 12 (see chapter 8).

(c) The Statement of Principles is **balance sheet orientated**. Gains and losses arise from a change in assets or liabilities. A profit and loss account based approach would concentrate on the transactions undertaken by a reporting entity and allocate them to the accounting period in which they belong. The balance sheet would then consist of residual amounts arising from this allocation.

This is another highly controversial idea and has caused a great deal of adverse comment from professional firms (notably Ernst and Young) and other interested parties.

The ASB has explained that in practice accounting will continue to allocate the effects of transactions to reporting periods. However, matching is not the main driver of the recognition process. For example, if an entity wishes to carry forward costs to a subsequent period to match income being earned in that period, these costs must meet the definition of an asset (and the relevant recognition criteria). In turn this means asking whether the costs to be deferred constitute future economic benefits.

FRS 5 already uses a similar approach to determine the substance of transactions and the way in which they should be reported in the financial statements.

5.9 Activity

The approach followed in the ASB's Statement of Principles is balance sheet orientated.

(a) Why is this approach controversial?
(b) Are there any advantages of a balance sheet based approach?

5.10 Activity solution

(a) **Reasons for controversy**

(i) The balance sheet is unsatisfactory in its present format. Most assets are included at historical cost; others may be included at a valuation, but not all companies revalue their assets. Internally generated intangible assets, such as brand names, may represent a significant part of the value of a company, but under current accounting practice they are not normally recognised.

(ii) Many commentators believe that a balance sheet based approach implies a move towards a system of current value accounting. (See Chapter 6 of the Statement of Principles, which is discussed in a later chapter of this text). This is likely to cause immense practical problems; the profession has been attempting to find a satisfactory system of inflation accounting for years, without success.

(iii) Investors are recognised as the most important users of accounts. Investors normally regard the level of profit as the most important information within the financial statements. This implies that the profit and loss account should be given primacy.

(b) **Advantages of a balance sheet based approach**

(i) Emphasis on the 'bottom line' encourages preparers of accounts to manipulate figures and users to adopt a simplistic approach to financial information. If the focus is on the balance sheet, it will be more difficult to manipulate the profit and loss account.

(ii) Financial statements are supposed to provide information on the stewardship of management. Stewardship implies the management of assets and liabilities, as well as the generation of profit. Management of working capital (for example) can be critical to the survival of a company. Focusing on the balance sheet allows a wider appreciation of the performance of management; 'growth' is a wider concept than profit.

(iii) It can be argued that the balance sheet is forward looking. Assets are rights to **future** economic benefits; liabilities will give rise to cash outflows **in the future**. Information in the balance sheet often has predictive value and should focus attention on the adaptability of an enterprise.

(iv) In theory, auditors may find a balance sheet based approach more helpful than a profit and loss account based approach. It is normally easier to audit a balance sheet than to audit a profit and loss account.

6 CHAPTER 7 – PRESENTATION OF FINANCIAL INFORMATION

6.1 The financial statements

Financial statements consist of primary financial statements and supporting notes. The primary financial statements are:

(a) the statement(s) of financial performance (profit and loss account and statement of total recognised gains and losses)

(b) the statement of financial position (balance sheet)

(c) the cash flow statement.

The presentation of information on **financial performance** focuses on the components of financial performance and their characteristics.

The presentation of information on **financial position** focuses on the types and functions of assets and liabilities held and on the relationships between them.

The presentation of **cash flow information** shows the extent to which the entity's various activities generate and use cash.

6.2 Presentation

Financial statements should communicate clearly and effectively and in as straightforward a manner as possible without loss of relevance or reliability and without unnecessarily increasing the length of the financial statements.

Structure and aggregation

The mass of detail would obscure the message if financial statements reported every single aspect of every relevant transaction and event. Greater knowledge results from an orderly **loss** of information. Aggregating information:

(a) conveys information that would otherwise have been obscured;
(b) highlights significant items and relationships between items;
(c) facilitates comparability between different entities; and
(d) is more understandable to users.

The notes and primary financial statements form an integrated whole. The notes amplify and explain the financial statements by providing:

(a) more detailed information on items recognised in the primary financial statements

(b) an alternative view of items recognised in the primary financial statements (for example, by disclosing a range of possible outcomes for a liability that is in dispute, or by disclosing segmental information)

(c) relevant information that it is not practicable to incorporate in the primary financial statements (for example, because of pervasive uncertainty).

Disclosure of information in the notes to the financial statements is not a substitute for recognition. It does not correct or justify any misrepresentation or omission in the primary financial statements.

Classification

Items that are similar should be presented together and distinguished from dissimilar items. Classification should consider the relationships between different classes of items, for example the relative sizes of profits and capital employed or debtors and sales.

Items that are similar or related should be presented in a manner that highlights that similarity or relationship. For example, different kinds of current assets are shown adjacent to each other and current liabilities are usually shown in a manner that highlights their relationship to current assets.

6.3 Financial performance

Information on financial performance should focus attention on the components of financial performance and on their key characteristics. This typically involves:

(a) recognising only gains and losses in the statement of financial performance;

(b) classifying components by reference to a combination of function (such as production, selling and administrative) and by the nature of the item (such as employment costs, interest payable and amounts written off investments);

(c) distinguishing amounts that are affected in different ways by changes in economic conditions or by business activity (for example, by providing segmental information or by presenting income from continuing and discontinued operations as separate components)

(d) identifying separately:

  (i) items that are unusual in amount or incidence judged by the experience of previous periods or expectations of the future

  (ii) expenses that have special characteristics, such as financing costs and taxation

  (iii) expenses that are related primarily to the profits of future, rather than current, accounting periods, such as some research and development expenditure.

Gains and losses are generally not offset in presenting information on financial performance.

6.4 Financial position

Information on financial position should be presented in a way that focuses attention on the types of assets and liabilities held and the relationship between them, and in the function of the various assets. This typically involves:

(a) recognising only assets, liabilities and ownership interest in the balance sheet;
(b) delineating the entity's resource structure and financial structure so that users can assess:

  (i) the nature, amounts and liquidity of available resources;

  (ii) the nature, amounts and timing of obligations that require or may require liquid resources for settlement.

(c) distinguishing assets by function (for example, assets held for sale are reported separately from assets held on a continuing basis for use in the entity's activities).

Assets are not offset against liabilities.

6.5 Cash flow statement

Cash flow information should show the extent to which the entity's activities generate and use cash. It should distinguish cash flows that are the result of operations from cash flows that result from other activities. For example, cash received from trading activities should be shown separately from cash used to repay debt, cash used to distribute dividends and cash reinvested.

6.6 Accompanying information

Financial statements are often accompanied by other information, for example, five year trend information, operating and financial reviews, directors' reports and statements by the chairman. This information should not be inconsistent with the financial statements.

The information provided has the same objective as financial statements, but is of a different kind. For example, it often includes:

(a) narrative disclosures describing and explaining the entity's activities;

(b) evolutionary or experimental disclosures that are not considered suitable for inclusion in the financial statements;

(c) historical summaries and trend information; or

(d) non accounting and non financial information.

The more complex an entity and its transactions become, the more users need an objective and comprehensive analysis and explanation of the main features underlying the entity's financial performance and position. These disclosures (normally included in the operating and financial review) are best presented in the context of a discussion of the business as a whole and are most useful if they discuss:

(a) the main factors underlying the reporting entity's financial performance, including the principal risks, uncertainties and trends involved in each of the main business areas and how the entity is responding to them;

(b) the dynamics of the reporting entity's financial position, including the strategies being adopted on capital structure and treasury policy; and

(c) the activities and expenditure (other than capital expenditure) of the period that can be regarded as a form of investment in the future.

6.7 Highlights and summary indicators

These may include amounts, ratios and other computations that attempt to distil key information about the reporting entity's financial performance and financial position. By itself, this type of information cannot adequately describe an entity's financial performance or financial position and as a result is not a basis for meaningful analysis or prudent decision making. The presentation of such information will therefore need to avoid exaggerating its importance.

6.8 Analysis

The 'presentation' chapter was one of the first chapters of the Statement to be developed and the original version was issued at the same time as the exposure draft of what became FRS 3 *Reporting financial performance*. FRS 3 provides users of the financial statements with information that assists them in analysing the components of an entity's financial performance.

The ideas in this chapter have also influenced the following:

- FRS 1 *Cash flow statements* (separate reporting of cash flows resulting from different activities)
- FRS 4 *Capital instruments* (analysis of shareholders' funds and long term debt)
- the Statement on the *Operating and Financial Review*.

6.9 Activity

What are the potential disadvantages of adopting a 'principles based' approach to standard setting?

6.10 Activity solution

(a) Accounting standards derived from a conceptual framework are likely to be complex and to rely on specialised terminology. The ASB has already been criticised for producing 'unintelligible' standards.

(b) Some users and preparers of accounts may prefer a prescriptive approach. There may be a belief that 'creative accounting' can only be prevented by a detailed 'cookbook' of rules.

(c) There are no definitive right answers to many accounting problems. Conflicts will always exist (for example, between accruals and prudence and between relevance and reliability) and choices will still have to be made. The existence of a conceptual framework, by itself, will not solve problems such as accounting for goodwill. It may, however, raise unrealistic expectations.

7 SSAP 2 - FUNDAMENTAL ACCOUNTING CONCEPTS

SSAP 2 is one of the few current accounting standards which sets out accounting principles. It was intended to be a practical guide, rather than a basic theory of accounting.

Definition Fundamental accounting concepts are broad basic assumptions which underlie the periodic financial accounts of business enterprises.

There are many such assumptions, but the four defined in *SSAP 2* are discussed here.

(a) **Going concern concept**

Sometimes referred to as the **continuity of existence** assumption. In the absence of information to the contrary, it is assumed that the business has an indefinite life. The going concern concept clearly excludes situations where the business is, or may be, going into liquidation in the near future, or where its operations are to be drastically reduced in scope.

(b) **Accruals concept**

Sometimes referred to as the **matching concept**, as it refers to the matching of costs and revenues. Revenue is usually recognised when it is **realised**. The **realisation** of revenue is usually taken to mean the date of sale rather than the date when the cash relating to the sale is received. It is thus logical to compare revenue reported in the period with the costs or expenses of earning that revenue. The operating profit determined in this way is supposed to indicate how efficiently the resources of the business have been utilised.

(c) **Consistency concept**

A business should be consistent in its accounting treatment of similar items, both within a particular accounting period, and between one accounting period and the next.

(d) **Prudence concept**

Revenues and profits are not reported and recognised in financial statements unless realised. Revenues and profits are not deemed realised until the likelihood of conversion to cash is high. In most cases, this means the date of sale. A business can provide for anticipated bad debts on credit sales as a separate exercise. By way of contrast, immediate provision is made for anticipated losses, even if such losses are unrealised. An example of the prudence concept is the valuation of stock at the lower of cost and net realisable value.

Where the prudence concept conflicts with the treatment required by another concept, it is the former which prevails. In particular, the accruals principle requires expenditure to be carried forward to be matched with related future income. Where there is significant uncertainty surrounding the realisation of this income, the prudence principle applies, and the related expenditure is written off in the period in which it arises.

8 FRED 21: ACCOUNTING POLICIES

8.1 Background to the FRED

FRED 21 addresses the selection, application and disclosure of accounting policies. It is intended to replace SSAP 2 *Disclosure of accounting policies*.

FRED 21 updates the discussion of the four fundamental accounting concepts (going concern, accruals, consistency and prudence) to be consistent with the Statement of Principles for Financial Reporting. It also clarifies some of the other aspects of SSAP 2.

8.2 Accounting policies

FRED 21 proposes the following requirements:

(a) An entity should adopt accounting policies that are, in the opinion of its directors, most appropriate to the particular circumstances for the purpose of giving a true and fair view and are consistent with the requirements of accounting standards and companies legislation.

This clarifies an implicit requirement in SSAP 2.

(b) If in exceptional circumstances compliance with the requirements of an accounting standard is inconsistent with the requirement to give a true and fair view, the requirements of the accounting standard should be departed from to the extent necessary to give a true and fair view.

Again, this clarifies existing practice.

(c) An entity should judge the appropriateness of accounting policies to its particular circumstances against the objectives of:

- relevance;
- reliability;
- comparability; and
- understandability.

An entity should take into account the following constraints:

- the need to balance the different objectives above; and
- the need to balance the cost of providing information with the likely benefit of such information to users of the entity's financial statements.

The objectives are the qualitative characteristics of useful financial information discussed in Chapter 3 of the Statement of Principles.

(d) An entity's accounting policies should be reviewed regularly to ensure that they remain the most appropriate to its particular circumstances. If an entity's accounting policy is no longer judged most appropriate, the entity should implement whichever accounting policy is now judged most appropriate.

8.3 The role of the fundamental accounting concepts

Unlike SSAP 2, FRED 21 does not emphasise the fundamental concepts of going concern, accruals, consistency and prudence. However, the Companies Acts and EC Directives still do require entities to observe the four fundamental concepts, unless there are special reasons for departing from them.

SSAP 2 stated that the four fundamental accounting concepts were to be regarded as working assumptions having general acceptance at the time. They were practical rules, rather than theoretical ideals. Since the standard was originally issued, nearly 30 years ago, financial reporting practice has developed and evolved and this is reflected in FRED 21.

Going concern and accruals

FRED 21 states that going concern and accruals play a pervasive role in financial statements. Where either of these notions is not appropriate to an entity, there will be fundamental implications for its selection of accounting policies. Therefore there is still an implicit requirement to observe them unless there are special reasons for not doing so.

FRED 21 does not contain formal definitions of going concern or accruals, but does describe them. Going concern is described in almost identical terms to the definition in SSAP 2. The FRED approaches accruals in a slightly different way from SSAP 2.

SSAP 2 defines accruals in terms of matching:

Definition The **accruals** concept: revenue and costs are accrued (that is, recognised as they are earned or incurred, not as money is received or paid), matched with one another so far as their relationship can be established or justifiably assumed, and dealt with in the profit and loss account of the period to which they relate.

FRED 21 defines accruals as follows:

Definition The non-cash effects of transactions and other events should be reflected, as far as possible, in the financial statements for the accounting period in which they occur, and not, for example, in the period in which any cash involved is received or paid. This is commonly referred to as the '**accruals** concept'.

This is consistent with the approach in the Statement of Principles. Suppose that an entity capitalises development costs in order to match them with income expected to be earned in a future period. Under SSAP 2 it applies the accruals concept because there is a relationship between the costs and the income; income is expected to arise as a result of incurring the costs. Under FRED 21 and the Statement of Principles, it applies the accruals concept because the development costs have given rise to an asset; access to future economic benefits (income from sales of a new product) as a result of past transactions or events (the development expenditure).

Consistency

FRED 21 takes the view that consistency is a desirable quality of financial information, rather than a concept as such. Consistency is an aspect of comparability, which is one of the qualitative characteristics of useful financial information. Consistency is important, but it should not be used to justify retaining an existing accounting policy when a new policy is more appropriate to an entity's circumstances. Again, this is consistent with the approach taken in the Statement of Principles.

Prudence

Like consistency, prudence is viewed as a desirable quality of financial information, rather than as a fundamental concept. Prudence is one aspect of the overall objective of reliability. Compare the two definitions:

Definition The concept of **prudence**: revenue and profits are not anticipated, but are recognised by inclusion in the profit and loss account only when realised in the form either of cash or of other assets the ultimate realisation of which can be assessed with reasonable certainty; provision is made for all known liabilities (expenses and losses) whether the amount of these is known with certainty or is a best estimate in the light of the information available. (SSAP 2)

Definition **Prudence** is the inclusion of a degree of caution in the exercise of the judgements needed in making the estimates required under conditions of uncertainty, such that gains and losses are not overstated and losses and liabilities are not understated. (Statement of Principles)

SSAP 2 defines prudence partly in terms of realisation. The ASB believes that this is out of date as markets have developed so that it is often possible to be reasonably certain that a gain exists, and to measure it with sufficient reliability, even if no disposal has occurred. Prudence is now much more concerned with uncertainty. A gain should be recognised only if there is reasonable certainty that it exists and if it can be measured reliably.

The Companies Act states that only profits realised at the balance sheet date should be included in the profit and loss account and these requirements continue to apply unless there are special reasons for departing from them. FRED 21 states that this may be the case if it is possible to be reasonably certain that, although a gain is unrealised, it nevertheless exists, and to measure it with sufficient reliability.

8.4 Estimation techniques

Definition **Estimation techniques** are the methods and estimates adopted by an entity to arrive at monetary values, corresponding to the measurement bases selected, for assets, liabilities, gains, losses and changes to shareholders' funds.

Examples of estimation techniques:

- methods of depreciation
- methods used to estimate the present value of a provision (eg, discounting)
- estimates of doubtful debts.

SSAP 2 does not cover the selection of estimation techniques (as opposed to accounting policies). FRED 21 makes the following proposals:

(a) Where estimation techniques are required to enable the accounting policies adopted to be applied, an entity should select estimation techniques that are, in the opinion of its directors, most appropriate to its particular circumstances and are consistent with the requirements of accounting standards and companies legislation.

(b) In judging the appropriateness of estimation techniques, an entity should take account of the same objectives and constraints that are taken into account in selecting accounting policies.

(c) Estimation techniques should be reviewed regularly and changed if a new technique is judged more appropriate to the entity's particular circumstances than the present technique.

(d) A change to an estimation technique should not be accounted for as a prior period adjustment (ie, it is **not** a change in accounting policy).

8.5 Applying the definitions in practice

A change in accounting policy gives rise to a prior period adjustment (as required by FRS 3), while a change in an estimation technique does not. This means that it is necessary to distinguish between the two in practice. FRED 21 gives the following examples:

- An entity has previously stated assets at historic cost and it now states them at replacement cost. This is a change in a measurement base and is therefore a change in accounting policy.

- An entity has previously measured the current disposal value of an asset by reference to recent disposals of similar assets and it now does this by reference to prices quoted in advertisements. This is a change in the method of estimation, not a change in accounting policy.

Different accounting policies present the same set of facts in different ways or different aspects of the same set of facts. Estimation techniques are used to arrive at the facts that are to be presented.

A change in the way in which an entity presents particular items is a change in accounting policy. However, if an entity merely presents additional disclosures, this is not a change in accounting policy.

8.6 Activity

Which of the following is a change in accounting policy as opposed to a change in estimation technique?

(1) An entity has previously capitalised interest incurred in connection with the construction of tangible fixed assets. It now writes off capitalised interest to the profit and loss account.

(2) An entity has previously depreciated vehicles using the reducing balance method at 40% per year. It now uses the straight line method over a period of five years.

(3) An entity has previously shown certain overheads within cost of sales. It now shows those overheads within administrative expenses.

(4) An entity has previously stated listed investments held as current assets at replacement cost. It now states these investments at net realisable value.

8.7 Activity solution

These examples are taken from an Appendix to FRED 21. For each of the items, ask whether this involves a change to:

- recognition?
- presentation?
- measurement basis?

If the answer to any of these is yes, the change is a change in accounting policy.

(1) The answer to all three is yes. Therefore this is a change in accounting policy.

(2) The answer to all three questions is no. This is only a change in estimation technique.

(3) This is a change in presentation and therefore a change in accounting policy.

(4) This is a change in measurement basis and therefore a change in accounting policy.

8.8 Disclosures

FRED 21 proposes the following disclosures, which are more extensive than those required by SSAP 2:

(a) a description of each of the accounting policies followed for material items;

(b) a description of estimation techniques used, where these are material;

(c) details of any changes to accounting policies that were followed in preparing financial statements for the preceding period;

(d) where the effect of a change to an estimation technique is material, the effect and a description of the change;

(e) if financial statements have been prepared on the basis of assumptions that differ from either the going concern assumption or the accruals concept, that fact should be stated prominently and an explanation provided.

The use of a particular estimation technique is material if:

(a) there is another estimation technique that is also relevant and reliable; and

(b) the figures presented in the financial statements would have been materially different if that technique had been adopted.

In addition, FRED 21 incorporates the disclosure requirements set out in UITF Abstract 7: *True and fair view override disclosures*.

8.9 Evaluation of the proposals

FRED 21 has been relatively non-controversial as most commentators appear to accept the need to replace SSAP 2 now that the Statement of Principles has been issued in its final form. SSAP 2 was originally issued at a time when there were few accounting standards and therefore it was intended to assist in developing accounting policies. However, this approach is now out of date. The emphasis in FRED 21 is on selecting accounting policies from those allowed by legislation and accounting standards.

FRED 21 also clarifies the distinction between accounting policies and estimation techniques. It abandons the SSAP 2 terminology of accounting bases, which some users and preparers of accounts found confusing in practice.

Most criticisms of the FRED reflect criticisms of the Statement of Principles itself, particularly the 'downgrading' of the prudence concept. It has been pointed out that the change to the definition of prudence (discussed above) implies that unrealised profits can be recognised and that this may not improve the reliability or understandability of the financial statements.

Other potential disadvantages of the proposals include the following:

(a) In practice there may be more than one appropriate accounting policy in a particular situation. For example, interest costs relating to the construction of fixed assets may be capitalised or written off to the profit and loss account as it is incurred. Some commentators have claimed that preparers of accounts will have difficulty in interpreting the requirement to select the 'most appropriate' policy in these circumstances.

(b) The FRED proposes that the materiality of estimation techniques should be judged by reference to the range of values that other acceptable techniques would have given. Only the technique, not the actual financial effect, would have to be disclosed, but in theory preparers of accounts would have to calculate the effect of all acceptable estimation techniques in order to assess whether they are material. This might be unnecessarily complicated and time consuming.

(c) Unlike SSAP 2, FRED 21 provides criteria by which the selection of accounting policies and estimation techniques should be judged. This means that preparers of financial statements will have to justify the policies and techniques used. This may put particular pressure on auditors, who may no longer be able to allow companies within the same industry to use different accounting policies.

Conclusion FRED 21 proposes that the requirements of SSAP 2 should be consistent with those in the Statement of Principles; this means that the way in which the fundamental concepts are applied would change if it became a standard.

9 STATEMENTS OF RECOMMENDED PRACTICE (SORPs)

Statements of Recommended Practice (SORPs) provide guidance on the application of accounting standards to specific industries. SORPs are not mandatory, although they indicate current best practice.

The ASC issued two SORPs on its own authority, both of which have now been replaced. In addition, it 'franked', (ie, approved) SORPs developed by particular industry groups. A few of these 'franked SORPs' are still in issue.

The ASB does not issue SORPs on its own authority. It recognises bodies for the purpose of issuing SORPs. It also issues 'negative assurance statements' to indicate that it is satisfied that the SORP has been properly developed and does not appear to contain any fundamental points of principle that are unacceptable in the context of current accounting practice. The ASB has issued Guidelines for determining whether a body is suitable to be recognised and all recognised bodies have to agree to apply by the ASB's Code of Practice.

The ASB has appointed specialist committees to advise it on recognising bodies that wish to develop SORPs and on whether negative assurance statements should be given on proposed SORPs:

- Financial Sector and other Special Industries Committee (which deals with the financial sector and other specialised industries in the private sector)
- Public Sector and Not-for-Profit Committee (which deals with the public sector and not-for-profit organisations)

An example SORP is SORP 1 *Financial Reports of Pension Schemes* (issued by the Pensions Research Accountants Group). The Pensions Act 1995 requires the accounts of pension schemes to comply with SORP 1. Under the Charities Act 1993 the accounts of charities must comply with SORP 2 *Accounting by charities* (issued by the Charity Commission).

Other SORPs cover housing associations, higher education institutions, authorised unit trust schemes, the oil industry, the insurance business, investment trust companies and some specialised aspects of banking.

In March 2000 the ASB issued an addition to FRED 21 clarifying the role of SORPs. It is proposed that, where an entity's activities fall within the scope of a SORP, the entity should state the title of the SORP and whether its financial statements have been prepared in accordance with it. If the SORP is not complied with, the difference in treatment should be described and the reasons explained.

10 DISCOUNTING IN FINANCIAL REPORTING

10.1 Introduction

In April 1997 the ASB published a Working Paper *Discounting in financial reporting*. The Working Paper sets out the ASB's approach to discounting.

A number of the ASB's recent projects (eg, provisions, pension costs and impairment of fixed assets) raise the issue of discounting. Some commentators have expressed concern about the apparently piecemeal introduction of discounting into financial reporting. The Working Paper has been issued in order to respond to this concern.

10.2 Discounting

Discounting is a method of reflecting the time value of money and risk in the value of an asset or a liability.

These factors can have a significant effect on long-term items in the balance sheet that are measured by future cash flows, for example, long-term provisions and impaired assets. If such items are recorded in the financial statements at an amount based on undiscounted cash flows, unlike items will appear alike. For example, a riskless cash inflow of £1 million due tomorrow, a riskless cash inflow of £1 million due in ten years and a risky cash inflow of £1 million due in ten years would all be recorded at £1 million. However, no company would regard these assets as equal, nor would they cost the same to acquire. If they are recorded at £1 million, relevant information is lost to the user of the financial statements and misleading information is given instead.

10.3 The ASB's approach

The ASB does not intend to make discounting a requirement for every balance sheet item. There is no need to discount the vast majority of current assets and current liabilities.

For this reason, the ASB does not intend to issue a general financial reporting standard on discounting. The decision on whether discounting will be prescribed in any specific circumstance will be considered as and when individual standards are developed.

In order to determine what discount rate should be used in any particular situation, it is necessary to consider:

(a) the implications of risk; and
(b) the accounting objective being sought.

11 SELF TEST QUESTIONS

11.1 How does the ASB work to achieve its aims? (1.3)

11.2 What does the FRC do? (1.5)

11.3 What are the objectives of the IASC? (1.11)

11.4 What are the six purposes of the Statement of Principles? (3.4)

11.5 What is the objective of financial statements? (4.2)

11.6 What are the qualitative characteristics of financial information? (4.8)

11.7 What is an asset? (5.2)

11.8 What are the recognition criteria for assets and liabilities? (5.4)

11.9 What are the primary financial statements? (6.1)

11.10 Does the ASB issue SORPs on its own authority? (9)

12 EXAMINATION TYPE QUESTION

12.1 Setting and monitoring

The setting and monitoring of accounting standards in the UK is now governed by the Financial Reporting Council, the Accounting Standards Board and the Review Panel.

You are required to describe the role of each of these bodies. **(20 marks)**

13 ANSWER TO EXAMINATION TYPE QUESTION

13.1 Setting and monitoring

(Tutorial note: a straightforward question that should present no problem to those students who have studied the current standard-setting process.*)*

Financial Reporting Council (FRC)

This Council generally oversees and guides the standard-setting process. It is made up of a chairman plus representatives from various sections of the community eg, industry, commerce, the accounting profession. These representatives are unpaid 'volunteers' and should ensure that matters of public and professional concern are brought to the attention of the standard-setters.

The FRC also appoints the members of the other standard-setting bodies and arranges the funding and general management of the standard-setting structure.

Accounting Standards Board (ASB)

This Board develops and publishes accounting standards. Members must therefore have the technical skills necessary to appreciate the accounting issues involved. The ASB will consider the views of the accounting profession, the business community and public at large, but it has the power to issue standards in its own name. The approval of the six UK accountancy bodies is not required; this approval was necessary for the ASB's predecessor, the Accounting Standards Committee (ASC), to issue Statements of Standard Accounting Practice (SSAPs). The extant SSAPs of the ASC were adopted by the ASB but these are gradually being replaced by the ASB's own Financial Reporting Standards (FRSs).

It is the ASB rather than the FRC which is involved in the day-to-day operation of the standard-setting process.

The ASB has established many sub-committees but one sub-committee deserves special mention - the Urgent Issues Task Force (UITF). This is designed to deal with material emerging issues not covered satisfactorily by an accounting standard or by legislation. Such issues usually arise where there are new developments in financial reporting or where controversial or conflicting interpretations of accounting practices are developing.

Financial Reporting Review Panel (FRRP)

This Panel is designed to accept the Secretary of State's delegation of power to challenge accounts which are not considered to comply with accounting standards and are not therefore true and fair.

The FRRP initially asks companies voluntarily to amend accounts that it considers to be unsatisfactory. Legal proceedings will be the ultimate sanction if voluntary action is not taken. Where accounting standards have not been followed, a note of this fact must be included in the accounts and the auditors must advise the FRRP of the situation. This will increase the detection work necessary to ensure that all departures from standards are adequately reviewed.

2 INTERNATIONAL ISSUES

INTRODUCTION & LEARNING OBJECTIVES

Chapter 1 emphasised the UK financial reporting environment. This chapter deals with international issues. The examiner has stated that students do not need to examine international accounting standards but may need to make a comparison of international accounting standards with the UK.

When you have studied this chapter you should be able to do the following:

- Discuss matters relating to the international harmonisation of accounting policies.
- Identify major differences from overseas accounts.
- Restate overseas accounts in line with UK accounting policies.
- Discuss in outline the work of the US FASB.

1 INTERNATIONAL HARMONISATION

1.1 Advantages of closer harmonisation

Increasingly businesses operate on a global scale and investors make investment decisions on a world-wide basis. There is thus a need for financial information to be presented on a consistent basis. In more detail, the advantages are as follows.

(a) **Multi-national companies**

Multi-national companies would benefit from closer harmonisation for the following reasons.

(i) Access to international finance would be easier. The international financial markets would understand the financial information presented to them more easily if the information is provided on a consistent basis between companies irrespective of their country of origin.

(ii) In a business which is operating in several countries, there would tend to be improved management control as internal financial information could more easily be prepared on a consistent basis if externally required financial information is required on a uniform basis.

(iii) There would be greater efficiency in accounting departments.

(iv) Consolidation of financial statements would be easier.

(b) **Investors**

If investors wish to make decisions based on the world-wide availability of investments then better comparisons between companies are required. At present most non-domestic investments are made by public investment companies and unit trusts which employ analysts skilled in the examination of financial statements from different countries.

An individual investor would have difficulty making an informed investment decision with the present differences in international financial reporting.

(c) **International economic groupings**

International economic groupings eg, the EU could work more effectively if there was international harmonisation of accounting policies. Part of the function of international economic groupings is to make cross-border trade easier. Similar accounting regulations would help this process.

1.2 Barriers to international harmonisation

Given that there are so many advantages, it may at first sight be surprising that there exist so many differences. Several factors influence the development of accounting practice in any one country and these influences may have been different or have been more dominant in one country compared to another. These influences will thus contribute to the lack of international accounting harmonisation.

(a) **Legal systems**

In the UK, company legislation has been written in general terms. Indeed prior to the implementation of the EC 4th Directive, there were no stipulated formats for company accounts. There was just the general principle that accounts should be presented on a 'true and fair' basis to shareholders and the accounting profession undertook the responsibility of stipulating appropriate accounting practices.

Many of the EU countries have had a long history of strict codification in law of accounting practices and disclosures and as a consequence it is the government rather than the accounting profession which has had a dominant influence.

(b) **Culture**

Cultural differences may result in different objectives for financial reporting. There may as a result be differences of emphasis given on the need for the regulation of companies by audit. Also, in a country with strong nationalistic tendencies, there may be a reluctance to accept accounting conventions used in other countries.

(c) **User groups**

Different user groups or a differing importance in the attention given to classes of user can result in financial information being presented in alternative ways. For example in some countries tax authorities may be the dominant user group. Therefore accounts may be biased to their needs with expenses charged to the profit and loss account only being those which are allowable for tax purposes. Depreciation rates may be computed in the financial accounts at the same rate at which the tax authority allows a 'capital allowance'.

(d) **Professional accounting bodies**

Professional accounting bodies have varying influence in countries and this point has already been touched upon earlier. It is often the case that if a country has a 'codified' system of law, the influence of the accounting profession will tend to be weak as a result.

1.3 Progress on harmonisation

There are a number of bodies part of whose function, or their main function, is the development of common accounting practices. We shall assess the progress on harmonisation by considering the work and achievements of these bodies.

1.4 IASC

The IASC has about 130 member organisations representing all the major countries in the world. The IASC has a small full-time secretariat and it has published 40 international accounting standards (IASs).

The objectives of the IASC are to:

> formulate and publish, in the public interest, standards to be observed in the presentation of audited financial statements and to promote their world-wide acceptance and observance.

Member organisations of the IASC undertake to support the work of the IASC by ensuring that published financial statements comply with IASs in all material respects and disclose the fact of such compliance.

Some countries, particularly those which had not started the process of formulating accounting standards of their own have adopted the IASs wholesale. Pakistan and Kenya are examples. Other countries have tried to ensure that the domestic accounting standards comply with the relevant IAS. In such a situation, companies tend to state that financial statements comply with domestic accounting standards and do not mention IASs.

1.5 Activity

In the previous chapter, the ASB's Explanatory Foreword to Accounting Standards was mentioned. If you can get access to a copy of this Foreword, look to see what it has to say about the relevance of IASs to FRSs.

1.6 Activity solution

'FRSs are formulated with due regard to international developments. The ASB supports the IASC in its aim to harmonise international financial reporting. As part of this support an FRS contains a section explaining how it relates to the International Accounting Standard (IAS) dealing with the same topic. In most cases, compliance with an FRS automatically ensures compliance with the relevant IAS.'

1.7 Other international bodies

International Federation of Accountants (IFAC)

The IFAC has the same membership as IASC and works closely with it. The IFAC does not set accounting standards but it does have committees that play a part in the process of harmonisation.

The main committee of relevance is the International Auditing Practices Committee (IAPC). Its objective is to produce generally accepted international standards on auditing. The standards effectively perform a similar function to IASs ie, they do not override national standards.

Organisation for Economic Co-operation and Development (OECD)

Membership of the OECD consists of most of the 'developed' countries. It has a 'Committee on International Investment and Multi-national enterprises' which has established guidelines regarding the disclosure of information for multi-national companies. It also has a 'Working group on accounting standards' which supports the efforts of the IASC and publishes reports on the harmonisation of accounting standards.

United Nations (UN)

The UN has a 'Commission on Transnational Reporting Corporations' which gathers information concerning the activities and reporting of multi-national companies. It seeks to improve the availability and comparability of information disclosed by multi-national companies and has initiated a number of special projects aimed at improving comparability.

There is some criticism of its work as to its political nature. The conclusions drawn may overly reflect the general suspicions that developing countries have to multi-national companies.

The 'G4 + 1' group

The 'G4 + 1' group consists of representatives of the ASB, the Financial Accounting Standards Board of the United States (FASB), the standard setting bodies of Canada, Australia and New Zealand and the IASC. The group has the objective of seeking common solutions to financial reporting issues, based on a common conceptual framework. It does not issue accounting standards, but through its Discussion Papers (called Position Papers) it seeks to influence the development of accounting standards of the member organisations. Position Papers reflect an agreed approach to reporting financial performance that each body represented in the Group intends to develop in its own country. In most cases this is expected to result in a new accounting standard or the revision of an existing standard.

The following Position Papers have been issued by the ASB as Discussion Papers:

- Business combinations
- Reporting financial performance: proposals for change (likely to lead to a revision of FRS 3)
- Leases: implementation of a new approach (main proposals likely to be developed into a new FRS to replace SSAP 21)

In addition to the G4+1 group, there are a number of other informal groupings of standard setters. These include the Joint Working Group on financial instruments (nine national standard setters, including the ASB, plus the IASC) and the E5+2 group (European members of IASC, plus the European Commission and the Federation des Experts Comptables Europeens).

1.8 Recent progress towards harmonisation

A number of interesting developments have occurred in recent years.

(a) **The European Union**

Early in 1995 the European Union (EU) announced plans to introduce accounting standards specifically for Europe. This was in response to concerns that the IASC was unduly influenced by US GAAP (which is very different from accounting practice in many European countries). It was thought that Europe's position within the IASC would be strengthened by the introduction of an identifiable set of European accounting rules which would be clearer and more prescriptive than the Fourth and Seventh Directives.

The UK profession did not welcome the idea of a third tier of accounting standards, which it saw as an unnecessary complication.

(b) **The IASC and the International Organisation of Securities Commissions (IOSCO)**

During 1995 the IASC and IOSCO agreed a timetable for IOSCO's endorsement of a core set of IASs. The core standards would cover topics such as intangibles, financial instruments, interim reporting, presentation, segments and leasing and they were to be produced by March 1998.

Following this development, the EU abandoned its plan to set up a standard setting body of its own. It agreed to support the work of the IASC and to allow companies to prepare their consolidated accounts in accordance with IASs when raising capital on international markets. It will also review all accounting directives with a view to resolving conflicts between the requirements of these and of IASs.

The IASC faced problems in developing a large number of standards in a very short time. Some of these standards, notably the one on financial instruments, are controversial and it was difficult to reach a consensus in a short time with so many different countries involved.

IOSCO's endorsement would greatly enhance the credibility and status of the IASC and its work. More importantly, it would mean that companies seeking a listing on most international stock exchanges (including the US) would be able to prepare their financial statements in accordance with IASs.

The IASC did not meet the original deadline for the completion of the core standards and this was subsequently extended to the end of 1998. IOSCO has now begun to review the standards, but this is likely to be a lengthy process. Many commentators believe that it could be several years before IASs are accepted as an alternative to US GAAP and at present unconditional acceptance of the core standards appears to be unlikely.

(c) **The influence of US GAAP**

At present, overseas companies seeking a listing in the US must prepare accounts in line with US Generally Accepted Accounting Principles (US GAAP), or reconcile their accounts to US GAAP. As US GAAP is both extremely prescriptive and very conservative, this can result in significant additional costs and other problems. In 1993 Daimler-Benz became the first German company to gain a listing on the New York Stock Exchange. However, it had to restate its accounts to comply with US GAAP which meant that a profit of DM168 million became a loss of DM949 million. Many European countries view IASs as a less onerous alternative to US GAAP.

The most powerful member of IOSCO is the US Securities and Exchange Commission (SEC). The SEC is heavily influenced by the FASB and is now reviewing the IASC's core standards in conjunction with IOSCO. It will not be possible for IOSCO to endorse the core standards unless they are accepted by the SEC. The SEC and the FASB have been consistently critical of the IASC's output.

Some commentators have pointed out that the SEC and the FASB have a vested interest in the failure of the IASC project, because if IASs become internationally acceptable, the influence of US GAAP will decline. The SEC has stated that it is looking for three key elements in IASs: comprehensiveness, high quality and rigorous application, but it is also known to be considering differences between IASs and US GAAP. Many people believe that IASs will need to be essentially 'US GAAP in different covers' if they are to be accepted by IOSCO. This may not be acceptable to some European countries.

Despite these problems, the prospect of endorsement by IOSCO has meant that the IASC now has a very high profile. Its output is regarded as increasingly important and influential.

In addition, recent developments have focused attention on the whole issue of international harmonisation. Many commentators now believe that international accounting standards (whether or not these are based on US GAAP) will eventually become more important than domestic standards.

2 MAJOR DIFFERENCES IN OVERSEAS ACCOUNTS

2.1 Introduction

We have considered in general terms the issues involved and work that has taken place in the international harmonisation of accounting standards. In this section we examine what the major differences are at the present time. You are not required to know what international practices are but if you have an appreciation of the differences, you will be better able to understand some of the current controversies being tackled by the ASB. You may also be required to restate overseas accounts to UK practice and here familiarity with international practice before the exam will help you in the examination.

Two major international influences on UK reporting practice are IASs and accounting standards developed in the USA by the Financial Accounting Standards Board (FASB). The latter are probably more important than the former due to the importance of the US economy in world trade, the long history of standard setting of the FASB and the development of a conceptual framework within which accounting standards are set.

Examples of differences between UK and US standards and IASs are shown below.

2.2 Examples

Goodwill	*IASC*	*US GAAP*	*UK GAAP*
Preferred treatment	Capitalise and amortise over a maximum period of 20 years	Capitalise and amortise over a maximum period of 40 years	Capitalise and amortise over useful economic life (maximum normally 20 years)
Allowed alternative treatment	-	-	-
Not allowed	Immediate write-off	Immediate write-off	Immediate write-off

Extraordinary items	*IASC*	*US GAAP and UK GAAP*
Preferred treatment	Definition is similar to FRS 3; extraordinary items should be disclosed on the face of the income statement.	Definitions are similar in the USA and the UK; FRS 3 in effectively abolishing extraordinary items brings the UK closer to the USA by establishing the rarity of extraordinary items.

Deferred tax	*IASC*	*US GAAP*	*UK GAAP*
Preferred treatment	Liability method, full provision	Liability method, full provision	Liability method, partial provision
Allowed alternative treatment	-	-	- (Note, however, the alternative of full provision for tax recoverable on pension provisions)
Not allowed	Deferral method, partial provision	Deferral method, partial provision	Deferral method

The UK has taken a more pragmatic view of deferred tax liabilities than in other countries. This is partly related to the considerable current tax savings given in the UK when 100% capital allowances were available in the year of expenditure. Potential deferred tax provisions were therefore very large.

Valuation of property	*IASC*	*US GAAP*	*UK GAAP*
Preferred treatment	Cost	Cost	No preferred treatment
Allowed alternative treatment	Valuation	-	Cost or valuation
Not allowed	-	Valuation	-

Capitalisation of development costs	*IASC*	*US GAAP*	*UK GAAP*
Preferred treatment	Recognise such costs as assets when specified criteria are met and write off as expense when the criteria are not met	Write off as incurred	May recognise as assets when specific criteria are met; choice of immediate write-off also permitted

Accounting for dividends	*IASC*	*US GAAP*	*UK GAAP*
Preferred treatment	Do not provide for dividends that are not declared at the year end	Do not provide for dividends that are not declared at the year end	Must provide for dividends relating to a financial year even though not declared until after the year end
Profits on long-term contracts	*IASC*	*US GAAP*	*UK GAAP*
Preferred treatment	Percentage of completion method	Percentage of completion and completed contract methods	Percentage of completion method
Not allowed	Completed contract method	-	Completed contract method
Borrowing costs	*IASC*	*US GAAP*	*UK GAAP*
Preferred treatment	Write off all borrowing costs as incurred	Capitalisation compulsory for certain assets	FRS 15 gives a choice. No preferred treatment under CA85
Allowed alternative treatment	Capitalisation permitted in specific circumstances	-	Capitalise or write off immediately
Not allowed	-	Immediate write-off for certain assets	-

2.3 Reconciliation statements

Due to the differences referred to, a company with a large group of international investors and, as a likely consequence, a listing on more than one stock exchange, may need to produce financial information which is expressed in terms of the domestic accounting policies of the investors.

UK companies with a listing on a US stock exchange are required to produce figures following US GAAP which consists of a reconciliation statement between UK and US GAAP. In addition a narrative statement summarising the differences in policies is required.

A relatively straightforward example is shown below and is taken from the Annual Report of Tomkins plc which describes itself as an 'international industrial management company'.

RECONCILIATION TO US ACCOUNTING PRINCIPLES

The following is a summary of the estimated adjustments to profit and shareholders' funds which would be required if US GAAP had been applied instead of UK GAAP.

PROFIT ATTRIBUTABLE TO SHAREHOLDERS

	1993 **£ million**	*1992* *£ million*	*1993* **$ million**	*1992* *$ million*
Profit attributable to shareholders as reported in the consolidated profit & loss account	**119.8**	92.6	**188.0**	145.3
Estimated adjustments:				
Goodwill amortisation	**(19.1)**	(10.8)	**(30.0)**	(16.9)
Deferred income taxes	**0.1**	0.1	**0.2**	0.2
Convertible redeemable preference share issue costs	**(0.1)**	(0.1)	**(0.2)**	(0.2)
Estimated profit attributable to shareholders (net income) as adjusted to accord with US GAAP	**100.7**	81.8	**158.0**	128.4

EARNINGS	***Per share***	*Per share*	***Per ADR***	*Per ADR*
Primary	**11.55p**	12.13p*	**$0.72**	$0.76*
Fully diluted	**11.10p**	11.20p*	**$0.70**	$0.70*

* As adjusted for the capitalisation issue in August 1992 and the two stage rights issue of November 1992 and January 1993.

SHAREHOLDERS' FUNDS	*1993* **£ million**	*1992* *£ million*	*1993* **$ million**	*1992* *$ million*
Shareholders' funds as reported in the consolidated balance sheet	**802.0**	449.8	**1,258.3**	705.7
Estimated adjustments:				
Goodwill	**1,235.5**	434.3	**1,938.5**	681.4
Cumulative amortisation of goodwill	**(59.4)**	(36.9)	**(93.2)**	(57.9)
Deferred income taxes	**0.3**	0.2	**0.5**	0.3
Dividends	**50.7**	22.9	**79.5**	35.9
Convertible redeemable preference shares	**(80.3)**	(129.6)	**(126.0)**	(203.5)
Estimated ordinary shareholders' funds as adjusted to accord with US GAAP	1,948.8	740.7	3,057.6	1,161.9

The exchange rate used to translate the above figures is that ruling at the 1993 balance sheet date (£1 = $1.5690)

Many large UK companies have to show such information. A recent report into this information revealed that profit under UK rules ranged from 34% below to 41 times higher than under US GAAP. Shareholders' investment based on UK GAAP ranged from 150% below to 150% above the US figures.

2.4 Restatement of overseas accounts in line with UK accounting policies

The examiner has stated that students do not need to know the content of international accounting standards but may need to restate overseas accounts in line with UK accounting policies. In the above example, the restatement has, of course, been the other way around and it is possible that the examiner could frame the question this way as well.

Irrespective of the conversion route, the approach to adopt is similar. The most likely requirement from the examiner is a reconciliation statement rather than a full balance sheet and profit and loss account. Even if full accounts are required a reconciliation statement is a good way to present your summary workings. Remember the examiner will need to tell you what the policies of the non-UK company are and if he does not stipulate the UK policy and it is an area where a UK company could have a choice, then you must clearly state your assumptions.

The two special problems you may have if the accounts presented in the examination question are non-UK are:

(a) The description and order of items in the financial statements may be different. Part of the mark allocation may be therefore for the reordering and change in narrative of the items.

(b) If the accounts are stated in a foreign currency (which is, of course, to be expected!), the easiest approach is to perform your workings and reconciliation statement in that currency so that the accounts will balance and then translate **all** items using a suitable and the same exchange rate. Look at the example above.

Attempt the activity below before looking at the solution.

2.5 Activity

The summarised financial statements of Exodus Inc., a company trading in Erewhon, are shown below.

	20X3	*20X2*
	$ million	*$ million*
Revenue	**4,231.4**	2,999.2
Income after tax	268.3	404.6
Assets	*$ million*	*$ million*
Cash	**435.9**	336.4
Marketable securities	-	51.8
Accounts receivable	**719.1**	427.4
Inventories	**522.0**	309.4
Prepaid expenses	**38.0**	16.3
Income taxes	**44.7**	25.9
Other receivables	77.3	17.4
Total current assets	**1,837.0**	1,184.6
Property, plant & equipment	**1,071.0**	291.8
Investment in associated companies	**6.1**	4.9
Goodwill	**116.4**	124.4
Total assets	**3,030.5**	1,605.7
Liabilities		
Bank loans & overdrafts	**113.3**	89.1
Short-term debt	**29.8**	12.0
Accounts payable	**518.7**	236.8
Other accounts payable & accrued expenses	**346.1**	155.3
Income taxes	**186.7**	95.9
Dividends	**82.2**	40.0
Total current liabilities	**1,276.8**	629.1
Long-term debt	**103.6**	62.1
Deferred income taxes	**16.5**	8.8
Other liabilities	**258.9**	79.6
Total liabilities	**1,655.8**	779.6

Equity share capital	**87.4**	22.1
Retained earnings	**1,287.3**	804.0
Total equity	1,374.7	826.1
Total liabilities & equity	**3,030.5**	1,605.7

The major accounting policies adopted and relevant figures are as follows.

(a) The goodwill relates to two acquisitions of subsidiaries. Goodwill is amortised over 20 years. The original amounts are $58 million and $102 million.

(b) Deferred tax has been provided on a full provision basis. If the partial provision basis had been used, the required year-end provisions would have been $3.4 million and $3 million in 20X3 and 20X2 respectively.

(c) Interest has been capitalised on certain properties which the group constructed for its own use. The total capitalised interest is $4.5 million and $3.1 million in 20X3 and 20X2 respectively. Interested capitalised in the period ended 20X3 was $900,000.

(d) Dividends to shareholders are accounted for in the year the directors propose to pay the dividends. Proposed dividends at 31 December 20X2 and paid in 20X3 were $48 million. Proposed dividends at 31 December 20X3 and paid in 20X4 were $56 million.

(e) The assets of the group are stated under the HC convention as required by local GAAP. Land is estimated to be worth $150 million more than its book value at both balance sheet dates.

Produce a statement reconciling profit after tax per the above financial statement to profit after tax under UK GAAP for 20X3 and a balance sheet as at 31 December 20X3 under UK GAAP. You are required to amortise goodwill over 20 years but to adjust for other items to present the highest amount of shareholders' funds.

Show the results in dollars.

2.6 Activity solution

Reconciliation of profit to UK accounting principles

	20X3 $ *million*
Profit after tax as reported	268.3
Adjustment:	
Deferred taxation on partial provision basis (W2)	7.3
Profit after tax under UK GAAP	275.6

(Tutorial note: interest may be capitalised under UK GAAP. As this increases assets and therefore shareholders' funds, no adjustment has been made.

Dividends require adjustments but the above statement is at the pre-dividend level.*)*

Balance sheet as at 31 December 20X3 under UK GAAP

	$ *million*	$ *million*	$ *million*
Fixed assets			
Intangible			116.4
Tangible (1,071 + 150)			1,221.0
Investment in associated undertakings			6.1
			1,343.5

Current assets			
Stocks		522.0	
Debtors			
Trade	719.1		
Prepayments	38.0		
Other (44.7 + 77.3)	122.0		
		879.1	
Cash at bank and in hand		435.9	
		1,837.0	
Creditors: amounts falling due within one year			
Bank loans and overdrafts	113.3		
Other loans	29.8		
Trade creditors	518.7		
Other creditors including taxation	186.7		
Accruals	346.1		
Dividends (82.2 + 56)	138.2		
		1,332.8	
Net current assets			504.2
Total assets less current liabilities			1,847.7
Creditors: amounts falling due after more than one year			
Loans		103.6	
Other		258.9	
			362.5
			1,485.2
Provisions for liabilities and charges			
Deferred taxation			3.4
			1,481.8
Capital and reserves			
Called up share capital			87.4
Revaluation reserve			150.0
Profit and loss account (W1)			1,244.4
			1,481.8

WORKINGS

		$ *million*
(W1)	Effect of adjustments on retained earnings	
	Per accounts	1,287.3
	Deferred tax (16.5 – 3.4)	13.1
	Dividends proposed not recorded	(56.0)
		1,244.4
(W2)	Deferred tax	
	Charge per accounts (16.5 – 8.8)	7.7
	Charge on partial provision basis (3.4 – 3.0)	0.4
	Credit	7.3

3 THE WORK OF THE FASB ON A CONCEPTUAL FRAMEWORK

3.1 The FASB Conceptual Framework Project

The Trueblood Report issued in 1973 formed the basis for the FASB's Conceptual Framework Project. Since that date the FASB has produced numerous discussion memoranda, exposure drafts and research reports which have resulted to date in the publication of 6 Statements of Financial Accounting Concepts (SFACs). Of these only 4 are comparable to the UK environment. These are:

- SFAC 1: Objectives of financial reporting by business enterprises
- SFAC 2: Qualitative characteristics of accounting information
- SFAC 5: Recognition and measurement in financial statements of business enterprises
- SFAC 6: Elements of financial statements

3.2 The IASC/ASB's view of a conceptual framework compared with that of the FASB

The FASB has been developing a conceptual framework since its creation in 1974. There has always been much more interest in a conceptual framework in the USA than in the UK mainly due to the large numbers of accounting academics in the USA and that most American accounting practitioners have a university degree in accounting. The practitioners as a consequence are more ready to accept the contribution of academics.

The conceptual framework in the USA was expected to achieve the following.

(a) Guide the body responsible for establishing standards.

(b) Provide a frame of reference for resolving accounting questions in the absence of a specific promulgated standard.

(c) Determine bounds for judgement in preparing financial statements.

(d) Increase financial statement users' understanding of and confidence in financial statements.

(e) Enhance comparability.

As can be seen from the objectives and the titles of the SFACs above, the ASB's view of a conceptual framework is similar to the FASB. This is not surprising as the ASB is relying heavily on the published documents of the FASB and the IASC. The IASC also relied extensively on the FASB documents so they all have similar features.

3.3 Assessment of the success or failure of the FASB's work

In order to be able to assess the success or failure of the FASB's conceptual framework project, one must refer back to the originally perceived benefits of the project and evaluate whether or not any of them has been achieved. Perhaps the central test may be found in analysing the extent to which the FASB have used the framework in the development of accounting standards. An analysis of the Appendices headed 'Basis for Conclusions' in recently issued FASs reveals few references to the fact that the members of the FASB have used the concepts statements to guide their thinking - and where reference is made it is generally to broad objectives or qualitative characteristics. On the other hand, it might be argued that the concepts statements have guided the thinking of FASB members without it being expressly stated.

There is also a view by some commentators that SFACs are merely a description of what current reporting practices are rather than objective sources of reference. As a result they can be conveniently ignored when accounting standards are developed.

The US experience does not augur well for the ASB.

4 THE IMPACT OF THE IASC ON UK ACCOUNTING PRACTICE

4.1 The ASB's position

The 1993 *Foreword to accounting standards* states the attitude of the ASB to international standards.

'FRSs are formulated with due regard to international developments. The ASB supports the IASC in its aim to harmonise international financial reporting. As part of this support an FRS contains a section explaining how it relates to the International Accounting Standard (IAS) dealing with the same topic. In most cases, compliance with an FRS automatically ensures compliance with the relevant IAS.'

Until very recently, it was relatively easy to ensure that most FRSs complied with the requirements of IASs. This was because IASs were very simple and permitted many alternative treatments. In only a very few cases were there differences between the requirements of a SSAP or FRS and the requirements of an IAS.

4.2 Conceptual frameworks

One of the most important ways in which the work of the IASC has influenced UK accounting practice is in the development of a conceptual framework. The ASB's *Statement of Principles* draws heavily upon the IASC *Framework for the Preparation and Presentation of Financial Statements.* Chapters 1 and 3 in particular are very similar to the IASC's conceptual framework.

There is no SSAP or FRS on revenue recognition, but IAS 18 *Revenue* is often consulted by UK accountants for guidance on this topic.

4.3 Joint projects and co-operation

During 1996 the ASB published two Discussion Papers, *Earnings per share* and *Segmental Reporting.* These sought the views of the UK accounting profession on exposure drafts issued by the IASC and the FASB. The IASC has now issued new standards on both topics. The ASB had not planned to review either SSAP 3 or SSAP 25 at that stage, but SSAP 3 was subsequently revised in an attempt to reflect international practice. FRS 14 *Earnings per share* was issued in 1998. However, the ASB has decided not to proceed to a revision of SSAP 25.

During 1996 the ASB became involved in a joint project with IASC on provisions and contingencies. The ASB is also a member of the 'G4 + 1' group. This consists of representatives of the standard setting bodies of the UK, the US, Canada, Australia and New Zealand plus the IASC. The group's current projects include topics such as leasing, financial instruments and accounting for business combinations. The 'G4 + 1' group is becoming increasingly influential.

There has been at least one joint project (on performance reporting) between the ASB and the FASB, which influences the IASC.

4.4 Current problems

There is growing pressure for UK accounting standards to reflect international practice. However, as IASs become more authoritative, they are also becoming more detailed and prescriptive, with fewer alternatives permitted. There is currently a debate as to the extent to which UK accounting practice should be influenced by the IASC (and in practice by the FASB).

The issues of deferred tax and pension cost accounting are particularly controversial at the present time. The IASC has recently issued a revised version of IAS 12 *Income taxes* which requires full provision for deferred tax. SSAP 15 requires partial provision. The IASC has also issued IAS 19 *Employee benefits*, which requires the use of fair value for pension scheme assets rather than actuarial value (as required by SSAP 24). Both these proposals are extremely unpopular with the UK accounting profession.

There are three choices open to the ASB. It can adopt all IASs. It can reject IASs outright and set standards independently. Or it can adopt IASs with some exceptions where there is very strong feeling against the international proposals.

The first option means that UK standards will effectively be set by outsiders. The second option has obvious disadvantages for companies seeking access to world-wide capital markets.

At the time of writing, the ASB appears to be intending to pursue the third option. Sir David Tweedie has recently stated that the ASB will adopt IASC proposals where it agrees with them, but where the ASB does not agree with the IASC's approach it will 'go it alone' and attempt to persuade other standard setting bodies to accept the UK standard. However, if the UK became isolated the ASB would eventually have to 'fall back into line with everybody else'.

The DTI is currently considering whether to allow UK companies to prepare domestic accounts under IASs, rather than FRSs. The ASB opposes this on two grounds:

- The authority of national standard setters must be maintained if the experience and insights of each country are to be reflected in the international debate.

- At present, UK GAAP is more rigorous than IASs (especially in the areas of reporting substance over form and fair values in acquisition accounting).

The ASB believes that UK companies should comply with UK standards but provide reconcilations to IASs if they wish.

4.5 The influence of the ASB

The UK is strongly represented on the IASC and is attempting to influence the international standard setting process. (One of the UK representatives is the Chairman of the ASB, Sir David Tweedie.) For example, by commenting on IASC exposure drafts the ASB is able to ensure that the views of the UK accounting profession are known and are passed on to the IASC. Joint projects also maintain the UK's influence.

In some areas, UK accounting practice is believed to be influencing international practice. For example, current UK practice on accounting for goodwill and intangible assets was initially rejected by the IASC and the FASB, but is now attracting considerable interest. The ASB has also been a pioneer in the use of the statement of total recognised gains and losses (introduced by FRS 3).

The ASB is also attempting to move its work programme ahead of the IASC's, so that it will be aware of and better able to represent the UK view. However, this may mean that the ASB's own programme for developing domestic standards will be influenced by the priorities of the IASC.

4.6 Small companies and the IASC

Compliance with international practice mainly influences the financial statements of large and listed companies. In the UK, small private companies are able to take advantage of a growing range of exemptions from Companies Act disclosure requirements. They are also exempt from the requirements of some accounting standards. The ASB has issued a Financial Reporting Standard for Smaller Entities (FRSSE), which effectively introduces a separate reporting regime for small companies.

There is no IASC equivalent of the FRSSE or any similar project. It remains to be seen whether small company accounts will continue to be influenced by the requirements of IASs.

5 CHAPTER SUMMARY

There are a number of advantages of international harmonisation to users and preparers of accounts. At present there are many instances where countries are pursuing accounting policies which are acceptable to the domestic reporting environment rather than being aimed at international harmonisation.

6 SELF TEST QUESTIONS

6.1 What four advantages are there for international companies of closer harmonisation? (1.1)

6.2 How is culture a barrier to harmonisation? (1.2)

6.3 What are the objectives of the IASC? (1.4)

6.4 What do the letters OECD stand for? (1.7)

6.5 Is UK policy on deferred tax similar to the USA? (2.2)

6.6 In what currency is a reconciliation statement prepared? (2.3)

6.7 What are the USA's conceptual framework documents called? (3.1)

6.8 How can the ASB influence the IASC? (4.5)

7 EXAMINATION TYPE QUESTION

7.1 Home Ltd

Home Ltd is the wholly-owned subsidiary of a parent company which is incorporated in the US. Since Home Ltd is required to publish financial statements in the UK, its financial statements are initially drawn up in accordance with Generally Accepted Accounting Practice prevailing in the UK (UK GAAP). However, in order to compile a set of financial statements which are suitable for use in the US consolidation, it is subsequently necessary to prepare a statement of adjustments to the UK accounts. A summary of adjustments to the profit before taxation for the year ended 31 December 20X6 is given below:

		£'000
Profit before taxation per UK GAAP		12,000
Adjustments to comply with US GAAP:		
(i)	Development costs incurred in the year written off (net of amortisation of development costs)	(900)
(ii)	Revaluation adjustments written back:	
	• excess depreciation	1,000
	• profit on sale	500
Profit before taxation per US GAAP		12,600

Requirements:

(a) Outline and evaluate the steps which have been taken in the UK and elsewhere to ensure international harmonisation of financial reporting practices. **(11 marks)**

(b) Explain, for EACH of the adjustments in the table given for Home Ltd,

- the difference in accounting practice between UK GAAP and US GAAP,
- the authority (company law and/or Accounting Standard) followed by Home Ltd in accounting for the relevant item in accordance with UK GAAP. **(9 marks)**

(Total: 20 marks)

8 ANSWER TO EXAMINATION TYPE QUESTION

8.1 Home Ltd

(a) Steps taken to ensure international harmonisation of financial reporting practice

The International Accounting Standards Committee (IASC)

The objectives of the IASC are 'to formulate and publish, in the public interest, standards to be observed in the presentation of financial statements and to promote their worldwide acceptance and observance'.

The IASC has approximately 130 member organisations representing most major countries in the world. It has published 40 accounting standards (IASs).

Member countries (which include the UK) undertake to support the work of the IASC by ensuring that published financial statements comply with IASs in all material respects. The ASB's Foreword to Accounting Standards states that FRSs will be formulated with due regard to international developments and that the ASB supports the IASC in its aim to harmonise international financial reporting.

The IASC encourages countries to adopt IASs where they have not developed accounting standards of their own. It also enters into discussions with other standard setting bodies, such as the Financial Accounting Standards Board (FASB) in the USA, in order to progress towards harmonisation.

The ASB's Statement of Principles is heavily based on the IASC's conceptual framework, which in turn is based on work done by the FASB. Standards based on what is effectively a common set of principles are likely to be broadly in harmony.

The IASC's influence is persuasive, but compliance with IASs is not mandatory. IASs cannot override national accounting standards. Until recently, IASs were drafted in very broad terms and allowed for alternative interpretations and treatments. This means that compliance with IASs has not necessarily resulted in international harmonisation. However, IASs are now becoming more detailed and prescriptive. This may encourage greater international harmonisation, but also may increase the possibility that countries may deliberately choose not to comply with IASs.

Organisation for Economic Co-operation and Development (OECD)

The OECD has a committee on International Investment and Multi-national Enterprises, which has established guidelines regarding the disclosure of information for multi-national companies. It also has a Working Group on accounting standards which supports the efforts of the IASC and publishes reports on the harmonisation of accounting standards.

Although the guidelines do promote international harmonisation, compliance is voluntary.

United Nations (UN)

The UN has a commission on Transnational Reporting Corporations, which gathers information concerning the activities and reporting of multi-national companies. It seeks to improve the availability and comparability of information disclosed by multi-national companies.

EU Directives

EU Directives are incorporated into national laws (the Companies Acts 1985 and 1989 in the UK). These have the effect of standardising the format of published accounts.

However, the directives make little provision for harmonisation of accounting principles and treatments.

(b) **Adjustments**

(i) *Development costs*

Home Ltd has followed SSAP 13 *Accounting for research and development*. SSAP 13 permits entities to defer development expenditure provided it meets a number of strict criteria (intended to ensure that expenditure is capitalised only if it is reasonably certain to generate income in future). Deferred development expenditure is amortised through the profit and loss account on a systematic basis when production begins.

US GAAP does not permit development expenditure to be carried forward. It must be written off through the profit and loss account in the period in which it was incurred.

(ii) *Revaluations*

The Companies Acts permit use of the Alternative Accounting Rules, which allow assets to be included in the balance sheet at valuation, rather than at historic cost. FRS 15 *Tangible fixed assets* requires depreciation to be based on the revalued amount.

Under FRS 3 *Reporting financial performance* the revaluation surplus is reported in the statement of total recognised gains and losses (STRGL), rather than the profit and loss account. FRS 3 requires the gain or loss of disposal on a revalued fixed asset to be calculated as the difference between the sale proceeds and the carrying amount (i.e. the net book value based on the depreciated revalued amount).

Revaluations are not permitted under US GAAP. All assets must be stated at historic cost. Therefore the excess depreciation on the revalued amount is written back to the profit and loss account. An adjustment must also be made for the difference between profit on disposal of a revalued asset based on its historic cost and profit based on the revalued amount.

3 TANGIBLE FIXED ASSETS

INTRODUCTION & LEARNING OBJECTIVES

There is, as yet, no single accounting standard on tangible fixed assets but rather a number of standards on particular types of fixed assets and items relating to fixed assets, such as depreciation.

This chapter brings together these standards.

When you have studied this chapter you should be able to do the following:

- Discuss revaluations of assets
- Explain and apply the provisions of FRS 15
- Explain and apply the provisions of SSAP 19
- Explain and apply the provisions of FRS 11

1 FIXED ASSETS

1.1 Alternative definitions of assets

Assets are defined in Chapter 4 of the Statement of Principles:

Definition Assets are rights or other access to future economic benefits controlled by an entity as a result of past transactions or events.

Go back to the earlier coverage of the Statement if you have forgotten how the various parts of the definition can be amplified.

Both the IASC and the FASB in their statements of concepts use similar definitions. The common features of all definitions are:

(a) There is a future economic benefit
(b) Control is in the hands of the entity.

1.2 Regulatory requirements relating to determination of cost and value

Accounting rules are contained in the *CA 1985*. They relate to the amount at which assets are stated in financial statements of companies. There are no statutory accounting rules for the measurement of liabilities.

Companies may use either HISTORICAL COST accounting rules or ALTERNATIVE accounting rules which are based upon current costs or market value. It is possible for a company to use a mixture of these rules as in the 'Modified Historical Cost Convention' when historical cost accounts are modified by the revaluation of certain fixed assets.

The accounting rules are contained in *Sch 4 CA 1985*. The table below summarises the rules.

ACCOUNTING RULES

Relate to amount at which ASSETS are stated in accounts

HISTORICAL COST ACCOUNTING RULES

Assets should be stated at the PURCHASE PRICE or PRODUCTION COST

These terms are defined, but with alternative rules for the identification of stock and fungible assets

Modifications to stating asset at purchase price/production cost:

FIXED ASSETS	CURRENT ASSETS
Reduce cost by provisions for depreciation with special rules for development costs and goodwill	Reduce cost to net realisable value.

ALTERNATIVE ACCOUNTING RULES

Any of the following assets may be stated at alternative amounts:

FIXED ASSETS

(i) Tangible fixed assets. Market value (at last valuation date) or current cost.

(ii) Intangible fixed assets (except goodwill). Current cost.

(iii) Investments. Market value (at last valuation date) or any other appropriate basis.

CURRENT ASSETS

(i) Investments. Current cost.

(ii) Stock. Current cost.

Application of the alternative accounting rules for any of the assets may result in:

(i) Amendment to the depreciation charge.

(ii) Additional disclosure of information.

(iii) Treatment of revaluations.

Definitions

Fungible assets: assets which are substantially indistinguishable from one another. Investments are specifically included within this term.

Purchase price: the actual price paid plus any expenses incidental to the acquisition.

Production cost: the total of the purchase price of the raw materials and consumables used and the amount of costs incurred which are directly attributable to the production of the asset. In addition there **may** be included a proportion of overhead expenditure and interest on capital borrowed to finance the production of the asset to the extent that it accrues in respect of the period of production.

2 FRS 15 - TANGIBLE FIXED ASSETS

2.1 Introduction

Definition **Tangible fixed assets** are assets that have physical substance and are held for use in the production or supply of goods or services, for rental to others, or for administrative purposes on a continuing basis in the reporting entity's activities. (FRS 15).

The main accounting standard relating to tangible fixed assets is now FRS 15 *Tangible fixed assets*, which has replaced SSAP 12 *Accounting for depreciation*. The main principles of accounting for depreciation remain the same. However, FRS 15 also addresses several other important topics that were not previously covered by accounting standards: initial measurement of fixed assets; capitalisation of borrowing costs; and revaluation of fixed assets.

FRS 15 does **not** apply to investment properties as defined by SSAP 19 *Accounting for investment properties*, which remains in force.

2.2 Initial measurement of fixed assets

FRS 15 recognises that fixed assets may be acquired in a number of ways. They may be purchased or the entity may construct them for its own use. Occasionally they may be donated to an entity (for example, if the entity is a charity).

FRS 15 states that:

(a) A tangible fixed asset should initially be measured at its cost.

In practice, an asset's cost is:

> its purchase price, **less** any trade discounts or rebates, **plus** any further costs directly attributable to bringing it into working condition for its intended use.

(b) Only those costs that are directly attributable to bringing the asset into working condition for its intended use should be included in its measurement.

Directly attributable costs are:

(i) labour costs of the entity's own employees arising directly from the construction, or acquisition, of the specific tangible fixed asset; and

(ii) incremental costs that would have been avoided only if the tangible fixed asset had not been constructed or acquired.

Administration and other general overhead costs should not be included, nor should abnormal costs (for example, costs caused by design errors, industrial disputes, idle capacity, wasted materials and production delays).

(c) Capitalisation of directly attributable costs should cease when substantially all the activities that are necessary to get the tangible fixed asset ready for use are complete, even if the asset has not yet been brought into use. A tangible fixed asset is ready for use when its physical construction is complete.

(d) The costs associated with a start up or commissioning period should be included in the cost of the tangible fixed asset only where the asset is available for use but incapable of operating at normal levels without such a start up or commissioning period.

Example

A machine has to be run in and tested before it can be used for producing goods. The costs associated with this are included in the cost of the machine.

After the machine has been run in, there is a further period during which it is operated below its capacity. The machine is capable of operating at full capacity, but demand for the product it makes has not yet built up. Costs associated with this period cannot be included in the cost of the machine.

(e) The initial carrying amount of tangible fixed assets received as gifts and donations by charities should be the current value of the assets at the date that they are received.

2.3 Activity

An entity incurred the following costs in constructing a building for its own use:

	£'000
Purchase price of land	250,000
Stamp duty	5,000
Legal fees	10,000
Site preparation and clearance	18,000
Materials	100,000
Labour (period 1 April 20X7 to 30 September 20X8)	150,000
Architect's fees	20,000
General overheads	30,000
	583,000

The following information is also relevant:

(1) Material costs were greater than anticipated. On investigation, it was found that material costing £10 million had been spoiled and therefore was wasted and a further £15 million was incurred as a result of faulty design work.

(2) As a result of these problems, work on the building ceased for a fortnight during October 20X7 and it is estimated that approximately £9 million of the labour costs relate to this period.

(3) The building was completed on 1 July 20X8 and occupied on 1 September 20X8.

Required

Calculate the cost of the building that will be included in tangible fixed asset additions.

2.4 Activity solution

Only those costs which are directly attributable to bringing the asset into working condition for its intended use should be included. You may find it helpful to remember the rules for stocks in SSAP 9: abnormal costs are not included, nor are general overheads.

Labour costs are only included for the period to 1 July 20X8. The building was available for use on that date, regardless of the fact that it was not actually in use until three months later.

	£'000
Purchase price of land	250,000
Stamp duty	5,000
Legal fees	10,000
Site preparation and clearance	18,000
Materials (100 – 10 – 15)	75,000
Labour (150 × 15/18 – 9)	116,000
Architect's fees	20,000
	494,000

Conclusion Fixed assets should initially be measured at cost. Only those costs that are directly attributable to bringing the asset into working condition for its intended use should be included in its measurement.

2.5 Finance costs

Interest on borrowings is often a very significant cost of acquiring or constructing an asset. Opinion is divided on whether or not finance costs should be included in the cost of a tangible fixed asset. Property companies are the most significant advocates of capitalisation - indeed, most of them capitalise interest on loans used to finance the construction of properties. Many supermarket chains have also capitalised finance costs relating to the construction of large 'superstores'.

Arguments for capitalising finance costs

(a) Finance costs are just as much a cost of constructing a tangible fixed asset as other directly attributable costs.

(b) Capitalising finance costs results in a tangible fixed asset cost that more closely matches the market price of completed assets. Treating the finance cost as an expense distorts the choice between purchasing and constructing a tangible fixed asset. Capitalisation also means that users of the financial statements can more easily compare companies which construct their fixed assets themselves and those which purchase them from third parties.

(c) The accounts are more likely to reflect the true success or failure of projects involving the construction of assets.

(d) Failure to capitalise borrowing costs means that profits may be reduced in periods when fixed assets are acquired. This is misleading as capital investment should increase profits in the long term.

Arguments against capitalising finance costs

(a) Borrowing costs are incurred in support of the whole of the activities of an enterprise. Any attempt to associate borrowing costs with a particular asset is necessarily arbitrary.

(b) Capitalisation of borrowing costs results in the same type of asset having a different carrying amount, depending on the method of financing adopted by the enterprise.

(c) Treating borrowing costs as a charge against income results in financial statements giving more comparable results from period to period. This provides a better indication of the future cash flows of an enterprise. Interest remains a period cost of financing the business and its treatment should not change merely as a result of the completion of a tangible fixed asset.

(d) Capitalisation leads to higher tangible fixed asset costs, which are more likely to exceed the recoverable amount of the asset.

Standard accounting practice

Capitalisation of finance costs is optional. FRS 15 does, however, set out rules that must be followed if interest is capitalised.

(a) If an entity adopts a policy of capitalising finance costs it should be applied consistently (ie, the entity cannot decide to capitalise finance costs in relation to some assets and not others).

(b) Only finance costs that are directly attributable to the construction of a tangible fixed asset should be capitalised as part of the cost of that asset. In other words, an entity should only capitalise those costs that would have been **avoided** if the asset had not been acquired or constructed.

(c) The total amount of finance costs capitalised during a period should not exceed the total amount of finance costs incurred during that period.

(d) Capitalisation should begin when:

(i) finance costs are being incurred; and
(ii) expenditures for the asset are being incurred; and
(iii) activities that are necessary to get the asset ready for use are in progress.

(e) Capitalisation should be suspended during extended periods in which active development is interrupted.

The basic principle here is that finance costs should only be capitalised while activity that will change the asset's condition is actually taking place. They cannot be capitalised while the asset is simply being held, for example for future development, or while partially completed. However, the activity need not be actual physical construction. Activities necessary to get the asset ready for use include technical and administrative work such as obtaining permits.

(f) Capitalisation should cease when substantially all the activities that are necessary to get the tangible fixed asset ready for use are complete.

(g) When construction of a tangible fixed asset is completed in parts and each part is capable of being used while construction continues on other parts, capitalisation of finance costs relating to a part should cease when substantially all the activities that are necessary to get that part ready for use are completed.

Example

On 1 January 20X8 A Ltd takes out a loan to finance the construction of a housing estate. There are to be six separate houses and construction begins immediately. Although work takes place on all six houses simultaneously, House 1 is completed and is capable of being occupied on 30 September 20X8. The house was actually occupied on 1 December 20X8. At 31 December 20X8 the remaining five houses were still under construction.

If interest on the loan for the year to 31 December 20X8 is £600,000, what is the amount that should actually be capitalised?

Solution

Assuming that the loan interest can be apportioned equally between the six houses, the loan interest relating to House 1 should only be capitalised for the nine months to 30 September 20X8. Note that capitalisation of costs must cease when the house is complete and capable of being occupied, regardless of when it actually is occupied. Therefore finance costs of £575,000 are capitalised for the year ended 31 December 20X8.

Disclosures

Where finance costs are capitalised, the following disclosures are required:

(a) the accounting policy adopted;
(b) the aggregate amount of finance costs included in the cost of tangible fixed assets;
(c) the amount of finance costs capitalised during the period;
(d) the amount of finance costs recognised in the profit and loss account during the period; and
(e) the capitalisation (interest) rate used to determine the amount of finance costs capitalised during the period.

Given that capitalisation of borrowing costs is optional, FRS 15 provides users of the financial statements with information to help them to compare the financial statements of different entities.

How to calculate the interest cost

In some cases, a loan is taken out specifically to construct an asset and therefore the amount to be capitalised is the interest payable on that loan.

Arriving at the interest cost is more complicated when the acquisition or construction of an asset is financed from an entity's general borrowings. In this situation it is necessary to calculate the finance cost by applying a notional rate of interest (the capitalisation rate) to the expenditure on the asset. FRS 15 provides the following guidance:

- the expenditure on the asset is the weighted average carrying amount of the asset during the period, including finance costs previously capitalised;
- the capitalisation rate is the weighted average of rates applicable to general borrowings outstanding in the period; and
- general borrowings should not include loans for other specific purposes such as constructing other fixed assets, finance leases and hedging foreign investments.

Where an entity has a lot of different loans this could be a very complex and quite subjective calculation and FRS 15 acknowledges that judgement will have to be used in determining which borrowings should be included.

Why capitalisation is still optional

The ASB would have preferred to either make capitalisation compulsory or to prohibit it altogether, and has been convinced that there are strong arguments for capitalisation.

However, if capitalisation became compulsory, there would be practical problems. Capitalisation of borrowing costs results in the same type of asset having a different carrying amount, depending on whether the entity is funded by debt or funded by equity. The ASB believes that equity funded entities should be allowed to include the cost of capital in the cost of an asset if debt funded entities are required to capitalise interest costs. The ASB is exploring the idea of capitalising notional interest on equity, but until a consensus can be reached as to how to do this, capitalisation of finance costs will continue to be optional.

Conclusion Capitalisation of finance (interest) costs remains optional.

2.6 Subsequent expenditure

As well as the initial cost of acquiring a fixed asset, an entity may also incur additional costs in relation to the asset during its life. There are two main categories of subsequent expenditure:

(a) expenditure to maintain or service the asset (an expense of the period)
(b) expenditure to improve or upgrade the asset (effectively an addition to fixed assets).

FRS 15 sets out three circumstances in which subsequent expenditure should be capitalised:

(a) where it provides an enhancement of the economic benefits of the tangible fixed asset in excess of its previously assessed standard of performance

Examples given in FRS 15:

- modification of an item of plant to extend its useful economic life or increase its capacity
- upgrading machine parts to achieve a substantial improvement in the quality of output

(b) where a component of the tangible fixed asset that has been treated separately for depreciation purposes and depreciated over its individual useful economic life is replaced or restored

(c) where it relates to a major inspection or overhaul of a tangible fixed asset that restores the economic benefits of the asset that have been consumed by the entity and have already been reflected in depreciation.

All other subsequent expenditure must be recognised in the profit and loss account as it is incurred.

Points (b) and (c) above deal with the situation in which an asset requires substantial expenditure every few years for overhauling and restoring major components. Examples include:

- the replacing of the lining of a blast furnace
- the dry docking of a ship
- the replacing of the roof of a building.

Previously, some entities dealt with this situation by setting up a provision for the expenditure, but FRS 12 *Provisions, contingent liabilities and contingent assets* has now prohibited this treatment (see later). Instead, the part of the asset that needs regular replacement should be depreciated separately over its individual useful economic life.

Example

An aircraft is required by law to be overhauled every three years. The cost of the overhaul is estimated at £150,000. How is this expenditure treated in the accounts?

Solution

The overhaul costs of £150,000 are depreciated separately from the rest of the aircraft, so that depreciation of £50,000 is charged each year until the next overhaul. When the expenditure is incurred, at the end of the three year period, it is capitalised and depreciated over the three years until the next major overhaul.

Note the requirement to depreciate major components of the asset separately before the refurbishment/restoration expenditure can be capitalised. Where a fixed asset is not accounted for as several different components, this kind of subsequent expenditure must be treated as normal repairs and maintenance and charged to the profit and loss account as it is incurred.

Conclusion Subsequent expenditure can only be capitalised if it enhances an asset or if it relates to restoration or replacement of a component of the asset (provided that the component has been separately depreciated).

3 VALUATION OF FIXED ASSETS

3.1 Introduction

One of the main reasons why a new accounting standard on fixed assets was believed to be necessary was the lack of available guidance on revaluation. The Companies Act 1985 allows tangible fixed assets to be carried either at historic cost or at a valuation (and also requires disclosure in the directors' report where the market value of land is substantially different from book value). However, until the issue of FRS 15 no accounting standard dealt with valuation, other than for investment properties as defined by SSAP 19.

This has resulted in a situation where some entities revalue some of their fixed assets (normally properties) and some entities continue to carry them at historic cost. In turn this has led to the following problems:

- valuations are not kept up to date (particularly if property prices are falling);
- entities 'cherry pick', ie, revalue certain assets and not others;
- some entities do not depreciate revalued fixed assets.

Despite these problems, there are strong arguments for carrying assets at current values. These are mainly related to the disadvantages of using historic cost (discussed in Chapter 12). The ASB wishes to encourage the use of current value in financial statements as it believes that this provides relevant information to users.

3.2 The basic rules

(a) Revaluation of fixed assets is **optional**.

(b) If one tangible fixed asset is revalued, all tangible fixed assets of the same class must be revalued. (This means that it is now impossible to 'cherry pick', for example, by revaluing some freehold properties and not others).

(c) Where an entity adopts a policy of revaluation it need not be applied to all classes of tangible fixed assets held by the entity.

Definition A **class of tangible fixed assets** is a category of tangible fixed assets having a similar nature, function or use in the business of the entity.

In practice a class of tangible fixed assets might be determined by the Companies Act balance sheet formats, for example: land and buildings; plant and machinery; and fixtures, fittings, tools and equipment. However, narrower classes are allowed, for example: specialised properties; non-specialised properties; and short leasehold properties.

(d) The carrying amount of a revalued fixed asset should be its **current value** at the balance sheet date.

Definition The **current value** of a tangible fixed asset to the business is the lower of replacement cost and recoverable amount.

Definition **Recoverable amount** is the higher of net realisable value and value in use.

This definition of current value is consistent with the value to the business model (see Chapter 12). It is also known as deprival value.

3.3 Frequency and basis of valuation

Frequency

FRS 15 does not insist on annual revaluations, but instead requires the following:

(a) Non-specialised properties:

- a full valuation every five years with an interim valuation in Year 3 or in other years where there has been a material change in value; *or*

- full valuation on a rolling basis over five year cycles with an interim valuation on the remaining portfolio where there has been a material change in value.

(b) Specialised properties: valuation at least every five years and in the intervening years where there has been a material change in value.

(c) Other tangible fixed assets:

- annual valuation where market comparisons or appropriate indices exist; *otherwise*
- valuation at least every five years and in the intervening years where there has been a material change in value.

Five yearly valuations should be carried out by a qualified external or internal valuer. If an internal valuer is used, the valuation should be reviewed by a qualified external valuer.

Definition An **internal valuer** is a director, officer or employee of the entity. An **external valuer** is not an internal valuer and does not have a significant financial interest in the entity.

Basis

The following valuation bases should be used for revalued properties that are not impaired:

(a) non-specialised properties: existing use value plus directly attributable acquisition costs if material. Disclose open market value where this is materially different

(b) specialised properties: depreciated replacement cost

(c) properties surplus to an entity's requirements: open market value less expected direct selling costs where these are material.

Tangible fixed assets other than properties should be valued using market value, where possible. Where market value is not obtainable, depreciated replacement cost should be used.

3.4 Reporting gains and losses on revaluation

Gains

(a) Revaluation gains should normally be recognised in the statement of total recognised gains and losses (this is also required by FRS 3). They cannot be recognised in the profit and loss account because they are not yet realised.

(b) Revaluation gains are only recognised in the profit and loss account if they reverse revaluation losses on the same asset.

Losses

A revaluation loss may be caused either:

- by a fall in prices (eg, a slump in the property market); or
- by consumption of economic benefits (eg, physical damage or deterioration).

Unless there is evidence to the contrary, it is assumed that a loss is caused by a fall in prices.

(a) Revaluation losses that are caused by a clear consumption of economic benefits should be recognised in the profit and loss account.

(b) Other revaluation losses should normally be recognised in the statement of total recognised gains and losses until the carrying amount reaches its depreciated historical cost. Thereafter they should be recognised in the profit and loss account.

(c) The exception to this rule is where the recoverable amount of the asset is greater than its revalued amount. The loss should then be recognised in the statement of total recognised gains and losses to the extent that the recoverable amount of the asset is greater than its revalued amount.

(d) In determining in which performance statement gains and losses on revaluation should be recognised, material gains and losses on individual assets should not be aggregated (in other words, gains and losses cannot be netted off against each other).

Losses caused by a fall in prices are valuation adjustments, are unrealised and are therefore reported in the statement of total recognised gains and losses. On the other hand, losses caused by a consumption of economic benefits are similar to depreciation and must therefore be reported in the profit and loss account. Where the recoverable amount of an asset is greater than its revalued amount the difference between the two amounts is not an impairment but a valuation adjustment and should therefore be recognised in the statement of total recognised gains and losses, rather than in the profit and loss account.

3.5 Activity

A property costing £500,000 was purchased on 1 January 20X4 and was depreciated over its useful economic life of 10 years. It had no residual value.

At 31 December 20X4 the property was valued at £540,000 and at 31 December 20X5 it was valued at £350,000.

How should these revaluations be treated in the accounts for the years ended 31 December 20X4 and 31 December 20X5 if at that date:

(a) the recoverable amount was £350,000?
(b) the recoverable amount was £380,000?

3.6 Activity solution

Year ended 31 December 20X4: a revaluation gain of £90,000 is reported in the statement of total recognised gains and losses.

Year ended 31 December 20X5: a revaluation loss of £130,000 occurs and is dealt with as follows:

		£'000	£'000
(a)	Recoverable amount £350,000		
	Statement of total recognised gains and losses (480 – 400)		80
	Profit and loss account		50
			130
(b)	Recoverable amount £380,000		
	Statement of total recognised gains and losses:		
	Net book value less depreciated historical cost (480 – 400)	80	
	Recoverable amount less revalued amount (380 – 350)	30	
			110
	Profit and loss account:		
	Depreciated historical cost less recoverable amount (400 – 380)	20	
			130

WORKING

	£'000
Cost at 1 January 20X4	500
Less: depreciation (500 ÷ 10)	(50)
	450
Revaluation gain	90
Valuation at 31 December 20X4	540
Less: depreciation (540 ÷ 9)	(60)
	480

Revaluation loss	(130)
Valuation at 31 December 20X5	350
Depreciated historic cost at 31 December 20X5 (500 – 100)	400

3.7 Reporting gains and losses on disposal

The profit or loss on the disposal of a revalued fixed asset should be calculated as the difference between the net sale proceeds and the carrying amount (this is also required by FRS 3). It should be accounted for in the profit and loss account of the period in which the disposal occurs and disclosed in accordance with FRS 3 *Reporting financial performance*.

The gain or loss on revaluation has already been included in the accounts (in the statement of total recognised gains and losses) when the asset was revalued. Unless the profit or loss on disposal is based on the carrying amount, the gain or loss on revaluation will be recognised twice.

Note that any unrealised revaluation gains are now realised and should be transferred from the revaluation reserve to the profit and loss account reserve as required by FRS 3.

3.8 Example of disposal of a revalued asset

Suggs Ltd sold one of its freehold properties on 30 June 20X4 (the last day of its accounting year). You are provided with the following information:

(1) Retained profit for the year, after charging depreciation on the above property, but before dealing with the gain on sale, is £797,000.

(2) Reserves at 30 June 20X3 comprised:

Profit and loss account	£1,852,000
Revaluation reserve	£937,000

(3)

	£
Original cost of property	700,000
Depreciation charged to date of revaluation (£700,000 × 2% = £14,000 pa for five years)	70,000
NBV at valuation	630,000
To revaluation reserve	270,000
Revaluation	900,000
Depreciation charge from date of revaluation to date of sale (£900,000 ÷ 45 = £20,000 pa for four years)	80,000
NBV at date of sale	820,000

(4) Annual transfers between the revaluation reserve and the profit and loss account have been made of the profits realised due to the additional depreciation charge.

(5) The property was sold for £932,000.

You are required to show the relevant extract from the profit and loss account and the reserves of Suggs Ltd for the year ended 30 June 20X4.

3.9 Solution

Step 1 Set up a proforma profit and loss account with extracts of the relevant items to be disclosed.

Profit on sale of property will be the difference between sale proceeds and NBV at date of sale.

Retained earnings will be as given plus gain on sale of property.

Profit and loss account for the year

	£
Operating profit	X
Profit on sale of property (932 – 820)	112,000
Tax, dividends, etc	X
Retained (797 + 112)	909,000

Step 2 Calculate the transfer to be made from the revaluation reserve of the amount realised on the sale of the property. This will comprise the original amount taken to the reserve on revaluation less annual transfers re the additional depreciation charge.

WORKING - **Transfer re sale**

	£
To revaluation reserve at date of revaluation	270,000
Less: Previously realised 4 × 6,000	24,000
	246,000

Step 3 Prepare a statement of reserves showing all movements on both the profit and loss account and the revaluation reserve. Transfers need to be made from the revaluation reserve of annual amounts realised due to the additional depreciation charge and the amount realised due to the sale of the property.

	Profit and loss account £	*Revaluation reserve* £
Balance at 1 July 20X3	1,852,000	937,000
Retained profit for year	909,000	
Transfer re additional depreciation charge (20,000 – 14,000)	6,000	(6,000)
Sale of property	246,000	(246,000)
Balance at 30 June 20X4	3,013,000	685,000

3.10 Disclosures where assets have been revalued

(a) For each class of revalued assets:

(i) name and qualifications of the valuer(s);
(ii) bases of valuation;
(iii) date and amounts of the valuation;
(iv) depreciated historic cost;
(v) whether the valuer(s) is (are) internal or external;

(vi) if the valuation has not been updated because the directors are not aware of any material change, a statement to that effect; and

(vii) date of the last full valuation (if not in the current period).

(b) For revalued properties:

(i) where properties have been valued as fully equipped operational entities having regard to their trading potential, a statement to that effect and the carrying amount of those properties; and

(ii) the total amount of notional directly attributable acquisition costs included in the carrying amount, where material.

Conclusion Revaluation of fixed assets is optional. Revaluation must be applied to all assets of the same class and must be kept up to date.

4 DEPRECIATION

4.1 Depreciable amount

Definition **Depreciation** is the measure of the cost or revalued amount of the economic benefits of the tangible fixed asset that have been consumed during the period.

There is a note to the main definition:

Consumption includes the wearing out, using up or other reduction in the useful economic life of a tangible fixed asset whether arising from use, effluxion of time or obsolescence through either changes in technology or demand for the goods and services produced by the asset.

FRS 15 requires that the depreciable amount of a tangible fixed asset should be allocated on a systematic basis over its useful economic life.

Definition The **depreciable amount** is the cost of a tangible fixed asset (or, where an asset is revalued, the revalued amount) less its residual value.

Definition **Residual value** is the net realisable value of an asset at the end of its useful economic life.

Definition The **useful economic life** of a tangible fixed asset is the period over which the entity expects to derive economic benefit from that asset.

The depreciation method used should reflect as fairly as possible the pattern in which the asset's economic benefits are consumed by the entity.

The depreciation charge for each period should be recognised as an expense in the profit and loss account unless it is permitted to be included in the carrying amount of another asset (for example, where it is part of development expenditure that is capitalised).

These definitions and requirements are very similar to those of the old SSAP 12. Depreciation continues to be an application of the accruals concept rather than a means of measuring value. Like SSAP 12, FRS 15 does not prescribe a method of depreciation.

4.2 Activity

A company revalues its buildings and decides to incorporate the revaluation into the books of account. The following information is relevant:

(a) Extract from the balance sheet at 31 December 20X7:

	£
Buildings:	
Cost	1,500,000
Depreciation	450,000
	1,050,000

(b) Depreciation has been provided at 2% per annum on a straight line.

(c) The building is revalued at 30 June 20X8 at £1,380,000. There is no change in its remaining estimated future life.

Show the relevant extracts from the final accounts at 31 December 20X8.

4.3 Activity solution

Profit and loss account – depreciation charge

	£
Based on original cost	30,000
Based on increase in valuation	5,000
Total	35,000

Balance sheet

	£
Buildings:	
Valuation 30 June 20X8	1,380,000
Accumulated depreciation	20,000
	1,360,000

WORKINGS

(a) **Buildings account (NBV)**

20X8		£	20X8		£
1 Jan.	Balance b/d	1,050,000	30 Jun.	Profit and loss depreciation first half year	15,000
30 Jun.	Revaluation surplus (Bal fig)	345,000	30 Jun.	Balance c/d	1,380,000
		1,395,000			1,395,000
30 Jun.	Balance b/d	1,380,000	31 Dec.	Profit and loss depreciation second half year	20,000
			31 Dec.	Balance c/d	1,360,000
		1,380,000			1,380,000

(b) **Depreciation calculations**

	£
First half year $0.5 \times 2\% \times 1{,}500{,}000$	15,000
Second half year $0.5 \times \frac{1{,}380{,}000}{34.5^{**}}$	20,000
	35,000

Had this building not been revalued, the charge for the year would have been £30,000.

** This is arrived at as follows:

		Years
Total number of years before building fully depreciated		50.0
Less: Depreciation in years to 31 December 20X7 $\frac{450{,}000}{30{,}000}$	15.0	
Depreciation 1 January 20X8 to 30 June 20X8	0.5	
		15.5
Number of years for depreciation to run		34.5

4.4 Change in method

A change from one method of providing depreciation to another is permissible only on the grounds that the new method will give a fairer presentation of the results and of the financial position.

This does not constitute a change in accounting policy. The carrying amount of the tangible fixed asset is depreciated using the revised method over the remaining useful economic life, beginning in the period in which the change is made.

4.5 Subsequent expenditure and impairment reviews

(a) Where a tangible fixed asset comprises two or more major components with substantially different useful economic lives, each component should be depreciated separately over its individual useful economic life.

(b) Subsequent expenditure on a tangible fixed asset that maintains or enhances the previously assessed standard of performance of the asset does not negate the need to charge depreciation.

(c) When either:

(i) a tangible fixed asset is not depreciated on the grounds that the charge would be immaterial (either because of the length of the estimated remaining useful economic life or because the estimated residual value of the tangible fixed asset is not materially different from the carrying amount of the asset); or

(ii) the estimated remaining useful economic life of the tangible fixed asset exceeds 50 years

the asset should be reviewed for impairment, in accordance with FRS 11, at the end of each reporting period. (This does not apply to non-depreciable land.)

These requirements are designed to deal with two particular problems. We have already looked at the first of these, the treatment of subsequent expenditure. FRS 12 has now prevented entities from providing for overhaul and servicing costs. Instead, where a major component of an asset has to be regularly replaced this component is depreciated separately.

The other problem is non-depreciation of revalued assets. Some entities in the past did not charge depreciation on revalued properties on the grounds that the assets were being maintained or refurbished regularly so that the economic life of the property was limitless. This treatment has been common in the hotel, brewing, public house and retail sectors.

It was widely expected that FRS 15 would require that all fixed assets were depreciated, thereby closing what many perceived to be a 'loophole' in SSAP 12. FRS 15 does state that subsequent expenditure does not remove the need to charge depreciation. However, the ASB has recognised that in rare cases, some tangible fixed assets may have very long useful economic lives. Entities can still avoid charging depreciation on the grounds that the charge is immaterial but they must carry out annual impairment reviews (FRS 11 is covered later in this chapter). This is likely to discourage non-depreciation as impairment reviews can be time consuming, complicated and costly and may result in reduced profits (if an impairment loss has to be recognised in the profit and loss account).

4.6 Split depreciation

The ASB has considered allowing 'split depreciation' (ie, charging depreciation based on historic cost to the profit and loss account and charging the extra depreciation on the revalued amount to the statement of total recognised gains and losses). Split depreciation has two main advantages:

(a) it increases the comparability of financial statements and removes a disincentive to revaluations; and

(b) depreciation charged to the profit and loss account represents an allocation of the actual cash outlay.

However, split depreciation would result in the profit and loss account not showing the full cost of the economic benefits consumed during the period. Depreciation based on current value reflects the cost that the entity could have avoided if it had not used the asset. Split depreciation would also be contrary to the Companies Act, which requires depreciation of revalued fixed assets to be calculated on the current cost or market value and based on the revalued amount. For these reasons, the ASB has concluded that split depreciation should not be allowed.

4.7 Review of useful economic life and residual value

(a) Useful economic life should be reviewed at the end of each reporting period and revised if expectations are significantly different from previous estimates. If a useful economic life is revised, the carrying amount of the asset at the date of revision should be depreciated over the revised remaining useful economic life.

(b) Where the residual value is material it should be reviewed at the end of each reporting period to take account of reasonably expected technological changes based on prices prevailing at the date of acquisition (or revaluation). Any change should be accounted for prospectively over the asset's remaining useful economic life.

There are several changes from SSAP 12:

- Useful economic lives of assets should be reviewed **annually** (SSAP 12 used the word 'regularly').
- SSAP 12 did not require the review of residual values.
- SSAP 12 permitted the depreciation adjustment arising on a change in useful economic life to be treated as an exceptional item where future results would be materially distorted. This is no longer allowed.

4.8 Activity

An asset was purchased for £100,000 on 1 January 20X5 and was depreciated over 5 years. Residual value was £10,000.

A general review of asset lives was undertaken in 20X7 and at 31 December 20X7 the remaining useful economic life was estimated at 7 years. Residual value was nil.

Calculate the depreciation charge for the year ended 31 December 20X7 and subsequent years.

4.9 Activity solution

	£
Net book value at 31 December 20X6 (100,000 – 36,000)	64,000
Annual depreciation charge (64,000 ÷ 8)	8,000

Note that the estimated remaining life is seven years from 31 December 20X7, but this information is used to compute the current year's charge as well.

4.10 Renewals accounting

Some entities, such as utility companies, own assets such as pipelines, roads, sewers, dams and tunnels, which they use to provide a service to the public. These assets are known as infrastructure assets. Many utility companies have not depreciated these assets, but instead have provided annually for the cost of maintaining them. FRS 12 has now prohibited the setting up of provisions for future costs.

Provided that certain conditions are met, FRS 15 allows 'renewals accounting' for infrastructure assets. Under renewals accounting, annual expenditure required to maintain the operating capacity of the infrastructure asset is charged as depreciation and is deducted from the carrying amount of the asset as accumulated depreciation. Actual expenditure is capitalised as part of the cost of the asset as it is incurred.

The conditions are as follows:

(a) the infrastructure asset is a system or network that as a whole is intended to be maintained at a specified level by the continuing replacement and refurbishment of its components; and

(b) the level of annual expenditure required to maintain the operating capacity of the asset is calculated from an asset management plan that is certified by a person who is appropriately qualified and independent; and

(c) the system or network is in a mature or steady state (that is, not being expanded or run down).

4.11 Disclosure

As well as the disclosures required by the Companies Act (the tangible fixed asset note) FRS 15 requires the following disclosures for each class of tangible fixed assets:

(a) the depreciation methods used;
(b) the useful economic lives or the depreciation rates used;
(c) total depreciation charged for the period; and
(d) the effect of a change in useful economic lives or residual value in the period, where material.

Where there has been a change in the depreciation method used in the period, the effect should be disclosed, if material. The reason for the change should also be disclosed.

Conclusion Depreciation should be charged on a systematic basis over the useful economic life of a tangible fixed asset. Tangible fixed assets must be reviewed for impairment annually if they are not depreciated or if their remaining useful economic life is more than 50 years.

4.12 FRS 15 in practice

On the whole, FRS 15 has been welcomed by users and preparers of financial statements. The requirement for regular revaluations has undoubted advantages in that it increases the comparability of financial statements and reduces opportunities for 'creative accounting'. (For example, many entities revalued assets during the 1980s and continued to use those valuations in their financial statements, despite the fact that property values subsequently fell).

The requirement to revalue all assets within a class means that entities will not be able to 'cherry pick' certain assets for revaluation while carrying others at historic cost. This will also increase comparability between entities.

Entities still have the choice of whether to revalue fixed assets. The ASB has accepted that enforcing the use of current values would not be practical, given that there is widespread resistance to the idea of current value accounting.

The most controversial aspect of the FRS has probably been its failure to prohibit non-depreciation of revalued fixed assets (although it discourages the practice by requiring impairment reviews). Many commentators are concerned that this failure will lead to 'creative accounting' abuses.

The ASB wishes to encourage the use of current values as this provides relevant information to users of the financial statements. However, a few commentators fear that some entities could revert to using historic cost in order to avoid costly annual revaluations and the other disadvantages associated with using current values (for example, the higher depreciation charge and the requirement to 'report the bad news as well as the good' if market values fall).

4.13 UITF Abstract 23: Application of the transitional rules in FRS 15

The issue

FRS 15 introduced a requirement (paragraph 83) that where a tangible fixed asset comprises two or more major components with different lives, each component should be accounted for separately for depreciation purposes and depreciated over its individual useful economic life.

For example a freehold property may be purchased. The acquisition cost would be split between the cost of land (not depreciated since its life is infinite), the cost of buildings (depreciated over, say, 50 years) and the cost of the lifts in the property (depreciated over, say, 10 years).

Paragraph 108 of FRS 15 explains the arrangements for introducing this rule. Where entities separate tangible fixed assets into different components on adopting FRS 15, the changes should be dealt with as prior period adjustments, as a change in accounting policy. However this requirement is slightly unclear, as there are two possible implications of introducing component accounting:

(a) identifying the various separate components with different lives, and
(b) amending the residual value and/or useful life of the remainder of the asset.

Should the effect of both (a) and (b) be combined into a single prior period adjustment; or should the prior period adjustment only incorporate item (a), with item (b) treated as normal in FRS 15 and therefore not giving rise to a prior period adjustment?

UITF Consensus

The UITF decided on the second of these options. When component accounting is first introduced to comply with FRS 15, the prior period adjustment should reflect the identification of the separate components. Any change to the useful economic life or residual value of the remainder of the asset should be accounted for prospectively as normally required by FRS 15, and should not give rise to a prior period adjustment.

5 SSAP 19 – INVESTMENT PROPERTIES

5.1 The requirements of SSAP 19 and the Companies Act

Under the general requirements of *FRS 15* all fixed assets having a finite useful life should be subject to a depreciation charge. Investment property companies objected to this requirement and as the ASC conceded they had reasonable grounds for objecting, the FRS 15 rules did not become effective for investment properties. *SSAP 19:* **Accounting for investment properties** provides a solution, and should be looked at as an addition to *FRS 15*.

SSAP 19 regards an investment property as an asset which is held as a disposable investment rather than an asset consumed in the business operations of a company over a number of years. With such a property the most useful information to give a user of the accounts is the current value of the investment. Systematic annual depreciation would be of little relevance.

SSAP 19 requires therefore that investment properties should not suffer a depreciation charge and must be stated at their current values.

There are no special requirement of the CA85 with respect to investment properties. The requirement is to depreciate assets with a finite useful life.

5.2 Standard accounting practice (as amended by the ASB in 1994)

(a) Investment properties should not be subject to periodic charges for depreciation on the basis set out in *FRS 15*, except for properties held on lease which should be depreciated on the basis set out in *FRS 15* at least over the period when the unexpired term is 20 years or less.

(b) Investment properties should be included in the balance sheet at their open market value.

(c) The names of the persons making the valuation, or particulars of their qualifications, should be disclosed together with the bases of valuation used by them. If a person making a valuation is an employee or officer of the company or group which owns the property this fact should be disclosed.

(d) Changes in the market value of investment properties should not be taken to the profit and loss account but should be taken to the statement of total recognised gains and losses (being a movement on an investment revaluation reserve), unless a deficit (or its reversal) on an individual investment property is expected to be permanent in which case it should be charged (or credited) in the profit and loss account of the period.

Definition An investment property is an interest in land and/or buildings:

(a) in respect of which construction work and development have been completed; and

(b) which is held for its investment potential, any rental income being negotiated at arm's length.

The following are exceptions from the definition:

(a) A property which is owned and occupied by a company for its own purposes is not an investment property.

(b) A property let to and occupied by another group company is not an investment property for the purposes of its own accounts or the group accounts.

5.3 Applying the requirements of SSAP 19 and the Companies Act

Industrial Ltd produces accounts to 31 December. On 1 January 20X8 it moved from its factory in Bolton to a new purpose-built factory in Rochdale (expected life of fifty years). The old premises were available for letting from 1 January 20X8 and a lease was granted on 30 September 20X8 to B Ltd at an annual rental of £8,000. A valuation of the old premises at 31 December 20X8 was £160,000.

Extracts from the balance sheet as at 31 December 20X7 were:

Fixed assets

	Cost	*Depreciation*	*NBV*
	£	£	£
Land and buildings:			
Old premises	200,000	80,000	120,000
New premises	450,000		450,000

5.4 Solution

Extracts from the balance sheet as at 31 December 20X8 would be:

Fixed assets

	Cost	*Depreciation*	*NBV*
	£	£	£
Land and buildings	450,000	9,000	441,000
Investment property at valuation			160,000

Reserves

Investment revaluation reserve	40,000

5.5 Treatment of annual valuations

SSAP 19 regards the total investment property revaluation reserve as being available to cover deficits. Amounts only need to be charged to the profit and loss account in respect of permanent deficits on revaluation.

5.6 Example

Newline Investment Co Ltd purchased three investment properties on 31 December 20X1, and the following valuations have been made during the period to 31 December 20X4:

	31 Dec 20X1	*31 Dec 20X2*	*31 Dec 20X3*	*31 Dec 20X4*
	£'000	£'000	£'000	£'000
Property A	200	180	120	90
Property B	300	330	340	340
Property C	400	440	450	450
Total	900	950	910	880

All revaluation deficits are expected to be temporary.

Show the balance on the investment revaluation reserve for each balance sheet date.

5.7 Solution

The investment revaluation reserve would be disclosed for the various years as follows:

	Year ended 31 December		
	20X2	*20X3*	*20X4*
	£'000	£'000	£'000
Balance b/d	Nil	50	10
Net revaluation	50	(40)	(10)
Balance c/d	50	10	Nil

The deficit of £20,000 not covered in the year ended 31 December 20X4 would normally be charged through the profit and loss account on the grounds of prudence, though SSAP 19 permits a debit balance on the investment revaluation reserve as long as it has arisen from temporary write-downs only.

5.8 Activity

State whether the following are investment properties and if so whether they should be depreciated.

(a) A freehold property bought for its investment potential and leased to an associated company at an arm's length rental.

(b) A leasehold property let to a third party. The leasehold has 18 years to run.

(c) An office building owned and occupied by a company.

(d) A leasehold property with 24 years left to run which is let to a subsidiary at an arm's length rental.

5.9 Activity solution

(a) This is an investment property. An associated company is not a group company. The property should not be depreciated under *SSAP 19*.

(b) This is an investment property. As the lease has less than 20 years to run it should be depreciated.

(c) This is not an investment property as it is used by the company for the purposes of its own business.

(d) This is not an investment property as it is occupied by a group company.

5.10 The conflict between SSAP 19 and the Companies Act

The legality of SSAP 19 is questioned as the requirement not to depreciate is in conflict with the requirement of the CA85 to depreciate assets with a finite useful life.

SSAP 19 states however that the treatment is necessary in order to show a true and fair view and thus use is made of the overriding provisions of the CA85 to show such a true and fair view.

SSAP 19 justifies the different accounting treatment for investment properties on the following grounds. It concludes that such assets are not held for consumption within the operations of the business but are held as investments. Therefore to the user of the financial statements, the most important information about such assets relates to their current value. Calculation of depreciation in such circumstances does not benefit the user from a balance sheet perspective nor a profit and loss account perspective as the asset is not consumed in the business operations.

Another way of justifying the special treatment is that the disposal of such an asset would not materially affect the trading operations of the business; it therefore cannot be relevant to depreciate such items.

5.11 Application of the CA 85 true and fair view override

Since SSAP 19 requires a routine use of the true and fair override, this is a useful point in the text to revise the disclosures that must be given when the override is invoked. These are laid down in UITF Abstract 7.

UITF Abstract 7: True and fair view override disclosures

The issue

The CA85 contains a true and fair override, so that any of the specific requirements of the Act may be ignored in the overriding interest of presenting a true and fair view. The Act requires that when the override has been invoked, the particulars, reasons and effect of the departure shall be given in a note to the accounts, but different companies have presented this information in different ways.

Principal requirements

The Abstract gives guidance on what is required when the override is invoked:

(a) Particulars - a statement of the treatment which the Act would normally require in the circumstances and a description of the treatment actually adopted.

(b) Reasons - a statement as to why the treatment prescribed would not give a true and fair view.

(c) Effect - a description of how the position shown in the accounts is different as a result of the departure, normally with quantification.

5.12 The weaknesses in SSAP 19

The justification of the different treatment of investment properties was explained earlier. Some commentators argue however that despite such arguments, SSAP 19 does not represent a valid treatment and is merely an example of the ASC giving way to the demands of pressure groups (ie, the property investment companies).

Other weaknesses relate to the subjective nature of the standard. No guidance is given on the distinction between temporary and permanent diminutions in value, nor whether the measurement of a deficit should be in relation to the revalued carrying amount.

FRED 17, which eventually became FRS 15, would have replaced SSAP 19, but did not propose any major changes in the accounting treatment of investment properties. The ASB has decided to consider the accounting treatment of investment properties in conjunction with the IASC's project on investment properties. Until this is complete, SSAP 19 will remain in force.

6 FRS 11: IMPAIRMENT OF FIXED ASSETS AND GOODWILL

6.1 Why a new accounting standard was needed

Definition **Impairment** is a reduction in the recoverable amount of a fixed asset or goodwill below its carrying amount.

It is accepted practice that a fixed asset should not be carried in financial statements at more than its recoverable amount, but there has been very little guidance as to how recoverable amount should be identified or measured.

The Companies Act requires provision to be made for permanent diminutions in the value of fixed assets, but does not include guidance as to:

(a) what constitutes a permanent (as opposed to a temporary) diminution; and
(b) the way in which diminutions should be presented in the financial statements.

SSAP 12 required that where there was a permanent diminution in value, the asset should be immediately written down to its recoverable amount and then depreciated over its remaining useful economic life. This meant that in most cases the diminution was charged immediately to the profit and loss account and was effectively treated as additional depreciation. However, the issue is more complicated where a fixed asset has been revalued.

Example

An asset costing £100,000 was purchased on 1 January 20X1 and has a useful economic life of 10 years. On 1 January 20X3 it was revalued to £150,000. On 1 January 20X5 it was estimated that the recoverable amount of the asset was only £100,000.

How could this impairment be treated in the financial statements for the year ended 31 December 20X5?

Solution

There are several possibilities. In theory (provided that the asset is not an investment property), the preparers of the financial statements could decide not to recognise the impairment on the grounds that it is temporary, but this would be unlikely to give a true and fair view.

In practice, there are two options:

(a) Treat the impairment as a fall in value:

Dr	Revaluation reserve	£12,500	
	Cr Fixed assets		£12,500

The impairment is recorded in the statement of total recognised gains and losses, but does not affect the results for the year. This is similar to the treatment of a temporary diminution required by SSAP 19.

(b) Treat the impairment as additional depreciation:

Dr	Depreciation expense	£12,500	
	Cr Fixed assets		£12,500

This is similar to the treatment of a permanent diminution required by SSAP 19 and results in a charge to the profit and loss account for the year.

From this we can see that this lack of guidance reduced the comparability of financial statements. In addition, impairment losses were not always recognised as soon as they occurred.

The need for guidance on how to calculate and recognise impairment has become more urgent with the issue of recent accounting standards:

- FRS 10 *Goodwill and intangible assets* requires annual impairment reviews where goodwill and intangible assets have a useful life exceeding twenty years.
- FRS 15 *Tangible fixed assets* requires annual impairment reviews where:
  - no depreciation charge is made on the grounds that it would be immaterial; or
  - the estimated remaining useful economic life of an asset is more than 50 years.

6.2 Scope

FRS 11 applies to purchased goodwill that is recognised in the balance sheet and all fixed assets except:

(a) investment properties as defined by SSAP 19

(b) fixed assets falling within the scope of FRS 13 (eg, investments)

(c) an entity's own shares held by an ESOP and shown as a fixed asset in the entity's balance sheet under UITF Abstract 13 *Accounting for ESOP trusts*.

Note that FRS 11 applies to investments in subsidiaries, associates and joint ventures because these are outside the scope of FRS 13.

6.3 The basic principle

Impairment is measured by comparing the carrying value of the asset with its recoverable amount. If the carrying amount exceeds the recoverable amount, the asset is impaired and should be written down. (Note that this effectively abolishes the distinction between temporary and permanent diminutions in value by treating all diminutions as permanent).

Definition **Recoverable amount** is the higher of the amounts that can be obtained from selling the asset (net realisable value) or using the asset (value in use).

Definition **Net realisable value** is the amount at which an asset could be disposed of, less any direct selling costs.

Definition **Value in use** is the present value of the future cash flows obtainable as a result of an asset's continued use, including those resulting from its ultimate disposal.

Value to the business

These definitions are based on the value to the business model in the ASB's draft Statement of Principles (sometimes known as **deprival value**). The reasoning behind it is that, when a fixed asset becomes impaired, the decision must be made whether to continue to use it or to sell it. This decision is based on the cash flows that can be generated by following each course of action, so that an entity will not continue to use the asset if it can realise more cash by selling it and vice versa. This means that when an asset is stated at the higher of net realisable value or value in use it is recorded at its greatest value to the entity.

The fair value approach

US GAAP measures impairment by reference to fair values rather than the higher of net realisable value and value in use.

The ASB has rejected the fair value approach because this cannot be applied easily unless there is an active market for the asset in question, which is unlikely in the case of most intangible assets.

6.4 Activity

The following information relates to three assets:

	A	*B*	*C*
	£'000	£'000	£'000
Net book value	100	150	120
Net realisable value	110	125	100
Value in use	120	130	90

(a) What is the recoverable amount of each asset?
(b) Calculate the impairment provision for each of the three assets.

6.5 Activity solution

(a) A: £120,000, B: £130,000, C: £100,000
(b) A: Nil, B: £20,000, C: £20,000

6.6 When to carry out an impairment review

Impairment reviews should be carried out if:

(a) events or changes in circumstances indicate that the carrying amount of an asset may not be recoverable; or

(b) when required by FRS 10 or by FRS 15.

They are **not** required otherwise.

Indications that assets may have become impaired include:

(a) a current period operating loss in the business in which the fixed asset or goodwill is involved or a net cash outflow from the operating activities of the business, combined with either past or expected future operating losses or net cash outflows from operating activities

(b) a significant decline in a fixed asset's market value during the period

(c) evidence of obsolescence or physical damage to the fixed asset

(d) a significant adverse change in the business or the market in which the fixed asset or goodwill is involved (eg, the entrance of a major competitor)

(e) a commitment by management to undertake a significant re-organisation

(f) a major loss of key employees

(g) a significant increase in market interest rates or other market rates of return that are likely to affect materially the fixed asset's recoverable amount.

6.7 Net realisable value

The net realisable value of an asset that is traded on an active market should be based on market value.

Net realisable value is the amount at which an asset could be disposed of, less any direct selling costs. Direct selling costs might include:

- legal costs
- stamp duty
- costs relating to the removal of a sitting tenant (in the case of a building).

Redundancy and reorganisation costs (eg, following the sale of a business) are **not** direct selling costs.

6.8 Value in use

Value in use is the present value of the future cash flows obtainable as a result of an asset's continued use.

Therefore there are two steps to the calculation:

1 estimate future cash flows
2 discount them to arrive at their present value.

Where possible, value in use should be estimated for individual assets. However, it may not always be possible to identify cash flows arising from individual fixed assets. If this is the case, value in use is calculated for income generating units (groups of assets that produce independent income streams).

Estimates of future cash flows

Estimates of future cash flows should be:

(a) based on reasonable and supportable assumptions;

(b) consistent with the most up to date budgets and plans that have been formally approved by management; and

(c) should assume a steady or declining growth rate for the period beyond that covered by formal budgets and plans.

Only in exceptional circumstances should:

(a) the period before the steady or declining growth rate is assumed extend to more than five years; or

(b) the steady or declining growth rate exceed the long term average growth rate for the country or countries in which the business operates.

Future cash flows should normally be estimated for individual fixed assets or income generating units in their current condition. They should not include future cash outflows or future capital expenditure (for example, the cost of future reorganisations). The exception to this rule is when a newly acquired income generating unit, such as a subsidiary, is being reviewed for impairment. In these cases, the cost of the asset (the purchase price) reflects the fact that the acquirer may have to bear the cost of future capital expenditure or future reorganisations. Therefore planned future expenditure may be taken into account up to the end of the first full year after acquisition.

The discount rate

The discount rate used to arrive at the present value of the expected future cash flows should be the rate of return that the market would expect from an equally risky investment. It should exclude the effects of any risk for which the cash flows have been adjusted and should be calculated on a pre-tax basis.

In practice, the discount rate can be estimated using:

(a) the rate implicit in market transactions of similar assets;

(b) the current weighted average cost of capital of a listed company whose cash flows have similar risk profiles to those of the income generating unit; or

(c) the weighted average cost of capital for the entity but only if adjusted for the particular risks associated with the income generating unit.

Conclusion Impairment is measured by comparing the carrying amount of an asset with its recoverable amount. Recoverable amount is the higher of net realisable value and value in use.

6.9 Income generating units

It may not be possible to estimate the value in use for individual fixed assets. If this is the case, it is necessary to base the calculation on income generating units.

Definition An **income generating unit** is a group of assets, liabilities and associated goodwill that generates income that is largely independent of the reporting entity's other income streams. The assets and liabilities include those directly involved in generating the income and an appropriate portion of those used to generate more than one income stream.

Income generating units are identified by dividing the total income of the entity into as many largely independent income streams as is reasonably practicable.

Income generating units should be as small as is reasonably practicable, but the income stream underlying the future cash flows of the unit should be largely independent of other income streams of the entity and should be capable of being monitored separately.

Where there is a large number of small income generating units, it may be appropriate to consider groups of units together.

Example

An entity has a chain of restaurants, each of which is an individual income generating unit. Impairment of individual restaurants is unlikely to be material, but a material impairment may occur if a number of restaurants are affected together by the same economic factors.

In practice, income streams can often be identified by reference to major products or services and unique intangible assets that generate income independently of each other, such as brands.

6.10 Allocating assets and liabilities to income generating units

Each of the identifiable assets and liabilities of the entity, excluding deferred tax balances, interest bearing debt, dividends payable and other items relating wholly to financing, are allocated to an income generating unit.

Central assets

Central assets (for example, assets used by the head office) may have to be apportioned across the units on a logical and systematic basis.

Example

An entity has three independent income streams. The net assets of the income streams are as follows:

A £500,000
B £750,000
C £1,000,000

In addition, there are head office net assets whose carrying amount totals £90,000. The income streams use head office resources in the proportion 2:3:4.

The income generating units are as follows:

	A	*B*	*C*	*Total*
	£'000	£'000	£'000	£'000
Net assets directly attributable to income generating unit	500	750	1,000	2,250
Head office net assets	20	30	40	90
Total	520	780	1,040	2,340

If there were an indication that a fixed asset in unit A was impaired, the recoverable amount of A would be compared with £520,000, rather than £500,000. The cash flows upon which the value in use of A is based should include the relevant portion of any cash outflows arising from central overheads.

Alternative approach to central assets

If it is not possible to apportion central assets meaningfully between income generating units, they may be excluded. If this approach is followed, an additional impairment review must be performed on the excluded central assets. In the example above, if the head office assets were not apportioned between units A, B and C, two separate impairment reviews would be necessary. The recoverable amounts of the individual units would be compared with the carrying amounts of £500,000, £750,000 and £1,000,000 respectively. The recoverable amount of the whole entity would then be compared with its total carrying value of £2,340,000.

Goodwill

Capitalised goodwill should be apportioned between income generating units in the same way as other assets. In practice, where several similar income generating units have been acquired as part of the same investment and are involved in similar parts of the business these may be combined to assess the recoverability of the goodwill.

Example

An entity acquires a business comprising three income generating units, D, E and F. After three years the carrying amount and the value in use of the net assets in the income generating units and the purchased goodwill are as follows:

	D	*E*	*F*	*Goodwill*	*Total*
	£'000	£'000	£'000	£'000	£'000
Carrying amount	240	360	420	150	1,170
Value in use	300	420	360		1,080

No reliable estimates of net realisable value are available.
An impairment loss of £60,000 is recognised on unit F. This reduces its carrying amount to £360,000 and the total carrying amount to £1,110,000 (1,170,000 – 60,000). A further impairment loss of £30,000 must then be recognised in respect of the goodwill (1,110,000 – 1,080,000).

6.11 Allocating impairment losses

Impairment losses may arise in relation to income generating units, rather than individual assets. Sometimes it may be obvious that specific assets are impaired (for example, they may be known to be damaged or obsolete). Otherwise, the loss is allocated to the assets in the income generating unit in the following order:

1. goodwill;
2. other intangible assets;
3. tangible assets (on a pro-rata or more appropriate basis).

This means that the loss is allocated to assets with the most subjective valuations first.

No intangible asset with a readily ascertainable market value should be written down below its net realisable value.

No tangible asset with a net realisable value that can be measured reliably should be written down below its net realisable value.

6.12 Activity

An impairment loss of £60,000 arises in connection with an income generating unit. The carrying amount of the assets in the income generating unit, before the impairment, is as follows:

	£'000
Goodwill	20
Patent (with no market value)	10
Tangible fixed assets	40
	70

6.13 Activity solution

The impairment loss is allocated as follows:

	Before impairment £'000	*Loss* £'000	*After impairment* £'000
Goodwill	20	(20)	–
Patent (with no market value)	10	(10)	–
Tangible fixed assets	40	(30)	10
	70	(60)	10

6.14 Allocation where acquired businesses are merged with existing operations

When an acquired business is merged with an existing business, this may result in an income generating unit that contains both purchased and (unrecognised) internally generated goodwill. In this case, the impairment loss should be allocated as follows:

(a) Estimate the value of the internally generated goodwill of the existing business at the date of merger and add it to the carrying amount of the income generating unit.

(b) Allocate any impairment arising on merging the businesses solely to purchased goodwill within the newly acquired business.

(c) Allocate subsequent impairments pro-rata between the goodwill of the acquired business and that of the existing business.

(d) The impairment allocated to the existing business should be allocated first to the (notional) internally generated goodwill.

(e) Only the impairments allocated to purchased goodwill (and, if necessary, to any other assets) should be charged in the profit and loss account.

Example

An entity has net assets with a carrying amount of £210,000. Value in use has been calculated as £240,000. Several years earlier, the entity had acquired another business. The carrying amount of the purchased goodwill arising on this acquisition is now £20,000. At the time of the acquisition, the original business had internally generated goodwill of £100,000.

Solution

Step 1 Calculate the impairment loss

	£'000
Carrying amount of net assets	210
Carrying amount of purchased goodwill	20
Notional carrying amount of internally generated goodwill	100
	330
Less: value in use	(240)
Impairment loss	90

Step 2 Allocate the loss

	Before impairment £'000	Loss £'000	After impairment £'000
Net assets	210		210
Purchased goodwill	20	(15)	5
Internally generated goodwill	100	(75)	25
	330	(90)	240

The impairment loss of £15,000 relating to purchased goodwill is recognised in the profit and loss account. The loss on internally generated goodwill does not affect the financial statements.

6.15 Subsequent monitoring of cash flows

For the five years following each impairment review where the recoverable amount has been based on value in use, the cash flows achieved should be compared with those forecast. If the actual cash flows are so much less than those forecast that use of the actual cash flows could have required recognition of an impairment in previous periods, the calculation should be re-performed using actual cash flows. Any impairment identified should be recognised in the current period.

6.16 Recognising impairment losses in the financial statements

(a) Assets carried at historic cost

Impairment losses are recognised in the profit and loss account. The impairment is effectively treated as additional depreciation.

(b) Assets which have been revalued

Impairment losses are normally recognised in the statement of total recognised gains and losses until the carrying value of the asset falls below depreciated historical cost. Impairments below depreciated historical cost are recognised in the profit and loss account. The impairment is treated as a downward revaluation.

Where a fixed asset has been revalued but the impairment is caused by a clear consumption of economic benefits (eg, because it is damaged) the loss is recognised in the profit and loss account. This type of impairment is treated as additional depreciation, rather than as a loss in value.

(c) Revision of useful economic life

The remaining useful economic life and residual value of the asset should be reviewed and revised if necessary. The revised carrying amount should be depreciated over the revised estimate of the remaining useful economic life.

Notice that these rules are the same as the rules for recognising revaluation gains and losses (FRS 15).

6.17 Activity

At 1 January 20X7 a fixed asset had a carrying value of £20,000, based on its revalued amount, and a depreciated historical cost of £10,000. An impairment loss of £12,000 arose in the year ended 31 December 20X7.

How should this loss be reported in the financial statements for the year ended 31 December 20X7?

6.18 Activity solution

Assuming that the loss is not a reduction in the service potential of the asset, a loss of £10,000 will be recognised in the statement of total recognised gains and losses and the remaining loss of £2,000 will be recognised in the profit and loss account.

6.19 Reversal of past impairments

After an impairment loss has been recognised, it may reverse. The reversal can only be recognised under certain conditions.

(a) **Tangible fixed assets and investments in subsidiaries, associates and joint ventures**

The reversal of past impairment losses should be recognised only when the recoverable amount of a tangible fixed asset has increased because of a change in economic conditions or in the expected use of the asset.

The reversal should be recognised in the current period's profit and loss account, unless it arises on a previously revalued fixed asset, in which case the reversal should be credited to the revaluation reserve and shown in the statement of total recognised gains and losses.

(b) **Goodwill and intangible assets**

The reversal of an impairment loss should be recognised in the current period, if and only if:

(a) the original loss was caused by an external event and subsequent external events clearly and demonstrably reverse the effects of that event in a way that was not foreseen in the original impairment calculations; or

(b) the loss related to an intangible asset with a readily ascertainable market value and this has increased to above the intangible asset's impaired carrying amount.

In all cases, the reversal of the loss should be recognised to the extent that it increases the carrying amount of the asset up to the amount that it would have been had the original impairment not occurred.

6.20 Activity

An impairment loss of £40 million has arisen in connection with an income generating unit and has been allocated to the net assets in the unit as follows:

	Before impairment	*Loss*	*After impairment*
	£m	£m	£m
Goodwill	20	(20)	–
Patent (with no market value)	10	(10)	–
Tangible fixed assets	40	(10)	30
	70	(40)	30

The original loss arose because the product made by the entity had been overtaken by a technologically more advanced model produced by a competitor. Three years later, the entity develops a technologically more advanced product of its own and the recoverable amount of the income generating unit increases to £45 million. The carrying amount of the tangible fixed assets would have been £35 million had the impairment not occurred.

How is the reversal of the impairment loss recognised in the financial statements?

6.21 Activity solution

The carrying amount of the tangible fixed assets is increased to £35 million, which is the amount that it would have been had the original impairment not occurred. A gain of £5 million is recognised in the profit and loss account.

No reversal of the impairment is recognised in relation to the goodwill and the patent, because the effect of the external event that caused the original impairment has not reversed. The original product has still been overtaken by a more advanced model.

6.22 Presentation and disclosure

(a) Impairment losses recognised in the profit and loss account should be included within operating profit under the appropriate statutory heading. They should be disclosed as an exceptional item if appropriate.

(b) Impairment losses recognised in the statement of total recognised gains and losses should be disclosed separately on the face of that statement.

(c) In the notes to the financial statements in the accounting periods after the impairment, the impairment loss should be treated as follows:

  (i) for assets held on a historical cost basis, the impairment loss should be included within cumulative depreciation: the cost of the asset should not be reduced

  (ii) for revalued assets held at a market value, the impairment loss should be included within the revalued carrying amount.

  (iii) for revalued assets held at depreciated replacement cost, an impairment loss charged to the profit and loss account should be included within cumulative depreciation: the carrying amount of the asset should not be reduced; an impairment loss charged to the statement of total recognised gains and losses should be deducted from the carrying amount of the asset.

(d) Other required disclosures include:

  (i) the discount rate applied (where the impairment loss is based on value in use)

  (ii) the reason for any reversal of an impairment loss recognised in a previous period, including any changes in the assumptions upon which the calculation of recoverable amount is based.

Conclusion Impairment losses are normally recognised in the statement of total recognised gains and losses if the asset has been revalued and the impairment is not due to a consumption of economic benefits. Otherwise impairment losses are recognised in the profit and loss account.

6.23 FRS 11 in practice

Most preparers and users of financial statements support the general principles of FRS 11. In particular, the recoverable amount test means that there is no need to judge whether a diminution is permanent or temporary. Users of financial statements will now be made aware of losses which otherwise might not have been recognised on the grounds that they were 'temporary'.

Impairment reviews may be complex, time consuming and subjective, as they involve forecasting future cash flows. However, the ASB believes that in practice they are likely to be comparatively rare for tangible fixed assets as they are only required if there is some indication of impairment. Where impairment reviews are required, it will only be necessary to calculate value in use if net realisable value is lower than the carrying amount. The impairment review procedures have been field tested by selected large companies as part of the development of the FRS.

However, FRS 11 has also been criticised on the following grounds:

(a) Impairments are classified as additional depreciation or as downward revaluations depending on their cause. This determines whether they are taken to the profit and loss account or to the statement of total recognised gains and losses. In practice, this distinction is likely to be extremely subjective.

(b) The allocation of assets and liabilities to income generating units is also bound to be subjective.

(c) Impairment must be assessed by reference to discounted cash flow. This implies that assets must be included in the balance sheet at amounts that are expected to earn at least a satisfactory rate of return. Some commentators have suggested that even profitable companies may have to write down their assets if they earn a poor rate of return, which seems illogical.

(d) There are inconsistencies with FRS 12 *Provisions, contingent liabilities and contingent assets* (discussed in a later chapter). FRS 12 prohibits the setting up of provisions for future losses (unless these are specifically required by another accounting standard). FRS 11 requires that future cash flows should be taken into account in calculating value in use. This means that projected future losses may be reflected in asset values.

(e) Some critics of the ASB believe that in practice impairment reviews will need to be far more common than it has suggested.

7 SSAP 4 – ACCOUNTING FOR GOVERNMENT GRANTS

7.1 Introduction

SSAP 4 was originally introduced following the advent of regional development grants under the *Industry Act 1972*. These grants were often related to capital expenditure and thus a standard was necessary to state how the grant should be accounted for.

Since the issue of *SSAP 4* the variety of forms of government assistance available to industry has greatly increased: many are discretionary in nature both as to whether they are given at all and as to the amount given. Frequently the terms on which grants are given do not make clear precisely the expenditure to which they are related. The problem facing accountants today is thus how to relate grants to specific expenditure.

An updated revised *SSAP* was therefore issued in July 1990.

Definition **Government** is widely defined to include national government and all tiers of local and regional government. It also includes EC bodies.

Definition **Grants** include cash or transfers of assets.

7.2 General principles

Grants should not be recognised in the profit and loss account until the conditions for receipt have been complied with and there is reasonable assurance that the grant will be received. (This is prudent.)

Subject to this condition, grants should be recognised in the profit and loss account so as to match them with the expenditure towards which they are intended to contribute. (Application of the accruals concept.)

7.3 Revenue grants

In the absence of evidence to the contrary, grants should be assumed to contribute towards the expenditure that is the basis for their payment. The explanatory foreword illustrates this principle by stating that if the grant is paid when evidence is produced that certain expenditure has been incurred, the grant should be matched with that expenditure.

However, if the grant is paid on a different basis, for example achievement of a non-financial objective, such as the creation of a specified number of new jobs, the grant should be matched with the identifiable costs of achieving that objective.

7.4 Capital grants

Grants for fixed asset purchases should be recognised over the expected useful lives of the related assets.

SSAP 4 permits two treatments. The explanatory foreword states that both treatments are acceptable and capable of giving a true and fair view:

(a) write off the grant against the cost of the fixed asset and depreciate the reduced cost; or

(b) treat the grant as a deferred credit and transfer a portion to revenue each year, so offsetting the higher depreciation charge on the original cost.

Method (a) is obviously far simpler to operate. Method (b), however, has the advantage of ensuring that assets acquired at different times and in different locations are recorded on a uniform basis, regardless of changes in government policy.

However, the *CA 1985* requires that fixed assets should be stated at purchase price and this is defined as actual price paid plus any additional expenses. Legal opinion on this matter is that companies should not deduct grants from cost. Thus method (a) may only be adopted by unincorporated bodies.

In practice, it remains to be seen whether companies will stop using method (a). The law was actually implemented in the *CA 1981*, but a large number of companies continue to use the method which contravenes the legislation.

7.5 Other grants

Purpose of grant	*Recognise in profit and loss account*
To give immediate financial support	When receivable
To reimburse previously incurred costs	When receivable
To finance general activities over a period	In relevant period
To compensate for a loss of income	In relevant period

7.6 Contingent liabilities

The explanatory foreword states that enterprises should consider regularly whether there is a likelihood of a breach of conditions on which the grant was made. If such a breach has occurred or appears likely to occur, the likelihood of having to make a repayment should be considered.

If repayment is probable then it should be provided for. It should be accounted for by setting off against any unamortised deferred income relating to the grant. Any excess should be immediately charged to profit and loss account.

7.7 Activity

A Ltd has been awarded government assistance in the form of a training grant. Suggest three ways in which the grant could be accounted for.

7.8 Activity solution

SSAP 4 requires that grants should be matched with expenditure to which it is intended to contribute.

Hence A Ltd could account for the training grant as follows:

(a) Match it against direct training costs.
(b) Match it against employee salary costs over the period of time training takes place.
(c) Take it to profit and loss account over the estimated period during which A Ltd or the employees are expected to benefit from the training.

7.9 Disclosure

The following information should be disclosed:

(a) accounting policy

(b) effects of government grants

- amount credited to profit and loss account
- balance on deferred income account

(c) if other forms of government assistance have had a material effect on the results

- the nature, and
- an estimate of those effects

(d) potential liabilities to repay grants should if necessary be disclosed in accordance with *FRS 12*.

8 INVESTMENTS

8.1 Regulations that come into effect as the status of an investment changes

Investments may be either fixed or current assets depending upon the intention of use by the entity purchasing the investment. The intention may change in time and thus the investment may need to be transferred from fixed to current or vice versa. UITF Abstract 5 may be relevant in this regard (see below).

In addition, the investment may represent equity shares in another company. The shareholding may be of a sufficient percentage to require the consolidation of a subsidiary in the group accounts or the inclusion of the investment under the equity method if it is an associate. Further, there are CA85 disclosure requirements to consider.

8.2 Companies Act requirements

(a) **Accounting principles**

The same principles for arriving at cost apply to all investments except that the purchase price of fungible assets (ie, those which are indistinguishable from one another) may be calculated using an appropriate method such as FIFO, LIFO or weighted average.

If the investment is a fixed asset provision for diminution in value may be made where an investment has fallen in value even though the fall may be temporary. Such a provision must be written back to the extent that it is no longer necessary.

If the investment is a current asset the lower of cost/NRV rule applies.

(b) **Disclosure**

For each category of investments there must be disclosure of the book amount of listed investments.

The market value of listed investments in each category must be given by way of note where it differs from the balance sheet amount. The stock exchange value of any investment must be disclosed where a market value has been taken which is higher than the stock exchange value.

Where at its balance sheet date a company:

(i) Holds 20% or more of any class of shares in another undertaking; or

(ii) Holds shares in another undertaking stated at an amount in excess of 20% of the investing company's total assets. Then it must disclose:

The name of the company;
Country of incorporation if outside Great Britain;
Class of shares and proportion held.

8.3 Transfers from current assets to fixed assets

UITF - Abstract 5

(a) **The issue**

Where at a date subsequent to its original acquisition a current asset is retained for use on a continuing basis in the company's activities it becomes a fixed asset and the question arises as to the appropriate transfer value. An example is a property which is reclassified from trading properties to investment properties.

Of particular concern is the possibility that companies could avoid charging the profit and loss account with write-downs to net realisable value arising on unsold trading assets. This could be done by transferring the relevant assets from current assets to fixed assets at above net realisable value, as a result of which any later write-down might be debited to revaluation reserve.

(b) **UITF consensus**

Where assets are transferred from current to fixed, the current asset accounting rules should be applied up to the effective date of transfer, which is the date of management's change of intent. Consequently the transfer should be made at the lower of cost and net realisable value, and accordingly an assessment should be made of the net realisable value at the date of the transfer and if this is less than its previous carrying value the diminution should be charged in the profit and loss account, reflecting the loss to the company while the asset was held as a current asset.

8.4 Current proposals relating to accounting for investments and their usefulness

ED 55 Accounting for investments was issued in 1990. *ED 55* proposed general rules for accounting for investments (both fixed and current assets). To some extent it has now been superseded by the ASB's financial instruments project (discussed in a later chapter) and it is now unlikely to be adopted in its present form. However, the general principles remain valid.

8.5 Accounting for fixed asset investments

ED 55 proposed that an asset could be stated at cost or valuation (as allowed by the Companies Acts). If an investment is revalued, annual valuations are subsequently required.

8.6 Accounting for current asset investments

The major proposal of *ED 55* was that **readily marketable investments** held as current assets should be included in the balance sheet at their current market value. Any movement in value between balance sheet dates should be included in the profit and loss account as part of income from investments.

This treatment known as **marking to market** is common in investment dealing companies but not in companies generally.

The arguments put forward in support of this policy are:

(a) marking to market provides the most objective means of measuring the financial effect of decisions taken to purchase, hold and sell investments during the period, in terms of both economic reality and consistency;

(b) it eliminates the scope afforded to management under the alternative method of accounting for investments at the lower of cost and net realisable value to manipulate the reported results for the period through decisions on the timing of the disposal of investments;

(c) the market value of an investment is the attribute of the asset that is of most significance both to the management of the enterprise and to those interested in the results or accounts of an enterprise.

Application of this policy involves a departure from the valuation rules of *CA 1985* but *ED 55* justified this on the grounds that it is necessary in order to give a true and fair view.

Other current asset investments follow the *CA 1985* rule, ie, stated at the lower of cost and net realisable value.

8.7 Future developments

The ASB is currently developing an FRS on the measurement of financial instruments. All investments other than investments in subsidiaries, associates and joint ventures will fall within the scope of the new standard.

The ASB's Discussion Paper *Derivatives and other financial instruments* is discussed in a later chapter. Its main proposal is that financial instruments should be measured at current values. In other words, all investments should be marked to market, including those that are not readily marketable and those which are held as fixed assets. The Paper proposes that in most cases movements in value should be taken to the profit and loss account.

9 CHAPTER SUMMARY

There is no single standard dealing with the general topic of fixed assets. The main practical problems arise as a result of the revaluation of assets.

There are two feasible approaches to the treatment of capital grants but companies need to use the deferred credit method.

An investment property is precisely defined and that definition needs to be carefully learned.

10 SELF TEST QUESTIONS

10.1 How is an asset defined in the Statement of Principles? (1.1)

10.2 When may subsequent expenditure be capitalised? (2.6)

10.3 How do FRS 3 and FRS 15 require the calculation of the profit/loss on disposal of a previously revalued asset to be performed? (3.7)

10.4 What happens when asset lives are revised? (4.7)

10.5 Investment properties should be included on the balance sheet at what value? (5.2)

10.6 What is the conflict between SSAP 19 and CA85? (5.10)

10.7 What is the definition of recoverable amount? (6.3)

10.8 How does the prudence principle affect the treatment of grants? (7.2)

10.9 Why should companies follow the deferred credit method of accounting for capital grants? (7.4)

10.10 What is the effect of UITF Abstract 5? (8.3)

11 EXAMINATION TYPE QUESTION

11.1 Properties (London) Ltd

Properties (London) Ltd formed a subsidiary company on 1 January 20X6 called Properties (Brighton) Ltd to purchase and renovate office premises.

During the year ended 31 December 20X6 Properties (Brighton) Ltd obtained a loan of £175,000 from its parent company and used part of these funds to acquire an office block at an address in Brighton.

It proposed to sub-divide this office block into 16 separate units. The following information was available at 31 December 20X6

(i) A loan was obtained from Properties (London) Ltd on 1 January 20X6 of £175,000.

(ii) The Brighton property was acquired for £100,000 of which £35,000 was the value of the land.

(iii) Ten units were renovated at a cost of £60,000.

(iv) Interest of £17,500 was paid to Properties (London) Ltd.

(v) The open market valuation of the partially renovated property in Brighton at 31 December 20X6 was £200,000 of which £50,000 was the value of the land.

(vi) It was estimated that a further £40,000 would be spent by 30 April 20X7 to complete the renovation of the remaining six units.

(vii) An additional loan had been agreed with Properties (London) Ltd of £65,000 receivable on 1 January 20X7 at 10% per annum interest.

(viii) There was estimated interest of £24,000 per year payable to Properties (London) Ltd for the years ended 31 December 20X7 and 20X8.

(ix) Agents advised that they could arrange tenancies for these units at a rental of £2,500 per annum per unit as follows

	4 units on 30 September 20X7
a further	6 units on 31 December 20X7
and the final	6 units on 30 April 20X8

(x) It is estimated that the open market value of the Brighton property will be £275,000 on 31 December 20X7 and £320,000 on 31 December 20X8.

(xi) The balance sheet of the holding company, Properties (London) Ltd as at 31 December 20X6 showed that the holding company had not raised any new finance from loans during the year. The directors of the holding company advise that they do not intend to raise additional loans during 20X7 and 20X8.

The assistant accountant was requested by the finance director to prepare profit and loss account and balance sheet entries on the basis that Properties (Brighton) Ltd would use the office premises in Brighton as its own head office accommodation. He prepared the following draft entries

Balance sheet entries as at 31 December 20X6

	Notes	£
Fixed assets		
Property at valuation	(1)	200,000
Less: Depreciation	(2)	2,500
		£197,500
Revaluation reserve		£40,000

Profit and loss entries for year ended 31 December 20X6

	£
Depreciation	2,500
Interest payable	17,500

Notes:

(1) The property was valued by Messrs Hews on 31 December 20X6.

(2) Depreciation is calculated at 2% of the cost of the buildings (£65,000 + £60,000).

(3) The company does not capitalise finance costs incurred in the construction of tangible fixed assets.

You are required:

(a) to say how far you agree with the draft entries prepared by the assistant accountant and calculate the appropriate entries for 20X6 and 20X7. **(6 marks)**

(b) (i) to show the appropriate entries that would appear in the profit and loss accounts for the years ended 31 December 20X6 and 20X7 and the balance sheets as at those dates in relation to

rental income
interest payable
depreciation
cost of acquisition
cost of renovation
revenue amounts
differences on revaluation.

Give a brief note to explain your treatment on the assumption that Properties (Brighton) Ltd decide to let the units and **not** use them for their own head office. **(13 marks)**

(ii) to draft the accounting policies for the accounting year ended 31 December 20X6 in respect of

income available for distribution
properties
depreciation

on the assumption that the units are let. **(6 marks)**

(Total: 25 marks)

12 ANSWER TO EXAMINATION TYPE QUESTION

12.1 Properties (London) Ltd

(a) If depreciation is charged in 20X6, then the balance sheet entries should be as follows

Either	£
Additions	160,000
Cost c/d	£160,000
Depreciation charge	2,500
Depreciation c/d	£2,500
or	
Additions	160,000
Revaluation	40,000
Valuation c/d	£200,000
Depreciation charge	2,500
Revaluation	(2,500)
Depreciation c/d	-

Since the property is an asset in the course of construction, depreciation need not be charged at all in 20X6.

Appropriate entries for 20X7 would be as follows

Either	£	
Cost b/d	160,000	
Additions	40,000	
Cost c/d	£200,000	
Depreciation b/d	2,500	
Depreciation charge	3,300	
Depreciation c/d	£5,800	
or		
Valuation b/d	200,000	
Additions	40,000	
Revaluation	35,000	
Valuation c/d	£275,000	
Depreciation b/d	-	
Depreciation charge	3,800	being 2% × (150,000 + 40,000)
Revaluation	(3,800)	
	-	

(b) (i) If the units are not used as a head office for Properties (Brighton) Ltd then, once completed, they will be investment properties and will not be subject to depreciation.

Any revaluation surpluses will be included in the investment property revaluation reserve.

	20X7	*20X6*
Profit and loss account	£	£
Rental income	2,500	-
Interest payable	(24,000)	(17,500)
Depreciation	-	-
Balance sheet		
Fixed assets in the course of construction	-	160,000
Fixed assets - investment properties	275,000	-
Investment property revaluation reserve	75,000	-

(ii) **Accounting policies for the year ended 31 December 20X6**

Income available for distribution

The balance on the profit and loss account is available for distribution. The investment property revaluation reserve is not available for distribution.

Properties and depreciation

Properties are included at cost. No depreciation has been charged as the properties are in the course of construction and are to be used as investment properties on completion.

(Tutorial note: *if an accounting policy note for 20X7 for properties and depreciation had been a requirement of this question, then it would state that no depreciation was charged on investment properties in accordance with SSAP 19 and that this was a departure from the requirements of the Companies Act 1985 so as to give a true and fair view.)*

4 INTANGIBLE FIXED ASSETS

INTRODUCTION & LEARNING OBJECTIVES

The accounting for intangible fixed assets has caused considerable problems for standard setters and is a prime area where the lack of a conceptual framework or statement of principles has not allowed specific standards to receive widespread acceptance. The ASB may now have resolved the problem by issuing FRS 10 *Goodwill and intangible assets*.

Goodwill and intangible assets are popular topics for examination questions. Questions on goodwill usually involve group accounting problems and examples of such examination questions will be seen later in the text.

When you have studied this chapter you should be able to do the following:

- Discuss the problems of accounting for goodwill.
- Discuss the issues involved in relation to intangible assets.
- Explain and apply the provisions of FRS 10.
- Explain and apply the provisions of SSAP 13.

1 PROBLEMS OF ACCOUNTING FOR GOODWILL

1.1 Nature of goodwill

FRS 10 contains the following definitions:

Definition **Purchased goodwill** is the difference between the cost of an acquired entity and the aggregate of the fair values of that entity's identifiable assets and liabilities.

Definition **Identifiable assets and liabilities** are the assets and liabilities of an entity that are capable of being disposed of or settled separately, without disposing of a business of the entity.

FRS 10 does not include a definition of fair value, but FRS 7 defines it as follows:

Definition **Fair value** is the amount at which an asset or liability could be exchanged in an arm's length transaction between informed and willing parties, other than in a forced or liquidation sale.

There is an important distinction between purchased and non-purchased goodwill (sometimes called inherent goodwill or internally generated goodwill).

Purchased goodwill arises as a result of a purchase transaction (eg, when one business acquires another as a going concern). The term therefore includes goodwill arising on the inclusion of a subsidiary or associate in the consolidated accounts. Purchased goodwill will be recognised within the accounts because at a specific point in time the fact of purchase has established a figure of value for the business as a whole which can be compared with the fair value of the individual net assets acquired, and this figure will be incorporated in the accounts of the acquiring company as the cost of the acquisition.

Non-purchased, or **inherent goodwill** is any other goodwill. It will not be recognised in the accounts because no event has occurred to identify the value of the business as a whole.

Goodwill has been described as an accounting anomaly. Purchased goodwill arises from a distinct transaction and must be accounted for, yet each method of accounting for it results in inconsistencies with other aspects of financial reporting. No single method is universally accepted as being the correct one.

1.2 Alternative accounting treatments

The possible ways of accounting for purchased goodwill with the major arguments for and against each of them are as follows:

(a) **Carry as an asset, amortised over useful life through the profit and loss account**

Arguments for:

(i) Goodwill is an asset on which capital has been expended in exchange for benefits which will materialise in future periods. Although different in quality and character from other assets, it does exist and can be purchased or sold, and as such it should be treated as an asset.

(ii) The expense of acquiring purchased goodwill should be matched against the extra earnings generated from its acquisition.

(iii) This treatment reflects the way in which purchased goodwill is gradually replaced by inherent goodwill following an acquisition.

Arguments against:

(i) Comparability is lost when one type of goodwill ('purchased') is treated as an asset while another ('non-purchased') is not recognised as such.

(ii) The life of goodwill is difficult to determine and hence the amortisation period is arbitrary.

(iii) Where large sums are spent on maintaining and developing the value of an acquired business, a requirement to amortise a significant part of the investment over an arbitrary period has no economic meaning.

(b) **Eliminate against reserves on acquisition**

Arguments for:

(i) Goodwill is not an asset in the normal sense of the word; it is not independently realisable and many of the factors contributing to it are beyond the control of management. Thus, it is not prudent to carry goodwill as an asset in the balance sheet and, as a once-and-for-all expense of acquisition, it should be written-off as it arises.

(ii) Goodwill will usually be worthless in a forced liquidation.

(iii) The treatment is consistent with that of inherent goodwill (ie, it is not recognised).

Arguments against:

(i) Since consideration has been given, then clearly an asset existed. If so, then it would seem excessively prudent to write it off immediately.

(ii) It is assumed that the accounts are prepared on a going concern basis, which renders point (ii) above irrelevant.

Immediate elimination against reserves was the preferred treatment under SSAP 22, which preceded FRS 10. Long experience of the method highlighted further disadvantages, which are listed in an Appendix to FRS 10:

(i) Immediate elimination of goodwill gives the impression that the acquirer's net worth has been depleted or even eliminated.

(ii) If goodwill is not included in the assets on which a return must be earned, management is not held accountable for the amount that it has invested in goodwill.

(iii) Costs attributed to building up internally generated goodwill are offset against profits in the profit and loss account. The costs of purchased goodwill are not charged in the profit and loss account. This means that companies that grow by acquisition may appear to be more profitable than those that grow organically.

(c) **Carry as a permanent asset unless impairment in value becomes evident**

Arguments for:

(i) Purchased goodwill does not lose value with the passage of time as it should be maintained in the normal course of business.

(ii) Following the principles of *FRS 15* that depreciation should be provided on the cost less the net residual value of an asset, if the goodwill is maintained then net residual value will be equal to or exceed cost so that no write-off will be appropriate.

(iii) The expenditure incurred in the normal course of business to generate inherent goodwill is charged to profit and loss. If purchased goodwill is also depreciated, there will be a double charge.

(iv) This approach recognises that purchased goodwill is neither an identifiable asset like other assets, nor an immediate loss in value. Although purchased goodwill is not in itself an asset, it is part of a larger asset, the investment in another business. Including goodwill as an asset reflects management's success (or otherwise) in maintaining its value and generating a return from its investment.

Arguments against:

(i) Purchased goodwill is not maintained, but over a period of time is consumed and replaced by newly generated inherent goodwill which is not accounted for.

(ii) The residual value of purchased goodwill is nil; it is the inherent goodwill by which it has been replaced which is subsequently valued.

(iii) The expense of maintaining inherent goodwill is a normal trading charge falling on any business; the depreciation of purchased goodwill is the consequence of a business acquisition.

(iv) To establish whether there has been a diminution in value it is necessary to carry out an impairment review. This relies on forecasts of future cash flows and may be subjective. Impairment reviews may also be time consuming and costly. Where goodwill has a finite life, amortisation would provide a much simpler method of reflecting depletion in value.

This method is also contrary to the *CA 1985*, which requires purchased goodwill of an individual company to be treated as an asset subject to depreciation.

(d) **The dangling debit**

Under this approach goodwill is shown as a deduction from the subtotal of share capital and reserves.

Advocates of the 'dangling debit' approach argue that goodwill is not an asset in the normal sense of the word, having no objective value. Goodwill arises only because of the accounting conventions of double entry bookkeeping, and should be presented in such a way as to balance the accounts without creating any accounting entries. The dangling debit gives the fullest possible disclosure and allows the user of accounts to treat it in any way considered appropriate. Investment analysts normally disregard goodwill, and the dangling debit presenting goodwill outside the normal framework of results is in line with this approach.

This method has been rejected by many commentators on the grounds of ambiguity; it is tantamount to writing-off goodwill against reserves while implying that the goodwill remains available as a form of asset. In addition, it is contrary to the *CA 1985*, which does not permit the setting-off of an asset with a liability.

(e) **The separate write off reserve**

This is a development of the dangling debit approach and is designed to overcome the legal problems associated with the dangling debit.

A reserve is created and named as a 'goodwill write-off reserve' or something similar. The goodwill is then charged against this reserve leaving a negative balance equivalent in amount to the goodwill. It is thus effectively the same as the dangling debit approach and thus the same advantages and disadvantages apply. However as it is a reserve there are no CA85 problems as an asset is not being offset against a liability.

1.3 The effect of alternatives on performance ratios

The alternatives in SSAP 22 (which preceded FRS 10) were immediate write off (therefore removing the asset from the balance sheet but no effect on earnings) and amortisation (therefore leaving the NBV of the asset on the balance sheet and reducing earnings).

(a) **Earnings per share**

Amortisation charges decrease the earnings per share.

Thus EPS will be lower if a policy of amortisation is adopted rather than a policy of immediate write off.

(b) **Return on capital employed**

Write off of purchased goodwill reduces capital employed and thus the return on capital employed is higher than when the goodwill is capitalised.

This effect is made more marked by amortisation charges reducing the return.

(c) **Net assets per share**

Net assets per share decreases when goodwill is written off directly to reserves. The ratio can be used as an indication of the extent to which the asset base supports the value of the shares. The goodwill write off can thus cause a misleading impression as the goodwill itself has not fallen in value.

Investment analysts normally overcame the lack of comparability between entities in the past by removing the effects of goodwill from the accounts ie, applying the preferred approach of SSAP 22 in all circumstances and eliminating goodwill in full.

1.4 Negative goodwill

Most purchased goodwill is positive goodwill, that is, the price paid for the entity is more than the total fair values of the net assets acquired. Negative goodwill arises where an entity is purchased for less than the total fair values of its identifiable net assets. This may occur for a number of reasons, for example, a business may be sold at a bargain price because the vendor needs to achieve a quick sale. Alternatively, the purchase price of a business may be reduced to take account of future reorganisation costs or probable future losses.

The possible methods of accounting for negative goodwill are as follows:

(a) **Recognise immediately as a gain in the profit and loss account or the statement of total recognised gains and losses**

The rationale for this treatment is that negative goodwill arises from a bargain purchase. The value of the business acquired is not less than the fair values of its net assets and therefore the purchaser has made a gain.

Arguments against:

(i) Recognition in the profit and loss account contravenes the Companies Acts as the gain is not realised until the assets acquired are depreciated or sold.

(ii) Recognition in the statement of total recognised gains and losses treats the negative goodwill as a revaluation gain, but recognition of a gain on non-monetary assets before they are realised is inconsistent with the requirements of other accounting standards.

(iii) Not all negative goodwill arises from bargain purchases; some is attributable to expected future losses and therefore should not be treated as an immediate 'gain'.

(b) **Take to a capital reserve**

The main argument for this treatment is that negative goodwill is not a liability or deferred income in the normal sense of the word and therefore it should not be treated as such.

The main argument against this treatment is that it artificially inflates reserves and shareholders' funds. Negative goodwill does not represent an actual reserve, and therefore should not be treated as one.

(c) **Eliminate against the fair value of assets acquired**

Arguments for:

(i) It is consistent with the principle that assets should initially be recognised at cost.

(ii) It helps to prevent unrealistically high fair values being assigned to assets whose values are very subjective. True bargain purchases are uncommon and cost may represent a realistic estimate of fair value.

(iii) This method is consistent with much international practice (eg, in the US).

Arguments against:

(i) Fair values can be different from cost and stating assets acquired at lower than their fair values would be inconsistent with FRS 7.

(ii) This method cannot be used where negative goodwill is attributable to future losses.

(d) **Include on the balance sheet and release to the profit and loss account over the periods expected to benefit**

The rationale for this treatment is that it matches negative goodwill with the costs that gave rise to it. It can be used for all negative goodwill, including that attributable to future losses.

The main argument against this method is that any 'amortisation' of negative goodwill is bound to be subjective.

2 PROBLEMS OF DEFINING, RECOGNISING, VALUING AND DEPRECIATING INTANGIBLES

2.1 The problem

To understand the debate it is necessary to consider the context which gave rise to it.

(a) Some companies, following an acquisition, have assigned fair values to intangible assets of various types rather than to goodwill.

Such assets might include brands, publication titles, business names, etc. Companies who make such a classification avoid having to apply the treatment normally required for accounting for goodwill to the assets thus identified, ie, the intangible asset could be carried forward in the balance sheet indefinitely.

(b) There is the possibility that it will become widespread practice to incorporate similar assets in the balance sheet by revaluation rather than by acquisition.

The balance sheet would thus include 'home-grown' intangibles as well as those which had been acquired at a known cost or an assigned fair value.

2.2 Definition

Definition **Intangible assets** are non-financial fixed assets that do not have physical substance but are identifiable and are controlled by the entity through custody or legal rights.

2.3 Brands

The term brand is generally used to mean a conjunction of characteristics which offer the expectation of a stream of enhanced future benefits.

The constituents of a brand include a recognised name, a product or range of products, an established operation and market position, marketing and other specialist know-how, and trading connections.

Brands are seldom traded as bare rights to trade names, rather a brand acquisition includes at least some of the integrated supporting functions.

Thus a brand is a combination of factors expected to produce enhanced earnings just like goodwill. This analysis is further supported by the fact that brands and goodwill are commonly valued using earnings multiples.

There is an argument that brands should be subsumed within goodwill and should not be separately recognised.

No one would deny that intangible assets are of real economic value to businesses, and in certain industry sectors they are of overwhelming importance to the success of the enterprise. The debate is not on that issue; it is on whether it is within the compass of our present accounting model to capture and convey useful information about such assets. By their nature many intangible assets have characteristics which cause accounting difficulty.

2.4 Activity

A case can be made for putting brands on to the balance sheet to disclose to shareholders and others the true value of the assets in the business.

What are the arguments for and against including a value for brand names in the balance sheet?

2.5 Activity solution

The recognition of a value attached to brand names is a recent development in financial reporting. It is a controversial area where arguments for and against the inclusion of brand names as an intangible fixed asset are likely to continue for some time.

There is an argument that brands should be subsumed under the general heading of 'goodwill' and should therefore be accounted for as such. This argument has a certain amount of substance because the brand names of certain companies, particularly in the food industry, will clearly have a bearing on the price that a predator may be prepared to pay for a company acquisition - this price when compared with the fair value of company's net assets will determine the value attached to goodwill. If this argument is accepted then the development of accounting for goodwill will automatically cover the development of accounting for brand names.

The main arguments in favour of including brand names in a company's balance sheet centre on the idea that inclusion will give a fairer presentation of the 'real' value of the company's assets. This inclusion is favoured by companies who consider that the following advantages will follow:

(a) they expect an increase in the share price *(**Note:** this is not true if the efficient market hypothesis is accepted, where the share price will already reflect the fact that a company has brand names of value)*;

(b) the risk of unwelcome take-over bids is reduced;

(c) the cost of raising new capital can be reduced (in 'cost of capital' terms);

(d) it is easier to borrow long term finance because the reserves created by the valuation of brand names reduce the gearing of a company; and

(e) the problems of having to account for what would inevitably be a higher goodwill value are avoided (in the case of purchased brand names).

The arguments against including a value for brand names in the balance sheet centre on two main points:

(a) it is not possible to comply with the basic accounting concepts in reaching a value for brand names, particularly for non-purchased brands. The methodology is likely to be too subjective and not verifiable;

(b) the balance sheet, as it is produced in normal historic cost accounting systems, does not purport to show the 'real' value of a company's net assets.

2.6 The Companies Act requirements relating to intangible fixed assets

Company law has special provisions relating to development expenditure (see later) and goodwill.

The amount of goodwill carried in the balance sheet is subject to special restrictive rules. Only goodwill which was purchased (rather than internally generated) may be carried as an asset. Goodwill cannot be restated under the alternative accounting rules.

As goodwill comes within the heading of fixed assets, it must be written off through the profit and loss account over its useful economic life. In addition the period over which it has been written off and the reasons for choosing that period must be disclosed in a note to the accounts.

3 FRS 10: GOODWILL AND INTANGIBLE ASSETS

3.1 Why a new accounting standard was necessary

FRS 10 was issued in December 1997 and replaced SSAP 22 *Accounting for goodwill.* Most commentators regarded SSAP 22 as unsatisfactory because it permitted a choice between two different accounting treatments. Entities chose the accounting treatment which gave the most favourable view of earnings and net assets. The preferred alternative, immediate elimination against reserves, was criticised for two main reasons:

(a) it gave the impression that the acquirer's net worth had been depleted or eliminated; and
(b) the financial statements overstated the rate of return on acquired investments.

In addition, there was clearly a need for an accounting standard which dealt with other intangible fixed assets. The similarities between goodwill and certain intangible assets such as brand names made it appropriate to consider the two together.

3.2 Objective

The objective of FRS 10 is to ensure that:

(a) capitalised goodwill and intangible assets are charged in the profit and loss account in the periods in which they are depleted; and

(b) sufficient information is disclosed in the financial statements to enable users to determine the impact of goodwill and intangible assets on the financial position and performance of the reporting entity.

Note that the FRS applies to all intangible assets with the exception of:

(a) oil and gas exploration and development costs;
(b) research and development costs (already covered by SSAP 13); and
(c) any other intangible assets that are specifically addressed by another accounting standard.

3.3 Goodwill

(a) Positive purchased goodwill should be capitalised and classified as an intangible fixed asset on the balance sheet.

(b) Internally generated goodwill should not be capitalised.

3.4 Other intangible assets

(a) An intangible asset purchased separately from a business should be capitalised at its cost.

Examples of assets which might be purchased separately from a business include copyrights, patents and licences.

(b) An intangible asset acquired as part of the acquisition of a business should be capitalised separately from goodwill if its value can be measured reliably on initial recognition. It should initially be recorded at its fair value.

(c) If its value cannot be measured reliably, an intangible asset purchased as part of the acquisition of a business should be subsumed within the amount of the purchase price attributable to goodwill.

Most purchased brand names are likely to be subsumed within goodwill, but the ASB has not specifically prohibited their recognition.

(d) An internally developed intangible asset may be capitalised only if it has a readily ascertainable market value.

In practice, very few internally generated intangibles have a readily ascertainable market value. The ASB does not believe that it is possible to determine a market value for unique intangible assets such as brands and publishing titles and so the recognition of internally generated brand names is effectively prohibited.

This treatment of internally generated intangible assets is consistent with the treatment of internally generated goodwill. If it is accepted that internally generated goodwill is never recognised because it cannot be valued objectively, it follows that internally generated brand names should not be recognised either.

3.5 Activity

How should the following intangible assets be treated in the financial statements?

(a) a publishing title acquired as part of a subsidiary company
(b) a licence to market a new product.

3.6 Activity solution

(a) The answer depends on whether the asset can be valued reliably. Although the ASB believes that unique intangible assets cannot have a market value it acknowledges that there are techniques that can be used for estimating values indirectly (eg, indicators based on multiples of turnover). If this is possible, the title will be recognised at its fair value, otherwise it will be treated as part of goodwill.

(b) Assuming that the licence has been purchased separately from a business, it should be capitalised at cost.

Conclusion Positive purchased goodwill should be included in the balance sheet as an intangible fixed asset. Other intangible assets may be recognised if they can be reliably valued.

3.7 Amortisation

Once they have been recognised, FRS 10 requires that intangible assets are treated in exactly the same way as goodwill. There are two reasons for this:

(a) Even if assets such as brand names are not part of goodwill, they are so similar to goodwill that they should be accounted for in the same way.

(b) If intangibles must be treated in the same way as goodwill, there is no longer any advantage in separately recognising brand names and similar assets.

Standard accounting practice

(a) Where goodwill and intangible assets are regarded as having limited useful economic lives, they should be amortised on a systematic basis over those lives.

(b) There is a rebuttable presumption that the useful economic lives of purchased goodwill and intangible assets are limited to 20 years or less.

(c) Where access to the economic benefits associated with an intangible asset is achieved through legal rights that have been granted for a finite period, the economic life of the asset may extend beyond that period only if the legal rights are renewable and renewal is assured.

(d) A residual value may be assigned to an intangible asset only if the residual value can be measured reliably. No residual value may be assigned to goodwill.

(e) The straight line method of amortisation should normally be used unless another method can be demonstrated to be more appropriate.

(f) The useful economic lives of goodwill and intangible assets should be reviewed at the end of each reporting period and revised if necessary.

(g) If a useful economic life is revised, the carrying value of the goodwill or intangible asset at the date of revision should be amortised over the remaining useful economic life.

3.8 Where useful economic life is longer than 20 years

In most cases, goodwill and intangible assets will probably be amortised over a period of less than 20 years. However, FRS 10 does recognise that they may occasionally have longer useful economic lives or that their lives may even be indefinite.

A useful economic life may be regarded as longer than 20 years or indefinite if:

(a) the durability of the acquired business or intangible asset can be demonstrated and justifies estimating the useful economic life to exceed 20 years; and

(b) the goodwill or intangible asset is capable of continued measurement (so that annual impairment reviews will be feasible).

Where goodwill and intangible assets are regarded as having indefinite useful economic lives, they should not be amortised.

Note that the Companies Acts do not allow purchased goodwill or intangible assets to be carried indefinitely as assets in the balance sheet. If goodwill and intangible assets are not amortised it will be necessary to make the additional disclosures required by UITF Abstract 7, as the 'true and fair view override' will be invoked.

3.9 Impairment reviews

Impairment reviews are required as follows:

(a) **Where goodwill and intangible assets are amortised over 20 years or less**

  (i) At the end of the first full financial year following the acquisition; and

  (ii) in other periods if events or changes in circumstances indicate that the carrying value may not be recoverable.

(b) **Where goodwill and intangible assets are amortised over more than 20 years**

  Impairment reviews are required at the end of each reporting period.

If the review indicates that there has been a diminution in value, the goodwill and intangible assets must be written down accordingly. The revised carrying value should be amortised over the current estimate of the remaining useful economic life (unless the asset is not being amortised because it has an indefinite life). This is similar to the treatment of tangible fixed assets where there has been an impairment in value.

The ASB has now issued FRS 11 *Impairment of fixed assets and goodwill.* Impairment reviews should be carried out in accordance with the requirements of this accounting standard.

3.10 Revaluation and restoration of past losses

Goodwill and intangible assets should not be revalued, either to increase the carrying value above original cost or to reverse prior period losses arising from impairment or amortisation, unless:

(a) the asset has a readily ascertainable market value; or

(b) an impairment loss was caused by an external event (eg, a change in economic conditions) and subsequent external events clearly and demonstrably reverse the loss in a way that was not foreseen in the original impairment calculations. (If the recoverable amount is increased above the asset's carrying value, the increase must be recognised in the current period.)

If one intangible asset is revalued, all assets of the same class should be revalued. Once an intangible asset has been revalued, further revaluations should be performed regularly.

The amortisation charge for revalued assets should be based on the revalued amount and the remaining useful economic lives (as for tangible fixed assets).

3.11 Negative goodwill

(a) Negative goodwill should be recognised and separately disclosed on the face of the balance sheet, immediately below the goodwill heading and followed by a subtotal showing the net amount of the positive and negative goodwill.

(b) Negative goodwill up to the fair values of the non-monetary assets (fixed assets and stocks) acquired should be recognised in the profit and loss account in the periods in which the non-monetary assets are recovered, whether through depreciation or sale.

(c) Any negative goodwill in excess of the fair values of the non-monetary assets acquired should be recognised in the profit and loss account in the periods expected to be benefited.

Negative goodwill is not expected to arise frequently.

3.12 Activity

On 1 January 20X6 A plc acquires the whole of the share capital of B Ltd for £100,000. The summarised balance sheet of B Ltd at the date of acquisition is as follows:

	£
Fixed assets (depreciated over 5 years)	130,000
Stocks	30,000
Other current assets	10,000
Current liabilities	(20,000)
	150,000

What is the credit to the profit and loss account for negative goodwill for the year ended 31 December 20X6?

3.13 Activity solution

Negative goodwill is £50,000 (150,000 – 100,000).

	£
Non-monetary assets recovered:	
Fixed assets (depreciated over 5 years)	26,000
Stocks (assumed sold during the year)	30,000
	56,000

Amortisation: $\frac{56}{160} \times 50{,}000 = £17{,}500$

Conclusion Goodwill and intangible assets should normally be amortised over a period of 20 years or less, but may be amortised over a longer period or maintained in the balance sheet indefinitely provided that certain conditions are met.

3.14 Disclosures

Recognition and measurement

Main disclosures:

(a) Describe the method used to value intangible assets.

(b) Disclose the following information separately for positive goodwill, negative goodwill and each class of intangible asset included on the balance sheet:

   (i) cost or revalued amount at the beginning of the financial period and at the balance sheet date;

   (ii) the cumulative amount of provisions for amortisation and impairment at the beginning of the financial period and at the balance sheet date;

   (iii) a reconciliation of the movements; and

   (iv) the net carrying amount at the balance sheet date.

(c) The profit and loss on each material disposal of a previously acquired business or business segment.

Amortisation

Disclose the following:

(a) Methods and periods of amortisation of goodwill and intangible assets and the reasons for choosing those periods.

(b) Details of changes in amortisation period or method.

(c) Grounds for amortising goodwill or intangible assets over a period that exceeds 20 years (if applicable).

Revaluation

Where assets have been revalued, disclose:

(a) the year in which the assets were valued, the values and the bases of valuation;

(b) the original cost or fair value and the amount of any provision for amortisation that would have been recognised if the assets had been valued at their original cost or fair value;

(c) the name and qualifications of the valuer (where the revaluation has taken place during the year).

Negative goodwill

(a) Disclose the periods in which negative goodwill is being written back in the profit and loss account.

(b) Where negative goodwill exceeds the fair values of the non-monetary assets, the amount and source of the 'excess' negative goodwill and the periods in which it is being written back should be explained.

FRS 6 *Acquisitions and mergers* requires the following additional disclosures:

(a) A table should be provided showing, for each class of assets and liabilities of the acquired entity:

(i) the book values, as recorded in the acquired entity's books immediately before the acquisition and before any fair value adjustments;

(ii) the fair value adjustments, analysed into

(1) revaluations
(2) adjustments to achieve consistency of accounting policies, and
(3) any other significant adjustments,

giving the reasons for the adjustments; and

(iii) the fair values at the date of acquisition.

The table should include a statement of the amount of purchased goodwill or negative goodwill arising on the acquisition.

(b) Where the fair values of the identifiable assets or liabilities, or the purchase consideration, can be determined only on a provisional basis at the end of the accounting period in which the acquisition took place, this should be stated and the reasons given. Any subsequent material adjustments to such provisional fair values, with corresponding adjustments to goodwill, should be disclosed and explained.

4 EVALUATION OF FRS 10

The issue of FRS 10 follows years of heated debate. Many people believed that the ASB would be unable to produce an accounting standard which would gain the support of preparers and users of accounts.

In order to attempt to obtain a consensus, the ASB discussed its proposals with interested parties at a series of public meetings. In addition, some large companies tested the proposed accounting treatments, including the impairment review procedures. Perhaps because of these attempts, FRS 10 has been cautiously welcomed.

Advantages

(a) FRS 10 recognises that purchased goodwill is neither an identifiable asset nor an immediate loss in value.

(b) In theory, goodwill can be carried forward indefinitely. It can be argued that this approach reflects economic reality. Entities can avoid an amortisation charge to the profit and loss account by carrying out impairment reviews.

(c) FRS 10 recognises that there are many different types of intangible asset with different characteristics. Some of these can be measured reliably and are clearly separable from goodwill.

(d) There is consistency between the treatment of goodwill and other intangible assets.

(e) The introduction of an accounting standard dealing with intangibles will reduce the scope for creative accounting. Entities will not be able to recognise internally generated intangibles.

Criticisms

(a) Only for large public companies will the benefit of maintaining goodwill on the balance sheet outweigh the costs and practical problems of carrying out annual impairment reviews. Smaller companies will almost certainly amortise goodwill. The ultimate success of the standard may depend on the effectiveness of the impairment review procedure if they are widely applied.

(b) The tests for impairment will also be subjective and might provide entities with scope for creative accounting.

(c) It will be difficult to compare the financial statements of entities which amortise goodwill and intangibles and those which carry out impairment tests.

(d) Where entities opt to carry out impairment tests, earnings may be volatile.

(e) The treatment of negative goodwill has been criticised in that it effectively creates a 'dangling credit' in the balance sheet. The 'amortisation' of negative goodwill may also be complicated to apply in practice.

5 RESEARCH AND DEVELOPMENT COSTS

5.1 SSAP 13 – Research and development

SSAP 13 was first issued in 1977 and revised in January 1989.

The term **research and development** can be used to cover a wide range of activity. *SSAP 13* follows the OECD classification in defining three broad areas of activity:

(a) **Pure (or basic) research:** experimental or theoretical work undertaken primarily to acquire new scientific or technical knowledge for its own sake rather than directed towards any specific aim or application.

(b) **Applied research:** original or critical investigation undertaken in order to gain new scientific or technical knowledge and directed towards a specific practical aim or objective.

(c) **Development:** use of scientific or technical knowledge in order to produce new or substantially improved materials, devices, products or services, to install new processes or systems prior to the commencement of commercial production or commercial applications, or to improving substantially those already produced or installed.

Development is therefore concerned with the introduction of new products or processes.

5.2 Classification of costs

Expenditure on research and development does not consist only of the salaries of scientists or the cost of test tubes. Many costs can properly be regarded as being incurred for research and development purposes. These include:

(a) Costs of materials.
(b) Salaries, wages, and other employment costs of workers involved in research and development.
(c) Depreciation of scientific and other equipment and land and buildings.
(d) A proportion of overhead costs.
(e) Related costs, such as patents, licence fees, etc.

5.3 Accounting problems

The problems in accounting for research and development revolve around two of the fundamental accounting concepts: accruals and prudence.

(a) **Pure and applied research**

Under the accruals concept, income is matched with the costs involved in generating that income. Yet how can expenditure on pure and applied research be matched with any particular period's income? There may be no direct benefit from the expenditure, or it may benefit many periods. Expenditure on pure and applied research can, therefore, be regarded as part of the continuing cost of running the business. Since no one period can be expected to benefit more than another, such expenditure should be written off as incurred. Carrying expenditure forward to future periods would conflict not only with the accruals concept, but with prudent accounting practice.

(b) **Development expenditure**

In the case of development expenditure, it is likely that future income, or cost reduction, can be directly attributable to a development project. An example of this is a motor car manufacturer who is developing a new model of car. He is incurring costs now in the expectation that they will be recovered from future sales of the car. On the accruals basis, such expenditure should not be written off against current year's income, but carried forward and set against income from the project in future years.

However, prudence dictates that it is impossible to determine whether future benefits will arise from a development project unless the project and its related expenditure are clearly identifiable. *SSAP 13* therefore concludes that development expenditure should normally be written off as incurred, but *may* be carried forward in certain circumstances.

5.4 SSAP 13 requirements

The cost of fixed assets acquired or constructed in order to provide facilities for research and development activities over a number of accounting periods should be capitalised and written off over their useful lives through the profit and loss account.

Expenditure on pure and applied research (other than that referred to in the previous paragraph) should be written off in the year of expenditure through the profit and loss account.

Development expenditure should be written off in the year of expenditure except in the following circumstances when it may be deferred to future periods:

(a) there is a clearly defined project; and

(b) the related expenditure is separately identifiable; and

(c) the outcome of such a project has been assessed with reasonable certainty as to:

   (i) its technical feasibility; and

   (ii) its ultimate commercial viability considered in the light of factors such as likely market conditions (including competing products), public opinion, consumer and environmental legislation; and

(d) the aggregate of the deferred development costs, any further development costs, and related production, selling and administration costs is reasonably expected to be exceeded by related future sales or other revenues; and

(e) adequate resources exist, or are reasonably expected to be available, to enable the project to be completed and to provide any consequential increases in working capital.

In the foregoing circumstances development expenditure may be deferred to the extent that its recovery can reasonably be regarded as assured.

If an accounting policy of deferral of development expenditure is adopted, it should be applied to all development projects that meet the criteria above.

Paras 23-27 SSAP 13

Development expenditure may also be carried forward where companies enter into a firm contract to carry out development work on behalf of third parties on such terms that the related expenditure is to be fully reimbursed (*para 17 SSAP 13*). Such expenditure should be included in work-in-progress.

5.5 Further problems with development expenditure

If development expenditure is deferred to future periods, three further problems arise:

(a) How and when should the expenditure be written off?
(b) What should be done if circumstances surrounding the project change?
(c) How should development expenditure be shown in the balance sheet?

These problems are considered in turn.

5.6 Writing off deferred development expenditure

The aim in carrying forward such expenditure is to match it against future benefits arising from the developed product. This can be in the form either of revenue from the sale of the product, or of reduced costs from improved production processes.

Deferred development expenditure should be matched against benefits in a sensible and consistent manner. It is not enough to write off the expenditure over an arbitrary number of years: writing off should start when the product begins to be produced commercially.

SSAP 13 states:

If development costs are deferred to future periods, they should be amortised. The amortisation should commence with the commercial production or application of the product, service, process or system and should be allocated on a systematic basis to each accounting period, by reference to either the sale or use of the product, service, process or system or the period over which these are expected to be sold or used.

Para 28 SSAP 13

5.7 Activity

I plc has deferred development expenditure of £600,000 relating to the development of Brand X. It is expected that the demand for the product will stay at a high level for the next three years. Annual sales of 400,000, 300,000 and 200,000 units respectively are expected over this period. Brand X sells for £10.

Suggest two possibilities for writing off the development expenditure.

5.8 Activity solution

(a) In equal instalments over the three year period, ie, £200,000 pa; or

(b) In relation to total sales expected (900,000 units):

				£
Year 1	$\frac{400,000}{900,000}$	× £600,000	=	266,667
Year 2	$\frac{300,000}{900,000}$	× £600,000	=	200,000
Year 3	$\frac{200,000}{900,000}$	× £600,000	=	133,333

5.9 Changing circumstances

Development expenditure should only be carried forward if there is a reasonable chance of setting it against income in the future, ie, if the conditions mentioned above are met. If circumstances change, it may be necessary to write off the expenditure at once, on the basis of prudent accounting.

This can occur in a number of situations, including:

(a) the arrival of possible competing products;
(b) changes in the general economic climate;
(c) changes in legislation, such as consumer or environmental changes.

If brought forward development expenditure is written off, it should not be regarded as a charge against prior years' profits.

SSAP 13 states that 'Deferred development expenditure should be reviewed at the end of each accounting period and where the circumstances which have justified the deferral of the expenditure no longer apply, or are considered doubtful, the expenditure, to the extent to which it is considered to be irrecoverable, should be written off immediately project by project.'

Para 29 SSAP 13

5.10 Accounting presentation

'The accounting policy on research and development expenditure should be stated and explained.

The total amount of research and development expenditure charged in the profit and loss account should be disclosed, analysed between the current year's expenditure and amounts amortised from deferred expenditure.

Movements on deferred development expenditure and the amount carried forward at the beginning and the end of the period should be disclosed. Deferred development expenditure should be disclosed under intangible fixed assets in the balance sheet.'

Paras 30-32 SSAP 13

The requirement to disclose the expenditure charged in the profit and loss account does *not* apply to 'small' unquoted companies. A small company here is one which satisfies the criteria (multiplied in each case by ten) for defining a medium-sized company under the *CA 1985* abbreviated accounts provisions.

Thus all quoted companies and large unquoted companies have to disclose the information.

5.11 Companies Act requirements

The *Companies Act 1985* requires deferred development expenditure to be included as an intangible fixed asset.

5.12 Applying SSAP 13 and CA85 disclosure requirements

An example of an appropriate note to the balance sheet would be as follows:

	£'000	£'000
Deferred development expenditure b/d		320
Expenditure incurred in the period	70	
Expenditure written off in the period	(64)	
		6
Deferred development expenditure c/d		326

The profit and loss account or a note to the profit and loss account would disclose the **total** amount of research and development expenditure. For example:

	£'000
Research and development expenditure:	
Expenditure charged in year	130
Development expenditure amortised	64
	194

The £130,000 does not include the £70,000 appearing in the balance sheet note as this has not been charged in the profit and loss account.

5.13 The conceptual validity of current practice of treating R&D expenditure

The current practice of allowing a choice can easily be criticised. Accounting standards should reduce/eliminate choice where appropriate. Users would be happier with being supplied with more information about R&D rather than the company complying with a set of formalised rules to decide whether development expenditure should be carried forward.

Companies are required to disclose the amounts spent each year. Further disclosures would be useful of the success or otherwise of past expenditure in creating new products and generating additional sales. Some companies' long-term survival is dependent on successful development of new products and therefore it would seem appropriate to have this information available to the investor.

6 CHAPTER SUMMARY

FRS 10 requires that positive purchased goodwill is included in the balance sheet as an intangible fixed asset. Other intangible assets may be included in the balance sheet if they can be reliably valued. Goodwill and intangible assets should normally be amortised over a period of 20 years or less, but may be amortised over a longer period or maintained in the balance sheet indefinitely provided that certain conditions are met.

SSAP 13 allows a choice of accounting treatment for development expenditure - immediate write off or carry forward if six conditions are satisfied.

7 SELF TEST QUESTIONS

7.1 What is the definition of identifiable assets and liabilities? (1.1)

7.2 How should non-purchased goodwill be accounted for? (1.1)

7.3 What is the 'dangling debit'? (1.2)

7.4 What is a brand? (2.3)

7.5 Why has the ASB decided that all intangible fixed assets should be treated in the same way as goodwill? (3.7)

7.6 How should negative goodwill be accounted for? (3.11)

7.7 What are the advantages of the requirements of FRS 10 ? (4)

7.8 What conditions must be satisfied before SSAP 13 allows the capitalisation of development costs? (5.4)

8 EXAMINATION TYPE QUESTION

8.1 Intangible assets

During recent years there has been a significant amount of debate regarding the accounting treatment of intangible assets.

You are required

(a) to state briefly the requirements of FRS 10 regarding the accounting treatment of intangible assets other than goodwill. **(5 marks)**

(b) to outline the main areas of concern regarding accounting for intangible assets. **(10 marks)**

(Total: 15 marks)

9 ANSWER TO EXAMINATION TYPE QUESTION

9.1 Intangible assets

(a) Purchased intangible assets should be capitalised as intangible fixed assets. Internally generated intangible assets should only be capitalised where they have a readily ascertainable market value.

Where intangible assets have limited lives (the usual situation), they must be amortised through the profit and loss account over their expected lives.

There is a general rebuttable presumption that the lives of intangible assets do not exceed 20 years. A longer (or even indefinite) life can be assigned only if the durability of the asset can be demonstrated and it is possible to remeasure its value each year (so that annual impairment reviews can be performed).

Amortisation is not required for assets that can be justified as having indefinite lives. They need be written down only if they are impaired ie, their recoverable amount (the higher of net realisable value and value in use) falls below their carrying value.

Impairment reviews must be performed annually where lives of more than 20 years are chosen. For lives of less than 20 years, they are required only in the year after acquisition, and in other years if there is some indication that the asset's value might have fallen below its carrying value.

(b) There are three main areas of concern regarding the accounting for intangible fixed assets:

(i) when such assets should be recognised.
(ii) the valuation to be adopted.
(iii) the period of amortisation to be adopted.

Recognition

It can be argued that users of financial statements need information on *all* the assets controlled by an entity. Financial statements which do not include intangible assets such as goodwill and brands do not show a true and fair view.

However, there is an essential difficulty because intangible assets have no physical substance. Therefore, judgement is required to determine whether they should be recognised in the financial statements. This is an argument against recognising some types of intangible fixed assets.

The ASB's Statement of Principles defines an asset as rights or other access to future economic benefits controlled by an entity as a result of past transactions or events. According to the Statement of Principles, an asset should be recognised if there is sufficient evidence that a change in assets and liabilities has occurred and if the asset can be measured at a monetary amount with sufficient reliability.

Most intangible assets would probably meet the definition of an asset. Only where the historic costs of creating or acquiring an asset are known is it capable of being measured with sufficient reliability. Purchased intangibles would therefore meet the recognition tests. Development expenditure meeting the criteria for deferral under SSAP 13 would also meet the recognition tests, although applying the criteria involves judgement about future events.

Under FRS 10, non-purchased goodwill and internally generated intangibles should not be recognised in the balance sheet.

Valuation

In order for an asset to be recognised in the financial statements, it is necessary to measure its value.

FRS 10 requires that purchased intangible assets should be recognised separately from purchased goodwill, provided their fair value can be measured reliably on initial recognition.

The recognition of intangibles such as brands has been controversial because the measurement of their value is often unavoidably subjective. For this reason, FRS 10 prohibits the recognition of internally generated intangibles.

FRS 7 *Fair values in acquisition accounting* gives guidance on arriving at the fair value of an intangible asset. This should be based on its replacement cost, which is normally its estimated market value. In practice, it is likely to be difficult to determine the replacement cost of (for example) a brand name.

One solution may be to value intangibles at their historic cost. However, it may be sometimes difficult to determine the cost of some intangible assets.

Some commentators believe that most intangible assets are indistinguishable from goodwill. Goodwill is defined as the difference between the value of the business as a whole and the aggregate of the fair values of its identifiable net assets. This means that the value of goodwill depends on the valuation of other assets, which may be subjective. The issue of FRS 7 has provided guidance on valuing assets in this situation and has greatly reduced the scope for manipulation of fair values (and therefore the manipulation of the valuation of goodwill).

Amortisation

The Companies Act states that all fixed assets having a finite economic life must be amortised.

Traditional accounting practice would prohibit entities from carrying intangible fixed assets indefinitely in the balance sheet. Amortisation is a means of matching the cost or value of the asset with the accounting periods expected to benefit from its existence. It can be argued that purchased intangibles diminish in value over time (they may be replaced by internally generated intangibles).

It can be argued that some types of intangibles do not have a finite economic life and that it would therefore be inappropriate to amortise them. Matching an intangible asset with the benefits arising from it may also be difficult in practice.

FRS 10 requires that intangible assets should normally be amortised over 20 years or less. Intangible assets may be amortised over a longer period, or carried in the balance sheet indefinitely, if their value is significant and is expected to be capable of continued measurement in future. If intangible assets are amortised over a period longer than 20 years impairment reviews should be performed annually to ensure that they are not carried at above their recoverable amounts.

5 STOCKS AND LONG-TERM CONTRACTS

INTRODUCTION & LEARNING OBJECTIVES

Stocks and WIP should be familiar to you from earlier studies. This chapter concentrates on long-term contracts which is the main area that will be tested at this level.

When you have studied this chapter you should be able to do the following:

- Explain the provisions of SSAP 9
- Perform calculations for items to appear in the financial statements for long-term contracts.

1 THE REQUIREMENTS OF SSAP 9 AND THE COMPANIES ACT FOR STOCK

1.1 SSAP 9

SSAP 9 was issued in 1975 and revised in 1988 in respect of the accounting treatment of long-term contracts.

The contents and principles of SSAP 9 for stocks excluding long-term contracts should be well known to you and thus only key points are included here.

1.2 Lower of cost and NRV

(a) **Cost**

(i) Cost of bringing stock to its present location and condition (cost of purchase and costs of conversion)

(ii) Cost of purchase comprises purchase price including import duties, transport and handling costs and any other directly attributable costs, less trade discounts, rebates and subsidies.

(iii) Cost of conversion comprises

(A) costs which are specifically attributable to units of production eg, direct labour, direct expenses and sub-contracted work.

(B) production overheads.

(C) other overheads, if any, attributable in the particular circumstances of the business to bringing the product or service to its present location and condition.

(iv) Production overhead must be based on a normal level of activity.

(b) **Net realisable value (NRV)**

Actual or estimated selling price less all costs to complete (ie, including all costs to be incurred in marketing, selling and distribution).

1.3 Valuation methods

(a) **Acceptable under SSAP 9**

1. FIFO
2. Unit cost
3. Average cost

In certain circumstances

4. Standard cost
5. Adjusted selling price

(b) **Unacceptable under SSAP 9**

1. LIFO
2. Replacement cost
3. Base cost

1.4 Disclosure

(a) Lower of cost/NRV of the separate items of stock or of groups of similar items

(b) Classify according to CA85 headings

1. Raw materials
2. Work-in-progress
3. Finished goods and goods for resale
4. Payments on account

1.5 The circumstances when net realisable values are likely to be relevant

The principal situations in which net realisable value is likely to be less than cost are where there has been:

(a) an increase in costs or a fall in selling price;
(b) physical deterioration of stocks;
(c) obsolescence of products;
(d) a decision as part of a company's marketing strategy to manufacture and sell products at a loss;
(e) errors in production or purchasing.

Furthermore, when stocks are held which are unlikely to be sold within the turnover period normal in that company (ie, excess stocks), the impending delay in realisation increases the risk that the situations outlined in (a) to (c) above may occur before the stocks are sold and needs to be taken into account in assessing net realisable value.

1.6 Activity

S Ltd trades in two products known as alpha and beta. The product alpha is purchased from abroad in a form suitable for resale. The product beta is raw material used in the construction of beta-flange.

You are given the following information relating to S Ltd for the year ended 30 September 20X8:

Alpha

Stock at 1 October 20X7	200 units @ £14 each		
	Receipts (units)	*Unit Price* (£)	*Issues (units)*
November 20X7	120	15	
January 20X8			150

February 20X8	150	18	
March 20X8			220
May 20X8	110	20	
July 20X8			80

At 30 September 20X8 it is estimated that an alpha could be sold for £19. S Ltd uses a FIFO method of stock valuation.

Beta

At 30 September 20X8 the company had 150 tons of beta in stock. This cost the company £26 per ton and could be resold in its raw state at £15 per ton or as part of a beta-flange which has a selling price of £12 per unit.

Beta-flange

At 30 September 20X8 there were 6,000 finished units of stock in hand but no work-in-progress. Each ton of beta forms 10 beta-flanges, after direct labour of 2 hours per ton of beta has been expended. Standard labour costs are £10 per hour. Factory overheads are absorbed at the rate of £4 an hour assuming normal output of 800,000 man hours. Due to industrial disputes and machine breakdowns only 550,000 man hours were worked during the year. In addition, the sales department incurs costs of £2 per hour relating to their advertising and customer liaison functions.

Compute the value of stock that would appear in the balance sheet of S Ltd at 30 September 20X8.

1.7 Activity solution

Stock of alpha

Units b/fwd	200
Receipts (120 + 150 + 110)	380
	580
Issues (150 + 220 + 80)	450
Units c/fwd	130

		Cost	*NRV*	*Lower*
		£	£	£
Units purchased May	110	2,200	2,090	2,090
Units purchased February	20	360	380	360
	130			2,450

Note: *SSAP 9* requires the lower of cost and NRV rule to be adopted for each item and not globally.

Stock of beta

150 tons at actual cost of £26 per ton	= £3,900

Stock of beta-flanges

Unit cost of a beta-flange

	£
Raw material (£26 per ton for 10 units)	2.60
Direct labour (£10 × 0.2 hours)	2.00

Overheads (£4 × 0.2 hours)	0.80
	5.40
Stock at cost 6,000 × £5.40	£32,400
NRV is above cost	£
Selling price per unit	12.00
Selling costs (£2 × 0.2)	0.40
	11.60

Summary

Stocks and work-in-progress

	£
Raw materials (2,450 + 3,900)	6,350
Finished goods	32,400
	38,750

2 LONG-TERM CONTRACT WORK-IN-PROGRESS

2.1 Introduction

Definition SSAP 9 defines a long-term contract as 'a contract entered into for the design, manufacture or construction of a single substantial asset or the provision of a service (or of a combination of assets or services which together constitute a single project) where the time taken substantially to complete the contract is such that the contract activity falls into different accounting periods.'

A contract that is required to be accounted for as long-term by *SSAP 9* will usually extend for a period exceeding one year. However, a duration exceeding one year is not an essential feature of a long-term contract. Some contracts with a shorter duration than one year should be accounted for as long-term contracts if they are sufficiently material to the activity of the period that not to record turnover and attributable profit would lead to a distortion of the period's turnover and results such that the financial statements would not give a true and fair view, provided that the policy is applied consistently within the reporting entity and from year to year.

In addition we need to recognise the nature of the assets and liabilities that arise during the contract period. The assets will change in nature from stocks to debtors (amounts recoverable on contracts). This change results in detailed accounting procedures and disclosure requirements.

The relevant parts of the standard are set out in full below together with some definitions. We will then see how the amounts to be shown in the financial statements are calculated.

2.2 Standard accounting practice for long-term contracts

(a) Long-term contracts should be assessed on a contract by contract basis and reflected in the profit and loss account by recording turnover and related costs as contract activity progresses. Turnover is ascertained in a manner appropriate to the stage of completion of the contract, the business and the industry in which it operates.

(b) Where it is considered that the outcome of a long-term contract can be assessed with reasonable certainty before its conclusion, the prudently calculated attributable profit should be recognised in the profit and loss account as the difference between the reported turnover and related costs for that contract.

(c) Long-term contracts should be disclosed in the balance sheet as follows:

(i) the amount by which recorded turnover is in excess of payments on account should be classified as 'amounts recoverable on contracts' and separately disclosed within debtors;

(ii) the balance of payments on account (in excess of amounts (i) matched with turnover; and (ii) offset against long-term contract balances) should be classified as payments on account and separately disclosed within creditors;

(iii) the amount of long-term contracts, at costs incurred, net of amounts transferred to cost of sales, after deducting foreseeable losses and payments on account not matched with turnover, should be classified as 'long-term contract balances' and separately disclosed within the balance sheet heading 'Stocks'. The balance sheet note should disclose separately the balances of:

- net cost less foreseeable losses; and
- applicable payments on account;

(iv) the amount by which the provision or accrual for foreseeable losses exceeds the costs incurred (after transfers to cost of sales) should be included within either provisions for liabilities and charges or creditors as appropriate.

Definition **Attributable profit** is that part of the total profit currently estimated to arise over the duration of the contract, after allowing for estimated remedial and maintenance costs and increases in costs so far as not recoverable under the terms of the contract, that fairly reflects the profit attributable to that part of the work performed at the accounting date. (There can be no attributable profit until the profitable outcome of the contract can be assessed with reasonable certainty.)

Definition **Foreseeable losses** are those losses which are currently estimated to arise over the duration of the contract (after allowing for estimated remedial and maintenance costs and increases in costs so far as not recoverable under the terms of the contract). This estimate is required irrespective of:

(a) whether or not work has yet commenced on such contracts;

(b) the proportion of work carried out at the accounting date;

(c) the amount of profits expected to arise on other contracts.

Definition **Payments on account** are all amounts received and receivable at the accounting date in respect of contracts in progress.

Turnover is not defined in *SSAP 9*. However Appendix 1 to *SSAP 9* states that turnover (ascertained in a manner appropriate to the industry, the nature of the contracts concerned and the contractual relationship with the customer) and related costs should be recorded in the profit and loss account as contract activity progresses. Turnover may sometimes be ascertained by reference to valuation of the work carried out to date. In other cases, there may be specific points during a contract at which individual elements of work done with separately ascertainable sales values and costs can be identified and appropriately recorded as turnover (eg, because delivery or customer acceptance has taken place).

For examination purposes, turnover is normally likely to represent the value of work done or certified as done.

2.3 Preparing financial statements in accordance with SSAP 9 for long-term contracts

Bloggs Builders undertakes a three year contract to build a bridge for £1 million. The following information is extracted from its books and records at the end of years 1, 2 and 3:

		Value of work done	*Costs*	*Payments on account Received*	*Invoiced*
		£'000	£'000	£'000	£'000
Year 1	To date	200	210	150	160
	To complete (estimated)	800	Not known	-	-
Year 2	To date	500	550	535	570
	To complete (estimated)	500	390	-	-
Year 3	To date (completed)	1,000	955	1,000	1,000

You are required to show how this information would be reflected in the accounts for each of the three years.

2.4 Solution

Step 1 A contract account accumulates the various costs incurred on each contract. By the end of year 1 the account will look as follows:

Contract account

	£		£
Bank/cash for:			
Material	X		
Labour, etc	X		
	210,000		

Step 2 Because a contract can continue for some time, there is normally provision for the contractor to invoice the customer for parts of the contract (often on a monthly basis). The part invoices are known as **progress payments**. They are credited to a progress payments account (it is thus a type of sales account) and debited to debtors.

By the end of year 1 the account will look as follows:

Progress payments account

	£		£
		Debtors	X
			X
			160,000

Step 3 Debtors are recorded in the normal way:

Debtors

	£		£
Progress payments account	160,000	Cash	150,000
		Balance c/d	10,000
	160,000		160,000

Step 4 At the end of year 1 a decision is required as to whether to take a proportion of profit. As the costs to completion are unknown at this stage, the profitable outcome cannot be assessed with reasonable certainty. Thus there can be no attributable profit.

The **value of work done** (given in the example) is recorded in the accounts:

Dr	Progress payments	£200,000	
Cr	Profit and loss account		£200,000

Step 5 The contract account is closed off to the profit and loss account up to the amount of recorded turnover.

Contract account

	£		£
Costs	210,000	Trading account	200,000
		Balance c/d (closing stock)	10,000
	210,000		210,000

Progress payments account

	£		£
Trading account	200,000	Debtors	160,000
		Balance c/d	40,000
	200,000		200,000

	£'000	£'000
Profit and loss account		
Turnover		200
Opening stock	-	
Purchases	210	
Closing stock (Bal fig)	(10)	
Cost of sales		200
Gross profit		-

Balance sheet

Stock:	
Net cost	10
Applicable payments on account	-
Debtors:	
Amounts recoverable on contracts	40
Progress payments receivable (debtor)	10

Step 6 In Year 2 similar entries are made but at this stage the profitable outcome of the contract can be foreseen. The attributable profit is calculated as follows:

	£'000
Contract price	1,000
Costs incurred	(550)
Estimated costs to complete	(390)
Anticipated total profit	60

Based on value of work done the contract is 50% complete (500/1,000). Therefore, the attributable profit is £30,000 (£60,000 × 50%).

Contract account

	£		£
(1) Balance b/d year 1	10,000	(4) Trading account	270,000
(2) Costs in year 2		Balance c/d	80,000
(550 – 210)	340,000		
	350,000		350,000

Progress payments account

	£		£
(1) Balance b/d year 1	40,000	(2) Debtors	
(3) Trading account		(570 –160)	410,000
(500 – 200)	300,000		
Balance c/d	70,000		
	410,000		410,000

Debtors

	£		£
(1) Balance b/d	10,000	(2) Cash (535 – 150)	385,000
(2) Progress payments		Balance c/d	35,000
account	410,000		
	420,000		420,000

Profit and loss account	£'000	£'000
Turnover (500 – 200)		300
Opening stock	10	
Purchases (550 – 210)	340	
Closing stock (Bal fig)	(80)	
Cost of sales		270
Gross profit (see step 6)		30

Balance sheet

Stock:	
Net cost	80
Applicable payments on account	(70)
Debtors:	
Progress payments receivable	35

Note on the sequence of entries

The numbers in the ledger accounts record the sequence of entries. At the end of the year the turnover figure (given in the example) can be transferred to the trading account from the progress payments account. The transfer of costs from the contract account to the trading account should be computed in **reverse**, ie,

(a) compute attributable profit (£30,000);
(b) deduct profit from turnover, giving cost of sales (£270,000).

Step 7 In year 3 the final outcome of the contract is known.

	£'000
The total profit on the contract is as follows:	
Contract price	1,000
Costs	955
Total profit	45

This profit has been recognised as follows:

Year 1	-
Year 2	30
Year 3	15
	45

Contract account

	£		£
Balance b/d	80,000	Trading account	485,000
Costs in year 3 (955 – 550)	405,000		
	485,000		485,000

Progress payments account

	£		£
Trading account	500,000	Balance b/d	70,000
		Debtors (1,000 – 570)	430,000
	500,000		500,000

Profit and loss account

	£'000	£'000
Turnover (1,000 – 500)		500
Opening stock	80	
Purchases (955 – 550)	405	
Closing stock	(-)	
Cost of sales		485
Gross profit		15

2.5 Activity

CS plc, building contractors, commenced trading on 1 January 20X6. As at 31 December 20X6, there were three contracts (numbers 3, 7 and 9) uncompleted. All other contracts had been completed before the year end at a profit and none had any retentions outstanding.

Details of the uncompleted contracts were as follows:

	Contract numbers		
	3	7	9
	£	£	£
Contract costs	26,000	31,200	15,300
Value of work completed	32,000	26,000	16,000

Progress payments	35,000	19,200	7,000
Estimate of final cost	32,000	36,000	50,000
Sales value	40,000	29,000	60,000

The estimate of final cost includes allowance for contingencies and provision for warranty work.

You are required to calculate the profit or loss applicable to each of the uncompleted contracts.

2.6 Activity solution

Calculation of profits and losses on uncompleted contracts:

	Contract numbers		
	3	7	9
	£	£	£
Costs incurred to date	26,000	31,200	15,300
Further costs to be incurred	6,000	4,800	34,700
Estimate of final cost	32,000	36,000	50,000
Sales value	40,000	29,000	60,000
Estimated total profit or loss	8,000	(7,000)	10,000

Contract 3

This contract is nearly complete. Attributable profit is:

£32,000/£40,000 × £8,000 = £6,400.

(***Tutorial note:***

Attributable profit has been computed on a 'sales' basis ie,

$$\frac{\text{Value of work completed}}{\text{Contract price}}$$

Alternative calculations are:

(a) $$\frac{\text{Costs to date}}{\text{Estimated total cost}} \quad \frac{26{,}000}{32{,}000} \times £8{,}000 = £6{,}500$$

(b) Progress payments invoiced basis

$$\frac{\text{Progress payments invoiced}}{\text{Contract price}} \quad \frac{30{,}000}{40{,}000} \times £8{,}000 = £6{,}000)$$

Contract 7

This contract is clearly in major difficulties. The whole of the foreseeable loss of £7,000 should be provided for and the contract will then be stated at net realisable value.

Contract 9

Assuming that the profitable outcome of this contract can be assessed with reasonable certainty, attributable profit is:

£16,000/£60,000 × £10,000 = £2,667

(***Tutorial note:***

The contract is in its early stages and thus it is equally valid to assume that the profitable outcome cannot be assessed with reasonable certainty. Assumptions must therefore be clearly stated in the answer.)

Conclusion Each contract must be assessed individually.

2.7 The problem areas that have not been resolved in relation to long-term contracts

The problem areas include the following.

(a) The changing in nature of an asset from WIP to debtor is not regarded as reasonable by some commentators. It is seen as an artificial device to overcome the problem of valuation resulting from the requirements of the CA85. From a user's point of view, the treatment does not allow the extent of investment in long-term contracts to be seen.

(b) There are still many areas of subjective judgements involved. For example in the calculation of attributable profit, different decisions can be made by entities as to the earliest time to take profit on a contract and different methods can be used to calculate the profit (ie, a sales or cost basis could be used).

3 CHAPTER SUMMARY

Long-term contracts require the calculation of attributable profit and the transfer of stocks and WIP to cost of sales in the profit and loss account.

Sales are matched with progress payments to determine balance sheet disclosures.

4 SELF TEST QUESTIONS

4.1 What classifications should stocks be disclosed under? (1.4)

4.2 What is the definition of a long-term contract? (2.1)

4.3 What is a payment on account? (2.2)

4.4 When is an estimate of foreseeable losses required? (2.2)

4.5 When invoices are issued to a customer on a long-term contract, what is the double entry? (2.4)

5 EXAMINATION TYPE QUESTION

5.1 Midas plc

Midas plc is a conglomerate that produces its accounts at 31 December. John Poor is the head office accountant responsible for the consolidation as at 31 December 20X2. He had been reviewing the accounts of Fencing Ltd, a recently acquired sub-subsidiary that carries on business as a fencing company, and considered the rate of stock and debtor turnover to be unexpectedly high.

In response to his enquiry, Fencing Ltd produced the following information concerning stock and debtors:

Stocks

Stocks were made up of raw materials at a cost of £86,000 and finished goods at a cost of £27,000.

The raw materials consisted of 8,600 metres of teak fencing at £10 per metre. The finished goods consisted of 10 security gates the company had manufactured in its own foundry in Scotland at a cost of £1,500 each and 1,000 metres of metal fencing manufactured in the foundry at a cost of £12 per metre.

Debtors

Debtors were made up of trade debtors at £55,000 and amounts recoverable on contracts at £24,000.

The trade debtors consisted of £25,000 for completed work that had been invoiced in the latter half of December 20X2. The amounts recoverable on contracts consisted of £19,000 due on a contract with Broad Rail plc and £5,000 due on a contract with Asda plc.

John Poor made some further enquiries and obtained the following additional information

Raw materials

Cheap supplies of teak had started coming into the country in January 20X3 from Indonesia at a list price of £5 per metre. The trade press had described these imports as dumping and had been making representations to government for the imports to be restricted.

Finished goods

Security gates could from mid January 20X3 be imported from Germany at £750 per gate. The German supplier had recently invested in advanced technology and the company could not match its costs at its own foundry in Scotland.

Amounts recoverable on contracts: Broad Rail plc contract

The contract with Broad Rail plc had been entered into on 1 July 20X1 and is due for completion on 30 June 20X2. The contract price was £120,000 and costs were estimated at £80,000 and were expected to accrue evenly over the period of the contract.

In the 20X1 accounts the amount due on contract was calculated as follows:

		£
Cost to 31.12.X1		20,000
Total profit on contract	£40,000	
Attribute 25% for six months	10,000	10,000
Turnover		30,000
Progress payments		25,000
Amount recoverable on contract		5,000

During 20X2 Fencing Ltd received progress payments of £50,000. The company had experienced difficulties in controlling the scheduling of the work and due to their inefficiency had incurred costs of £16,000 during the year.

It was normal industry practice for the customer to hold a 5% retention. The company explained that the high rate of retention had been stipulated by the customer because in 20X1 Fencing Ltd had only just been listed as an approved supplier and had little experience of managing large contracts. It was expected that the management problems that had arisen in 20X2 had been overcome and that the costs of 20X3 would be in line with the original estimate.

Applying paragraph 23 of SSAP 9, the amount recoverable on contracts had been calculated at 31 December 20X2 as follows:

	£	£
Cost in 20X2		56,000
Total profit on contract	40,000	
Less: Cost escalation	16,000	
Revised profit	24,000	
Attribute 75% for 18 months	18,000	
Less: 20X1 profit taken in 20X1	10,000	
		8,000
Turnover		64,000
Progress payments		50,000
Amount recoverable on contract		14,000
Amount recoverable 20X1		5,000
		19,000

Amounts recoverable on contracts: Asda plc contract

The contract with Asda plc had been entered into on 1 October 20X2 and was due for completion on 31 March 20X3.

The contract price was £10,000 and costs were estimated at £7,500 and were expected to accrue evenly over the period of the contract.

		£
Cost to 31.12.X2		3,750
Total profit on contract	£2,500	
Attribute 50% for three months	1,250	1,250
Turnover		5,000
Progress payments		-
Amount recoverable on contract		5,000

You are required:

(a) to discuss whether you consider that the figure of £19,000 that had been calculated as the amount due on contract from the Broad Rail plc contract gave a true and fair view. **(7 marks)**

(b) to state, with clear reasons, the amounts at which you consider the following items should appear in the accounts of Fencing Ltd as at 31 December 20X2 together with any notes to the accounts:

(i) Stock

(ii) Debtors

(13 marks)
(Total: 20 marks)

6 ANSWER TO EXAMINATION TYPE QUESTION

6.1 Midas plc

(Tutorial note: the question breaks down into several individual components. Take one component at a time and 'build up' an answer. Use the following 'break-down':

Long-term contract	Discussion Calculation
Short-term stocks	Raw materials, comment and calculation Finished goods, comment and calculation
Debtors	£25,000 normal sales Asda plc contract)

(a) The figure of £19,000 does not fairly reflect the amount recoverable on the contract as at 31 December 20X2. Although the addition for the balance at 31 December 20X1 is in order, the amount attributed to the year 20X2 is unsuitable.

While paragraph 9 of SSAP 9 confirms that 'profit taken up needs to reflect the proportion of the work carried out', and therefore some turnover/cost of sales should be incorporated for the year, the same paragraph also states that the profit taken up 'take into account any known inequalities of profitability in the various stages of a contract'. The £16,000 additional costs need therefore to be attributed to 20X2 together with any costs to be matched with the turnover recognised.

If the contract can be considered to be half complete as at 31 December 20X2 (18 months done, 18 months still to do) then turnover recognised should be £60,000, cost of sales matched of £40,000 plus the £16,000 additional cost. Profit for 20X2 on the contract would therefore be £4,000.

The amount recoverable on the contract at 31 December 20X2 would be

	£
Amount recoverable for 20X1	5,000
Turnover recognised in 20X2	60,000
	65,000
Progress payments received	50,000
Amount recoverable	15,000

This would give a fairer reflection of the periodic profitability of the long-term contract.

(b) (i) **Raw materials**

It is necessary to consider whether the information concerning the cheap teak imports constitutes a 'post balance sheet event' requiring adjustments to the accounts at 31 December 20X2. SSAP 17 *Accounting for post balance sheet events* gives an indication in its appendix that "... evidence concerning the net realisable value of stocks" would constitute an adjusting event. If therefore the net realisable value is likely to be reduced to £5 per metre by market forces then the raw materials stock of teak should be carried at a valuation of (8,600 × £5) £43,000.

Finished goods

There appears to be nothing that indicates that the valuation of the 1,000 metres of metal fencing should be adjusted - the value of £12,000 would therefore be retained.

The security gates however present another post balance sheet event problem. If market forces are likely to reflect the price reduction of the competitor it would seem prudent to reflect the lower value of £750 per gate in the stock valuation. The finished goods of 10 such items would therefore be valued at £7,500.

The total finished goods valuation would be £19,500 and the total stock valuation would be £62,500.

(ii) The debtors of £25,000 for completed work appear to be correctly included in the accounts, assuming there are no bad or doubtful debts at the balance sheet date.

The other debtors figure would currently include an amount of £5,000 for the Asda plc contract on the grounds that it should be reported in line with SSAP 9 as a long-term contract. If it is usual for Fencing Ltd to report such contracts in this manner then consistency would require the adopted accounting practice. However, if the contract is *not* considered to be a long-term contract then it should be reflected as WIP, at cost of £3,750.

TAX IN COMPANY ACCOUNTS

INTRODUCTION & LEARNING OBJECTIVES

SSAPs 5 and 15 are covered in earlier stages of the examination system and thus much of the contents of this chapter should be revision to you. SSAP 15 does however cause difficulty to many students and is thus thoroughly covered in this chapter, together with proposals for its revision. Full questions on deferred taxation can be set in the examination and may be either computational or narrative.

This chapter also covers FRS 16 *Current tax* which has replaced SSAP 8.

When you have studied this chapter you should be able to do the following:

- Apply the requirements of SSAP 5
- Apply the requirements of FRS 16
- Apply the requirements of SSAP 15
- Record entries relating to deferred tax in the accounting records.

---

1 SSAP 5: ACCOUNTING FOR VALUE ADDED TAX

1.1 Taxable, zero-rated and exempt items

A clear distinction needs to be made between the treatment of traders in taxable, zero-rated and exempt items:

(a) **Taxable items**

Because traders in taxable items are charged VAT on their purchases and can pass it on to their customers in sales, they do not suffer it as an expense. Consequently, VAT should have no effect on the profit and loss account. The only exceptions to this rule are non-deductible inputs, such as motor cars and certain business entertaining expenses. Because VAT on these items cannot be recovered, it should be included as part of the cost of the items.

(b) **Zero-rated items**

These include exports, food, travel fares and construction. Traders in these items do not charge VAT on outputs, but can recover VAT on their inputs. Therefore, again, VAT should have no effect on the profit and loss account.

(c) **Exempt items**

These include land transactions, insurance premiums, postal and health services, betting, education and small businesses. Although such traders do not charge VAT on their outputs, they have no right (unlike zero-rated traders) to recover VAT on their inputs. In such cases the irrecoverable VAT will be added to the trader's costs.

1.2 Standard accounting practice

SSAP 5 requires that:

(a) Turnover shown in the profit and loss account should exclude VAT on taxable outputs.

(b) Irrecoverable VAT on fixed assets and other items disclosed separately in published accounts (eg, capital commitments) should be included in their cost.

1.3 Activity

A company trading in goods which are subject to VAT at standard rate (17.5%) has a turnover of £2,156,780 inclusive of VAT. What figure for turnover should be disclosed in its published accounts?

1.4 Activity solution

The VAT exclusive figure should be disclosed

$$\frac{100}{117.5} \times £2,156,780 = £1,835,557.$$

2 CURRENT TAX

2.1 Accounting for corporation tax

The double entry to record the corporation tax charge for the year is:

		£	£
Dr	Corporation tax charge (profit and loss account)	X	
	Cr Corporation tax creditor (balance sheet)		X

This amount is normally an estimate as in most cases the actual tax liability for the period is not known at the time that the financial statements are prepared. If the estimate is incorrect, the under or over provision is dealt with by increasing or decreasing the following year's tax charge.

Following the passing of the Finance Act 1998, 'large' companies (defined as those with profits chargeable to corporation tax of more than £1.5 million) must pay their corporation tax in four quarterly instalments based on their anticipated profits for the current year.

Small and medium sized companies continue to pay their corporation tax liability nine months after the end of their accounting period.

Therefore corporation tax payable is included in the balance sheet under 'Creditors: Amounts payable within one year'.

2.2 Accounting for income tax

(a) **The company as a collecting agent**

Just as a company acts as a collecting agent for VAT, it acts as a collecting agent for income tax (IT). Certain payments by companies are made under deduction of income tax at source

(i) loan stock and debenture interest
(ii) patent and mineral output royalties
(iii) covenants
(iv) annuities.

The income tax is paid over to the Inland Revenue on the fourteenth day after the end of the quarter in which the payment is made. The quarter ends are 31 March, 30 June, 30 September and 31 December. If the company year end does not correspond with one of these quarter ends, then that year end forms a fifth quarter end.

(b) **Unfranked investment income (UFII)**

A company in receipt of debenture interest will receive it net of income tax which the paying company will have deducted at source. This income is known as unfranked investment income.

		£	£
Dr	Cash (net receipt)	x	
Cr	Debenture interest received		x

It follows that the company (which suffers corporation tax, not income tax) may reclaim the income tax deducted at source from the Inland Revenue. The double entry is to gross up the receipt using an income tax account

		£	£
Dr	Income tax account	x	
Cr	Debenture interest received		x

The gross debenture interest is therefore credited to profit and loss account. Where a company both pays interest and receives unfranked investment income

(i) Income tax on the excess of interest paid over interest received is paid to the Inland Revenue. If this is unpaid at the year end, it forms part of the tax creditor. Alternatively,

(ii) Income tax on the excess of interest received over interest paid is repayable to the company. This is done by offset against the corporation tax (CT) liability.

2.3 Example

	£'000
Loan interest received (net of income tax deducted at 20%)	21,000
Loan interest paid (net of income tax deducted at 20%)	36,000

The income tax account is as follows

Income tax account

	£		£
Interest received account (20/80 × £21,000)	5,250	Interest paid account (20/80 × £36,000)	9,000
Balance c/d	3,750		
	£9,000		£9,000

£3,750 is subsequently paid to the Inland Revenue.

2.4 Activity

	£
Loan interest received (net)	21,000
Loan interest paid (net)	12,000

Show the income tax account, assuming that income tax has been deducted at 20%.

2.5 Activity solution

Income tax account

	£		£
Interest received account (20/80 × £21,000)	5,250	Interest paid account (20/80 × £12,000)	3,000
		Corporation tax account	2,250
	£5,250		£5,250

The IT recoverable is therefore offset against the CT payable.

2.6 FRS 16: Current tax

FRS 16 was issued to replace SSAP 8 *The treatment of taxation under the imputation system in the accounts of companies*. This was necessary because most of the requirements of SSAP 8 became obsolete as a result of the abolition of Advance Corporation Tax (ACT) in April 1999 and the introduction of withholding taxes in the Republic of Ireland. The objective of FRS 16 is to ensure that reporting entities recognise current taxes in a consistent and transparent manner.

Definition **Current tax** is the amount of tax estimated to be payable or recoverable in respect of the taxable profit or loss for a period, along with adjustments to estimates in respect of previous periods.

Definition **Taxable profit or loss** is the profit or loss for the period, determined in accordance with the rules established by the tax authorities, upon which taxes are assessed.

Standard accounting practice

(a) Current tax should be recognised in the profit and loss account for the period.

(b) The exception to this is where a gain or loss has been directly recognised in the statement of total recognised gains and losses (STRGL). Tax attributable to that gain or loss must also be recognised in the STRGL. (SSAP 8 did not include this requirement; the STRGL had not been introduced when it was originally issued.)

(c) Current tax should be measured at the amounts expected to be paid (or recovered) using the tax rates and laws that have been enacted or substantively enacted by the balance sheet date. This represents a change from SSAP 8, which simply required tax to be measured at the latest known rate. The change has been made to increase consistency and to align UK practice with the requirements of IAS 12 *Income taxes*.

2.7 Dividends and interest

FRS 16 requires that outgoing dividends paid or proposed, incoming dividends, interest payable or receivable and other income receivable should be recognised at an amount that:

- includes any withholding taxes; but
- excludes attributable tax credits.

Withholding tax suffered on income should be taken into account as part of the tax charge.

Definition **Withholding tax** is tax on dividends or other income that is deducted by the payer of the income and paid to the tax authorities wholly on behalf of the recipient.

The recipient suffers tax on the **gross** amount of the income (ie, the dividend or interest including the withholding tax). Therefore it is appropriate to 'gross up' the amount payable or receivable in the profit and loss account so that it includes the withholding tax deducted.

At present dividends from UK companies are not subject to withholding tax and SSAP 8 did not address its treatment.

Neither SSAP 8 nor FRS 16 specifically mentions UK income tax on debenture interest and similar items (see section 2.2 above). However, this appears to fall within the definition of a withholding tax. The practical effect of this is that items received or paid under deduction of income tax must be included in the profit and loss amount at the **gross** amount. As this was the normal accounting treatment under SSAP 8, there is no change to present practice.

Definition A **tax credit** is given under UK tax legislation to the recipient of a dividend from a UK company. The credit is given to acknowledge that the income out of which the dividend has been paid has already been charged to tax in the company that earned it.

As the recipient of a dividend from a UK company has no further tax to pay and cannot reclaim the tax credit it would not be logical to recognise it in the profit and loss account. This is the main change from SSAP 8, which required dividends receivable to be 'grossed up' to include the tax credit. Until 1997 tax credits on dividends received could be reclaimed.

2.8 Income and expenses subject to non-standard rates of tax

Some transactions are deliberately structured so that some or all of the income or expenditure is non taxable or taxable at a different rate from the standard rate. This structure makes the transaction profitable. Examples include some leasing transactions and advances and investments made by financial institutions. One possible method of presenting these transactions in the profit and loss account is to 'gross up' to reflect the notional amount of tax that would have been payable if the transaction had been taxable on a different basis. Note that 'grossing up' only affects the presentation of the profit and loss account, not the actual amount of tax payable.

FRS 16 states that income and expenses other than dividends, interest and similar items should be included in the pre-tax results on the basis of the income and expenses **actually receivable or payable**. No adjustment should be made to reflect a notional amount of tax that would have been paid or relieved in respect of the transaction if it had been taxable, or allowable for tax purposes, on a different basis. (This was previously required by UITF Abstract 16, which is now superseded.)

'Grossing up' is prohibited because it fails to reflect the true nature of the transactions that have occurred in the period.

2.9 Disclosure of current tax

An Appendix to FRS 16 illustrates the required disclosures.

Tax on profit on ordinary activities (note to the profit and loss account)

	£'000	£'000
UK corporation tax		
Current tax on income for the period	X	
Adjustments in respect of prior periods	X	
	—	
	X	
Double taxation relief	(X)	
	—	
		X
Foreign tax		
Current tax on income for the period	X	
Adjustments in respect of prior periods	X	
	—	
		X
		—
Tax on profit on ordinary activities		X
		—

The Companies Act and FRS 3 require disclosure of special circumstances affecting the tax liability in respect of profits, income or capital gains for the current year or succeeding years.

A similar analysis note is required if any current tax is recognised in the STRGL.

Investment income

(a) Dividends received from UK companies are shown **net** (ie, the actual cash amount received).

(b) Unfranked investment income (eg, interest received) is shown **gross** (ie, inclusive of income tax).

(c) Any income received subject to a withholding tax is shown **gross** (ie, inclusive of the withholding tax).

Annual charges (e.g. debenture interest payable)

These are shown **gross**.

Dividends paid and proposed

These are appropriated **net** in the profit and loss account.

2.10 Activity

Apricot Ltd had trading profits of £500,000 for the year ended 31 December 20X1. The estimated tax liability for the year is £165,000. During the year to 31 December 20X1 the following transactions occurred:

(a) Payment of corporation tax of £160,000 for the year ended 31 December 20X0. The actual amount provided in the accounts for that year was £155,000.

(b) Receipt of a dividend of £30,000 from another UK company.

(c) Dividend of £138,000 proposed for the year. This was paid on 31 March 20X2.

Required

Prepare the relevant extracts from the financial statements for the year ended 31 December 20X1. The tax credit relating to dividends from UK companies is 10/90.

2.11 Activity solution

Profit and loss account for the year ended 31 December 20X1 (extract)

	£
Operating profit	500,000
Investment income received	30,000
Profit on ordinary activities before taxation	530,000
Tax on profit on ordinary activities (Note)	(170,000)
Profit on ordinary activities after taxation	360,000
Dividends proposed	(138,000)
Retained profit for the year	222,000

Note to the profit and loss account: Tax on profit on ordinary activities

	£
UK corporation tax:	
Current tax on income for the period	165,000
Adjustments in respect of prior periods	5,000
	170,000

Balance sheet at 31 December 20X1 (extract)

	£
Creditors: Amounts falling due within one year:	
Taxation	165,000
Proposed dividends	138,000

Conclusion FRS 16 deals with the way in which current tax is presented in the profit and loss account and in the STRGL. It requires that investment income received and dividends and interest payable are included in the profit and loss account inclusive of withholding tax but excluding attributable tax credits.

3 ACCOUNTING FOR DEFERRED TAXATION

3.1 Calculation of taxable profit

The essential problem that the remainder of this chapter deals with is the alternative methods which can be adopted in determining the tax charge and thus the after tax profit.

There are three possibilities - to charge profit and loss account with

(a) tax on the taxable profit (the basic liability for corporation tax for the year), or
(b) tax on the accounting profit (profit before tax multiplied by the appropriate percentage), or
(c) tax on a figure of profit somewhere between the taxable and accounting profits.

It is therefore necessary to consider why taxable and accounting profits are different.

There are two types of difference

(a) permanent, and
(b) timing.

3.2 Permanent differences

These are items where the tax treatment will *always* differ from the accounting treatment. An example is the cost of entertaining customers.

Example

Two companies are both subject to corporation tax at 30%. Both have profits of £100,000 which are identical for taxation and accounting purposes except that Company 1 has debited disallowable entertaining expenses of £60,000 against these profits while Company 2 has not.

Show pre-tax profit, the tax charge and post-tax profit.

	Company 1 £'000	*Company 2* £'000
Pre-tax profit	100	100
Taxation (30% of £160/30% of £100)	(48)	(30)
	52	70

It would appear that these two companies are subject to two very different levels of taxation and the reality is that they are. Because Company 1 incurs a large amount of non-allowable expenditure, it is effectively taxed at 48% whereas Company 2 is taxed at 30% - the expected rate. It would clearly be necessary in the case of Company 1 to indicate the 'special circumstances' which have affected the tax charge *(Companies Act* requirement). However it would not be appropriate to make any further accounting entry because there is no possibility of change in the tax liability for this year in the future.

Other examples of permanent differences are

(a) fines and certain legal costs
(b) capital expenditure charged to revenue (ie, improvement as opposed to repair expenditure)
(c) interest on overdue tax.

A company will always pay corporation tax on the income used to pay the disallowable expenditure.

3.3 Timing differences

Timing differences arise where the taxation rules allocate an item of expenditure or income to a different period from that used in the accounts. Thus the expenditure or income will be allowed for or charged to tax but in a different period from that in which it is dealt with in the financial accounts.

The most common item giving rise to timing differences is the difference between capital allowances and depreciation.

The entire deferred taxation debate developed during a period when capital allowances were much more rapid in amortising the cost of an asset than the corresponding depreciation provision. This led to very substantial differences between profit shown by the accounts and those computed for tax purposes.

At that time 100% first year allowances were resulting in low corporation tax charges. However when the system of capital allowances was changed, some companies were faced with large tax liabilities for which they had made no provision (the effect was twofold: new assets received reduced allowances, old assets had been fully relieved).

The leasing industry, in particular, found itself facing unprovided tax liabilities.

Similar increases or reductions in provisions could result from future radical changes in the tax system.

3.4 Deferred taxation

Deferred taxation arises because of the existence of timing differences. It represents tax which will become payable when a present deferral of tax is reversed and the potential liability crystallises. The following simple example demonstrates the basic concepts.

Example

A company purchases a single item of plant for £240,000. It is entitled to writing down allowances of 25% per annum. It is estimated that the plant will have a useful life of four years after which it will be sold for £76,000. Depreciation will be on a straight-line basis.

Pre-tax profits for the next four years are

Year	*Profit*
	£'000
1	100
2	120
3	140
4	150

Show pre-tax profit, tax charge and post-tax profit on the alternative bases of

(a) providing only for the tax payable in each period
(b) allocating the total tax charge equitably over the four accounting periods.

Assume corporation tax at 35%.

(a) **Tax payable basis**

Year	*1*	*2*	*3*	*4*	*Total*
	£'000	£'000	£'000	£'000	£'000
Pre-tax profit	100	120	140	150	510
Tax payable	(28)	(41)	(51)	(58)	(178)
Post-tax profit	72	79	89	92	332
Effective tax %	28	34	36	39	35

WORKINGS

Year	*1*	*2*	*3*	*4*
	£'000	£'000	£'000	£'000
Profit after depreciation	100	120	140	150
Add: Depreciation	41	41	41	41
	141	161	181	191
Less: Capital allowances	(60)	(45)	(34)	(25)
	81	116	147	166
Tax at 35%	28	41	51	58

Capital allowances

Cost/written down value	240	180	135	101
WDA (25%) (Balancing allowance in year 4)	(60)	(45)	(34)	(25)
	180	135	101	76

Note: the balancing allowance in year 4 is the difference between the tax WDV and the sale proceeds on disposal.

(b) **Tax allocation basis**

Year	*1*	*2*	*3*	*4*	*Total*
	£'000	£'000	£'000	£'000	£'000
Pre-tax profit	100	120	140	150	510
Tax charge					
Current tax payable	(28)	(41)	(51)	(58)	(178)
Deferred tax	(7)	(1)	2	6	-
Post-tax profit	65	78	91	98	332
Effective tax %	35	35	35	35	35

WORKINGS

Depreciation	41	41	41	41
Capital allowances	(60)	(45)	(34)	(25)
Timing difference	(19)	(4)	7	16
Tax at 35%	(7)	(1)	2	6

Note: when first year allowances were at the rate of 100%, the effect seen above was far greater.

At first sight the above example represents a plausible argument for the practice of comprehensive allocation of the tax liability on a strict accruals basis. The constant rate of tax in part (b) is much more attractive than the violent fluctuations in part (a) and common-sense dictates that the benefit of capital allowances should be spread over the period which benefits from them. Before examining this assertion further, it is appropriate to consider terminology.

(a) The timing difference of £(19,000) in year 1 is referred to as an *originating* timing difference. In this case it represents an amount of tax payable which is deferred to a later period. This will not always be the case. For example, a company creating a provision for deferred repairs of £50,000 for the first time would have an originating timing difference of this amount but it would represent future tax recoverable rather than payable (ie, the amount deducted in the financial accounts this year is greater than the deduction in the tax computations).

(b) The timing difference in year 3 of £7,000 is termed a *reversing* timing difference. In this case it represents the crystallisation of a previously deferred liability. In the case of a deferred repairs provision, a subsequent reversal would represent the recovery of prepaid tax.

The above example demonstrated the concept of full provision (or comprehensive allocation). When the benefit of the first year capital allowance was taken, provision was made for tax on the resulting timing difference. This tax was then credited to profit and loss account in later years. However, it is not difficult to imagine a situation where the reversal will never take place. This is illustrated in the activity below.

3.5 Activity

A company commences business on 1 January 20X1. It makes the following purchases of fixed assets in the first five years of its life

Year to 31 December	£'000
20X1	100
20X2	120
20X3	180
20X4	300
20X5	500

All purchases are entitled to writing down allowances of 25%. Depreciation is provided at 15% straight line on cost.

The company is very successful and intends to continue an aggressive expansion programme involving substantial capital expenditure after 20X5 (each year's expenditure substantially exceeding that for the previous year).

Compute the timing difference arising in each year.

3.6 Activity solution

Year to 31 December		*20X1* £'000	*20X2* £'000	*20X3* £'000	*20X4* £'000	*20X5* £'000	*Total* £'000
Depreciation of	20X1 asset	15	15	15	15	15	
	20X2 asset	-	18	18	18	18	
	20X3 asset	-	-	27	27	27	
	20X4 asset	-	-	-	45	45	
	20X5 asset	-	-	-	-	75	
		15	33	60	105	180	393
Capital allowances (W1)		(25)	(49)	(82)	(137)	(226)	(519)
Timing differences		(10)	(16)	(22)	(32)	(46)	(126)

WORKINGS

Capital allowances

		20X1 £'000	*20X2* £'000	*20X3* £'000	*20X4* £'000	*20X5* £'000
WDA of	20X1 asset	25	19	14	11	8
	20X2 asset	-	30	23	17	12
	20X3 asset	-	-	45	34	25
	20X4 asset	-	-	-	75	56
	20X5 asset	-	-	-	-	125
		25	49	82	137	226

In the above activity there are net originating timing differences in every year which lead to an increasing future liability. However, the company's future plans point to a continuance of this situation, at least as long as substantial and increasing capital expenditure occurs. Of course, any slow down in the level of expansion could lead to a crystallisation of liabilities because there would be insufficient tax allowances to cover the depreciation charge in any year.

By the end of the fifth year, the company has been able to defer tax on timing differences of £126,000. The key question is whether or not provision should be made for the amount of tax which *might* be payable *if* these timing differences reverse. To provide for deferred tax (at the current rate of 30%) would mean reducing profits to establish the following provisions

Year to 31 December	*20X1* £'000	*20X2* £'000	*20X3* £'000	*20X4* £'000	*20X5* £'000
Deferred tax	3.0	4.8	6.6	9.6	13.8

However, will this tax ever be paid? If crystallisation of a liability is unlikely, can there be any logic in making provision for it? The effect will be to reduce profits unnecessarily and to create a liability in the balance sheet which is never likely to crystallise. On the other hand, if crystallisation of tax liabilities is likely, the amounts are clearly substantial and provision should be made for them.

4 THREE POSSIBLE BASES FOR ACCOUNTING FOR DEFERRED TAX

4.1 Introduction

Arising from the above dilemma, there are three possible approaches to providing for deferred tax. These are

(a) flow-through (also known as nil provision or cash basis) method
(b) full provision (or comprehensive allocation) method
(c) partial provision (or true rate) method.

Each will be considered in turn.

4.2 Flow-through method

This approach is based on the argument that tax is more of an appropriation of profit than a cost. Accordingly, whatever tax happens to be payable in a period should be debited against those profits. Under this approach, no attempt is made to 'smooth' tax liabilities over various periods and therefore no liability is set up in the balance sheet for deferred taxation.

This concept has not gained favour in the UK. It is argued that investors and other users of accounts look to the after-tax profit figure as a measure of performance and it is therefore very important to ensure that the tax charge is realistic in relation to profits for a period.

4.3 Full provision method

This is based on making provision for all timing differences whether or not they are ever likely to crystallise. It is based on a rigid application of the accruals concept. It is an attractive approach because the amount of the provision can be ascertained with complete certainty and requires no subjective assessment of the likely future crystallisation of liability.

4.4 Partial provision method

The profession has come, by a tortuous route, to the concept of only providing for that deferred tax which can reasonably be expected to create a liability in the foreseeable future. This is seen by some as being unsatisfactory because it requires the application of subjective judgement in assessing the extent to which liabilities will crystallise. It will be seen that, unlike the full provision method, partial provision requires the preparation of budgets in order to establish the likelihood of future crystallisation of the liability. This creates a particular problem for the auditor, trying to establish if the provision is 'true and fair'.

The original SSAP 15 required provision for deferred tax arising on short-term timing differences and on all other timing differences unless it could be demonstrated with reasonable certainty that they would not reverse within the foreseeable future.

After being in operation for some time, the standard was reviewed in the light of the Companies Act 1981 and of some criticism concerning the apparent flexibility which permitted companies to

(a) provide for no deferred tax
(b) provide for all deferred tax, or
(c) provide for some deferred tax

according to their interpretation of the standard!

A revised version of SSAP 15 was issued in May 1985. This still requires provision for deferred tax using the partial provision method but has tightened up the definition of when provision should be made. The revised standard also requires disclosure of the deferred tax not provided. *It is thus necessary to calculate the full potential liability as well as that which is actually expected to arise.*

4.5 Full provision

In computing the full potential liability for deferred tax, it is necessary to consider the historical position. This involves identifying all items in the accounts to date which give rise to a timing difference.

Example

Patler plc prepares accounts to 31 December annually. At 31 December 20X8 a full provision for deferred tax had been made and the account comprised the following balances

	Timing differences	*Tax*
	£'000	£'000
Excess of capital allowances claimed over depreciation (for periods up to 31 December 20X8)	150 (30%)	45
Chargeable gain, on sale of freehold, rolled over	100 (30%)	30
	250	75

(Note that the accumulated timing difference on fixed assets is the difference between accounting NBV and tax WDV).

For the year ended 31 December 20X9 the timing differences comprise

	£'000
Excess capital allowances for the year	20

The company's budgets etc show that it is probable that a liability will arise on reversal of the timing differences.

Produce the deferred taxation account for 20X9.

Solution

Deferred taxation account

	Memo timing differences	*Tax*		*Memo timing differences*	*Tax*
	£'000	£'000		£'000	£'000
Balance c/d			Balance b/d (accelerated capital allowances		
(ACAs (150 + 20))	170	51	(ACAs))	150	45
(gain rolled over)	100	30	(gain rolled over)	100	30
				250	75
			P&L a/c 20X9 - (charge for deferred tax excess capital allowances)	20	6
	270	81		270	81

Computing the full provision is relatively straightforward because it involves analysing actual transactions to identify the liability. For example, the total timing difference in respect of accelerated capital allowances is simply the difference between the tax written down value and the net book value of the relevant assets. Items such as revaluation surpluses will be obvious from the accounts and the tax computation should disclose other items with differing accounting and tax treatments.

Some analysts use full provision for EPS purposes because of its objectivity. Because SSAP 15 requires disclosure of amounts not provided, the information is readily available to allow analysts to adjust a company's deferred tax charge from a partial to a full provision basis.

As explained later SSAP 15 is currently being reviewed and a return to full provision in the future seems likely. Again this is because it is objective and also because timing differences are smaller now that 100% first year allowances have been dropped and inflation is low.

4.6 Applying SSAP 15

By contrast, the computation of the partial deferred tax provision is more problematic because it involves the assessment of expected future transactions in order to assess the likelihood of the crystallisation of tax liabilities.

Example

Pedlar plc commenced to trade on 1 January 20X1. At 31 December 20X1 the taxation computation shows

	£
Accounting profit	200,000
Depreciation charged	80,000
	280,000
Capital allowances	(200,000)
Taxable profit	£80,000
Tax at 30%	£24,000

There are no other timing differences and budgets prepared show the following

	Accounting profit	*Depreciation*	*Capital allowances*	*Timing differences*	
				Originating	*Reversing*
	£	£	£	£	£
20X2	280,000	90,000	50,000	-	40,000
20X3	360,000	140,000	120,000	-	20,000
20X4	420,000	80,000	95,000	15,000	-

No further reversing timing differences are anticipated after 20X4 due to an annually increasing investment in qualifying assets.

Produce the deferred taxation account and profit and loss account for 20X1.

Step 1 **The future position**

The profit figures budgeted ensure that any relief for allowances will be covered by taxable income.

Thus the budgeted timing differences can be assessed as follows

		Originating	*Reversing*	*Cumulative*
		£'000	£'000	£'000
Year	20X2	-	40	(40)
	20X3	-	20	(60)
	20X4	15	-	(45)
	20X5/on	All		

The *cumulative* column shows the *maximum* total £60,000 in respect of which a liability will crystallise and this is the amount upon which tax must be provided.

Step 2 **The deferred taxation account will show**

	Memo timing differences £'000	Tax £'000		Memo timing differences £'000	Tax £'000
Balance c/d	60	18	P&L a/c (20X1) (provision for future liability)	60	18
	60	18		60	18

Step 3 **The profit and loss account for the year to 31 December 20X1 will show**

	£	£
Profit on ordinary activities before tax		200,000
UK taxation		
Corporation tax based on profit (30%)	24,000	
Transfer to deferred tax	18,000	(42,000)
		158,000

Note: the tax still does not equal 30% of accounting profit as only a partial provision has been made. The deferred tax not provided is

	£'000	£'000
Accelerated capital allowances (200 – 80)	120	
Provision for reversal	60	
	60 (30%)	18

Step 4 **Future accounting (assuming budget = actual)**

(i) **Tax payable**

	20X2 £'000	*20X3* £'000
Budgeted profit	280	360
Excess depreciation	40	20
Taxable profit	320	380
Tax payable (30%)	96	114

(ii) **Profit and loss account**

	20X2 £'000	£'000	*20X3* £'000	£'000
Profit before taxation		280		360
UK taxation				
CT based on profit	(96)		(114)	
Transfer *from* deferred tax account	12		6	
		(84)		(108)
Profit after taxation		196		252

Note: at the end of 20X3 the deferred tax account would be emptied as the reversals are now complete.

Budgets and capital asset purchasing intentions will, for most companies, form the 'reasonable assumptions' on which the decision will be based.

4.7 Activity

At 31 December 20X2 the written-down value of fixed assets ranking for capital allowances exceeds tax WDV by £1,400,000. C plc has in the past as a policy not provided for deferred tax. Relevant information is as follows:

Year		*Capital allowances*	*Depreciation*
		£'000	£'000
Actual	20X2	1,500	1,200
Forecast	20X3	1,100	1,670
Forecast	20X4	1,600	1,400
Forecast	20X5	1,750	1,600
Forecast	20X6 onwards - CA always in excess of depreciation.		

Show the deferred tax charges for 20X2 to 20X5 on a new accounting policy following the requirements of *SSAP 15*, and the provisions required in the balance sheet as at 31 December 20X1 to 20X5, assuming that there are no other timing differences to be considered and the corporation tax rate is 50%. Identify separately the amount of unprovided deferred tax for 20X1 to 20X5.

4.8 Activity solution

Timing differences

	Originating/(reversing)
	£'000
20X2	300
20X3	(570)
20X4	200
20X5	150
20X6	originating
After	exceed reversing in all years

Provisions required (to cover net future reversals)

		£
20X1	50% × (570 – 300)	135,000*
20X2	50% × 570	285,000
20X3		Nil
20X4		Nil
20X5		Nil

* prior year adjustment.

(***Tutorial note:***

The additional expected current tax liability occurs in 20X3. The £285,000 must therefore be provided in accounting periods **before** 20X3. Originating positive timing differences arising after 20X3 are only of relevance in showing that no further reversals are required.)

Profit and loss charge (difference between opening and closing provision required)

		£
20X2	285,000 – 135,000	150,000 Dr
20X3	0 – 285,000	285,000 Cr
20X4		Nil
20X5		Nil

Unprovided deferred tax

	ACAs b/d	Timing difference	ACAs c/d	At 50%	Provided	Unprovided
	£'000	£'000	£'000	£'000	£'000	£'000
20X1			1,100	550	135	415
20X2	1,100	300	1,400	700	285	415
20X3	1,400	(570)	830	415	-	415
20X4	830	200	1,030	515	-	515
20X5	1,030	150	1,180	590	-	590

5 THE REQUIREMENTS OF SSAP 15

5.1 Standard accounting practice

(a) **Method of computation**

Deferred tax should be computed under the liability method.

(b) **When does one need to account for deferred taxation?**

Para **Extracts from SSAP 15**

25 *Tax deferred or accelerated by the effect of timing differences should be accounted for to the extent that it is probable that a liability or asset will crystallise.*

26 *Tax deferred or accelerated by the effect of timing differences should not be accounted for to the extent that it is probable that a liability or asset will not crystallise.*

(c) **The criteria for deciding the amount of the provision**

Para **Extracts from SSAP 15**

27 *The assessment of whether deferred tax liabilities or assets will or will not crystallise should be based upon reasonable assumptions.*

28 *The assumptions should take into account all relevant information available up to the date on which the financial statements are approved by the board of directors, and also the intentions of management. Ideally, this information will include financial plans or projections covering a period of years sufficient to enable an assessment to be made of the likely pattern of future tax liabilities. A prudent view should be taken in the assessment of whether a tax liability will crystallise, particularly where the financial plans or projections are susceptible to a high degree of uncertainty or are not fully developed for the appropriate period.*

SSAP 15 is deliberately vague as to the time period the projections and financial plans should cover. Each case needs to be looked at on its own merits. The old SSAP 15 referred to a minimum period of three years. In practice, this was interpreted as a sufficient period to look ahead, rather than merely as a minimum. The appendix to SSAP 15 does, however, give advice on the period of years to be covered by financial plans. Where the pattern of timing differences is expected to be regular, forecasts for three to five years may be sufficient. However it may need to be longer for an enterprise with an irregular pattern of timing differences.

5.2 Disclosures

The emphasis is on full disclosure of deferred tax provided for and equally full disclosure of amounts unprovided. The point is that providing for deferred tax is at best highly subjective and therefore amounts unprovided should also be shown.

Para	***Profit and loss account***
33	*Deferred tax relating to the ordinary activities of the enterprise should be shown separately as a part of the tax on profit or loss on ordinary activities, either on the face of the profit and loss account or in a note.*
34	*Deferred tax relating to any extraordinary items should be shown separately as part of the tax on extraordinary items, either on the face of the profit and loss account or in a note.*
35	*The amount of any unprovided deferred tax in respect of the period should be disclosed in a note, analysed into its major components.*
36	*Adjustments to deferred tax arising from changes in tax rates and tax allowances should normally be disclosed separately as part of the tax charge for the period.*
	Balance sheet
37	*The deferred tax balance, and its major components, should be disclosed in the balance sheet or notes.*
38	*Transfers to and from deferred tax should be disclosed in a note.*
39	*Where amounts of deferred tax arise which relate to movements on reserves (eg, resulting from the expected disposal of revalued assets) the amounts transferred to or from deferred tax should be shown separately as part of such movements.*
40	*The total amount of any unprovided deferred tax should be disclosed in a note, analysed into its major components.*
41	*Where the potential amount of deferred tax on a revalued asset is not shown because the revaluation does not constitute a timing difference (as defined in the standard), the fact that it does not constitute a timing difference and that tax has, therefore, not been quantified should be stated.*
42	*Where the value of an asset is shown in a note because it differs materially from its book amount, the note should also show the tax effects, if any, that would arise if the asset were realised at the balance sheet date at the noted value.*

5.3 Further points

(a) **Losses**

Losses constitute a timing difference - they can be carried forward to reduce tax payable in the future. There are special rules in SSAP 15 on the recognition of losses as a deferred tax asset because prudence should be exercised.

(b) **Revaluation of assets**

A revaluation constitutes a timing difference where a taxable profit is foreseen on disposal. This will not be the case when the company intends to take advantage of rollover relief.

(c) **Retention of overseas earnings**

A share of an overseas subsidiary's retained earnings is included in the consolidated financial statements. If the subsidiary intends to distribute these earnings and that distribution would be taxable in the parent company's books, the tax that would become payable should be provided for as deferred tax ie, the retained overseas earnings constitute a timing difference.

(d) **Change in tax rates**

SSAP 15 is based on a balance sheet approach ie, deferred tax is provided for where it is expected to crystallise. The liability in the balance sheet is a fair reflection of what will be payable. Thus if there are changing tax rates, deferred tax should be provided at the rate of tax that will be payable not at the current rate. The assessment of the deferred tax not provided is also performed at the long-term rate.

6 METHODS OF COMPUTING DEFERRED TAXATION

There are two possible methods of dealing with deferred taxation

(a) the *liability* or *accrual* method
(b) the *deferral* method (of which there are several variants).

The methods differ as to the treatment of changes in the tax rate, and of reversing timing differences which were created when the rate was different from the current rate.

(a) **Liability method**

The liability method is a method of computing deferred tax whereby it is calculated at the rate of tax that it is estimated will be applicable when the timing differences reverse. Usually the current tax rate is used as the best estimate, unless changes in tax rates are known in advance. As a result, deferred tax provisions are revised to reflect changes in tax rates. Thus, the tax charge or credit for the period may include adjustments of accounting estimates relating to prior periods.

(b) **Deferral method**

The deferral method shows deferred tax at the amount of the benefit to the company, in historic cost terms, of being able to defer taxation.

Under this method the deferred taxation account records the originating timing differences at the rates of taxation in operation when those originating timing differences occurred. Unlike the liability method, no adjustment is made to the existing deferred taxation account when changes in taxation rates occur.

(c) **Which method is acceptable**

In the various EDs and SSAPs issued on deferred taxation, there has been a number of changes of mind as to the appropriateness of the two methods. The current SSAP 15 requires the use of the liability method, as it is consistent with the aim of partial provision ie, how much tax is expected to be paid?

7 DEFERRED TAX - QUESTION TECHNIQUE

7.1 Introduction

So far, in the context of deferred tax examples we have concentrated on the impact of ACAs. There are however, other timing differences between the tax computation and the accounts profit. Any examination question is likely to involve other timing differences in addition to ACAs and SSAP 15 requires disclosure to be made by category of timing difference.

This section has been designed to demonstrate a suitable question technique. The workings include tutorial notes which would not of course normally appear.

7.2 Question

Parrot plc has been trading for a number of years. You ascertain the following as at 1 January 20X1.

	£'000
Fixed assets	
Tax written down value	190
Net book value	250
Provision for deferred taxation	14

The following information refers to the year ended 31 December 20X1

(a) Depreciation charged in the financial statements was £50,000. Capital allowances in the tax computation were £70,000.

(b) Budgeted expenditure on fixed assets over the next few years is expected to give rise to capital allowances and depreciation as follows

	CA £'000	*Depreciation* £'000
20X2	60	50
20X3	90	100
20X4	100	120
20X5	90	60

Thereafter it is anticipated that capital allowances will continue to exceed depreciation.

(c) During the year Parrot plc issued convertible loan stock. On an accruals basis, loan stock interest included in the financial statements was £20,000. However, because interest was paid in arrears, cash paid was only £10,000. Assume for this question that only interest paid is allowed against tax, so that a timing difference will arise.

(d) During the year Parrot plc invested in the debentures of another company. Cash received as interest amounted to £30,000, but the financial statements, drawn up on an accruals basis included £45,000. This investment is considered to be long term. Assume again that only interest received is charged to tax.

Corporation tax is at the rate of 35%.

Show extracts from the financial statements for Parrot plc relating to deferred taxation.

7.3 Question technique

Generally, three standard workings are necessary in these questions

(a) a table of timing differences (TDs)
(b) a working to find the maximum cumulative reversal of ACAs
(c) a table of tax on the TDs.

Step 1 **Timing differences**

	Full b/d £'000	*Partial b/d* £'000	*Partial c/d* £'000	*Full c/d* £'000	*Tutorial note*
ACAs	60	40	20	80	(i)
Interest paid	-	-	(10)	(10)	(ii)
Interest received	-	-	-	15	(iii)
	60	40	10	85	

(Tutorial note:

(i) The Full b/d will be the difference at the beginning of the year between capital allowances to date and depreciation to date. Alternatively, this is given by the difference between tax WDV and accounts NBV ie, £250,000 – £190,000 = £60,000.

By the end of the year (Full c/d) this cumulative difference will have increased by the difference arising in the year (£70,000 – £50,000 = £20,000) and will therefore be £60,000 + £20,000 = £80,000.

To complete the Partial b/d column there must be some means of calculating the TDs on which deferred tax (DT) was provided at the start of the year. Here we are given the opening DT provision so this can be grossed up to find TDs

$$= £14{,}000\ \frac{100}{35} = £40{,}000.$$

Finally, we need the working to find the maximum cumulative reversal of ACAs, by looking ahead to future budgets.

The first step is to fill in the table of TDs. This working has four columns which will eventually allow calculations to be made to meet SSAP 15's disclosure requirements. It also has a line for each type of TD.)

Step 2 **Maximum cumulative reversal of ACAs**

	CA	*Depreciation*	*Originating TD/ (reversing TD)*	*Cumulative*
	£'000	£'000	£'000	£'000
20X2	60	50	10	10
20X3	90	100	(10)	-
20X4	100	120	(20)	(20)
20X5	90	60	30	10

The maximum cumulative reversal is £20,000 and this goes into working (a).

(Tutorial notes:

(ii) Since the loan stock was issued during the year there are no TDs to bring forward.

The cumulative difference by the end of this year is (£20,000 – £10,000) £10,000. This is the total difference to date and therefore goes into the Full c/d column.

Relief has been given in the tax computation to a lesser extent than an expense has gone through the profit and loss account. When this cash is paid, more relief will be obtained and therefore less tax paid. This TD therefore potentially gives rise to a DT asset and the TD has accordingly been shown in brackets (as opposite to the potential liability formed by the ACAs).

We now have to decide whether this difference will ever crystallise. For the moment, the way to consider this is to consider what will happen in future years with the loan stock interest. In this first year the cash received and the accruals basis produce different figures. However, for all future years until the year of conversion, we would expect in any year to make two half year loan stock payments equivalent in total to the full year's profit and loss account charge. For all these years then our total TD will remain at the current £10,000.

Reversal will occur in the year of conversion when the arrears of cash will catch up. Because conversion is anticipated the reversal is therefore anticipated and the £10,000 TD also goes in the Partial c/d column.

(iii) The process for debenture interest receivable is almost identical

Full b/d) Partial b/d)	Nil since debentures purchased during the year
Full c/d	Cumulative TD to date = £45,000 – £30,000 = £15,000. This may potentially form a tax liability as when the difference is received there will be tax to pay. The £15,000 is therefore shown in the table in the same direction as TDs on ACAs.
Partial c/d	No reversal is anticipated as the investment is to be held for the long term. There will be no 'catching up' effect as with the interest paid. No provision is therefore necessary on the partial basis.)

Step 3 The final step is to complete the DT table (working (c)) by multiplying TDs in working (a) by the appropriate tax rate(s). Here all are calculated at 35%.

Deferred tax

	Full b/d	*Partial b/d*	*Partial c/d*	*Full c/d*
	£'000	£'000	£'000	£'000
ACAs	21	14	7.0	28.00
Interest paid	-	-	(3.5)	(3.50)
Interest received	-	-	-	5.25
	21	14	3.5	29.75

The above working allows us to calculate all necessary figures for the financial statements.

7.4 Solution

Extracts from the financial statements

Note:

(1) **Taxation**

	£'000
Corporation tax	x
Deferred tax (3.5 – 14)	(10.5)
	x

The tax charge above would have increased by £19,250 if deferred tax had been fully provided for. [Full provision charge (29,750 – 21,000) 8,750 less partial provision credit (10,500) = £19,250]

(2) **Provisions for liabilities and charges**

Deferred tax

(a) **Movement**

	£'000
At 1 January 20X1	14.0
Profit and loss account credit	(10.5)
At 31 December 20X1	3.5

(b) **Analysis by major component**

	Provided £'000	Not provided £'000
Accelerated capital allowances	7.0	21.00 (28 – 7)
Interest paid	(3.5)	-
Interest received	-	5.25
	3.5	26.25 (29.75 – 3.5)

8 PROBLEMS IN ACCOUNTING FOR DEFERRED TAX

8.1 Why partial provision is unsatisfactory

SSAP 15 has been coming under increasing criticism, mainly because of problems arising from the fact that it requires deferred tax to be accounted for using the partial provision basis:

- SSAP 15 was originally issued at a time when generous capital allowances and high inflation meant that many entities had a 'core' of timing differences that would never reverse and therefore partial provision reflected economic reality. Since then, conditions have changed, and there is now a far greater likelihood that timing differences will reverse.

- Partial provision is subjective and potentially complicated to apply because it involves predicting future events, such as changes in the taxation system, capital expenditure and the useful economic lives of assets.

There are other problems:

- There are inconsistencies within the SSAP. Full provision is required for timing differences in respect of post-retirement benefits, but partial provision is required for all other timing differences.

- There are inconsistencies in the application of partial provision (eg, some entities provide deferred tax on fair value adjustments on acquisition while some do not). There is evidence that some entities make full provision on grounds of simplicity and this reduces the comparability of financial statements.

However, arguably the most important disadvantage of partial provision is that it is inconsistent with international practice. Almost all other major standard setters (including the FASB and the IASC) now require full provision.

8.2 Full provision and nil provision

As we have seen, the 'full provision' basis is based on the principle that financial statements for a period should recognise the tax effects, whether current or deferred, of all transactions occurring in that period.

Advantages of the full provision basis:

- It is straightforward to apply and objective.

- It has the effect of smoothing out distortions in the tax charge caused by timing differences. This means that it may provide more useful information for users of the financial statements because it is easier to make inter-temporal comparisons.

- It can be argued that the full provision basis matches the tax liability against the revenue to which it relates.

- It is consistent with international practice.

- There are also important conceptual arguments for full provision:

- Every tax difference represents a real liability since every one reverses. Whatever else happens, an entity will pay more tax in future as a result of the reversal than it would have done in the absence of the timing difference.

- Only the impact of new timing differences arising in future prevents the total liability from reducing. Partial provision takes account of these future differences, but this is inconsistent with the principle that only past transactions and events can be taken into account when measuring a liability. (The Statement of Principles defines a liability as an obligation arising from *past* transactions and events and FRSs 5 and 12 are based on this definition.)

- Partial provision relies on management intentions regarding future events. This is inconsistent with the principle that a liability can only arise from an obligation, rather than management decisions or intentions.

The main disadvantage of the full provision basis is that it may lead to the build up of large balances which never crystallise. Full provision is unpopular with many preparers of accounts because it can distort key performance measures. In particular, it increases gearing and reduces the amount available for dividend payments.

The ASB has rejected nil provision (the flow through basis). Nil provision has the advantages of straightforwardness and objectivity, and normally produces a tax liability which is closer to the 'real' liability than either full or partial provision. However, nil provision can also result in large fluctuations in the tax charge. It may understate tax liabilities. It does not allow tax relief relating to long term liabilities such as pension costs to be recognised in the same period as the costs themselves. It is also inconsistent with international practice.

8.3 Possible approaches to full provision

Full provision could, in theory, be implemented in different ways.

Timing differences and temporary differences

Earlier in this chapter we saw that there are two types of differences between profit before tax in the financial statements and the profit chargeable for tax: permanent differences and timing differences. In the UK, deferred tax has not been provided on permanent differences, but only on timing differences. In contrast, IAS 12 *Income Taxes* and the US accounting standard require deferred tax to be provided on 'temporary differences'. Temporary differences are the differences between the carrying values of the assets and liabilities in the balance sheet at the end of the period and the amounts that will actually be taxable or recoverable in respect of these assets and liabilities in future.

Most temporary differences are timing differences, but they can include permanent differences, for example:

- non-taxable grants received for the purchase of fixed assets that are deferred and recognised as income over the lives of the fixed assets

- foreign exchange differences on consolidation under the temporal method (non-monetary assets of foreign subsidiaries are translated at historic rates).

One obvious advantage of adopting this approach would be international harmonisation. However, there are several disadvantages. The main one is that identifying and measuring temporary differences is difficult in practice. For example, temporary differences can arise where the financial statements of an overseas subsidiary are consolidated. These can be difficult to quantify because some assets are eliminated on consolidation and others may or may not be taxable.

Other disadvantages of the 'temporary differences' approach include the following:

(a) It is believed to be conceptually wrong. In theory, deferred tax would have to be provided as soon as assets or liabilities were recognised.

Example

An entity acquires an asset for £100. This asset is subject to tax at 30% and therefore a deferred tax provision of £30 is recognised. The net value of the asset is understated, and this is misleading, because the entity would not have acquired the asset if its value had been less than its cost. The asset should still be recognised at its cost of £100.

(b) Because of the problems described in point (a), in practice there would have to be exceptions for at least some permanent differences. It is more logical to require deferred tax to be provided on timing differences only.

(c) It would lead to the build up of liabilities that would only crystallise in the distant future, if ever.

Therefore the ASB does not favour the temporary differences approach.

Liabilities and valuation adjustments

There are two very distinct views as to how full provision based on timing differences should be provided in practice:

(a) Timing differences should be recognised only if they represent rights or obligations at the balance sheet date, that is, only if the critical events that will cause their future reversal have occurred by the balance sheet date.

(b) Timing differences should be recognised even if the critical events causing their reversal have not occurred by the balance sheet date. This view holds that timing differences are similar to valuation adjustments, even though they may not be liabilities in their own right. A deferred tax liability is recognised in respect of accelerated capital allowances on a fixed asset because that fixed asset is worth less than an otherwise equivalent fixed asset that is still fully tax deductible.

The choice of approach is important, because it determines which timing differences are recognised.

8.4 Should deferred tax be provided on revalued assets?

Under SSAP 15, deferred tax is only recognised when it is likely that the asset will be disposed of and that the disposal will result in a chargeable gain after taking roll-over relief into account.

There are two points of view, which reflect the two views held as to the nature of deferred tax.

If deferred tax is regarded as an increase or decrease in a future tax liability it is argued that deferred tax should not be provided on a revaluation gain unless there is a commitment to dispose of the asset. If there is no commitment to dispose of the asset the revaluation gain is a permanent difference, rather than a timing difference, and will never affect taxable profit.

If deferred tax is regarded as a valuation adjustment it is argued that deferred tax should be provided on all revaluations. This reflects the difference in value between an asset which carries a potential tax liability and one which does not.

For example, if a company revalues land costing £1 million to £1.5 million that land cannot be worth as much to the company as land acquired separately for £1.5 million (which would be fully tax deductible). Because the historic cost of the land is only £1 million, the tax cost must only be £1 million.

8.5 Should deferred tax be provided on fair value adjustments?

FRS 7 *Fair values in acquisition accounting* requires the assets and liabilities of an acquired entity to be stated at fair values. Again, there are two points of view.

If deferred tax is viewed as an increase or decrease in a future tax liability it is believed that deferred tax should not be provided for on fair value adjustments. This is because the new reporting entity's actual tax liability is not altered as a result of the acquisition.

For example, if a company attributes a fair value of £600,000 to the stock of an acquired company whose cost to the acquired company was £500,000, the cost of the stock for tax purposes will always be £500,000 and the actual amount of tax that will be payable by the acquired entity on the sale of the stock is not altered as a result of the acquisition.

If deferred tax is viewed as a valuation adjustment it is believed that deferred tax should generally be provided for on fair value adjustments, where these relate to assets or liabilities that are expected to be realised or settled.

Taking the same example as above, the stock which has a fair value of £600,000 and a tax cost of £500,000 cannot be worth as much to the company as stock acquired separately for £600,000 (which would be fully tax deductible).

8.6 Deferred tax and post retirement benefits

SSAP 24 *Accounting for pension costs* requires pension costs to be accounted for on an accruals basis. This results in either an asset or a liability in the balance sheet. Pension costs are allowable for tax only when actually paid by the company. Therefore any balance sheet amount recorded under SSAP 24 is a timing difference on which deferred tax would be provided under the full provision method.

Those who regard deferred tax as an increase or decrease in a future tax liability would argue that as a result of the company's decision to pay and claim tax relief for pension costs in previous periods, its tax assessments in future periods will be higher or lower than they would have been otherwise, irrespective of the effect of any future transactions. Therefore any resulting deferred tax asset or liability should be recognised immediately.

Those who regard deferred tax as a valuation adjustment would argue that a pension asset must be worth less to the business than an asset whose cost will be fully deductible for tax purposes (eg, a new machine). Likewise, a pension liability that attracts tax relief when settled must be a lower burden to the reporting entity than an otherwise equivalent liability that does not (eg, a trade creditor). Therefore it is appropriate to recognise a deferred tax asset or liability.

8.7 Discounting deferred tax

The main disadvantage of the full provision method is that it may give rise to large liabilities that are never significantly reduced. It gives no indication of when (or whether) the liability will be paid. Discounting deferred tax balances would be a possible method of mitigating the effect of full provision.

Deferred tax can be discounted only if it represents a future cash flow. If deferred tax is an increase or decrease in future tax assessments (which will result in future cash flows), it represents an increase in future cash flows that can be discounted.

The 'valuation adjustment' approach to deferred tax is based on the premise that an asset that is not fully tax deductible must be worth less than an asset that is tax deductible. Therefore future tax payments are affected and result in future cash flows which can be discounted.

Discounting will always reduce the balance sheet liability for deferred tax. However, it will not necessarily reduce the tax charge in the profit and loss account. If interest on the brought forward items is greater than the discount arising on new items during the period, the tax charge for the period will be increased.

9 FRED 19: DEFERRED TAX

9.1 The main proposal

FRED 19 *Deferred tax* was issued in 1999 and if its proposals are adopted it will replace SSAP 15.

FRED 19 proposes that **full provision** should be made for all deferred tax assets and liabilities arising from timing differences.

Deferred tax assets or liabilities would only arise if the transactions or events that increase or decrease future tax charges have occurred by the balance sheet date. This means that deferred tax would be recognised on timing differences arising from:

- accelerated capital allowances;
- accruals for pension costs that will be deductible for tax purposes only when paid;
- elimination of unrealised intra group profits on consolidation;
- unrelieved tax losses; and
- other sources of short term timing differences.

Deferred tax would not be recognised on timing differences arising:

- on gains on revaluing assets, unless the entity has entered into a binding agreement to sell the asset by the balance sheet date;

- following the sale of assets, on gains that have been rolled over onto replacement assets if it is more likely than not that the taxable gain will be rolled over into replacement assets;

- on unremitted earnings of subsidiaries, associates and joint ventures, unless at the balance sheet date:

  – dividends have been accrued as being payable or receivable; or

  – the subsidiary, associate or joint venture has entered into a binding agreement to distribute past earnings in future.

The principle behind this is that deferred tax is only provided where it represents an asset or a liability in its own right. This is called the incremental liability approach. The Statement of Principles defines a liability as an obligation to transfer economic benefit as the result of a past transaction or event.

For example, if an entity has capital allowances in excess of depreciation it has an **obligation** to pay more tax in future. It cannot avoid this obligation. Therefore it has a liability. In contrast, if an entity revalues a fixed asset, it will not have an obligation to pay more tax unless it enters into a binding agreement to sell the asset. Therefore it does not have a liability.

Although the ASB has accepted the need for full provision, it has not adopted the same approach as the IASC. Unlike FRED 19, IAS 12 requires deferred tax to be provided on revaluation gains and retained profits of associates and joint ventures. This is similar to the 'valuation adjustment' approach to full provision discussed earlier. The ASB has rejected the valuation adjustment approach because:

(a) it is not consistent with the Statement of Principles and with FRS 12, which both base provisions on obligations;

(b) it is more difficult to apply and interpret;

(c) in some circumstances it creates and reverses provisions simply to standardise the tax charge rather than to reflect tax actually paid (for example, deferred tax provided on the revaluation of an asset that is not sold but depreciated is simply released to the profit and loss account over the life of the asset); and

(d) it is not appropriate in a mixed valuation system (ie, the current system where some assets are measured at historic cost and some at current value).

9.2 Deferred tax assets

Deferred tax assets should be recognised to the extent that they are regarded as recoverable. They should be regarded as recoverable if it is more likely than not that there will be suitable taxable profits from which the future reversal of the underlying timing differences can be deducted.

The FRED gives the following guidance:

(a) The existence of unrelieved tax losses at the balance sheet date is strong evidence that there might not be suitable tax profits against which deferred tax assets can be recovered. In these circumstances, deferred tax assets should only be recognised if there is other persuasive and reliable evidence that suitable tax profits will be generated in future.

(b) In the case of unrelieved trading losses, such evidence will exist only if the loss resulted from an identifiable and non-recurring cause and the reporting entity has otherwise been consistently profitable over a considerable period, with any past losses being more than offset by income in later periods.

FRED 19 appears to be less stringent than SSAP 15, which states that deferred tax assets resulting from tax losses should only be recognised if the availability of future taxable profits against which the losses can be offset is 'assured beyond reasonable doubt'. The ASB believes that it is more appropriate to emphasise how unlikely it is that the 'more likely than not' criteria will be met than by setting a recognition threshold that is higher than that set for other assets. This is consistent with the ASB's definition of prudence as a degree of caution where there is uncertainty.

9.3 Other proposals of FRED 19

These include the following:

(a) Deferred tax attributable to gains or losses recognised in the statement of total recognised gains and losses (STRGL) should also be recognised in the STRGL. (This is consistent with the requirements of FRS 16.)

(b) Deferred tax should be measured at the average tax rates that are expected to apply in the periods in which the timing differences are expected to reverse, based on tax rates and laws that have been enacted or substantively enacted by the balance sheet date. (This is also consistent with the requirements of FRS 16.)

In practice this means that there would be no change from the liability method required by SSAP 15. However, SSAP 15 does not stipulate that enacted rates must be used.

The ASB proposes that enacted rates should be used because:

(i) these are likely to be the best estimates of future tax rates because these will be influenced by political and economic factors which are very difficult to predict;

(ii) where there is evidence of possible future changes (eg, where proposals are announced in green papers for further consultation) it is very difficult to predict the likelihood that these changes will actually be enacted; and

(iii) this is consistent with the requirements of IAS 12.

9.4 Discounting

FRED 19 proposes that:

(a) Deferred tax assets and liabilities should be discounted if:

(i) the timing differences on which they are based have been measured by reference to undiscounted cash flows; and

(ii) the effect of discounting is material.

(b) Deferred tax assets and liabilities should be discounted according to the expected years of reversal of the timing differences existing at the balance sheet date.

(c) The discount rates used should be the post-tax yields to maturity that could be obtained at the balance sheet date on government bonds with similar maturity dates and in similar currencies to those of the deferred tax assets or liabilities.

These proposals have been included in an attempt to mitigate the effects of the increased liabilities and reduced earnings that would result from a change to full provision. (The Statement of Principles states that discounting should be used where carrying amounts are based on future cash flows.)

FRED 19 proposes that the 'full reversal' approach to discounting should be used. The future cash flows are treated as occurring when the timing differences constituting the deferred tax balance at the year-end are expected to reverse. This is consistent with the reasoning behind the full provision basis: every individual timing difference reverses and when it does so it has an incremental effect on future cash flows.

The alternative is the 'net reversal' approach. This treats the future cash flows as occurring when the timing differences as a whole (ie, after taking account of new timing differences to replace those that reverse) are expected to reverse. The ASB has rejected this approach because it is not consistent with full provision but with partial provision (which also views deferred tax as a whole, rather than as being made up of individual timing differences).

9.5 Activity

A company purchases a fixed asset for £500,000 on 1 January 20X0. The asset has a useful economic life of five years and no residual value. Capital allowances of 50% of cost can be claimed for each of the first two years of the asset's life. The rate of corporation tax is 30% and the post-tax discount rate is expected to be 5% throughout the life of the asset.

Calculate the deferred tax provision at 31 December 20X0 assuming that the proposals in FRED 19 are implemented.

9.6 Activity solution

Timing difference at 31 December 20X0:

	£'000
Net book value (500 – 100)	400
Written down value (500 × 50%)	(250)
	150

This will reverse as follows:

Years from now	*1*	*2*	*3*	*4*	*Total*
	£'000	£'000	£'000	£'000	£'000
Depreciation	100	100	100	100	400
Capital allowances	(250)	–	–	–	(250)
	(150)	100	100	100	150
Deferred tax liability (30%) (undiscounted)	(45)	30	30	30	45
Discount factor	0.952	0.907	0.864	0.823	
Deferred tax liability (discounted)	(43)	27	26	25	35

9.7 Presentation and disclosure

FRED 19 includes a number of proposals, of which the most important are:

(a) Deferred tax assets and liabilities should not normally be offset.

(b) Deferred tax liabilities should be classified as 'provisions for liabilities and charges' in the balance sheet (as at present). Deferred tax assets should be classified as debtors, under a separate subheading where material.

(c) Deferred tax assets and liabilities should be separately disclosed on the face of the balance sheet if the amounts are so material in the context of the total net current assets or net assets that readers might misinterpret the accounts otherwise.

(d) If deferred tax assets or liabilities have been discounted, the unwinding of the discount recorded at the previous balance sheet date and any movements attributable to changes in discount rates since the previous balance sheet date should be included as financial items next to interest in the profit and loss account. They should be disclosed separately either on the face of the profit and loss account or in a note.

(e) All other deferred tax recognised in the profit and loss account should be included within tax on profit or loss on ordinary activities (as at present).

(f) Information should be disclosed about factors affecting current and future tax charges. This should include a reconciliation of the current tax charge for the period to the profit before tax on ordinary activities multiplied by the standard rate of corporation tax.

9.8 Evaluation of the proposals

The ASB has admitted that it is not wholly convinced by the arguments for the full provision method. Nevertheless, it does not believe that this is one of the areas where a good case can be made for going against international opinion. It believes that continuing with the partial provision method would damage the credibility of UK financial reporting.

There are many advantages of full provision and these have been discussed earlier in the chapter. One possible view of FRED 19 is that it would achieve broad consistency with international practice while mitigating some of the disadvantages of full provision by adopting the incremental liability approach and discounting. FRED 19 is also consistent with the Statement of Principles and other recent FRSs such as FRS 12.

However, full provision is likely to be unpopular because it will reduce profits and increase gearing. Most respondents to the ASB's earlier Discussion Paper *Accounting for tax* were in favour of the retention of partial provision. They believed that partial provision gave the most realistic estimate of future tax payments and the most accurate reflection of a company's ongoing effective tax rate.

Criticisms of FRED 19 have included the following:

(a) It is necessarily a compromise. It introduces a version of full provision, ostensibly for the sake of international harmonisation. Yet it is not consistent with IAS 12 and in practice may very well produce similar results to the partial provision basis under SSAP 15.

(b) The proposals are unnecessarily complicated. In particular, discounting deferred tax balances is likely to cause practical problems. (The ASB has stated that it is particularly interested in responses to the proposals for discounting for this reason.)

(c) The 'full reversal' basis of discounting deferred tax liabilities may turn them into *assets* in the early years of an asset's life (because capital allowances exceed depreciation before the timing differences reverse). This may confuse users of the financial statements.

(d) It could be argued that nil provision, or 'flow through' accounting is the only method of providing deferred tax that is consistent with the Statement of Principles as it is questionable whether deferred tax is a present obligation as a result of a past event.

Conclusion FRED 19 proposes that full provision should be made for deferred tax.

10 CHAPTER SUMMARY

FRS 16 covers the presentation and disclosure of items relating to current tax in the financial statements.

Deferred taxation arises due to timing differences and the need to apply the matching revenues with the full costs of earning those revenues.

SSAP 15 requires the use of the partial provision basis ie, provide deferred tax to the extent it is expected that additional corporation tax liabilities will arise in the foreseeable future.

11 SELF TEST QUESTIONS

11.1 What happens if there is an excess of interest paid over interest received in the accounting period? (2.2)

11.2 Are annual charges shown gross or net in the profit and loss account? (2.9)

11.3 What are permanent differences? (3.2)

11.4 What are the three possible bases for providing deferred tax? (4.1)

11.5 Should deferred tax be accounted for under the liability method or the deferral method? (5.1)

11.6 What should be disclosed in the profit and loss account in respect of deferred tax? (5.2)

12 EXAMINATION TYPE QUESTIONS

12.1 Bimbo Ltd

(a) Bimbo Ltd was incorporated on 1 April 20X1. In the year ended 31 March 20X2 the company made a profit before taxation of £100,000 (depreciation charged of £10,000) and made the following capital additions

Plant	£48,000
Motor vehicles	£12,000

Corporation tax is chargeable at the rate of 30%. Writing down allowances are available at 25%.

You are required to compute the following

(i) the corporation tax payable for the year ended 31 March 20X2

(ii) the deferred tax charge for the year on the basis that full provision is made for all originating timing differences, showing also the relevant extracts from the financial statements.

(b) Using the information in (a) above calculate the deferred tax provision required at the balance sheet date on the basis that provision is made only if it is probable that a liability or asset will crystallise (ie, on the SSAP 15 (revised) basis).

The company has prepared capital expenditure budgets at 31 March 20X2 which reveal the following pattern of capital allowances and depreciation

	Capital allowances	*Depreciation*
	£	£
Year to 31 March 20X3	17,000	16,000
Year to 31 March 20X4	23,000	19,000
Year to 31 March 20X5	21,000	19,000
Year to 31 March 20X6	15,000	21,000
Year to 31 March 20X7	24,000	29,000
Year to 31 March 20X8	25,000	20,000

From 1 April 20X8 capital allowances are expected to exceed depreciation charges each year.

(c) Continuing from the facts in (b), for the year ended 31 March 20X3 the following information is relevant in respect of capital allowances and depreciation

Depreciation	£14,000
Capital allowances	£16,000

The budgets for capital expenditure and depreciation are as previously stated for the years 20X4 to 20X8.

In addition the following further information may be relevant for the deferred tax calculation:

In preparing the financial statements for the year to 31 March 20X3 the financial director has decided to set up a deferred repairs provision. An amount of £1,200 will be set aside from profits of the current year and for each of the next three years, at which point it is anticipated that a major refurbishment programme will be undertaken at an estimated cost of £4,800.

You are required to prepare the extracts from the financial statements for the year ended 31 March 20X3 in respect of taxation. An accounting policy note is **not** required. **(20 marks)**

12.2 Partial plc

Partial plc was established as a company that manufactured replacement keys. It had started with the manufacture of replacement metal keys for antique boxes where the original keys had been lost and had become recognised as specialists within this field. Their expertise has since extended to the provision of electronic, as well as mechanical, entry devices. This has resulted in the need for an ongoing capital asset investment programme. The draft profit and loss account for the year ended 30 November 20X0 showed a pre-tax profit of £375,000 and it was forecast that the profit for 20X1 would increase by 20% to £450,000.

The following information was available concerning the company's fixed assets as at 30 November 20X0.

	£
Gross cost of fixed assets	1,000,000
Accumulated depreciation	400,000
Capital allowances	525,000

The following forecast information was available as at 30 November 20X0 relating to depreciation charges and capital allowances for the next five years on the assumption that they go ahead with the capital investment programme.

Year ending	*Depreciation charge*	*Capital allowances*
	£	£
30.11.X1	234,000	265,000
30.11.X2	253,000	303,000
30.11.X3	276,000	193,000
30.11.X4	278,000	192,000
30.11.X5	248,000	262,000

The forecast depreciation charge of £234,000 and capital allowance of £265,000 were amended in the accounts prepared for the year ended 30 November 20X1 to £250,000 and £289,000 respectively.

The following forecast information was available as at 30 November 20X1 relating to depreciation charges and capital allowances for the next five years

Year ending	*Depreciation charge*	*Capital allowances*
	£	£
30.11.X2	250,000	289,000
30.11.X3	278,000	197,000
30.11.X4	275,000	193,000
30.11.X5	253,000	265,000
30.11.X6	254,000	278,000

Assume a corporation tax rate of 30%.

You are required:

(a) (i) to explain why permanent differences are not treated in the same way as timing differences in calculating a deferred taxation provision and

(ii) to state the requirements set out in SSAP 15 *Accounting for deferred tax* relating to the disclosure of the deferred taxation provision in the balance sheet and

(iii) to explain how the deferred tax provision should be calculated for inclusion in the balance sheet. **(12 marks)**

(b) (i) to prepare the balance sheet entry for Partial plc as at 30 November 20X0 for deferred tax to comply with the provisions of SSAP 15 *Accounting for deferred tax*.

(ii) to prepare the profit and loss account and balance sheet entries for deferred taxation for Partial plc for the year ended 30 November 20X1 to comply with the provisions of SSAP 15 *Accounting for deferred tax*. **(12 marks)**

(c) to discuss how the revaluation of fixed assets on which capital allowances are received could be dealt with when calculating the deferred taxation provision. **(6 marks)**

(Total: 30 marks)

13 ANSWERS TO EXAMINATION TYPE QUESTIONS

13.1 Bimbo Ltd

(a) (i) **Corporation tax payable year ended 31 March 20X2**

	£
Profit per accounts	100,000
Add: Depreciation	10,000
	110,000
Less: WDA 25% of £60,000	15,000
Taxable profits	£95,000
Tax payable @ 30%	£28,500

(ii)

	£
Tax WDV	45,000
Accounts NBV	50,000
	£(5,000)
Deferred tax provision required @ 30%	£1,500

Extract from balance sheet and notes

Provisions for liabilities and charges

	Amount provided £	*Amount not provided* £
Deferred taxation	1,500	-

Extract from profit and loss account

	£	£
Profit before taxation		100,000
Taxation		
UK corporation tax at 30% on profits	28,500	
Deferred taxation	1,500	
		(30,000)
Profit after taxation		£70,000

(b) Deferred tax charge £1,200 (amount not provided for year £300)
Balance sheet provision £1,200 (amount not provided for year £300)

WORKINGS

(W1) **Maximum cumulative reversal of originating timing differences in respect of accelerated capital allowances**

	CA	*Depreciation*	*Difference OTD/(RTD)*	*Cumulative*
	£	£	£	£
20X3	17,000	16,000	1,000	1,000
20X4	23,000	19,000	4,000	5,000
20X5	21,000	19,000	2,000	7,000
20X6	15,000	21,000	(6,000)	1,000
20X7	24,000	29,000	(5,000)	(4,000)
20X8	25,000	20,000	5,000	1,000

(W2) **The basic deferred taxation working is**

	(A) Full basis b/d	*(B) Partial basis b/d*	*(C) Partial basis c/d*	*(D) Full basis c/d*
	£	£	£	£
Timing differences				
ACAs	-	-	(4,000)	(5,000)
Deferred tax provision required @ 30%	-	-	(1,200)	(1,500)

(c) **Extracts from the financial statements in relation to taxation (31 March 20X3)**

Profit and loss account

	£
Taxation	
UK corporation tax at 30% on profits	x
Deferred taxation credit	(60)
Profit and loss account tax charge	x

An amount of £300 has not been provided during the year in respect of deferred taxation because it is not foreseen that the related liabilities will crystallise.

Balance sheet

Provisions for liabilities and charges	
Deferred taxation *(Note 1)*	£1,140

Note 1

	Brought forward	*Movement*	*Carried forward*	*Amount not provided*
	£	£	£	£
ACAs	(1,200)	(300)	(1,500)	(600)
Deferred repairs	-	360	360	-
	£(1,200)	£60	£(1,140)	£(600)

WORKINGS

(W1) **Maximum cumulative reversal of OTD in respect of ACAs**

	CA	*Depreciation*	*Difference OTD/(RTD)*	*Cumulative*
	£	£	£	£
20X4	23,000	19,000	4,000	4,000
20X5	21,000	19,000	2,000	6,000
20X6	15,000	21,000	(6,000)	-
20X7	24,000	29,000	(5,000)	(5,000)
20X8	25,000	20,000	5,000	-

(W2)

	(A) Full basis b/d	*(B) Partial basis b/d*	*(C) Partial basis c/d*	*(D) Full basis c/d*
	£	£	£	£
Timing differences				
ACAs	(5,000)	(4,000)	(5,000)	(7,000)
Deferred repairs	-	-	1,200	1,200
	(5,000)	(4,000)	(3,800)	(5,800)
Deferred tax @ 30%	(1,500)	(1,200)	(1,140)	(1,740)

	£
Profit and loss	
Credit (C – B)	60
Balance sheet provision (C)	(1,140)
Amount unprovided	
Balance sheet (D – C)	(600)
P&L account (D – A) – (C – B)	300

13.2 Partial plc

(Tutorial note: overall a question which fully examines the requirements of SSAP 15. It is a good test of knowledge of the standard and will be very difficult for those students who have not studied the standard **in full.**

Use the breakdown of the question to construct your answer and be careful not to answer more than the requirements of each section. Avoid general answers that merely repeat the requirements of SSAP 15.*)*

(a) (i) The differences between accounting profit and taxable profit can be categorised into those which are permanent and those which can be attributed to timing. Permanent differences arise for two main reasons

(1) Certain types of income recognised in the accounts are not assessed for taxation purposes.

(2) Certain types of expenditure which are recognised in the accounts following generally accepted accounting principles are not allowed as an expense against taxable income.

These differences will always exist and therefore the increase or decrease in tax liability cannot be deferred or accelerated. They are therefore not relevant to any assessment of deferment or acceleration.

Timing differences arise because certain items are included in the accounts for a period which is different from that in which they are dealt with for tax purposes.

There is no permanent reduction or increase in the amount of tax payable. In an effort to match the tax charge in the accounts with the taxable profit reported in the accounts, adjustments are made for such timing differences through a deferred taxation provision. No such matching is possible with permanent differences, therefore no account is taken of such differences in the calculation of the deferred taxation provision.

(ii) **Balance sheet disclosure requirements**

(1) Any deferred tax balance, and its major components, should be disclosed either in the balance sheet or in the notes to the accounts. The notes should also disclose transfers to and from the deferred tax provision.

(2) Transfers to and from deferred tax accounted for as movements on reserves should be shown separately as part of such movements.

(3) Where the value of an asset is shown in a note because it differs materially from its book amount, the tax implications of its sale at the revalued amount should be shown by way of a note to the accounts.

(4) Any unprovided deferred tax should be shown in the notes, analysed into its major components.

(iii) SSAP 15 requires that deferred tax be calculated on the partial provision basis. This basis requires deferred tax to be accounted for in respect of the net amount by which it is probable that any payment of tax will be temporarily deferred or accelerated by the operation of timing differences that will reverse in the foreseeable future without being replaced. If they will be replaced, and therefore will not crystallise, the timing differences should not result in a provision for deferred tax. Accurate forecasts are required for assessments of possible reversals.

(b) (i) At 30 November 20X0 the full provision of deferred tax would be

	£'000
Capital allowances	525
Accumulated depreciation	400
Difference	125
@ 30%	37.5

Forecast differences

	Depreciation £'000	*Capital allowances* £'000	*Differences* £'000
20X1	234	265	31
20X2	253	303	50
20X3	276	193	(83)
20X4	278	192	(86)
20X5	248	262	14

On a partial provision basis the provision required is calculated by reference to the maximum reversal ie, £83,000 + £86,000. With increases in the differences of £81,000 in years 20X1 and 20X2 the maximum reversal of the differences at the end of 20X0 is £169,000 – £81,000.

Provision = £88,000 × 30% = £26,400.

Balance sheet entry

	£
Provisions for liabilities and charges	
Taxation including deferred taxation	26,400

Note would include details of:

Deferred tax provided re accelerated capital allowances	26,400
Deferred tax not provided re accelerated capital allowances (£37,500 – £26,400)	11,100

(ii) At 30 November 20X1 the full provision for deferred tax would be

	£'000
Capital allowances (525 + 289)	814
Accumulated depreciation (400 + 250)	650
	164
@ 30%	49.2

Forecast differences

	Depreciation £'000	*Capital allowances* £'000	*Differences* £'000
20X2	250	289	39
20X3	278	197	(81)
20X4	275	193	(82)
20X5	253	265	12
20X6	254	278	24

On a partial provision basis the provision required is calculated by reference to the maximum reversal ie, £81,000 + £82,000 = £163,000. With the increase of £39,000 in 20X2 only £124,000 of the difference at 30.11.20X1 is likely to reverse. Therefore provision required is £124,000 × 30% = £37,200.

Balance sheet entry

	£
Provisions for liabilities and charges	
Taxation including deferred taxation	37,200

Notes would include details of

Deferred tax provided re accelerated capital allowances	37,200
Deferred tax not provided re accelerated capital allowances (£49,200 – £37,200)	12,000

Profit and loss account would include a debit entry of £10,800 to increase the provision from £26,400 (at 30.11.20X0) to the £37,200 required at 30.11.20X1.

(c) When an asset which attracts capital allowances (and is assumed to depreciate) is revalued a deferred tax problem arises. Timing differences caused by the depreciation/capital allowance differences will originally be calculated on the cost of the asset. After revaluation, the capital allowances will be unchanged but the depreciation will be based on the revalued amount. The differences between the two will therefore change. It is possible to deal with this problem in one of two ways

(i) Ignore the additional depreciation because there is no corresponding capital allowance adjustment and therefore it does not constitute a timing difference. No adjustment to deferred tax arises.

(ii) The revaluation is considered to be a write-back of past depreciation and therefore reverses the deferred tax effect of charging that past depreciation. Timing differences thereafter are based on the comparison of depreciation of the revalued asset with the original capital allowances.

Both methods appear to be acceptable providing that the one chosen is applied consistently.

7 ACCOUNTING FOR PENSION COSTS

INTRODUCTION & LEARNING OBJECTIVES

Pension costs can be a difficult area to study due to the lack of familiarity with the terms used to describe the type of schemes and the means by which the schemes are funded. You will need to spend some time mastering the meaning of these terms.

When you have studied this chapter you should be able to do the following:

- Describe the regulations relating to the treatment of pension costs.
- Explain and apply the provisions of SSAP 24.

1 THE CONCEPTUAL NATURE OF PENSION RIGHTS AND PENSION COSTS

1.1 Pension rights

Pension schemes fall into two basic categories

(a) **Defined benefit schemes**

Definition Under these schemes employees' pension benefits are specified, typically as a percentage of final salary.

An actuary will calculate, on the basis of a set of carefully chosen assumptions, the size of the fund required on retirement to provide the specified pensions and hence the contributions required to ensure that on the retirement of each employee the required fund exists. Traditionally defined benefit schemes comprise the lion's share of the larger UK employee pension schemes.

(b) **Defined contribution schemes**

Definition Under these schemes the contributions made by employer and employee are specified amounts, normally set percentages of current salary, and no fixed commitments are made as to the pension level which the employee will eventually receive.

The contributions are simply invested, and the size of the fund accumulated by the retirement date, including investment income, will determine the size of the pension payable. The great advantage of such schemes is that it is possible to identify a pool of funds attributable to each individual member, therefore greatly enhancing the portability of the pension. The portability advantage is the reason why an increasing number of employee schemes, particularly in smaller firms, are defined contribution schemes.

1.2 The main problems

The provision of pensions creates two separate decisions for a company

(a) **Funding**

This is the level and pattern of cash contributions to provide for the eventual payment of pensions. The decision as to funding would generally be a matter to be decided between an employer and a professional actuary.

(b) **Costing**

This is the way in which the expense of pensions is charged to the company's profit and loss account and is the matter in which the accountant is directly involved.

It is imperative, however, to understand from the outset that the two decisions are separate and consequentially that the charge in the profit and loss account is not necessarily the same as the cash contributions made. You are already familiar with that principle in many areas of accounting since the profit and loss account is drawn up on an accruals rather than a cash basis.

2 FUNDING

This section deals with the ways in which contributions to pension funds are calculated.

2.1 Funded and unfunded schemes

There are two approaches to the provision of pensions, the choice of which is very important to the security of the future benefits

(a) **Unfunded pensions**

Definition In such schemes the employer pays pensions due directly out of the company's assets, and thus does not maintain a separate pension fund.

In some cases the employer will appropriate a certain level of funds each year to a separate pool of assets earmarked for the payment of pensions, whereas in other cases he will simply pay pensions due out of current revenues. In either case the pension is directly vulnerable to downturns in the fortunes of the company.

(b) **Funded pensions**

Definition These schemes involve the employer making regular contributions to an external pension fund which is legally separate from the employer company.

Such a fund will either be administered by trustees, or, as in the case of many smaller funds, will be administered by an insurance company. Funded schemes have the great advantage over unfunded ones that contributions are accumulated externally to the employing company and thus will not be lost if the company hits trouble.

2.2 Calculation of contributions: defined contribution schemes

Definition In defined contribution schemes the liability of the employer is for a set level of contributions and no further liability accrues.

The precise amount of the contributions is therefore a matter for negotiation between employer and employee.

2.3 Calculation of normal contributions: defined benefit schemes

(a) **Actuarial involvement**

In these schemes the liability of the employer is to provide a set level of pension benefits, typically a percentage of final pre-retirement salary, and is therefore a very long term commitment. In view of this, an actuary will be employed to calculate the contributions which will be required to ensure that sufficient funds will have been accumulated to meet pension liabilities as and when they fall due.

(b) **Actuarial assumptions**

The calculation of contributions entails taking into account a number of uncertain future factors and thus the actuary will have to make assumptions concerning them. These assumptions will cover factors including the following

(i) future rates of inflation and pay increases
(ii) increases to pensions already being paid
(iii) earnings on investments
(iv) the number of employees joining the scheme
(v) the age profile of the employees, and
(vi) the probability that employees will die or leave the company's employment before reaching retirement age.

(c) **Actuarial objectives**

In choosing the level and pattern of contributions the actuary will have in mind two major objectives

(i) to build up assets in the scheme in a prudent and controlled manner in advance of the retirement of the members of the scheme, and

(ii) to avoid undue distortion of the employer's cash flows.

(d) **Available methods**

The actuarial methods commonly used divide broadly into two categories although the detail of these is outside the syllabus.

(i) **Accrued benefits methods**

Definition These methods look at the estimated ultimate pension benefits of the employees in the scheme (based necessarily on future salary levels) and attempt to provide for that proportion of those benefits accrued to date.

These methods will tend to produce increasing contributions relating to each employee as his/her service life progresses, as later contributions will be invested for shorter periods than earlier ones. In spite of this the actuary will be able to specify the contributions as a level percentage of total payroll costs, on the assumption that the overall age profile of the members of the scheme remains constant (due to new entrants joining the scheme).

(ii) **Prospective benefits methods**

Definition These methods once again regard the estimated ultimate pension benefits but simply try to spread the cost of providing for these benefits over the service lives of the employees currently in the scheme, typically as a level percentage of payroll costs, without considering what proportion of the benefits has actually accrued.

Prospective benefits methods will therefore tend to build up assets earlier in an employee's service life as they take into account the ageing of the work force.

2.4 Surpluses and deficiencies in defined benefit schemes

As the chosen funding plan is based on assumptions about the future, it is essential that the adequacy of the chosen plan is regularly reviewed. Accordingly, most pension schemes undergo a formal valuation on a triennial basis to compare the actuarial value of the assets and the liabilities and to reveal any deficiencies or surpluses.

(a) **Valuations**

There are a number of different actuarial methods of valuation. These are outside the syllabus. It is however worth appreciating that if there are different methods of valuation, identical companies, to which different methods are being applied, could end up with very different amounts in their books.

(b) **Reasons for surpluses and deficits**

The main causes of surpluses and deficits are as follows

(i) Variations between reality and the assumptions made at the last valuation. Surpluses and deficits on this basis are referred to as *experience* surpluses or deficits.

(ii) The effect of changes in actuarial assumptions on the actuarial valuation of accrued benefits.

(iii) Retroactive changes in benefits or in conditions for membership.

(iv) Increases to pensions in payment or to deferred pensions for which provision has not previously been made.

(c) **Elimination of surpluses and deficits**

Surpluses and deficits need to be eliminated to the extent that they are not expected to be offset by future deficits and surpluses, as they represent respectively needlessly idle funds and a potential threat to the security of pension payments. Actions which the actuary may recommend to rectify the position include

(i) **Correction of surpluses**

- improvement of benefits
- refunds to the employer (subject to deduction of tax at source of 40%)
- contribution holidays (periods of reduced or nil contribution although the scope of these is limited due to the provisions of the Social Security Act 1991 (outside the syllabus))

(ii) **Correction of deficits**

- an increase in the normal contribution rate
- additional special payments over a limited period
- lump sum contributions

The decision as to which method to use is made on the advice of the actuary taking into account the cash flow position of the employer company. For instance a refund would be very suitable for a company in a situation of financial stringency but less so for one which already has cash surpluses.

3 COSTING

3.1 Introduction

This section deals with the way in which pensions are dealt with in the financial statements of a company. Accounting in this area is dealt with by SSAP 24 *Accounting for pension costs*.

The standard applies to all situations when an employer has a legal or contractual commitment under a pension scheme or one implicit in the employer's actions, to provide for or contribute to pensions for his employees and applies irrespective of whether the scheme is funded or unfunded.

3.2 Basic principles

The Standard is based on the concept that the provision for or contribution to a pension represents deferred remuneration and applies the accruals concept of SSAP 2 to produce the following *accounting objective*

> "The employer should recognise the expected cost of providing pensions on a systematic and rational basis over the period during which he derives benefit from the employee's services".

The methods by which this is pursued are examined in the following sections.

3.3 Defined contribution schemes

Under defined contribution schemes the liability of an employer for meeting pension costs is restricted to the amount of contributions payable (normally specified as a percentage of annual salary), and therefore the pension cost charged to profit and loss account is simply the amount of contributions payable in respect of the relevant accounting period.

3.4 Defined benefit schemes

As discussed previously the liability for meeting pension costs of an employer in respect of a defined benefit scheme cannot be finally determined until the date of retirement and therefore the charge to profit and loss account (as with the contributions) must be calculated using actuarial methods. The standard divides the pension cost charged into two elements: the regular pension cost and variations from the regular cost.

3.5 Regular pension cost

Definition This is the consistent ongoing cost as calculated under the chosen actuarial method.

The actuarial method should be chosen so as to give the cost as a substantially level percentage of current and expected future pensionable payroll in the light of the current actuarial assumptions. This satisfies the accounting objective as the level of the pensionable payroll gives a good measure of the benefits the company derives from its workforce. The question therefore becomes which actuarial method to use.

As discussed earlier both prospective benefits methods and accrued benefits methods (assuming a constant age profile in the scheme) will normally give contributions as a level percentage of payroll. In this case the same actuarial method can be used for the calculation of the regular cost. However, in situations when the actuarial method used for funding purposes does not suit the accounting objective, a separate actuarial calculation will have to be performed for costing purposes.

3.6 The accounting treatment for over and under funded schemes

An overfunded scheme has, by definition, a surplus in the pension scheme. Conversely an underfunded scheme is in deficit. Changes will need to be made in accounting for the costs of the pension scheme to reflect the surplus or deficiency. SSAP 24 refers to these changes as **variations from the regular cost**.

As the regular pension cost is calculated on actuarial methods the causes of these surpluses or deficiencies will be the same as those which caused funding surpluses and deficits as discussed earlier, namely

(i) variations of assumptions from reality (experience surpluses and deficits)
(ii) the effects of changes in actuarial assumptions on accrued benefits
(iii) retroactive changes in benefits or in conditions for membership, and
(iv) increases to pensions in payment or to deferred pensions for which provision has not previously been made.

3.7 Usual treatment

The basic treatment prescribed by the Standard for variations from the regular cost is that they should be allocated over the expected remaining service lives of current employees in the scheme (a period representing the average remaining service lives may be used if desired).

The reasoning for this treatment is that surpluses and deficits are (in most situations) part of the ongoing process of revising the estimate of the ultimate liability which will fall on the employer on the retirement of employees. They therefore cannot be treated as prior period adjustments (in accordance with FRS 3) as they relate to the employees currently in the scheme.

3.8 Example

Boris plc operates a defined benefit scheme with a regular pension cost of £400,000 per annum. A surplus of £1,020,000 has been identified by the actuary at 31 December 20X0. The actuary recommends a three year contribution holiday. The average remaining service lives of members is ten years.

Show how the surplus should normally be accounted for. (Ignore tax)

3.9 Solution

P&L charge will be regular cost of £400,000 less the surplus* spread over 10 years (£400,000 × 3 ÷ 10 = £120,000) = £400,000 – £120,000 = £280,000.

* Note that the surplus to be spread is the reduction in payments needed to clear the surplus identified by the actuary at 31 December 20X0. The difference arises because of the time value of money.

Year	*Funding* £'000	*Accounting* £'000	*Accruals and deferred income* £'000
20X1	-	280	280
20X2	-	280	560
20X3	-	280	840
20X4	400	280	720
20X5	400	280	600
20X6	400	280	480
20X7	400	280	360
20X8	400	280	240
20X9	400	280	120
20X10	400	280	–
	2,800	2,800	

3.10 Exceptions

The Standard, however, specifies the following exceptions

(a) **Significant reduction in number of employees in the scheme**

When a significant reduction in the number of employees covered by the scheme occurs (for example due to redundancies in a reorganisation), a significant surplus may arise which does not relate to the remaining employees in the scheme. In such cases the surplus should be recognised in the profit and loss account in the same period as the effects of the elimination of the surplus (by means of refund, contribution holiday, or reduced normal contributions) are felt in the cash contributions to the scheme.

Example

Suppose the £1,020,000 surplus in the first Example was caused by a significant reduction in the number of employees during 20X0.

Show how the surplus should be accounted for. (Ignore tax)

Year	*Funding* £'000	*Accounting* £'000
20X1	–	–
20X2	–	–
20X3	–	–
20X4	400 pa	400 pa

Under FRS 3 where the significant reduction in the number of employees *is related to the sale or termination of an operation,* the associated pension cost or credit should be recognised immediately to the extent necessary to comply with the requirements of paragraph 18 of FRS 3. This means that the deficit or surplus should be included as part of the profit or loss on sale or termination.

Example

Suppose the £1,020,000 surplus in the first Example was caused by a reduction in the number of employees because of the disposal of a business segment.

Show how the surplus should be accounted for. (Ignore tax)

Year	*Funding* £'000	*Accounting* £'000		*Prepayment* £'000
20X0	400	400		
		(1,020)	to profit or loss on disposal of business segment	1,020
20X1	–	340		680
20X2	–	340		340
20X3	–	340		–
20X4	400 pa	400 pa		–

Note that the effect of the above (in the same way as when the surplus was part of an extraordinary event) has been not to defer recognition of the pension credit.

(b) **Major event outside the scope of actuarial assumptions**

In very limited circumstances, a major event or transaction has occurred which is outside the scope of, and has not been allowed for in the actuarial assumptions. This may have caused a material deficit requiring significant additional contributions to the pension fund, so that prudence may require that the deficit is recognised over a period shorter than the expected remaining service lives of the employees in the scheme.

(c) **Refund**

When a refund is made to the employer (subject to deduction of tax at source 40%) then the company *may* recognise the refund in the profit and loss account in the period in which it is received.

Example

Suppose that the £1,020,000 surplus in the first Example was cleared by a refund at the start of 20X1 instead of a contribution holiday.

Show how the surplus may be accounted for. (Ignore tax)

Year	Funding	Accounting
	£'000	£'000
20X1	(1,020)	(1,020)
	400	400
20X2	400 pa	400 pa

Alternatively

Year	Funding	$\left(400 - \frac{1{,}020}{10}\right)$ Accounting	Accruals and deferred income
	£'000	£'000	£'000
20X1	(1,020)		1,020
	400	298	918
20X2	400	298	816
20X3	400	298	714
20X4	400	298	612
20X5	400	298	510
20X6	400	298	408
20X7	400	298	306
20X8	400	298	204
20X9	400	298	102
20X10	400	298	–
	2,980	2,980	

3.11 Ex gratia pensions and discretionary and ex gratia increases

(a) When ex gratia pensions are granted, the capital cost, to the extent not covered by a surplus, should be recognised in the profit and loss account in the accounting period in which they are granted.

(b) Where allowance for discretionary or ex gratia increases in pensions is not made in the actuarial assumptions the capital cost of the increases (when not covered by surpluses) should be recognised in the profit and loss account in the accounting period in which they are initially granted.

3.12 Balance sheet amounts

As can be seen from the preceding sections and examples, SSAP 24 is primarily concerned with the profit and loss account. The balance sheet amounts produced are residual items and represent the difference between the cumulative cost charged to profit and loss account and the cumulative payments made by the company in respect of pensions. This is one of the major criticisms of SSAP 24.

3.13 Activity

The actuarial valuation as at 31 December 20X1 of the defined benefit pension scheme of a company showed a deficit of £30 million. The actuary recommended that the deficit be eliminated by lump sum payments of £15 million per annum for two years, in addition to the regular cost of £5 million per annum. The average remaining service life of employees in the scheme was estimated as eight years.

What will be the entries in the accounts over the years 20X2 to 20X9?

3.14 Activity solution

The pension cost charge for the next eight years should be:

$$£5 \text{ million} + \frac{£30 \text{ million}}{8} = £8.75 \text{ million}$$

The funding and accounting policies will therefore be as follows:

	Funding £m	*Accounting* £m	*Prepayment* £m
20X2	20	8.75	11.25
20X3	20	8.75	22.50
20X4	5	8.75	18.75
20X5	5	8.75	15.00
20X6	5	8.75	11.25
20X7	5	8.75	7.50
20X8	5	8.75	3.75
20X9	5	8.75	–
	70	70.00	

The prepayment will be disclosed on the balance sheet.

4 ACCOUNTING REGULATIONS RELATING TO PENSION COSTS

4.1 Standard accounting practice of SSAP 24

Para

80 Subject to the provisions of paragraphs 81 to 83, variations from the regular cost should be allocated over the expected remaining service lives of current employees in the scheme. A period representing the average remaining service lives may be used if desired.

81 The provisions of paragraph 80 should not be applied where, and to the extent that, a significant change in the normal level of contributions occurs because contributions are adjusted to eliminate a surplus or deficiency resulting from a significant reduction in the number of employees covered by the enterprise's pension arrangements. Where the significant reduction in the number of employees is related to the sale or termination of an operation, the associated pension cost or credit should be recognised immediately to the extent necessary to comply with FRS 3. In all other cases where there is a reduction in contributions arising from a significant reduction in employees the reduction of contributions should be recognised as it occurs. Amounts receivable may not be anticipated; for example, the full effect of a contribution holiday should not be recognised at the outset of the holiday, but rather spread over its duration.

82 In strictly limited circumstances prudence may require that a material deficit be recognised over a period shorter than the expected remaining service lives of current employees in the scheme. Such circumstances are limited to those where a major event or transaction has occurred which has not been allowed for in the actuarial assumptions, is outside the normal scope of those assumptions and has necessitated the payment of significant additional contributions to the pension scheme.

83 Where a refund that is subject to deduction of tax in accordance with the provisions of the UK Finance Act 1986, or equivalent legislation, is made to the employer, the enterprise may depart from the requirements of paragraph 80 and account for the surplus or deficiency in the period in which the refund occurs.

84 Where ex gratia pensions are granted the capital cost, to the extent not covered by a surplus, should be recognised in the profit and loss account in the accounting period in which they are granted.

85 Where allowance for discretionary or ex gratia increases in pensions is not made in the actuarial assumptions, the capital cost of such increases should, to the extent not covered by a surplus, be recognised in the profit and loss account in the accounting period in which they are initially granted.

Paras 80-85 SSAP 24

4.2 Disclosure requirements

The following disclosures should be made in respect of a **defined contribution** scheme:

(a) the nature of the scheme (ie, defined contribution);
(b) the accounting policy;
(c) the pension cost charge for the period;
(d) any outstanding or prepaid contributions at the balance sheet date.

The following disclosures should be made in respect of a **defined benefit** scheme:

(a) the nature of the scheme (ie, defined benefit);

(b) whether it is funded or unfunded (ie, assets held outside or inside the employer's business);

(c) the accounting policy and, if different, the funding policy;

(d) whether the pension cost and provision (or asset) are assessed in accordance with the advice of a professionally qualified actuary and, if so, the date of the most recent formal actuarial valuation or later formal review used for this purpose. If the actuary is an employee or officer of the reporting company, or of the group of which it is a member, this fact should be disclosed;

(e) the pension cost charge for the period together with explanations of significant changes in the charge compared to that in the previous accounting period;

(f) any provisions or prepayments in the balance sheet resulting from a difference between the amounts recognised as cost and the amounts funded or paid directly;

(g) the amount of any deficiency on a current funding level basis, indicating the action, if any, being taken to deal with it in the current and future accounting periods;

(h) an outline of the results of the most recent formal actuarial valuation or later formal review of the scheme on an ongoing basis.

This should include disclosure of:

(i) the actuarial method used and a brief description of the main actuarial assumptions;
(ii) the market value of scheme assets at the date of their valuation or review;
(iii) the level of funding expressed in percentage terms;
(iv) comments on any material actuarial surplus or deficiency indicated by (iii) above;

(i) any commitment to make additional payments over a limited number of years;

(j) the accounting treatment adopted in respect of a refund made in accordance with the provisions of paragraph 83 where a credit appears in the financial statements in relation to it;

(k) details of the expected effects on future costs of any material changes in the group's and/or company's pension arrangements.

4.3 UITF - Abstract 6

Accounting for post-retirement benefits other than pensions

The aim of UITF 6 is to give guidance on the accounting treatment and disclosure of post-retirement health care and other benefits. UK groups with operations in countries where the provision of such benefits is particularly significant, such as the United States, are faced with the question of how they should be treated and disclosed.

The UITF concludes that they are liabilities that should be recognised in financial statements and that the principles of SSAP 24 *Accounting for pension costs* are applicable.

4.4 Amendment to SSAP 15

This document dated December 1992 entitled 'Amendment to SSAP 15 *Accounting for deferred tax*' has its place in this chapter because it is concerned with the interaction between SSAP 15 and SSAP 24.

You have seen above that pensions are usually accounted for on an accruals rather than a cash basis. Clearly, this has deferred tax implications since taxation relief is generally granted in respect of payments made to the pension fund. However, when SSAP 15 was issued and subsequently revised pensions were normally accounted for on a cash basis and consequently there were few significant deferred tax implications.

Three additional paragraphs have now been inserted into SSAP 15.

(a) *Either* the full *or* partial provision basis may be used in accounting for deferred tax on pensions and other post-retirement benefits, with the policy adopted to be disclosed.

The normal treatment under SSAP 15 would be to use the partial provision basis. This is inconsistent with SSAP 24 since pensions themselves are accounted for on a full provision basis, even though in many cases it is likely that the obligations will continually roll over (ie, as one obligation is settled another will arise). The justification for this proposed amendment to SSAP 15 is that it is difficult to justify a prohibition, as the current provisions of SSAP 15 would require, on the related deferred tax being treated on a similar basis if it, too, continually rolls over.

(b) The same *recognition criteria* to be used for the tax implications of pensions and other post-retirement benefits as in accounting for the obligations to provide those benefits.

The idea of recognition criteria is discussed in the Statement of Principles. This would not have been permissible under SSAP 15.

(c) In contemplating the recognition of a deferred tax asset with regard to pensions or other post-retirement benefits, the normal rules regarding the recoverability of assets in SSAP 2 and the Companies Act 1985 apply.

4.5 UITF Abstract 18: Pension costs following the 1997 tax changes in respect of dividend income

Following the Finance (No 2) Act 1997, pension schemes are no longer able to reclaim a tax credit on dividend income. Most pension schemes will experience a reduction of the actuarial value of their net assets. It will therefore be necessary to account for a loss in the financial statements of employers sponsoring defined benefit schemes.

This loss should be spread forward over the expected remaining service lives of the employees in the scheme.

This is because the change to tax legislation does not fall outside the normal scope of the actuarial assumptions (SSAP 24 para 82). It is simply a change in the expected return on assets. This means that there is no case for a departure from the normal principle of spreading forward deficiencies and surpluses.

5 OTHER MATTERS

5.1 How future regulation of pension costs and funds might avoid recent scandals

In this chapter we have been concerned with the accounting treatment of the employer company rather than the pension fund. The implicit assumption has therefore been made that the pension fund is run properly and is adequately funded so that pension commitments are met. There are however cases where the pension fund has run into difficulties due to the close relationship between the employer company and the pension fund. The major example was the Mirror Group Newspapers Pension Fund which lost about £300 million of its assets due to the influence and control of the owner of the Mirror Group, Robert Maxwell. Monies were extracted from the fund as loans to businesses within the Maxwell empire. When that empire crumbled, there was the problem that there were insufficient assets to pay creditors and the pension fund was one of those creditors. As a consequence, pensioners and potential pensioners had severely reduced pension rights.

In November 1993, the Government published **Pension Law Reform**, the report of the Pension Law Review Committee (known as the Goode Report). Many of the report's recommendations were incorporated in the Pensions Act 1995.

5.2 The Pensions Act 1995

The purpose of the Act is to learn from the Robert Maxwell affair and put pensions on a more secure footing for the new century. The key changes are summarised below.

(a) A new regulatory body, the Occupational Pensions Regulatory Authority (OPRA), has wide-ranging powers to intervene in the running of occupational pension schemes. OPRA replaces the previous Occupational Pensions Board. The scheme actuary and the scheme auditor must report immediately to OPRA if they believe that the employer or the trustees or any of the scheme's advisers are not performing their proper duties.

(b) Trustees can face unlimited fines and/or a prison sentence for not performing their duties properly, and can be removed from office by OPRA.

(c) At least one third of the trustees of every company pension scheme should be nominated by the members of the scheme, thus ensuring that members' interests are properly represented.

(d) From April 1997 all final salary pension schemes have been subject to a minimum funding requirement (MFR), that the value of their assets is at least equal to their liabilities. Where funding falls to below 90% of the MFR, the employer has one year to restore it to above this limit.

(e) A new Compensation Scheme has been set up. Where a pension scheme has become insolvent because of theft or fraud committed after 6 April 1997, the scheme may apply to the new Pensions Compensation Board if the employer is also insolvent. Compensation will be paid up to 90% of the missing assets.

(f) New rules have been introduced for divorces. UK courts are now required to take pension rights into account when making financial provision orders in divorce settlements.

(g) New rules have been introduced for calculating SERPS rebates. The rebate given to those who contract out of the State Earnings Related Pension Scheme (SERPS) is now related to age, so that the older one is, the bigger the rebate that is available. The object is to stop older people from judging it worthwhile to contract back into SERPS.

It is hoped that the three major new pillars of the Act (member-nominated trustees, the MFR and the Compensation Scheme) overseen by OPRA should ensure that another Robert Maxwell scenario cannot happen.

6 CURRENT DEVELOPMENTS

6.1 Weaknesses of SSAP 24

The ASB has undertaken a review of SSAP 24. This review has highlighted the following problems:

- Too many options are permitted, leading to inconsistency between companies. This also provides companies with flexibility to adjust results on a short term basis.

- Its disclosure requirements are insufficient to explain the pension cost and related amounts in the balance sheet.

6.2 Valuing pension scheme assets

As we have seen, in order to arrive at the cost of providing pensions under a defined benefit scheme, the scheme assets and liabilities must be valued. There are two main methods:

- The actuarial method: assets and liabilities are valued by an actuary on the basis of estimates of future interest rates, salary increases and service lives of employees.

- The market value method: assets and liabilities are stated at their market values or fair values.

SSAP 24 requires the use of the actuarial method.

When the ASB began its review of accounting for pension costs, valuation was not a major issue. Most respondents to the ASB's earlier Discussion Papers were in favour of revising SSAP 24, but retaining the actuarial method. However, the IASC then issued IAS 19 *Employee benefits* which requires the use of market values to measure pension scheme assets, on the grounds that these give the most objective and comparable information. Most other major standard setters also require the use of market values.

The ASB has now issued FRED 20 *Retirement benefits*, which covers pensions and other forms of retirement benefit, eg, the provision of post-employment medical care. It has been developed from proposals in the ASB's Discussion Paper *Aspects of accounting for pension costs* and will eventually replace SSAP 24 *Accounting for pension costs* if its proposals are adopted.

The proposals in FRED 20 affect **defined benefit schemes only**. Accounting for defined contribution schemes will not change.

6.3 Measurement of scheme assets and liabilities

FRED 20 proposes that:

(a) scheme assets should be measured at **fair value** (instead of on an actuarial basis); and

(b) scheme liabilities should be measured on an actuarial basis using the projected unit method. Scheme liabilities comprise:

   (i) any benefits promised under the formal terms of the scheme; and

   (ii) any constructive obligations for further benefits where past practice by the employer has created a valid expectation in employees that such benefits will be granted.

In theory, scheme liabilities should also be valued at fair value, but this is not possible as there is no active market for most defined benefit scheme liabilities. Fair value must therefore be estimated using actuarial techniques. Unlike SSAP 24, FRED 20 stipulates the method to be used.

FRED 20 also proposes that:

(a) Scheme liabilities should be discounted at a rate that reflects the time value of money and the characteristics of the liability. Such a rate should be assumed to be the current rate of return on an AA corporate bond of equivalent currency and term to the scheme liability.

Scheme liabilities are normally long-term. The requirement to discount them is consistent with other recent FRSs and FREDs and with the Statement of Principles.

(b) Full actuarial valuations by a professionally qualified actuary should be obtained for a defined benefit scheme at intervals not exceeding three years. At each balance sheet date the actuary should review the most recent actuarial valuation and update it to reflect current conditions.

6.4 Recognition in the balance sheet

Under SSAP 24 actuarial gains and losses are recognised over the future service lives of employees and the focus is on the profit and loss account. The amount recognised in the balance sheet does not represent the surplus or deficit of the scheme. It arises as a result of the 'spreading' approach and represents the difference between the contributions paid and the amount recognised in the profit and loss account.

FRED 20 takes a very different approach:

(a) A surplus in a scheme should be recognised as an asset to the extent that the employer is able to recover the surplus either through reduced contributions in the future or through refunds from the scheme.

(b) A deficit should be recognised as a liability to the extent of the employer's legal or constructive obligation to fund it.

(c) Contributions overpaid or underpaid should be disclosed as debtors or creditors due within one year.

(d) The remaining defined benefit asset or liability should be presented separately on the face of the balance sheet after other net assets.

An Appendix to FRED 20 gives an example of the presentation:

	20X1	*20X0*
	£m	£m
Net assets excluding pension asset	700	650
Net pension asset	335	143
Net assets including pension asset	1,035	793

6.5 Recognition in the performance statements

Periodic costs

The pension 'cost' is the change in the defined benefit asset or liability in the period (other than that arising from contributions paid). FRED 20 proposes that this is analysed into its components:

(a) Current service cost is recognised in the profit and loss account as part of operating results.

Definition **Current service cost** is the increase in the actuarial liability expected to arise from employee service in the current period.

(b) The interest cost and the expected return on assets are recognised in the profit and loss account as a net figure adjacent to interest (ie, as a financing item).

Definition **Interest cost** is the expected increase during the period in the present value of the actuarial liability because the benefits are one period closer to settlement.

Definition The **expected return on assets** is the expected rate of return multiplied by the market value of the scheme assets. The **expected rate of return on assets** is the average rate of return (including both income and changes in market value) expected over the remaining life of the related obligation on the actual assets held by the scheme.

(c) Actuarial gains and losses are recognised immediately in the statement of total recognised gains and losses (STRGL). Once they have been recognised in the STRGL, they are not subsequently recognised in the profit and loss account.

Definition **Actuarial gains and losses** are changes in actuarial deficits or surpluses that arise because events have not coincided with the actuarial assumptions made for the last valuation (experience gains and losses) or the actuarial assumptions have changed.

Each component of the pension cost is presented in a way that reflects its characteristics. This approach reflects the ASB's current thinking on reporting financial performance, which is that items with similar characteristics should be grouped together in the statements of financial performance. The ASB's Discussion Paper on this subject is discussed in a later chapter.

The ASB accepts that a major disadvantage of the market value approach is that it leads to volatile results. This problem should be avoided because actuarial gains and losses would be treated in a similar way to revaluation gains and losses. The profit and loss account would not be distorted by movements in the value of scheme assets.

Past service costs

Past service costs arise when scheme benefits are improved, for example, an employer might decide to extend the scheme to provide pension benefits for employees' spouses. An increase in scheme liabilities arises in the current period but it relates to employee services in prior periods. FRED 20 proposes that these should be recognised in the profit and loss account over the period in which the increases in benefits vest. If the benefits vest immediately, the past service cost should be recognised immediately.

Settlements and curtailments

A settlement is an irrevocable action that relieves the employer or the scheme of the primary responsibility for meeting an obligation to provide a pension. Settlements include:

(a) a lump sum cash payment to scheme members in exchange for their rights to receive specified pension benefits

(b) the purchase of an irrevocable annuity contract sufficient to cover vested benefits.

A curtailment is an event that reduces the expected years of future service of present employees or reduces for a number of employees the accrual of defined benefits for some or all of their future service. Curtailments include:

(a) termination of employees' services earlier than expected, for example as a result of closing a factory or discontinuing a segment of a business, and

(b) termination of, or amendment to the terms of, a defined benefit scheme so that some or all future service by current employees will no longer qualify for benefits or will qualify only for reduced benefits.

Settlements and curtailments often arise when individual employees retire or transfer out of the scheme and these are normally allowed for in actuarial assumptions. Where they arise from major changes in the circumstances of the scheme they will not have been allowed for in the actuarial assumptions. In this case they are treated in the same way:

(a) Losses should be recognised in the profit and loss account in the period in which the employer becomes demonstrably committed to the transaction.

(b) Gains should be recognised in the profit and loss account in the period in which all parties whose consent is required are irrevocably committed to the transaction.

6.6 Disclosure

FRED 20 proposes extensive disclosures of which the main ones are as follows:

(a) the main assumptions underlying the scheme;

(b) an analysis of scheme assets into broad classes and the expected rate of return on each class;

(c) an analysis of the amounts included:
 (i) within operating profit;
 (ii) as a financial item adjacent to interest; and
 (iii) within the statement of total recognised gains and losses

(d) a five year history of:
 (i) the difference between expected and actual return on assets;
 (ii) experience gains and losses on scheme liabilities; and
 (iii) the total actuarial gain or loss.

(e) an analysis of the movement in the surplus/deficit in the scheme over the period;

(f) a reconciliation of the surplus/deficit to the balance sheet asset/liability.

6.7 The reasons for the proposed changes

The proposals in FRED 20 are unpopular. Nevertheless, the ASB believes that UK financial reporting must be consistent with international practice in this area. This is arguably the most important reason for the proposed changes.

There are two other reasons:

(a) The effect of SSAP 24 is potentially confusing. A surplus often gives rise to a creditor in the balance sheet (particularly where a contribution holiday is taken) while a deficit may result in a prepayment (because contributions are increased to meet it before they are recognised in the profit and loss account). The ASB believes that the proposed new approach, whereby surpluses are treated as assets and deficits are treated as liabilities, would be more understandable.

(b) Although the actual assets and liabilities of a pension scheme do not belong to the employing company, pension scheme surpluses and deficits meet the definitions of assets and liabilities in the Statement of Principles. A surplus is an asset of the employer because the employer has the ability to receive economic benefits from that surplus (e.g. to reduce contributions). A deficit is a liability because the employer has an obligation to transfer economic benefits (increase contributions) to the scheme.

6.8 Criticisms of the proposals

These have been as follows:

(a) Market values may be volatile. Even though actuarial gains and losses bypass the profit and loss account there may be significant fluctuations in the balance sheet.

(b) Market values are not relevant to the economic reality of most pension schemes. Under the proposals in FRED 20, assets and liabilities would be valued at short term amounts, but most pension scheme assets and liabilities are held for the long term. Actuarial valuation would better reflect the long term costs of funding a pension scheme.

(c) The treatment of pension costs in the profit and loss account and STRGL is complex and may not be easily understood by users of the financial statements. It has been argued that all the components of the pension cost are so interrelated that it does not make sense to present them separately. One commentator has said that the ASB's approach would report 'budgeted figures in the profit and loss account and variances in the STRGL and pretend that they have nothing to do with each other'. If actuarial gains and losses are taken to the STRGL it is possible that the profit and loss account will not reflect the true cost of providing pensions.

(d) Actuarial gains and losses are treated in a similar way to revaluation gains and losses on fixed assets. It has been argued that they are more similar to long term provisions, such as those for environmental rectification costs. FRS 12 requires that all adjustments to provisions are taken to the profit and loss account.

(e) A pension scheme surplus meets the ASB's definition of an asset and so FRED 20 treats it as if it 'belongs' to the employer. However, in practice the situation is that the surplus 'belongs' to the members of the scheme and must be applied for their benefit. FRED 20 does not reflect the legal and economic reality of the situation.

Conclusion FRED 20 proposes major changes to current practice. The main proposal is that scheme assets should be measured at fair value rather than on an actuarial basis.

7 CHAPTER SUMMARY

Defined benefit schemes present accounting problems due to the long term nature of the potential liabilities. The opinion on the sufficiency of the funding of the scheme is however the province of the actuary.

The accounting method used for costing should be one which recognises the expected cost of providing pensions over the employees' periods of service. If funding is on a different basis, accruals or prepayments will arise.

8 SELF TEST QUESTIONS

8.1 What is a defined benefit scheme? (1.1)

8.2 What is a funded scheme? (2.1)

8.3 What are actuarial assumptions? (2.3)

8.4 What is an experience surplus? (2.4)

8.5 What is the accounting objective of SSAP 24? (3.2)

8.6 How are variations from regular cost usually treated? (3.7)

8.7 What are the three exceptions from the usual treatment? (3.10)

8.8 What needs to be disclosed in the financial statements for a defined contribution scheme? (4.2)

8.9 What topic does UITF Abstract 6 cover? (4.3)

8.10 What report recently reviewed the law on occupational pension schemes? (5.1)

9 EXAMINATION TYPE QUESTIONS

9.1 Pension costs I

(a) A company's defined benefit pension scheme had a surplus of £510,000 as at 31 December 20X0. The regular pension cost is £200,000 per annum. The actuary recommends a three year contribution holiday. The average remaining service life of members is ten years.

You are required to show how the surplus should normally be accounted for. (Ignore tax).

(b) A company's defined benefit pension scheme had a deficit of £450,000 as at 31 December 20X0. The regular pension cost is £100,000 per annum. The actuary recommends annual lump sum payments of £270,000 in 20X1 and 20X2 in addition to the regular cost. The average remaining service life of members is twelve years.

You are required to show how the deficit should normally be accounted for. (Ignore tax).

(c) Suppose the £510,000 in (a) were caused by a substantial reduction in the number of employees during 20X0 unrelated to the sale or termination of an operation.

You are required to show how the surplus should normally be accounted for. (Ignore tax).

9.2 Pension costs II

The requirements that follow relate to the accounting treatment of pension costs in accordance with the provisions of SSAP 24 *Accounting for pension costs.*

You are required:

(a) to explain how the Standard provides for the matching process. **(8 marks)**

(b) to discuss whether the implementation of the Standard has made the accounts of different companies comparable in respect of their treatment of pension costs for a defined benefit scheme and give **two** examples to support your discussion. **(9 marks)**

(c) to explain how provisions and prepayments might arise in the balance sheet. **(3 marks)**

(Total: 20 marks)

10 ANSWERS TO EXAMINATION TYPE QUESTIONS

10.1 Pension costs I

(a)

Year	*Cash*	*Accounting*	*Accrual*
	£'000	£'000	£'000
20X1	–	140	140
20X2	–	140	280
20X3	–	140	420
20X4	200	140	360
20X5	200	140	300
20X6	200	140	240
20X7	200	140	180
20X8	200	140	120

20X9	200	140	60
20X10	200	140	–
	1,400	1,400	

(b)

Year	*Cash* £'000	*Accounting* £'000	*Accrual* £'000
20X1	370	145	225
20X2	370	145	450
20X3	100	145	405
20X4	100	145	360
20X5	100	145	315
20X6	100	145	270
20X7	100	145	225
20X8	100	145	180
20X9	100	145	135
20X10	100	145	90
20X11	100	145	45
20X12	100	145	–
	1,740	1,740	

(c)

Year	*Cash* £'000	*Accounting* £'000
20X1	–	–
20X2	–	–
20X3	–	–
20X4	200 pa	200 pa

10.2 Pension costs II

(Tutorial notes:

(1) A straightforward question on SSAP 24.

(2) Use the requirements of the question to guide your answer. Do not put in your answer all that you know about SSAP 24 - keep your comments to the point.*)*

(a) The matching process requires that the cost of providing a pension to a company's employees (ie, the company's contributions to an employee pension fund) should be attributed to the period when the company 'profits' from the activities of the employees. SSAP 24 is based on the underlying concept that companies should recognise and charge the costs of providing pensions for its employees as such costs accrue. This accounting policy may differ from the policy adopted by the company in actually funding the pensions but the accounting objective, based on the matching process, should guide the recording and recognition of the pension cost.

With the publication of SSAP 24 some companies had to change from the more traditional approach of accounting for pension costs at the time that the actual cash payments were made to the pension fund. The problems of cash injections to commence a pension fund, make good underfunded schemes and cover discretionary additional pension awards were often dealt with on a cash basis rather than an accruals basis. No thought was given to the effect on periodic profit measurement by the use of such accounting methods. With the adoption of the accounting provisions of SSAP 24 more suitable profit and loss account charges for pension costs will result.

(b) The implementation of SSAP 24 by all companies should help harmonise the accounting practices adopted for pension costs but it will not eliminate subjective judgement and choice in certain areas. The SSAP will not therefore standardise the accounting practices but may eliminate variability. Eliminating subjectivity would be an unrealistic, and possibly inappropriate, objective for the standard. The standard does, however, require extensive disclosures for defined benefit schemes which will prove to be useful to the reader in trying to compare the accounts of different companies.

Two problems are accounting for variations from the regular pension costs and the application of the prudence concept

(i) **Accounting for variations from the regular pension costs**

These variations by definition will be different for a company from one period to another and from one company to another. Accounting for such variations will often be dependent on the cause for the variation. Such causes include experience surpluses/deficiencies, changes in assumptions and retroactive changes in benefits/conditions for membership. Accounting for such variations will differ, making inter-company comparisons difficult.

(ii) **Application of the prudence concept**

The problems caused by variations from the regular pension costs are significant even if all companies chose to spread these additional costs over the remaining useful working lives of its employees. This problem can be further complicated by the prevalence of the prudence concept which means that some companies may choose a shorter write-off than would apply if the matching process were to prevail.

(c) An accrual or prepayment will arise if the cash payments made under the funding policy differ from the charges made in the profit and loss account following the matching process.

REPORTING THE SUBSTANCE OF TRANSACTIONS

INTRODUCTION & LEARNING OBJECTIVES

Off balance sheet finance is a form of creative accounting ie, the manipulation of items in the financial statements so that they are excluded or changed in amount so as to present a more favourable picture of the entity.

FRS 5 *Reporting the substance of transactions* is concerned with reducing or eliminating creative accounting. This chapter also looks at FRS 12 *Provisions, contingent liabilities and contingent assets*, which was issued in 1998.

When you have studied this chapter you should be able to do the following:

- Understand and apply the requirements of FRS 5.
- Understand the issues involved in accounting for provisions.
- Understand and apply the requirements of FRS 12.

1 OFF BALANCE SHEET FINANCE

1.1 The advantages perceived from schemes of off balance sheet finance

Definition Off balance sheet finance is the organisation of transactions such that financial commitments are not included in the balance sheet of a company or a group.

The perceived benefits include the following:

(a) Perceived lower level of gearing.

(b) There may be a breach of loan covenants if further liabilities are recorded on balance sheet.

(c) In most cases, off balance sheet finance schemes result in assets also being reduced. Therefore a higher ROCE may result.

(d) Specialised activities eg, leasing and financial services (which have high gearing) can be removed from a group balance sheet.

1.2 The concept of substance over form

Definition Substance over form requires that transactions and other events should be accounted for and presented in accordance with their substance and financial reality and not merely with their legal form.

The concept prevents off balance sheet finance because if the commercial reality is that the company has a financial commitment, that commitment should be included on the balance sheet.

The first major area where an accounting standard introduced a change from legal form to substance was SSAP 21. This standard is examined in detail in the next chapter but should already be familiar.

Finance leases give rights over the use of assets for a period which covers all or a substantial part of their useful life. Such leases are effectively an alternative to hire purchase and loan financing. Hence failure to capitalise such leases would give rise to a disparity of accounting treatment which could distort comparisons between companies. In particular, comparisons of:

(a) return on capital employed;
(b) debt/equity ratio

could be misleading.

Substance over form is at the heart of *SSAP 21*.

Under a finance lease, the lessee acquires substantially all the benefits of use of an asset for the substantial majority of its useful economic life. The lessee also takes on the risks of ownership – repairs, maintenance and insurance. A finance lease is therefore similar to the purchase of an asset on credit terms.

Since the introduction of SSAP 21, companies have developed other means of providing off balance sheet finance, some of which were stopped by the revised definition of a subsidiary under the CA89 (quasi-subsidiaries) and the rest (it is hoped by the ASB) by the issue of FRS 5.

1.3 Common forms of off balance sheet finance

Ways in which companies have tried to keep items off the balance sheet in the past include the following.

(a) **Leasing of assets**

Prior to the issue of SSAP 21 leases were not capitalised ie, the asset and its related financial commitment were not shown on the lessee's balance sheet.

(b) **Controlled non-subsidiaries**

Prior to the CA89 and FRS 2 under the old, looser definition of a subsidiary, companies could control other companies but, as they were not technically subsidiaries, they were not consolidated in the group accounts. We have yet to cover consolidated accounts in this text, but the effect of non-consolidation is that the assets and liabilities of the subsidiary were not included within the total assets and liabilities of the group.

Since the CA89 companies have become more ingenious in arranging their affairs so that off balance sheet arrangements continue to occur in entities which were not classified as subsidiaries under the new legislation. FRS 5 tackles these issues.

(c) **Innovations in the financial markets**

A number of (often complex) arrangements were developed for which the accounting entries were not immediately obvious. It was the growth in these arrangements which resulted in the determination of the ASB to issue an accounting standard on the substance of transactions. We refer to some of these innovations in our coverage of FRS 5 below.

2 REFLECTING THE SUBSTANCE OF TRANSACTIONS IN FINANCIAL STATEMENTS

2.1 FRS 5: Reporting the substance of transactions

FRS 5 was issued in April 1994.

Its main thrust is to ensure that financial statements report the substance of transactions and not merely their legal form. The view held by the ASB was that, previously, users could be left unaware of the total assets employed in a business and of its overall financing. Detailed disclosures in the notes are no substitute for inclusion in the accounts.

2.2 General principles

FRS 5 sets out general principles covering the following areas

(a) what is excluded from the scope of the Standard
(b) how to determine the substance of a transaction
(c) whether any resulting assets and liabilities should be included in the balance sheet
(d) at what point there should be changes in previously recognised assets
(e) what disclosures are necessary

(f) whether any 'vehicle' companies incorporated into a transaction should be consolidated
(g) under what circumstances is a 'linked' presentation appropriate.

The FRS also contains notes showing how its requirements are to be applied to six specific transaction types - consignment stock, sale and repurchase agreements, factoring, securitised assets, loan transfers and Private Finance Initiative contracts.

2.3 Scope of the standard

Certain transactions are excluded from the standard because of the special nature of the transactions. The main exclusions relate to financing arrangements such as forward contracts, futures, foreign exchange and interest rate swaps. The ASB has issued FRS 13, which requires entities to disclose information about financial instruments, and is developing a further accounting standard on their measurement.

Where the general principles of the standard seem to apply to an asset or liability which is subject to the requirements of a more specific standard (eg, SSAP 9 covers stocks), the specific requirements of the other standard apply.

2.4 Determining the substance of a transaction

Common features of transactions whose substance is not readily apparent are

(a) the separation of the legal title to an item from the ability to enjoy the principal benefits and exposure to the principal risks associated with it

(b) the linking of a transaction with one or more others in such a way that the commercial effect cannot be understood without reference to the series as a whole and

(c) the inclusion in a transaction of one or more options whose terms make it highly likely that the option will be exercised.

A key step in determining the substance of a transaction is to identify its effect on the assets and liabilities of the entity.

Assets are, broadly, rights or other access to future economic benefits controlled by an entity. Liabilities are, broadly, an entity's obligations to transfer economic benefits.

Risk often indicates which party has an asset. Risk is important, as the party which has access to benefits (and hence an asset) will usually also be the one to suffer or gain if the benefits ultimately differ from those expected.

These points are considered in detail in Chapters 4 and 5 of the ASB's *Statement of Principles*.

2.5 Inclusion of assets and liabilities in the balance sheet

Assets and liabilities should be included in the balance sheet where there is both

(a) sufficient evidence that an asset or liability exists, and
(b) the asset or liability can be measured at a monetary amount with sufficient reliability.

2.6 Transactions in previously recognised assets

An asset should cease to be recognised only where two conditions are both fulfilled - that the entity retains no significant access to material benefits, and any risk it retains is immaterial in relation to the variation in benefits likely to occur in practice.

2.7 Disclosures

Disclosure of a transaction should be sufficiently detailed to enable the user of the financial statements to understand its commercial effect.

A transaction may need to be disclosed whether or not it results in additional assets and liabilities being recognised. Where assets or liabilities are recognised but their nature differs from that of items usually found under the relevant balance sheet heading, the differences should be explained. For example certain assets may not be available for use as security for liabilities.

To the extent that a transaction has not resulted in the recognition of assets or liabilities it is still necessary to consider whether disclosure of its nature and effect is required in order to give a true and fair view. For example the transaction may give rise to guarantees or other obligations.

2.8 'Vehicle' companies

Some off balance sheet financing arrangements include the use of another entity (a 'vehicle') to house certain assets and liabilities. Normally, the arrangement will be structured so that the vehicle does not meet the legal definition of a subsidiary. Where the commercial effect is no different from that which would result were the vehicle a subsidiary, the vehicle will meet FRS 5's definition of a 'quasi subsidiary'. FRS 5 requires such quasi subsidiaries to be included in consolidated accounts in the same way as if they were subsidiaries.

2.9 Linked presentation and offset

Parts of FRS 5 require certain assets and liabilities to be linked together (ie, the gross amount of assets and liabilities are shown but are also netted off) or offset (ie, only the net amount is shown).

2.10 Linked presentation

The linked presentation is available for certain non-recourse finance arrangements. Non-recourse finance involves selling an asset such as a debtor to a third party. If the seller does not have to make any payments to the purchaser if the debtor does not eventually pay the debt, the seller no longer has an asset (ie, the debtor) as it does not meet the recognition criteria in the FRS (all significant benefits and risks have been transferred).

In some non-recourse finance arrangements however, an entity retains significant benefits and risks associated with a specific item, but the maximum loss it can suffer is limited to a fixed monetary amount. In such circumstances a 'linked' presentation is required to present the nature of such an arrangement.

Example

Extract from balance sheet	£	£
Debtor	80,000	
Less: Non-returnable amounts received on sale of debtor	80,000	
		–

Pressure for the above approach came from certain financial institutions (eg, banks) which wanted to show their gross 'assets' (eg, mortgages advanced) even though they had passed on the assets, in this particular form, to another entity.

2.11 Offset

Offsetting of an asset and liability is generally not allowed, but here also the FRS is attempting to respond to special cases. It allows offset when the items do not constitute 'separate assets and liabilities'. Its main area of use would be certain types of bank balances and overdrafts.

2.12 Employee share ownership plans

Questions have arisen following FRS 5 as to the appropriate accounting for employee share ownership plans (ESOPs). ESOP trusts are designed to encourage employee shareholdings and are often used as vehicles for distributing shares to employees under remuneration schemes. In particular, should the sponsoring company recognise assets and liabilities in its own accounts in respect of the trust? UITF Abstract 13 **Accounting for ESOP trusts** deals with these issues.

UITF consensus

The principles of FRS 5 require the sponsoring company of an ESOP trust to recognise the assets and liabilities of the trust as its own whenever it has de facto control of the shares held by the ESOP trust and bears their benefits or risks.

3 APPLYING FRS 5

3.1 Introduction

FRS 5 includes detailed application notes on the most common types of 'special purpose' transactions:

(a) consignment stock
(b) sale and repurchase agreements
(c) factoring of debts
(d) securitised mortgages
(e) loan transfers
(f) private finance initiative (PFI) and similar contracts.

The notes are meant to clarify, rather than to override, the general principles of the FRS but they are mandatory.

This is not an exhaustive list and there are other transactions which may come within the scope of the standard. The business environment is now so complex that it is impossible to prescribe for every situation.

3.2 Consignment stock

Consignment stock is stock held by one party but legally owned by another, on terms which give the holder the right to sell the stock in the normal course of his business, or at his option to return it unsold to the legal owner. Legal title may pass when one of a number of events has occurred, for example, when the dealer has held the stock for a specified period such as six months, or when the dealer has sold the goods. The sales price may be determined at the date of supply, or it may vary with the length of the period between supply and purchase, or it may be the manufacturer's factory price at sale.

Other terms of such arrangements include a requirement for the dealer to pay a deposit, and responsibility for insurance. The arrangement should be analysed to determine whether the dealer has in substance acquired the stock before the date of transfer of legal title.

FRS 5 states that the key factor will be who bears the risk of slow moving stock. The risk involved is the cost of financing the stock for the period it is held. In a simple arrangement where stock is supplied for a fixed price that will be charged whenever the title is transferred and there is no deposit, the manufacturer bears the slow movement risk. If, however, the price to be paid increases by a factor that varies with interest rates and the time the stock is held, then the dealer bears the risk. If the price charged to the dealer is the manufacturer's list price at the date of sale, then again the risks associated with the stock fall on the manufacturer. Whoever bears the slow movement risk should recognise the stock on the balance sheet.

Consignment stock arrangements are most common in the motor trade.

Example

On 1 January 20X6 Gillingham plc, a manufacturer, entered into an agreement to provide Canterbury plc, a retailer, with machines for resale. Under the terms of the agreement Canterbury plc pays a fixed rental per month for each machine that it holds and also pays the cost of insuring and maintaining the machines. The company can display the machines in its showrooms and use them as demonstration models.

When a machine is sold to a customer, Canterbury plc pays Gillingham plc the factory price at the time the machine was originally delivered. All machines remaining unsold six months after their original delivery must be purchased by Canterbury plc at the factory price at the time of delivery.

Gillingham plc can require Canterbury plc to return the machines at any time within the six month period. In practice, this right has never been exercised. Canterbury plc can return unsold machines to Gillingham plc at any time during the six month period, without penalty. In practice, this has never happened.

At 31 December 20X6 the agreement is still in force and Canterbury plc holds several machines which were delivered less than six months earlier. How should these machines be treated in the accounts for the year ended 31 December 20X6?

Solution

The key issue is whether Canterbury plc has purchased the machines from Gillingham plc or whether they are merely on loan. It is necessary to determine whether Canterbury plc has the benefits of holding the machines and is exposed to the risks inherent in those benefits.

Gillingham plc can demand the return of the machines and Canterbury plc is able to return them without paying a penalty. This suggests that Canterbury plc does not have the automatic right to retain or to use them.

Canterbury plc pays a rental charge for the machines, despite the fact that it may eventually purchase them outright. This suggests a financing arrangement as the rental could be seen as loan interest on the purchase price. Canterbury plc also incurs the costs normally associated with holding stocks.

The purchase price is the price at the date the machines were first delivered. This suggests that the sale actually takes place at the delivery date. Canterbury plc has to purchase any stocks still held six months after delivery. Therefore the company is exposed to slow payment and obsolescence risks. Because Canterbury plc can return the stocks before that time, this exposure is limited.

It appears that both parties experience the risks and benefits. However, although the agreement provides for the return of the machines, in practice this has never happened.

Conclusion: the machines are assets of Canterbury plc and should be included in the balance sheet.

3.3 Sale and re-purchase agreements

Sale and re-purchase arrangements are arrangements under which assets are sold by one party to another on terms that provide for the seller to re-purchase the assets in certain circumstances. The sale may be at market value or at some agreed percentage of market value. The re-purchase arrangement may take a number of forms, for example, an unconditional commitment for both parties, an option granted to the seller to repurchase (a call option) or an option granted to the buyer to require re-purchase (a put option). The arrangements often contain provisions to enable the seller to make use of the asset during its ownership by the buyer.

The re-purchase price may be variable (depending on the original price and the period during which the asset has been held by the purchaser), agreed at the time of re-purchase or subject to market price movements. The re-purchase price may also be designed to permit the purchaser to recover incidental holding costs if these do not continue to be met by the seller.

FRS 5 states that the key question is whether the commercial effect is that of a sale or of a secured loan. A secured loan transaction will usually have the following features

(a) the seller will secure access to all future benefits inherent in the asset, often through call options

(b) the buyer will secure adequate return on the purchase (interest on the loan, often through adjustment of the re-purchase price) and appropriate protection against loss in value of the asset bought (often through put options).

The analysis should look at all features of the agreement that are likely to have a commercial effect in practice.

Sale and re-purchase arrangements are common in property development and in maturing whisky stocks.

3.4 Debt factoring

Factoring of debts is a well established method of obtaining finance. In most forms of factoring, debts are sold to the factor, but the latter's degree of control over, and responsibility for those debts will vary from one arrangement to another. A significant accounting question is only likely to arise where the factoring arrangement leads to the receipt of cash earlier than would have been the case had the debts been unfactored. If this is so, the question to be answered is whether the seller has in substance received either a loan on the security of his debtors or receipts that are appropriately credited to reduce a debtor.

If the seller is in essence a borrower, and the factor a lender, then the arrangements will be such as to provide that the seller pays the equivalent of interest to the factor on the timing difference between amounts received by him from the factor and those collected by the factor from the debtor. Such payment would be in addition to any other charges.

FRS 5 states that the key factor in the analysis will be who bears the risk (of slow payment) and the benefit (of early payment) from the debtors. If the finance cost reflects events subsequent to transfer, then the transfer is likely to be equivalent to obtaining finance because the seller is bearing the risks and rewards of the debtors. If the cost is determined when the transfer is made, with no other variable costs, then it is likely to be a straightforward sale.

The risk of bad debts is unlikely to be relevant to the analysis, as the exposure to such risk is agreed between the seller and the factor and charges will reflect this, just as in a normal credit insurance contract.

Example

On 1 January 20X6 Lewis plc entered into an agreement with Factoring plc whereby it transferred title to its debtors to Factoring plc subject to a reduction in bad debts based on past experience. Lewis plc received a payment of 90% of the total of net debtors. Under the terms of the agreement, the company had the right to a future sum the amount of which depended on whether and when the debtors paid. Factoring plc had the right of recourse against Lewis plc for any additional losses up to an agreed maximum amount.

At 31 December 20X6, title had been transferred to debtors with an invoice value of £10 million less a bad debt provision of £300,000 and Lewis plc was subject under the agreement to a maximum potential debit of £100,000 to cover losses.

What is the appropriate accounting treatment for this transaction in the balance sheet of Lewis plc at 31 December 20X6?

Solution

As Lewis plc retains the risk of slow payment and bad debts the substance of the transaction is that of a financing arrangement and the company has not disposed of the debtors.

Under the terms of the factoring agreement, finance will be repaid only from the proceeds generated by the debtors. There appears to be no possibility of any claim against Lewis plc being made other than against proceeds generated from the debtors. The finance appears to be non-returnable. There is only recourse for losses up to a fixed amount. These are indications that linked presentation is appropriate.

Balance sheet (extract)

	£m	£m
Current assets		
Gross debts (after providing for bad debts)	9.7	
Less: non returnable proceeds ((90% × 9.7) – 0.1)	(8.63)	
		1.07
Cash		8.73
Creditors: amounts falling due within one year		
Recourse under factored debts		0.1

3.5 Securitised assets

Securitisation involves the transfer of assets to a special purpose 'vehicle' which finances their purchase by the issue of debt, for example loan notes. The assets act as security for the loan notes, although the note holders are not exposed to any risks associated with the assets.

The assets transferred may be property, or stock or receivables such as trade debts. However this type of arrangement is most common in the UK for mortgages.

Suppose Company A issues mortgages to home buyers. It is responsible for setting the mortgage rate and term and for credit control. A is known as the 'originator' as it originates the mortgages.

A packages together a group of mortgages and 'sells' them to Company B. B issues loan notes offering the mortgages as security. Then B uses the proceeds from issuing the loan notes, to settle with A. B is known as the 'issuer'.

B usually has negligible equity, and the shares that it has are usually owned by a charitable trust or by a 'friend' of A. A does not control the friendly party and thus B is not a legal subsidiary of A.

A will usually continue to service the mortgages and will extract profit from B by a servicing fee.

Where the originator retains significant benefits or risks then the mortgages remain as an asset and the money it received is shown as a liability.

The amounts may be shown under a linked presentation (see above) if the necessary conditions are satisfied.

Derecognition of the asset is only appropriate where the originator has not retained any significant benefits.

3.6 Loan transfers

Loan transfers involve transferring the benefits and risks of a loan to a third party. Effectively the loan is 'sold' like a tangible asset.

The same principles apply here as for securitised assets.

3.7 Quasi-subsidiaries

Identifying quasi-subsidiaries is very similar to identifying assets. As for other types of 'special purpose' transaction, the key factors are risks and benefits.

The flow of benefits from the other entity is not normally the critical factor. Benefits obtained from subsidiaries (eg, dividends) may not differ substantially from those obtained from other forms of investment.

Evidence of which party is exposed to benefits and risks is often given by determining which party stands to suffer or gain from the financial performance of an entity.

Control is also a key factor. Control is defined as the ability to direct the financial and operating policies of an entity with a view to gaining economic benefit from its activities. The existence of control normally distinguishes a quasi-subsidiary from other forms of investment.

If one party controls another, but does not obtain benefits from the other's net assets, it is effectively managing that party on behalf of another. There must be a flow of benefits in order to distinguish control from management.

Where the operating and financial policies of an entity have been determined in advance, then the company which obtains the benefits will be deemed to have control on those grounds alone.

It is important to look at the situation that arises in practice and not merely at the notional rights that may be held by various investors.

Example

On 1 January 20X6 Sarton plc sold a factory that it owned to Bypass plc, a wholly owned subsidiary of the National Investment Bank plc. The sale proceeds were £15 million. The factory had a book value of £12 million. Bypass plc was financed by a loan of £15 million from the National Investment Bank plc. Sarton plc was paid a fee by Bypass plc to continue to operate the factory. This fee represented the balance of profit remaining after Bypass plc had paid its parent company loan interest set at a level that represented current interest rates. If there was an operating loss, Sarton plc would be charged a fee that would cover the operating losses and interest payable.

How should these transactions be treated in the financial statements of Sarton plc for the year ended 31 December 20X6?

Solution

Sarton plc manages the factory, which means that it controls its policies. Sarton plc also very clearly stands to suffer or gain from the financial performance of Bypass plc. The bank's return is limited to that of a secured lender. The commercial effect of the arrangement is exactly the same as if Bypass plc were a subsidiary of Sarton plc.

Bypass plc should be consolidated by Sarton plc. All transactions between the two companies should be eliminated from the accounts. The factory should be included in the consolidated balance sheet at its cost to the group (£12 million) and the loan should also be included in the consolidated balance sheet. The loan interest should be included in the consolidated profit and loss account.

3.8 Joint ventures

An entity may enter into joint ventures with other entities, in order to carry out specific projects. A joint venture may be a quasi-subsidiary of one of the venturers. Only if the two parties are genuine equals will a quasi-subsidiary relationship not exist.

Again, it is necessary to look at both control and benefits.

The key factor which dictates the substance of a joint venture arrangement is normally the identity of the two investors and their objectives in entering into the arrangement. If one of the parties to the venture is a bank or other financial institution, seeking a lender's return on the venture, it is likely that the joint venture is a quasi-subsidiary of the other party.

If one of the parties stands to gain or lose more than the other from the financial performance of the venture, then the venture is probably a quasi-subsidiary of that party. Gains and losses do not only arise from actual profit sharing. They may arise through interest, management charges, guarantees or options to transfer assets. As usual, it is important to look at the situation which is likely to arise in practice.

3.9 The Private Finance Initiative (PFI) and similar contracts

In September 1998 the ASB issued a further Application Note to FRS 5. This Application Note covers transactions subject to the Private Finance Initiative (PFI).

Government departments have no legal obligation to comply with rules in FRSs. However, the existence of 'best practice' laid down by the ASB will put pressure on them to do so.

Under a typical PFI contract, a private sector 'operator' constructs a capital asset (eg, a road, bridge, hospital, school) and uses that asset to provide services to a public sector 'purchaser'. The accounting issues are:

(a) whether the purchaser has an asset (the property used to provide the contracted services) and a corresponding liability to pay the operator for it; or

(b) whether the operator has an asset of the property used to provide the contracted services and a debt due from the purchaser.

A PFI contract should be analysed in two stages:

(i) Exclude any separable elements of the contract that relate only to services (these are not relevant to deciding which party has the asset);

(ii) Assess the remainder of the contract.

Where all that remains is payments for the property that are akin to a stand alone lease, SSAP 21 should be applied. This means that where the purchaser has substantially all of the risks and rewards of ownership of the property, the purchaser has an asset and a liability to pay for it.

In all other cases, FRS 5 should be applied. This means that the asset is recorded by the party that bears the profits or losses (risks and rewards) relating to the asset.

These requirements have proved controversial, the main issue being the separation of the services from the remainder of the contract. The Treasury view of PFI contracts is that they are essentially contracts for services rather than buildings and that the property and the service elements must be considered as a whole. This view normally results in the assets and liabilities being kept off the purchaser's balance sheet.

The ASB view is that transactions which give rise to assets and liabilities for the government should be reported as such.

4 CREATIVE ACCOUNTING

4.1 Definition and examples of creative accounting

Definition Creative accounting is the legal manipulation of items in the financial statements so that they are excluded or changed in amount so as to present a more favourable picture of the entity.

Examples are as follows:

(a) Off balance sheet financing

(b) Window dressing (entering into transactions shortly before the year end to improve the balance sheet)

(c) Merger or acquisition accounting

(d) Use of provisions on the acquisition of a subsidiary

(e) Choice of goodwill write offs

(f) Inclusion of brands on the balance sheet

(g) Issuing debt as equity

(h) Avoiding interest charges on debt by issuing low interest stock at discount.

Note that fraudulent transactions are not included within the scope of creative accounting.

4.2 How the current regulations and pronouncements of the ASB would treat these

Off balance sheet finance has been the main type of creative accounting and we have already considered the various standards and company law provisions that have been introduced to counter such schemes culminating in the issue of FRS 5.

With window dressing, companies may enter into transactions shortly before the year end to 'improve' the look of the balance sheet. These transactions reverse shortly after the year end. Such transactions are covered by SSAP 17 but it only required disclosure in the notes, not changes in the financial statements. The general provisions of FRS 5 should be helpful in cutting down on abuses in this area by requiring assets and liabilities to be recognised if certain criteria are met and not derecognised unless further conditions are met.

Items (c) to (e) involve the manipulation of existing accounting standards on group accounts. These issues are examined in later chapters on group accounts as they require a detailed understanding of consolidation techniques but are also briefly mentioned here.

The use of merger and acquisition accounting was regulated for many years by SSAP 23, although there was much criticism of the definition of a merger in the standard, and of the fact that merger accounting was optional rather than compulsory if the conditions for a merger were satisfied. The ASB hope that these problems have been resolved now that SSAP 23 has been replaced by FRS 6 in this area of accounting.

Provisions for reorganisations and losses following an acquisition have long had the effect of increasing goodwill on consolidation and improving post acquisition profits when the provisions are released to the profit and loss account. The ASB attempted to ban such provisions in FRS 7 but some preparers of financial statements strongly disapproved of the ASB's actions in this area and the ASB has tried to clarify the position by issuing FRS 12 (see below).

Accounting for goodwill and intangible assets has been discussed in an earlier chapter. The issue of FRS 10 is expected to resolve the problems associated with these areas.

Items (g) and (h) are the subject of FRS 4 which is dealt with in a later chapter.

5 FRS 12: PROVISIONS, CONTINGENT LIABILITIES AND CONTINGENT ASSETS

5.1 The problem

Provisions may be made for items such as environmental liabilities, reorganisation costs, litigation and future losses. Although FRS 3 (discontinued operations), FRS 7 (reorganisation costs and future losses) and SSAP 18 (contingencies) partly addressed the problem, there was no accounting standard covering the general topic of provisions.

This led to various problems:

(a) Provisions were often recognised as a result of an intention to make expenditure, rather than on an obligation to do so.

(b) Several items were aggregated into one large provision that was reported as an exceptional item (the 'big bath').

(c) Inadequate disclosure meant that in some cases it was difficult to ascertain the significance of the provisions and any movements in the year.

FRS 12 has been issued to prevent abuses and to ensure that users of the financial statements are provided with sufficient information to understand the nature, timing and amount of provisions. It replaces SSAP 18 *Accounting for contingencies.*

5.2 What is a provision?

Definition A **provision** is a **liability** of **uncertain** timing or amount.

This definition means that provisions are a sub-class of liabilities.

Definition A **liability** is an obligation to transfer economic benefits as a result of past transactions or events. Uncertainty is what distinguishes a provision from another type of liability (such as a trade creditor or an accrued expense).

Note that the FRS 12 definition is narrower than the Companies Act definition. The Companies Act defines provisions as 'amounts retained as **reasonably necessary** to cover any liability or loss which is either **likely** or certain to be incurred'. For a provision to be recognised under FRS 12 there must be an **obligation** to incur expenditure.

Although 'provisions' are often made for items such as depreciation and doubtful debts strictly speaking these are not provisions, but normal accounting estimates.

5.3 Contingent liabilities and contingent assets

Definition A **contingent liability** is:

(a) a possible obligation that arises from past events and whose existence will be confirmed only by the occurrence of one or more uncertain future events not wholly within the entity's control; or

(b) a present obligation that arises from past events but is not recognised because:

  (i) it is not probable that a transfer of economic benefits will be required to settle the obligation; or

  (ii) the amount of the obligation cannot be measured with sufficient reliability.

Definition A **contingent asset** is a possible asset that arises from past events and whose existence will be confirmed only by the occurrence of one or more uncertain future events not wholly within the entity's control.

There are two important changes from SSAP 18:

- The SSAP 18 definition of contingency included probable gains and losses. Under FRS 12, if a gain or loss is probable it is not a contingency.

- The FRS 12 definition of a contingent liability is narrower than the SSAP 18 definition. For there to be a contingent liability there must be an **obligation**.

5.4 Recognition

Provisions

A provision should only be recognised when:

(a) an entity has a present obligation (legal or constructive) as a result of a past event; and
(b) it is probable that a transfer of economic benefits will be required to settle the obligation; and
(c) a reliable estimate can be made of the amount of the obligation.

Definition A **legal obligation** is an obligation that derives from:

(a) a contract;
(b) legislation; or
(c) other operation of law.

Definition A **constructive obligation** is an obligation that derives from an entity's actions where:

(a) by an established pattern of past practice, published policies or a sufficiently specific current statement, the entity has indicated to other parties that it will accept certain responsibilities; and

(b) as a result, the entity has created a valid expectation on the part of those other parties that it will discharge those responsibilities.

FRS 12 explains that:

- A past event gives rise to a present obligation if, taking account of all available evidence, it is **more likely than not** that a present obligation exists at the balance sheet date.

- A transfer of economic benefits is regarded as probable if it is **more likely than not** to occur.

- Where there are a number of similar obligations (eg, product warranties) the probability that a transfer will be required in settlement is determined by considering the **class of obligations as a whole**. For example, if an entity guarantees to refund the cost of faulty goods, the chance of having to make a refund in respect of one specific item is extremely small, but the entity will almost certainly need to make some refunds in respect of its goods as a whole.

- Only in extremely rare cases will it not be possible to make a reliable estimate of the obligation. If it is not possible to make a reliable estimate, the item is disclosed as a contingent liability.

Contingent liabilities

Contingent liabilities should not be recognised. They should be disclosed unless the possibility of a transfer of economic benefits is remote.

Contingent assets

Contingent assets should not be recognised. (Recognition of contingent assets could result in the recognition of profit that may never be realised). If the possibility of an inflow of economic benefits is probable they should be disclosed.

Only if a gain is virtually certain should it be recognised (because it cannot then be a contingency).

5.5 Activity

How should the following items be treated in the financial statements?

(a) A manufacturer gives warranties at the time of sale to purchasers of its product. Under the terms of the contract for sale the manufacturer undertakes to make good manufacturing defects that become apparent within three years from the date of sale. On past experience it is probable that there will be some claims under the warranties.

(b) A retail store has a policy of refunding purchases by dissatisfied customers, even though there is no legal obligation to do so. Its policy of making refunds is generally known.

(c) During 20X5 A gives a guarantee of certain borrowings of B, whose financial condition at that time is sound.

(d) A furnace has a lining that needs to be replaced every five years for technical reasons. At the balance sheet date, the lining has been in use for three years.

(e) New laws have been passed that require an entity to fit smoke filters to its factories by 30 June 20X6. At 31 December 20X5 (the balance sheet date) the entity has not yet fitted the smoke filters.

5.6 Activity solution

These items are taken from the Appendix to FRS 12. For each of the items, ask two questions:

(i) Is there a present obligation as the result of a past event?
(ii) Is a transfer of economic benefits in settlement probable?

A provision is recognised if the answer to both questions is yes.

(a) Present obligation? - Yes. The past (obligating) event is the sale of the product, which gives rise to a legal obligation (under the contract).

Transfer of benefits probable? - Yes. There will probably be claims **for the warranties as a whole.**

Conclusion - Recognise a provision.

(b) Present obligation? - Yes. The past event is the sale of the product, which gives rise to a constructive obligation (see the definition above).

Transfer of benefits probable? - Yes.

Conclusion - Recognise a provision.

(c) Present obligation? - Yes. The giving of the guarantee has given rise to a legal obligation.

Transfer of benefits probable? - No.

Conclusion - Do not recognise a provision. Disclose the guarantee as a contingent liability unless the probability of having to honour it is remote.

(d) Present obligation? - No. No obligation exists independently of the entity's future actions. There is a realistic alternative to incurring the expenditure - the entity could decide not to continue operating the furnace.

Conclusion - Do not recognise a provision. Instead, the cost of the furnace lining should be capitalised and depreciated over five years.

(e) Present obligation? - No. The obligating event would be either the fitting of the filters (which has not happened) or the illegal operation of the factory without the filters (which has not happened because the filters are not yet legally required).

Conclusion - Do not recognise a provision.

5.7 Measurement

General rules

(a) The amount recognised as a provision should be the best estimate of the expenditure required to settle the present obligation at the balance sheet date. (This is the amount that an entity would pay to settle the obligation at the balance sheet date or to persuade a third party to assume it).

(b) In measuring a provision, an entity should take into account:

- (i) the risks and uncertainties surrounding the event (but uncertainty does not justify the creation of excessive provisions or overstatement of liabilities)
- (ii) future events (eg, technological developments) where there is sufficient objective evidence that they will occur.

(c) Where the effect of the time value of money is material (for example, where a liability will be settled in several years' time), the amount of a provision should be discounted. The rate used should be a pre-tax rate that reflects current market assessments of the time value of money and the risk specific to the liability. The discount rate should not reflect risks for which future cash flow estimates have been adjusted.

(d) Gains from the expected disposal of assets should not be taken into account in measuring a provision, even if the disposal is linked to the event giving rise to the provision (for example, where assets are sold when a division is closed down).

(e) Provisions should be reviewed at each balance sheet date and adjusted to reflect the current best estimate. They should be reversed if the transfer of economic benefits is no longer probable.

(f) A provision should only be used for expenditures for which it was originally recognised. (This requirement effectively prevents entities from using 'big bath accounting'.)

Reimbursements

A **reimbursement** is an amount received from a third party to pay part or all of the expenditure required to settle a provision (for example, through an insurance contract).

(a) A reimbursement should be recognised only when it is virtually certain to be received.

(b) The reimbursement should be treated as a separate asset (ie, it should not be netted off against the provision to which it relates).

(c) In the profit and loss account, the expense relating to a provision may be presented net of the income recognised for a reimbursement.

Methods of dealing with uncertainties

These include:

- weighting the cost of all probable outcomes according to their probabilities ('expected value'); and
- considering a range of possible outcomes.

Example - expected value

An entity sells goods with a warranty covering customers for the cost of repairs of any defects that are discovered within the first two months after purchase. Past experience suggests that 90% of the goods sold will have no defects, 5% will have minor defects and 5% will have major defects. If minor defects were detected in all products sold, the cost of repairs would be £10,000; if major defects were detected in all products sold, the cost would be £100,000.

The expected value of the cost of repairs is £5,500 (5% × 10,000 + 5% × 100,000).

Example - possible outcomes

An entity has to rectify a serious fault in an item of plant that it has constructed for a customer.

In this case, the most likely outcome is that the repair will succeed at the first attempt at a cost of £400,000, but a provision for £500,000 is recognised because there is a significant chance that a further attempt will be necessary.

The most likely outcome may be the best estimate of the liability, but other possible outcomes must be considered. Where other possible outcomes are either mostly higher or mostly lower than the most likely outcome, the best estimate will be a higher or lower amount.

5.8 Recognising an asset when recognising a provision

When a provision or change in a provision is recognised, an asset should only be recognised when the expenditure provides access to future economic benefits; otherwise the setting up of the provision should be charged immediately to the profit and loss account.

FRS 12 gives the following example:

When an oil rig is commissioned, an obligation for decommissioning costs is incurred. The commissioning also gives access to oil reserves over the years of the oil rig's operation. Therefore an asset representing future access to oil reserves is recognised at the same time as the provision for decommissioning costs (ie, the double entry is Debit Assets, Credit Provisions rather than Debit Profit and loss account, Credit Provisions).

5.9 Future operating losses

Provisions should not be recognised for future operating losses.

However, note that FRS 12 only covers provisions which are not covered by another accounting standard. This means that there are still situations in which entities are required to make provisions for future losses (eg, discontinued operations (FRS 3), foreseeable losses on long term contracts (SSAP 9)).

5.10 Onerous contracts

Definition An **onerous contract** is a contract in which the unavoidable costs of meeting the obligation exceed the economic benefits expected to be received under it.

An example: a lease contract for a property that is no longer required and where the lease cannot be cancelled.

If an entity has an onerous contract, a provision should be recognised for the present obligation under the contract (for example, for the best estimate of unavoidable lease payments).

5.11 Restructuring

Definition A **restructuring** is a programme that is planned and controlled by management and materially changes either

(a) the scope of a business undertaken by an entity; or
(b) the manner in which that business is conducted.

Examples

(a) sale or termination of a line of business

(b) the closure of business locations in a country or region or the relocation of business activities from one country or region to another

(c) changes in management structure, for example, eliminating a layer of management

(d) fundamental reorganisations that have a material effect on the nature and focus of the entity's operations.

When does an entity have an obligation to restructure?

Provisions for restructuring costs can only be recognised where an entity has a constructive obligation to carry out the restructuring. A Board decision on its own is **not** sufficient to create an obligation.

This requirement is designed to prevent entities from recognising provisions where there is only an intention to restructure and also from making unnecessary provisions which can then be used to artificially enhance profits in subsequent periods. However, critics of the ASB have argued that in practice most Boards of Directors do not take decisions to restructure lightly.

A constructive obligation to restructure arises only when the entity:

(a) has a detailed formal plan for the restructuring identifying at least

   (i) the business or part of the business concerned;

   (ii) the principal locations affected;

   (iii) the location, function, and approximate number of employees who will be compensated for terminating their services;

   (iv) the expenditures that will be undertaken; and

   (v) when the plan will be implemented; and

(b) has raised a valid expectation in those affected that it will carry out the restructuring by starting to implement the plan or announcing its main features to those affected by it.

For an entity to have an obligation to sell an operation there must be a binding sale agreement.

Expenses of restructuring

A restructuring provision should include only the direct expenditures arising from the restructuring, which are those that are both:

(a) necessarily entailed by the restructuring; and
(b) not associated with the ongoing activities of the entity.

The provision should not include costs that relate to the future conduct of the business such as the cost of:

(a) retraining or relocating staff who will continue with the business;
(b) marketing; or
(c) investment in new systems and distribution networks.

5.12 Activity

On 1 December 20X8 the board of an entity decided to close down a division on 31 March 20X9. On 31 January 20X9 a detailed plan for closing down the division was agreed; letters were sent to customers informing them of the decision and redundancy notices were sent to the staff of the division.

Should a provision be recognised in the accounts for the year ended 31 December 20X8?

5.13 Activity solution

No provision should be recognised. There was no present obligation at the balance sheet date. The obligating event is the announcement of the plan, which creates a constructive obligation. This did not take place until after the balance sheet date.

5.14 Disclosure

Provisions

For each class of provision, disclose:

(a) carrying amount at the beginning and end of the period

(b) additional provisions made in the period

(c) amounts used during the period

(d) unused amounts reversed during the period

(e) effect of discounting during the period

(f) a brief description of the nature of the obligation and expected timing of any resulting transfers of economic benefit

(g) an indication of the uncertainties about the amount or timing of those transfers of economic benefit

(h) the amount of any expected reimbursement.

Contingent liabilities

For each class of contingent liability (unless remote) disclose:

(a) an estimate of its financial effect
(b) an indication of the uncertainties relating to the amount or timing of any outflow
(c) the possibility of any reimbursement.

Contingent assets

For contingent assets (only where probable) disclose:

(a) a brief description of their nature
(b) where practicable, an estimate of their financial effect.

Prejudicial information

In extremely rare cases, some of the above disclosures may prejudice an entity in a dispute with other parties about the subject of the provision or contingency. If this is the case, the entity need not disclose the information, unless it is required by law, but should disclose the general nature of the dispute, together with the fact that, and reason why, the information has not been disclosed.

Unwinding of discounts

Where a provision is discounted, its present value increases as time passes. This means that the provision has to be increased accordingly and the profit and loss account charged with the expense. This expense is called 'unwinding of the discount' and should be included in the profit and loss account as a financial item adjacent to interest (ie, below operating profit). It should be shown separately from other interest either on the face of the profit and loss account or in a note. The reasoning behind this is that unwinding of the discount is similar to interest because it relates to the time value of money, but it is not 'true' interest.

Illustrations

FRS 12 includes examples of disclosures:

Example 1

Warranties

A manufacturer gives warranties at the time of sale to purchasers of its three product lines. Under the terms of the warranty the manufacturer undertakes to repair or replace items that fail to perform satisfactorily for two years from the date of sale. At the balance sheet date a provision of £60,000 has been recognised. The provision has not been discounted as the effect of discounting is not material. The following information is disclosed:

'A provision of £60,000 has been recognised for expected warranty claims on products sold during the last three financial years. It is expected that most of this expenditure will be incurred in the next financial year, and all will be incurred within two years of the balance sheet date.'

Example 2

Decommissioning costs

In 2000 an entity involved in nuclear activities recognises a provision for decommissioning costs of £300 million. The provision is estimated using the assumption that decommissioning will take place in 60–70 years' time. However, there is a possibility that it will not take place until 100–110 years' time, in which case the present value of the costs will be significantly reduced. The following information is disclosed:

'A provision of £300 million has been recognised for decommissioning costs. These costs are expected to be incurred between 2060 and 2070. However, there is a possibility that decommissioning will not take place until 2100–2110. If the costs were measured based upon the expectation that they would not be incurred until 2100–2110 the provision would be reduced to £136 million. The provision has been estimated using existing technology, at current prices, and discounted using a real discount rate of 2 per cent.'

Example 3

Disclosure exemption

An entity is involved in a dispute with a competitor, who is alleging that the entity has infringed patents and is seeking damages of £100 million. The entity recognises a provision for its best estimate of the obligation, but discloses none of the information required by FRS 12. The following information is disclosed:

'Litigation is in process against the company relating to a dispute with a competitor which alleges that the company has infringed patents and which is seeking damages of £100 million. The information usually required by FRS 12 is not disclosed on the grounds that it can be expected to prejudice seriously the outcome of the litigation. The directors are of the opinion that the claim can be successfully resisted by the company.'

5.15 FRS 12 in practice

FRS 12 is likely to prevent the abuses that have taken place in the past, such as 'big bath' accounting. It should also provide users of the financial statements with much more extensive information about provisions and contingencies.

However, the standard has not been welcomed enthusiastically. Because there must be an obligation before a provision can be recognised, entities will not be allowed to recognise provisions in many situations where they would probably have done so in the past. Critics of the ASB claim that this represents a move away from the fundamental concept of prudence. There may be difficulties for auditors, because management may have an excuse to avoid making provisions.

This move away from prudence is evident in the way in which provisions are measured, as well as in the criteria for their recognition. The FRS states that uncertainty does not justify the creation of excessive provisions or overstatement of liabilities and that care is needed to avoid duplicating adjustments for risk and uncertainty so that a provision is overstated.

Conclusion A **provision** is a **liability** of **uncertain** timing or amount. A provision should only be recognised when:

(a) an entity has a present obligation as a result of a past event; and
(b) it is probable that a transfer of economic benefits will be required; and
(c) a reliable estimate can be made of the amount of the obligation.

The amount recognised as a provision should be the best estimate of the expenditure required to settle the present obligation at the balance sheet date.

6 UITF ABSTRACT 17: EMPLOYEE SHARE SCHEMES

6.1 Background

Share option schemes are used as part of employee remuneration either as a management incentive or through SAYE ('save as you earn') schemes that are available to all employees. A more recent development is the increasing use of share awards, either through annual bonuses or longer term incentive schemes as an alternative or addition to share option plans.

The Abstract is concerned with the measurement and timing of the charge to be recognised by companies in the profit and loss account. It applies to all employee share schemes, including share option schemes. It does not apply to SAYE schemes.

6.2 UITF Consensus

(a) The costs of awards to employees that take the form of shares or rights to shares should be recognised over the period to which the employee's performance relates. In the case of annual bonuses, this is the year to which the bonus relates. In the case of long-term incentive schemes, this is the period to which the performance criteria relate.

(b) The amount recognised should be based on the fair value of the shares at the date an award has been made to participants in the scheme.

(c) Where an award takes the form of shares, or rights to shares, the minimum amount recognised should be the difference between:

(i) **either** the fair value of the shares at the date the award is made to participants in the scheme;

or the book value of shares that are available for the award (where purchases have been made by an ESOP trust and treated in accordance with UITF Abstract 13); and

(ii) the amount of the consideration, if any, that participants may be required to pay for the shares.

(d) In the case of a long term incentive scheme, the amount initially recognised should be based on a reasonable expectation of the extent that performance criteria will be met. The amount should be charged in the profit and loss account on a straight line basis (or another basis that more fairly reflects the services received) over the period to which the performance criteria relate.

(e) Where there are no performance criteria and the award is clearly unrelated to past performance, the period over which the cost is recognised should be that from the date of the award to the date at which the employee becomes unconditionally entitled to the shares.

(f) Where new shares are issued under an employee share scheme the credit entry for the charge to the profit and loss account should be reported in the reconciliation of movements in shareholders' funds. It should not be reported in the statement of total recognised gains and losses.

7 CHAPTER SUMMARY

FRS 5 is a complex standard. The principle is that the substance of any transaction should be recorded in the financial statements. This may mean that an asset or liability is recorded which otherwise would not be or an asset or liability is removed from the financial statements when otherwise it would not be. A special linked presentation is allowed in certain circumstances.

FRS 12 states that a **provision** is a **liability** of **uncertain** timing or amount and requires that a provision should only be recognised when:

(a) an entity has a present obligation as a result of a past event; and
(b) it is probable that a transfer of economic benefits will be required; and
(c) a reliable estimate can be made of the amount of the obligation.

The amount recognised as a provision should be the best estimate of the expenditure required to settle the present obligation at the balance sheet date.

8 SELF TEST QUESTIONS

8.1 What is off balance sheet finance? (1.1)

8.2 Which documents have been issued to restrict the use of controlled non-subsidiaries? (1.3)

8.3 What are the common features of transactions whose substance is not readily apparent? (2.4)

8.4 What is the general definition of an asset? (2.4)

8.5 What is the difference between 'linking' and 'offset'? (2.9)

8.6 Where is 'window dressing' covered in an accounting standard? (4.2)

8.7 What is a 'big bath'? (5.1)

8.8 What is the definition of a provision? (5.2)

8.9 When should a provision be recognised? (5.4)

8.10 When does an entity have a constructive obligation to transfer economic benefits? (5.4)

9 EXAMINATION TYPE QUESTION

9.1 S Ltd

FRS 5 - *Reporting the substance of transactions* - requires that a reporting entity's financial statements should report the substance of the transactions into which it has entered.

You are the management accountant of S Ltd. During the most recent financial year (ended 31 August 20X8), the company has entered into a debt factoring arrangement with F plc. The main terms of the agreement are as follows:

1. On the first day of every month S Ltd transfers (by assignment) all its trade debts to F plc, subject to credit approval by F plc for each debt transferred by S Ltd.

2. At the time of transfer of the debtors to F plc, S Ltd receives a payment from F plc of 70% of the gross amount of the transferred debts. The payment is debited by F plc to a factoring account which is maintained in the books of F plc.

3. Following transfer of the debts, F plc collects payments from debtors and performs any necessary follow-up work.

4. After collection by F plc, the cash received from the debtor is credited to the factoring account in the books of F plc.

5. F plc handles all aspects of the collection of the debts of S Ltd in return for a monthly charge of 1% of the total value of the debts transferred at the beginning of that month. The amount is debited to the factoring account in the books of F plc.

6. Any debts not collected by F plc within 90 days of transfer are regarded as bad debts by F plc and re-assigned to S Ltd. The cash previously advanced by F plc in respect of bad debts is recovered from S Ltd. The recovery is only possible out of the proceeds of other debtors which have been assigned to S Ltd. For example, if, in a particular month, S Ltd assigned trade debts having a value of £10,000 and a debt of £500 was identified as bad, then the amounts advanced by F plc to S Ltd would be £6,650 [70% × £10,000 - 70% × £500].

7. On a monthly basis, F plc debits the factoring account with an interest charge which is calculated on a daily basis on the balance on the factoring account.

8. At the end of every quarter, F plc pays over to S Ltd a sum representing any credit balance on its factoring account with S Ltd at that time.

Requirement:

Write a memorandum to the Board of Directors of S Ltd which outlines

(a) how, under the principles set out in FRS 5, the substance of a transaction should be determined; **(10 marks)**

(b) how the debt factoring arrangement will be reported in the financial statements of S Ltd. **(10 marks)**

(Total: 20 marks)

10 ANSWER TO EXAMINATION TYPE QUESTION

10.1 S Ltd

MEMORANDUM

To: The Board of Directors

From: The Management Accountant

Subject: How the debt factoring arrangement will be reported in the financial statements

Date: 25 November 20X8

(a) **Determining the economic substance of a transaction**

FRS 5 *Reporting the substance of transactions* states that in order to determine the economic substance of a transaction it is necessary to identify its effect on the assets and liabilities of the entity.

FRS 5 defines assets and liabilities very widely. Assets are 'rights or other access to future economic benefits controlled by an entity as a result of past transactions or events'. Control means the ability to obtain the future economic benefits relating to an asset and to restrict the access of others to those benefits. Evidence of whether an entity has benefits (and therefore has an asset) is given by whether it is exposed to the risks inherent in those benefits. A liability is 'an obligation to transfer economic benefits as a result of past transactions or events'. If an entity cannot avoid an outflow of resources, it has a liability.

Therefore to determine the substance of a transaction it is necessary to identify the asset or assets involved and then to identify the risks and benefits associated with them. The details of the transaction or arrangement are then analysed to establish which party is actually exposed to the risks and benefits in practice, regardless of the legal position. Provided that the asset(s) can be measured reliably in monetary terms and that there is sufficient evidence of their existence, the party exposed to the risks and benefits recognises the asset in its financial statements.

(b) **How the debt factoring arrangement will be reported in the financial statements**

The legal form of the transaction is that S Ltd has transferred the title to the debtors to the factor, F plc. However, the key issue is whether S Ltd has actually assigned its debtors to F plc in practice or whether S Ltd has merely raised a secured loan from F plc. In order to determine the substance of the arrangement it is necessary to establish which party bears the risks and enjoys the benefits associated with the debtors.

The main benefit of holding debtors is normally an eventual cash inflow, while the main risks are slow payment and non-recovery (ie. bad debts).

The terms of the agreement can be analysed as follows:

- F plc only accepts debts subject to credit approval, so that S Ltd bears the risk of slow payment and bad debts.
- S Ltd receives only 70% of the debts at the time of assignment. The remaining sums, less interest charged by F plc, are only paid to S Ltd after the debtors have been collected by F plc. Again, S Ltd bears slow payment risk.
- Although F plc administers the scheme and collects the debts, S Ltd must pay a fee for this service. Additionally, all debts not paid within 90 days are re-assigned to S Ltd

and S Ltd must repay any monies advanced in respect of those debts. S Ltd is bearing the risk of bad debts.

- F plc charges further interest based on the balance on the factoring account, the size of which depends on the speed with which debts are collected. S Ltd is bearing slow payment risk.

From this analysis it is clear that S Ltd is bearing all the risks associated with the debtors and that the commercial substance of the relationship is that F plc has provided a loan secured on the debtors. The risks to S Ltd are mitigated to some extent, because F plc can only recover bad debts out of the proceeds of other debtors assigned to it.

S Ltd should recognise the debtors as an asset until they have been collected by F plc. The sum advanced from F plc should be treated as a loan, but a linked presentation is appropriate, so that the loan is deducted from the debtors on the balance sheet. S Ltd should record expenses for interest, administration charges and bad debts in its profit and loss account.

9 LEASING CONTRACTS

INTRODUCTION & LEARNING OBJECTIVES

The issue of accounting for the substance of a transaction as opposed to its form has mainly involved the desire by companies to organise some of their finance so that it does not appear on the balance sheet (ie, off balance sheet financing). The standard setters have taken a long time to counteract balance sheet schemes, apart from the early issue of SSAP 21.

Lessee accounting should be revision to you. Lessor accounting is complex but can be the subject of a full question. You must therefore understand how the calculations are derived.

When you have studied this chapter you should be able to do the following:

- Demonstrate your understanding of the accounting and disclosure requirements of *SSAP 21* for both lessees and lessors.
- Perform calculations to implement the *SSAP 21* accounting requirements.

1 BACKGROUND AND DEFINITIONS

1.1 The growth of leasing business

The increasing trend towards obtaining use of fixed assets by means of finance leases in the 1970s emphasised the urgent need for considering the implications for financial reporting. After much delay, *ED 29* on accounting for leases and hire purchase contracts was issued in 1981 and *SSAP 21* in September 1984.

1.2 Types of leases

Before *SSAP 21* most lessees treated all leases in the same way, rentals paid were charged to profit and loss account, and no asset and finance obligation appeared in the balance sheet.

SSAP 21 distinguishes between two types of leases:

(a) finance leases, which in substance are considered similar to hire purchase contracts; and
(b) operating leases which are essentially leases of a short-term nature.

(The definitions are considered in detail below.)

1.3 Legal requirements

Although there is no explicit requirement to disclose leasing commitments, *Sch 4 Companies Act 1985* requires particulars to be given of financial commitments which:

(a) have not been provided for; and
(b) are relevant to assessing the company's state of affairs.

If such commitments are material, then this requirement, together with the overriding true and fair view requirement, will mean disclosure of significant non-cancellable leasing commitments.

1.4 Definitions in SSAP 21

A **lease** is a contract between a lessor and a lessee for the hire of a specific asset. The lessor retains ownership of the asset but conveys the right to the use of the asset to the lessee for an agreed period of time in return for the payment of specific rentals. The term 'lease' as used in this statement also applies to other arrangements in which one party retains ownership of an asset but conveys the right to the use of the asset to another party for an agreed period of time in return for specific payments.

Definition A **finance lease** is a lease that transfers substantially all the risks and rewards of ownership of an asset to the lessee. It should be presumed that such a transfer of risks and rewards occurs if at the inception of a lease the present value of the minimum lease payments, including any initial payment, amounts to substantially all (normally 90 per cent or more) of the fair value of the leased asset. The present value should be calculated by using the interest rate implicit in the lease (as defined below). If the fair value of the asset is not determinable, an estimate thereof should be used.

Notwithstanding the fact that a lease meets these conditions, the presumption that it should be classified as a finance lease may in exceptional circumstances be rebutted if it can be clearly demonstrated that the lease in question does not transfer substantially all the risks and rewards of ownership (other than legal title) to the lessee. Correspondingly, the presumption that a lease which fails to meet these conditions is not a finance lease may in exceptional circumstances be rebutted.

Definition An **operating lease** is a lease other than a finance lease.

Definition A **hire purchase contract** is a contract for hire of an asset which contains a provision giving the hirer an option to acquire legal title to the asset upon the fulfilment of certain conditions stated in the contract.

Definition The **lease term** is the period for which the lessee has contracted to lease the asset and any further terms for which the lessee has the option to continue to lease the asset, with or without further payment, which option it is reasonably certain at the inception of the lease that the lessee will exercise.

Definition The **minimum lease payments** are the minimum payments over the remaining part of the lease term (excluding charges for services and taxes to be paid by the lessor) and:

(a) in the case of the lessee, any residual amounts guaranteed by him or by a party related to him; or

(b) in the case of the lessor, any residual amounts guaranteed by the lessee or by an independent third party.

Definition The **interest rate implicit in a lease** is the discount rate that at the inception of a lease, when applied to the amounts which the lessor expects to receive and retain, produces an amount (the present value) equal to the fair value of the leased asset. The amounts which the lessor expects to receive and retain comprise (a) the minimum lease payments to the lessor (as defined above), plus (b) any unguaranteed residual value, less (c) any part of (a) and (b) for which the lessor will be accountable to the lessee. If the interest rate implicit in the lease is not determinable, it should be estimated by reference to the rate which a lessee would be expected to pay on a similar lease.

Definition **Fair value** is the price at which an asset could be exchanged in an arm's length transaction less, where applicable, any grants receivable towards the purchase or use of the asset.

2 THE REQUIREMENTS OF SSAP 21 IN THE LESSEE'S ACCOUNTS

2.1 The effect on the financial statements of treating a lease as a finance or operating lease

SSAP 21 requires capitalisation of finance leases by lessees. No major change in accounting treatment is required for operating leases. The effect on financial statements may be summarised as follows:

	Hire purchase	*Finance leases*	*Operating leases*
P/L account	(a) Depreciation (b) Finance charge	(a) Depreciation (b) Finance charge	Rental payments
Balance sheet - asset	Fixed asset less depreciation	Fixed asset less depreciation	-
- liability	Obligations under hire purchase contracts	Obligations under finance leases.	-

2.2 Applying the requirements to given situations to classify leases as finance or operating

A finance lease is defined as a lease that transfers substantially all the risks and rewards of ownership of an asset to the lessee. To decide whether there is a presumption of transfer of risks and rewards of ownership it is necessary to complete the following steps:

Step	*Comment*
(1) Calculate minimum lease payments (MLPs) inclusive of initial payment.	MLPs = minimum payments plus any residual amounts guaranteed by lessee.
(2) Discount (1) to determine present value of MLPs.	Discount factor is either: (i) rate of interest implicit in lease (if known) or (ii) a commercial rate of interest (for a similar lease)
(3) Calculate fair value of asset at beginning of lease.	Fair value = arm's length price less any government grants receivable by lessor.
(4) Presumption is satisfied if (2) amounts to 90% or more of (3).	

2.3 Finance leases – initial entries

At the start of the lease:

(a) the present value of the MLPs should be included as a fixed asset, subject to depreciation;
(b) the obligation to pay rentals should be included as a liability.

In practice the fair value of the asset or its cash price will often be a sufficiently close approximation to the present value of the MLPs and therefore can be used instead.

2.4 Finance leases – depreciation

The related fixed asset should be depreciated over the shorter of:

(a) the economic useful life of the asset (as in FRS 15); and

(b) the lease term.

The lease term is essentially the period over which the lessee has the use of the asset. It includes:

(i) the primary (non-cancellable) period; plus

(ii) any secondary periods during which the lessee has the contractual right to continue to use the asset, provided that it is reasonably certain at the outset that this right will be exercised.

2.5 Finance leases – allocation of finance charges

(a) Over the period of the lease, the total finance charge is the amount by which the rentals paid to the lessor exceed the present value of the MLPs.

(b) Each individual rental payment should be split between:

(i) finance charge (P/L account item); and
(ii) repayment of obligation to pay rentals (thus reducing the balance sheet liability).

(c) How should finance charges be allocated over the term of the lease? The basic aim is to allocate the charge in such a way as to produce a reasonably constant periodic rate of return on the remaining balance of liability. There are three main methods:

(i) actuarial method;
(ii) sum of the digits (rule of 78) method;
(iii) straight-line method.

Of the above methods the actuarial method gives the most accurate result.

2.6 Example of the actuarial method

A company has two options. It can buy an asset for cash at a cost of £5,710 or it can lease it by way of a finance lease. The terms of the lease are as follows:

(1) primary period is for four years from 1 January 20X2 with a rental of £2,000 pa payable on the 31 December each year;

(2) the lessee has the right to continue to lease the asset after the end of the primary period for an indefinite period, subject only to a peppercorn (nominal) rent;

(3) the lessee is required to pay all repair, maintenance and insurance costs as they arise;

(4) the interest rate implicit in the lease is 15%.

The lessee estimates the useful economic life of the asset to be eight years. Depreciation is provided on a straight-line basis.

2.7 Solution

Step 1 Is the lease a finance lease?

Referring to the steps in the earlier paragraph:

(1) MLPs = 4 × £2,000 = £8,000

(2) Present value of MLPs:

From discount tables – present value of four annual sums – first receivable at the end of the first year:

£2,000 × 2.855 = £5,710

(3) Fair value of asset is £5,710.

(4) Present value of MLPs is more than 90% of fair value of asset.

The lease is then a finance lease.

Step 2 The asset is shown in the balance sheet at £5,710 (subject to depreciation). Depreciation is over eight years (presumably no residual value to the asset at the end of eight years).

Annual depreciation charge = 1/8 × £5,710 = £714

Step 3 The liability is shown in the balance sheet at £5,710 but subsequently reduced by the capital portion of the leasing payments.

The total finance charge is £(8,000 – 5,710) = £2,290. The allocation of this to each rental payment and the consequent capital sum outstanding is calculated as follows:

Period (year ended 31 December)	*Capital sum at start of period*	*Finance charge at 15% pa*	*Sub-total*	*Rental paid*	*Capital sum at end of period*
	£	£	£	£	£
20X2	5,710	856	6,566	(2,000)	4,566
20X3	4,566	685	5,251	(2,000)	3,251
20X4	3,251	488	3,739	(2,000)	1,739
20X5	1,739	261	2,000	(2,000)	-
		2,290		8,000	

Step 4 The effect on the financial statements of the lessee may be summarised as follows:

	Profit and loss account		*Balance sheet*			
				Obligation		
Year ended 31 December	*Finance charge*	*Depn.*	*Fixed asset (NBV)*	*Total*	*Non-current*	*Current*
	£	£	£	£	£	£
20X2	856	714	4,996	4,566	3,251	1,315
20X3	685	714	4,282	3,251	1,739	1,512
20X4	488	714	3,568	1,739	-	1,739
20X5	261	714	2,854	-	-	-
20X6	-	714	2,140	-	-	-
20X7	-	714	1,426	-	-	-
20X8	-	714	712	-	-	-
20X9	-	712	-	-	-	-
	2,290	5,710				

The finance charge each year is a constant periodic rate of return (15%) on the remaining balance of liability, eg, £856 is 15% of £5,710, etc.

2.8 The sum of the digits (or rule of 78) method

This method is an approximation to the actuarial method. Although not as theoretically precise as the actuarial method, the sum of the digits method has the advantage of being easier to operate.

Using the figures from the previous example, the finance charge may be allocated as follows:

$$\text{Sum of digits:} = \frac{N\ (N+1)}{2} = \frac{4\ (4+1)}{2} = 10$$

Year ended 31 Dec.		£
20X2	4/10 × 2,290	916
20X3	3/10 × 2,290	687
20X4	2/10 × 2,290	458
20X5	1/10 × 2,290	229
		2,290

The liability at the end of each year may be calculated by slotting the above figures into the table.

2.9 Straight-line method

Under the straight-line method, a finance charge of $\frac{2,290}{4}$ = £572 would be allocated to each period from 20X2 to 20X5. This is the simplest of the methods. It does not attempt to produce a constant periodic rate of charge, but if used in connection with a relatively small lease it may produce figures which in any year are not significantly different from those which would be produced by one of the other methods. What is a small lease will depend on the size of the company.

It is sometimes argued that, in order to establish whether the straight-line method provides a reasonable approximation, it is necessary to calculate the finance charge allocation on two or more bases. This is not necessarily so. In some cases the **total** finance charges may not be material in which case the straight-line method may be used: there will be no need to compare the allocation under the straight-line method with that under any other method.

2.10 Hire purchase contracts

The depreciation and the finance chargeS should be allocated in the same way as for finance leases.

2.11 Operating leases

Rentals under operating leases should be charged to the profit and loss account on a straight-line basis over the term of the lease unless another systematic and rational basis is more appropriate. Any difference between amounts charged and amounts paid should be adjusted to debtors or creditors.

2.12 Activity

P Ltd entered into a five year lease on 1 January 20X3 for a machine with a fair value of £20,000. Rentals are £5,200 pa payable in advance and the residual value at the end of the lease is calculated as £4,200 which will be returned to P Ltd.

P Ltd is responsible for insurance and maintenance costs. The rate of interest implicit in the lease is 15.15%. You are required to show the allocation of finance charges on a sum of the digits basis and on an actuarial basis and comment on the result.

2.13 Activity solution

Step 1 Calculate the finance charge.

	£
5 × £5,200	26,000
Fair value	20,000
Finance charge	6,000

Step 2 Allocate finance charge on a sum of the digits basis.

$$\text{Finance charge pa} = \frac{\text{Number of rentals not yet due} \times \text{total finance charge}}{\text{Sum of number of rentals}}$$

Year	*No of rentals not yet due*		*Finance charge* £
20X3	4		2,400
20X4	3		1,800
20X5	2	6,000/10	1,200
20X6	1		600
20X7	-		
	10		6,000

Step 3 Allocate finance charge on an actuarial basis.

Year	*Capital b/d*	*Lease payment*	*Capital outstanding*	*Finance charge*	*Capital c/d*
	£	£	£	£	£
20X3	20,000	5,200	14,800	2,242	17,042
20X4	17,042	5,200	11,842	1,794	13,636
20X5	13,636	5,200	8,436	1,278	9,714
20X6	9,714	5,200	4,514	686	5,200
20X7	5,200	5,200	-	-	-

Conclusion Where the lease term is relatively short and the interest rate is not high the two methods of interest allocation produce very similar results.

3 DISCLOSURE REQUIREMENTS

3.1 Disclosure – finance leases and hire purchase contracts

For disclosure purposes finance leases and hire purchase agreements are treated as one group.

(a) **Balance sheet: assets**

There is a choice of disclosure for assets. Either:

(i) show by each major class of asset the gross amounts of assets held under a finance lease and related accumulated depreciation; or

(ii) integrate the finance lease assets with owned fixed assets and disclose the **net** amount of assets held under finance leases.

(b) **Balance sheet: obligations under finance leases**

The amounts of obligations related to finance leases (net of finance charges allocated to future periods) should be disclosed separately from other obligations and liabilities, either on the face of the balance sheet or in the notes to the accounts.

These net obligations under finance leases should then be analysed between amounts payable in the next year, amounts payable in the second to fifth years inclusive from the balance sheet date, and the aggregate amounts payable thereafter. This analysis may be presented either:

(i) separately for obligations under finance leases; or
(ii) where the total of these items is combined on the balance sheet with other obligations and liabilities, by giving the equivalent analysis of the total in which it is included.

If the analysis is presented according to (i) above, a lessee may, as an alternative to analysing the net obligations, analyse the gross obligations, with future finance charges being separately deducted from the total.

(c) **Profit and loss account**

The total depreciation charge and the aggregate finance charges for the period in respect of finance leases should be disclosed.

3.2 Disclosure - Operating leases

(a) **Balance sheet: obligations under operating leases**

In respect of operating leases, the lessee should disclose the payments which he is committed to make during the next year, analysed between those in which the commitment expires within that year, in the second to fifth years inclusive and over five years from the balance sheet date, showing separately the commitments in respect of leases of land and buildings and other operating leases.

(b) **Profit and loss account**

Total operating lease rentals charged as an expense in the profit and loss account - split between hire of plant and machinery rentals and other operating leases.

3.3 Accounting policies

Disclosure should be made of the policies adopted for accounting for operating and finance leases.

3.4 Illustration of disclosure requirements – finance leases

Using the earlier illustration and the calculations under the actuarial method the following disclosure would be appropriate:

Extracts from balance sheet

	31 Dec 20X2
	£
Assets:	
Leased property under finance leases	5,710
Less: Accumulated depreciation	714
	4,996

Alternatively, the above figures could be included within the overall totals of fixed assets and disclose merely the NBV of £4,996.

Extracts from balance sheet

	£
Liabilities:	
Non-current obligations under finance leases	3,251
Current obligations under finance leases	1,315
	4,566

The above figures may be disclosed separately on the face of the balance sheet or aggregated with other items (eg, bank loans and overdrafts). In the latter situation the notes to the accounts would reveal the above figures.

Notes to the accounts – Obligations under finance leases

The future minimum lease payments to which the company is committed as at 31 December 20X2 are:

	£
Amounts payable next year	2,000
Amounts payable in the second and third years	4,000
	6,000
Less: Finance charges allocated to future periods	1,434
	4,566

An alternative disclosure would be:

The future net obligations to which the company is committed as at 31 December 20X2 are:

	£
Amounts due within one year	1,315
Amounts due in the second and third years	3,251
	4,566

Notes to the accounts – Profit and loss account

Profit is stated after charging:

	£
Depreciation of owned assets	X
Depreciation of assets held under finance leases (and hire purchase contracts – if relevant)	714
Finance charges payable:	
Finance leases (and hire purchase contracts)	856
Hire of plant and machinery – operating leases	X
Hire of other assets – operating leases	X

Extract from statement of accounting policies

Where assets are financed by leasing agreements that give rights approximating to ownership ('finance leases'), the assets are treated as if they had been purchased outright at the present value of the total rentals payable during the primary period of the lease. The corresponding leasing commitments are shown as obligations to the lessor.

Charges are made to profit and loss account in respect of:

(a) depreciation – which is provided on a straight-line basis over the economic useful life of the asset;

(b) the total finance charge which is allocated over the primary period of the lease using the actuarial method.

3.5 Illustration of disclosure requirements - operating leases

The commitments should be analysed as follows:

At 31 December 20X2 the company had annual commitments under non-cancellable operating leases as set out below:

	Land and buildings	*Other*
	£	£
Operating leases which expire:		
Within one year	x	x
In the second to fifth years inclusive	x	x
Over five years	x	x

This disclosure is not requiring the total sums which will actually be paid in future, but merely for how long a particular lease will require payments. For example, a company uses two offices, both leased:

Lease A expires in three years – Annual rental £30,000
Lease B expires in forty five years – Annual rental £20,000

The disclosure would be:

	Land and buildings
	£
Operating leases which expire:	
In the second to fifth years inclusive	30,000
Over five years	20,000
Total annual commitment as at the current year-end	50,000

3.6 Activity

Gills Ltd has entered into three agreements to acquire three machines, X, Y and Z.

The agreement details were as follows

Agreement date	*Subject of agreement*	*Length of lease*	*Lease terms*	*Payable*
1 March 20X8	Machine X	18 months	£15,000 pa	Six months in advance
1 January 20X7	Machine Y	6 years	£12,025 pa	Annually in advance
1 January 20X8	Machine Z	5 years	£3,700 pa	Annually in arrears

The accountant of Gills Ltd made further enquiries and discovered that at the time of entering into the agreements the following information was correct

	Age when leased	*Useful remaining life at date of agreement*	*Cost to purchase at date of agreement*
Machine X	3 years	6 years	£92,500
Machine Y	New	6 years	£46,250
Machine Z	New	5 years	Cost not available

Assume

(a) that Gills Ltd could borrow funds throughout 20X7 and 20X8 at 12% per annum
(b) that interest is allocated using the sum of the digits method.

You are required:

(a) to prepare calculations to show the effect on the profit and loss account of Gills Ltd for the year ended 31 December 20X8 and the balance sheet as at 31 December 20X8 of treating the three leases in accordance with the provisions of SSAP 21 *Accounting for leases and hire purchase contracts.*

(b) to prepare calculations to show the effect on the profit and loss account of Gills Ltd for the year ended 31 December 20X8 and the balance sheet as at 31 December 20X8 if the leases were not being treated in accordance with SSAP 21 but were being treated as operating leases.

12% discount factors are shown below

Years (t)	*Present value of £1 to be received after t years*	*Present value of £1 per year for each of t years*
1	0.893	0.893
2	0.797	1.690
3	0.712	2.402
4	0.636	3.038
5	0.567	3.605
6	0.507	4.112

3.7 Activity solution

(a) **Machine X**

Treat as an operating lease.

Profit and loss account	10 months' rental charge	=	£12,500
Balance sheet	Prepayment, 2 months' rental charge	=	£2,500

Disclosure in notes to the accounts, operating lease commitment of £7,500 for next year under heading of lease with a commitment finishing next year.

Machine Y

Treat as a finance lease.

Workings re interest allocation

	£
Total purchase price, 6 years × £12,025	72,150
'Cash' purchase price	46,250
Interest	£25,900

Sum of digits = 5 + 4 + 3 + 2 + 1 + 0 = 15

For year 20X8 interest allocated to profit and loss account would be

$$\frac{4}{15} \times £25,900 = £6,907$$

Depreciation charged (straight line) to profit and loss account would be

$$\frac{£46,250}{6 \text{ years}} = £7,708$$

This would give a fixed asset value of £46,250 less accumulated depreciation of £15,416 in the balance sheet.

Other balance sheet figures would be

Obligations under finance lease

Less than one year	$£12,025 - \left(\frac{3}{15} \times £25,900\right)$	=	£6,845
More than one year	$(£12,025 \times 3) - \left(\frac{2+1+0}{15} \times £25,900\right)$	=	£30,895

Machine Z

Treat as a finance lease.

Workings using discounted rentals to calculate fair value at time of purchase

£3,700 × 3.605 = £13,338.50

Interest allocation

	£
Total purchase price, 5 years × £3,700	18,500.00
Fair value	13,338.50
Interest	£5,161.50

Sum of digits = 5 + 4 + 3 + 2 + 1 = 15

For year 20X8 interest allocated to profit and loss account would be

$$\frac{5}{15} \times £5,161.50 = £1,720.50$$

Depreciation charged (straight line) to profit and loss account would be

$$\frac{£13,338.50}{5 \text{ years}} = £2,667.70$$

This would give a fixed asset value of £13,338.50 less accumulated depreciation of £2,667.70 in the balance sheet.

Other balance sheet figures would be

Less than one year	$£3{,}700 - \left(\frac{4}{15} \times £5{,}161.50\right)$	=	£2,323.60
More than one year	$(£3{,}700 \times 3) - \left(\frac{3+2+1}{15} \times £5{,}161.50\right)$	=	£9,035.40

(b) **Machine X**

No change, as per answer to part (a) above.

Machine Y

Profit and loss account charge of £12,025 annual rental.

Disclose, in the notes to the accounts, operating lease commitment of £12,025 for next year under heading of lease with a commitment expiring after five years.

Machine Z

Profit and loss account charge of £3,700 annual rental.

Disclose, in notes to the accounts, operating lease commitment of £3,700 for next year under heading of lease with a commitment finishing in the second to fifth years.

4 ACCOUNTING FOR LESSORS AND FINANCE COMPANIES

4.1 Introduction

From the viewpoint of the lessor, the substance over form argument regards a finance lease as being equivalent to the provision of finance, rather than the hiring out of a fixed asset. Conversely an operating lease should be accounted for by capitalising and depreciating the leased asset.

The two types of lease may be compared for the lessor as follows:

	Finance leases	*Operating leases*
Balance sheet	Net investment in finance lease	Property held for operating leases (cost - depreciation)
Profit and loss account	Finance charge (allocated on basis which gives constant periodic return on net cash investment)	Rental income (straight-line basis) Depreciation

4.2 Accounting for finance leases

The standard deals with calculation of the carrying value of the finance lease receivables and with lessors' profit recognition. It requires the receivables to be carried on a balance sheet at an amount based on the net investment in the lease. Conversely, it requires that profit recognition should normally be based on the lessor's net *cash* investment.

The net investment in a lease is initially the cost of the asset to the lessor, less any government or other grants receivable (ie, the fair value).

The rentals paid by the lessee should be apportioned by the lessor between (a) gross earnings (ie, the lessor's interest earned) and (b) a repayment of capital.

Over the period of the lease the net investment in the lease (ie, the carrying value of the receivables) will therefore be the fair value of the asset less those portions of the rentals which are apportioned as a repayment of capital.

For the purposes of profit recognition, however, the total gross earnings should normally be allocated to accounting periods to give a constant periodic rate of return on the lessor's net **cash** investment (NCI) in the lease in each period. The NCI is based on the funds which the lessor has invested in the lease. The amount of funds invested in a lease by a lessor is different from the net investment in the lease because there are a number of other cash flows which affect the lessor in addition to those which affect net investment. In particular, tax cash flows are an important component of the NCI.

The standard permits a reasonable approximation to be made in arriving at the constant period rate of return. Hence there are a number of different methods of profit recognition which may comply with the standard. Traditionally, the two main methods used have been the actuarial method after tax and the investment period method, but following changes to UK tax law these are rarely used in practice and are unlikely to be examined. Instead, the 'pre-tax' methods used in lessee accounting (ie, the straight line method, the sum of the digits method and the actuarial method) will usually give an acceptable answer.

4.3 The lessor's profit and loss account

A simple outline of the lessor's profit and loss account might appear as follows:

	£	£	*Note*
Rentals received		X	1
Capital repayments		(X)	
Finance income		X	2
Interest	X		3
Overheads	X		3
Bad debts	X		4
		(X)	
Profit before tax		X	
Tax		(X)	3
Profit after tax		X	
Dividends		(X)	3
Retained profit		X	

Notes:

(1) Rentals received is the aggregation of rental income for all leases.

(2) To compute this figure it is necessary to calculate, for each major type of leasing arrangement that the lessor enters into, the finance income within the total rental receipts using one of the methods which will approximate to the constant period rate of return.

Item 2 is the total of the finance income calculated for all leases for an accounting period.

(3) All these items are the normal expenses incurred by the lessor in the accounting period.

(4) This is assessed in the usual way.

4.4 Illustration of lessor accounting for a finance lease

The lessor in the example in paragraph 2.6 above will account for the leased asset as follows:

(a) Confirm that the terms of the lease satisfy the conditions to be a finance lease. This is the same as in 2.7 above.

(b) Recognise the £5,710 value of the asset as a receivable (debtor), 'investment in finance lease'.

(c) Recognise the finance income receivable each year on the same basis that the lessee recognised the finance charge payable:

Year	*Finance income receivable*
	£
20X2	856
20X3	685
20X4	488
20X5	261
	2,290

(d) At the end of the primary period of the lease, the total lease payments received (4 × £2,000) will exactly equal the original receivable (£5,710) plus the total finance income recognised (£2,290).

4.5 Accounting for hire purchase contracts

In the case of hire purchase, profit recognition should also, in principle, be based on net cash investment. However, since the capital allowances under a hire purchase contract accrue to the hirer, the finance company's net cash investment is often not significantly different from its net investment; hence allocation of gross earnings (ie, finance charges) based on net investment will again in most cases be a suitable approximation to allocation based on net cash investment.

This will have the result that the entries in the finance company's accounts will be a mirror image of the entries in the hirer's accounts if the hirer is using the actuarial method before tax.

4.6 Presentation in accounts

The standard requires disclosure of the net investment in (a) finance leases and (b) hire purchase contracts at each balance sheet date. The amounts should be described as receivables. Whereas in lessee accounting the figures in respect of leases and hire purchase contracts may be aggregated, in the case of lessors and finance companies the amounts in respect of each should be shown separately.

For companies subject to *Sch 4 CA 1985* the net investment in finance leases and hire purchase contracts should be included in current assets under the heading 'debtors' and described as 'finance lease receivables' and/or 'hire purchase receivables' as appropriate. It should be analysed in the notes to the accounts between those amounts receivable within one year and those amounts receivable thereafter.

A suitable form of disclosure would be:

Balance sheet as at 31 December 20X7

		20X6
	£	£
Current assets:		
Finance lease and hire purchase receivables	1,200	1,100

Notes to the accounts

(1) The amounts receivable under finance leases and hire purchase contracts comprise:

	£	£
Finance leases	900	820
Hire purchase contracts	300	280
	1,200	1,100

Included in the totals receivable is £900 (20X6 £850) which falls due after more than one year.

The standard requires that the gross amounts (ie, original cost or revaluation) and accumulated depreciation of assets held for use in operating leases should be disclosed. This information could be incorporated into tables showing the amounts for other fixed assets or could be shown as a separate table. It is recognised that, for banks, assets held for use in operating leases are different in nature from a bank's infrastructure (eg, its own premises). Hence it may not be appropriate to combine assets held for use in operating leases with a bank's infrastructure for capital adequacy purposes.

4.7 Manufacturer/dealer lessor

A manufacturer or dealer may offer customers the option of either outright purchase or rental of an asset. The rental option is thus a means of encouraging sales and may be packaged to appear attractive, eg, cars sold with 0% finance option.

The question then arises as to whether the total profit on a transaction is split into a trading profit (and thus recognised at the date the agreement is signed) and finance income (spread over the lifetime of the agreement).

SSAP 21 states 'A manufacturer or dealer/lessor should not recognise a selling profit under an operating lease. The selling profit under a finance lease should be restricted to the excess of the fair value of the asset over the manufacturer's or dealer's cost less any grants receivable by the manufacturer or dealer towards the purchase, construction or use of the asset.'

The fair value of the asset can be taken to be the cash selling price as long as the credit terms reflect a reasonable level of interest. However where, for example, a car dealer is offering 0% finance deals it is not reasonable to record all the profit as trading profit and no finance income. Clearly the trader in this situation is reducing the fair value of the car. An approach that could be taken in this situation is to discount the lease payments using a reasonable estimate of the implicit rate of interest. The PV of the MLPs thus becomes the fair value for determining trading profit.

4.8 Tax free grants to lessors

Lessors may be able to obtain tax free grants against the purchase price of assets acquired for leasing.

One possible method of accounting for tax free grants is 'grossing up'. The pre-tax profit and the tax charge are changed by the same amount so that a standard tax charge is reported. 'Grossing up' fails to reflect the true nature of the transactions that have occurred in the period.

SSAP 21 prohibits the grossing up of tax free grants to lessors. It requires that the grants should be spread over the period of the lease. The grant is treated as non-taxable income.

5 SALE AND LEASEBACK TRANSACTIONS

5.1 Introduction

A sale and leaseback transaction takes place when an owner sells an asset and immediately reacquires the right to use the asset by entering into a lease with the purchaser. A common example is a company selling the freehold interest in its office/factory to a financial institution.

Before dealing with the accounting for the sale and leaseback transaction itself, the carrying value of the asset in question should be reviewed. If the asset has suffered an impairment in value below its carrying amount it should be written down immediately to its fair value. This is nothing to do with sale and leaseback specifically, but is a step which should be taken so that the sale and leaseback accounting is not distorted.

The subsequent steps will depend on whether the leaseback is an operating lease or a finance lease.

If the asset is land and buildings then it is likely to be an operating lease.

5.2 Operating lease

If the leaseback is an operating lease, the seller-lessee **has** disposed of substantially all the risks and rewards of ownership of the asset and so has realised a profit or loss on the disposal. Provided that the transaction is established at fair value, the profit or loss should be recognised. However, it is possible that a sale and leaseback transaction can be arranged at other than fair value. If the sale price is above fair value, the excess will not be genuine profit, but will arise solely because the operating lease rentals payable in the ensuing years will also be at above fair value. The standard therefore provides that the excess of sale price over fair value should not be recognised as profit in the year but should be credited to income, over the shorter of the remainder of the lease term and the period to the next rent review (if any) so as to reduce the rentals payable to a level consistent with the fair value of the asset.

Illustration

The NBV of an asset is £70,000, the fair value is £100,000. Alternative sale prices and annual rentals (for five years) are:

	(a) £	*(b)* £
Sale price	120,000	100,000
Rental pa	28,000	23,000

The recognition of the profit will be as follows:

Recognise profit on sale (100,000 – 70,000)	30,000	30,000
Excess proceeds	20,000	
Credit excess proceeds to P & L account over five years	(4,000)	
Rentals	28,000	23,000
Net rental	24,000	23,000

The net rentals charged to P & L account in (a) are higher than (b) reflecting the interest cost of the 'loan' of £20,000, (ie, the artificially higher selling price).

If the sale price is below fair value then, if a bad bargain (because seller/lessee had to raise cash quickly) the profit/loss should be recognised immediately. If the price is artificially low to compensate for lower than market value rentals, any book profit should be recognised immediately and any book loss should be deferred and amortised over the lease term.

Continuing the previous illustration alternative figures for the sale/leaseback deal are:

	(c) £	*(d)* £
Sale price	80,000	60,000
Rental pa	19,000	15,000

Solution

Profit (80,000 – 70,000)	10,000	Loss (60,000 – 70,000)	(10,000)
No recognition of difference between sale price and fair value		Debit P & L account over five years with	2,000

5.3 Finance lease

If the leaseback is a finance lease, the seller-lessee is in effect re-acquiring substantially all the risks and rewards of ownership of the asset. In other words, he never disposes of his ownership interest in the asset, and so it would not be correct to recognise a profit or loss in relation to an asset which (in substance) never was disposed of.

However, it is possible that a sale and leaseback resulting in a finance lease may be arranged on terms reflecting a higher or lower capital value than the book value of the asset (ie, so as to reflect an **apparent** profit or loss).

For example, an asset which has a carrying value of £70 may be sold at £120 and leased back on a finance lease. In such a case, the lease payments would (other things being equal) be higher than if the sale and leaseback had been arranged at carrying value. The standard therefore provides that the £50 apparent profit should be deferred and amortised (ie, credited to income) over the lease term: this will have the effect of reducing the rentals – which are shown as interest and depreciation of the leased-back asset – to a level consistent with the previous carrying value of the asset.

Where the asset is carried at below fair value, it may be appropriate to revalue it. If, in the same example, the fair value of the asset were £100, the asset could be revalued to that amount, and there would remain only £20 of apparent profit to be deferred and amortised over the lease term. The effect would then be to reduce the rentals to a level consistent with the fair value of the asset.

As an alternative to calculating the apparent profit and deferring and amortising that amount, the same result can be achieved by leaving the previous carrying value unchanged, setting up the amount received on sale as a creditor, and treating the lease payments partly as principal and partly as a finance charge. This treatment will reflect the substance of the transaction, namely that it represents the raising of finance secured on an asset which is held and not disposed of. Following the issue of FRS 5 this second method should arguably now always be used.

6 TERMINATION OF LEASES

6.1 Termination payments

Most lease contracts provide for a payment to the lessor in the event of early termination. This payment is normally equivalent to most or all of the rentals that the lessor would have received if the agreement had proceeded as planned.

6.2 Operating leases

Accounting for the termination of an operating lease is straightforward. The termination payment is treated as income in the accounts of the lessor and an expense in the accounts of the lessee.

6.3 Termination of a finance lease in the books of the lessee

(a) **Early termination**

This gives rise to the following:

(i) disposal of the capitalised asset by the lessee;
(ii) a termination payment made to the lessor by the lessee.

The termination payment reduces the lease creditor. The difference between the termination payment and the lease creditor is treated as a gain or loss on disposal of the leased asset.

(b) **Residual value**

Some leases provide for the lessee to guarantee the residual value of an asset on termination. This will apply if the lease terminates at the expected date.

The accounting treatment is very similar to the treatment on early termination.

Example

A Ltd leases a motor vehicle under a finance lease. The vehicle is capitalised at its fair value of £16,000. Under the terms of the lease agreement, A Ltd must guarantee the vehicle's residual value of £4,000. This guarantee will be called upon if the vehicle's actual residual value is less than £4,000.

The lease term is four years and A Ltd depreciates the vehicle using the straight line method.

At the end of the lease period, A Ltd is required to make a payment of £2,000 to the lessor.

Show the journal entry to record the disposal of the vehicle.

Solution

	£	£
Dr Motor vehicles: Accumulated depreciation	12,000	
Cr Motor vehicles: Cost		16,000
Dr Lease obligation: Guarantee	2,000	
Dr Loss on disposal	2,000	

The motor vehicle is depreciated down to its estimated residual value.

6.4 Termination of a finance lease in the books of the lessor

The lessor will receive a termination payment, which will reduce the net investment in the lease. The difference between the net investment in the lease and the termination receipt is treated as a gain or a loss in the profit and loss account.

The treatment of the leased asset depends on the course of action to be taken by the lessor. If the lessor expects to sell the asset or to re-lease it under a finance lease it is treated as a current asset. If the lessor expects to lease the asset under an operating lease, it is treated as a fixed asset.

7 THE USEFULNESS OF SSAP 21

7.1 Introduction

SSAP 21 has been useful in cutting down the use of off balance sheet financing through the use of lease finance. It should be appreciated that by the time of the issue of SSAP 21, leasing was a very important method of obtaining the use of fixed assets in a business. Leasing remains an important method, but is now largely fairly shown in the financial statements. Its main usefulness has been to disclose the true liabilities of a business.

7.2 The definition of finance leases

There has been some manipulation of the 90% test so that leases have been classified as operating rather than finance leases. The main ploy has been to write the lease agreement leaving a significant residual payment at the end of the lease but the residual payment is not a guaranteed sum. As a consequence, the present value of the expected residual payment does not fall within the definition of the lessee's minimum lease payments.

A further consequence of this may be that the lease may still be defined as a finance lease in the books of the lessor (which is probably what the lessor company would prefer). Some examples will illustrate this point.

7.3 Examples

Peanuts Ltd has entered into a lease with Almond Ltd for plant with a fair value of £70,000. The lease term is 5 years, and the agreement specifies 5 annual payments of £10,000 each. Peanuts Ltd has not contracted to pay any other amounts to Almond Ltd under the lease.

This lease is an operating lease for Peanuts Ltd as the minimum lease payments are £50,000 and the fair value of the plant is £70,000 ie, the minimum lease payments are less than 90% of the value of the asset even before discounting. (The present value of the minimum lease payments is not known here as we cannot calculate the interest rate implicit in the lease, but it is clearly less than £50,000).

Using the facts above, suppose also that Almond Ltd has a guarantee for the residual value of £30,000 from the manufacturer of the plant. There is no unguaranteed residual value.

Amounts receivable

Under the lease	£50,000
Guaranteed residual value	£30,000

There is no unguaranteed residual value, so if these amounts were discounted at the interest rate implicit in the lease, the result would be the fair value of the asset ie, the lease is a finance lease for the lessor.

Using the original facts above, suppose that the manufacturer of the plant has made a guarantee of £25,000 against the residual value of £30,000.

In this case the minimum lease payments include

Under the lease	£50,000
Guaranteed residual value	£25,000

These amounts should be discounted to present value and compared with the fair value of £70,000 to assess whether or not the lease is a finance lease.

An alternative method is to consider the unguaranteed residual value. If this is less than 10% of the fair value of the asset (even before discounting) then the lease will be a finance lease because so little of the value of the asset is unguaranteed.

In this example the present value of the unguaranteed residual value, which must be less than £5,000, is also less than 10% of the fair value. Hence the lease is a finance lease.

The examples above illustrated that the 90% test can result in different answers for the lessee and the lessor. This occurred because the lessor receives a significant guarantee against the residual value of the asset by a party other than the lessee.

7.4 Further problems of classification

In practice a further problem arises because the lessee may not have adequate information to classify the lease. The difficulties relate to

(a)	fair value	-	lessee may be unaware of the cost of the leased asset, and will have to use an estimate; and
(b)	implicit interest rate	-	lessee may have no estimate of residual value or simply uses a known interest rate for a similar lease.

7.5 Property transactions

SSAP 21 applies to property transactions in the same way as for other leases. Many property leases are classified as operating leases due to the long expected life of the building compared to the length of the lease. The FRRP recently noted in reviewing a case that the existing standard did not provide unequivocal guidance for reverse premiums and the UITF has now developed an Abstract on this topic. This is covered below.

Property transactions are also the major type of asset subject to sale and leaseback arrangements. Some commentators feel that these transactions are too open to manipulation by the lessee company.

7.6 UITF Abstract 12: Lessee accounting for reverse premiums and similar incentives

The issue

An operating lease agreement may include incentives for the lessee to sign the lease. Such incentives may take various forms, such as an up front cash payment to the lessee (a reverse premium), a rent-free period or a contribution to certain lessee costs (such as fitting out or relocation), but are not limited to these examples. The question arises as to how such incentives should be accounted for in the accounts of the lessee.

UITF Consensus

The Task Force reached a consensus that benefits received and receivable by the lessee, whatever form they may take, as an incentive for the lessee to sign a lease should be spread by the lessee on a straight line basis over the lease term, or over the period to the date on which the rent is first adjusted to the prevailing market rate if shorter than the full lease term.

8 CURRENT DEVELOPMENTS

8.1 Introduction

The ASB has published a Discussion Paper: *Leases: Implementation of a new approach*, which reproduces the text of a Position Paper that has been developed by the 'G4 + 1' group of accounting standard setters. The proposals in the Discussion Paper will eventually form the basis of a new standard to replace SSAP 21.

8.2 The problem

As we have seen, SSAP 21 states that a lease should be presumed to be a finance lease if, at the inception of the lease, the present value of the minimum lease payments amounts to 90% or more of the fair value of the leased asset. The remainder of the definition implies that even if the lease fails to meet the '90% test' it should be treated as a finance lease if it clearly transfers the risks and rewards of ownership of the asset to the lessee.

Despite this, agreements that are in substance finance leases are often deliberately structured so that they narrowly fail the '90% test'. The leased asset and the obligation to make future payments can therefore be kept off the balance sheet.

One possible solution to this problem would be to redraft the definitions so that the threshold for treating a lease as a finance lease was lower. Another would be to bring leases within the scope of FRS 5, so that leases would have to be treated according to the substance of the agreement.

The ASB and other standard setters believe that any attempt to redefine the difference between operating and finance leases would still be arbitrary. It is unsatisfactory because it is an 'all or nothing' approach. In theory, a lessee recognises all of an asset if the minimum lease payments amount to 91% of its value, but nothing at all if the minimum lease payments are 89% of its value.

Instead, the ASB proposes to abolish the distinction between operating leases and finance leases.

8.3 The main proposal

The main proposal is that **all** material leases should give rise to assets and liabilities for lessees, and these must be recognised on the balance sheet:

(a) Assets and liabilities should be recognised by a lessee when the lessor has substantially performed its obligation to provide the lessee with access to the leased property for the lease term. This is normally when the leased property is delivered or made available to the lessee.

(b) Until the lease is recognised, a lessee should account for a lease contract in a similar way to any contract to purchase property that has not yet been delivered.

(c) At the beginning of the lease term, lessees should record the fair value of the rights and obligations that are conveyed by the lease. Fair value is measured by the fair value of the consideration given, except where the fair value of the asset received is more clearly evident.

(d) The fair value of the rights obtained by a lessee would normally be the present value of the minimum payments required by the lease. It cannot be less than this amount.

What is recognised in the balance sheet would not be the leased asset itself, but the right to use the leased asset for the term of the lease. According to the Statement of Principles and other conceptual frameworks used by 'G4+1' group members, these rights in themselves are an asset.

Definition An **asset** is rights or other access to future economic benefits controlled by an entity as a result of past transactions or events (Statement of Principles).

The amount recognised would not necessarily be the full value of the asset. Under many leases that are at present classified as operating leases, an asset is leased for only a small part of its useful economic life. Only the value of that part would be recognised in the lessee's balance sheet. The obligation to make the future payments required by the lease would be recognised as a liability.

After the lease was recognised in the lessee's balance sheet, it would be treated in a similar way to a finance lease under SSAP 21.

8.4 The scope of a revised standard

Executory contracts and take or pay contracts

An **executory contract** is a contract under which both parties are still to perform to an equal degree the actions promised by and required of them under the contract.

One example of an executory contract is a **take or pay contract**. Under a take or pay contract, one party undertakes to supply goods or services over the life of the contract and the other party undertakes to pay the contracted amount, even if the goods and services are not required. Take or pay contracts are executory contracts throughout their term, because each party has the right and obligation to participate in the exchange, or to compensate or be compensated for the consequences of not doing so.

All contracts cease to be executory once significant performance has occurred. Under a lease contract, a lessor substantially completes its performance early in the term of the lease by delivering the leased item to the lessee. Therefore leases are distinct from executory contracts.

Therefore the Discussion Paper proposes that executory contracts, including take or pay contracts, should be outside the scope of any new standard. Executory contracts would continue to fall within the scope of FRS 5 *Reporting the substance of transactions.*

Contracts for services

Where a lease contains a contract for services the two elements should be accounted for separately.

Where contracts for services in substance incorporate leases of the service provider's property, these should be accounted for as leases.

Short leases

There would be no specific exemption for short leases. Any exemption based on a material lease term would be arbitrary and therefore open to abuse. If the assets and liabilities arising from a short lease were not material they would not have to be recognised.

8.5 Renewal and purchase options

A lease may include options to extend the minimum term of the lease or to purchase the asset at the end of the lease term. The Discussion Paper proposes that the exercise of these should not be anticipated when the assets and liabilities are recognised by the lessee at the inception of the lease. Options should only give rise to additional assets and liabilities when they are exercised. This is because the fair value of the options will be reflected in the minimum payments required by the lease.

In circumstances where the fixed non-cancellable term of the lease is clearly unrepresentative of the time period that the lessee is compelled to occupy or possess the property, the asset and liability recognised at the beginning of the lease term should reflect the rights and obligations that exist on the assumption that the lease is renewed (or not cancelled).

8.6 Accounting by the lessor

The main proposals are:

(a) Two separate assets should be reported on the balance sheet:

- amounts receivable from the lessee (under debtors); and
- an interest in the residual value of the asset (under fixed assets).

This presentation reflects the fact that these amounts are subject to quite different risks.

(b) Amounts receivable from the lessee would be recorded initially at fair value and would normally be the converse of the amounts reported as liabilities by lessees.

The Discussion Paper does not address the method by which lessors should recognise income from leases. The ASB proposes that the net cash investment method should continue to be used.

8.7 Leases of land and buildings

Under SSAP 21, leases of land and buildings are almost always treated as operating leases, because the lessor retains a significant interest in the residual value of the property.

Abolishing the distinction between finance leases and operating leases would be particularly contentious for leases of land and buildings. Land and buildings are normally held on long leases and therefore lessees would have to recognise significant additional assets and liabilities in their balance sheets.

The Discussion Paper recommends that leases of land and buildings should not be exempt from the proposed new approach and the ASB supports this recommendation. The Paper points out that a lessee's interest in a leased property could be revalued and would also come within the scope of accounting standards on impairment. This would be a considerable improvement on current financial reporting practice.

The proposals would also mean that the financial statements of lessors would be more understandable. In particular, there would be two assets in the lessor's financial statements: a financial asset representing the payments required by the lease and an interest in the residual value of the property. This would enable users of the financial statements to appreciate the extent to which the lessor is primarily at risk from default by the lessee and the extent to which the lessor is at risk from (and may benefit from) future changes in the value of the property.

SSAP 19 *Accounting for investment properties* would continue to apply to residual interests in investment properties held by lessors. These would be reported as the difference between the amount of the lease receivable and the fair value of the property.

8.8 Implications of the proposals

The ASB believes that abolishing the distinction between finance leases and operating leases would improve the consistency and comparability of financial statements.

Further arguments for abolishing the distinction between operating and finance leases include:

(a) analysts now commonly adjust financial statements to show the effect of recognising the fair values of rights and obligations under operating leases;

(b) many leases are now extremely complex and difficult to classify because they have characteristics of both types of lease; and

(c) it avoids the use of an arbitrary threshold that can be manipulated by preparers of accounts.

However, the proposals have some disadvantages:

(a) Many lessees' gearing will increase significantly if these proposals are adopted. Some commentators believe that leasing may become less attractive as a result.

(b) Recognising rights to assets, rather than actual assets, may make financial statements less understandable to users.

(c) Some commentators claim that the proposals can be exploited to leave most leased assets off the balance sheet. For example, suppose that a lessee leases an asset for one year, a very small proportion of its useful economic life. The lessee has an option to renew the lease each year, which it exercises, so that in practice it uses the asset for the whole of its useful economic life. The lessee clearly has the risks and benefits relating to the asset, but because the renewals are not anticipated, the assets and liabilities are deemed immaterial and are kept off the balance sheet. Applying FRS 5 to leases would avoid the possibility of abuses such as this.

Conclusion A recent Discussion Paper proposes that the distinction between finance leases and operating leases should be abolished. All material leases should give rise to assets and liabilities for lessees and these should be recognised on the balance sheet.

9 CHAPTER SUMMARY

You should be prepared to answer both written and computational questions on *SSAP 21* to demonstrate your understanding of the accounting requirements of this standard.

The disclosure requirements of the standard and *CA85* could well be tested as part of a general published accounts question.

10 SELF TEST QUESTIONS

10.1 What are the CA85 requirements for leasing transactions? (1.3)

10.2 What is the definition of the lease term? (1.4)

10.3 What is the definition of fair value under *SSAP 21*? (1.4)

10.4 Over what period is an asset which has been capitalised under a finance lease depreciated? (2.4)

10.5 Name three methods of allocating the lessee's finance charge over the term of a lease. (2.5)

10.6 How should assets held under finance leases be disclosed in the lessee's balance sheet? (3.1)

10.7 To a lessor what is the net investment in a lease? (4.2)

10.8 How does *SSAP 21* require a manufacturer or dealer/lessor to recognise a selling profit under a finance lease? (4.7)

10.9 Under what circumstances can a profit on sale be recognised when the related leaseback is an operating lease? (5.2)

11 EXAMINATION TYPE QUESTION

11.1 Trendy Clothes

Trendy Clothes plc manufactures a machine that prints on sports shirts at a cost of £126,000. It either sells the machine for £160,748 cash or leases the machine on a three year lease.

Lease with Sporty Shirts plc

On 1 January 20X9 Trendy Clothes plc entered into a three year non-cancellable lease with Sporty Shirts plc on the following terms

(i) lease rentals were £56,000 payable annually in advance

(ii) initial direct costs of £8,400 incurred in commission and legal fees were borne by Trendy Clothes plc and charged to the profit and loss account on a systematic basis

(iii) there was a guaranteed residual value of £28,000

(iv) the interest rate implicit in the lease with Sporty Shirts plc was 18%.

Transaction with Optimistic Sales Ltd

On 1 January 20X9 Trendy Clothes plc entered into an arrangement with Optimistic Sales Ltd. Optimistic Sales Ltd had purchased a machine from Trendy Clothes plc but, having run into cash flow problems, the company arranged a sale and lease-back of the machine to Trendy Clothes plc.

The arrangement was that Optimistic Sales Ltd sold the machine to Trendy Clothes plc for £124,575 and immediately leased it back for four years at a rental of £37,500 payable yearly in advance. At the time of the sale the book value of the machine was £75,000 which was arrived at after the provision of depreciation on the company's normal straight-line basis. It was agreed that the machine should revert to Trendy Clothes plc at the end of the four year period when its scrap value was estimated to be nil. The lease is non-cancellable and Trendy Clothes plc is reasonably confident that the lease payments will be met. The interest rate implicit in the lease with Optimistic Sales was 14%. For the purpose of this question, taxation is ignored and therefore the net cash investment in the lease is equivalent to the net investment.

You are required:

(a) In respect of the lease with Sporty Shirts plc

(i) to draft the entries that would appear in the profit and loss account of Trendy Clothes plc for the year ended 31 December 20X9 **(8 marks)**

(ii) to draft the entries that would appear in the balance sheets of Trendy Clothes plc as at 31 December 20X9 and 20X10. **(4 marks)**

(b) In respect of the transaction with Optimistic Sales Ltd draft the journal entries to record the transaction in the books of **Optimistic Sales Ltd** for the year ended 31 December 20X9. **(8 marks)**

(Total: 20 marks)

Present value factors to discount from end of the year

End of year	*14%*	*16%*	*18%*
1	0.877	0.862	0.848
2	0.769	0.743	0.718
3	0.675	0.641	0.609
4	0.592	0.552	0.516
5	0.519	0.476	0.437

12 ANSWER TO EXAMINATION TYPE QUESTION

12.1 Trendy Clothes

(Tutorial notes:

(1) Part (a) is a straightforward leasing question once it is recognised that Trendy Clothes is a manufacturer/lessor and is thus entitled to take immediate credit for 'normal' trading profit provided that the lease is a finance lease.

(2) Part (b) is a sale and leaseback transaction. Before the issue of FRS 5, the finance arrangement would have resulted in a profit to the lessee which would have been spread over the life of the lease to reduce the lease rentals to those that would have (roughly) applied had the asset been 'sold' at its current net book value. However, the substance of the agreement is that Optimistic Sales Ltd has taken out a loan to finance its continued use of the asset.*)*

(a) The lease is a finance lease if the present value of the minimum lease payments (MLPs) is more than 90% of the fair value of the asset.

The gross investment in the lease is the MLPs either guaranteed (£28,000) or rentals payable (£56,000 × 3 years = £168,000) plus any unguaranteed residual value (for this lease, nil) ie, £196,000. These MLPs should be discounted, at the implicit interest rate of 18%, to give the net investment in the lease

£		*Discount factor*	*Present value* £
56,000	×	1.000	56,000
56,000	×	0.848	47,488
56,000	×	0.718	40,208
28,000	×	0.609	17,052
		Net investment in finance lease	£160,748

PV of MLPs is therefore 100% of fair value.

Trendy Clothes should take immediate credit for trading element of profit

	£
PV of MLPs	160,748
Less: Cost	126,000
Trading profit	£34,748

Gross earnings allocated over the period of the lease are (£196,000 – £160,748) = £35,252. Allocation based on finance provided is as follows

Period (year)	*Net cash investment at start of period*	*'Cost'*	*Rentals*	*Average cash investment in period*	*Interest (18%)*	*Net cash investment at end of period*
	£	£	£	£	£	£
20X9	-	(160,748)	56,000	(104,748)	18,855	(123,603)
20X10	(123,603)	-	56,000	(67,603)	12,169	(79,772)
20X11	(79,772)	-	56,000	(23,772)	4,228 *	(28,000)
					£35,252	

* figure rounded.

(i) **Profit and loss account extracts (year ended 31 December 20X9)**

	£
Turnover	160,748
Cost of sale	(126,000)
Gross profit	34,748
Interest receivable under finance lease	18,855
Direct lease expense (straight line allocation over three year lease period)	(2,800)

(ii) **Balance sheet extracts (as at 31 December)**

	20X9	*20X10*
	£	£
Investment in finance lease		
Current	43,831	51,772
Non-current	79,772	28,000
Prepaid expenses	5,600	2,800

(b) Given the value of the rentals compared to a reasonable estimate of fair value the lease appears to be a finance lease. Although the seller/lessee appears to have made a 'profit' of £49,575 (124,575 - 75,000) the substance of the arrangement is that the seller/lessee has taken out a loan of £124,575 on which it will pay finance charges. The asset remains in the balance sheet at £75,000.

Relevant journal entries in books of Optimistic Sales Ltd

	£	£
Dr Bank account	124,575	
Cr Obligations under finance lease account		124,575

being sale of asset under leaseback agreement and recognition of liability under such contract.

Dr Obligations under finance lease account	25,309	
Dr Profit and loss account	12,191	
Cr Bank account		37,500
being rental paid, to pay interest and part clear liability under lease contract.		

Dr Profit and loss account	18,750	
Cr Accumulated depreciation account		18,750
being the depreciation charge for the year (75,000 ÷ 4)		

WORKINGS

	£
'Sale'	124,575
Net book value	75,000
Profit on 'sale'	£49,575

Total finance charges = (£37,500 × 4) – £124,575	=	£25,425
Average cash invested in lease for 20X9 = £124,575 – £37,500	=	£87,075
Finance charge = 14% × £87,075	=	£12,191

10 REPORTING FINANCIAL PERFORMANCE

INTRODUCTION & LEARNING OBJECTIVES

FRS 3 is a very important standard as it affects the layout of the profit and loss account and introduced a new primary statement - the Statement of Total Recognised Gains and Losses.

Earnings per share is of importance due to the stress placed on it as a performance indicator by the financial community. It remains to be seen whether its importance will diminish following the issue of FRS 3 and FRS 14 as earnings now includes all 'distorting' items of income and expense.

You need to ensure that you are fully conversant with the arithmetic in calculating EPS.

When you have studied this chapter you should be able to do the following:

- Demonstrate your understanding of *FRS 3*.
- Prepare a profit and loss account showing the analysis between continuing operations, acquisitions and discontinued operations.
- Prepare a statement of total recognised gains and losses.
- Prepare the other statements required in the notes by *FRS 3*: a reconciliation of movements in shareholders' funds and a note of historical cost profits and losses for the year.
- Compute and disclose EPS in accordance with FRS 14.

---

1 THE REQUIREMENTS OF FRS 3

1.1 Introduction

FRS 3, issued in October 1992, radically reformed the presentation of the profit and loss account and added a new primary statement to the annual financial statements, the **Statement of total recognised gains and losses**. In addition it virtually eradicated extraordinary items and changed the earnings per share calculation to earnings after extraordinary items.

1.2 Objective of FRS 3

The objective of the FRS is to require companies to highlight a range of important components of financial performance to aid users in understanding the performance achieved by a reporting entity in a period and to assist them in forming a basis for their assessment of future results and cash flows.

It attempts to achieve the objective by requiring all gains and losses recognised in the financial statements for the period to be included in the profit and loss account or the statement of total recognised gains and losses.

Gains and losses may be excluded from the profit and loss account only if they are specifically permitted or required to be taken directly to reserves by an accounting standard or by law.

1.3 Format of the profit and loss account

A layered format is to be used for the profit and loss account to highlight a number of important components of financial performance:

(a) results of continuing operations (including the results of acquisitions);
(b) results of discontinued operations;
(c) profits or losses on the sale or termination of an operation, costs of a fundamental reorganisation or restructuring and profits or losses on the disposal of fixed assets; and
(d) extraordinary items.

The thrust of this approach can be illustrated diagrammatically as follows:

CONTINUING	**DISCONTINUED**
Normal operations	Normal operations
The items listed in (c) above	The items listed in (c) above

Extraordinary items - being unusual items outside ordinary activities

Note that exceptional items will comprise the items listed in (c) above, which are disclosed separately on the face of the profit and loss account, and other items which are disclosed separately by way of note only (and are thus within the normal operations boxes).

A sample format is shown below:

Profit and loss account for the year ended 30 June 20X3

	Continuing operations		*Discontinued*		
		Acquisitions	*operations*	*Total*	*Total*
	20X3	*20X3*	*20X3*	*20X3*	*20X2*
					as restated
	£m	£m	£m	£m	£m
Turnover	550	50	175	775	690
Cost of sales	(415)	(40)	(165)	(620)	(555)
Gross profit	135	10	10	155	135
Net operating expenses	(85)	(4)	(25)	(114)	(83)
Less: 20X2 provision			10	10	
Operating profit	50	6	(5)	51	52
Profit on sale of properties	9			9	6
Provision for loss on operations to be discontinued					(30)
Loss on disposal of discontinued operations			(17)	(17)	
Less: 20X2 provision			20	20	
Profit on ordinary activities before interest	59	6	(2)	63	28
Interest payable				(18)	(15)
Profit on ordinary activities before taxation				45	13
Tax on profit on ordinary activities				(14)	(4)
Profit on ordinary activities after taxation				31	9
Minority interests				(2)	(2)
Extraordinary items (included only to show positioning)				-	-
Profit for the financial year				29	7
Dividends				(8)	(1)
Retained profit for the financial year				21	6
Earnings per share				39p	10p

1.4 Continuing and discontinued operations

The analysis between continuing operations, acquisitions (as a component of continuing operations) and discontinued operations should be disclosed to the level of operating profit. The analysis of turnover and operating profit is the **minimum** disclosure required in this respect on the **face** of the profit and loss account.

The example above thus provides more than the minimum disclosure. The minimum disclosures for the top section of the profit and loss account could be shown as follows:

	20X3	*20X3*	*20X2 as restated*
	£m	£m	£m
Turnover			
Continuing operations	550		500
Acquisitions	50		
	600		
Discontinued operations	175		190
		775	690
Cost of sales		(620)	(555)
Gross profit		155	135
Net operating expenses		(104)	(83)
Operating profit			
Continuing operations	50		40
Acquisitions	6		
	56		
Discontinued operations	(15)		12
Less: 20X2 provision	10		
		51	52

Note the following points

(a) In either example, as the full statutory headings have not been shown, a note to the accounts needs to show an analysis of the statutory cost headings between continuing operations, acquisitions (as a component of continuing operations) and discontinued operations.

(b) The analysis in respect of continuing operations, acquisitions and discontinued operations is required only to the profit before interest level because interest payable is usually a reflection of a company's overall financing policy, involving both equity and debt funding considerations on a group wide basis, rather than an aggregation of the particular types of finance allocated to individual segments of the reporting entity's operations. Any allocation of interest would involve a considerable degree of subjectivity that could leave the user uncertain as to the relevance and reliability of the information.

(c) The comparative figures should be based on the status of an operation in the financial statements of the period under review and should, therefore, include in the continuing category only the results of those operations included in the current period's continuing operations. The comparative figures appearing under the heading 'continuing operations' may include figures which were shown under the heading of acquisitions in that previous period. No reference needs to be made to the results of those acquisitions, since they are not required to be presented separately in the current year.

The comparative figures for discontinued operations will include both amounts relating to operations discontinued in the previous period and amounts relating to operations discontinued in the period under review, which in the previous period would have been included as part of continuing operations.

The analysis of comparative figures between continuing and discontinued operations is not required on the face of the profit and loss account.

1.5 Definition of discontinued operations

The separate analysis of discontinued operations is one of the routes by which the ASB is attempting to restrict the ambit of extraordinary items. The definition of discontinued operations is however quite strict so as to encourage preparers of financial statements to leave the results of parts of the business being reorganised under the heading of continuing operations.

Definition Discontinued operations are those operations of the reporting entity that are sold or terminated and that satisfy all of the following conditions

(a) The sale or termination is completed either in the period or before the earlier of three months after the commencement of the subsequent period and the date on which the financial statements are approved.

(b) If a termination, the former activities have ceased permanently.

(c) The sale or termination has a material effect on the nature and focus of the reporting entity's operations and represents a material reduction in its operating facilities resulting either from its withdrawal from a particular market (whether class of business or geographical) or from a material reduction in turnover in the reporting entity's continuing markets.

(d) The assets, liabilities, results of operations and activities are clearly distinguishable, physically, operationally and for financial reporting purposes.

Operations not satisfying all these conditions are classified as continuing.

Note the timing restriction. If the termination is not completed within the time stated, the turnover and costs of the operations remain in continuing operations.

This does **not** mean, however, that an exceptional item should not be shown in respect of the actual profit/loss or anticipated loss on disposal. This point is discussed below after the definition of exceptional items has been considered.

Note also part (c) of the definition. The nature and focus of a reporting entity's operations refers to the positioning of its products or services in their markets including the aspects of both quality and location. For example, if a hotel company which had traditionally served the lower end of the hotel market sold its existing chain and bought luxury hotels then, while remaining in the business of managing hotels, the group would be changing the nature and focus of its operations. A similar situation would arise if the same company were to sell its hotels in (say) the United States of America and buy hotels in Europe.

The regular sales and replacements of material assets which are undertaken by a company as part of the routine maintenance of its portfolio of assets should not be classified as discontinuances and acquisitions. In the example the sale of hotels and the purchase of others within the same market sector and similar locations would be treated as wholly within continuing operations.

1.6 Definition of continuing operations

Continuing operations are all operations other than discontinued operations.

2 CLASSIFICATION OF ITEMS

2.1 Exceptional items

Definition Material items which derive from events or transactions that fall within the ordinary activities of the reporting entity and which individually or, if of a similar type, in aggregate, need to be disclosed by virtue of their size or incidence if the financial statements are to give a true and fair view.

All exceptional items, other than those stated below, should be included under the statutory format headings to which they relate. They should be separately disclosed by way of note or, where it is necessary in order that the financial statements give a true and fair view, on the face of the profit and loss account.

There are in effect two types of exceptional items; those that are exceptional but are still included in the statutory format headings and those which are separately identified.

The view of the ASB is that exceptional items should not be transferred to a single heading of 'exceptional', because profit before exceptional items could then become the focus of financial statement presentations, with the implication that no exceptional items are expected in the future.

2.2 Items to be shown separately

The following items, including provisions in respect of such items, should be shown separately on the face of the profit and loss account after operating profit and before interest:

(a) profits or losses on the sale or termination of an operation;
(b) costs of a fundamental reorganisation or restructuring; and
(c) profits or losses on the disposal of fixed assets.

Note that these items may or may not be exceptional. Thus a disposal of a fixed asset may be a normal trading transaction but it may also due to its size be an exceptional item. The practical effect of the distinction is that details of each exceptional item need to be disclosed in the notes to the profit and loss account.

Each of the three specific items will be examined in turn.

2.3 Profits or losses on the sale or termination of an operation

The 'sale or termination of an operation' is not defined in *FRS 3*. It encompasses but is not restricted to the term 'discontinued operation'. Thus the item may be part of continuing operations or discontinued operations and therefore needs to be disclosed under its correct heading. It is likely to be an exceptional item as well.

Often the sale or termination straddles two accounting periods. In the first period a provision may have been established for losses expected to arise in the following period (under the prudence concept). However, there has been much criticism in recent years on the 'excessive' use of provisions by companies and thus *FRS 3* imposes the following restrictions:

(a) a provision should not be made unless the company is demonstrably committed to the sale or termination, eg, public announcement of specific plans or a binding contract for sale has been entered into after the balance sheet date;

(b) The provision should cover only:

  (i) the direct costs of the sale or termination;

  (ii) operating losses up to the sale date;

  (iii) less anticipated trading profits (if any).

2.4 Example of the termination of an operation

X plc has a calendar year end. On 30 October 20X7 the board of directors decide to withdraw from a market which is a significant part of the company's existing business. Plans are disclosed to the workforce on 30 November with a termination set at 31 March 20X8.

Actual and projected results of the operation are:

	Actual to 31 December 20X7 £'000	*Projected to 31 March 20X8* £'000
Sales	45,000	8,000
Operating costs	44,000	12,000
Redundancy and other costs		3,000

The accounts for the year ended 31 December 20X7 are expected to be approved by 18 March 20X8.

Therefore in the accounts for the year ended 31 December 20X7 the operation is not classified as a discontinued operation (due to the timing of the date on which the accounts are approved). A provision should however be disclosed (as an exceptional item) totalling:

	£'000
Projected loss	4,000
Redundancy	3,000
	7,000

If in the 20X8 accounting period actual results of the operation are:

	£'000
Sales	9,400
Operating costs	11,600
Redundancy	3,000

the profit and loss account for the year ended 31 December 20X8 would show:

	Continuing operations 20X8 £'000	*Discontinued operations 20X8* £'000	*Continuing operations 20X7* £'000	*Discontinued operations 20X7* £'000
Turnover	X	9,400	X	45,000
Operating costs:	X	(11,600)		(44,000)
Less: 20X7 provision		4,000		
Operating profit	X	1,800		1,000
Provision for loss on operations to be discontinued				(7,000)
Loss on termination of discontinued operation		(3,000)		
Less: 20X7 provision		3,000		
Profit (loss) on ordinary activities before taxation	X	1,800		(6,000)

2.5 Costs of a fundamental reorganisation

As the title of this item implies it is only a reorganisation or restructuring having a material effect on the nature and focus of the company's operation that qualifies for separate disclosure. This item will therefore be classified as exceptional as well.

2.6 Disposals of fixed assets

This heading is not intended to include profits and losses that are no more than marginal adjustments to depreciation previously charged.

If an asset has previously been revalued, *FRS 3* has now ruled on the method of computation of the profit or loss.

Examples of the computation were shown in an earlier chapter.

2.7 Activity

Do the following situations meet the definition of discontinued operations as defined by *FRS 3*?

(a) X plc, an office furniture and equipment manufacturer runs separate divisions of approximately equal size for the two activities. It has now decided to sell the less profitable equipment division and use the funds received to expand the furniture division by growth and acquisition. The decision to sell was made in October 20X5 and the sale completed on 21 March 20X6. The accounts for the year 20X5 were approved on 15 March 20X6.

(b) Y plc as a result of the recession has suffered a down turn in demand and now has productive over capacity. In order to reduce costs Y plc has decided to transfer production into one of its two factories and to 'moth-ball' the other factory. This decision was made in April 20X3 and the transfer completed in August 20X3. The company has a September year end.

(c) Z plc a printing company also carries out specialised book binding. This part of the business is carried out in a separate workshop and comprises approximately 0.5% of the total assets of the company and contributes approximately the same proportion of profits.

During 20X4 Z plc sold the bookbinding business to a consortium of the workforce and sold the workshop to the local council. The profit arising from this transaction amounted to £100,000 on profits of £2,400,000 for 20X4.

2.8 Activity solution

(a) This situation meets three of the four criteria laid down by *FRS 3* but fails to meet the timing restriction. *FRS 3* states that the sale should be completed before the earlier of three months after commencement of the subsequent period and the date on which the financial statements are approved.

(b) This would not be treated as a discontinued operation as the activities have not ceased permanently. The purpose of this decision is to reduce productive capacity temporarily until there is an upturn in the market.

(c) This situation appears to meet the *FRS 3* criteria for discontinued operations except that the loss of this part of the business will have no material effect on the operations of Z plc. Therefore it will not be treated as a discontinued operation.

(The size of the profit arising on the sale is not taken into account in the *FRS 3* criteria).

2.9 Extraordinary items

Definition Material items possessing a high degree of abnormality which arise from events or transactions that fall outside the ordinary activities of the reporting entity and which are not expected to recur. They do not include exceptional items nor do they include prior period items merely because they relate to a prior period.

As discontinued activities are shown as ordinary activities and exceptional items include profit/loss on disposals of operations, extraordinary items should become extremely rare. Indeed the ASB contemplated removing extraordinary items completely but did not do so because company law includes extraordinary items in its formats.

To emphasise the change Sir David Tweedie, Chairman of the ASB has stated:

> 'Martians walking down the street will be extraordinary, everything else is exceptional.'

2.10 Prior period adjustments

Definition Material adjustments applicable to prior periods arising from changes in accounting policies or from the correction of fundamental errors. They do not include normal recurring adjustments or corrections of accounting estimates made in prior periods.

Prior period adjustments are extremely rare. An entity may change its accounting policy only if the new policy will give a fairer presentation of its results and of its financial position. To be fundamental, an error must be so significant that it destroys the true and fair view and hence the validity of the financial statements.

The following are **not** prior period adjustments and should be dealt with in the profit and loss account of the period in which they are identified:

(a) corrections and adjustments to estimates made in prior periods (eg, provisions for doubtful debts)

(b) modifications of an existing accounting treatment which are necessary because the entity is undertaking different transactions.

FRS 3 requires the following accounting treatment:

(a) Restate the comparative figures for the preceding period in the primary statements and the notes.

(b) Adjust the opening balance of reserves for the cumulative effect of the adjustments. This adjustment should be clearly disclosed in the reserves note and should also be disclosed in the reconciliation of movements in shareholders' funds (see below).

(c) Disclose the effect of prior period adjustments on the results for the preceding period where practicable.

(d) Disclose the cumulative effect of the adjustments at the foot of the statement of total recognised gains and losses for the current period (see below).

2.11 UITF Abstract 14: Disclosure of changes in accounting policy

(a) **The issue**

The Companies Act requires accounting policies to be applied consistently within the same accounts and from one financial year to the next. A change of policy is permitted if it appears to the directors that there are special reasons for a departure from this principle. Particulars of the departure, the reasons for it and its effect must be disclosed in a note to the accounts. The

(b) **UITF Consensus**

Where there is a change in accounting policy, the disclosures made must include an indication of the effect of the change on the current year's results, in addition to the disclosures required by FRS3 (see above). In those cases where the effect on the current year is either immaterial or similar to the quantified effect on the prior year a simple statement saying this is sufficient. Where it is not practicable to give the effect on the current year, that fact, together with the reasons, should be stated.

3 OTHER STATEMENTS REQUIRED

3.1 The contents and purpose of a Statement of total recognised gains and losses

The statement of total recognised gains and losses is a **primary statement** as defined by the ASB's **Statement of principles**, ie, it is required for a true and fair view.

The statement shows items taken straight to reserves as well as the profit and loss account. This primary income statement has been designed to further discourage users of the financial statements from focusing only on the profit and loss account whilst ignoring reserve movements which could hide a multitude of sins.

The statement is not intended to reflect the realisation of gains recognised in previous periods nor does it deal with transfers between reserves.

Thus, when for example an asset is sold which has previously been revalued, the revaluation gain merely changes from an unrealised reserve to a realised reserve. It is not therefore accounted for in the current year's statement of total recognised gains and losses.

An illustrative statement is shown below:

Statement of total recognised gains and losses for the year ended 30 June 20X3

	20X3	*20X2 as restated*
	£m	£m
Profit for the financial year	29	7
Unrealised surplus on revaluation of properties	4	6
Unrealised (loss)/gain on trade investment	(3)	7
	30	20
Currency translation differences on foreign currency net investments	(2)	5
Total recognised gains and losses relating to the year	28	25
Prior year adjustment (as explained in note X)	(10)	
Total gains and losses recognised since last annual report	18	

3.2 Other statements

FRS 3 requires two other statements to be shown as **notes** to the accounts. The second of these notes, 'Historical cost profits and losses' must however be presented immediately following the profit and loss account or the statement of total recognised gains and losses.

(a) Reconciliation of movements in shareholders' funds

The reconciliation of movements in shareholders' funds brings together the performance of the period, as shown in the statement of total recognised gains and losses, with all the other changes in shareholders' funds in the period, including capital contributed by or repaid to shareholders.

Illustration

Reconciliation of movements in shareholders' funds for the year ended 30 June 20X3

	20X3	*20X2 as restated*
	£m	£m
Profit for the financial year	29	7
Dividends	(8)	(1)
	21	6
Other recognised gains and losses relating to the year (net)	(1)	18
New share capital subscribed	20	1
Net addition to shareholders' funds	40	25
Opening shareholders' funds (originally £375m before deducting prior year adjustment of £10m)	365	340
Closing shareholders' funds	405	365

(b) Note of historical cost profits and losses

The note of historical cost profits and losses is a memorandum item, the primary purpose of which is to present the profits or losses of companies that have revalued assets on a more comparable basis with those of entities that have not. It is an abbreviated restatement of the profit and loss account which adjusts the reported profit or loss, if necessary, so as to show it as if no asset revaluation had been made.

Note of historical cost profits and losses for the year ended 30 June 20X3

	20X3	*20X2 as restated*
	£m	£m
Reported profit on ordinary activities before taxation	45	13
Realisation of property revaluation gains of previous years	9	10
Difference between a historical cost depreciation charge and the actual depreciation charge of the year calculated on the revalued amount	5	4
Historical cost profit on ordinary activities before taxation	59	27
Historical cost profit for the year retained after taxation, minority interests, extraordinary items and dividends	35	20

3.3 Critical evaluation of FRS 3

FRS 3 adopts an 'information set' approach. Users of the financial statements are encouraged to analyse and interpret the profit and loss account as a whole, rather than concentrating on the profit on ordinary activities.

FRS 3 is generally believed to have improved financial reporting in the following ways:

(a) Reporting entities are required to highlight a range of important components of financial performance. Operating profit is placed in the context of the profit and loss account (and financial performance) as a whole.

(b) Analysing the profit and loss account between continuing operations, acquisitions and discontinued operations enables users to assess the future performance of an entity. For example, turnover and costs arising from a discontinued operation will not occur in the future.

(c) Disclosure of exceptional items also provides useful information. Profits or losses from non-trading activities (such as the sale of fixed assets or restructuring costs) can have a dramatic impact on the overall performance of a company. The disclosure draws attention to the fact that they will not recur.

(d) The statement of total recognised gains and losses combines information about operating and related performance with other aspects of financial performance and provides information that is useful for assessing the return on investment.

(e) Standardisation of treatment and disclosure of items (including the note of historical cost profits and losses) has made it easier to compare the performance of different companies.

(f) The extensive disclosure requirements and the virtual elimination of extraordinary items mean that the profit on ordinary activities is far less likely to be manipulated by preparers of accounts.

However, FRS 3 has been criticised for the following reasons:

(a) Elimination of extraordinary items means that profit on ordinary activities may fluctuate from year to year and it may be difficult to interpret trends.

(b) Some commentators believe that the definition of discontinued items is too restrictive and therefore unhelpful. Others believe that preparers of financial statements may still try to manipulate the profit and loss account by arranging sales and terminations so that they fit (or do not fit) the definition.

(c) It has been argued that the profit and loss account does not highlight operating exceptional items such as stock write downs or bad debt provisions. In addition, there is no analysis of the components of the tax charge or the minority interest.

(d) The extensive disclosures required may actually obscure the view given by the profit and loss account and make it more difficult to understand, particularly for less sophisticated users. There is evidence that users may want to concentrate on a single performance figure and may be unwilling or unable to analyse financial information in detail.

4 REPORTING FINANCIAL PERFORMANCE: CURRENT DEVELOPMENTS

4.1 Background

The ASB has issued a Discussion Paper *Reporting financial performance: proposals for change*. This has been developed by the 'G4+1' group of standard setters and in the UK its proposals will almost certainly lead to a revision of FRS 3.

The reasons for reviewing FRS 3 centre on the operation of the statement of total recognised gains and losses (STRGL):

(a) Since FRS 3 was first issued, financial reporting practice has developed. The ASB's recent and current projects on derivatives, impairment and pensions have highlighted the need to reconsider the purpose of the STRGL. When fixed assets, financial instruments or pension scheme assets and liabilities change in value some gains and losses arise that could in theory be reported in either the profit and loss account or in the STRGL. On what basis should the distinction be made?

(b) There is also some evidence that users and preparers of accounts are confused by the existence of two performance statements. Therefore they concentrate on the profit and loss account and largely ignore the STRGL.

4.2 New statement of performance

Some standard setters, including the ASB, have adopted a second performance statement (the STRGL) in addition to the income statement or profit and loss account. This approach has several advantages:

(a) it enables entities to provide more detail about financial performance than they could in only one statement;

(b) the second statement completes the picture given in the first; it improves financial reporting without disrupting the existing income statement/profit and loss account.

A significant drawback of the two-statement approach is that undue significance may be attached to one statement at the expense of the other (as in the UK) and greater significance may be given to the distinction between the two statements than is justified.

Therefore the central proposal of the Discussion Paper is that there should be a single performance statement with three main components:

- Results of operating (or trading) activities
- Results of financing and other treasury activities
- Other gains and losses

The Discussion Paper includes an illustration of how a 'typical' performance statement might appear (subject to adaptation to comply with the requirements of the Companies Act in the UK):

Statement of financial performance

	£'000	£'000
Operating (trading) activities		
Revenues		775
Cost of sales		(620)
Other expenses		(104)
Operating income		51
Financing and other treasury activities		
Interest on debt	(26)	
Gains and losses on financial instruments	8	
Financing income		(18)
Operating and financing income before taxation		33
Taxation on income		(12)
Operating and financing income after taxation		21
Other gains and losses		
Profit on disposal of discontinued operations	3	
Profit on sale of properties in continuing operations	6	
Revaluation of long term assets	4	

Exchange translation differences on foreign currency net investments	(2)	
Other gains and losses before taxation	11	
Taxation on other gains and losses	(4)	
Other gains and losses after taxation		7
Total recognised gains and losses		28

All three components of the statement can be broken down into subcomponents of continuing activities, acquisitions and discontinued activities, shown either on the face of the statement or by way of a note.

The main principle behind the statement of financial performance is that items with similar characteristics are grouped together.

Possible criteria for deciding in which component to report gains and losses include:

- realised *v* unrealised
- caused by internal events (eg, value adding activities) *v* caused by external events (eg, price changes)
- certain *v* uncertain
- high predictive value *v* less predictive value
- operating *v* holding

The Paper suggests that the characteristics typical of each group are as follows:

Characteristics more typical of operating items	**Characteristics more typical of other gains and losses**
Operating activities	Non-operating activities
Non-holding items	Holding items
Recurring	Non-recurring
Internal events (eg value adding activities)	Caused by external events (eg, price changes)

Items that predominantly have the characteristics listed on the left would be reported as operating items and those which predominantly have the characteristics listed on the right would be reported as 'other gains and losses'. No one characteristic should be used as a classification criterion to the exclusion of the others.

Broadly speaking, items that currently appear in the profit and loss account would be shown under operating activities or financing and other treasury activities, while items that currently appear in the STRGL would be shown under 'other gains and losses'. There are some exceptions and these are addressed later.

The Discussion Paper does not address the contents of the 'financing/treasury' section of the statement in depth as these are likely to be determined by the international project on financial instruments. They may include interest expense and gains and losses on financial instruments.

The 'G4+1' group proposes that national standard setters should prescribe the content of 'other gains and losses' and possibly 'financing and other treasury activities' with 'operating/trading activities' being the default section.

4.3 Gains and losses on fixed assets

The Discussion Paper proposes some changes to present practice which would be implemented by changes to FRS 11 *Impairment of fixed assets and goodwill* and FRS 15 *Tangible fixed assets.*

Operating activities would include:

(a) depreciation based on carrying value (as at present);

(b) impairment losses and their reversal (losses on revalued assets are currently reported in the STRGL, which is broadly equivalent to 'other gains and losses' in the single performance statement);

(c) gains and losses on disposal representing adjustments to depreciation (as at present); and

(d) disposal losses that are impairments (as at present).

Other gains and losses would include:

(a) revaluation gains (these are currently reported in the STRGL);

(b) disposal gains that do not represent adjustments to depreciation or reversals of impairments (these are currently reported under operating activities); and

(c) revaluation and disposal losses where these do not represent impairments or adjustments to depreciation (as at present).

4.4 Recycling

Definition **Recycling** is the reporting of an item of financial performance in more than one accounting period because the nature of the item is deemed to have changed in some way over time.

Recycling is an issue where there are two performance statements. For example, a gain could be recognised in the STRGL when a fixed asset is revalued and the same gain could be reported in the profit and loss account when the asset is sold. FRS 3 and FRS 15 prohibit recycling by requiring that a gain on disposal of a revalued asset is calculated as the sales proceeds less the net carrying amount.

Recycling continues to be an issue where there is a single performance statement because gains and losses reported in one component of the statement could in theory be reported again in another component in a later accounting period.

There are two possible views:

(a) the 'other gains and losses' section of a single statement (or the second performance statement where there are two statements) is a type of 'holding tank' for certain items pending the occurrence of a specific event that changes them in some way, when they will be reported again, as part of operating or financing activities; or

(b) each item is reported only once, when recognised, within the appropriate component of the statement of financial performance.

The 'holding tank' approach

This approach emphasises a bottom line 'earnings' figure, through which all items of financial performance must pass at some time. There are three main arguments for this approach:

(a) There is a long standing convention that realised profits must be recognised within the income statement. Unrealised items should be reported either in the second performance statement (where one exists) or as part of movements in shareholders' funds. If this approach were adopted, unrealised items would have to be recycled to the income statement as they became realised.

(b) The second performance statement can be used to cope with the uncertainty surrounding the measurement of a gain or loss. Uncertain items can be recognised immediately in the second statement and then recycled into the income statement as subsequent valuations confirm or change the estimated amounts of the gains and losses.

(c) All items are ultimately part of operations and therefore all items of financial performance should appear in operating activities at some point.

The components approach

This approach envisages that the characteristics of the items allocated to the different components of financial performance are permanent. The statement(s) of financial performance are designed to assist users of the financial statements by classifying together items that have a similar effect on the entity. This purpose would be obscured if items were being transferred between headings to reflect changes in their nature.

Conclusion

The Paper concludes that there is no conceptual justification for recycling. Therefore it should be prohibited. Once an item has been recognised in a statement of financial performance, it should not be recognised again in a future period in a different component. However, it is appreciated that there may be some situations where recycling may be permitted or required by individual standard setters in the short term.

This means that there will be no change to existing practice.

4.5 Exceptional items

The Discussion Paper proposes changes to the way in which exceptional items are disclosed. At present, FRS 3 requires three types of exceptional item to be separately disclosed on the face of the profit and loss account below operating profit. These would still be disclosed on the face of the performance statement, but in different positions:

- Profits and losses on sale or termination of an operation in 'other gains and losses'.
- Profits and losses on disposal of fixed assets in 'other gains and losses'.
- Costs of a fundamental reorganisation or restructuring in 'operating activities'.

If exceptional items are grouped together, this implies that these items have more in common with each other than with the line item to which they relate. Undue significance may also be given to 'pre exceptional' results. However, it is appropriate to disclose large or unusual items separately on the face of the performance statement, so that users of the financial statements can assess their significance.

4.6 Continuing and discontinued activities

The Paper proposes that the results of discontinued/discontinuing activities and acquisitions made during the period should be disclosed separately from continuing activities. There would be no change to present practice.

The Paper notes that there are differences between the definitions of discontinued/discontinuing activities between 'G4+1' members. Some members, including the ASB, disclose discontin*ued* operations and require a discontinuation to be completed by or shortly after the year-end. Others disclose discontin*uing* activities and merely require the sale or termination to be planned.

The Paper does not stipulate a preferred definition. Each has advantages:

(a) Disclosure of discontinuing activities reflects the economic decision making process of management and gives timely information to users of the financial statements.

(b) Disclosure of discontinued activities removes the potential for management to manipulate the reporting of results by identifying activities as 'discontinued' in a loss making period then retaining the activities and including them again in 'continuing activities' when the loss making period is over. Activities which an entity intends to discontinue can be included in the notes to the financial statements or elsewhere in the annual report.

4.7 Tax expense

Tax expenses could be reported in several different ways, ranging from one single line at the foot of the statement to allocating tax expense to each individual reported line. Both these extremes have been rejected:

(a) If tax expense is reported as a single line this implies that tax expense is different from all other revenues and expenses. This is not consistent with a 'full provision' approach (where tax is assumed to arise from, and be allocable to, individual transactions).

(b) Allocating tax expense to each individual line would provide too much detail to be helpful to users.

The Paper proposes that tax expense should be allocated to two amounts: one for the total of operating/trading activities and financing and other treasury activities; and one for other gains and losses. A note of breakdown of the tax effect of each item in 'other gains and losses' should be required. This approach leaves the statement of financial performance relatively uncluttered and avoids the possibly arbitrary effects of a more detailed allocation of tax expense.

4.8 Other proposed changes to FRS 3

(a) Some entities voluntarily disclose 'pre exceptional results'. This would remain optional, but where they are disclosed, details of pre exceptional results, exceptional items and post exceptional results would be required for each of the past five years.

(b) **All** material errors would require correction by prior period adjustment (FRS 3 requires prior period adjustments only where there have been fundamental errors).

Most other requirements of FRS 3 would remain unchanged.

4.9 Dividends paid and proposed

The ASB believes that dividends paid are an appropriation of profit, not part of financial performance and proposes that they should no longer be disclosed in the statement of financial performance but as part of changes in equity. Legal issues will have to be addressed as the Companies Act 1985 requires that dividends paid and proposed are disclosed on the face of the profit and loss account as a deduction from profit.

4.10 Evaluation of the proposals

The Discussion Paper is not primarily responding to problems with FRS 3 and similar standards, but refining them further. There are four main benefits:

(a) the purpose of the STRGL is clarified;

(b) developments in accounting for pension costs and derivatives are anticipated;

(c) the new performance statement will make it even harder for users of the financial statements to rely on a single 'bottom line' figure; and

(d) the new performance statement matches the way in which the cash flow statement has evolved.

Criticisms of the proposals have included:

(a) They concentrate on presentation and do not address the fundamental question 'what is financial performance?';

(b) Financial performance is taken to be all changes in equity other than transactions with owners in their capacity as owners. This definition is flawed, because items such as revaluation gains and exchange differences arising from the retranslation of foreign subsidiaries under the closing rate method can be viewed as capital maintenance adjustments rather than components of performance.

(c) All material errors give rise to prior period adjustments. This may provide greater potential for the manipulation of results. It may also highlight errors to a greater extent than before and this might cast doubt on the efficiency of preparers and auditors and might be confusing to users.

Conclusion A recent Discussion Paper proposes that the profit and loss account and the STRGL should be amalgamated into a single performance statement with three headings: operating/trading activities; financing and other treasury activities; and other gains and losses.

5 THE ACCOUNTING AND DISCLOSURE REQUIREMENTS OF FRS 14

5.1 FRS 14 - Earnings per share

Earnings per share is a widely used measure of a company's performance, particularly over a number of years, and is a component of the very important Stock Exchange yardstick – the price/earnings (P/E) ratio.

The objective of FRS 14 *Earnings per share* is to improve the comparison of the performance of different entities in the same period and of the same entity in different accounting periods by prescribing methods for determining the number of shares to be included in the calculation of earnings per share and other amounts per share and by specifying their presentation.

FRS 14 has replaced SSAP 3. The ASB had not originally planned to issue a new accounting standard on earnings per share at this stage. However, the IASC has now issued a new standard on earnings per share and the ASB believed that UK practice should be brought into line with the new IAS.

FRS 14 applies to public companies. Private companies that voluntarily disclose earnings per share must also comply with FRS 14.

5.2 The basic calculation

$$\text{Earnings per share (in pence)} = \frac{\text{net profit or loss for the period attributable to ordinary shareholders}}{\text{weighted average number of ordinary shares outstanding in the period}}$$

The net profit or loss attributable to ordinary shareholders is the net profit or loss after deducting dividends and other appropriations in respect of non-equity shares (normally preference shares).

5.3 Shares in issue

Where several classes of shares are in issue, then earnings should be apportioned according to dividend rights.

5.4 When to include shares in the calculation

Where there has been an issue of shares during the period, shares are normally included in the weighted average number of shares from the date consideration is receivable, which is generally the date of their issue. For example:

- ordinary shares issued in exchange for cash are issued when cash is receivable;
- ordinary shares issued as a result of the conversion of a debt instrument are included as of the date that interest ceases accruing;
- ordinary shares issued as part of the purchase consideration for an acquisition are included as of the date of the acquisition;
- ordinary shares issued as part of the purchase consideration for a business combination accounted for as a merger are included for all periods presented.

Ordinary shares that are issuable upon the satisfaction of certain conditions (contingently issuable shares) are not included in the computation until all the necessary conditions have been satisfied.

5.5 Issue at full market price

Earnings should be apportioned over the weighted average equity share capital (ie, taking account of when shares are issued during the year).

Example

A company issued 200,000 shares at full market price (£3.00) on 1 July 20X8.

Relevant information

	20X8	*20X7*
Ordinary profit attributable to the ordinary shareholders for the year ending 31 Dec.	£550,000	£460,000
Number of ordinary shares in issue at 31 Dec.	1,000,000	800,000

Calculation of earnings per share

20X7 $= \frac{£460{,}000}{800{,}000} = 57.5\text{p}$

20X8 $= \frac{£550{,}000}{800{,}000 + (\frac{1}{2} \times 200{,}000)} = 61.11\text{p}$

Conclusion Since the 200,000 shares have only contributed finance for half a year, the number of shares is adjusted accordingly. Note that the solution is to use the earnings figure for the period without adjustment, but divide by the average number of shares weighted on a time basis.

5.6 Bonus issues

When there has been an event that has changed the number of ordinary shares outstanding without a corresponding change in resources (inflow or outflow of cash), the comparative earnings per share figure should also be adjusted.

Example

A company makes a scrip issue of one new share for every five existing shares held on 1 July 20X8.

Relevant information

	20X8	*20X7*
Ordinary profit attributable to the ordinary shareholders for the year ending 31 Dec.	£550,000	£460,000
Number of ordinary shares in issue at 31 Dec.	1,200,000	1,000,000

Calculation of earnings per share

$$20X7 = \frac{£460{,}000}{1{,}200{,}000} = 38.33p$$

$$20X8 = \frac{£550{,}000}{1{,}200{,}000} = 45.83p$$

In the 20X7 accounts, the EPS for the year would have appeared as 46p (£460,000 ÷ 1,000,000). In the example above, the computation has been reworked from scratch. However, to make the changes required it would be simpler to adjust directly the EPS figures themselves.

Since the old calculation was based on dividing by 1,000,000 while the new is determined by using 1,200,000, it would be necessary to multiply the EPS by the first and divide by the second. The fraction to apply is, therefore,

$$\frac{1{,}000{,}000}{1{,}200{,}000} \text{ or } \frac{5}{6}$$

Consequently $46p \times \frac{5}{6} = 38.33p$.

Given that the scrip issue has not increased the assets in the company, similarly the market value of each share would be expected to be only 5/6 of the former price, since for every five shares previously held, the shareholder now has six.

Assuming a pre-issue market price of £3.00, five shares would have a market value of £15.00.

After the issue six shares would, other things being equal, have the same value. Therefore, one share would have a theoretical post-issue price of £15.00 ÷ 6 = £2.50. The new EPS could in consequence equally well have been calculated by multiplying the old EPS by the theoretical new share price divided by the actual old price

$$\left(\frac{£2.50}{£3.00} = \frac{5}{6}\right)$$

Since there are now six shares in issue for every five previously held, the number of shares after the issue is similarly

$$1{,}000{,}000 \times \frac{6}{5} = 1{,}200{,}000$$

or alternatively

$$1{,}000{,}000 \times \frac{3.00}{2.50} = 1{,}200{,}000$$

These interrelationships are important when considering a rights issue.

5.7 Rights issues

Rights issues present special problems, because they are normally below full market price and therefore combine the characteristics of issues at full market price and bonus issues above. Determining the weighted average capital, therefore, involves two steps:

Step 1 Adjust for bonus element in rights issue, by multiplying capital in issue before the rights issue by:

$$\frac{\text{Actual cum rights price}}{\text{Theoretical ex rights price}}$$

Step 2 Calculate the weighted average capital in issue as above.

Example

A company issued one new share for every two existing shares held by way of rights at £1.50 per share on 1 July 20X8. Pre-issue market price was £3.00 per share.

Relevant information

	20X8	*20X7*
Ordinary profit attributable to the ordinary shareholders for the year ending 31 Dec	£550,000	£460,000
Number of ordinary shares in issue at 31 Dec	1,200,000	800,000

Calculation of earnings per share

20X7 Original per 20X7 accounts:

$$\frac{£460{,}000}{800{,}000} = 57.5\text{p}$$

Adjusted for rights issue:

$$57.5\text{p} \times \frac{2.50}{3.00} = 47.92\text{p}$$

20X8 Based on weighted average number of shares:

1st half-year – actual in issue 800,000

– adjusted for bonus element $800{,}000 \times \frac{3.00}{2.50}$

= 960,000

2nd half-year – actual in issue, including bonus element, 1,200,000

Therefore, EPS = $\frac{£550{,}000}{(960{,}000 + 1{,}200{,}000) \div 2}$

= 50.92p

Notes on solution

(1) 20X7

Pre-rights, two shares would be worth £6.00. Ex-rights, three shares would theoretically be worth £6.00 + £1.50 = £7.50, or £2.50 each. The appropriate fraction for the adjustment of comparatives is, therefore, £2.50 divided by £3.00.

The revised EPS figure could have been obtained by dividing the earnings figure of £460,000 by a share number adjusted for the bonus element, ie:

$$800{,}000 \times \frac{3.00}{2.50} = 960{,}000$$

$$(\frac{£460{,}000}{960{,}000} = 47.92\text{p})$$

(2) 20X8

The calculation must take account of the quasi-capitalisation. The share number used must, therefore, reflect the bonus element for the whole year and the increase in the fund of capital for the half year.

(3) Relationship of rights issue to issue at full market price and capitalisation

Each of the examples used a pre-issue share price of £3.00. Both the rights issue and the issue at full market price raised £600,000 from shareholders. However, after the rights issue there were 1,200,000 shares in issue, whereas following the issue at full market value there were only 1,000,000.

If the latter had been followed immediately by a capitalisation to bring the number of shares issued up to 1,200,000, the EPS figures would have become:

20X7 $\quad 57.5\text{p} \times \frac{2.50}{3.00} = 47.92\text{p}$

20X8 $\quad 61.11\text{p} \times \frac{2.50}{3.00} = 50.92\text{p}$

These are, as would be expected, the same as those calculated for the rights issue.

5.8 The reasoning behind, and the effect of, disclosing the nil basis of EPS

For the purpose of FRS 14, earnings are the profit of the period after tax. Problems arise in determining the tax charge, because in some circumstances, this is a variable dependent on the amount of dividends paid.

Major parts of the tax charge are constant, eg, corporation tax on income. Variable elements may arise (for example in the past in relation to irrecoverable ACT).

There are two ways of dealing with this problem:

(a) **net** basis – taking account of all the tax elements above, both constant and variable;
(b) **nil** basis – taking account of only the constant tax elements, ie, the position if no dividends were paid.

(There is in fact a third possibility, the **full** distribution basis. This is the charge if the company paid dividends up to the theoretical maximum current profits allowed. It is used in the *Financial Times* to calculate **times covered**, ie, the ratio of profit as thus defined to the gross dividend. However, the approach would not be suitable for calculating EPS.)

The nil basis produces a figure which is independent of the level of dividends, and thus arguably a better indicator of underlying profitability.

SSAP 3 required the calculation and disclosure of earnings per share on the nil basis where this was materially different from the net basis.

FRS 14 does not require the nil basis. The original reasoning behind this was that the nil basis can be calculated from other disclosures in the financial statements. Following the abolition of ACT it will be very unusual for the nil basis to be materially different from the net basis.

Conclusion FRS 14 requires EPS to be calculated using the net basis ie, using the actual tax charge in the profit and loss account.

6 DILUTED EARNINGS PER SHARE

6.1 The existing circumstances that will cause a company's future EPS to be diluted

As well as basic earnings per share, FRS 14 requires entities to disclose diluted earnings per share. To calculate diluted earnings per share, the net profit attributable to ordinary shareholders and the weighted average number of shares outstanding are adjusted for the effect of all dilutive potential ordinary shares.

Definition A **potential ordinary share** is a financial instrument or a right that may entitle its holders to ordinary shares.

Examples of potential ordinary shares:

- convertible loan stock
- convertible preference shares
- share warrants and options
- rights granted under employee share schemes
- rights to ordinary shares that are conditional upon the satisfaction of conditions.

Diluted earnings per share shows to what extent the amount available for ordinary dividends per share would have been affected if all the potential ordinary shares had been issued under the worse possible dilution.

To calculate diluted earnings per share:

- the net profit or loss for the period attributable to ordinary shareholders is adjusted for:
  - dividends on potential shares (eg, on convertible preference shares)
  - interest (eg, on convertible loan stock)
  - any other changes in income and expense that would result from the conversion
- the weighted average number of ordinary shares that would be issued if all the potential ordinary shares were converted is added to the weighted number of ordinary shares. (Potential ordinary shares should be assumed to have been converted at the beginning of the period, or, if they were not in existence at the beginning of the period, the date of issue.)

6.2 Convertibles

The principles of convertible loan stock and convertible preference shares are similar and will be dealt with together.

Example

On 1 April 20X1, the company issued £1,250,000 8% convertible unsecured loan stock for cash at par. Each £100 nominal of the stock will be convertible in 20X6/20X9 into the number of ordinary shares set out below:

On 31 December 20X6	124 shares
On 31 December 20X7	120 shares
On 31 December 20X8	115 shares
On 31 December 20X9	110 shares

Relevant information

Issued share capital:

£500,000 in 10% cumulative preference shares of £1;
£1,000,000 in ordinary shares of 25p = 4,000,000 shares.

Corporation tax is 30%.

Trading results for the year ended 31 December

	20X2	20X1
	£	£
Profit before interest and tax	1,100,000	991,818
Interest on 8% convertible unsecured loan stock	100,000	75,000
Profit before tax	1,000,000	916,818
Corporation tax	300,000	275,045
Profit after tax	700,000	641,773

Calculation of earnings per share

			20X2		20X1
(1)	**Basic earnings per share**		£		£
	Profit after tax		700,000		641,773
	Less: Preference dividend		50,000		50,000
	Earnings		650,000		591,773
	Earnings per share based on 4,000,000 shares		16.2p		14.8p
(2)	**Diluted earnings per share**				
	Earnings as above		650,000		591,773
	Add: Interest on the convertible unsecured loan stock	100,000		75,000	
	Less: Corporation tax	30,000		22,500	
			70,000		52,500
	Adjusted earnings		720,000		644,273
	Earnings per share based on 5,550,000 shares (20X1 – 5,162,500)		13.0p		12.5p

Notes:

(A) Up to 20X5 the **maximum** number of shares issuable after the end of the financial year will be at the rate of 124 shares per £100, viz: 1,550,000 shares, making a total of 5,550,000.

(B) The weighted average number of shares issued and issuable for 20X1 would have been one-quarter of 4,000,000 plus three-quarters of 5,550,000, ie, 5,162,500.

6.3 Options and warrants

The total number of shares issued on the exercise of the option or warrant is split into two:

(i) the number of shares that would have been issued if the cash received had been used to buy shares at fair value (using the average price of the shares during the period); and

(ii) the remainder, which are treated like a bonus issue (ie, as having been issued for no consideration).

The number of shares issued for no consideration is added to the number of shares when calculating the diluted earnings per share.

Example

On 1 January 20X7 a company issues 1,000,000 shares under option. The net profit for the year is £500,000 and the company already has 4,000,000 ordinary shares in issue at that date.

During the year to 31 December 20X7 the average fair value of one ordinary share was £3 and the exercise price for the shares under option was £2.

Solution

Basic earnings per share: $\dfrac{£500,000}{4,000,000} = 12.5\text{p}$

Diluted earnings per share:	
Number of ordinary shares in issue	4,000,000
Number of shares under option	1,000,000
Number of shares that would have been issued at fair value: (1,000,000 × 2/3)	(666,667)
	4,333,333

Earnings per share: $\dfrac{£500,000}{4,333,333} = 11.5\text{p}$

(Note that this calculation is not the same as the calculation required by SSAP 3. Under SSAP 3, earnings were increased by the amount of interest which would have been earned if the subscription monies received on exercise of the option had been invested in 2.5% consolidated stock.)

6.4 Employee share schemes

Share option and similar schemes are becoming increasingly common. The accounting treatment of these is covered by UITF Abstract 17 (see Chapter 8).

For the purpose of calculating diluted EPS, there are two types of scheme:

(a) where the award is based on performance
(b) other schemes.

Performance based awards are treated as contingently issuable shares (see 6.5 below). All other awards are treated as options. The assumed proceeds of the potential ordinary shares may need to be adjusted to reflect the fact that they have been earned by past services. This will be the case for those schemes to which UITF Abstract 17 applies. The assumed proceeds consist of the consideration (if any) that the employee must pay upon exercise of the award and the cost of the shares calculated in accordance with UITF Abstract 17 and not yet recognised.

Example

A company operates an employee share option scheme that awards share options to employees and their dependants on the basis of period of service with the company. The shares were granted on 1 January 20X7 and are due to vest in the employees at 31 December 20X9. The company has 5 million ordinary shares in issue at 1 January 20X7. The following details are also relevant:

(a) The market price of the shares at 1 January 20X7 was £2.00.
(b) The exercise price of the option is £1.25.
(c) There are 1 million shares under option.
(d) The net profit for the year ended 31 December 20X7 is £600,000.
(e) The average fair value of an ordinary share during 20X7 is £2.50.

Calculate basic and diluted EPS for the year ended 31 December 20X7.

Solution

Step 1 Calculate the assumed proceeds per option

UITF Abstract 17 requires that the cost of the shares to the company is recognised over the period of the scheme. This is calculated as follows:

	£
Market price at 1 January 20X7	2.00
Less: Exercise price	(1.25)
	0.75

This is allocated over the life of the scheme so that 25p per option per year is charged to the profit and loss account. Therefore the assumed proceeds per option are:

	£
Exercise price	1.25
Compensation cost attributable to future service, not yet recognised (2 × 25p)	0.50
	1.75

Step 2 Calculate earnings per share

Basic earnings per share: $\frac{£600,000}{5,000,000} = 12p$

Diluted earnings per share:

Number of ordinary shares in issue	5,000,000
Number of shares under option	1,000,000
Number of shares that would have been issued at fair value: (1,000,000 × 1.75/2.50)	(700,000)
	5,300,000

Earnings per share: $\frac{£600,000}{5,300,000} = 11.3p$

The dilution will become greater over time. Suppose that net profits for the year ended 31 December 20X8 were also £600,000. Diluted EPS would be based on assumed proceeds of £1.50 (exercise price of £1.25 plus costs not yet charged to the profit and loss account of 25p).

Number of ordinary shares in issue	5,000,000
Number of shares under option	1,000,000
Number of shares that would have been issued at fair value: (1,000,000 × 1.50/2.50)	(600,000)
	5,400,000

Earnings per share: $\frac{£600,000}{5,400,000} = 11.1p$

6.5 Contingently issuable shares

Contingently issuable shares are included in the calculation of diluted earnings per share from the beginning of the period, or, if they were not in existence at the beginning of the period, from the date of the relevant financial instrument or the granting of the rights.

The number of shares to include in the calculation is based on the number of shares that would be issuable if the end of the accounting period was the end of the contingency period. For example:

- Where a condition is expressed as an average over a period the performance achieved to date is deemed to be that achieved over the whole of the contingency period. For example, if the number of shares to be issued depends on whether profits average £100,000 over a three year period, the condition is expressed as a cumulative target of £300,000 over the three year period. If at the end of the first year, profits are £150,000, no additional shares are brought into the calculation.
- Where the number of shares to be issued depends on the market price of the shares of the issuing company, the number of shares to be included in the calculation is based on the number that would be issued based on the market price at the end of the current accounting period or the average over a specified period, depending on the terms of the underlying contract.
- If the contingency is based on a condition other than earnings or market price, it should be assumed that the status of the condition at the end of the reporting period will remain unchanged until the end of the contingency period. For example, if a further issue of shares is generated on the opening of the tenth new retail outlet and at the year end only five have been opened, no additional shares are included in the calculation.

Example

A company has 500,000 ordinary shares outstanding at 1 January 20X7. It has agreed to issue additional shares as follows:

(a) 10,000 additional ordinary shares for every new retail outlet opened in each of the three years 20X7 to 20X9;

(b) 1,000 additional ordinary shares for each £1,000 of total net profit in excess of £350,000 over the three years ending 20X9.

The company opened one new retail outlet on 1 July 20X7 and another on 1 January 20X9. Net profit for the three years was £150,000, £240,000 and £175,000 respectively.

Calculate basic and diluted earnings per share for each of the three years ended 31 December 20X9.

Solution

Basic earnings per share

One retail outlet is opened during 20X7 and another during 20X9. Therefore 10,000 additional shares are issued in each of those two years. Because the earnings condition is not actually met until the last day of 20X9, no further additional shares are issued.

20X7 $\frac{£150,000}{505,000}$ = 29.7p

(Number of shares: 500,000 × 6/12 + 510,000 × 6/12)

20X8 $\frac{£240,000}{510,000}$ = 47.1p

20X9 $\frac{£175,000}{520,000}$ = 33.7p

Diluted earnings per share

Contingently issuable shares are included in the diluted earnings per share calculation from the beginning of the period in which the condition is met. Therefore a further 5,000 potential shares are included in 20X7 as a result of the opening of the retail outlet on 1 July.

Additional shares are included in respect of the earnings contingency:

20X7 Earnings for the period were less than £350,000, therefore no additional shares.

20X8 Cumulative earnings for the two years are £390,000, therefore 40,000 additional shares are included.

20X9 Cumulative earnings for the three years are £565,000, therefore a further 175,000 additional shares are included (565,000 – 390,000).

Number of shares:

	20X7	*20X8*	*20X9*
Basic	505,000	510,000	520,000
Retail outlet contingency	5,000	–	–
Earnings contingency	–	40,000	215,000
	510,000	550,000	735,000

Earnings per share:

20X7 $\frac{£150,000}{510,000}$ = 29.4p

20X8 $\frac{£240,000}{550,000}$ = 43.6p

20X9 $\frac{£175,000}{735,000}$ = 23.8p

6.6 The order in which to include dilutive securities in the calculation

Only potential ordinary shares that would dilute basic earnings per share should be taken into account when computing the diluted figure.

Where there is more than one issue of dilutive share the calculation is in two stages:

1. For each issue, calculate earnings per incremental share.
2. Adjust basic earnings per share for each issue from the most dilutive to the least dilutive.

Example

The net profit attributable to ordinary shareholders is £500,000. There are 100,000 ordinary shares in issue. The average fair value of one ordinary share during the year was £50.

The following potential ordinary shares must be taken into consideration:

(i)	Options	5,000 shares with an exercise price of £40 per share.
(ii)	Convertible preference shares	40,000 shares entitled to a cumulative dividend of £8 per share. Each preference share is convertible to 2 ordinary shares.
(iii)	5% convertible bond	nominal amount £5,000,000. Each £1,000 bond is convertible to 20 ordinary shares.

The tax rate is 40%.

Solution

Step 1 Calculate the increase in earnings attributable to ordinary shareholders on conversion of potential ordinary shares.

	Increase in earnings £	*Increase in number of ordinary shares*	*Earnings per incremental share* £
Options			
Increase in earnings	NIL		
Shares issued for no consideration:			
(5,000 × (50 – 40)/50)		1,000	NIL
Convertible preference shares			
Increase in earnings (40,000 × 8)	320,000		
Increase in shares (2 × 40,000)		80,000	4.00
5% convertible bonds			
Increase in earnings (5,000,000 × 5% × 60%)	150,000		
Incremental shares (5,000 × 20)		100,000	1.50

The lower the incremental earnings per share, the higher the dilutive effect. This calculation shows that the most dilutive potential ordinary shares are the options, followed by the 5% convertible bonds and then the convertible preference shares. This is the order in which they should be considered in the earnings per share calculation.

Step 2 Calculate diluted earnings per share.

	Net profit attributable £	*Ordinary shares*	*Earnings per share* £
Basic earnings per share	500,000	100,000	5.00
Options	–	1,000	
	500,000	101,000	4.95

5% convertible bonds	150,000	100,000	
	650,000	201,000	3.23
Convertible preference shares	320,000	80,000	
	970,000	281,000	3.45

Because diluted earnings per share is increased when taking the convertible preference shares into account, the convertible preference shares are antidilutive and are therefore ignored.

The diluted earnings per share is £3.23.

6.7 Presentation

(a) Basic and diluted earnings per share should be presented on the face of the profit and loss account for each class of ordinary share.

(b) Basic and diluted earnings per share must be presented with equal prominence.

(c) Basic and diluted earnings per share should be presented even if the amounts are negative (ie, a loss per share).

(Note that these requirements represent another change from SSAP 3. SSAP 3 only required the disclosure of diluted earnings per share when the dilution was more than 5% of basic earnings per share. Under FRS 14, diluted earnings per share must **always** be disclosed.)

The following information should be disclosed for both basic and diluted earnings per share:

(a) the amounts used as numerators and a reconciliation of those amounts to the net profit or loss for the period; and

(b) the weighted average number of ordinary shares used as the denominator and a reconciliation of the denominators to each other.

If an alternative measure of earnings per share is disclosed this should be:

(a) calculated using the weighted average number of ordinary shares determined in accordance with FRS 14;

(b) presented consistently over time;

(c) reconciled to the amount required by FRS 14. The reconciliation must list the items for which an adjustment is being made and disclose their individual effect on the calculation;

(d) not presented more prominently than the version required by FRS 14; and

(e) the reason for calculating the additional version should be explained.

The reconciliation and explanation should appear adjacent to the earnings per share disclosure, or a reference should be given to where they can be found.

Where ordinary share transactions or potential ordinary share transactions occur after the balance sheet date, a description of these should be disclosed where they are of such importance that non-disclosure would affect the ability of the users of the financial statements to make proper evaluations and decisions.

6.8 The usefulness of FRS 14

The 'Earnings per share' (EPS) figure is used to compute the major stock market indicator of performance, the Price Earnings ratio (PE ratio). The calculation is:

$$\text{PE ratio} = \frac{\text{Market value of share}}{\text{EPS}}$$

Rightly or wrongly, the stock market places great emphasis on the earnings per share figure and the PE ratio. FRS 14 sets out a standard method of calculating EPS, which enhances the comparability of the figure.

However, EPS has limited usefulness as a performance measure. Many of these limitations are inherent in the calculation itself.

(a) An entity's earnings are affected by its choice of accounting policies. Therefore, it may not always be appropriate to compare the EPS of different companies.

(b) Where new shares are issued for cash or as consideration for an acquisition, FRS 14 requires the additional shares to be taken into account from the date of issue. In practice, it may be years before the additional capital begins to generate earnings. A new share issue is often accompanied by a decrease in EPS.

(c) EPS is not an appropriate measure of performance for a small owner-managed company. This is because earnings may be materially affected by policy decisions, for example, as to the level of directors' remuneration.

(d) EPS does not take account of inflation. Apparent growth in earnings may not be true growth.

(e) EPS does not provide predictive value. High earnings and growth in earnings may be achieved at the expense of investment which may generate increased earnings in the future.

(f) EPS cannot be used as a basis of comparison between companies as the number of shares in issue in any particular company is not related to the amount of capital employed. For example, two companies may have the same amount of capital employed, but one company has 100,000 £1 shares in issue and reserves of £4,900,000. Another company may have 5 million 50p shares in issue and reserves of £2,500,000. The same level of earnings will produce different EPS.

(g) EPS is based on historic information, yet it is used to calculate the PE ratio, which is a forward-looking figure.

(h) The diluted EPS (DEPS) is a theoretical measure of the effect of dilution on the basic EPS. There is no evidence to suggest that even the most sophisticated analysts use DEPS. This is because of its hypothetical nature.

In theory, diluted EPS serves as a warning to equity shareholders that the return on their investment may fall in future periods. However, diluted EPS as currently required by FRS 14 is not intended to be forward looking but an additional past performance measure. For example, when calculating diluted EPS where there are warrants or options, fair value is based on the average price of an ordinary share for the period, rather than the market price at the period end. Therefore diluted EPS is only of limited use as a prediction of future EPS.

(i) EPS is a measure of profitability. Profitability is only one aspect of performance. Concentration on earnings per share and 'the bottom line' arguably detracts from other important aspects of an entity's affairs, for example, cash flow and stewardship of assets.

6.9 Earnings per share and FRS 3

The issue of FRS 3 has had a significant impact on the usefulness of EPS.

Under FRS 3, EPS is computed on earnings after extraordinary items. This means that EPS is now much more volatile than previously and may fluctuate significantly from year to year, for example, following reorganisations or sales of property.

FRS 3 and FRS 14 permit companies to publish more than one EPS figure. This means that EPS can be calculated at different levels of profit.

The ASB believes that it is not possible to distil the performance of a complex organisation into a single measure. It wishes to shift the emphasis away from profit after tax and EPS and to encourage more analysis of the profit and loss account as a whole. The standard EPS figure is the starting point for this analysis.

In practice, many companies do publish an additional version of EPS.

The Institute of Investment Management and Research (IIMR) reacted to the issue of FRS 3 by developing their own alternative to the standard EPS. This is set out in SOIP 1 *The definition of IIMR headline earnings*. It suggested that the figure should be calculated as follows:

(a) Include:

- trading profits and losses (including exceptional items)
- interest
- trading results of acquired or discontinued operations as reported
- tax and minority interest adjustments to reflect other adjustments made.

(b) Exclude:

- profits and losses on sales and terminations
- provisions for exceptional items required to be disclosed on the face of the profit and loss account
- profits and losses on the sale of fixed assets
- exceptional profits and losses on the reorganisation or redemption of long-term debt
- any impact of goodwill
- pension cost impact of discontinuations
- extraordinary items (if any) net of tax.

The IIMR figure has now been widely adopted by financial institutions, including the Financial Times and Extel. It appears that, despite the efforts of the ASB, users of accounts still want to concentrate on a single measure of performance.

6.10 Evaluation of the changes from SSAP 3

The change to the method of calculating diluted earnings per share where there are options is an improvement on the SSAP 3 method which could be criticised as being arbitrary.

Users of the financial statements are provided with additional information in order to assess the effect of dilution.

Treating diluted earnings per share as a measure of past performance may not address the needs of investors, who are primarily concerned with the effect of potential dilution in the future. Arguably, the FRS 14 calculation is too prudent and also potentially complicated to apply.

7 CHAPTER SUMMARY

FRS 3 requires the operations of a company to be analysed between continuing and discontinued operations. Continuing operations are further split to show acquisitions in the accounting period.

All gains and losses are collected together in a statement of total recognised gains and losses.

EPS is calculated and disclosed for all listed companies. Complications arise if there has been a change in the amount of ordinary share capital in the period. Where there are dilutive potential ordinary shares, diluted EPS must also be calculated and presented.

8 SELF TEST QUESTIONS

8.1 What components of financial performance should be highlighted in the layered format for the profit and loss account required by *FRS 3*? (1.3)

8.2 In order to qualify as a discontinued operation, *FRS 3* has introduced a timing restriction for the sale or termination to be completed. What is this restriction? (1.5)

8.3 What is an exceptional item? (2.1)

8.4 What three categories of items does FRS 3 require to be shown separately on the face of the profit and loss account? (2.2)

8.5 The statement of total recognised gains and losses is what kind of statement? (3.1)

8.6 What is the denominator of the basic EPS calculation? (5.2)

8.7 When is the weighted average method used in an EPS calculation? (5.5)

8.8 Does a bonus issue reduce or increase EPS? (5.6)

8.9 What is the ratio used after a rights issue in calculating the EPS for the year? (5.7)

8.10 What are three examples of potential dilutions in EPS? (6.1)

9 EXAMINATION TYPE QUESTION

9.1 Pilum

Draft profit and loss account for year ended 31 December 20X4

	£	£
Profit before tax		2,438,000
Less: Taxation		
Corporation tax	1,035,000	
Under provision for 20X3	23,000	
		1,058,000
		1,380,000
Less: Transfer to reserves	115,000	
Dividends		
Paid - Preference interim dividend	138,000	
Paid - Ordinary interim dividend	184,000	
Proposed - Preference final dividend	138,000	
Proposed - Ordinary final dividend	230,000	
		805,000
Retained		575,000

On 1 January 20X4 the issued share capital of Pilum plc was 4,600,000 6% preference shares of £1 each and 4,140,000 ordinary shares of £1 each.

You are required to calculate the earnings per share (on basic and diluted basis) in respect of the year ended 31 December 20X4 for each of the following circumstances. (Each of the five circumstances (a) to (e) is to be dealt with separately):

(a) On the basis that there was no change in the issued share capital of the company during the year ended 31 December 20X4.

(b) On the basis that the company made a bonus issue on 1 October 20X4 of one ordinary share for every four shares in issue at 30 September 20X4.

(c) On the basis that the company made a rights issue of £1 ordinary shares on 1 October 20X4 in the proportion of 1 of every 5 shares held, at a price of £1.20. The middle market price for the shares on the last day of quotation cum rights was £1.80 per share.

(d) On the basis that the company made no new issue of shares during the year ended 31 December 20X4, but on that date it had in issue £1,150,000 10% convertible loan stock 20X6 to 20X9. This loan stock will be convertible into ordinary £1 shares as follows:

20X6	90	£1	shares for £100 nominal value loan stock
20X7	85	£1	shares for £100 nominal value loan stock
20X8	80	£1	shares for £100 nominal value loan stock
20X9	75	£1	shares for £100 nominal value loan stock

(e) On the basis that the company made no issue of shares during the year ended 31 December 20X4, but on that date there were outstanding options to purchase 460,000 ordinary £1 shares at £1.70 per share. The fair value of ordinary £1 shares was £2.00 per share throughout the year.

Assume where appropriate that the corporation tax rate is 50%.

10 ANSWER TO EXAMINATION TYPE QUESTION

10.1 Pilum

	Working	
(a)	(W1)	26.7p
(b)	(W2)	21.3p
(c)	(W3)	24.4p
(d)	(W4)	22.4p
(e)	(W5)	26.2p

WORKINGS

(W1)

	£'000
Profit on ordinary activities after tax	1,380
Preference dividends 138 × 2	276
Earnings	1,104

EPS $\frac{1,104}{4,140} \times 100 = 26.7\text{p}$

(W2) Five shares in issue for every four before, multiply answer to (a) by 0.8.

(W3)

				Value £
Before	5	shares at	£1.80 =	9
Rights	1	at	£1.20 =	1.20
After	6			10.20

Theoretical ex rights price = $\frac{£10.20}{6} = £1.70$

Weighted ave no of shares = $\left(\frac{9}{12} \times 4{,}140 \times \frac{1.8}{1.7}\right) + \left(\frac{3}{12} \times 4{,}140 \times \frac{6}{5}\right)$

(in 000s)

$= 3{,}288 + 1{,}242$

$= 4{,}530$

Multiply answer to (a) by $\frac{4{,}140}{4{,}530}$

(Tutorial note: the last part of the calculation is substituting the new denominator for the old denominator which is a quicker way of producing the figures***)***

(W4)

	£'000
Earnings in working 1	1,104.0
Add: After tax interest saved if converted 1,150 × 10% × 50%	57.5
	1,161.5

Calculate dilution as if conversion took place issuing the highest number of shares possible ie, 90 per £100.

No of shares (in 000s) $= 4{,}140 + \left(\frac{90}{100} \times 1{,}150\right) = 5{,}175$

Diluted EPS $= \frac{1{,}161.5}{5{,}175} \times 100 = 22.4\text{p}$

(W5)

Number of ordinary shares in issue	4,140,000
Number of shares under option	460,000
Number of shares that would have been issued at fair value: (460,000 × 1.70/2.00)	(391,000)
	4,209,000

Earnings per share (earnings as in (a)): $\frac{1{,}104}{4{,}209} \times 100 = 26.2\text{p}$

11 REALISED AND LEGALLY DISTRIBUTABLE PROFIT

INTRODUCTION & LEARNING OBJECTIVES

This chapter should be revision of earlier studies.

The profit and loss account is the starting point for determining the profits which may legally be distributed as dividends as the law assumes 'normal' accounting conventions have been applied.

Distributable profits are maximised for private companies with public companies facing further restrictions. Certain types of investment companies have relieving provisions from the normal plc rules.

When you have studied this chapter you should be able to do the following:

- Outline the principles of realised profits.
- Discuss the rules relating to the distribution of profits.

1 REALISED PROFITS IN ACCORDANCE WITH THE COMPANIES ACT AND UK GAAP

1.1 The legal framework

The term 'realised profits' was introduced into UK company law in the Companies Acts 1980 and 1981. The CA80 imposed restrictions on the distribution of profits by companies, including a prohibition on the distribution of unrealised profits. The CA81 required that only profits realised at the balance sheet date should be included in the profit and loss account.

Both these provisions are now in the CA85.

Para 12(a) Sch 4 CA85 states that only realised profits may be included in a profit and loss account.

Definition Realised profits are defined as such profits which fall to be treated as realised profits in accordance with principles generally accepted with respect to the determination for accounting purposes of realised profits at the time when those accounts are prepared.

1.2 UK GAAP

As can be seen from the CA85 definition of realised profits, generally accepted principles need to be applied ie, UK GAAP. However UK GAAP does not provide a definition of realised profit. In order to assist in the interpretation of what is realised, the CCAB issued a technical release in September 1982 on 'The determination of realised profits and disclosure of distributable profits in the context of the *Companies Acts 1948-1981'(TR 481)*.

The technical release gives the following guidance.

(a) A profit which is required by statements of standard accounting practice to be recognised in the profit and loss account should normally be treated as a realised profit unless the SSAP specifically indicates that it should be treated as unrealised.

(b) Profit may be recognised in the profit and loss account in accordance with an accounting policy which is not the subject of a SSAP, or, exceptionally, which is contrary to a SSAP. Such a profit will normally be a realised profit if the accounting policy adopted is consistent with the accruals and prudence concepts as set out in SSAP 2 and Sch 4.

(c) Where, in special circumstances, a true and fair view could not be given, even if additional information were provided, without including in the profit and loss account an unrealised profit, the effect of the true and fair view requirement of S228 CA85 is to require inclusion of that unrealised profit. Moreover, para 15 Sch 4 CA85 allows the directors to include an unrealised profit in the profit and loss account where there are special reasons for doing so.

1.3 The contribution of SSAPs/FRSs to the definition of realised profits

SSAPs which refer to realised profits include the following.

(a) SSAP 2 refers to realised profits in explaining the prudence concept.

Revenues and profits are not anticipated, but are recognised by inclusion in the profit and loss account only when realised in the form either of cash or of other assets the ultimate cash realisation of which can be assessed with reasonable certainty.

SSAP 2 should be used when an item is not dealt with by a more specific accounting standard.

(b) SSAP 9 states that profit recognised in the profit and loss account is realised as profits are only recognised on long-term contracts if the outcome of the contract is 'reasonably certain'.

(c) SSAP 20 states that gains on the retranslation of long-term liabilities are unrealised but are included in the profit and loss account in order to show a true and fair view.

Conclusion Most items are realised if they are included in the profit and loss account under specific accounting standards or the fundamental concepts of SSAP 2.

1.4 Future developments

Within the next year, SSAP 2 will probably be replaced by a new standard based on the proposals in FRED 21 *Accounting policies*. FRED 21 has been discussed in detail in an earlier chapter. Unlike SSAP 2, it regards prudence as a desirable quality of financial information rather than a fundamental concept and it does not define prudence in terms of realisation.

However, the Companies Act states that 'the amount of any item shall be determined on a prudent basis and in particular only profits realised at the balance sheet date shall be included in the profit and loss account'. The Companies Act definition of prudence is similar to the SSAP 2 definition and it will continue to apply for the purposes of arriving at distributable profit.

2 DISTRIBUTABLE PROFITS IN ACCORDANCE WITH THE COMPANIES ACT

2.1 Profits available for dividend: rules for all companies

All companies, including private companies, are prohibited from paying dividends (making a distribution) except out of profits available for that purpose.

Profits available for dividend are

Definition Accumulated, realised profits, so far as not previously utilised (whether by distribution or capitalisation), less the accumulated, realised losses, so far as not previously written off: S263(3) CA85

This definition permits the distribution as dividend of a *capital profit* ie, a surplus over book value realised on sale of a fixed asset. But the key words are

(a) *Accumulated* - which means that the balance of profit or loss from previous years must be brought into account in the current period, and

(b) *Realised* - which prohibits the inclusion of unrealised profits arising from eg, the revaluation of fixed assets retained by the company.

Note that distributions are made by *individual companies* and not by groups.

2.2 Detailed rules

There are the following detailed rules in CA85.

(a) A revaluation surplus is an unrealised profit.

(b) If fixed assets are revalued and as a result more has to be provided for depreciation than would have been necessary if the original value had been retained, the additional depreciation may be treated as part of the realised profit for dividend purposes. This effectively means the depreciation based on the revaluation surplus can be added back notionally to the profit and loss account for the determination of realised profits. This adjustment can be put through the accounts as a transfer between reserves.

Example

A Ltd purchased freehold land and buildings on 30 June 20X4 for £200,000 (land £60,000, buildings £140,000). The net book value of the buildings at 31 December 20X7 is £121,386. On 1 January 20X8 the land was revalued to £75,000 and the buildings to £135,000. Depreciation on buildings is computed at 4% reducing balance. Accounts are prepared on a calendar year basis.

The entries to the revaluation reserve should be

	£
Re land	15,000
Re buildings £(135,000 - 121,386)	13,614
	£28,614

The depreciation charge for the year ended 31 December 20X8 = 4% × £135,000 = £5,400. This amount is the charge to P&L account (FRS 15) although CA85 requires only the HC depreciation (4% × £121,386 = £4,855).

However, to show the realised part of the revaluation reserve a transfer from the reserve to distributable reserves may be made

Revaluation reserve

	£
Balance at 1 January 20X8	28,614
Transfer to distributable reserves £(5,400 - 4,855)	545
Balance at 31 December 20X8	28,069

(c) On the disposal of a revalued asset any unrealised surplus or loss on valuation immediately becomes realised.

(d) If there is no available record of the original cost of an asset, its cost may be taken as the value put on it in the earliest available record.

(e) If it is impossible to establish whether a profit or a loss brought forward was realised or unrealised, any such profit may be treated as realised and any such loss as unrealised: S263 CA85.

2.3 Provisions and distributable profits

Generally, any provision which has been charged to the profit and loss account will be a realised loss and will reduce the balance of distributable profits (S275 of CA 1985). So, for example, a provision established against a doubtful debt or damaged stock would reduce a company's distributable profits.

In 1998 the ASB issued FRS 12 *Provisions, contingent liabilities and contingent assets* to provide mandatory guidance on when and at what amount provisions should be set up in the financial statements (see chapter 8 of this text for detailed consideration of FRS 12). Requirements such as the banning of the establishment of provisions for future operating losses will have the effect of reducing the amount of provisions in the accounts and thereby increasing the balance of distributable profits available to a company.

2.4 Revaluation deficits

Company legislation has enshrined in law the principles of distributable profits and losses decided in a series of court cases in the late nineteenth and early twentieth centuries. These principles were, in part, based on sound accounting concepts. However, in the treatment of provisions for losses on assets, the judgements of the courts were very difficult to reconcile with any accounting principles.

The CA85 stipulates the following

(a) A provision made in the accounts is a realised loss. A revaluation deficit is a provision for a loss in value and is therefore a realised loss.

(b) If a revaluation deficit arises on a revaluation of all fixed assets (or on a revaluation of all fixed assets except for goodwill) the revaluation deficit is an *unrealised* loss.

Consequently, where a company undertakes a partial revaluation of fixed assets, a deficit on one asset is a realised loss and cannot therefore be offset against a surplus on another asset (an unrealised profit) for the purposes of arriving at distributable profits. This is despite the fact that all surpluses and deficits can be accounted for in the revaluation reserve.

(c) A partial remedy to this problem is contained in the CA85. Deficits arising on an asset where there has been a partial revaluation of the assets are to be treated as unrealised losses provided that

(i) the directors have 'considered' the aggregate value of the fixed assets which have not been revalued at the date of the partial revaluation, and

(ii) the directors are satisfied that their aggregate value is not less than their aggregate book value, and

(iii) a note to the accounts states the above two facts.

2.5 Example

X Ltd has the following balance sheet

	£'000
Net assets	
Share capital	100
Share premium	50
Revaluation reserve	70
Profit and loss account	80

Two of the company's assets were revalued during the year, one giving rise to a surplus of £100,000, the other a deficit of £30,000.

The profits available for dividend are

	£'000
Net realised profits - Profit and loss account	80

Less: Realised losses - Revaluation deficit	30
	50

If all the company's assets had been revalued or the directors had 'considered' the value of the assets not revalued, the revaluation deficit would be unrealised and therefore the profits available for distribution would be £80,000.

2.6 Revaluation surpluses

Revaluation surpluses are unrealised profits in the accounting period in which the revaluation takes place. The only exception to this rule is where the *same* asset was

(a) previously revalued giving rise to a deficit, and

(b) the deficit was treated as a realised loss. In such a case, the revaluation surplus will be a realised profit *to the extent* that it makes good the realised loss. It should be noted that company law does not specify this but best accounting practice would require this treatment.

It should also be remembered that revaluation surpluses can eventually *become* realised profits when the asset is either depreciated or sold.

2.7 Why unrealised profits or losses can affect the distributable profits of public companies

In addition to the rules set out above, a public company may not pay a dividend unless its net assets are at least equal to the aggregate amount of its called-up share capital and undistributable reserves. It may not pay a dividend so as to reduce its net assets below that aggregate amount: S264 CA85. It must *maintain* its called-up share capital and undistributable reserves.

Undistributable reserves are

(a) Share premium account

(b) Capital redemption reserve

(c) Unrealised profits (less unrealised losses unless previously written off)

(d) Any other reserve which the company is prohibited from distributing by any statute or by its memorandum or articles of association.

The effect of this provision is that any excess of unrealised losses over unrealised profits must be deducted from realised profits in arriving at the amount available for distribution.

2.8 Calculation of the distributable profits of both companies

A public company has the following balance sheet.

	£'000
Share capital	100
Unrealised profits	60
Unrealised losses	(80)
Realised profits	35
Net assets	115

Net assets must not be reduced below

Share capital	100
Undistributable reserves	-
	100

ie, maximum distribution is £15,000 being

Realised profits	35
Less: Excess of unrealised losses over unrealised profits	(20)
	15

For a private company the maximum distribution would be £35,000.

2.9 Activity

State whether each of the following are realised or unrealised profits (or losses) for the purpose of calculating distributable profits

(i) Depreciation charged on a revalued fixed asset.

(ii) Development expenditure in the profit and loss account which was previously capitalised in the balance sheet.

(iii) The share of profits from an associated company to an investing company which does not prepare consolidated financial statements.

(iv) The profit on the disposal of a fixed asset which had been revalued in a previous year.

(v) A provision for libel damages in a forthcoming court case.

2.10 Activity solution

(i) Depreciation is generally a realised loss. However the part related to the revalued amount above cost turns an equivalent amount of the revaluation reserve into a realised profit. Therefore, it is only the depreciation on the original cost element which effectively reduces distributable profits.

(ii) Development expenditure is generally written off in the year it is incurred and is a realised loss. If previously capitalised the amount will be a realised loss in the year of the original expenditure unless the notes to the accounts state that it is not so treated (this is a CA85 provision). If the notes state this fact, then the expenditure only becomes a realised loss in the year it is written off.

(iii) Only dividends received and receivable are realised profits. To the extent that the associate has not distributed its profits, they are unrealised from the viewpoint of the investing company.

(iv) A revaluation is an unrealised profit. The sale of the asset turns the unrealised profit into a realised profit.

(v) As the provision has been made in the accounts (rather than a contingent liability note) it is a realised loss. The CA85 states that provisions are realised losses.

2.11 Distributable profit of investment companies

There are special rules for certain types of investment companies, due to the restrictions they are required to place upon themselves as to the distribution of profits.

For the purposes of the special distribution rules an investment company is a *public* company which has complied with the following requirements:

(a) that the business of the company consists of investing its funds mainly in securities, with the aim of spreading investment risk and giving members of the company the benefits of the results of the management of its funds

(b) that none of the company's holdings in companies (other than those which are for the time being in investment companies) represents more than 15% by value of the investing company's investments

(c) that distribution of the company's capital profits is prohibited by its memorandum or articles of association

(d) that the company has not retained in any accounting reference period more than 15% of the income it derives from securities.

The key part of the requirements is point (c): an investment company is precluded from distributing all capital profits (including realised). Thus, if the company had to maintain capital in the same way as any other public company, this would result in a deficit on revaluation of the investments (an unrealised loss) reducing the profit available for distribution, without the benefit of capital profits being taken into account.

Investment companies may make a distribution on the basis of the capital maintenance test for public companies (excluding capital profits) or on the basis of an asset ratio test.

Under the asset ratio test distribution can be made up to the total of

Accumulated *realised* revenue profits
Less: Accumulated revenue losses *(whether realised or not)*
provided that after the distribution
Total assets exceed 150% of liabilities.

2.12 Example

The balance sheets of two investment companies are as follows

	A plc	*B plc*
	£	£
Share capital	100	100
Unrealised capital profits	100	
Unrealised capital losses		(70)
Unrealised revenue profits		30
Unrealised revenue losses	(50)	
Realised capital profits	100	
Realised capital losses		(120)
Realised revenue profits	200	250
	£450	£190
Assets	800	400
Liabilities	(350)	(210)
	£450	£190

	A plc	*B plc*
	£	£
Capital maintenance test		
'Private company' rules		
Net realised profits (not capital profits)	200	
(250 – 120)		130
'Public company' rules		
Less: Unrealised losses	50	40 (70 – 30)
	£150	£90

Asset ratio test		
A plc £(200 – 50)	150	
(Assets would fall to £650 which is more than one-and-a-half times liabilities, so distributable profit is £150.)		
B plc		250
(Assets would fall to £150 which is less than one-and-a-half times liabilities. One-and-a-half times liabilities is £315, thus assets may only fall by £85 so distributable profit is £85 on this basis. Thus B plc will not opt for the asset ratio test. It can make the distribution on the capital maintenance test of £90.)		

2.13 Relevant accounts: S270 CA85

The basis of calculation of what is available for dividend is the *relevant accounts*

(a) Usually the relevant accounts are the latest audited annual accounts laid before the company in general meeting as required by S270 CA85.

When the annual accounts are the basis of calculation the rules are

(i) The accounts must have been properly prepared and also audited.

(ii) The report of the auditors must either be unqualified or, if qualified, accompanied by a statement by the auditors as to whether in their opinion the subject of their qualification is material to the determination of distributable profits. In this context an unqualified report is one which states without qualification that the accounts have been *properly prepared.*

(b) If figures derived from the latest annual accounts would preclude the payment of a dividend, interim accounts may be used but they must be *such as are necessary to enable a reasonable judgement to be made.*

(c) If the company has not yet produced its first annual accounts, interim accounts (as described in (b) above) may be used.

When annual accounts are used under (a) or interim accounts are used under (b) or (c) above, they must be *properly prepared* ie, they must comply with the various rules on statutory accounts and they must give a true and fair view. It is not necessary, however, that they should deal with matters which are not material to the dividend rules. In case (c) the auditors must report whether in their opinion the accounts have been properly prepared.

2.14 Why distributable profits need to be defined

Distributable profits need to be defined in order to set an upper limit on dividend payments. This has the effect of protecting the original capital for the payment of creditors.

However, creditors cannot be protected from the loss of capital arising from poor trading. That is if a loss is made, capital is depleted.

The rules regarding the computation of distributable profits are generally sensible except that the rules regarding revaluation deficits are fairly easily circumvented.

3 CHAPTER SUMMARY

The profit and loss account balance on the balance sheet is the starting point for determining the profits which may legally be distributed as dividends. The law assumes 'normal' accounting conventions have been applied.

Distributable profits can be larger for private companies than public companies since plcs face further restrictions. Certain types of investment companies have relieving provisions from the normal plc rules.

4 SELF TEST QUESTIONS

4.1 What is the CA85 definition of realised profits? (1.1)

4.2 Can an unrealised profit ever be credited to profit and loss account? (1.2)

4.3 What are the profits available for dividend for a limited company? (2.1)

4.4 Is a provision a realised or unrealised loss? (2.2)

4.5 If a company revalues some of its assets and there is a deficit on one of the assets, how do the directors act so that it is not treated as a realised loss? (2.4)

4.6 What are included in undistributable reserves? (2.7)

4.7 What is included in the investment companies' asset ratio test? (2.11)

5 EXAMINATION TYPE QUESTION

5.1 Omega

The balance sheet of Omega as at 30 September 20X5 contained the following balances and notes:

		£'000
Share capital		10,000
Reserves:		
Share premium	*Note 1*	1,000
Revaluation reserve	*Note 2*	1,780
Other reserves:		
Merger reserve	*Note 3*	550
Profit and loss account - 20X5	*Note 4*	1,940
Profit and loss account b/d		(200)
Capital and reserves		15,070
Liabilities		15,070
Total assets		30,140

Note 1 The share premium arose on the issue of shares on 1 October 20X2.

Note 2 The revaluation reserve arose as a result of a revaluation of certain of the fixed assets on 1 October 20X4. It comprises a gain of £2,000,000 on the revaluation of plant and machinery, which is the balance remaining after the transfer to the profit and loss account of £200,000 representing the depreciation on the revaluation surplus; and a loss of £220,000 arising from the revaluation of office premises. The directors propose to revalue the remaining fixed assets which currently appear at historic cost in a subsequent financial year.

Note 3 The merger reserve represented the premium of £550,000 on shares issued on the acquisition on 1 October 20X4 of a subsidiary, Alpha plc in accordance with the merger provisions of the CA85.

Note 4 The profit and loss account balance is the balance after:

(i) creating a provision of £1,200,000 representing an impairment in the value of a subsidiary, Gamma plc.

(ii) the transfer of the £200,000 mentioned in ***Note 2*** from the revaluation reserve to the profit and loss account representing the amount by which the total depreciation charge for the year exceeded the amount that would have been provided if the plant had not been revalued.

(iii) crediting an exchange gain of £38,000 that arose on the translation of a long-term loan taken out in French francs on 1 October 20X4. The loan was taken out to use in the United Kingdom because the interest rate was favourable at the date the loan was raised.

You are required:

(a) to calculate the amount of distributable profit for Omega on the basis that it is:

(i) a public company
(ii) an investment company. **(10 marks)**

(b) to explain briefly:

(i) the disclosure requirements relating to distributable profits in a single company and group context

(ii) the effect on the distributable profits of the holding company if the group has sufficient distributable profits in aggregate to make a distribution to the holding company's shareholders but the holding company itself has insufficient distributable profits

(iii) the effect on the distributable profits of the holding company if the holding company has sold one subsidiary company to another subsidiary for a consideration that exceeds the carrying value of the investment in the holding company's accounts

(iv) the effect on the distributable profits of the holding company if a subsidiary company which has a coterminous accounting period declares a dividend after the end of the holding company's year end. **(10 marks)**

(Total: 20 marks)

6 ANSWER TO EXAMINATION TYPE QUESTION

6.1 Omega

(Tutorial note: although part (a) requires only a calculation, it is sensible to include a short justification as to why you have treated certain items as realised or unrealised.

This is particularly relevant as for some of the points the distinction between realised and unrealised is not clear cut.*)*

(a) (i) **Rules for all companies**

Realised profits less realised losses

	£'000
Per profit and loss account (1,940 – 200)	1,740
Revaluation deficit *(note 1)*	(220)
Exchange gain *(note 2)*	(38)
	1,482

Notes:

(1) Deficit arose on piecemeal revaluation of fixed assets and the directors have not 'considered' the value of the assets. Therefore realised loss.

(2) SSAP20 states that the gain arising on a long term monetary item is unrealised.

Further rule for plc

Maintain share capital and undistributable reserves ie, deduct excess of unrealised losses over unrealised profits.

There are no unrealised losses.

Therefore distributable profits are	£1,482,000

(ii) **Exclude capital profits from net realised profits**

There are no realised capital profits

Distributable profits are	£1,482,000

or Asset ratio test

Realised revenue profits less revenue losses

	£'000
Distributable profits as per private company rules	1,482
Add back realised capital loss (offices)	220
Distribution	1,702

Subject to assets exceeding 150% of liabilities

Assets per balance sheet	30,140
Liabilities 15,070 × 1.5	22,605
Excess	7,535

Therefore distributable profits are £1,702,000

(b) (i) There is no statutory requirement that requires a company to identify the division between distributable and non-distributable reserves. However, in practice, some companies do include a statement with the reserve movements.

The calculation of distributable profits only relates to an individual company and not to a group. Where consolidated accounts are presented, the relevant distributable profits will be the holding company's realised profits.

(ii) This situation mainly arises where the subsidiary companies have not paid dividends to the holding company. As the rules of distribution only apply in an individual context, the subsidiaries will have to declare a dividend which then becomes additional distributable profit to the holding company.

(iii) If the sale is at arm's length and is supported by appropriate documentation, then the surplus on sale would appear to be realised. The fact that the transaction has taken place between companies in the same group need not prevent the profit on the transaction being realised, and therefore distributable. If the transaction is artificial it may be unlawful to make a distribution from the resulting profit. If the arrangement were to have been made through inter-company arrangements, it might be argued that the profit had not been realised.

(iv) If the dividends receivable from a subsidiary are accrued in the holding company's accounts, the dividend would be regarded as realised even if declared after the holding company's year end whether paid or passed through a current account.

12 ACCOUNTING FOR THE EFFECTS OF CHANGING PRICES

INTRODUCTION & LEARNING OBJECTIVES

This chapter covers the two main alternatives to historic cost accounting. Neither approach has been the subject of much discussion in recent years partly due to the lower rates of inflation and partly to the failure of previous attempts to implement an accounting standard.

It is to be expected however that the ASB will raise the importance of changing prices in the context of the balance sheet valuation of assets. Chapter 6 of the Statement of Principles is covered at the end of this chapter.

When you have studied this chapter you should be able to do the following:

- Discuss the development of accounting for the effects of changing prices in the UK to the present day.
- Demonstrate your understanding of how CPP accounts are prepared.
- Show what adjustments need to be made to convert HC accounts to CC accounts.
- Discuss the limitations of CPP and CC accounts.

1 HISTORIC COST ACCOUNTS

1.1 Analysis of reported historic cost profits into their different types of gains/losses

HC accounts are the prevalent form of financial statements in the UK. The strict HC convention is often modified to include the selective revaluation of fixed assets.

Total gains are expressed under FRS 3 in the statement of total recognised gains and losses. Total gains accruing to shareholders are thus the difference between the opening and closing balance sheets after adjusting for changes in capital contributions and dividends. These total gains can be split between:

(a) Revaluation gains arising from the occasional revaluation of fixed assets and
(b) Operating gains which comprise all the other gains reported in the financial statements.

As we shall see, current cost accounting (CCA) and current purchasing power accounting (CPP) recognise some gains and losses not reported under HC accounting and also split the operating gains into different types of gains.

1.2 The deficiencies of a historic cost balance sheet

The pure HC balance sheet ignores the current value of assets and thus the amounts reported are unlikely to be realistic up-to-date measures of the resources employed by the business. The main problems will be unrecorded assets such as goodwill and undervalued assets such as land and buildings.

There is a general consensus that users of financial statements would like details of the current worth of assets which is why many balance sheets do include revaluations.

As no account is taken of the changing value of money over time, it is also difficult to interpret trends.

1.3 The ways in which historic cost accounts can be misleading for decision making purposes

HC accounts can be misleading in a period of changing prices in a number of ways.

(a) **Matching current revenues with out of date costs**

If a business buys an item of stock for £10 and sells it for £20, historic cost accounting would allow distribution of the profit of £10. However if the replacement cost of that item has now risen to £13 that would leave insufficient funds to remain in business.

The concept of operating capital maintenance would only distribute a maximum of £7, arrived at by comparing the current cost of sales of £13 with the current revenue of £20. This would leave £13, sufficient to continue in business.

(b) **Distorted ratios**

With profits overstated in (a) and the balance sheet understated (see above) key ratios such as ROCE can be misleading.

(c) **Fixed monetary items**

No attempt is made to recognise the loss that arises through holding assets of fixed monetary value and the gain that arises through holding liabilities of fixed monetary value.

(d) **Time series information**

If no account is taken of changes in the real value of money a misleading impression may be given by trend information. A company may appear to be increasing turnover and profits but this may only be in monetary, not in real terms.

1.4 Why, despite their limitations, modified historic cost accounts still prevail

Modified HC accounts still prevail because of the past difficulties in finding a suitable alternative. There have been a number of proposals, EDs and SSAPs setting out alternatives and all have foundered.

HC accounts are generally accepted by the business community and thus any dramatic alternative is going to face a significant problem in being implemented. Alternatives tend to require much subjective judgement to be made and the sole advantage of HC accounting - that it is relatively objective - seems to win the day.

1.5 General and specific price changes

The argument for an alternative to HC accounting has revolved around the question of whether accounting for the effects of inflation should be directed towards:

(a) presenting accounts in the same real terms from one year to another; or
(b) protecting the operating capabilities of companies; or
(c) some combination of the two.

Option (a) involves accounting for general price changes. The owners of the business are shareholders who may suffer from general inflation as the purchasing power of their investment in the business declines. Changes in general prices are thus used to record the effect.

Option (b) involves the consideration of specific price changes. Here the perspective of the business as a separate entity is paramount. The effects of price changes on the specific assets owned by the business are therefore used.

The dispute is made more complex by a lack of basic agreement on a definition of the concept of profit.

This is best illustrated by a simple example.

1.6 Example

Alan sets up in business on 1 January with £1,000, which he immediately uses to buy goods for resale. On 31 January he sells these goods for £1,500. At this date the replacement price of the goods to Alan is £1,200. During January the Retail Price Index (RPI) has risen by 30%.

1.7 Solution

In historic cost terms the results of his trading are:

	£
Sales	1,500
Cost of goods sold	1,000
Profit	500

However, if Alan wishes to continue in business at the same level, he must presumably replace the goods he has sold with new stock costing £1,200. If the profit and loss account is to show the amount which can be reasonably distributed while maintaining the operating capability of his business, the profit could more sensibly be stated on a current cost basis as follows:

	£
Sales	1,500
Cost of goods sold (replacement cost)	1,200
Profit	300

But in real terms how much better off is Alan? He began with £1,000 in cash. To maintain his general purchasing power ability he would have needed to have increased this by 30% (rise in the Retail Price Index 1 January to 31 January) to £1,300 by 31 January. In fact, he has £1,500. He is therefore £200 better off in terms of his general purchasing power ability on 31 January than when he started.

Conclusion The profit could variously be argued to be £500 (historical cost), £300 (current cost) or £200 (current purchasing power). The decision as to which (if any) is the correct figure requires basic agreement as to a definition of profit.

1.8 Current purchasing power accounting

Despite the widespread academic support for current value approaches, the first proposals of the ASC were based on current purchasing power accounting.

The ASC's preference for CPP accounting appears to have been based on its relative ease of preparation, its use of basic historic cost records, and its consequential verifiability. It was not demonstrated that the system best met the needs of either internal or external users of accounting information.

1.9 Current value accounting

Although the ASC produced a standard based on CPP accounting *(PSSAP 7)* this was only accorded provisional status because of the appointment of the Sandilands Committee. The Committee reviewed a vast amount of academic and professional evidence on a variety of systems including CPP accounting, economic income and current value systems. Although it appears to have been well aware of the theoretical basis of the various current value systems it was strongly influenced by the fact that Philips NV already operated a system of replacement cost accounting. The origins of this system seem to lie with Bonbright (USA 1936), but were developed by German and Dutch academics between the wars.

The Sandilands Committee's proposals for CCA were developed by the ASC in *ED 18*. However, its original proposals were rejected by the profession. A compromise proposal for a supplementary statement was developed **(Hyde Guidelines)** which eventually formed the basis of *SSAP 16* (1979). These proposals were largely based on the Sandilands system, but extended the definition of operating capital to include monetary working capital, and included an adjustment to CC operating profit to take account of the capital structure/gearing of the firm.

1.10 Recent developments

SSAP 16 was introduced for a trial period, during which the ASC monitored its progress. At the end of this period certain refinements to the standard were advocated *(ED 35)* but drew so much criticism that they were withdrawn. In the light of the decline in the rate of inflation and the considerable hostility to CCA, *SSAP 16* was deemed voluntary. Attempts to produce a replacement have not yet borne fruit. The ASC has published a handbook containing its suggested system, and recent academic discussion has centred on a combination of CCA and CPP known as real terms accounting.

2 CURRENT PURCHASING POWER ACCOUNTING

2.1 Introduction

Under current (or constant) purchasing power (CPP) accounting the accounts are adjusted so that all figures are shown in terms of money with the same purchasing power. It is thus necessary to adjust items by means of a general price index. In the UK the index used for these purposes is the Retail Price Index (RPI) and items are generally restated in terms of the purchasing power at the end of the financial period. This approach formed the basis of *PSSAP 7*, which was proposed by the ASC in 1974, but withdrawn following the report of the Sandilands Committee.

2.2 Gains or losses caused by the impact of general inflation on a company's net monetary position

In converting the figures in the basic historical cost accounts into those in the supplementary current purchasing power statement a distinction is drawn between:

(a) monetary items; and
(b) non-monetary items.

Monetary items are those whose amounts are fixed by contract or otherwise in terms of numbers of pounds, regardless of changes in general price levels. Examples of monetary items are cash, debtors, creditors and loan capital.

Holders of monetary assets lose general purchasing power during a period of inflation to the extent that any income from the assets does not adequately compensate for the loss; the converse applies to those having monetary liabilities.

Non-monetary items include such assets as stock, plant and buildings. The retention of the historical cost concept requires that holders of non-monetary assets are assumed neither to gain nor to lose purchasing power by reason only of changes in the purchasing power of the pound.

The owners of a company's equity capital have the residual claim on its net monetary and non-monetary assets. The equity interest is therefore neither a monetary nor a non-monetary item.

2.3 Preparation of CPP adjusted financial statements

CPP accounts are prepared by adjusting all monetary amounts in the accounts to reflect the value of money at one point in time. Thus, the unit of measurement is the 'CPP unit' rather than the monetary unit. In principle the CPP unit can be based on the value of money at any point in time. In practice the value of money at the balance sheet date is used, in which case CPP can be termed **current** purchasing power accounting rather than constant purchasing power accounting.

CPP accounts are prepared by updating all items in the profit and loss account, and all non-monetary items in the balance sheet, by the CPP factor:

$$\frac{\text{Index at the balance sheet date}}{\text{Index at date of entry in account}}$$

Depreciation is adjusted by reference to the date of acquisition of the related fixed asset item.

Monetary items in the balance sheet are not adjusted, because their value in CPP units is their monetary amount.

In the CPP accounts it is necessary to compute a gain or loss from holding monetary items in times of inflation. In principle this can be found by adjusting all entries in the accounts for each monetary item by the CPP factor, so that the difference between the 'CPP balance' and the actual monetary balance represents the gain or loss on holding that item.

2.4 Example of the preparation of CPP accounts

W Ltd was formed on 1 January 20X8, with a fully-subscribed share capital of £200,000. On the same date a loan of £100,000 was raised.

On 31 March 20X8, storage facilities with a twenty-year life and no residual value were purchased for £150,000. On the same date 1,000 widgets were purchased for £100,000. On 30 June 20X8, 600 widgets were sold for £90,000. Expenses of £10,000 were paid on 30 June 20X8. All transactions were for cash.

The company provides a full year's depreciation in the year of acquisition of an asset.

A general price index moved:

1	January	20X8	660
31	March	20X8	715
30	June	20X8	780
31	December	20X8	858

Assuming straight-line depreciation, you are required to:

(a) prepare historical cost accounts for the year to 31 December 20X8; and
(b) prepare CPP accounts for the year to 31 December 20X8.

2.5 Solution

Step 1 Remember you need to update **all** of the items in the profit and loss account by the CPP factor:

$$\frac{\text{Index at the balance sheet date}}{\text{Index at date of entry in account}}$$

You also need to calculate the loss or gain on monetary items. These calculations are shown in detail in Workings 1 and 2.

W Ltd
Profit and loss account for the year ended 31 December 20X8

	HC £	£	*CPP factor*	*CPP* CPP £	CPP £
Sales		90,000	$\frac{858}{780}$		99,000
Purchases	100,000		$\frac{858}{715}$	120,000	

Less: Closing stock	40,000		$\frac{858}{715}$	48,000	
Cost of sales		60,000			72,000
Gross profit		30,000			27,000
Depreciation	7,500		$\frac{858}{715}$	9,000	
Expenses	10,000		$\frac{858}{780}$	11,000	
		17,500			20,000
					7,000
Loss on monetary items (48,000(W1) – 30,000(W2))					(18,000)
Net profit/(loss)		12,500			(11,000)

Step 2 In the balance sheet it is only the non-monetary items which are adjusted.

Balance sheet as at 31 December 20X8

	£	£		CPP £	CPP £
Plant:					
Cost		150,000	$\frac{858}{715}$		180,000
Depreciation		7,500	$\frac{858}{715}$		9,000
		142,500			171,000
Current assets:					
Stock	40,000		$\frac{858}{715}$	48,000	
Bank	130,000		-	130,000	
		170,000			178,000
		312,500			349,000
Loan		(100,000)			(100,000)
		212,500			249,000
Share capital		200,000	$\frac{858}{660}$		260,000
Retained profit/(loss)		12,500			(11,000)
		212,500			249,000

WORKINGS

			HC £	CPP factor	CPP CPP £
(W1)	**Bank movements**				
	1 January 20X8	Shares issued	200,000	$\frac{858}{660}$	260,000
	1 January 20X8	Loan raised	100,000	$\frac{858}{660}$	130,000
	31 March 20X8	Storage	(150,000)	$\frac{858}{715}$	(180,000)
	31 March 20X8	Purchases	(100,000)	$\frac{858}{715}$	(120,000)
	30 June 20X8	Sales	90,000	$\frac{858}{780}$	99,000
	30 June 20X8	Expenses	(10,000)	$\frac{858}{780}$	(11,000)
	Loss on monetary items (Bal fig)				48,000
	31 December 20X8	Balance c/f	130,000		130,000
(W2)	**Loan movement**				
	1 January 20X8	Loan raised	100,000	$\frac{858}{660}$	130,000
	Gain on monetary item (Bal fig)				(30,000)
	31 December 20X8	Balance	100,000		100,000

Note that this is a simple example designed to illustrate the principles of CPP. In practice, with more complex examples, less detailed translation methods are used, particularly to avoid the amount of analysis of monetary items that would be necessary with the example above.

2.6 The strengths and weaknesses of the CPP model

CPP accounting has the great merit that it leaves unchanged the basic historic cost accounting records of the company. Therefore, it is verifiable and said to be 'objective'. Some argue that the use of the RPI to measure the effect of changing purchasing power is inappropriate, because it does not represent the effect of specific price changes on the company. However, it may be argued that it is consistent with proprietorship theory in that it measures the impact on the company in terms of shareholders' purchasing power. This argument rests upon the assumption that the RPI is representative of the expenditure pattern of typical shareholders.

The Sandilands Committee rejected CPP statements stating they 'do not attempt to provide a comprehensive statement of the 'value to the business' of net assets. The use of the RPI as a measure of the change in the 'purchasing power' of money gives a poor indication of the effects of inflation on companies'. The Committee argued that presentation as a supplementary set of statements would be likely 'to detract significantly from any usefulness the CPP method may have'. It was also suggested that the system was 'complicated and conceptually the most difficult'. The Committee concluded that 'If UK company accounts are to show more adequately than at present the effects of changing prices, it is accounting practices that must be changed, not the unit of measurement in which amounts are expressed.'

2.7 Activity

U plc buys and sells sprocket-flanges. During the three months ended 31 March 20X6 the company enters into the following transactions:

1 Jan 20X6	Buy 500 units costing £750.
31 Jan 20X6	Sell 400 units for £2,000. Replace them with units costing £1,400.
28 Feb 20X6	Sell 200 units for £1,000. Buy 50 units costing £200.
31 Mar 20X6	Sell 200 units for £1,100. Buy 100 units costing £500.

The retail price index during the period was as follows:

1 Jan 20X6	200
31 Jan 20X6	220
28 Feb 20X6	230
31 Mar 20X6	240

You are required to prepare a trading account using CPP accounting.

2.8 Activity solution

			CPP £
Sales			
31 Jan		$2{,}000 \times \frac{240}{220}$	2,182
28 Feb		$1{,}000 \times \frac{240}{230}$	1,043
31 Mar			1,100
			4,325
Cost of sales			
Purchased	1 Jan	$750 \times \frac{240}{200}$	900
	31 Jan	$1{,}400 \times \frac{3}{4} \times \frac{240}{220}$	1,145
			2,045
Gross profit			2,280

Conclusion All profit and loss items must be adjusted by the CPP factor.

3 CURRENT COST ACCOUNTING

3.1 The Sandilands Committee – Appointment and terms of reference

On 21 January 1974, shortly before the issue of *PSSAP 7,* the Government appointed a Committee on Inflation Accounting under the chairmanship of Sir Francis Sandilands. The terms of reference of the Committee were:

To consider whether, and if so how, company accounts should allow for changes (including relative changes) in costs and prices, having regard to established accounting conventions based on historic costs, the proposal for current general purchasing power accounting put forward by the Accounting Standards Steering Committee, and other possible accounting methods of allowing for price changes, and to make recommendations.

The Committee reviewed evidence from a wide range of bodies and academics and experience of accounting for inflation gained in other countries. It was strongly influenced by evidence concerning the system of replacement cost accounting operated by Philips NV and its subsidiaries. The report, which advocated a similar system, referred to as current cost accounting, was published in 1975.

3.2 Conclusions of the Committee

The Committee identified the following principles of a useful (relevant) accounting system:

(a) Money should be the unit of measurement.

CPP accounting falls outside this framework because it does not utilise the £ as a monetary unit. The Committee drew the conclusion that the most useful method of accounting for inflation in the longer term is a system based on the use of the monetary unit as the unit of measurement.

(b) The current cost accounts should be the main accounts to be published.

(c) Assets should be shown at their **value to the business**. In the majority of cases this will be their written down current replacement cost but may in some cases be their net realisable value or 'economic value' (see below).

(d) Liabilities should be measured generally on the same basis as assets although in practice this may cause difficulties.

(e) A figure of **operating profit** should be regarded as the profit for the year. It is arrived at by charging against the amounts realised for a company's output during the year the 'value to the business' of the assets consumed in generating those amounts.

Holding gains and extraordinary gains, which would be excluded from operating profit, should be shown separately.

Definition A holding gain is a gain made in monetary terms simply by holding an asset in a period of rising prices. Holding gains may be **realised**, ie, the assets have been used up in the business or sold or **unrealised**, ie, the item has increased in value but the gain is only a book gain.

(f) A cash flow statement for the year should be attached to the accounts.

(g) Accounting statements, as far as possible, should meet seven general qualifications: objectivity, realism, prudence, comparability, consistency, intelligibility and ease and economy in preparation.

3.3 The concept of deprival value

Determination of value to the business (alternatively known as deprival value)

In cases where:	*The correct basis of valuation is:*
1 NRV > PV > RC	RC
2 NRV > RC > PV	RC
3 PV > RC > NRV	RC
4 PV > NRV > RC	RC
5 RC > PV > NRV	PV
6 RC > NRV > PV	NRV

Key:

NRV = Net realisable value.

PV = Present value of net cash flows derived from the expected use of the asset. Also known as **economic value** or **value in use**.

RC = Replacement cost.

Deprival value is derived in two stages:

(i) Recoverable amount = The **higher** of net realisable value and economic value

This is because if management own an asset, they have control over the choice between use and disposal, and if it is economically rational they will choose the option having the highest value.

(ii) Deprival value = The **lower** of replacement cost and recoverable amount

This is because if deprived of an asset, management have a choice as to whether or not to replace it. If it is economically rational they will replace the asset only if they can generate a surplus either by resale or by use.

3.4 Developments after Sandilands

A working party under Sir Douglas Morpeth was established by the ASC to implement CCA. It produced *ED 18*, published in October 1976, which contained detailed proposals for a system of current cost accounting to replace historic costs within a short timetable for all but the smallest companies. The proposals met considerable opposition, most notably from smaller practitioners, and, following an EGM of the ICAEW in June 1977, were withdrawn. Following the rejection of *ED 18* the ASC established a committee under Mr William Hyde to develop interim proposals. The guidelines developed recommended a voluntary supplementary CCA statement for listed and other large companies. These provisions formed the basis of *SSAP 16* issued in 1980. In contrast to the Sandilands proposals, *SSAP 16*:

(a) retained HC accounts, but required a CCA supplementary statement;
(b) only applied to large companies;
(c) contained adjustments for monetary working capital and gearing.

Although *SSAP 16* is not now an accounting standard, the principles of CCA are part of the syllabus for the examination.

3.5 SSAP 16: Current cost accounting – basic approach

The CCA system is based upon a concept of capital which is represented by the **net operating assets** of the business – ie, the **operating capability**. A change in the input prices of goods and services used and financed by the business will affect the amount of funds required to **maintain the operating capability** of the net operating assets. CCA, in contrast to HCA, is designed to reflect this in the determination of profit and in the balance sheet.

3.6 Operating capability

For a manufacturing company the balance sheet may be expressed diagrammatically as follows:

OPERATING CAPABILITY (represented by net operating assets)	FINANCING
Fixed assets	**Shareholders' Funds**
Working capital (a) Stock (b) Monetary working capital (debtors less creditors)	**Borrowings**

SSAP 16 highlights attention on the impact of **input price changes** on the funds required to maintain a business's operating capability.

Definition Operating capability is the amount of goods and services which the business is able to supply in the period, with its existing resources. In accounting terms, it is represented by net operating assets.

Definition Input prices mean prices of goods and services used by a business, and include direct costs such as raw materials and wages, as well as costs of production overheads and fixed assets.

3.7 Capital maintenance concept

SSAP 16 emphasises two CCA profit figures:

(a) **Current cost operating profit**

(i) Surplus arising from ordinary activities of the business after allowing for impact of price changes on funds needed to continue the business and maintain its operating capability.

(ii) Determined **before** interest and tax.

(iii) Takes no account of the way operating capability is financed between shareholders' funds and borrowings.

(b) **Current cost profit attributable to shareholders**

(i) Surplus arising after allowing for impact of price changes on funds needed to maintain shareholders' proportion of operating capability (takes gearing into account).

(ii) Determined **after** interest, tax and extraordinary items.

3.8 The four main current cost adjustments

There are four main adjustments to the historical cost profit and loss account:

(a) depreciation adjustment (additional depreciation);

(b) cost of sales adjustment (COSA);

(c) monetary working capital adjustment (MWCA);

(d) gearing adjustment.

Their relationship to the two CCA profit figures may be shown as follows, assuming prices are rising throughout the period:

	£	£
Historical cost profit before interest and tax		X
Less: Depreciation adjustment	X	
Cost of sales adjustment	X	
Monetary working capital adjustment	X	
		X
Current cost operating profit		X
Less: Interest payable	X	
Tax	X	
	X	
Add: Gearing adjustment	(X)	
		X
Current cost profit attributable to shareholders		X
Less: Dividends		(X)

The purpose of each of these adjustments and their method of calculation is described later in this chapter.

3.9 Current cost balance sheet

In drawing up the current cost balance sheet, the following principles are observed:

(a) **Fixed assets**

These are stated at **value to the business**. In the case of non-specialist buildings, this is the estimated market value of the building. In the case of other fixed assets, value to the business is defined as net current replacement cost or, if an impairment to below net replacement cost has been recognised, recoverable amount.

Net current replacement cost is normally derived from gross current replacement cost by reference to the proportion of the total working life that remains. It therefore represents the cost of purchasing a similar asset of the same age. The most convenient method of calculating the gross current replacement cost is normally through the application of relevant indices to existing gross book values.

The recoverable amount is calculated by taking the greater of the estimated amounts, at current price levels, which can be recovered either through the continued use of the asset in the business for a limited period, or through its disposal, if this is envisaged.

(b) **Stock**

This is also stated at value to the business, ie, the lower of replacement cost (generally calculated by revaluing to the balance sheet date by means of indices) and recoverable amount.

(c) **Other items**

Most other items appear as in the historical cost balance sheet, with the addition of a current cost reserve.

3.10 Calculation of current cost figures – Example

Set out below is a detailed example of the application of *SSAP 16* to historical cost accounts. The methods of calculation of current cost figures and the format of the statements are not compulsory, but are based on the guidance notes issued with the standard. Variations are acceptable provided they accord with the principles outlined.

3.11 Example

IP Ltd is an established manufacturing company. The following draft historical cost accounts have been prepared for the year to 31 December 20X5.

Trading and profit and loss account for the year ended 31 December 20X5

	£'000	£'000
Sales		8,000
Opening stock	520	
Purchases	6,400	
	6,920	
Closing stock	720	
		6,200
Gross profit		1,800
Depreciation	420	
Expenses (including interest payable – £75,000)	318	
		738
Net profit before taxation		1,062
Corporation tax		510
		552
Dividends: Interim paid	100	
Final proposed	200	
		300
Retained profit for the year		252

Balance sheet as at 31 December 20X5

	20X5		*20X4*	
	£'000	£'000	£'000	£'000
Fixed assets		3,580		3,200
Current assets:				
Stock	720		520	
Trade debtors	2,180		1,700	
Cash	15		180	
	2,915		2,400	
Current liabilities				
Trade creditors	1,228		985	
Final dividend	200		150	
Corporation tax	510		260	
	1,938		1,395	
Net current assets		977		1,005
		4,557		4,205
Ordinary shares of £1 each, authorised, issued and fully paid		1,500		1,500
Revenue reserves		2,057		1,805
		3,557		3,305

10% Debenture stock	750	750
Deferred taxation	250	150
	4,557	4,205

Additional information

(1) Fixed assets:

	31 December 20X5	*31 December 20X4*
	£'000	£'000
Cost	4,800	4,000
Accumulated depreciation	1,220	800
	3,580	3,200

The company acquired additional plant and machinery on 30 September 20X5. There were no disposals in 20X5 and the assets held on 1 January 20X5 were originally acquired on 1 January 20X3. The company depreciates at a rate of 10% on a straight line basis.

(2) Sales, purchases and expenses have occurred evenly during the year.

(3) Both opening and closing stock represent two months' purchases.

(4) Debtors and creditors at each balance sheet date represent three months' sales and purchases.

(5) The following index numbers are considered appropriate:

	Plant and machinery	*COSA & MWCA*
20X2 December	104.5	-
20X3 January	105.5	-
20X4 October	-	173.3
November	-	175.4
December	114.5	177.4
20X5 January	115.5	179.6
August	121.4	193.6
September	121.8	195.6
October	122.2	197.9
November	123.3	200.0
December	124.7	202.4
20X6 January	125.3	204.4
20X5 Average for year	120.0	190.8

Each index is appropriate to the middle of the month concerned.

Show the supplementary current cost accounts in accordance with SSAP 16.

3.12 Solution: Current cost profit and loss account

Under the accruals concept of *SSAP 2* revenue is determined for a particular period and then the applicable costs are matched against that revenue to determine the profit. In historical cost accounts the costs are based on historical values. Current cost accounting follows the same matching principle, but requires the matching to be at the same price level as the sales revenue. This can be achieved either by allocating individual costs to particular sales on the basis of costs ruling at the date of the sale or, more practically, by some method of averaging.

Step 1 **Cost of sales adjustment**

The averaging adjustment attempts to put all items in the trading account on the same index as the sales.

Trading account

	£		£
Opening stock	X	Sales	X
Purchases	X		
	X		
Less: Closing stock	(X)		
Cost of goods sold	X		
Gross profit	X		
	X		X

The purpose of the cost of sales adjustment is to eliminate that part of the gross profit which is purely a holding gain, ie, an inflationary increase in value of goods held in stock prior to sale.

Assuming the sales are evenly spread, they will be centred around the middle of the year and will be at a price level which is the average for the year.

If the sales are evenly spread and any increase in stock occurs evenly over the year, purchases will also be evenly spread and will therefore also be at an average price level for the year.

However, the opening and closing stock, according to the question, arose in November and December of each year. To obtain the current cost of goods sold, the stocks must therefore be restated at an average price for the year.

The index applicable to opening stock is:

$$\frac{175.4 + 177.4}{2} = 176.4$$

The index applicable to closing stock is:

$$\frac{200.0 + 202.4}{2} = 201.2$$

The average index for the year is given as 190.8.

The stock can, therefore, be restated as follows:

	Historical cost £'000	*Index adjustment*	*Current cost* £'000	*Adjustment* £'000
Opening stock	520	$\frac{190.8}{176.4}$	562.4	42.4
Closing stock	720	$\frac{190.8}{201.2}$	682.8	37.2
				79.6

The debit for opening stock in the trading account is increased by £42,400. The credit for closing stock is reduced by £37,200. The effect is to increase the cost of goods sold by the total of these two, £79,600.

Step 2 **Depreciation adjustment**

Historic cost depreciation charged in the accounts amounted to £420,000. From the fixed asset note it can be easily determined that this comprises:

		£'000
(i)	On assets owned for whole year – 10% × £4,000,000	400
(ii)	On assets purchased at beginning of last quarter – 1/4 × 10% × £800,000	20
		420

This requires to be restated at the average cost for the period of assets' use during the year. The above figures are based on the prices at which the assets were purchased. The indices applicable are:

(i) 1 January 20X3 $\frac{104.5 + 105.5}{2} = 105$

(ii) 30 September 20X5 $\frac{121.8 + 122.2}{2} = 122$

(*Note:* the indices given in the illustration are stated as relating to the middle of each month.)

Averages for periods of use during the year are:

(i) Average for year $= 120.0$

(ii) Average for last quarter $\frac{122.2 + 123.3 + 124.7}{3} = 123.4$

The depreciation charge can therefore be restated as follows:

	Historical cost £'000	*Index adjustment*	*Current cost* £'000	*Adjustment* £'000
Assets owned all year	400	$\frac{120}{105}$	457.1	57.1
Assets bought 30 September	20	$\frac{123.4}{122}$	20.2	0.2
				57.3

The depreciation charge increases by £57,300 when based on current costs.

Step 3 **Monetary working capital adjustment**

Monetary working capital is the aggregate of:

(i) trade debtors, prepayments and trade bills receivable; plus

(ii) stocks not subject to a cost of sales adjustment because such an adjustment is considered inappropriate; less

(iii) trade creditors, accruals and trade bills payable in so far as they arise from the day-to-day transactions of the business as distinct from transactions of a capital nature.

Bank balances and overdrafts may fluctuate with the volume of stock or the items in (i), (ii) or (iii) above. That part of bank balances or overdrafts arising from such fluctuations should be included in monetary working capital, together with any cash float required to support the day-to-day operations of the business if doing so has a material effect on the current cost operating profit.

The adjustment is intended to reflect:

(1) the inflationary cost of maintaining those monetary assets which are considered to be an essential component in the operating capability of the business; and

(2) the effective contribution that inflationary increases in those liabilities which arise directly from trading make towards the cost of (1) and the cost of replacing stock at current cost represented by the cost of sales adjustment.

The adjustment can be calculated in a number of ways, but *SSAP 16* suggested that when the averaging method is used for the cost of sales adjustment, as above, the same method could be used for the MWC adjustment.

The index applicable to opening MWC is:

$$\frac{173.3 + 175.4 + 177.4}{3} = 175.4$$

The index applicable to closing MWC is:

$$\frac{197.9 + 200.0 + 202.4}{3} = 200.1$$

The average index for the year is given as 190.8.

Restatement of MWC at mid-year prices produces the following differences:

	Historical cost	*Index adjustment*	*Current cost*	*Adjustment*
	£'000		£'000	£'000
Opening MWC	715	$\frac{190.8}{175.4}$	777.8	62.8
Closing MWC	952	$\frac{190.8}{200.1}$	907.8	44.2
				107.0

The £107,000 represents the inflationary cost of maintaining the average volume of MWC during the year. If the opening volume of MWC was maintained until the middle of the year, it would have risen by £62,800 as a result of price increases. Similarly, if the closing volume of MWC originated at the middle of the year, the closing figure includes £44,200 resulting from price increases.

Step 4 **Gearing adjustment**

This is based on the average relative proportions of **shareholders' interest** and **other monetary items** applicable to the year.

Shareholders' interest includes:

(i) ordinary share capital;
(ii) preference share capital;
(iii) reserves at current cost;
(iv) minority interest;
(v) dividends payable.

To calculate the reserves to be included, it is necessary to add to the historical cost reserves the increases which will result from stating fixed assets and stock at current cost at the balance sheet dates. Where these valuations are to be based on an index, they are obtained by multiplying the historical cost **net book values** by:

$$\frac{\text{Index at balance sheet date}}{\text{Index at origin of historical cost figure}}$$

The bottom line has already been determined for use in the depreciation and cost of sales adjustments. In the illustration the top line is the average of the mid-December and mid-January indices provided. The calculation may best be set out as follows:

		20X5			*20X4*	
		£'000	£'000		£'000	£'000
Per HC balance sheet:						
Ordinary shares			1,500.0			1,500.0
Reserves			2,057.0			1,805.0
Dividends payable			200.0			150.0
Increases in non-monetary assets to current cost at balance sheet date:						
Fixed assets:						
Purchased in 20X5						
HC NBV		780.0				
CC NBV	$(\times \frac{125}{122})$	799.2				
			19.2			
Purchased 1 January 20X3						
HC NBV		2,800.0			3,200.0	
CC NBV	$(\times \frac{125}{105})$	3,333.3		$(\times \frac{115}{105})$	3,504.8	
			533.3			304.8
Stock:						
HC		720.0			520.0	
CC	$(\times \frac{203.4}{201.2})$	727.9		$(\times \frac{178.5}{176.4})$	526.2	
			7.9			6.2
Shareholders' interest at current cost			4,317.4			3,766.0

The average is therefore $\frac{4,317.4 + 3,766.0}{2} = 4,041.7$

Other monetary items are those which have not been treated as monetary working capital or shareholders' interest. They therefore include:

(i) loans;
(ii) deferred taxation;
(iii) current taxation;
(iv) all amounts of cash or overdrafts not included in monetary working capital.

The total in the example is:

	20X5	*20X4*
	£'000	£'000
Debentures	750	750
Deferred taxation	250	150
Corporation taxation	510	260
	1,510	1,160
Less: Cash	15	180
	1,495	980

The average is therefore $\frac{1,495 + 980}{2} = 1,237.5$

The gearing adjustment adds back the proportion of the depreciation, cost of sales and monetary working capital adjustments which can be expected to be financed by the other monetary items and is calculated by multiplying the net total of the three adjustments by:

$$\frac{\text{Average other monetary items}}{(\text{Average other monetary items} + \text{average shareholders' interest})}$$

In the example this becomes:

$$1,000 \times (57.3 + 79.6 + 107.0) \times \frac{1,237.5}{1,237.5 + 4,041.7} = £57,200$$

No adjustment is required where other monetary items amount to a net asset, since in those circumstances the cash is considered to be surplus to operations, not having been included in MWC.

Step 5 The current cost profit and loss account may now be prepared:

IP Ltd
Current cost profit and loss account for the year ended 31 December 20X5

	£'000	£'000
Turnover		8,000
Profit before interest and taxation on the historical cost basis		1,137
Less: Current cost operating adjustments (see note)		244
Current cost operating profit		893
Gearing adjustment	(57)	
Interest payable	75	
		18
Current cost profit before taxation		875
Taxation		510
Current cost profit attributable to shareholders		365
Dividends		300
Retained current cost profit of the year		65
Current cost earnings per share		24.3p

Note:

Adjustments made in deriving current cost operating profit:

	£'000
Cost of sales	80
Monetary working capital	107
Working capital	187
Depreciation	57
Current cost operating adjustments	244

3.13 Solution: Current cost balance sheet

This is the same as the historical cost balance sheet except that:

(a) the retained profit figure is reduced by the net total of all current cost adjustments made in the current cost profit and loss account;

(b) the non-monetary assets are shown at net current cost at balance sheet date, as calculated for the gearing adjustment; and

(c) the total of the adjustments in (a) and (b) is shown as the **current cost reserve**.

Step 1 **Retained profit**

20X4 £'000	*20X4* £'000		*20X5* £'000	*20X5* £'000
	1,805.0	Per HC accounts		2,057.0
		Less: CC adjustments made to date in current cost profit and loss account		
-		Depreciation adjustment	57.3	
-		Cost of sales adjustment	79.6	
-		Monetary working capital adjustment	107.0	
-		Gearing adjustment	(57.2)	
				186.7
	1,805.0			1,870.3

Step 2 **Current cost reserve**

20X4 £'000	*20X4* £'000		*20X5* £'000	*20X5* £'000
		CC adjustments above		186.7
		Unrealised surpluses arising on restatement of historical cost at 31 December 20X5 as per gearing adjustment:		
-		Fixed assets	19.2	
304.8			533.3	
	304.8			552.5
	6.2	Stock		7.9
	311.0	Total for current cost balance sheet		747.1

Step 3 **Current cost balance sheet as at 31 December 20X5**

20X4			*20X5*	
£'000	£'000		£'000	£'000
		Assets employed:		
	3,505	Fixed assets		4,132
		Net current assets:		
526		Stock	728	
715		Monetary working capital	952	
1,241		Total working capital	1,680	
(150)		Proposed dividends	(200)	
(80)		Other current liabilities (net of cash)	(495)	
	1,011			985
	4,516			5,117
		Financed by:		
		Share capital and reserves:		
1,500		Share capital	1,500	
311		Current cost reserve	747	
1,805		Retained profit	1,870	
	3,616			4,117
	750	Loan capital		750
	150	Deferred taxation		250
	4,516			5,117

Note that the only assets restated to current cost are those which are non-monetary, ie, fixed assets and stock. Monetary assets and liabilities will be realised or paid at their contractual amount, ie, their historical cost. Cash is netted against current liabilities.

Note also that the revaluation of fixed assets and stock is intended to show them at net current cost at the balance sheet date, not the average values used for the current cost adjustments in the profit and loss account.

Conclusion It should now be evident that the double entry for the current cost profit and loss adjustments is effectively between retained profit and current cost reserve. The adjustments do not therefore change the total reserve balance shown in the historical cost balance sheet. This is only affected in total by the net balance sheet revaluations of fixed assets and stock. The current cost profit and loss adjustments were therefore ignored when determining shareholders' interest for the gearing adjustment.

3.14 The strengths and criticisms of the current cost deprival value model

SSAP 16 has been criticised on a number of grounds:

(a) The inclusion of a monetary working capital adjustment and a gearing adjustment:

 (i) Causes problems of definition, particularly in relation to cash and overdrafts.

 (ii) Treats preference share capital like equity, although it is, in reality, nearer to borrowings in terms of sources of finance. This is due to the need to show profit attributable to all shareholders, ordinary and preference, as required by the Companies Acts.

The guidance notes suggest that where a company has a material amount of preference shares with fixed repayment rights, it may wish to show in a note the effect of including preference share capital in net borrowings.

(iii) Includes in borrowings such disparate items as taxation and debentures. While the latter might be expected to be maintainable in a constant ratio to equity (excluding preference shares), the former will, under *SSAP 15* vary in relation to taxable profit.

(b) It can be argued that the monetary working capital and gearing adjustments reflect some of the benefit of borrowing in a period of inflation, by allowing for the netting off or adding back of that portion of the realised holding gains financed by monetary liabilities.

However, there is still no indication given of the real effect, in general purchasing power terms, of inflation on the investor's stake.

(c) Profits are not comparable in real terms from year to year, nor from company to company within any one year.

(d) Treatment of backlog depreciation: it is debited to current cost reserve (reducing the unrealised holding gain on fixed assets). Would it be better to treat it as under-provision for depreciation in earlier years and set it against cumulative retained current cost profits? Otherwise cumulative retained current cost profit will not represent the amount which can be distributed without depleting the operating capability.

To counter the problems raised in (b) and (c) above *SSAP 16* suggested that additional voluntary disclosures could be made.

In particular the standard did not deal with the maintenance of financial capital in general purchasing power terms. Some users of accounts may be interested in a statement of the change in shareholders' equity interest after allowing for the change in the general purchasing power of money.

SSAP 16 also recognised that as with accounts drawn up on the historical cost basis the CCA figures for profit and capital employed in different years are not comparable unless they are adjusted to a common price basis.

3.15 Practical problems in operating current cost accounting

Amongst the practical problems encountered in operating current cost accounting are the following:

(a) **Selection of a suitable index**

It is not always easy to obtain an index which is perfectly suitable for measuring the movement in the current cost of a particular type of asset. This need not be an insuperable problem because the company may be able to construct its own index, or to apply one which gives results which do not materially distort the result.

(b) **Overseas assets**

It is often difficult to obtain a suitable index for use with overseas assets. Once again a proxy is often possible.

(c) **Valuation of specialist plant and buildings**

It is often difficult to obtain a suitable market value for specialist items, but indices may be constructed as an alternative.

(d) **There may be no intention to replace an asset, possibly due to a change in the nature of the business**

In such a case the current cost of the existing asset was not given a relevant adjustment. Where a company is trying to maintain its operating capacity in a different area it should use a suitable index based on a possible replacement in the new field of activity.

(e) **There may be no modern equivalent asset due to the advance of technology**

In such a case it is necessary to calculate what proportion of the cost of a new asset is required in order to maintain the volume of output and determine the current cost of the old equivalent therefrom. That part of the charge which gives added output or cost advantages should be disregarded.

(f) **It may be difficult to audit some of the adjustments**

In practice it is generally no more difficult to verify these areas than other subjective aspects of accounting.

4 THE 'REAL TERMS' SYSTEM

4.1 The review of SSAP 16

Between 1977 and 1984 most major companies included a supplementary current cost statement in their accounts. From 1980 it was a requirement of *SSAP 16*. During this latter period the CCA Monitoring Working Party (the Neville Committee) undertook a review of experience gained in operating the standard. As its deliberations were drawing to a close the ICAEW Research Directorate completed a (somewhat hurried) study known as the **Carsberg Report**.

The Neville Committee concluded that CC accounts were little used in practice, and their value was doubtful in relation to specialised industries such as oil, shipping and property. There was no support for an extension of CC accounting to small firms. Although the committee lacked enthusiasm for CC accounts it considered that they should be retained as a note to the accounts rather than as a supplementary statement.

Carsberg suggested that in view of their comparatively recent introduction CC accounts were surprisingly widely used. He found that adjusting for current costs was generally beneficial and cost effective for large firms. He also suggested the continuation of CCA, subject to a number of alterations to the standard, whilst research continued in an attempt to find an ideal system of adjustment for changing prices.

4.2 The search for a successor to SSAP 16

In developing a successor to *SSAP 16* the ASC sought a standard which would be 'universal'. It was considered that this was essential since all registered companies are covered by the same obligation to show a true and fair view. However, the strong opposition to CCA by small companies meant that compliance with an inflexible standard was likely to be minimal.

On this basis the ASC issued *ED 35*. This specified that certain current cost information should be shown as a note to the accounts (if not the main accounts) and not as a supplementary statement. The requirement applied to listed companies. Smaller companies were to be covered by alternative provisions in due course.

ED 35 did not meet with success and was withdrawn followed in 1988 by the withdrawal of *SSAP 16*.

4.3 The ASC Handbook – Accounting for the effects of changing prices

Following the suspension of *SSAP 16* the ASC recognised that none of the proposals for showing the effects of changing prices had gained universal acceptance and noted that there remained disagreement as to the appropriate method. Nonetheless it was felt valuable to publish a handbook in which the objective was to identify those methods which may be adopted and to identify those which the ASC considered most appropriate.

The committee began by arguing that historical cost accounting has considerable weaknesses. It stated:

'Historical cost accounting is a universally recognised accounting convention which continues to be the method of financial reporting preferred by most business enterprises, and is an accepted basis for the legal accounts of enterprises throughout the European Community. However, the ASC considers that, by their nature, historical cost accounts cannot give fully up-to-date information about a company's results and financial position, and this is especially so in times of volatile prices. While the ASC does not assert that historical cost accounting is 'wrong', it does believe that it has serious limitations in times of changing prices.'

The Handbook identifies three variables in the alternative approaches to measuring profit:

(a) the basis to be adopted for valuing assets;
(b) the capital maintenance concept to be used; and
(c) the unit of measurement to be used.

These three variables may be manipulated to produce eight alternative accounting systems, of which four are practicable possibilities.

Asset valuation (cost)	*Capital maintenance concept*	*Unit of measurement*	*System of accounting*
1 HC	FCM	£	HCA
2 HC	FCM	CPP	CPP
3 HC	OCM	£	
4 HC	OCM	CPP	
5 CC	FCM	£	RTA
6 CC	FCM	CPP	
7 CC	OCM	£	CCA
8 CC	OCM	CPP	

The crucial distinction between real terms accounting (RTA) and CCA lies in the use of a financial capital maintenance concept (FCM) in the former, and an operating capital maintenance concept (OCM) in the latter.

Operating capital maintenance can be expressed in a number of ways but it is usual to express it as the productive capacity of the company's assets in terms of goods and services capable of being produced (the volume concept). A number of practical points of difficulty arise:

(a) Defining operating capital – various definitions have been proposed embracing only tangible items (stock/work-in-progress), and tangible items plus some (net) monetary assets.

(b) The impact of technological and market changes on operating capacity.

(c) The irrelevance of 'operating capacity' to certain types of firm.

The OCM approach was adopted by the Sandilands Committee and formed the basis of all ASC proposals up to *SSAP 16*. The difficulties referred to above have led to recognition of the merits of the FCM approach and of real terms accounting.

4.4 Preparation of current cost accounts in accordance with the ASC's Handbook

The basic approach to profit measurement under the real terms system is to:

(a) calculate the shareholders' funds at the beginning of the period based on current cost asset values;

(b) restate that amount in terms of pounds of the reporting date (by adjusting (a) by the relevant change in a general index such as the RPI); and

(c) compare (b) with the shareholders' funds at the end of the year based on current cost asset values.

This comparison indicates whether or not the real financial capital has been maintained. If the year-end figure is larger than the restated opening figure, a real terms profit has been made.

(Introductions and withdrawals of capital, including dividends, need to be allowed for in the three steps set out above.)

Since, under the real terms system, profit results from a comparison of opening and closing shareholders' funds (ie, net assets) at current cost (after adjusting for additions to capital and distributions of profit or repayment of capital), any real increase or decrease in the current costs of assets forms part of reported total gains. This contrasts with most versions of the operating capital maintenance approach in which such gains or losses are taken direct to a current cost reserve – as advocated by *SSAP 16*.

Although a real terms total gains figure is considered to be a useful piece of information about a company's performance, it does not necessarily follow that the total gains could be fully distributed if the company wishes to continue in business at the same level of activity. This is so because the maintenance of a company's real financial capital does not guarantee the maintenance of its operating capital.

4.5 Basic layout using the real terms system

While the simple comparison of opening and closing balance sheets is a way of expressing how profit is determined, it is not an adequate way of reporting profitability as it gives insufficient information about the components of the profit figure. Information on a real terms system can be presented in a number of ways, as shown below. However, total real gains are usually determined by making the following two adjustments to historical cost profit:

(a) adding holding gains, that is the amount by which the current cost of a company's assets has increased during the year; and

(b) deducting the amount by which general inflation has eroded the purchasing power of the shareholders' funds during the year.

Component (a) is the total nominal increase in asset values; this amount is unrealised (realised gains being included in historical cost profit). Component (b) deducts from that amount a charge for the effect of general inflation, leaving the 'real' (but unrealised) gain or loss.

The simplest layout of results under the real terms system focuses on these two adjustments.

4.6 Example

The current cost valuations as computed for IP Ltd provide the figures for unrealised holding gains. The retail price index would normally be used to compute the general inflation adjustment. During the year ended 20X5 the RPI has risen from 175 to 200.

IP Ltd
Adjusted earnings statement year ended 20X5

	£'000	£'000
Historical cost profit after taxation		552
Add: (a) Unrealised holding gains arising during the year (W1)	249	
Less: (b) Inflation adjustment to shareholders' funds (W2)	516	
Real holding loss		(267)
Total real gains		285

WORKINGS

(W1) Unrealised holding gains arising during the year.

Step 4 above shows the amounts within the current cost reserve at the beginning and end of the year. Realised holding gains are essentially **transfers** between the profit and loss account and the current cost reserve and do not increase the **total** gains arising in the year.

The unrealised holding gains arising during the year are the difference between:

	£'000	£'000
UHG at year end:		
Fixed assets	552.5	
Stock	7.9	
		560.4
UHG at beginning of year:		
Fixed assets	304.8	
Stock	6.2	
		311.0
		249.4

(W2) Opening shareholders' funds

Must reflect current cost values of assets at the beginning of the year.

	£'000
Share capital	1,500
HC reserves at 1 January 20X5	1,805
Unrealised holding gains at 1 January 20X5 (W1)	311
	3,616

Adjustment $3,616,000 \times \frac{25}{175}$ 516.6

Conclusion This presentation emphasises real asset appreciation, by focusing on whether or not the specific price changes of assets held were greater than or less than the effect of general inflation on the shareholders' funds. In this example prices of the specific assets held have not increased more than prices generally.

5 THE ASB'S CONTRIBUTION TO THE DEBATE

5.1 Measurement systems

Chapter 6 of the ASB's Statement of Principles considers measurement in financial statements. The first draft of this chapter was issued as part of an Exposure Draft in 1995. The chapter began by contrasting historic cost with the alternatives: a system of measurement based on current values; and adjustments for the effects of general inflation.

Historic cost

The chapter set out the advantages of the historic cost basis: objectivity, reliability, familiarity and understandability. The main disadvantage is its lack of relevance to the current state of the business, because:

- the balance sheet does not provide an accurate representation of the current financial position; and
- the profit and loss account reports gains on holding assets when they are realised rather than when they occur: one effect is that no distinction is drawn between gains that have been made in past periods but are realised in the current period and those that are both made and realised in the current period.

Current value

The most important advantage of current value is its relevance to users who wish to assess the current state or recent performance of the business.

The main disadvantages of current value are its possible greater subjectivity and lower reliability than historical cost. A further disadvantage is its lack of familiarity.

Adjusting for the effects of general inflation

The ASB rejected CPP on three grounds:

- its complexity;
- its failure to capture economic substance when specific and general price movements diverge; and
- the unfamiliarity of information stated in terms of constant purchasing power units.

5.2 The ASB's initial conclusions

The ASB drew the following conclusions:

- The use of current values for both assets and liabilities provides the information that is most relevant to the decisions of users.
- In the case of assets, the appropriate current value is stated according to the value to the business rule. In the case of liabilities, market values may be used.
- A real terms capital maintenance system improves the relevance of information because it shows current operating margins as well as the extent to which holding gains and losses reflect the effect of general inflation, so that users of real terms financial statements are able to select the particular information they require.

- Practice should develop by evolving in the direction of greater use of current values to the extent that this is consistent with the constraints of reliability and cost.

5.3 The ASB's current position on measurement

The chapter on measurement in financial statements was arguably the most controversial part of the initial draft of the Statement of Principles. Many commentators interpreted the conclusions, particularly the final one, to mean that the ASB intended to reintroduce a form of current cost accounting.

The ASB subsequently denied this and stated that it accepts that the existing modified historical cost system will be used for the foreseeable future. Significant changes were made to this part of the Statement before the second draft was issued in 1998. The final version of the Statement emphasises the need to choose the most appropriate basis of measurement in specific circumstances. It no longer suggests that current values should be used in preference to historic cost.

The basic principles

(a) There is a choice between a measurement system that requires:

   (i) a single measurement basis (eg, historic cost or current value) to be used for all assets and liabilities; or

   (ii) the measurement basis to be selected separately for each category or assets or liabilities so that it fits the circumstances surrounding that particular category (for example, the 'modified historic cost' system where some fixed assets are stated at current value while the rest are stated at historic cost).

   It is envisaged that the latter approach (the mixed measurement system) will be used.

(b) A measurement basis (historic cost or current value) must be selected for each category of assets or liabilities. The basis selected should be the one that best meets the objective of financial statements and the demands of the qualitative characteristics of financial information, bearing in mind the nature of the assets or liabilities concerned and the circumstances involved.

(c) An asset or liability being measured using the historical cost basis is recognised initially at transaction cost. An asset or liability being measured using the current value basis is recognised initially at its current value at the time it was acquired or assumed.

(d) Subsequent remeasurement will occur if it is necessary to ensure that:

   (i) assets measured at historic cost are carried at the lower of cost and recoverable amount;

   (ii) monetary items denominated in foreign currency are carried at amounts based on up-to-date exchange rates; and

   (iii) assets and liabilities measured on the current value basis are carried at up to date current values.

(e) Such remeasurements are only recognised if:

   (i) there is sufficient evidence that the monetary amount of the asset or liability has changed; and

   (ii) the new amount of the asset or liability can be measured with sufficient reliability.

Choosing a measurement basis

(a) The carrying amounts of assets and liabilities need to be sufficiently reliable. If only one of the measures available is reliable, it should be the one used if it is also relevant. If both historic cost and current value are reliable, the better measure to use is the one that is most relevant.

(b) Current value is not necessarily less reliable than historic cost. For example, debtors stated at historical cost may need to be adjusted to allow for bad or doubtful debts and this involves a degree of estimation similar to that involved in estimating current values not derived from an active market. The hurdle that a measure must clear to be deemed reliable is set at the same height for current value measures as for historical cost measures.

Measurement issues

(a) The value to the business rule should be used to select from alternative measures of current value. This is the same as deprival value (discussed earlier in this chapter).

(b) When basing carrying amounts on future cash flows, those cash flows should be discounted.

(c) The only way to determine an appropriate monetary amount for an asset or liability may be through estimates. This is acceptable provided that a generally accepted estimation method is used and the measure is supported by a reasonable amount of confirmatory evidence.

Capital maintenance and changing prices

(a) In almost all cases, the capital maintenance model adopted by an entity will be financial capital maintenance and ownership interest will be measured in nominal amounts.

(b) When general or specific price changes are significant this approach is open to criticism.

 (i) General price changes can affect the significance of reported profits and of ownership interest. If this problem is acute, profit should only be recognised after adjustments have been made to maintain the purchasing power of the entity's financial capital.

 (ii) Specific price changes can affect the significance of reported profits and financial position. If this problem is acute, the user should be informed of the significance of specific price changes for the entity's financial performance and financial position.

Although the ASB has denied that a return to current cost accounting as such is on its agenda, it has evidently not ruled out this possibility if the inflation rate rises in the future.

5.4 The influence of the Statement of Principles on recent standards

Many recent financial reporting standards and exposure drafts reflect the ASB's wish to encourage greater use of current values and its thinking on measurement issues, particularly subsequent remeasurement (revaluation and impairment).

- FRS 10 *Goodwill and intangible assets* and FRS 11 *Impairment of Fixed Assets and Goodwill* require that assets are not stated at more than their recoverable amount.
- FRS 15 *Tangible Fixed Assets* was introduced to overcome many of the problems associated with the modified historical cost basis. It requires that once an asset has been revalued, it must continue to be stated at current value.
- The definition of recoverable amount in FRS 11 and the definition of current value in FRS 15 are based on the value to the business model.

- FRS 7 *Fair values in acquisition accounting* and FRS 12 *Provisions, contingent liabilities and contingent assets* require the use of discounted cash flows in some circumstances. FRED 19 *Deferred tax* proposes that deferred tax liabilities should be discounted if the effect is material.
- The ASB is expected to propose that derivatives and other financial instruments should be stated at current value.

6 CHAPTER SUMMARY

This chapter has outlined two alternatives to historic cost accounting – CPP and CCA. Whilst you should be able to carry out the basic adjustments to convert historic cost accounts to these two accounting conventions, it is more important to be able to comment on the alternatives and the development of inflation accounting generally.

7 SELF TEST QUESTIONS

7.1 Does ROCE tend to be overstated or understated by HC accounts? (1.3)

7.2 What are the advantages of CPP accounting which led to the publication of *PSSAP 7*? (1.8)

7.3 What is the system suggested in the ASC handbook which is a combination of CCA and CPP? (1.10)

7.4 Is equity capital a monetary or a non-monetary item under CPP? (2.2)

7.5 What is the CPP factor for adjusting non-monetary values? (2.3)

7.6 What capital maintenance concept is the CCA system based on? (3.5)

7.7 What are the two CCA profit figures recognised in *SSAP 16*? (3.7)

7.8 How is stock stated in CCA accounts? (3.9)

7.9 What is monetary working capital? (3.12)

7.10 What were the three variables identified by the ASC handbook in the alternative approaches to measuring profit? (4.3)

8 EXAMINATION TYPE QUESTION

8.1 Forge Manufacturing plc

The accountant of Forge Manufacturing plc had partly completed a worksheet to convert the historic cost accounts for the year ended 31 December 20X9 to current cost accounts. The worksheet contained the following information

	Historic cost 20X9		*Adjustments 20X9*	
			Dr	*Cr*
	£	£	£	£
Sales		300,000		
Cost of sales		147,500	9,665 (1)	
Gross profit		152,500		
Expenses	64,000			
Interest	11,000			11,000 (7)
Depreciation	40,000		20,000 (4c)	
MWC	-		3,365 (3)	
		115,000		
Gearing adjustment				18,265 (5)
Interest			11,000 (7)	
		37,500		

Retained profit b/d	37,500
	75,000
Less: Dividends paid	25,000
Retained profit c/d	£50,000

	Current cost	Historic cost		Adjustments 20X9	
	20X8	20X8	20X9	Dr	Cr
	£	£	£	£	£
Land	125,000	100,000	100,000	25,000 (6) 5,750 (4a)	
Equipment	250,000	200,000	200,000	50,000 (6) 50,000 (4a)	
Aggregate depreciation	(100,000)	(80,000)	(120,000)		20,000 (6) 20,000 (4b) 20,000 (4c)
Stock	75,000	72,500	75,000	2,500 (6) 625 (2)	
Debtors	100,000	100,000	125,000		
Cash	7,500	7,500	20,000		
	£457,500	£400,000	£400,000		
Capital	125,000	125,000	125,000		
Retained profit	37,500	37,500	50,000		
Current cost reserve	57,500	-	-	20,000 (4b) 18,265	57,500 (6) 9,665 (1) 625 (2) 3,365 (3) 55,750 (4a)
Non-current loan	137,500	137,500	137,500		
Creditors	62,500	62,500	75,000		
Bank overdraft	37,500	37,500	12,500		
	£457,500	£400,000	£400,000		

The stock indices relating to 20X9 are as follows

Index at date closing stock was acquired	1,500
Index at 31 December 20X9	1,562.5
Average for year	1,475

The equipment indices relating to equipment are as follows

Index when acquired	800
Index at 31 December 20X8	1,000
Index at 31 December 20X9	1,200

The land indices relating to land are as follows

Index when acquired	1,147.2
Index at 31 December 20X9	1,500

Depreciation has been calculated in the historic accounts at 20% of cost with £40,000 charged in 20X7, 20X8 and 20X9 on the equipment costing £200,000 on 1 January 20X7.

Note relating to adjustments in the worksheet

(1) £9,665 - This is the cost of sales adjustment made to increase the historic cost of £147,500 to bring it up to replacement cost.

Unfortunately the accountant has been transferred to deal with an urgent assignment and has been unable to complete the preparation of the current cost accounts.

You are required:

(a) to state which capital maintenance concept has been applied and the advantage of using this particular concept. **(6 marks)**

(b) to show the calculations to support the stock adjustment of £625. **(3 marks)**

(c) to briefly explain the five adjustments made in respect of equipment and aggregate depreciation. **(8 marks)**

(d) to draft a current cost profit and loss account for the year ended 31 December 20X9. **(3 marks)**

(Total: 20 marks)

9 ANSWER TO EXAMINATION TYPE QUESTION

9.1 Forge Manufacturing plc

(Tutorial note:

For part (c) show how the adjustments would have been calculated and explain what these adjustments are claimed to do.

The summary current cost profit and loss account should include a sub-total of the historic cost profit with the current cost adjustments being made to this profit.*)*

(a) The adjustments by the accountant have been made by applying an operating capital maintenance concept. The current cost accounts that would result from the adjustments being proposed to the 20X9 historic cost accounts would reflect the basic concept of CCA which is the maintenance of the operating capability of the company. For Forge Manufacturing plc this would be the amount of goods and services which the business would be able to supply with its existing resources in a particular period.

From a conceptual point of view, it may be stated that CCA is concerned with the business - it is entity-based. This contrasts with other forms of accounting system which purport to reflect the effects of changing prices on a business from the point of view of the owner/shareholder - this orientation is proprietor-based.

The advantage of the entity-based concept is that it concentrates on maintaining the business's ability to function at its current output level. The adjustments made to the profit and loss account should help ensure that distributions to shareholders, in the form of dividends, are not so big that the business would be unable to replace the stock that has been sold or the assets that have been used. In addition, the use of replacement cost under this concept should result in more realistic values being attributed to a company's assets in the balance sheet.

(b) Using the stock-related indices the value of closing stock for the 20X9 balance sheet would be

$$£75{,}000 \times \frac{1{,}562.5}{1{,}500.0} = £78{,}125$$

An adjustment of £3,125 is required at that date. The same adjustment at 31 December 20X8 would have been £2,500 ie, £(75,000 – £72,500). The increase of £625 is therefore credited to the current cost reserve in 20X9.

(c) **Adjustment ref (6)**

Dr	Equipment	£50,000	
Cr	Current cost reserve		£50,000

This represents the increase from the historic cost of £200,000, when the index was 800, to an estimated current cost, when the relevant index had moved to 1,000, of £250,000 (31 December 20X8) ie, £200,000 × $\frac{1,000}{800}$ = £250,000. £(250,000 – 200,000) = £50,000.

Adjustment ref (4a)

Dr	Equipment	£50,000	
Cr	Current cost reserve		£50,000

This represents the adjustment required to bring the current cost of the asset up to the 31 December 20X9 level of £300,000 when the index was 1,200 ie, £250,000 × $\frac{1,200}{1,000}$ = £300,000. £(300,000 – 250,000) = £50,000.

Both the £50,000 adjustments above represent unrealised holding gains.

Adjustment ref (6)

Dr	Current cost reserve	£20,000	
Cr	Equipment account depreciation		£20,000

This is required to bring the accumulated depreciation provision up to the level that reflects the current cost of the asset used. Again the equipment indices would be used. £80,000 × $\frac{1,000}{800}$ = £100,000. £(100,000 – 80,000) = £20,000. This adjustment is effectively an adjustment to the opening balance on the current cost reserve.

Adjustment ref (4b)

Dr	Current cost reserve	£20,000	
Cr	Equipment account depreciation		£20,000

This is the backlog depreciation to bring the provision at 31 December 20X8 up to the required balance on that account at that time but calculated at 31 December 20X9. The depreciation at 31 December 20X8 should be based on £300,000, not £250,000.

The required accumulated provision should therefore be £300,000 × $\frac{£100,000}{£250,000}$ = £120,000. £(120,000 – 100,000) = £20,000.

Adjustment ref (4c)

Dr	Profit and loss account	£20,000	
Cr	Equipment account depreciation		£20,000

The depreciation charge in the historic cost profit and loss account would have been based on the historic cost of £200,000. The current cost depreciation charge for the year should be based on £300,000. This adjustment will raise the depreciation charge for the period to the required £60,000.

(d) **Draft current cost profit and loss account for the year ended 31 December 20X9**

	£	£
Sales		300,000
Historic cost of sales		(147,500)
Gross profit		152,500
Expenses	(64,000)	
Depreciation	(40,000)	
		(104,000)
Historic cost operating profit		48,500
Current cost operating adjustments:		
Depreciation	(20,000)	
Stock	(9,665)	
MWCA	(3,365)	
		(33,030)
Current cost operating profit		15,470
Interest	(11,000)	
Gearing adjustment	18,265	
		7,265
		22,735
Dividends paid		(25,000)
Current cost loss for the year		(2,265)

Note: there appears to be no tax charge for the year!

13 CONSOLIDATED ACCOUNTS - SIMPLE GROUPS

INTRODUCTION & LEARNING OBJECTIVES

There will normally be a computational consolidation question in the examination. The question will probably also require some comment as to the significance of the figures produced.

Group accounts are dealt with in several chapters.

This chapter details the legal and professional requirements for the preparation of consolidated accounts. However it does not start from basics and thus you may find that you need to revise the techniques learned from earlier exams.

When you have studied this chapter you should be able to do the following:

- Demonstrate your understanding of the requirements of, and definitions in, *FRS 2* and *CA85* relating to group accounts.
- Deal with unrealised inter-company profits in group accounts.

1 COMPANIES ACT AND FRS 2 DEFINITIONS

1.1 Definition of subsidiary undertaking

The *CA89* extended the definition of a subsidiary beyond the previous *(CA85)* definition to implement the *EC Seventh Directive. FRS 2* assists in interpreting the legal definition.

It is important to note that the new definitions for accounting purposes refer to a subsidiary **undertaking** rather than a subsidiary company. A subsidiary undertaking may include a partnership or an unincorporated business.

Definition An undertaking is the subsidiary of another undertaking where:

(a) The parent holds a majority of the rights to vote at general meetings of the undertaking/company on all or substantially all matters; or

(b) The parent is a member and has a right to appoint or remove directors having a majority of the rights to vote at board meetings of the undertaking/company on all or substantially all matters; or

(c) The parent is a member and has the right to control alone a majority of the rights to vote at general meetings of the undertaking/company pursuant to an agreement with other shareholders; or

(d) The parent has a right to exercise a **dominant influence** over the undertaking by virtue of provisions in the memorandum or articles or by a lawful contract; or

(e) The parent has a **participating interest** and **actually exercises** a **dominant influence** or the parent and subsidiary undertaking **are managed on a unified basis.**

For definition (d) above the existence of a **dominant influence** is only deemed to apply if the parent has a right to give directions on operating or financial policies and the subsidiary directors are obliged to comply with those directions whether or not they are for the benefit of the subsidiary.

Definition A **participating interest** means an interest in shares, held for the long term, to secure a contribution to its activities by the exercise of control or influence. A holding of 20% or more is presumed to be a participating interest unless the contrary can be shown.

Definition A parent company is a company which owns a subsidiary undertaking.

FRS 2 gives guidance on the meaning of the *CA 1989* definitions.

(i) For definition (e) the result of the **actual exercise of dominant influence** is that major decisions will be taken in accordance with the wishes of the dominant party whether these are expressed or perceived. Two or more undertakings **are managed on a unified basis** if the whole of their operations are integrated and managed as a single unit. An interest should be considered as **held on a long-term basis** where it is held other than exclusively with a view to subsequent resale.

(ii) For definition (d) the phrase **dominant influence** is defined in the Act and is a more restrictive definition than the interpretation given for **the actual exercise of dominant influence** in definition (e). *FRS 2* makes it clear that they are two separate definitions.

1.2 Discuss the reasons why the definitions need to be so complex

The definitions of a subsidiary under the old *CA85* applied when either:

(a) more than 50% of the equity shares were held; or
(b) there was control over the composition of the board of directors.

These definitions caused difficulties mainly due to the possibilities of creating a dependent company which was not legally a subsidiary and which could then be used for various 'off balance sheet' activities.

The *CA89* fundamentally changed the definitions and brought most of these dependent companies into the group accounts.

1.3 Compare the definitions of subsidiaries internationally

The CA89/FRS 2 definition corresponds to the EC definition which is included in the 7th Directive. There is however, an optional method in the 7th Directive which was not included in the UK legislation. This option covers a horizontal group.

A horizontal group may exist where there is no relationship between two entities but they are managed on a unified basis and the same persons form the majority on the board of both companies. Such 'groups' are in fact quite common in practice; for example an entrepreneur may start one company with himself as the major shareholder and create further companies (once again with himself as the main shareholder). If he manages these on a 'unified basis', a horizontal group exists under the 7th Directive.

It was considered in the UK however that there was little public need for the preparation of group accounts in such circumstances.

In the USA the definition of a subsidiary is based on the existence of a controlling financial interest. The usual condition is for 50% or more of the voting stock to be held.

1.4 Statement of Principles – Accounting for interests in other entities

Chapter 8 of the ASB's Statement of Principles covers the accounting treatment of subsidiaries, associates, joint ventures and simple investments. The main points are summarised below.

(a) Single entity financial statements and consolidated financial statements present the reporting entity's interests in other entities from different perspectives.

(b) In single entity financial statements, interests in other entities are dealt with by focusing on the income and capital growth arising from the interest (eg, dividends received and changes in market value).

(c) In consolidated financial statements, the way in which interests in other entities are dealt with depends on the degree of influence involved.

- An interest in another entity that involves control of that other entity's operating and financial policies is dealt with by incorporating the controlled entity as part of the reporting entity (ie, by consolidation).

- An interest in another entity that involves joint control of, or significant influence over, that other entity's operating and financial policies is dealt with by recognising the reporting entity's share of that other entity's results and resources in a way that does not imply that they are controlled by the reporting entity (eg, by the equity method or gross equity method).

- Other interests in other entities (simple investments) are dealt with in the same way as any other asset.

(d) Although consolidated financial statements are the financial statements of the group as a whole, they are prepared from the perspective of the parent's shareholders. As a result, they ultimately focus on the parent's ownership interest in its subsidiaries. The effect on benefit flows of any outside equity interest in the subsidiaries (minority interest) is therefore separately identified.

(e) Consolidated financial statements reflect the whole of the parent's investment in its subsidiaries, including purchased goodwill.

(f) A business combination is reflected in the consolidated financial statements in accordance with its character. Therefore, a transaction that is in the character of:

- an acquisition is reflected in the consolidated financial statements as if the acquirer purchased the acquiree's assets and liabilities as a bundle of assets and liabilities on the open market.

- a merger is reflected in the consolidated financial statements as if a new reporting entity, comprising all the parties to the transaction, had been formed.

The Statement of Principles effectively restates generally accepted accounting principles.

2 REQUIREMENTS RELATING TO THE PREPARATION OF CONSOLIDATED ACCOUNTS

2.1 FRS 2's regulations in relation to acquisition accounting

In most cases, group accounts should be presented as consolidated accounts which may be prepared under the acquisition or merger methods (these methods are dealt with in FRS 6. See later).

FRS 2 covers such matters as the following.

(a) Purpose of group accounts.
(b) Definition of group members (see above).
(c) Exemptions from preparing group accounts.
(d) Exclusions of subsidiaries from consolidation.
(e) Consolidation adjustments.
(f) Changes in composition of a group and changes in stake.

Items (a), (c), (d) and (e) are dealt with in this chapter. Item (f) is covered in the next chapter.

2.2 Purpose of consolidated accounts

The *CA85* requires group accounts to be in the form of consolidated accounts which give a 'true and fair' view.

FRS 2: **Accounting for subsidiary undertakings** states the purpose of consolidated accounts is to

> 'present financial information about a parent undertaking and its subsidiary undertakings as a single economic entity to show the economic resources controlled by the group, the obligations of the group and the results the group achieves with its resources.'

2.3 The usefulness and problems of the current requirements

It is generally accepted that consolidated accounts provide useful information to users of the financial statements. They reflect the economic substance of the group as a single economic entity rather than the individual accounts of the group companies as separate legal entities.

Consolidated accounts reflect the fact that the group controls 100% of the assets and liabilities of the subsidiaries because group assets and liabilities are included. They also show the proportion of shareholders' funds and the result for the year owned by the group. This is reflected by the disclosure of minority interest in the consolidated profit and loss account and the consolidated balance sheet. Intra-group transactions are eliminated, meaning that distortion of the view of the group's financial performance is avoided.

However, the requirement to prepare consolidated accounts may also cause problems. Consolidated accounts may obscure information about the separate assets, liabilities and results of individual subsidiaries. (The parent undertaking does not have to present its own profit and loss account if group accounts are prepared.) For example, consolidated accounts may hide a situation in which one subsidiary is making losses because the other subsidiaries are making profits or a situation in which one subsidiary has a dangerous liquidity problem.

Following the issue of FRS 6 *Acquisitions and mergers* the acquisition method of consolidation must be used in almost all cases. This results in the 'freezing' of the pre-acquisition reserves of subsidiaries and means that shareholders' funds in the consolidated accounts may be very much lower than the aggregate of shareholders' funds in the individual accounts. Because consolidated accounts include all the liabilities of the group, it may appear very much more highly geared than any of the individual companies.

2.4 Consolidation techniques

The *CA89* introduced into the law various rules on consolidation accounting. *FRS 2* confirms the rules or reduces the choice in some instances. There are three main areas:

(a) **Accounting policies**

Uniform group accounting policies should be used for determining the amounts to be included in the consolidated financial statements. In exceptional cases different policies may be used with disclosure.

Clearly if the aggregate figures are to make sense they should have been derived using common policies.

(b) **Accounting periods and dates**

The accounts of all subsidiaries to be used in preparing consolidated financial statements should have the same financial year-end and be for the same accounting period as those of the parent company. Where the financial year of a subsidiary differs from that of the parent company, interim financial statements for that subsidiary prepared to the parent company's accounting date should be used. If this is impracticable, earlier financial statements of the subsidiary undertaking may be used, provided they are prepared for a financial year that ended not more than three months earlier.

(c) **Intra-group transactions**

In the past there has been a variety of methods adjusting for the effect of intra-group transactions. Such transactions may result in profits or losses being included in the book value of assets in the consolidation. This area is dealt with in detail in the next section.

3 ADJUSTMENTS FOR INTRA-GROUP TRADING

3.1 Reasons for adjustments

Presenting information about the economic activities of the group as a single economic entity in consolidated financial statements requires adjustment for intra-group transactions of the amounts reported in the individual financial statements of the parent and its subsidiary undertakings. Intra-group transactions may result in a profit or loss that is included at least temporarily in the book value of group assets. To the extent that such assets are still held in the undertakings included in the consolidation at the balance sheet date, the related profits or losses recorded in the individual financial statements have not arisen for the group as a whole and must therefore be eliminated from group results and asset values. The elimination should be in full, even where the transactions involve subsidiary undertakings with minority interests.

3.2 Situations where intra-group profits occur

Intra-group profits occur in two situations.

(a) Goods are sold by one member of the group to another and the items are used as raw materials in the receiving company or sold on by the receiving company.

(b) Goods are sold by one member of the group to another and the items are used as fixed assets by the receiving company.

Each situation is dealt with below.

3.3 Stock

Where goods have been sold by one group company to another at a profit and some of these goods are **unsold** at the year end, then the profit loading on these goods is **unrealised** from the viewpoint of the group as a whole.

(a) **Wholly-owned subsidiary**

Where goods are sold by S Ltd (a wholly-owned subsidiary) to H Ltd (its parent company), or by H Ltd to S Ltd, and some of the goods are in stock at the year end, there are two steps:

(i) calculate the unrealised profit in closing stock; and

(ii) Dr Consolidated revenue reserves
    Cr Consolidated stock

with the unrealised profit. This reduces stock to cost and removes unrealised profit from the group reserves.

(b) **Partly-owned subsidiary**

Suppose H Ltd owns 90% of S Ltd. During the year S Ltd sells goods to H Ltd at cost plus 25%. At the year end the closing stock of H Ltd includes £8,000 of goods, at invoice value, acquired originally from S Ltd. What adjustments are required in the consolidation working papers?

In the past this was an area in which opinions differed. The *CA 1989* requires intra-group profits to be eliminated but where a subsidiary is partly owned it allows the elimination to be either of the whole of the profit or in proportion to the group's shareholding in the subsidiary.

3.4 The treatment of intra-group profits as required by FRS 2

FRS 2 removes the choice as to who should suffer the deduction of intra-group profit and requires that 'the profits should be eliminated against both the group's interest and the minority's interest in proportion to their interest in the company whose individual accounts recorded the profits'.

Thus, sales from the parent company to the subsidiary produce profits in the parent company. Any unrealised profits should be charged against the group. Sales from the subsidiary to the parent company produce profits in the subsidiary company. The unrealised profits should be split between the group and the minority.

Returning to the above example of H Ltd and S Ltd, the **total** unrealised profit is:

$$\frac{25}{125} \times £8,000 = £1,600$$

(Note the denominator in the fraction. The £8,000 is at **selling** price to S Ltd, ie, 100 + 25)

Consolidated stock must be reduced (credited) with £1,600.

The debit to this credit is split between consolidated reserves and minority interest as the subsidiary recorded the original profit. The journal entry required is thus:

	£	£
Dr Consolidated revenue reserves 90% × 1,600	1,440	
Dr Minority interests 10% × 1,600	160	
Cr Consolidated stock		1,600

A note to the accounts would show 'Provision has been made for the whole of the unrealised profit in stock.' This note should appear in the statement on accounting policies.

If H Ltd had sold the goods to S Ltd the journal entry required would be

	£	£
Dr Consolidated revenue reserves	1,600	
Cr Consolidated stock		1,600

Note that when the adjustment is made, the effect is to reduce group reserves or minority interests directly. An alternative way of achieving the same overall adjustment is to amend the stock and reserves values of the selling company on the balance sheet as given in the question. This is merely a working for the purposes of the consolidation: the actual stock and reserves of the individual company are unaffected. Subsequently, when the figures are picked up in the group reserves and minority interest calculations, the group and the minority will receive their respective share of the reduced reserves. Similarly, when the group stock is calculated, the reduction in its value due to the provision for unrealised profit will not be forgotten.

3.5 Fixed assets

The problems involved are similar to those considered under stock, but there is the added complication of depreciation on the fixed assets.

3.6 Example - fixed assets

At the beginning of the year S Ltd (60% owned by H Ltd) sells goods costing £20,000 to H Ltd. H Ltd pays £25,000 for the goods and uses them as fixed assets, depreciating over five years with a nil scrap value at the end of the period using the straight line basis.

3.7 Solution

There are two points here:

(a) There is an unrealised profit of £5,000 in the transfer price of the fixed asset.

(b) During the first year in which the fixed asset is used H Ltd is incurring a depreciation charge of 20% of £25,000. Had the goods been transferred at cost, the depreciation charge would have been only £4,000. This, of course, works in the opposite direction to (a) from the group's viewpoint.

Step 1 Calculate the cost and accumulated depreciation on the transferred asset as it stands in the balance sheet.

	Per balance sheet
	£
Cost	25,000
Accumulated depreciation	5,000
NBV	20,000

Step 2 Compare these figures with how the fixed asset would appear had there been no transfer (ie, how the asset should appear).

	Per balance sheet	*Should be*
	£	£
Cost	25,000	20,000
Accumulated depreciation	5,000	4,000
	20,000	16,000

Step 3 Calculate the adjustments required.

	Per balance sheet	*Should be*	*Adjustment*
	£	£	£
Cost	25,000	20,000	5,000 (a) Unrealised profit
Accumulated depreciation	5,000	4,000	1,000 (b) Depreciation overcharge
NBV	20,000	16,000	

Step 4 Deal with the adjustments

(a) Unrealised profit on transfer

A provision for unrealised profit will be made, which reduces the cost of the fixed asset from its transfer value to the original cost to the group. The debit will either be wholly to consolidated reserves or shared between the group and minority interest depending upon where the original profit was recorded. In this case:

	£	£
Dr: Consolidated profit and loss account (60% × 5,000)	3,000	
Dr: Minority interest (40% × 5,000)	2,000	
Cr: Fixed asset cost (provision for unrealised profit)		5,000

(b) Each year the provision for unrealised profit will be reduced by £1,000 to adjust for the excess depreciation charged. The consolidated reserves, and minority interest when appropriate, will be credited. After five years, at the end of the useful life of the asset, the provision for unrealised profit will be fully written back. In this particular case, the depreciation is charged in H Ltd, and therefore the profit adjustment is wholly attributable to the group:

	£	£
Dr: Provision for depreciation (provision for unrealised profit)	1,000	
Cr: Consolidated profit and loss account		1,000

Again, these adjustments can be carried using the balance sheets given in the question as working papers, if preferred. The double entries would be:

			£	£
(i)	Dr:	Profit and loss account	5,000	
	Cr	Fixed asset cost		5,000

In the balance sheet of the company which made the profit on transfer (S Ltd in this case).

			£	£
(ii)	Dr:	Provision for depreciation	1,000	
	Cr	Profit and loss account		1,000

In the balance sheet of the company which is depreciating the asset.

These adjusted figures would then be picked up for the calculation of group reserves and minority interest and would give the same overall effect.

Step 5 The fixed assets section of the balance sheet will show:

		Cost	*Depn*	
		£	£	£
Fixed assets				
Plant	(25,000 – 5,000)	20,000		
	(5,000 – 1,000)		4,000	16,000

3.8 Activity

A plc owns 80% of the equity shares in Z Ltd. During the year ended 31 December 20X4 Z Ltd sold goods to A plc for £100,000 making a profit of 20% on selling price.

At the balance sheet date £30,000 of these goods remained in the stocks of A plc.

What is the unrealised profit in stock at 31 December 20X4 and how will this be dealt with in the consolidated accounts?

3.9 Activity solution

Step 1 Calculate the unrealised profit

£30,000 × 20% = £6,000.

Step 2 Calculate minority share of unrealised profit

£6,000 × 20% = £1,200.

Step 3 Show adjustments in consolidated accounts

	£	£
Dr Consolidated reserves	4,800	
Minority interest	1,200	
Cr Consolidated stocks		6,000

3.10 Alternative treatments for eliminating intra-group unrealised profits

The alternative treatments that have been used in the past include the following.

(a) Eliminating the unrealised profit from group reserves in all circumstances.
(b) Eliminating the group share only.

Using the above activity, the adjustments would therefore be as follows.

(a)	Dr	Consolidated reserves	6,000	
		Cr Consolidated stocks		6,000
(b)	Dr	Consolidated reserves	4,800	
		Cr Consolidated stocks		4,800

The second alternative is easier to criticise than the first.

Transactions between undertakings included in the consolidation deal with the assets and liabilities that are wholly within the group's control, even if they are not wholly owned. From the perspective of the group as a single entity no profit or loss arises on intra-group transactions because no increase or decrease in the group's net assets has occurred.

The treatment leaves stock at a value which is above cost to the group.

The first alternative has the support of some commentators on the grounds of prudence. Legally the minority interest have made a profit on the transaction as the goods have been properly sold to the other company. The group should therefore suffer the full adjustment. However FRS2 views the adjustment on a matching basis. Group accounts are being prepared and from a group perspective the transaction is deemed not to have taken place. If it is so deemed then profit must be removed from where it has been included.

4 EXEMPTIONS FROM PREPARING GROUP ACCOUNTS

4.1 Exemptions for intermediate parent companies

An intermediate parent company is a company which has a subsidiary but is also itself a subsidiary of another company.

For example:

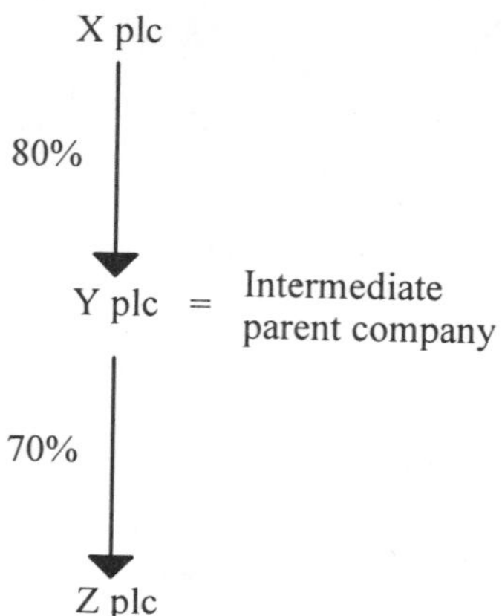

An intermediate parent company is exempt from the requirement to prepare group accounts if:

(a) none of its securities is listed anywhere in the EC; and
(b) its immediate holding company is incorporated in the EC.

Providing that:

(a) it is wholly owned by that immediate parent; or

(b) its immediate parent holds more than 50% and notice for the preparation of group accounts has not been served from shareholders owning either more than one half of the remaining shares or 5% of the total shares.

Various detailed conditions apply for this exemption including the need for the intermediate parent company to be included in the group accounts of an EC parent. A copy of these accounts must be filed with the Registrar of Companies together with an English translation.

4.2 Exemptions for small and medium-sized groups

A parent company need not prepare group accounts if the group headed by that parent satisfies at least two of the following conditions:

Annual turnover	£13.44m gross or £11.2m net
Balance sheet assets	£6.72m gross or £5.6m net
Average employees	250

The 'gross' figures are those calculated prior to any consolidation adjustments whereas the 'net' figures are those after the consolidation adjustments, such as the elimination of intra-group balances, have been made. A company may satisfy the relevant limits on either a net or a gross basis or by a mixture of the two.

The purpose of allowing the calculations to be made using the higher gross figures is to prevent a parent company from having to prepare group accounts in order to discover that it does not need to prepare group accounts.

Surprisingly, if the accounting period is more or less than one year the turnover limit specified is **not** adjusted on a pro-rata basis as it is for individual company abbreviated accounts limits.

The right to the exemption from preparing group accounts does not apply if any company in the group is:

(a) a public company; or
(b) a banking or insurance company; or
(c) a company authorised under the *Financial Services Act*.

5 THE EXCLUSION OF SUBSIDIARY UNDERTAKINGS FROM CONSOLIDATION

5.1 Introduction

Under the *Companies Act 1985* there are cases where subsidiary undertakings **need not** or **must not** be included in the consolidation. Where all of the subsidiaries fall within the exclusions, group accounts are not required.

FRS 2 is based on the premise that the value of the information provided by the consolidated accounts depends on the extent to which the information about the group is complete ie, all undertakings are consolidated. Thus a subsidiary should only be excluded in **exceptional** circumstances. Where such exceptional circumstances are identified *FRS 2* makes exclusions mandatory rather than optional.

5.2 Different activities

Subsidiaries **must be** excluded from consolidation where their activities are so different from other undertakings in the consolidation that their inclusion would be incompatible with the obligation to give a true and fair view. The exclusion does not apply merely because some of the undertakings are industrial, some commercial and some provide services or because they carry on industrial or commercial activities involving different products or providing different services.

This is the only mandatory exclusion under the *Companies Act*.

Where a subsidiary is excluded because of dissimilar activities, the group accounts should include separate financial statements for that subsidiary. They may be combined with the financial statements of other subsidiaries with similar operations if appropriate.

In the group accounts the investment in the subsidiary should be stated using the **equity method** of accounting.

5.3 Materiality

The *Companies Act* states that a subsidiary undertaking **may** be excluded from the consolidation where its inclusion is not material for the purpose of giving a true and fair view.

Two or more undertakings may be excluded on these grounds only if they are not material when taken together.

FRS 2 (like any Accounting Standard) does not deal with immaterial items and therefore does not cover this exclusion.

5.4 Severe long-term restrictions

A subsidiary **should** be excluded from the consolidation where severe long-term restrictions substantially hinder the exercise of the rights of the parent company over the assets or management of that undertaking.

Subsidiaries excluded from consolidation are to be treated as fixed asset investments. They are to be included at their carrying amount when the restrictions came into force, subject to any write down for impairment in value, and no further accruals are to be made for profits or losses of those subsidiary undertakings, unless the parent undertaking still exercises significant influence. In the latter case they are to be treated as associates.

5.5 Disproportionate expense or undue delay

In the *CA85* a subsidiary **may** be excluded from the consolidation where the information necessary for the preparation of group accounts cannot be obtained without disproportionate expense or undue delay. Whether the expense is disproportionate or the delay undue should be judged in the context of that information to the group accounts.

FRS 2, however, states that neither reason can justify excluding a subsidiary.

5.6 Temporary investment

A subsidiary should be excluded from the consolidation where the interest of the parent company is held exclusively with a view to subsequent resale and the undertaking has not previously been included in consolidated group accounts prepared by the parent company.

The investment in the subsidiary will be shown as a **current asset** at the lower of cost and net realisable value.

5.7 Summary

Reason	*CA 1989*	*FRS 2*	*Treatment*
Different activities	Mandatory	Mandatory (in exceptional circumstances only)	Equity accounting
Severe long-term restrictions	Optional	Mandatory	If restrictions in force at date of acquisition carry initially at cost. If restrictions came into force at a later date equity account at date when restrictions came into force. Consider need for provisions for impairment in value.
Immaterial	Optional	Not applicable	-
Disproportionate expense or undue delay	Optional	Not permissible	-
Temporary investment	Optional	Mandatory	Current asset at the lower of cost and NRV

5.8 Activity

(a) X plc, an international manufacturing group, has a subsidiary undertaking, Z Ltd, which is an insurance company. Can the group be exempted from consolidating Z Ltd on the grounds of different activities?

(b) A plc owns a subsidiary undertaking, P Ltd, which is located in an African state where the Government has for a number of years frozen all remittances out of the country by private individuals and companies.

Does A plc need to include P Ltd in its consolidated accounts?

(c) The N group has the following group figures at its current year end.

Annual turnover £14.5m gross and net.
Balance sheet assets £4.9m net £6.5m gross.
Average employees 245.

Do group accounts need to be prepared?

Answer the above giving reasons.

5.9 Activity solution

(a) Z Ltd must be included unless to do so would impair the true and fair view.

(b) P Ltd can be said to be operating under severe long-term restrictions. Its results should not be consolidated and it should be equity accounted at the date restrictions came into force.

(c) No group accounts need to be prepared as the group meets two of the three size criteria for exemption.

5.10 The validity of the arguments for non-consolidation of subsidiary undertakings

FRS 2 requires the consolidation of subsidiaries in situations based on full control of the net assets of the subsidiary and the intention to hold the subsidiary as a long-term investment. If there is no or insufficient control, it is misleading to prepare group accounts on a basis which implies full control as does the consolidation basis. Similarly if there is no intention to retain the subsidiary, it is misleading to treat it as an integral part of the group by consolidation of its assets and liabilities.

The main area where it is arguable whether a subsidiary should be excluded from consolidation relates to dissimilar activities. Consolidation does not imply that all businesses within the group are in similar trades. The consolidation accounts merely show the collective assets under the control of the holding company. Segmental analysis shows the split between different activities where appropriate. Therefore, it could be argued that there are no situations in which this exclusion is merited.

FRS 2 does however stress that cases of different activities are exceptional. For example it states in its explanatory notes that the contrast between banking and insurance companies and other companies is not sufficient of itself to justify non-consolidation.

5.11 Disclosures applying to subsidiary undertakings that have not been consolidated

The Companies Act 1985 and FRS 2 require the following disclosures in respect of each subsidiary not consolidated:

(a) name;

(b) the reason for excluding the subsidiary from consolidation;

(c) country of incorporation (if outside the UK);

(d) the class of shares held;

(e) the proportion of shares held, distinguishing direct and indirect holdings;

(f) the aggregate amount of capital and reserves at the year-end and its results for the year (unless it is equity accounted);

(g) details of any audit qualifications applying to the subsidiary's accounts for the relevant financial year;

(h) particulars of balances between the subsidiary and the rest of the group;

(i) the nature and extent of transactions of the subsidiary with the rest of the group;

(j) if the subsidiary is not equity accounted, amounts included in the consolidated financial statements in respect of dividends received and receivable and any write-down in the period in respect of the investment in the subsidiary or amounts due from it; and

(k) if the subsidiary is excluded because of different activities, the separate financial statements of the undertaking.

6 CHAPTER SUMMARY

The CA89 definition of a subsidiary undertaking is supported by FRS 2 as to interpretation. There are five alternative tests.

FRS 2 requires the consolidation of subsidiaries in most circumstances. Unrealised profits need to be eliminated on the basis that the transaction never happened.

There are two main situations in which a parent company is exempted from the preparation of group accounts and four reasons why a subsidiary may or must be excluded from consolidation.

7 SELF TEST QUESTIONS

7.1 What is a participating interest? (1.1)

7.2 What are the five alternative definitions of a subsidiary undertaking? (1.1)

7.3 What is the purpose of consolidated accounts? (2.2)

7.4 What does FRS2 require regarding group accounting policies? (2.4)

7.5 What does the CA89 require in relation to intra-group profits? (3.3)

7.6 What does FRS2 require in relation to intra-group profits? (3.4)

7.7 What are the two main exemptions from preparing group accounts? (4.1, 4.2)

7.8 What grounds for exclusion of a subsidiary are mandatory? (5.7)

8 EXAMINATION TYPE QUESTIONS

8.1 Hiding or providing information

"The consolidation of financial statements hides rather than provides information".

You are required to discuss this statement. **(10 marks)**

8.2 Barker Ltd

You are supplied with the following information in relation to Barker Ltd and its 100% owned subsidiary Morgan Ltd

	Barker Ltd	*Morgan Ltd*
Turnover	£11m	£3m
Balance sheet total	£2.5m	£2.1m
Employees	150	110

During the year Barker Ltd sold goods to Morgan Ltd for £3m taking a profit of £1m. At the year end half of these goods were unsold; all amounts due have been settled. Both companies are UK incorporated. Barker Ltd is an 80% owned subsidiary of Hollis Gmbh, a company incorporated in Germany.

You are required to write a memorandum to the board of Barker Ltd, assuming that you are a consultant, advising on factors to take into consideration in deciding whether or not Barker Ltd should file consolidated accounts. **(12 marks)**

9 ANSWERS TO EXAMINATION TYPE QUESTIONS

9.1 Hiding or providing information

Consolidated accounts were introduced as a legal requirement in order to show a true and fair view of the assets, liabilities, income and expenses attributable to the shareholders of the holding company.

The accounts of the parent company do not give sufficient information to its shareholders because:

(a) Its balance sheet merely records the cost of investment in subsidiary companies. It therefore fails to reveal the underlying assets and liabilities of the subsidiary.

(b) Its profit and loss account merely records the dividends receivable from the subsidiary companies. To the extent that a subsidiary does not distribute all its profit then there is no information on the profits accruing to the parent company shareholders. Even if all profits are distributed there will be no information of the size of the revenues and costs of the subsidiaries.

However, although the total assets and profits attributable to the parent company shareholders are known as a result of consolidations, the shareholders can require more information than merely an aggregate total. If the group is diversified both in terms of its products and its geographical markets, the shareholders may need to know the split of sales, profits and assets between the constituent parts of the group. If the full accounts of the subsidiaries were given to the holding company shareholders then much of this information would be provided.

Such an approach may well overload the shareholders with information and thus a better approach is to provide segmental information on the group's industrial and geographical components. The *Companies Act 1985* goes some way to provide such disclosure, which is expanded in SSAP 25.

(***Tutorial note:*** Arguments should be given for and against the statement if possible, but as the consolidation process has been a feature of law of many western countries for decades, the argument for consolidation is very strong.)

9.2 Barker Ltd

MEMORANDUM

To The Board of Barker Ltd

From Consultant

Date X-X-20XX

Re **Eligibility of Barker Ltd for exemptions from filing consolidated accounts**

Barker Ltd has two possible options to consider when determining its exemption from filing accounts.

Intermediate holding company

Barker Ltd is a direct subsidiary of an EC incorporated parent company. There are certain provisions which must be satisfied

(a) Hollis Gmbh (or an EC parent company above Hollis) must prepare audited financial statements incorporating Barker Ltd (it is necessary to check that these audited financial statements will be available for filing within ten months of the year end)

(b) the financial statements must comply with the Seventh Directive (it is necessary to check that the Directive has been incorporated into German legislation), and

(c) the financial statements must be drawn up to the same date.

Furthermore, the minority in Barker Ltd have the right to request the preparation of consolidated financial statements by serving notice on the company within six months of the end of the previous year.

It is necessary to appreciate that in order to take advantage of this exemption the financial statements of Hollis Gmbh (or the ultimate EC parent) must be translated into English (and certified). This expense must be compared with the cost of consolidating the wholly owned subsidiary.

Medium-sized group

	Gross		*Net*	
	Actual	*Limit*	*Actual*	*Limit*
Turnover	£14m	£13.44m	£11m	£11.2m
Balance sheet total	£4.6m	£6.72m	not necessary	
Employees	260	250		

The Barker Ltd group satisfies two out of three of the conditions and is thus medium-sized. If the group was also medium-sized in the previous year then Barker Ltd is eligible for the exemption.

Barker Ltd itself may file abbreviated accounts for a medium-sized company.

Barker Ltd will need to incur extra audit costs as the auditors are required to provide a report stating that in their opinion Barker Ltd is eligible for the exemption.

14 CONSOLIDATED ACCOUNTS - MORE COMPLEX GROUPS

INTRODUCTION & LEARNING OBJECTIVES

Until now, you have only dealt with simple group structures in which one parent owns one or more subsidiaries. This chapter covers more complex group structures in which subsidiaries themselves have investments in subsidiary companies.

When you have studied this chapter you should be able to do the following:

- Determine whether one company is a subsidiary of another.
- Prepare consolidated accounts in a complex situation.

1 MIXED AND VERTICAL GROUPS

1.1 The different possible structures of a group

More complex group structures exist where a subsidiary of a parent company owns all or part of the shareholding which makes another company also a subsidiary of the parent company. The structures can be classified under two headings:

(a) Vertical groups
(b) Mixed groups.

Examples of both are illustrated below.

1.2 Vertical groups

(a) Suppose H Ltd owns 70% of A Ltd. A Ltd is thus a subsidiary of H Ltd.

(b) If, in addition, A Ltd owns 60% of B Ltd, then B Ltd is a subsidiary of A Ltd. Furthermore, B Ltd is said to be a sub-subsidiary of H Ltd.

(c) H Ltd has a direct interest in A Ltd and an **indirect** interest in B Ltd (exercised via A Ltd's holding in B Ltd). H Ltd has an effective interest of only 42% (70% × 60%) in B Ltd. Nevertheless, B Ltd is a sub-subsidiary of H Ltd because H Ltd has a controlling interest in A Ltd and A Ltd has a controlling interest in B Ltd. There is now a 'vertical group' consisting of H Ltd, A Ltd and B Ltd.

H's interest in B Ltd:

H Ltd
↓ 70%
A Ltd
↓ 60%
B Ltd

70% × 60%
= 42%

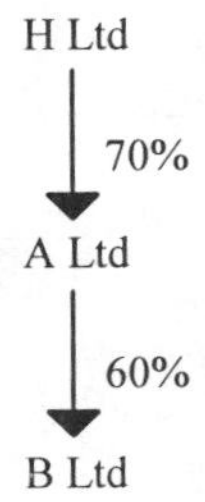

Where a parent company owns a controlling interest in a subsidiary which in turn owns a controlling interest in a sub-subsidiary, then the group accounts of the ultimate parent company must disclose the parent company's share of the underlying net assets and earnings of both the subsidiary and the sub-subsidiary companies.

1.3 Mixed groups

In a mixed group situation the parent company has a controlling interest in at least one subsidiary. In addition, the parent company and the subsidiary together hold a controlling interest in a further company.

For example, H Ltd owns 80% of S Ltd, H Ltd owns 40% of W Ltd, S Ltd owns 30% of W Ltd.

This is a mixed group situation.

(a) S Ltd is a subsidiary of H Ltd; and

(b) H Ltd and S Ltd between them own more than 50% of W Ltd (the fact that S Ltd is not a wholly-owned subsidiary of H Ltd is irrelevant).

W Ltd is thus a member of the H Ltd group and must, therefore, be included in the consolidated balance sheet.

Diagrammatically, the situation is as follows:

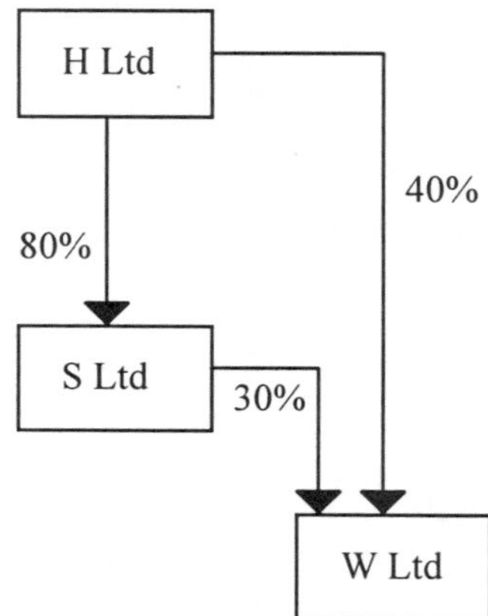

H Ltd's interest in W Ltd = (80% × 30%) + 40% = 64%

1.4 Example

H Ltd owns 35% of S Ltd, S Ltd owns 40% of W Ltd and H Ltd owns 40% of W Ltd.

1.5 Solution

This is **not** a mixed group situation. Neither S Ltd nor W Ltd is a member of the H Ltd group, although S Ltd and W Ltd may both be 'associates' of H Ltd.

H Ltd's interest in W Ltd might be calculated as before as (35% × 40%) + 40% = 54%. Although H Ltd has an arithmetic interest in W Ltd which is more than 50%, it does not have parent company control of W Ltd, as it does not control S Ltd's 40% stake in W Ltd.

1.6 Activity

H Ltd owns 60% of S Ltd, S Ltd owns 25% of W Ltd, H Ltd owns 30% of W Ltd.

Is W Ltd a subsidiary company of H Ltd?

1.7 Activity solution

Diagrammatically, the situation is as follows:

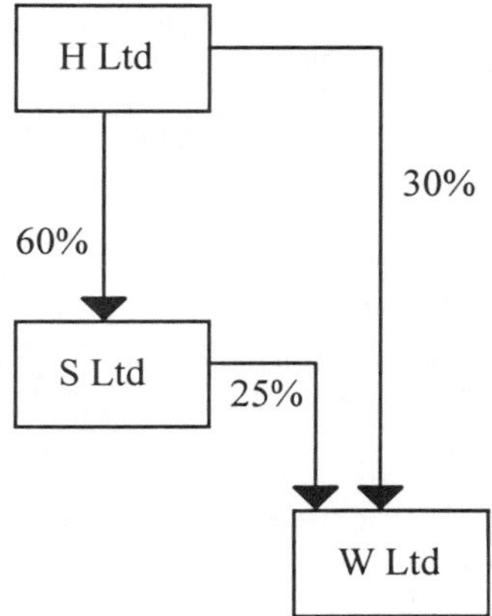

H Ltd's arithmetic interest in W Ltd = (60% × 25%) + 30% = 45%.

W Ltd is a subsidiary of H Ltd. H Ltd effectively controls S Ltd, and thus S Ltd's use of all its shares in W Ltd. Added to its own shares, H Ltd is then able to control the voting of 25% (through S Ltd) plus 30% of W Ltd's shares, ie, 55%. For computational purposes, however, the group interest must be taken as 45% with a minority interest, as always the difference between 100% and the group interest, of 55%.

2 THE DIRECT AND INDIRECT METHODS TO CONSOLIDATE SUB-SUBSIDIARIES

2.1 Methods of consolidation

Calculations of the goodwill on consolidation, the minority shareholders' interest and so on become more complicated. Nevertheless, the normal approach is used, subject to certain modifications.

There are two methods which can be used for dealing with sub-subsidiaries, each giving different results for particular items

(a) **The direct method**

This approach will be followed here.

(b) **The indirect method**

This requires sub-consolidations to be made. In the example in the previous section B Ltd would be consolidated with A to produce the A group accounts. H Ltd and the A group would then be consolidated.

This method is generally more time consuming (in an examination question).

Two situations will be considered in turn

(a) Situation 1 - where the subsidiary is acquired first and then the sub-subsidiary

(b) Situation 2 - where the subsidiary acquires the sub-subsidiary first and is subsequently taken over by the parent company.

2.2 Example 1 – Subsidiary acquired first

The draft balance sheets of H Ltd, S Ltd and T Ltd, as at 31 December 20X4, are as follows:

	H Ltd	*S Ltd*	*T Ltd*		*H Ltd*	*S Ltd*	*T Ltd*
	£'000	£'000	£'000		£'000	£'000	£'000
Net assets	180	80	80	Share capital	200	100	50
Shares in subsidiary	120	80		Profit and loss a/c	100	60	30
	300	160	80		300	160	80

You ascertain that H Ltd acquired 75,000 £1 shares in S Ltd on 1 January 20X4 when the revenue reserves of S Ltd amounted to £40,000. S Ltd acquired 40,000 £1 shares in T Ltd on 30 June 20X4 when the revenue reserves of T Ltd amounted to £25,000; they had been £20,000 on the date of H Ltd's acquisition of S Ltd. Goodwill is amortised over 5 years from the date of acquisition, with a full year's charge in the year of acquisition.

2.3 Solution

Step 1 Draw a diagram of the group structure and then set out the respective interests of the parent company and the minority, distinguishing between direct (D) and indirect (I) interests:

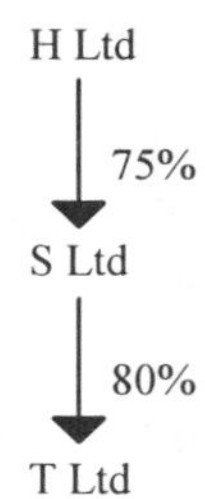

	S Ltd			*T Ltd*
Interest of:				
H Ltd shareholders	75% (D)	75% × 80% =		60% (I)
Minority shareholders	25% (D)		20% (D)	
		25% × 80% =	20% (I)	
				40%
	100%			100%

Make sure that you understand the above calculations. The main difficulty lies in the calculation of the minority interest in T Ltd. The **effective** figure of 40% consists of two distinct elements:

(i) The direct minority of 20% – ie, the 20% of the share capital of T Ltd not owned by S Ltd.

(ii) 25% of S Ltd is not owned by H Ltd. This 25% minority of S Ltd thus have a stake in T Ltd via their company's holding in T Ltd, equivalent to 25% of 80%, ie, 20%. This is the indirect minority in T Ltd.

Step 2 Draw a diagram setting out the relationship between the various companies, and show the revenue reserves at key dates:

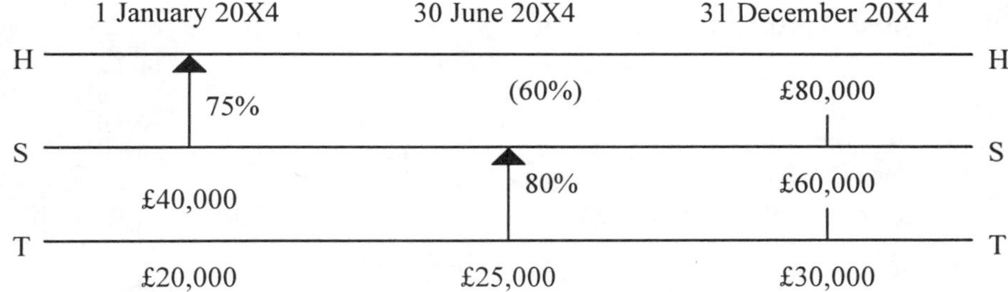

Step 3 Goodwill

Two calculations are required, one for each subsidiary. They are performed separately as goodwill/negative goodwill is determined for each subsidiary.

	Notes	*S Ltd*		*T Ltd*	
		£'000	£'000	£'000	£'000
Cost of investment					
(75% × 80)	(1)		120		60
Less: Share of net assets at acquisition date					
Share capital		100		50	
Profit and loss account	(2)	40		25	
	(3)	140 (75%)	(105)	75 (60%)	(45)
	(4)		15		15
Amortisation			(3)		(3)
			12		12

Notes

(1) The cost of H Ltd's investment in S Ltd is £120,000, and this figure is used in the calculation. The cost of S Ltd's investment in T Ltd is £80,000. However, H Ltd owns only 75% of S Ltd, so the 'effective' cost to H Ltd of its indirect holding is T Ltd is £60,000 (75% × £80,000).

(2) Care must be taken in determining the date for the split between post-acquisition and pre-acquisition reserves. In the previous case, the parent company acquired control of S Ltd on 1 January 20X4, so this is the relevant date: but what about S Ltd's acquisition of shares in T Ltd? When talking about the pre-acquisition/post-acquisition split, the problem is considered from the viewpoint of the ultimate parent company, H Ltd. The test is to ask the question 'When did T Ltd become a member of the H Ltd group?'

The answer is 30 June 20X4. Profits of T Ltd arising after this date are post-acquisition as regards the H Ltd group. The information given regarding T Ltd's reserves at 1 January 20X4 is irrelevant in this context.

(3) The interest of H Ltd is S Ltd and the effective interest of H Ltd in T Ltd are taken from the table in Step 1. Whilst S Ltd owns 80% of T Ltd's share capital and reserves, H Ltd only owns 75% of S Ltd. Thus, the effective interest of 60% (75% × 80%) is used.

Step 4 Consolidated profit and loss account

	£'000
H Ltd	100
S Ltd 75% (60 – 40) (see note 3 above)	15
T Ltd 60% (30 – 25) (see notes 2 and 3 above)	3
Less: Goodwill amortised (30 ÷ 5)	(6)
	112

Step 5 Minority interest

	Notes	£'000		£'000
S Ltd: Net assets at balance sheet date				
Share capital		100		
Profit and loss account		60		
		160		
Less: Cost of investment in T Ltd	(5)	(80)		
	(6)	80	(25%)	20
T Ltd: Net assets at balance sheet date				
Share capital		50		
Profit and loss account		30		
	(6)	80	(40%)	32
				52

Notes

(5) The minority shareholders in S Ltd are entitled to their share of the net assets of S Ltd. However, one of the assets of S Ltd is the cost of the investment in T Ltd which, in the consolidation process, is replaced with the net assets of T Ltd. The minority shareholders in S Ltd are entitled to their share of these also. They receive their share of T Ltd's net assets as the minority interest in S Ltd form the indirect minority interest in T Ltd. So, the minority in S Ltd receive their share of the net assets of S Ltd after having deducted the cost of the investment in T Ltd, and their share of the net assets of T Ltd as they form the indirect part of the minority interest in T Ltd.

(6) The percentage interests are taken from the table in Step 1.

Step 6 The consolidated balance sheet can now be prepared:

Summarised consolidated balance sheet of H Ltd and its subsidiary companies as at 31 December 20X4

	£
Goodwill	24,000
Net assets	340,000
Minority interests	(52,000)
	312,000
Capital and reserves:	
Called up share capital	200,000
Profit and loss account	112,000
	312,000

2.4 Activity

The balance sheets of H Ltd, S Ltd and M Ltd as at 31 December 20X5 were as follows:

	H Ltd	*S Ltd*	*M Ltd*
	£	£	£
Ordinary share capital (£1 shares)	120,000	60,000	40,000
Reserves	95,000	75,000	35,000
	215,000	135,000	75,000
45,000 shares in S Ltd	72,000		
16,000 shares in M Ltd	25,000		
12,000 shares in M Ltd		20,000	
Sundry net assets	118,000	115,000	75,000
	215,000	135,000	75,000

All shares were acquired on 31 December 20X2 when S reserves amounted to £30,000 and M reserves amounted to £10,000.

You are required to calculate the goodwill arising on the consolidation of S Ltd and M Ltd.

2.5 Activity solution

Step 1 Calculate group shareholdings.

In S Ltd

$$\frac{45,000}{60,000} \times 100\% = \qquad 75\%$$

In M Ltd

Direct $\frac{16,000}{40,000} \times 100\% =$	40%
Indirect $75\% \times \frac{12,000}{40,000} \times 100\% =$	22.5%
	62.5%

Step 2 Calculate goodwill arising on S Ltd.

	£	£
Cost of investment		72,000
Less: Share of net assets acquired:		
Share capital	60,000	
Profit and loss account	30,000	
	90,000 (75%)	67,500
Goodwill		4,500

Step 3 Calculate goodwill arising on M Ltd.

	£	£
Cost of investment		
In H Ltd		25,000
In S Ltd		
75% × £20,000		15,000
		40,000

Less: Share of net assets acquired:		
Share capital	40,000	
Profit and loss account	10,000	
	50,000 (62.5%)	31,250
		8,750

2.6 Example – Subsidiary acquires sub-subsidiary first

The draft balance sheets of H Ltd, S Ltd and T Ltd as at 31 December 20X4 are as follows:

	H Ltd	*S Ltd*	*T Ltd*		*H Ltd*	*S Ltd*	*T Ltd*
	£'000	£'000	£'000		£'000	£'000	£'000
Net assets	180	80	80	Share capital	200	100	50
Shares in subsidiary	120	80		Revenue reserves	100	60	30
	300	160	80		300	160	80

S Ltd acquired 40,000 £1 shares in T Ltd on 1 January 20X4 when the revenue reserves of T Ltd amounted to £25,000. H Ltd acquired 75,000 £1 shares in S Ltd on 30 June 20X4 when the revenue reserves of S Ltd amounted to £40,000 and those of T Ltd amounted to £30,000. Goodwill is amortised over 5 years from the date of acquisition, with a full year's charge in the year of acquisition.

2.7 Solution

The main area of difficulty lies in the allocation of the reserves of the subsidiary companies between pre-acquisition and post-acquisition. (Remember that the object of the exercise is to prepare a consolidated balance sheet of the **H Ltd group**.)

(a) **Revenue reserves of S Ltd**

When did S Ltd become a member of the H Ltd group? Answer: 30 June 20X4 – so only revenue reserves of S Ltd arising after 30 June 20X4 can be regarded as post-acquisition from the viewpoint of the H Ltd group.

(b) **Revenue reserves of T Ltd**

Care must be taken here! When did T Ltd become a member of the H Ltd group? Certainly not on 1 January 20X4, because S Ltd was not a subsidiary of H Ltd at that time. The answer is 30 June 20X4, because only from that time was T Ltd a subsidiary of S Ltd **and** a member of the H Ltd group. Hence, only revenue reserves of T Ltd arising after 30 June 20X4 can be viewed as post-acquisition as regards the H Ltd group.

The same procedures as outlined above can now be performed for the consolidation, dealing with the two acquisitions separately. The detailed workings are left for the student to do.

The only difference from the earlier example is that the revenue reserves of T Ltd were £5,000 more at the date when H Ltd became T Ltd's ultimate parent company. Hence, 'goodwill on consolidation' will be reduced by £3,000 (H's interest in T × £5,000) = £3,000.

Goodwill (at cost)	£27,000
Consolidated reserves	£115,000

2.8 The effect on the group financial statements of using the direct and indirect methods

As we have seen, the direct method computes the group accounts of the holding company using the effective interest of the parent company in the subsidiary to allocate share capital and reserves. The indirect method would consolidate the sub-subsidiary with the subsidiary to produce the group accounts of the subsidiary and then the accounts of the parent company and the accounts of the subsidiary group can be consolidated (ie, by this stage the subsidiary group can be dealt with as one accounting entity).

The two approaches will not make any difference to the assets and liabilities recorded in the parent company group balance sheet, nor a difference in the gross turnover and costs in the consolidated profit and loss account.

There may however be differences in the amounts of goodwill, minority interests, and group reserves due to the different way in which the reserves of the sub-subsidiary are allocated. The nature and size of the differences will depend on the precise circumstances of each case.

3 THE CONSOLIDATION OF MIXED GROUPS

3.1 Approach

The approach is similar to the direct method of dealing with sub-subsidiaries ie, an effective interest is computed and used to allocate share capital and reserves. The approach will be illustrated by the following example.

The following are the summarised balance sheets of T Ltd, P Ltd and A Ltd as at 31 December 20X4:

	T Ltd	*P Ltd*	*A Ltd*
	£	£	£
Fixed assets	140,000	61,000	170,000
Investments (see notes)	200,000	65,000	-
Net current assets	10,000	14,000	10,000
	350,000	140,000	180,000
Ordinary shares of £1 each	200,000	80,000	100,000
Profit and loss account	150,000	60,000	80,000
	350,000	140,000	180,000

You ascertain that:

(a) On 1 January 20X3 P Ltd acquired 35,000 ordinary shares in A Ltd at a cost of £65,000 when the revenue reserves of A Ltd amounted to £40,000.

(b) On 1 January 20X4 T Ltd acquired 64,000 ordinary shares in P Ltd at a cost of £120,000 and 40,000 shares in A Ltd at a cost of £80,000. The revenue reserves of P Ltd and A Ltd amounted to £50,000 and £60,000 respectively on 1 January 20X4.

You are required to prepare the consolidated balance sheet of the T Ltd group as at 31 December 20X4. Goodwill is amortised over 4 years from the date of acquisition, with a full year's charge in the year of acquisition.

3.2 Solution

Step 1 The basic approach is similar to that used in vertical groups.

Group structure

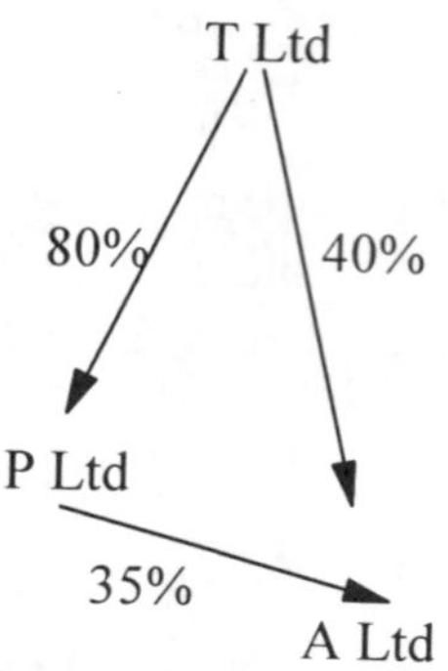

Respective interest in P Ltd and A Ltd:

	P Ltd				*A Ltd*	
T Ltd shareholders	80%	(D)	Direct	=	40%	
			Indirect 80% × 35%	=	28%	
						68%
Minority shareholders	20%	(D)	Direct	=	25%	
			Indirect 20% × 35%	=	7%	
						32%
	100%					100%

Notes:

(a) T Ltd effectively owns 68% of A Ltd. This comprises a direct holding of 40% and an indirect holding (exercised through T Ltd's controlling interest in P Ltd) of 28%.

(b) A Ltd is a member of the T Ltd group because T Ltd and P Ltd (a subsidiary of T Ltd) together own more than 50% of the share capital of A Ltd (in fact, together they hold 75%).

Diagrammatic representation of shareholdings and revenue reserves:

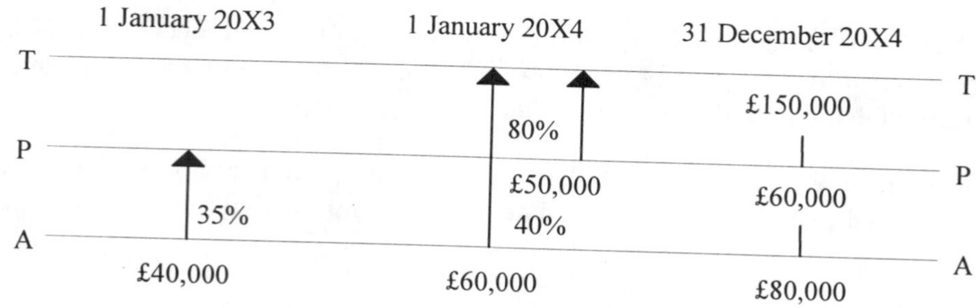

Step 2 Prepare consolidation schedules:

Goodwill

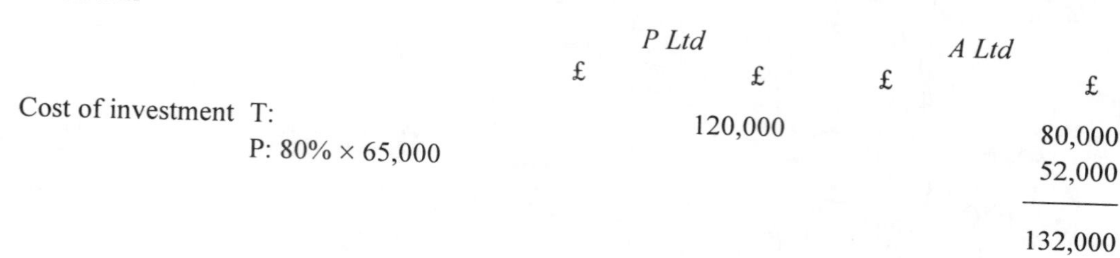

	P Ltd		*A Ltd*	
	£	£	£	£
Cost of investment T:		120,000		80,000
P: 80% × 65,000				52,000
				132,000

Less: Share of net assets acquired				
Share capital	80,000		100,000	
Profit and loss account	50,000		60,000	
	130,000 (80%)	(104,000)	160,000 (68%)	(108,800)
Goodwill		16,000		23,200
Amortisation charge		(4,000)		(5,800)
		12,000		17,400

Consolidated profit and loss account reserve

		£
T Ltd:		150,000
P Ltd: 80% (60,000 – 50,000)		8,000
A Ltd: 68% (80,000 – 60,000)		13,600
Less: Goodwill amortised	P	(4,000)
	A	(5,800)
		161,800

Minority interest

	£	£
P Ltd: Share capital	80,000	
Profit and loss account	60,000	
	140,000	
Less: Cost of investment in A	(65,000)	
	75,000 (20%)	15,000
A Ltd: Share capital	100,000	
Profit and loss account	80,000	
	180,000 (32%)	57,600
		72,600

Step 3 **Consolidated balance sheet of T Ltd and its subsidiary companies as at 31 December 20X4**

	£	£
Fixed assets:		
Intangible assets		29,400
Tangible assets		371,000
Net current assets		34,000
Total assets less current liabilities		434,400
Minority interests		72,600
Capital and reserves:		
Called up share capital, allotted and fully paid	200,000	
Profit and loss account	161,800	
		361,800
		434,400

Having worked through the solution to this question, try working it on your own.

4 CHAPTER SUMMARY

There are two types of complex groups - vertical and mixed. Similar techniques can be applied to the consolidation of both types by working out an effective interest of the holding company in each subsidiary and using this interest to allocate share capital and reserves.

5 SELF TEST QUESTIONS

5.1 What is a vertical group? (1.2)

5.2 What is a mixed group? (1.3)

5.3 What are the two methods of dealing with sub-subsidiaries? (2.1)

5.4 Do the methods make any difference to the consolidated assets of the group? (2.8)

6 EXAMINATION TYPE QUESTION

6.1 H Ltd

The balance sheets of H Ltd, S Ltd and T Ltd, as at 31 December 20X8 were as follows:

	H Ltd	*S Ltd*	*T Ltd*
	£	£	£
Ordinary share capital (£1 shares)	100,000	75,000	50,000
Reserves	120,000	60,000	40,000
	220,000	135,000	90,000
60,000 shares in S Ltd	95,000		
30,000 shares in T Ltd		48,000	
Sundry net assets	125,000	87,000	90,000
	220,000	135,000	90,000

The investments were acquired as follows:

		Balances on	
		S Ltd Reserves	*T Ltd Reserves*
		£	£
(a)	Both investments acquired 31 December 20X1	10,000	8,000
(b)	H Ltd in S Ltd on 31 December 20X2	12,000	15,000
	S Ltd in T Ltd on 31 December 20X4	20,000	18,000
(c)	S Ltd in T Ltd on 31 December 20X5	30,000	25,000
	H Ltd in S Ltd on 31 December 20X7	40,000	32,000

You are required to prepare the consolidated balance sheet of H Ltd and its subsidiary companies, as at 31 December 20X8 for each of the three possible situations. **(25 marks)**

Show goodwill as a permanent asset.

7 ANSWER TO EXAMINATION TYPE QUESTION

7.1 H Ltd

Group structure

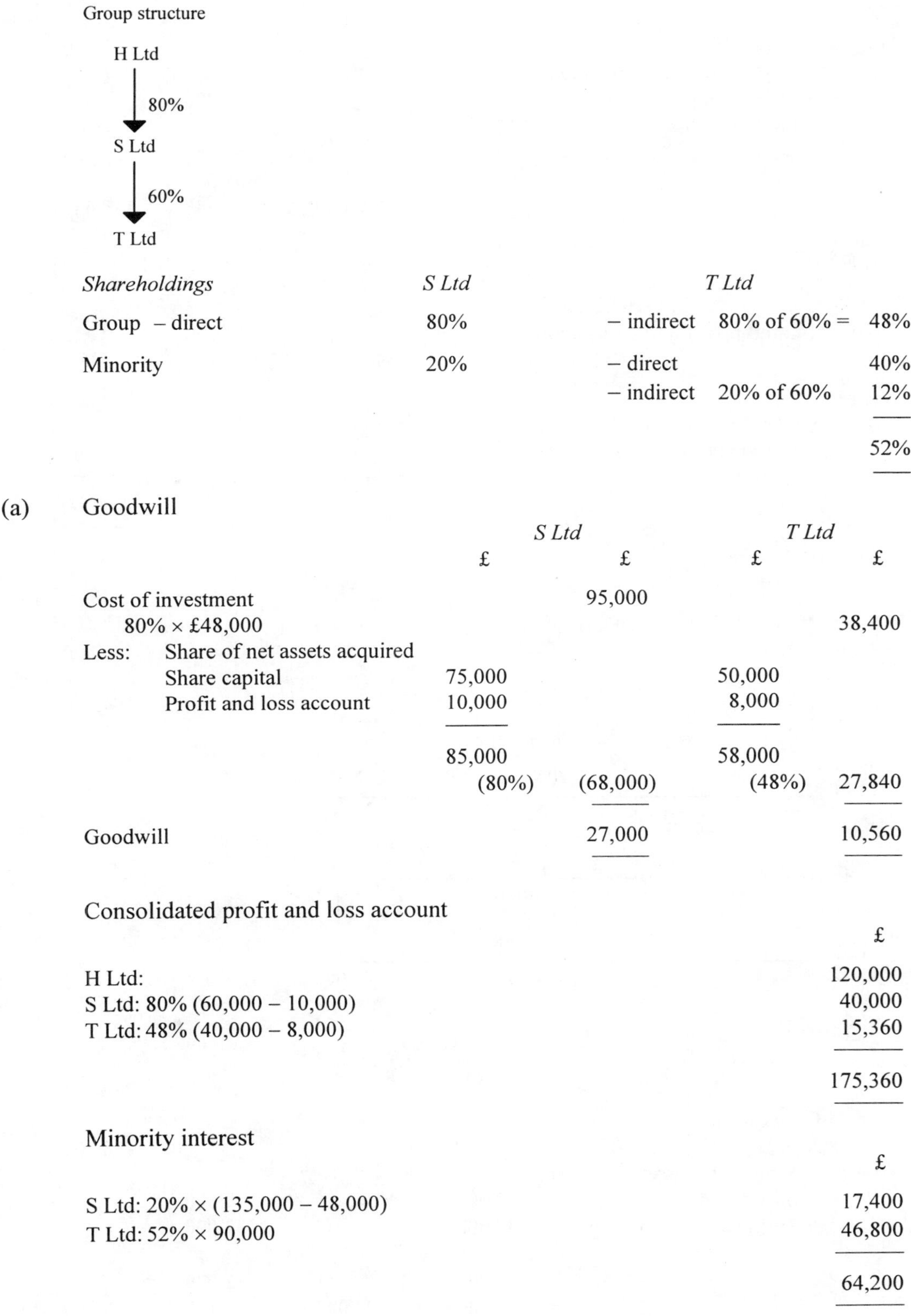

Shareholdings	*S Ltd*		*T Ltd*	
Group – direct	80%	– indirect	80% of 60% =	48%
Minority	20%	– direct		40%
		– indirect	20% of 60%	12%
				52%

(a) Goodwill

	S Ltd		*T Ltd*	
	£	£	£	£
Cost of investment		95,000		
80% × £48,000				38,400
Less: Share of net assets acquired				
Share capital	75,000		50,000	
Profit and loss account	10,000		8,000	
	85,000		58,000	
	(80%)	(68,000)	(48%)	27,840
Goodwill		27,000		10,560

Consolidated profit and loss account

	£
H Ltd:	120,000
S Ltd: 80% (60,000 – 10,000)	40,000
T Ltd: 48% (40,000 – 8,000)	15,360
	175,360

Minority interest

	£
S Ltd: 20% × (135,000 – 48,000)	17,400
T Ltd: 52% × 90,000	46,800
	64,200

(b) Goodwill

		S Ltd		T Ltd	
		£	£	£	£
Cost of investment			95,000		
80% × £48,000					38,400
Less:	Share of net assets acquired				
	Share capital	75,000		50,000	
	Profit and loss account	12,000		18,000	
		87,000		68,000	
		(80%)	(69,600)	(48%)	(32,640)
Goodwill			25,400		5,760

Consolidated profit and loss account

	£
H Ltd:	120,000
S Ltd: 80% (60,000 – 12,000)	38,400
T Ltd: 48% (40,000 – 18,000)	10,560
	168,960

Minority interest

	£
S Ltd: 20% × (135,000 – 48,000)	17,400
T Ltd: 52% × 90,000	46,800
	64,200

(c)

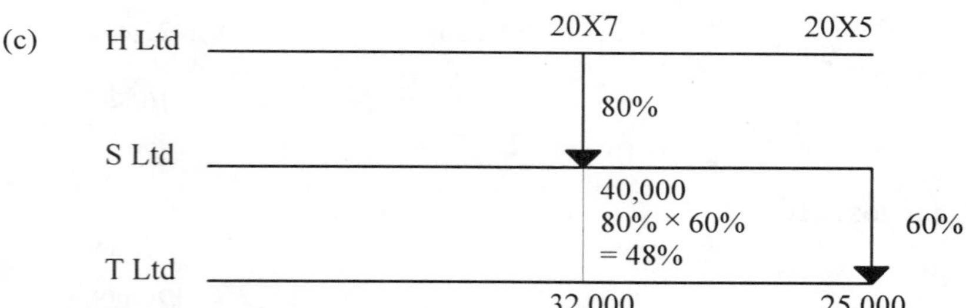

Goodwill

		S Ltd		T Ltd	
		£	£	£	£
Cost of investment			95,000		
80% × £48,000					38,400
Less:	Share of net assets acquired				
	Share capital	75,000		50,000	
	Profit and loss account	40,000		32,000	
		115,000		82,000	
		(80%)	92,000	(48%)	39,360
Goodwill/(negative goodwill)			3,000		(960)

Consolidated profit and loss account

	£
H Ltd:	120,000
S Ltd: 80% (60,000 – 40,000)	16,000
T Ltd: 48% (40,000 – 32,000)	3,840
	139,840

Minority interest

	£
S Ltd: 20% × (135,000 – 48,000)	17,400
T Ltd: 52% × 90,000	46,800
	64,200

Consolidated balance sheets as at 31 December 20X8

	(a) £	*(b)* £	*(c)* £
Goodwill on consolidation	37,560	31,160	2,040
Sundry net assets	302,000	302,000	302,000
Minority interests	(64,200)	(64,200)	(64,200)
	275,360	268,960	239,840
Capital and reserves			
Called up share capital	100,000	100,000	100,000
Consolidated revenue reserves	175,360	168,960	139,840
	275,360	268,960	239,840

15 CONSOLIDATED ACCOUNTS - CHANGES IN A GROUP

INTRODUCTION & LEARNING OBJECTIVES

Acquisitions and disposals of subsidiaries trigger off special accounting problems mainly in the accounting period in which the change occurs. FRS 2 states the considerations which apply when a change occurs although it does not deal with the consolidation method to use (see FRS 6 in the next chapter) nor the problems of attributing fair values in acquisition accounting (see FRS 7 in the next chapter).

When you have studied this chapter you should be able to do the following:

- Account for piecemeal acquisitions.
- Account for disposals or part disposals of subsidiaries.
- Understand the principles of demerger.

1 CHANGES OF PARENT COMPANY INTEREST

1.1 Date of change in composition of a group

The date on which an undertaking becomes or ceases to be another undertaking's subsidiary undertaking marks the point at which a new accounting treatment for that undertaking is applied. The relevant date is the date on which **control** passes. This date should also be the one on which an undertaking begins or ceases to qualify as a parent or subsidiary undertaking under CA89. The date on which control passes is a matter of fact and cannot be backdated or otherwise altered.

Where control is transferred by a public offer, the date control is transferred is the date the offer becomes unconditional, usually as a result of a sufficient number of acceptances being received. For private treaties, the date control is transferred is generally the date an unconditional offer is accepted.

Where an undertaking becomes or ceases to be a subsidiary undertaking as a result of the issue or cancellation of shares, the date control is transferred is the date of issue or cancellation.

The date that control passes may be indicated by the acquiring party commencing its direction of the operating and financial policies of the acquired undertaking or by changes in the flow of economic benefits. The date on which the consideration for the transfer of control is paid is often an important indication of the date.

1.2 Acquisition of subsidiaries

When a subsidiary is first consolidated, the acquisition or merger method may be used depending upon the terms of the combination. FRS2 covers the accounting problems where the combination is made in stages. By implication, these problems only arise if acquisition accounting is used (ie, merger accounting would not be appropriate). These problems are dealt with below.

Other aspects of dealing with acquisitions under acquisition accounting include the allocation of fair values on acquisition to the net assets of the subsidiary and the choice of accounting for any goodwill arising. Fair values are dealt with in the next chapter. Goodwill has already been covered.

1.3 Disposal of subsidiaries

During the year, a parent company may decide to sell all or part of its shareholding in an individual company. Possible situations may include:

(a) the disposal of all the shares held in the subsidiary;

(b) the disposal of part of the shareholding, still leaving a controlling interest after the sale;

(c) the disposal of part of the shareholding, leaving a residual holding after the sale which is regarded either as an associated company investment or a trade investment.

Each of the situations will be examined in this chapter. In each case it has been assumed that acquisition accounting was originally used for the business combination. Disposals of subsidiaries which have previously been consolidated using merger accounting are not considered by *FRS 2*.

1.4 The problems caused by piecemeal acquisitions

A step-by-step or piecemeal acquisition arises when shares in the subsidiary are acquired over a period of time. The question arises as to whether goodwill should be computed by reference to each slice of share capital acquired, ie, whether the fair value of assets is considered on each acquisition of shares.

FRS 2 takes the simpler approach: the computation of goodwill will be one computation by reference to the fair value of the net assets of the subsidiary at the date the subsidiary becomes part of the group. This complies with Sch 4A para 9 CA85.

However, when a group increases its interest in an undertaking that is already its subsidiary, the identifiable assets and liabilities of that subsidiary should be revalued to fair value and goodwill arising on the increase in interest should be calculated by reference to that fair value. This revaluation is not required if the difference between fair values and carrying amounts of the identifiable assets and liabilities attributable to the increase in stake is not material.

1.5 Prepare consolidated financial statements incorporating piecemeal acquisitions

An example will illustrate the adjustments involved.

Company X acquires an 80% holding in Company Y over a number of years as shown below

Holding acquired %	*Fair value of net assets of Y* £m	*Price paid* £m
10	8	1.00
20	10	2.50
25	12	3.10
25	16	5.95
80		12.55

The investee's balance sheet at the consolidation date shows:

	£m
Net assets	20
Share capital	4
Reserves	16
	20

The amount of issued share capital has remained unchanged.

What amounts will be included in the consolidated balance sheets?

1.6 Solution

Step 1 Determine whether the company is a subsidiary at the date of consolidation and, if so consolidate assets and liabilities with minority being allocated their share of share capital and reserves at that date.

MI 20% × £20m = £4m

Step 2 Perform separate calculations of goodwill as at

(a) date investee became associate (if applicable)
(b) date investee became subsidiary
(c) date further investments made.

Goodwill computations

	Transaction 2	3	4	*Total*
	£m	£m	£m	£m
Cost of investment	3.5	3.1	5.95	
Share of net assets acquired at each relevant date:				
30% × £10m	3.0			
25% × £12m		3.0		
25% × £16m			4.00	
Goodwill	0.5	0.1	1.95	2.55
Post acquisition reserves				
30% × (16 – (10 – 4))	3.0			
25% × (16 – (12 – 4))		2.0		
25% × (16 – (16 – 4))			1.0	6.0

Step 3 Effect on group balance sheet

	£m
Goodwill	2.55
Consolidated net assets	20
MI	(4)
	18.55
Addition to group reserves	(6.00)
Elimination of cost of investment	12.55

1.7 The effects of a subsequent bonus issue or a capital reduction of a subsidiary company

The examiner refers to two types of changes in share capital of a subsidiary following its acquisition. Either may appear as a complication in an examination question.

(a) **Bonus issue**

A bonus issue is a transfer of reserves to share capital. It therefore should not affect the financial statements of the group. The net assets of the group are the same and the parent company has the same percentage interest in the subsidiary. Care needs to be taken to consider properly the 'reserves at acquisition' figure supplied to you in the question however.

If the bonus issue is less than the amount of reserves which existed at the date of acquisition, then reduce the reserves at acquisition by the bonus issue when calculating goodwill. Goodwill remains the same as the share capital increases by the group share of the bonus issue.

If the bonus issue is more than the amount of reserves which existed at the date of acquisition, then as far as the group is concerned, the post acquisition profits recorded in group reserves should be the same as before the issue. Therefore the group share of all the remaining reserves of the subsidiary need to go to consolidated reserves and **in addition** the group share of the post-acquisition profits which have been turned into share capital need to be included in consolidated reserves rather than the goodwill calculation.

(b) **Capital reduction**

A capital reduction normally arises when a company has got into financial difficulties and the detail of reconstruction schemes is covered later in the text. The normal feature is that some of the share capital is written off so that a debit balance on the profit and loss account is eliminated. In addition however, further write offs may be required due to the write down in value of assets.

It is thus similar to a bonus issue to the extent that it effectively represents a transfer from share capital **to** reserves. There should thus be no effect on the consolidated balance sheet. It will however be easier to compute goodwill which arose on the original acquisition by using the original figures for share capital and reserves.

If there has been an asset write down, then the group share of the asset write down must be charged against group reserves.

The easiest way to account for the effect on the group financial statements is generally to compute the allocation of share capital and reserves before the effect of the capital reduction on these items as the following example demonstrates.

1.8 Example

A plc has an 80% interest in Y Ltd which is undertaking a capital reduction scheme. The balance sheet before the capital reduction is as follows

	£
Net assets	500,000
Share capital	650,000
Profit and loss	(150,000)
	500,000

The capital reduction scheme will eliminate the debit balance on the profit and loss account and reduce assets by £100,000.

A plc paid £800,000 for its investment when the reserves of Y Ltd were £200,000. Goodwill arising on the acquisition has been fully amortised.

Show how the relevant items would be included in the consolidated balance sheet.

Step 1 Put through the capital reduction scheme

	£
Net assets	400,000
Share capital	400,000

Profit and loss	-
	400,000

Step 2 Minority interests

20% × 400,000 = £80,000

Step 3 Goodwill

Calculate using original figures

	£	£
Cost of investment		800,000
Less: Share of net assets acquired		
Share capital	650,000	
Reserves	200,000	
	850,000 (80%)	680,000
Goodwill - fully amortised		120,000

Step 4 Compute post acquisition reserves to go to group reserves.

	£
Reserves at acquisition	200,000
Loss at time of capital reduction	150,000
Post acquisition loss	350,000
Add asset write down	100,000
	450,000
Loss to group reserves 80%	360,000
Add goodwill fully amortised	120,000
	480,000

Effect on consolidated balance sheet

	£
Net assets	400,000
MI	(80,000)
	320,000
Group reserves reduced by	480,000
Elimination of cost of investment	800,000

2 DISPOSALS OF SUBSIDIARIES

2.1 FRS 2's accounting and disclosure requirements

Where there is a material disposal (ie, sale of a substantial shareholding), the consolidated profit and loss account should include:

(a) the appropriate proportion of the results (ie, turnover and profit) of the subsidiary up to the date of sale. The results of the subsidiary are likely to be separately disclosed on the face of the profit and loss account as they may constitute a 'discontinued operation' under *FRS 3;*

(b) the gain or loss (usually treated as an exceptional item) on the sale of the investment. The calculation of the gain or loss is rather tricky. It is the difference between:

(i) the proceeds of sale, and

(ii) the parent company share of the net assets of the subsidiary, at the date of sale, plus the goodwill on consolidation to the extent that it has not been written off (amortised) through the profit and loss account.

2.2 Preparing group accounts following a disposal of shares

First we shall examine the situation where a parent company disposes of its entire shareholding in a subsidiary (a 'total disposal'). Consider the following balance sheets.

Balance sheet at 31 December 20X8

	H Ltd	*S Ltd*
	£'000	£'000
Shares in S Ltd at cost (75%)	82.5	-
Other sundry assets	257.5	100
	340.0	100
Called up share capital – £1 ordinary	200.0	60
Profit and loss account	140.0	40
	340.0	100

H Ltd acquired the shares in 20X3 when S Ltd's profit and loss account stood at £10,000. The whole holding was sold for £115,000 on 31 December 20X8.

Assume that goodwill is carried as a permanent item.

Ignore taxation.

Prepare the consolidated balance sheet before the disposal and analyse the gain which will be reported on the sale.

2.3 Solution

Consolidated balance sheet before disposal

	£'000	£'000
Goodwill on consolidation (82.5 – 75% × (60 + 10))		30.0
Other sundry net assets		357.5
		387.5
Called-up capital – £1 ordinary		200.0
Consolidated reserves		
H Ltd	140.0	
S Ltd (75% × (40 – 10))	22.5	162.5
		362.5
Minority interests (25% × 100)		25.0
		387.5

The gain on sale would be computed

		£'000
(a)	Separate accounts of H Ltd	
	Proceeds	115.0
	Carrying amount – cost	(82.5)
		32.5

		£'000
(b)	Consolidation	
	Proceeds	115.0
	Less: Share of net assets (75% × 100)	(75.0)
	Goodwill not yet written off	(30.0)
		10.0

The difference between the gains represents the profits relating to the shares sold retained in the subsidiary, ie £22,500 which are already included in consolidated reserves.

Thus the gains may be computed using an alternative method

		£'000
(a)	Separate accounts of H Ltd (as above)	32.5
	Less: Post-acquisition profits to date of disposal	(22.5)
(b)	Gain to group	10.0

2.4 Example illustrating FRS 3 disclosure

Balance sheets as in the example in para 2.2. The profit and loss accounts for the year ended 31 December 20X8 are as follows

	H Ltd Group £'000	*S Ltd* £'000
Turnover	300	200
Cost of sales	(190)	(120)
Gross profit	110	80
Administrative expenses	(30)	(25)
Distribution costs	(20)	(15)
Profit before taxation	60	40
Taxation	(21)	(14)
Profit after taxation	39	26
Dividends payable	(10)	-
Retained for the year	29	26
Brought forward	111	14
Carried forward	140	40

The entire holding in S Ltd is sold on 30 September 20X8 for £135,000. Taxation on any gain is to be ignored. Goodwill arising on consolidation is carried as a permanent item in the consolidated balance sheet. H Ltd has not yet accounted for the disposal. H Ltd has other, 100%, subsidiaries.

Prepare the consolidated profit and loss account for the year in accordance with FRS 3, incorporating the gain on the disposal.

Work to the nearest £.

2.5 Solution

Step 1 The gain on sale would be computed as follows

H Ltd's accounts

		£	£
Proceeds			135,000
Cost			(82,500)
Gain to H Ltd			52,500

Consolidated accounts

		£	£
Proceeds			135,000
Less:	Share of net assets at disposal		
	B/d (60 + 14 [40 – 26])	74,000	
	In year up to disposal (26 × 9/12)	19,500	
	Group share (75%)	93,500	(70,125)
			64,875
Less:	Goodwill not yet written off		(30,000)
Gain to group			£34,875

Step 2 The consolidated profit and loss account would be as follows

H Ltd Consolidated profit and loss account for the year ended 31 December 20X8

	Continuing operations £	*Discontinued operations* £	*Total* £
Turnover (200,000 × 9/12)	300,000	150,000	450,000
Cost of sales (120,000 × 9/12)	(190,000)	(90,000)	(280,000)
Gross profit	110,000	60,000	170,000
Administrative expenses (25,000 × 9/12)	(30,000)	(18,750)	(48,750)
Distribution costs (15,000 × 9/12)	(20,000)	(11,250)	(31,250)
Operating profit	60,000	30,000	90,000
Profit on disposal of discontinued operations	-	34,875	34,875
Profit on ordinary activities before taxation	60,000	64,875	124,875
Tax on profit on ordinary activities (21,000 + 9/12 × 14,000)			(31,500)
Profit on ordinary activities after taxation			93,375
Minority interest (25% × £26,000 × 9/12)			(4,875)
Profit for the financial year			88,500
Dividends			(10,000)
Retained profit for the financial year			78,500

Note to the financial statements

Reserves

	Profit and loss account H Ltd	*Profit and loss account* Group
	£	£
At beginning of year	111,000	114,000
Transfer from profit and loss account of the year (29,000 + 52,500)	81,500	78,500
At end of year	192,500	192,500

The split of the operating expenses could be shown as a note rather than on the face of the profit and loss account as illustrated in FRS 3, but for exam purposes the above method is the quickest.

2.6 Effect of goodwill

(a) Goodwill carried as a permanent item

In the example above it was assumed that goodwill arising on consolidation had been carried as a permanent item in the consolidated balance sheet. FRS 10 allows goodwill to be retained in the balance sheet, provided that certain conditions are met and subject to annual impairment reviews.

However, remember that the gain to the group was calculated as follows

	£	*Consolidated* £
Proceeds		135,000
Less: Share of net assets at disposal		
B/d (60 + 14)	74,000	
In year up to disposal (26 × 9/12)	19,500	
Group share 75%	93,500	(70,125)
		64,875
Less: Goodwill		(30,000)
Gain to group		34,875

At the moment of disposal, the goodwill relating to that part (all) of the original holding disposed of was written off as part of the gain on sale, thereby passing through the consolidated profit and loss account.

(b) Goodwill amortised over time

In accordance with FRS 10, purchased goodwill is normally amortised through the profit and loss account over its useful economic life. If only part of the goodwill has been written off prior to disposal only part will have passed through the consolidated profit and loss account. The **remainder** should be made to pass through the profit and loss account as part of the gain on sale.

For example, if in the example above, £18,000 out of the total goodwill of £30,000 had been written off by the date of disposal the group gain on disposal would be calculated as

		Consolidated £
Proceeds		135,000
Less:	Share of net assets at disposal (as above)	(70,125)
Less:	Goodwill not written off relating to disposal (30,000 – 18,000)	(12,000)
		52,875

This is clearly a different figure. Whereas previously £30,000 was written off as part of the group gain on sale, here £12,000 has been written off as part of the gain on sale and the other £18,000 as part of the amortisation of goodwill. Nevertheless the total amount passing through the consolidated profit and loss account is still £30,000.

(c) **Goodwill written off immediately to reserves**

Under SSAP 22 this was the preferred treatment for purchased goodwill. FRS 10 has now effectively outlawed this method, although it is included here for completeness.

In this situation no goodwill has been written off through the consolidated profit and loss account. In order to prevent purchased goodwill from by-passing the consolidated profit and loss account altogether FRS 2 requires the gain or loss on disposal to be determined by including the attributable amount of purchased goodwill which has previously been eliminated **against reserves** as a matter of accounting policy. In order to meet this requirement the goodwill eliminated against reserves must be reinstated on disposal of the interest in the subsidiary.

Facts as previously, except that group policy is to eliminate goodwill arising on consolidation by immediate write off to reserves.

The consolidated gain would be computed as follows giving exactly the same gain as when the policy was to carry goodwill as a permanent item.

		Consolidated £
Proceeds		135,000
Less:	Share of net assets at date of disposal (as above)	(70,125)
		64,875
Less:	Goodwill reinstated	(30,000)
		34,875

The 'other side' of the entry to reduce the gain above (a Dr) is a Cr to Consolidated Reserves reinstating that goodwill

	Consolidated £
At 1 January 20X8 (114 – 30)	84,000
Retained for year (as above)	78,500
Goodwill reinstated	30,000
At 31 December 20X8	192,500

Overall total goodwill of £30,000 has passed through the consolidated profit and loss account once again, leading to equality of treatment whatever accounting policy has been chosen with regard to goodwill.

2.7 Partial disposal – subsidiary to associate

In this situation the disposal will reduce the shareholding below 50%. The entity will be consolidated up to the date of disposal and equity accounted from the date of disposal. Any gain or loss is computed as previously.

2.8 Example

Profit and loss accounts for the year ended 31 December 20X9

	H Ltd	*S Ltd*	*A Ltd*
	£	£	£
Profit before tax	100,000	80,000	30,000
Corporation tax	35,000	28,000	10,500
	65,000	52,000	19,500
Proposed dividend	20,000		
Retained for year	£45,000		

H Ltd acquired its investments

Company	*%*	*Date*	*Cost*	*Share capital*	*Reserves at acquisition*	*Goodwill on consolidation*
			£	£	£	£
S Ltd	80	20X0	110,000	100,000	12,000	20,400
A Ltd	60	20X5	60,000	70,000	10,000	12,000

One third of H Ltd's shares in A Ltd were sold on 31 March 20X9 for £35,000. Goodwill on consolidation has been fully amortised. A Ltd's reserves at 1 January 20X9 amounted to £25,000.

2.9 Solution

Step 1 The gain on sale would be computed as follows

		£	£
H Ltd			
Proceeds			35,000
Cost 20/60 × £60,000			(20,000)
			£15,000
Group			
Proceeds			35,000
Share of net assets at date of disposal			
Brought forward – share capital		70,000	
– reserves		25,000	
In year up to disposal 3/12 × £19,500		4,875	
	20% ×	£99,875	(19,975)
Group gain			15,025

Step 2 A consolidation schedule could be prepared as follows

	H Ltd		*S Ltd*		*A Ltd Subsidiary (3/12)*	*A Ltd As associate (9/12 × 40%)*	*Consolidated*
	£		£		£	£	£
Profit before tax	100,000		80,000		7,500		187,500
Share of associate						9,000	9,000
							196,500
Corporation tax	(35,000)		(28,000)		(2,625)		(65,625)
Share of associate						(3,150)	(3,150)
	65,000		52,000		4,875	5,850	127,725
Minority		(20%)	(10,400)	(40%)	(1,950)		(12,350)
			41,600		2,925		£115,375

Step 3 The consolidated profit and loss account would be as follows

H Ltd Consolidated profit and loss account for 20X9

	£	£
Profit before tax		187,500
Income from interests in associated undertakings		9,000
Profit on disposal of continuing operations		15,025
		211,525
Taxation		
Group	(65,625)	
Share of associated undertaking	(3,150)	
		(68,775)
Profit after tax		142,750
Minority interests		(12,350)
Profit attributable to members of H Ltd		130,400
Proposed dividend		(20,000)
Retained for year		£110,400

Since all operations are continuing, the disclosure is considerably simplified.

2.10 Accounting for a partial disposal of shares in a remaining subsidiary

Although there will be a gain on sale, the subsidiary will be consolidated for the whole year, only the % holding will change, not the entity's status as a subsidiary.

2.11 Example

Facts as in example 2.8 except that only 5% of A Ltd's issued shares were sold on 31 March 20X9 for £12,000.

2.12 Solution

Step 1 The gain on sale would be computed as follows

H Ltd	£	£
Proceeds		12,000
Cost $^{5}/_{60}$ × £60,000		(5,000)
		7,000

Group

Proceeds			12,000
Share of net assets at date of disposal			
Brought forward – share capital		70,000	
– reserves		25,000	
In year up to disposal $^{3}/_{12} \times$ £19,500		4,875	
	5% ×	99,875	(4,994)
Group gain			7,006

Step 2 A consolidation schedule could be prepared as follows

	H Ltd	*S Ltd*	*A Ltd*	*Consolidated*
	£	£	£	£
Profit before tax	100,000	80,000	30,000	210,000
Tax	(35,000)	(28,000)	(10,500)	(73,500)
PAT		52,000	19,500	

Minority interest		£
In S Ltd	20% × 52,000	10,400
In A Ltd	40% × $^{3}/_{12} \times$ £19,500	1,950
	45% × $^{9}/_{12} \times$ £19,500	6,581
		18,931

Step 3 The consolidated profit and loss account would be as follows

H Ltd Consolidated profit and loss account for 20X9	£
Profit before tax	210,000
Profit on disposal of continuing operations	7,006
	217,006
Taxation	(73,500)
Profit after tax	143,506
Minority interests	(18,931)
Profit attributable to members of H Ltd	124,575
Proposed dividend	(20,000)
Retained for year	104,575

Again, since all operations are continuing, the disclosure is considerably simplified.

2.13 Treatment of dividends

The treatment is straightforward and does not involve any pro-rating calculations. There are two alternatives

(a) the dividend has been **paid** prior to disposal, then the net assets of the subsidiary will have been reduced by the cash payment. Thus the full amount paid is taken out.

(b) the dividend is paid after the date of disposal or it is merely proposed. In either of these cases, the net assets have not been reduced by a cash payment prior to disposal. Therefore the dividend may be ignored.

2.14 Example

S Ltd has the following summary profit and loss account for year ended 31 December 20X8.

	£'000
Profit after tax	240
Dividend paid in April	(50)
Dividend proposed	(70)
Retained profit	120
Retained profit b/d	580
Retained profit c/d	700

H Ltd acquired 80% of S Ltd 4 years ago when S Ltd had share capital of £200,000 and reserves of £250,000. Ignore goodwill.

H Ltd disposed of half of its holding in S Ltd on 1 July 20X8 for £400,000.

Calculate the profit on disposal for the group.

Ignore taxation.

2.15 Solution

		£	£
Sale proceeds			400,000
Share of net assets at disposal			
Brought forward (580 + 200)		780,000	
In year (½ × £240,000) – *50,000		70,000	
	40% ×	850,000	(340,000)
			£60,000

* The dividend paid is deducted from the profits for the first half of the year and the proposed dividend is ignored.

2.16 Taxation

The corporation tax payable on the gain is based on the gain in the parent company books, not the gain in the group accounts.

	£
Sale proceeds	X
Less: Cost	X
Gross gain	X
Tax computed as corporate tax rate × gross gain	X

This tax is then included in the tax charge relating to the discontinued activity.

2.17 Activity

H Ltd purchased 80% of the ordinary share capital of S Ltd on 30 September 20X4 for £15,000. S Ltd's share capital and reserves at that date were as follows:

	£
Share capital	10,000
Reserves	5,000
	15,000

Goodwill arising on consolidation was amortised over 10 years from the date of acquisition. On 30 September 20X8, H Ltd sold 25% of its holding in S Ltd for £10,000. S Ltd's profit after tax for the year ended 31 December 20X8 is £6,000, its opening reserves for 20X8 being £24,000.

What is the profit or loss arising on the disposal of S Ltd to be included in the consolidated accounts for the year ended 31 December 20X8?

2.18 Activity solution

Step 1 Calculate consolidated goodwill.

	£
Cost	15,000
80% net assets acquired	12,000
Goodwill	3,000
Amortisation (3,000 ÷ 10 × 4)	(1,200)
	1,800

Step 2 Calculate gain/loss.

	£	£
Proceeds		10,000
Less: Share of net assets at 1.1.X8 (10 + 24) × 20%	6,800	
Share of profit for year to disposal 20% × 6,000	1,200	
		(8,000)
		2,000
Less: Goodwill not yet amortised (1,800 × 25%)		(450)
		1,550

Conclusion Gain to be included in the consolidated accounts is £1,550.

3 CHANGES IN THE INTERNAL STRUCTURE OF A GROUP

3.1 The reasons why groups change their internal structures

Definition The internal structure of a group is the number of companies and/or divisions that exist and the legal, accounting and reporting relationships between the companies/divisions.

The legal structure tends to reflect the way the group wants to manage the total operations and the way the individual sections report.

Thus a group may have a pyramid structure as below.

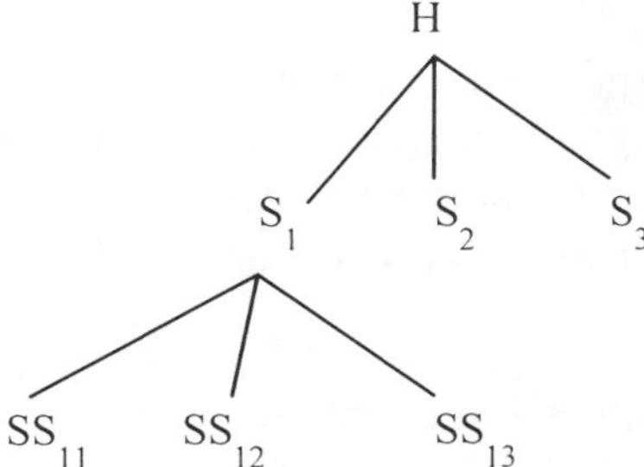

The bottom level companies (sub-subsidiaries) report to the next level (subsidiaries) which in turn report to the holding company. This structure supports a hierarchical style of management.

Other groups may prefer a flatter organisational structure with perhaps the number of subsidiaries being reduced and most subsidiaries being directly owned by the holding company.

Clearly with changes in management at the top of a group or changes in the operating environment for a group, changes may be thought necessary in the legal structure of a group. It is of course possible for the reporting and management structure to operate in a different way from the legal structure but, in the long run, it is easier if the two coincide.

Further reasons why a group may change its structure include taxation (the total taxation borne by the group can be affected by the legal structure of the group) and overseas operations (which may need to be operated as separate subsidiaries to comply with local laws).

3.2 The effects of changes in the direct ownership of subsidiaries

In principle the reorganisation of the group should result in no changes in the group financial statements. The reorganisations are achieved by transferring the shareholdings from one group company to another. No assets leave or are added to the group as a result.

Accounting problems may arise, however, in the individual company(ies) which originally held the investment(s). The transferor company will be making a disposal of an asset. These problems can largely be overcome by the purchasing company paying consideration which equals the book value of the investment.

3.3 Why a company may demerge some of its subsidiaries

Definition A demerger is the splitting of a group into two or more parts, each of which continues to be owned by the original shareholders but with no legal relationship with the former other parts of the group.

A major example was the demerger of ICI into ICI and Zeneca in 1993.

A demerger is an extreme form of internal restructuring. The group becomes two groups but from the shareholders' point of view it is a restructuring as they retain the same effective interest in the two groups as they had in the original group.

The main reason given for demergers is to 'enhance shareholder value'. In the view of the directors making the decision, the stock market has a history of placing a value on the old group which does not equal the true value of the group. Splitting the group results in two publicly quoted groups which may be valued by the stock market at more than the former combined entity. This seems to have been the case with the demergers that have been done in the past but it is not a common type of reorganisation.

The impetus for demerging may be an unwanted bid by another company and is thus a means of defending the group from take-over. This appears to have been the case with ICI as the Hanson group was building up a stake.

3.4 Preparing the financial statements after a demerger

The preparation of financial statements after a demerger is quite straightforward providing you understand the nature of the transactions. In accounting terms a group is giving some of its assets ie, investments in subsidiaries, to its shareholders by distributing the shareholdings to them. This may be done directly or through the medium of another company. The end effect to the shareholders is the same.

A direct distribution of the investment is a distribution *in specie* as in the illustration below.

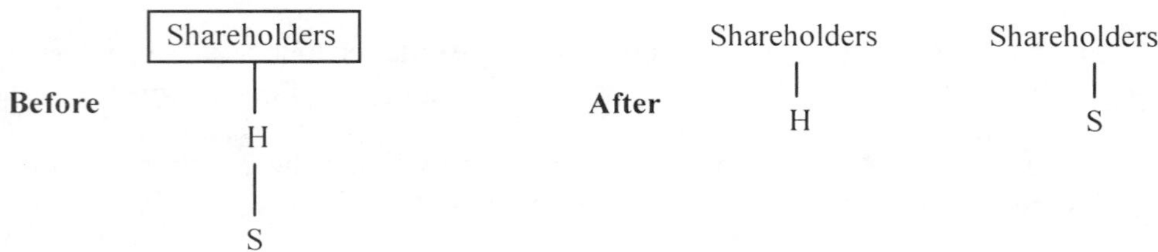

In accounting terms, the company is paying a dividend in the form of shares rather than cash. The entry in the holding company books is therefore:

Dr Profit and loss account (or directly to reserves)
Cr Cost of investment

with the (probably) book value of the investment.

Alternatively a new company may be formed and the shares issued to the shareholders in the existing group. The investment (or subsidiary) is transferred to the new company as below.

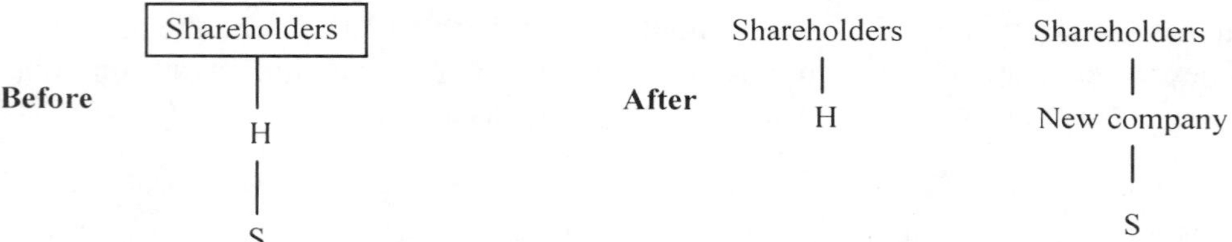

In the old parent company, the transaction is dealt with in the same way as for a direct distribution ie, a 'dividend' is being paid to the shareholders, the value of which is (probably) made to be equivalent to the book value of the net assets transferred to the new company or the cost of investment of the subsidiary being transferred.

3.5 Example

The summarised consolidated balance sheet of the X Group is shown below, together with the individual summarised balance sheets of X plc and its wholly owned subsidiary Y Ltd at 31 December 20X6.

	X Group £'000	*X plc* £'000	*Y Ltd* £'000
Investment in Y Ltd	-	800	-
Other net assets	3,600	2,200	1,400
	3,600	3,000	1,400
Share capital	2,000	2,000	800

Profit and loss account	1,600	1,000	600
	3,600	3,000	1,400

On 1 January 20X7, X plc forms a new company, Z Ltd. Z Ltd issues 800,000 £1 ordinary shares to the shareholders of X plc in exchange for X plc's investment in Y Ltd, so that Y Ltd is demerged.

Prepare the summarised financial statements of X plc and the X Group immediately after the demerger.

3.6 Solution

(Tutorial note: X plc has effectively made a distribution of £800,000 to its shareholders. The group's net assets are reduced by £1,400,000 and X plc's net assets by £800,000. The reduction is disclosed as a movement on retained earnings.*)*

	X Group £'000	*X plc* £'000
Net assets	2,200	2,200
Share capital	2,000	2,000
Profit and loss account b/f	1,600	1,000
Demerger	(1,400)	(800)
	2,200	2,200

4 CHAPTER SUMMARY

Piecemeal acquisitions are dealt with by waiting for the date the subsidiary becomes part of the group and performing a fair value exercise at that date.

Disposals require the calculation of a gain on disposal by reference to the book value of the net assets of the subsidiary at the date of disposal and goodwill originally purchased to the extent that it has not been written off through the consolidated profit and loss account.

Changes in the internal structures of groups do not generally affect the financial statements of the group but only the individual companies within the group.

5 SELF TEST QUESTIONS

5.1 What is the date when a subsidiary is acquired? (1.1)

5.2 How is a piecemeal acquisition dealt with? (1.4)

5.3 How should the reserves at acquisition be dealt with when there is a bonus issue in the subsidiary? (1.7)

5.4 How does FRS3 affect the disposal of subsidiaries? (2.4)

5.5 What happens in the computation of a gain on sale if goodwill was written off on acquisition? (2.6)

5.6 What adjustment is required if a dividend has been paid by the subsidiary before the date of disposal? (2.13)

5.7 How is taxation dealt with on disposal? (2.16)

5.8 What is a demerger? (3.3)

6 EXAMINATION TYPE QUESTION

6.1 Argent plc

Argent plc acquired the whole of the issued capital of 20,000,000 ordinary shares of £1 each in Plated plc some years ago for £64,125,000. At that date the reserves of Plated plc were £38,050,000.

During 20X9 Plated plc had been involved in litigation over claims that the company's processing methods were causing serious environmental pollution. Although the company had been successful in its legal action, the management were concerned about the possible adverse effect on the group. Therefore, on 31 December 20X9 the directors of Argent plc were considering three alternative courses of action in relation to its investment in Plated plc.

The three alternative courses of action were:

Alternative No. 1

This was to sell the 20,000,000 ordinary shares to a competitor, Maple Leaf plc for £90,000,000. At the date of the proposed sale on 31 December 20X9 the post-acquisition reserves of Plated plc were £28,350,000.

Alternative No. 2

This was to transfer the business and net assets of Plated plc to Argent Finance plc, which was another company within the Argent Group, for £92,475,000 and to liquidate Plated plc.

Alternative No. 3

This was to transfer the business and net assets of Plated plc to Silver Shine plc, a company that was not a member of the group, for £88,525,000 and to liquidate Plated plc.

Goodwill has not been amortised on the grounds that it has an indefinite useful economic life.

You are required:

(a) to show the entries to be made in the books of Argent plc on 31 December 20X9 on the assumption that:

   (i) all of the shares in Plated plc were sold to Maple Leaf plc for £90,000,000;

   (ii) the business and net assets of Plated plc were transferred to Argent Finance plc for £92,475,000;

   (iii) the business and net assets were transferred to Silver Shine plc for £88,525,000.

(6 marks)

(b) to show how the individual items in the consolidated accounts will be affected by:

   (i) the sale of the shares to Maple Leaf plc;
   (ii) the transfer of the business and net assets to Argent Finance plc;
   (iii) the transfer of the business and net assets to Silver Plating plc. **(10 marks)**

(c) to state how the individual items in the consolidated accounts will be affected by the sale to Maple Leaf Ltd if it has been the group policy to amortise the goodwill on consolidation over twenty years of which fifteen years has been charged to date. **(4 marks)**

(Total: 20 marks)

7 ANSWER TO EXAMINATION TYPE QUESTION

7.1 Argent plc

(Tutorial notes:

(1) A much simpler question than it first appears.

(2) For part (a) put down what you 'feel' is the right answer, even if you think it is too simplistic. It will probably be correct!

(3) For part (b) remember it is the **group** effect that is important. Take into account the increase in assets represented by retained post-acquisition profits.

(4) For part (c) remember that goodwill amortisation will be through the profit and loss account.*)*

			£'000
(a)	(i)	Sale proceeds	90,000
		Cost	64,125
		Gain to profit and loss account	25,875
	(ii)	Due from Argent Finance plc	92,475
		Cost	64,125
		Gain to profit and loss account	28,350
	(iii)	Sale proceeds	88,525
		Cost	64,125
		Gain to profit and loss account	24,400

(Tutorial note: the question gives no tax rates. Therefore, the answers above are the gains recorded in the individual accounts of Argent plc before tax.*)*

			£'000	£'000
(b)	(i)	Sale proceeds		90,000
		Cost	64,125	
		Post-acquisition profits	28,350	
				92,475
		Loss to group		(2,475)
		Of which goodwill not yet amortised		6,075

(Tutorial note: to the extent that goodwill has not been amortised through the profit and loss account it should be recognised in order to calculate the gain/loss (FRS 2).*)*

An alternative calculation of the overall gain is:

	£'000
Sale proceeds	90,000
Net assets at date of disposal (£20,000,000 + £38,050,000 + £28,350,000)	(86,400)
	3,600
Adjustment re goodwill not yet amortised	(6,075)
Loss to group	(2,475)

(ii) With an internal transfer of net assets there is *no* change to the position of the group. The profit achieved by Argent plc and the increases/decreases in asset and liability values will be eliminated upon consolidation of the group's profit and loss account and balance sheet.

(iii)

	£'000	£'000
Sale proceeds		88,525
Cost	64,125	
Post-acquisition profits	28,350	
		92,475
Loss to group		(3,950)
Of which goodwill is		6,075

In cases (b)(i) and (b)(iii) the post-acquisition profits of £28,350,000 will be incorporated in either the balance brought forward on the profit and loss account or the profit and loss account for the year (line-by-line), with the loss on disposal probably being shown as an exceptional item.

WORKING

Assuming the consideration was in cash, then acquisition accounting would have applied. Goodwill on consolidation would be valued as follows:

	£'000
Fair value of assets at acquisition:	
Capital	20,000
Reserves	38,050
	58,050
Consideration	64,125
Goodwill on consolidation	6,075

(c) If the goodwill has been amortised for fifteen of its expected twenty year 'life', the goodwill on consolidation at the year-end before disposal would have been:

	£'000	£'000
Original goodwill value		6,075
Fifteen years' amortisation (in round £'000)		4,556
Written down value		1,519
Sales proceeds		90,000
Net assets at date of acquisition		(86,400)
Goodwill	6,075	
Goodwill written off	4,556	
		(1,519)
Profit to group		2,081

(Tutorial note: as the goodwill of £4,556,000 has already passed through the profit and loss account it should not be treated as part of the cost to be set against sale proceeds.*)*

16 CONSOLIDATED ACCOUNTS - MERGERS AND ACQUISITIONS

INTRODUCTION & LEARNING OBJECTIVES

Merger accounting and acquisition accounting are alternative methods of recording the acquisition of a subsidiary by a parent undertaking. Merger accounting is only appropriate if certain conditions are satisfied. The CA 1989 contains one set of conditions; these are tightened still further by the provisions of FRS 6.

Acquisition accounting is open to abuse unless the fair values of the consideration issued and net assets acquired are 'fairly' arrived at. The central point of the debate is whether the perspective of the purchaser should be used in arriving at those values. The ASB has now issued FRS 7 to deal with the problems that have arisen in this area in the past.

When you have studied this chapter you should be able to do the following:

- State and understand the requirements of FRS 6 for merger accounting and acquisition accounting.
- Discuss the means by which fair values are arrived at in an acquisition, including knowledge of FRS 7.

1 MERGERS AND TAKEOVERS

1.1 The conceptual difference between an acquisition and a merger

Business combinations arise when one or more companies become subsidiaries of another company. Two different methods have been developed to account for business combinations – acquisition accounting and merger accounting.

In an acquisition, one party to the combination can be identified as having the role of an acquirer. FRS 6 requires the use of acquisition accounting in such circumstances.

In a merger, two or more companies are combining to pool their interests on an equal footing, and no acquirer can be identified. FRS 6 requires the use of merger accounting in such circumstances.

One key criterion employed to determine the appropriate method or methods of accounting is whether or not the combination is based principally on a share for share exchange. Merger accounting is considered to be an appropriate method of accounting when two groups of shareholders continue, or are in a position to continue, their shareholdings as before but on a combined basis. Acquisition accounting is, therefore, required when there is a transfer of the ownership of at least one of the combining companies, and substantial resources leave the group as consideration for that transfer. Conversely, when only limited resources leave the group, merger accounting may be used.

We will consider the other criteria later.

1.2 The requirements of the Companies Act and FRS 6 relating to merger accounting

FRS 6 **Acquisitions and mergers** deals only with accounting in the consolidated accounts and not with accounting in the individual company accounts (although some guidance is provided in an appendix to the standard). However, the entries at the individual company stage can affect the entries at the consolidated accounts stage and thus the accounts of the parent company are dealt with first.

1.3 Accounts of the parent undertaking – basic situation

The investment in a new subsidiary will be shown as a fixed asset investment in the parent company's own accounts. The amount at which this investment will be stated will depend upon which method of accounting is to be used on consolidation:

(a) If acquisition accounting is to be used, then the investment will be recorded at cost, which will normally be the fair value of the consideration given.

(b) If merger accounting is to be used, then the investment will be recorded at the nominal value of the shares issued as purchase consideration plus the fair value of any additional consideration.

1.4 Example

A plc makes an offer to all the shareholders of B plc to acquire their shares on the basis of one new £1 share (market value £3) plus 25p for every two £1 shares (market value £1.10 each) in B plc. The holders of 95,000 shares in B plc (representing 95% of the total shares) accept this offer.

1.5 Solution

The investment in B plc will be recorded in the books of A plc as follows:

(a) If acquisition accounting is to be used on consolidation:

	£	£
Dr Investment in B plc	154,375	
Cr £1 ordinary shares		47,500
Cr Share premium		95,000
Cr Cash		11,875
	154,375	154,375

(b) If merger accounting is to be used on consolidation:

	£	£
Dr Investment in B plc	59,375	
Cr £1 ordinary shares		47,500
Cr Cash		11,875
	59,375	59,375

1.6 Accounts of the parent undertaking – the effect of merger relief

S130 CA85 states that if a company issues shares at a premium, whether for cash or otherwise, a sum equal to the aggregate amount or value of the premium on those shares shall be transferred to a share premium account.

S131 CA85 provides that where a company has, by an arrangement including the exchange of shares, secured at least a 90% equity holding in another company then *S130 CA85* shall not apply to the premium on any shares which are included in the purchase consideration. This provision is known as the 'merger relief' provision.

In the example above A plc did, by an arrangement including the exchange of shares, secure at least a 90% equity holding in another company and hence would not transfer £95,000 to the share premium account, and could then record the investment in B plc at £59,375 – exactly the same figure as arrived at if merger accounting were to be used on consolidation. If however A plc has decided that acquisition accounting is to be used on consolidation, the holding company would credit the share premium to a merger reserve, thus:

	£	£
Dr Investment in B plc	154,375	
Cr £1 ordinary shares		47,500
Cr Merger reserve		95,000
Cr Cash		11,875
	154,375	154,375

A plc is relieved by S131 from setting up a share premium account, but wants to state the investment at its fair value, in order to use acquisition accounting on consolidation. The merger reserve is therefore set up to enable the investment to be stated at its fair value.

1.7 Conditions necessary to apply merger accounting methods

Both CA 1989 and FRS 6 allow merger accounting to be used only in specified circumstances. These circumstances are listed below and should be learnt.

CA 89 conditions

(a) The subsidiary was acquired by an arrangement providing for the issue of equity shares by the parent company or its subsidiaries.

(b) The group has obtained at least 90% of the 'relevant shares' in the subsidiary (being shares with unrestricted rights to participate in distributions and on liquidation).

(c) The fair value of consideration given other than equity shares does not exceed 10% of the nominal value of the equity shares issued.

(d) The adoption of merger accounting complies with generally accepted accounting principles or practice.

If these conditions are met, the CA89 permits that the merger method of accounting may be used.

FRS 6 criteria

FRS 6 contains five criteria that must be satisfied before merger accounting can be used:

(a) No party to the combination is portrayed as either acquirer or acquired, either by its own board or management or by that of another party to the combination.

(b) All parties to the combination participate in establishing the management structure for the combined entity and in selecting the management personnel.

(c) The relative sizes of the combining entities are not so disparate that one party dominates the combined entity by virtue of its relative size.

(d) The consideration received by the equity shareholders of each party to the combination, in relation to their equity shareholding, comprises primarily equity shares in the combined entity. Any non-equity consideration represents an immaterial proportion of the fair value of the consideration received by the equity shareholders of that party.

(e) No equity shareholders of any of the combining entities retain any material interest in the future performance of only part of the combined entity.

If a business combination meets all five of these criteria, and the use of merger accounting is not prohibited by companies legislation, FRS 6 requires that merger accounting must be used for that combination.

The following points can be made:

(a) Condition (d) of the CA89 effectively gives statutory backing to FRS 6 or any other revised standard on this topic in the future.

(b) FRS 6 explains criterion (c) by stating that one party would be presumed to dominate if it is more than 50% larger than each of the other parties to the combination, judged by considering the proportion of the equity of the combined entity attributable to the shareholders of each of the combining parties. However this presumption may be rebutted if it can be clearly shown that there is no such dominance.

(c) No further guidance is given on the interpretation of 'immaterial proportion' in criterion (d) of FRS 6.

1.8 Activity

P is a parent company about to make an offer to acquire another company S.

The initial proposal is to issue 1,000 ordinary shares of £1 each worth £3 per share together with £200 cash.

Demonstrate whether these proposals meet the *CA 1989* conditions for merger accounting.

1.9 Activity solution

The proposals do not meet the requirements of CA 1989 as the cash element is more than 10% of the nominal value of the equity shares.

	Nominal value	
	£	%
Equity shares 1,000 @ £1	1,000	100
Cash	200	20

This problem could be overcome by P making a bonus issue of 1 for 1 held and then offering to issue 2,000 equity shares worth £1.50 each to the shareholders of S.

	Nominal value	
	£	%
Equity shares 2,000 @ £1	2,000	100
Cash	200	10

1.10 Consolidated accounts – acquisition accounting

Where a business combination is accounted for as an acquisition, the fair value of the purchase consideration should, for the purpose of consolidated financial statements, be allocated between the underlying net tangible and intangible assets other than goodwill, on the basis of the fair value to the acquiring company in accordance with the requirements of *FRS 2*.

Any difference between the fair value of the consideration and the aggregate of the fair values of the separable net assets including identifiable intangibles such as patents, licences and trade marks will represent goodwill, which should be accounted for in accordance with the provisions of FRS 10.

In an acquisition the results of the acquired company should be brought into the group accounts from the date of acquisition only.

1.11 Consolidated accounts – merger accounting

In merger accounting it is not necessary to adjust the carrying values of the assets and liabilities of the subsidiary to fair value either in its own books or on consolidation. However, appropriate adjustments should be made to achieve uniformity of accounting policies between the combining companies.

In the group accounts for the period in which the merger takes place, the profits or losses of subsidiaries brought in for the first time should be included for the entire period without any adjustment in respect of that part of the period prior to the merger. Corresponding amounts should be presented as if the companies had been combined throughout the previous period and at the previous balance sheet date.

A difference may arise on consolidation between the carrying value of the investment in the subsidiary (which will normally be the nominal value of the shares issued as consideration plus the fair value of any additional consideration) and the nominal value of the shares transferred to the issuing company.

(a) Where the carrying value of the investment is less than the nominal value of the shares transferred, the difference should be treated as a reserve arising on consolidation.

(b) Where the carrying value of the investment is greater than the nominal value of the shares transferred, the difference is the extent to which reserves have been in effect capitalised as a result of the merger and it should therefore be treated on consolidation as a reduction of reserves.

1.12 Comparison of consolidated financial accounts prepared under merger accounting and acquisition accounting

On 31 December 20X6 F plc purchased 29,000 shares in B Ltd by issuing 58,000 shares as consideration. The market value of F plc's shares on that date were £2.50 each.

The balance sheets of the two companies immediately before the share exchange were as follows:

	F plc £'000	*B Ltd* £'000
£1 ordinary shares	100	30
Profit and loss account	120	90
	220	120
Sundry net assets	220	120

As at 31 December 20X6, the fair value of B Ltd's sundry net assets was £15,000 in excess of their book value.

You are required to prepare consolidated balance sheets as at 31 December 20X6 reflecting the above information, on the basis of:

(a) acquisition accounting; and
(b) merger accounting.

Solution

(a) **Acquisition accounting**

Step 1 For consolidation purposes the investment in B Ltd must be recorded at its fair value:

	£	£
Dr Cost of investment	145,000	
Cr £1 ordinary shares (58,000 @ £1)		58,000
Cr Merger reserve (58,000 @ £1.50)		87,000
	145,000	145,000

Alternatively the merger reserve would be established as a consolidation adjustment only.

Step 2 If acquisition accounting is to be used, assets must be recorded at their fair value:

	£	£
Dr Sundry net assets	15,000	
Cr Revaluation reserve		15,000

This may be done in the subsidiary's books or as a consolidation adjustment.

Step 3 Consolidation schedules:

Goodwill

	£	£
Cost of investment		145,000
Less: Share of net assets acquired:		
Share capital	30,000	
Revaluation reserve	15,000	
Profit and loss account	90,000	
	135,000 (29/30)	130,500
Goodwill		14,500

Consolidated profit and loss account reserve

	£
F plc:	120,000
B Ltd: 29/30 (90,000 – 90,000)	0
	120,000

Minority interest

	£	£
Share of net assets:		
Share capital	30,000	
Revaluation reserve	15,000	
Profit and loss account	90,000	
	135,000 (1/30)	4,500

Step 4 **Consolidated balance sheet as at 31 December 20X6**

	£'000
Sundry net assets	355.0
Goodwill	14.5
	369.5
£1 ordinary shares	158.0
Consolidated revenue reserves	120.0
Merger reserve	87.0
Minority interests	4.5
	369.5

(b) **Merger accounting**

Step 1 The investment in B Ltd is recorded as the nominal value of shares issued by F plc:

	£	£
Dr Cost of investment	58,000	
Cr £1 ordinary shares		58,000

Assets are not restated to their fair value.

Step 2 Consolidation schedules:

'Difference' on consolidation

	£
Nominal value of shares issued	58,000
Less: Nominal value of shares acquired	29,000
Positive difference - write off to consolidated reserves	29,000

Consolidated profit and loss account

	£
F Ltd:	120,000
B Ltd: 29/30 × £90,000	87,000
Less: Difference on consolidation written off	(29,000)
	178,000

Minority interest

	£
1/30 × £120,000	4,000

Step 3

Consolidated balance sheet as at 31 December 20X6

	£'000
Sundry net assets	340
£1 ordinary shares	158
Consolidated revenue reserves	178
Minority interests	4
	340

Notes:

(i) Although consolidated revenue reserves have been recorded as £178,000 under merger accounting and £120,000 under acquisition accounting, this does not mean that distributable reserves are greater. Distributions are made from the profits of individual companies, not by groups.

(ii) Differences on consolidation can arise in merger accounting, but these differences are not goodwill as they are not based on the fair values of the consideration given and the separable net assets acquired. Such differences should always be adjusted against consolidated reserves.

1.13 Activity

The summarised balance sheet of G Ltd at 28 February 20X6 was as follows:

	£		£
Fixed assets	180,000	Ordinary share capital	
Current assets	565,000	(25p ordinary shares)	245,000
		Reserves	300,000
		Current liabilities	200,000
	745,000		745,000

At that date the company acquired the whole issued share capital of C Ltd by the issue of 120,000 new ordinary shares at the day's market price of 80p.

The summarised balance sheet of C immediately prior to acquisition was as follows:

	£		£
Fixed assets	40,000	Ordinary share capital	
Current assets	55,000	(£1 ordinary shares)	20,000
		Reserves	50,000
		Current liabilities	25,000
	95,000		95,000

The fixed assets of C were revalued two weeks before the acquisition at £50,000 but no entry had yet been made in the books of C.

You are required to prepare the consolidated balance sheet at 28 February 20X6 using:

(a) acquisition accounting;
(b) merger accounting.

1.14 Activity solution

(a) **Acquisition accounting balance sheet**

	£	£
Fixed assets (230,000 + 16,000)		246,000
Current assets	620,000	
Creditors – amounts falling due within one year	225,000	
		395,000
Total assets less current liabilities		641,000
Capital and reserves:		
Called up share capital (W3)		275,000
Merger reserve (W1)		66,000
Profit and loss account		300,000
		641,000

WORKINGS

(W1) **Issue of shares at a premium**

	Dr £	*Cr* £
Dr Cost of investment 120,000 × 80p	96,000	
Cr Ordinary share capital		30,000
Cr Merger reserve		66,000

(W2) **Calculation of goodwill on consolidation**

	£	£
Cost of investment		96,000
Net assets at acquisition:		
Equity interest	70,000	
Surplus on revaluation	10,000	
		80,000
Goodwill		16,000

(W3) **Share capital**

	£
Previously in issue	245,000
Consideration for acquisition	30,000
	275,000

(b) **Merger accounting balance sheet**

	£	£
Fixed assets		220,000
Current assets	620,000	
Creditors – amounts falling due within one year	225,000	
Net current assets		395,000
Total assets less current liabilities		615,000
Capital and reserves:		
Called up share capital		275,000
Profit and loss account		340,000
		615,000

WORKINGS

	£
Nominal value of ordinary shares issued	30,000
Nominal value of ordinary shares acquired	20,000
	10,000
Less: Reserves of C Ltd at date of merger	50,000
Add to group reserves	40,000

1.15 UITF Abstract 15 - Disclosure of substantial acquisitions

FRS 6 requires detailed disclosures in respect of substantial acquisitions arising during the accounting period. For listed companies FRS 6 defines 'substantial' by reference to Class 1 or Super Class 1 transactions under the Stock Exchange Listing Rules. These classify transactions by assessing their size relative to that of the company making the transaction. It does this by ascertaining whether any of a number of ratios (eg, the net assets of the target to the net assets of the offeror) exceeds a given percentage.

UITF Abstract 15 was issued in order to clarify the definition of 'substantial' in respect of listed companies, as the Listing Rules have changed since FRS 6 was issued. An acquisition is now defined as substantial if it is a transaction in which any of the ratios set out in the London Stock Exchange Listing Rules defining Class 1 transactions exceeds 15%.

For other entities, an acquisition is 'substantial':

(a) where the net assets or operating profits of the acquired entity exceed 15% of those of the acquiring entity, or

(b) where the fair value of the consideration given exceeds 15% of the net assets of the acquiring entity.

For substantial acquisitions, the following information must be disclosed:

(a) the summarised profit and loss account and statement of total recognised gains and losses of the acquired entity for the period from the beginning of its financial year to the effective date of acquisition, giving the date on which this period began; and

(b) the profit after tax and minority interests for the acquired entity's previous financial year.

2 DISCUSSION PAPER: BUSINESS COMBINATIONS

2.1 Background

The ASB has issued a Discussion Paper which looks at the various methods of accounting for business combinations. The Discussion Paper is based on a paper issued by the 'G4 + 1' group of standard setters of which the ASB is a member. The ASB has issued the Paper in order to give preparers of accounts in the UK the opportunity to influence the international debate.

The Paper considers three methods:

(a) the acquisition method;

(b) the merger method; and

(c) the fresh start method. This assumes that a completely new entity emerges from the combination and measures all the assets and liabilities of the combined entity (including goodwill) at their fair values; the method is not currently used in any major standard setting country.

2.2 Recommendations

A single method

The use of a single method of accounting for business combinations is preferable to two or more methods. This is because:

(a) The future cash flows that will result from a particular combination are generally the same, regardless of the method used. Relevance is impaired, rather than enhanced, if more than one method is used, particularly if different methods produce dramatically different results. Reliability requires that similar transactions be accounted for in similar ways and comparability may be impaired by the use of two methods.

(b) The costs of using two methods exceed the benefits.

(c) There are practical difficulties in distinguishing between the circumstances in which the acquisition method and the merger of interests method should be applied. A single method avoids these difficulties and also avoids the possibility of manipulation by preparers of the financial statements.

The acquisition method

The acquisition method is the most appropriate method to use. This is because:

(a) an acquirer can be identified in virtually all business combinations; and

(b) the method produces information that is comparable to other accounting information and is familiar to preparers, users and auditors.

The merger method

There are several criticisms of the merger method:

(a) There is lack of broad agreement on the circumstances in which it should be applied.

(b) It is based on the notion that the combination results from a transaction between owners, but in practice the transaction is between the combining companies themselves.

(c) Although it results in the continuation of ownership interests these interests are not the same interests after the combination, because the risks and rewards that the shareholders have after the combination are not the same risks and rewards that they had prior to it.

(d) Even if an acquirer cannot be identified, there is no reason for not revaluing the assets and liabilities of the combining companies to fair value. The merger method is an exception to the general rule that exchange transactions should be accounted for in terms of fair values rather than book values. For this reason, the merger method provides information that is less relevant than that provided by the other methods. The information is also less reliable, because the method records assets and liabilities from the perspective of the combining companies, rather than the combined entity.

The fresh start method

The use of the fresh start method would overcome some of these problems, as assets and liabilities are recorded at fair values. Therefore there is a case for using it in circumstances where no acquirer can be identified, or where the acquirer is substantially modified as a result of the combination. However, the Paper rejects it because:

(a) There are many uncertainties involved, for example, how should goodwill be determined? Should it only be applied to combinations in which no acquirer can be identified?

(b) The two methods would produce different accounting results and therefore entities would still have incentives to prefer one method rather than the other.

(c) Combinations in which no acquirer can be identified are extremely rare. When they occur it is still possible to account for them using the purchase method because there are arbitrary methods of overcoming this problem (eg, by treating the larger of the two companies as the acquirer).

2.3 Responses to the Paper

Most respondents to the Paper opposed the proposal to ban merger accounting and there was widespread support for the present system. There are two different kinds of business combination and therefore two distinct methods are needed in order to reflect them fairly.

Some commentators have pointed out that the opposition to the merger method reflects the situation in the US, where the criteria for merger accounting are based on conditions rather than principles. Merger accounting is relatively common in the US and many combinations accounted for as mergers would not qualify as mergers in the UK. In the UK, FRS 6 has largely resolved the problems of 'creative accounting'.

The ASB appears to have no immediate plans to implement the proposals in the Paper. However, it has announced that it will monitor international developments with a view to possible changes to FRS 6. In addition, the changes introduced by FRS 10 *Goodwill and intangible assets* may result in more companies trying to use the merger method in future.

Because international harmonisation of financial reporting is becoming increasingly important, if one or more of the 'G4+1' group were to prohibit merger accounting, the ASB would be under pressure to do the same.

Conclusion A Position Paper issued by the 'G4+1' group proposes that the merger method should be prohibited. At present the ASB does not intend to ban merger accounting in the UK.

3 FAIR VALUE IN THE CONTEXT OF ACQUISITION ACCOUNTING

3.1 Introduction

In order to account for an acquisition, the acquiring company must measure the cost of what it is accounting for, which will normally represent:

(a) the cost of the investment in its own balance sheet; and

(b) the amount to be allocated between the identifiable net assets of the subsidiary and goodwill in the consolidated financial statements.

For acquisition accounting, the *CA89, FRS 2* and *FRS 6* require the cost of investment to be based on the fair value of the consideration given, but they do not elaborate on how this is to be determined. FRS 7 *Fair values in acquisition accounting* was issued in 1994 to give guidance in this area.

The ASB describe the objective of FRS 7 as 'to ensure that when a business entity is acquired by another, all the assets and liabilities that existed in the acquired entity at the date of acquisition are recorded at fair values reflecting their condition at that date; and that all changes to the acquired assets and liabilities, and the resulting gains and losses, that arise after control of the acquired entity has passed to the acquirer are reported as part of the post-acquisition financial performance of the acquiring group.'

This emphasises the two key issues addressed by the FRS:

(a) the principles for making 'fair value adjustments' on consolidation to the values of assets acquired and liabilities assumed in a business combination that is accounted for as an acquisition

(b) the treatment of provisions established for future operating losses and for post-acquisition reorganisation and integration costs.

3.2 FRS 7: Fair values in acquisition accounting

FRS 7's main requirements are that

(a) The assets and liabilities recognised in the allocation of fair values should be those of the acquired entity that existed at the date of acquisition. They should be measured at fair values that reflect the conditions at the date of the acquisition.

(b) The liabilities of the acquired entity should not include provisions for future operating losses. Changes in the assets and liabilities resulting from the acquirer's intentions or from events after the acquisition should be dealt with as post-acquisition items. Similarly, costs of reorganisation and integrating the business acquired, whether they relate to the acquired entity or the acquiring group, should be dealt with as post-acquisition costs and do not affect the fair values at the date of acquisition.

(c) Fair values should be based on the value at which an asset or liability could be exchanged in an arm's length transaction. The fair value of monetary items should take into account the amounts expected to be received or paid and their timing.

(d) Unless they can be measured at market value, the fair values of non-monetary assets will normally be based on replacement cost, but should not exceed their recoverable amount as at the date of acquisition. The recoverable amount reflects the condition of the assets on acquisition but not any impairments resulting from subsequent events.

The FRS also describes the application of these principles to determine initial fair values for particular categories of assets and liabilities, including fixed assets, stocks, pension schemes and deferred taxation. A period of investigation of an acquired company for the purpose of fixing adjustments to fair values and purchased goodwill is established which ends on the date at which the first set of financial statements following the acquisition are approved by the directors.

3.3 The problems of more contentious items

Previous practice has been to make a provision for reorganisation costs/future losses at the time of the acquisition. This had two main effects:

(a) As the provision was a reduction from the net asset value of the acquired business, goodwill (the balancing figure) was increased. As goodwill was then written off to reserves (the preferred accounting treatment under SSAP 22), the provision had not been set up through the profit and loss account of the year.

(b) As costs were incurred in reorganising the business in the post acquisition period, they were set off against the provision. They therefore bypassed the profit and loss account.

Sir David Tweedie's (Chairman of the ASB) response to this was, 'The contention that reorganisation expenses or losses to be incurred following an acquisition should be deemed to be existing liabilities of the acquired company is perverse; the amount of goodwill arising on the acquisition actually goes up, and usually nothing gets charged to the profit and loss account. Accounting in this way for a gleam in the acquirer's eye is simply not rational.'

'FRS 7 is wholly consistent with the information set approach underlying FRS3. The accounts should disclose what actually happens after new acquisitions enter the group. The costs of digesting acquisitions should, like future losses, be charged through the profit and loss account when they occur and be separately disclosed if necessary. Post-acquisition performance should not be masked by the creation and release of provisions that were not liabilities of the acquired company before it was purchased.'

Although FRS 10 has now effectively prohibited elimination of goodwill against reserves, these requirements of FRS 7 are still very necessary. If goodwill is amortised over a long period, the effect of the charge on each year's results may be relatively small. Without FRS 7 it would still be possible for preparers of financial statements to use provisions in order to artificially enhance post acquisition results in the short term.

Conclusion Provisions for future reorganisation costs/losses should not be established as part of the fair values of the net assets of a subsidiary acquired. The costs/losses relate to the post-acquisition period and no 'liability' exists at the acquisition date which complies with the definition of a liability in the Statement of Principles.

3.4 The fair values of purchase consideration, assets and liabilities generally

First stage

The allocation of fair values gives rise to the following sources of differences from book values as reported in the separate financial statements of the acquired business prior to the acquisition, which should be recorded as fair value adjustments in the table required to be disclosed by FRS 6, dealt with earlier in this text.

(a) Revaluations of assets and liabilities to current values, for example the revaluation of fixed assets and stocks to replacement costs.

(b) Adjustments to harmonise accounting policies, for example changes to the basis for the inclusion of overheads in stocks and work-in-progress

(c) Adjustments to asset values arising from different estimates of net realisable value, for example changes to bring the carrying value of debtors and stocks to estimated net realisable value where the acquirer's estimates of net realisable value differ from those previously made by the management of the acquired company.

It is necessary to distinguish between the effect of different estimates of existing values (fair value adjustments) and the effect of different commercial intentions that an acquirer may have for the acquired company (post-acquisition items).

Second stage

Amounts attributed to fair values at the point of acquisition should not anticipate the financial costs of the acquirer's future plans for making changes to the acquired company's activities or, as a result of the acquisition, to the acquirer's own activities.

Similarly any gains that might result from an asset or liability identified by the first stage realising a greater or lower value as a result of the acquirer's post-acquisition efforts should not be anticipated. In particular, the recognition of expected costs or losses that are not liabilities of the acquired business at the date of acquisition would not be permitted as fair value adjustments, even though they may have been taken into account by the acquirer in its investment appraisal.

3.5 Activity

X plc acquired 80% of the ordinary share capital of Y Ltd on 30 September 20X4 for £320,000.

The net assets in the draft accounts of Y Ltd at that date were £350,000.

The following information is relevant:

(a) Y Ltd's freehold factory is included in the accounts at £100,000 and no adjustment has been made to recognise the valuation of £120,000 put on the property when it was professionally revalued on 15 September 20X4.

(b) The fair value of Y Ltd's stock at 30 September 20X4 is estimated to be £4,000 less than its book value at that date.

(c) In August 20X4 Y Ltd made a decision to close down a small workshop with the loss of some jobs. The net costs of closure are estimated at £10,000. No provision has been made at 30 September 20X4.

What is the goodwill arising on the acquisition of Y Ltd?

3.6 Activity solution

Step 1 Adjust the value of Y Ltd's net assets at 30 September 20X4 to fair value.

	£
Net assets per question	350,000
Revaluation of property	20,000
Write-off of stock	(4,000)
Provision for reorganisation costs*	(10,000)
	356,000

* Note that it is Y Ltd who have decided to close the workshop, and that this decision was made prior to the year-end, so a provision can be established correctly for this item.

Step 2 Calculate goodwill.

	£
Fair value of consideration	320,000
Net assets acquired 80% × £356,000	284,800
Goodwill arising	35,200

3.7 Investigation period and goodwill adjustments

The timing and complexity of an acquisition may lead to a provisional allocation of fair values in the first post-acquisition financial statements of the acquirer. Adjustments to those fair values and to purchased goodwill should be fixed by the date that the financial statements for the first full financial year following the acquisition are approved by the directors; thereafter, any adjustments, except for the correction of fundamental errors that should be accounted for as prior period adjustments, should be recorded as gains or losses when they are recognised.

3.8 Examples of fair value

(a) The fair value of a tangible fixed asset should be based on:

(i) market value, if assets similar in type and condition are bought and sold on an open market, or

(ii) depreciated replacement cost, reflecting the acquired business's normal buying process and the sources of supply and prices available to it.

The fair value should not exceed the recoverable amount of the asset.

(b) The fair value of an intangible fixed asset should be based on its replacement cost, which is normally its estimated market value.

(c) Stocks, including commodity stocks, that the acquired entity trades on a market in which it participates as both a buyer and a seller should be valued at current market prices.

Other stocks and work-in-progress should be valued at the lower of replacement cost and net realisable value.

(d) The fair value of a deficiency or, to the extent that it is reasonably expected to be realised, a surplus in a funded pension scheme should be recognised as a liability or an asset of the acquiring group.

3.9 Fair value of the cost of acquisition

In order to apply the requirements of FRS 7, it is necessary to determine the fair values of the constituent parts of the purchase consideration. The purchase consideration may comprise:

(a) cash or other monetary items, including the assumption of liabilities by the acquirer;

(b) capital instruments issued by the acquirer, including shares, debentures, loans and debt instruments, share warrants and other options relating to the securities of the acquirer; or

(c) non-monetary assets, including securities of another entity.

Any of these elements can give rise to difficulties of valuation. Some of these difficulties are summarised below.

(a) When settlement of cash consideration is deferred, fair values are obtained by discounting to their present value the amounts expected to be payable in the future. The appropriate discount rate is the rate at which the acquirer could obtain a similar borrowing, taking into account its credit standing and any security given.

(b) Where shares (and other capital instruments) issued by the acquirer are quoted on a ready market, the market price on the date of acquisition would normally provide the most reliable measure of fair value.

Where, owing to unusual fluctuations, the market price on one particular date is an unreliable measure of fair value, market prices for a reasonable period before the date of acquisition, during which acceptances could be made, would need to be considered.

(c) Where securities issued by the acquirer are not quoted or, if they are quoted, the market price is unreliable owing, for example, to the lack of an active market in the quantities involved, it would be necessary to make a valuation of those securities. The fair value would be estimated by taking into account items such as:

(i) the value of similar securities that are quoted;
(ii) the present value of the future cash flows of the instrument issued;
(iii) any cash alternative to the issue of securities; and
(iv) the value of any underlying security into which there is an option to convert.

4 CHAPTER SUMMARY

Merger accounting and acquisition accounting are alternative methods of recording the acquiring of a subsidiary by a parent company. Merger accounting is only permitted if certain conditions laid down in CA 89 and FRS 6 are satisfied.

Acquisition accounting is open to abuse unless the fair values of the consideration issued and net assets acquired are 'fairly' arrived at. The ASB has now acted to issue FRS 7 to standardise accounting in this area.

5 SELF TEST QUESTIONS

5.1 What is the simple difference between an acquisition and a merger? (1.1)

5.2 At what amount is an investment in a subsidiary recorded in the parent company's accounts? (1.3)

5.3 What does S131 CA85 state? (1.6)

5.4 What are the four conditions for merger accounting to be permitted under CA 89? (1.7)

5.5 What are the five criteria for merger accounting to be permitted under FRS 6? (1.7)

5.6 In merger accounting what happens if the nominal value of shares issued is less than the nominal value of shares acquired? (1.11)

5.7 What are the two key issues addressed by FRS 7 on fair values? (3.1)

5.8 How should the fair values of non-monetary assets generally be calculated? (3.2)

5.9 Would a provision for future reorganisation costs comply with the definition of a liability in the Statement of Principles? (3.3)

6 EXAMINATION TYPE QUESTION

6.1 Charlie plc

Charlie plc is negotiating to acquire all the issued equity and voting shares of Alex Ltd. It is proposed that the consideration offered to the shareholders of Alex Ltd comprises a 2 for 1 share for share exchange and 25 pence cash per share. The current share price of Charlie plc is £3.

Although the two companies are in competition, both management teams have agreed that by merging the two companies the new entity will be in a better position to counter increased foreign competition. It is expected that the two management teams will be able to work together.

The shareholders of Alex Ltd are not hostile to the combination as it will improve the liquidity of their share price.

Inevitably as a result of the combination there will be some reorganisation to eliminate common overheads. At present, rationalisation plans would result in the closure of Alex Ltd's regional distribution network at an estimated cost of £4,500,000, including redundancy costs of £500,000 and losses on the disposal of various fixed assets of £3,750,000.

The balance sheets of both companies as at 31 December 20X5 are set out below.

	Charlie plc		*Alex Ltd*	
	£'000	£'000	£'000	£'000
Fixed assets				
Tangible		9,715		14,250
Current assets				
Stock	8,000		2,000	
Long-term debtors	-		1,500	
Investments	-		500	
Debtors	600		875	
	8,600		4,875	
Current liabilities	(1,100)		(3,200)	
Net current assets		7,500		1,675
Long-term liabilities		(1,000)		(4,000)
		16,215		11,925
Called up share capital (ordinary shares of £1)		12,000		5,000
Reserves		4,215		6,925
		16,215		11,925

The following information relates to Alex Ltd.

(1) *Fixed assets*

These comprise:

	Freehold offices	*Plant*
Net book value	£8,000,000	£6,250,000

The freehold offices have a market value of £10 million.

A lot of the plant will be scrapped under the reorganisation plans and has an estimated value on that basis of £2,500,000. The net replacement cost of the plant is £5 million. The amount Alex Ltd would have expected to recover from its future use is at least £5 million.

(2) *Stock*

Stocks are carried at the lower of cost and net realisable value.

	£'000
Cost	2,000
Net realisable value	6,000
Replacement cost	2,500

(3) The long-term debtors are receivable at the 20X7 year end.

(4) The investments are carried in the balance sheet at the lower of cost and net realisable value. They cost £500,000 and have a net realisable value of £980,000.

(5) The long-term liability is a loan carrying 10% pa interest and is repayable on 31 December 20X8. The current interest rate available on loans is 12%.

You are required to:

(a) explain whether the combination should be treated as an acquisition or a merger, according to the conditions set out in the Companies Act 1985 and in FRS 6;

(b) prepare the consolidated balance sheet of the Charlie plc group at 31 December 20X5 together with a table of fair values as required by FRS 6 *Acquisitions and mergers*;

(c) explain your treatment of the reorganisation costs which are expected to arise as a result of the combination.

Assume a corporation tax rate of 40%.

Present value factors to discount from end of year:

End of year	*10%*	*11%*	*12%*	*13%*	*14%*
1	0.909	0.901	0.893	0.885	0.877
2	0.826	0.812	0.797	0.783	0.769
3	0.751	0.731	0.712	0.693	0.675
4	0.683	0.659	0.636	0.613	0.592
5	0.621	0.593	0.567	0.543	0.519

7 ANSWER TO EXAMINATION TYPE QUESTION

7.1 Charlie plc

(a) The proposed combination must be accounted for as a merger if the criteria set out in both the Companies Act 1985 and FRS 6 are met.
The Companies Act conditions are:

(i) The subsidiary was acquired by an arrangement providing for the issue of equity shares by the parent company.

(ii) The group has obtained at least 90% of the equity shares in the subsidiary.

(iii) The fair value of the consideration other than equity shares does not exceed 10% of the nominal value of the equity shares issued.

(iv) The adoption of merger accounting complies with generally accepted accounting principles or practice.

The first two conditions are clearly met and the last condition helps give weight to the criteria set out in FRS 6.

Let us consider whether condition (iii) is met. The fair value of the non-equity consideration (in this case cash, but it could be preference shares or debentures for example) is £1.25 million, whereas the nominal value of the shares issued is £10 million and so the criteria that the non-equity consideration does not exceed 10% of the nominal value of the equity shares issued is not met.

Cash consideration	5,000,000 × 25p	= £1,250,000
Nominal value of shares issued	2 × 5,000,000	= £10,000,000

$$\frac{1,250,000}{10,000,000} = 12.5\%$$

(***Tutorial note:*** it would be wrong now not to discuss the FRS 6 criteria and whether they are met just because the CA 1985 criteria are not met.)

The FRS 6 criteria are as follows:

(1) No party to the combination is portrayed as either acquirer or acquired, either by its own board or management.

Both management teams appear to regard the combination as a merger, to counter foreign competition. However no indication is given of what the new entity will be called and as the only proposed rationalisations concern Alex Ltd, this criteria appears not to be met.

(2) All parties to the combination participate in establishing the management structure for the combined entity and in selecting the management personnel.

The proposed redundancies affect Alex Ltd only, an indication that this criteria has not been met.

(3) The relative sizes of the combining entities are not so disparate that one party dominates the combined entity by virtue of its relative size.

The shareholders of Alex Ltd will be issued with 10 million shares, and therefore after the share issue will control 45% ($^{10}/_{22}$ × 100%). It would appear this criteria is met.

(4) The fair value of the consideration received by equity shareholders will only contain an immaterial proportion of non-equity consideration.

$$\frac{\text{Cash}}{\text{Cash + Fair value of shares}} = \frac{1,250,000}{1,250,000 + £3 \times 10,000,000} = 4\%$$

ie, 96% of the consideration received by equity shareholders in relation to their shareholding comprises equity shares. This criteria appears to be met.

(5) No equity shareholders of any of the combining entities retain a material interest in the future performance of only part of the combined entity.

In the absence of any minority interest and no earn out clauses this criteria is definitely met.

Conclusion

This combination must be accounted for as an acquisition. It neither meets the statutory nor FRS6 criteria.

(b) **The Charlie plc group balance sheet as at 31 December 20X5**

	£'000	£'000
Fixed assets		
Intangible		17,708
Tangible (9,715 + 10,000 + 5,000)		24,715
		42,423
Current assets		
Stock (8,000 + 2,500)	10,500	

Long-term debtors (W1)	1,196	
Investments (W2)	980	
Debtors (600 + 875)	1,475	
	14,151	
Creditors: Amounts falling due within one year (1,100 + 3,200 + 1,250) (W5)	(5,550)	
		8,601
Total assets less current liabilities		51,024
Creditors: Amounts falling due after more than one year (1,000 + 3,809) (W3)		(4,809)
		46,215
Called up share capital (12,000 + 10,000)		22,000
Merger reserve (W5)		20,000
Reserves		4,215
		46,215

Note: fair value table

Acquisition - Alex Ltd - 31 December 20X5

	Book value £'000	*Revaluations* £'000	*Provisions* £'000	*Fair value* £'000
Fixed assets				
Freehold offices (i)	8,000	2,000		10,000
Plant (ii)	6,250		(1,250)	5,000
Current assets				
Stock (iii)	2,000	500		2,500
Long-term debtors (iv)	1,500		(304)	1,196
Investments (v)	500	480		980
Debtors	875			875
Total assets	19,125	2,980	(1,554)	20,551
Current liabilities	(3,200)			(3,200)
Long-term liabilities (vi)	(4,000)		191	(3,809)
Total liabilities	(7,200)		191	(7,009)
Net assets	11,925	2,980	(1,363)	13,542

Explanation of adjustments

(i) Increases in value of freehold property since last revaluation
(ii) Write down of plant to its net replacement cost
(iii) Adjustment of stock to its net replacement cost
(iv) Write down of long-term debtors to their present value
(v) Revaluation of investments to their market value
(vi) Adjustment to long-term liabilities to their present value

WORKINGS

(W1) **Long-term debtors**

The fair value is the present value of the amount expected to be received; two years at a discount rate of 12%. The discount rate of 12% is relevant as it is the current interest rate.

1,500 × 0.797 = 1,196

(W2) **Current asset investments**

	£
Market value	980,000
Cost	500,000
Fair value adjustment	480,000

(W3) **Long-term liabilities**

The fair value of the long-term liability is the present value of the amount expected to be paid. Where the current rate of interest commanded by the new group (in this question 12%) is materially different to the coupon rate (in this question 10%) a fair value adjustment is required.

			£'000
31.12.X6	Interest	400 × 0.893	357
31.12.X7	Interest	400 × 0.797	319
31.12.X8	Interest and capital	4,400 × 0.712	3,133
			3,809

(W4) **Calculation of goodwill**

	£'000
Cost of investment (5,000 × 2 × £3) + (25p × 5,000)	31,250
Less: Group share of the fair value of the net assets at acquisition (100% × 13,542) (see fair value table)	(13,542)
Premium arising on consolidation/goodwill	17,708

(*Note:* The combination is treated as taking place on 31 December 20X5, and so no amortisation of goodwill has yet occurred.)

(W5) Charlie plc will record the cost of the investment in Alex

		£'000	£'000
Dr	Cost of investment	31,250	
Cr	Share capital		10,000
	Merger reserve (in lieu of share premium)		20,000
	Bank (25p × 5,000)		1,250

(c) Prior to the introduction of FRS 7 it was relatively common for acquirers to evaluate the fair value of the net assets acquired from their perspective, ie, after making provision for post combination reorganisation costs and losses and writing down assets which they considered to be of little value in the light of integration/reorganisation plans.

This had the beneficial effect of reducing the fair value of the net assets acquired thus increasing the goodwill, which was then normally written off immediately against reserves under SSAP 22.

When the post combination reorganisation costs were incurred, etc, they were charged not against the profit and loss account for the period, but against the provision.

FRS 7 has effectively curtailed this creative accounting practice. Therefore if FRS 7 had not been in force the plant could have been written down by £3,750,000 to £2,500,000 and provision made for the other costs of closing Alex Ltd's regional distribution network.

17 ASSOCIATED COMPANIES

INTRODUCTION & LEARNING OBJECTIVES

In most cases, the consolidation of a subsidiary under the single entity concept is the main way in which group accounts are prepared. In this chapter we examine alternative methods which are sometimes used, the equity and proportional consolidation methods. The equity method is, in fact, most commonly used for companies which are not in the group - associated undertakings.

When you have studied this chapter you should be able to do the following:

- Compare alternative methods of dealing with investments in the group accounts.
- Deal with associates and joint ventures under FRS 9.

1 ALTERNATIVE METHODS OF SHOWING THE INVESTMENT IN ANOTHER COMPANY

1.1 Comparing the equity method of accounting with proportional consolidation

Definition Under the **equity method** accounts record the share of profits attributable to the investing company from the investee and the company's **share** in the net assets of the investee. Thus, minority shareholders' interest in the net assets is not shown.

Definition In the **proportional consolidation method** the share of individual assets and liabilities of the investee are included in the relevant totals. Thus minority shareholders' interest in the net assets is not shown.

These two methods are illustrated in the following example together with normal consolidation so that the differences are highlighted.

1.2 Example - Comparison of consolidation and equity methods

The separate summarised accounts for the year to 31 December 20X2 of H and S are:

Balance sheets as at 31 December 20X2

	H	*S*
	£	£
Fixed assets	2,200	10,000
Cost of investment	1,800	-
Net current assets	1,000	1,000
	5,000	11,000
Share capital	2,000	1,000
Reserves	3,000	2,000
Long-term debt	-	8,000
	5,000	11,000

Profit and loss accounts for year ended 31 December 20X2

	H	*S*
	£	£
Sales	4,000	20,000
Cost of sales	3,500	18,900
Operating profit	500	1,100
Interest payable	-	800
	500	300
Tax	270	160
Retained profit for year	230	140

H acquired an 80% interest in S four years ago when the reserves of S were £500.

Show the group balance sheets and profit and loss accounts under the consolidation method, the equity method, and the proportional consolidation method. Assume that goodwill is written off in equal instalments over six years.

1.3 Solution

Step 1 **Goodwill** - This will be the same under each method.

	£
Share capital and reserves of S at acquisition	1,500
H Ltd share 80% × £1,500	1,200
Cost of investment	1,800
Goodwill	600
Less: Written off over four years	400
	200

Step 2 **Minority interest at 31 December 20X2** - only included under the consolidation method.

	£
Net assets of S Ltd at 31 December 20X2	3,000
Minority interest 20% × £3,000	600

Step 3 **Group reserves** - The same amount of profit is dealt with under any of the methods.

	£
H Ltd reserves	3,000
S Ltd post-acquisition reserves 80% £(2,000 – 500)	1,200
	4,200
Less: Goodwill written-off	400
	3,800

Group balance sheet of H Ltd and subsidiary as at 31 December 20X2

	Consolidation	*Equity*	*Proportional consolidation*
	£	£	£
Net assets			
Fixed assets	12,200	2,200	10,200
Goodwill arising on acquisition of investment in subsidiary	200	200	200
Share of net assets in subsidiary (80% × £3,000)	-	2,400	-
Net current assets	2,000	1,000	1,800
	14,400	5,800	12,200
Capital employed			
Share capital	2,000	2,000	2,000
Reserves	3,800	3,800	3,800
	5,800	5,800	5,800
Minority interests	600	-	-
Long-term debt	8,000	-	6,400
	14,400	5,800	12,200

Group profit and loss accounts of H Ltd for the year ended 31 December 20X2

	Consolidation	*Equity*	*Proportional consolidation*
	£	£	£
Sales	24,000	4,000	20,000
Cost of sales	22,400	3,500	18,620
Operating profit	1,600	500	1,380
Share of profit of subsidiary (80% × £300)		240	
Interest payable	800		640
Goodwill written off	100	100	100
	700	640	640
Tax £(270 + 160)	430		
£(270 + (80% × 160))		398	398
	270	242	242
Minority interest 20% × £140	28		
Profit attributable to H Ltd Group	242	242	242

1.4 The benefits and weaknesses of using equity accounting

The group balance sheets are completely different in form, and give contrasting images of the financial stability of the group. The equity group balance sheet appears to show a safe state of affairs. The consolidated balance sheets, however, reveal the considerable long-term debt incurred by the subsidiary.

It is because the equity method fails to reveal the underlying assets and liabilities that its use is not regarded as a valid method of showing group accounts in the majority of situations, and it is therefore only used when, for some reason, consolidation is regarded as inappropriate. The equity method is, however, used in accounting for **associates and joint ventures**.

The benefit of the equity method for associates is that it allows the group balance sheet to record the current share of net assets of the associate but does not mislead the user into thinking that the associate is a part of the group as the assets are not combined with the group assets.

The proportional consolidation method does show the underlying assets and liabilities although it implies that all of each asset is not under the control of the investing company. This is why it has not found favour in the UK when accounting for subsidiaries. Similarly it has not found favour in dealing with associates as the assets are not kept separate from the group assets.

1.5 Situations requiring the use of equity accounting or proportional consolidation

The equity method may be found in three situations.

(a) Associates under FRS 9
(b) Exclusion of subsidiaries from consolidation under FRS 2 (see earlier)
(c) Joint ventures under FRS 9.

Proportional consolidation may only be used for **unincorporated** joint ventures. Under the CA 89, joint ventures which are incorporated must be dealt with using the equity method of accounting if they are associated undertakings.

There is no prescribed method of proportional consolidation.

FRS 9 has now effectively prohibited the use of proportional consolidation for joint ventures.

2 ASSOCIATED UNDERTAKINGS – INTRODUCTION

2.1 Introduction

Where a company owns more than 50% of the share capital of another company, the *CA 1985* requires group accounts. The law in effect recognises the influence which a parent company may exert over a subsidiary company and the existence of an economic unit, the **group**. If a parent company's accounts were to show only dividends received or receivable from subsidiaries, the shareholders of the parent company would not be given sufficient information regarding the underlying profitability of the unit, the group. Consequently, group accounts normally include the parent company's share of the post-acquisition profits of subsidiaries.

However, if a company, H Ltd, which has subsidiaries, owns (say) 40% of the ordinary share capital of another company, A Ltd, then A Ltd does not come within the legal definition of subsidiary company. H Ltd **may** nevertheless be able to exert considerable influence over A Ltd. It would thus seem sensible to allow H Ltd to show information in its accounts about its share of the profits of A Ltd.

FRS 9 provides rules for accounting for associated companies, ie, companies which fall into the position described above.

The *CA89* introduced into law the requirement for associated **undertakings** to be included in group accounts under the **equity** method. The equity method is the method detailed by FRS 9.

The term **undertakings** includes companies and unincorporated businesses. *FRS 9* also applies to all undertakings (not just companies). As the *CA89* requires the word 'undertaking' to be used in the published accounts, the rest of this section will follow the *CA89* terminology, where it is sensible to do so.

2.2 What is an 'associated undertaking'?

(a) **Company law**

An associated undertaking will come within the definition of a **participating interest** in the investing company's **individual** accounts.

Definition A participating interest is an interest held in the shares of another undertaking, held for the long term, with a view to exercising control or influence to secure a benefit to the investor's own activities. Where an investor holds 20% or more of the shares there is a presumption that this is a participating interest.

In the group accounts participating interests are split into **interests in associated undertakings** and **other participating interests**.

Definition An associated undertaking means an undertaking in which an undertaking included in the consolidation has a **participating interest** and over whose operating and financial policy it exercises a significant influence, and which is not –

(i) a subsidiary undertaking, or

(ii) a joint venture dealt with in the group accounts by proportional consolidation (NB Only **unincorporated** undertakings can be dealt with using proportional consolidation).

Where an undertaking holds 20 per cent or more of the voting rights in another undertaking, it shall be presumed to exercise such an influence over it unless the contrary is shown.

To summarise, most participating interests are associated undertakings. The difference between the two terms mainly relates to the type of share capital held. A participating interest arises when 20% of **any** type of share capital is held. An associated undertaking requires a 20% or more **equity** voting shareholding.

(b) **FRS 9**

The FRS 9 definition is quite complex, but is essentially similar to the company law definition.

Definition An **associate** is an entity (other than a subsidiary) in which another entity (the investor) has a **participating interest** and over whose operating and financial policies the investor exercises a **significant influence**.

Definition A **participating interest** is an interest held in the shares of another entity on a long term basis for the purpose of securing a contribution to the investor's activities by the exercise of control or influence arising from or related to that interest.

Definition The exercise of **significant influence** means that the investor is actively involved and is influential in the direction of its investee through its participation in policy decisions covering aspects of policy relevant to the investor, including decisions on strategic issues such as:

(a) the expansion or contraction of the business, participation in other entities or changes in products, markets and activities of its investee; and

(b) determining the balance between dividend and reinvestment

The main thing to note is that the emphasis of the FRS 9 definition is different to that in the Companies Act. Under the Companies Act, a holding of 20% or more is presumed to be an associate unless it can clearly be demonstrated otherwise. SSAP 1 (which preceded FRS 9) used a similar definition. In practice, this meant that the 20% threshold was normally the only factor taken into account, so that many investments were treated as associates when the investee did not actually exercise significant influence.

The FRS 9 definition centres on the actual substance of the relationship between the parties, (ie, whether significant influence is exercised in practice) rather than its strict legal form (the size of the shareholding).

An investing company's ability to exercise significant influence may depend on the other shareholdings as well as its own. For example, if A Ltd holds 30% of the shares in B Ltd, but the remaining 70% of the shares in B Ltd are held by C plc, then A Ltd is extremely unlikely to be able to exercise significant influence over B Ltd.

However, in questions you should assume that a shareholding of between 20% and 50% is an associate unless you are given information which suggests otherwise.

Conclusion A company is an associated undertaking if the investing company exercises significant influence over it. A shareholding of between 20% and 50% normally gives significant influence.

3 GROUP FINANCIAL STATEMENTS INCORPORATING ASSOCIATED UNDERTAKINGS

3.1 Introduction

Definition **Equity accounting** is a method of accounting that brings an investment into its investor's financial statements initially at its cost, identifying any goodwill arising. The carrying amount of the investment is adjusted in each period by the investor's share of the results of its investee less any amortisation or write-off for goodwill, the investor's share of any relevant gains or losses, and any other changes in the investee's net assets including distributions to its owners, for example by dividend.

The equity method of accounting is used to account for an associated undertaking in the *consolidated* financial statements. Where the investing company does not prepare group accounts (perhaps because it has no subsidiaries) the associate is accounted for as an ordinary trade investment ie, dividends received/receivable in the profit and loss account and cost or valuation less amounts written off in the balance sheet.

3.2 Equity accounting in the consolidated balance sheet

(a) **Calculation**

The investment in the associate is stated at

	(i)	cost
plus	(ii)	group share of retained post-acquisition profits
less	(iii)	amounts written off (eg, goodwill).

Where goodwill has been fully amortised, the valuation will be equal to the investing company's share of net assets in the associate.

Example

Eagle plc acquired 25% of the ordinary share capital of Hawk plc for £640,000 when the reserves of Hawk plc stood at £720,000. Eagle plc appointed two directors to the board of Hawk plc and the investment is regarded as long term. Both companies prepare accounts to 31 December each year. The summarised balance sheet of Hawk plc on 31 December 20X4 is as follows

	£'000
Sundry net assets	2,390
Capital and reserves	
Called up share capital	800
Share premium	450
Profit and loss account	1,140
	2,390

Hawk plc has made no new issues of shares nor has there been any movement in the share premium account since Eagle plc acquired its holding.

Show at what amount the investment in Hawk plc will be shown in the consolidated balance sheet of Eagle plc as on 31 December 20X4. Assume that goodwill arising on the acquisition has been fully amortised.

Investment in associated undertaking

	£
Cost	640,000
Add: group share of post acquisition reserves	
25% × £(1,140 – 720)	105,000
Less: goodwill fully amortised (W1)	(147,500)
Alternatively 25% × £2,390,000	£597,500

(W1) **Goodwill**

		£	£
Cost			640,000
Less: Share of net assets at acquisition			
Share capital		800,000	
Share premium		450,000	
Reserves		720,000	
	25% ×	£1,970,000	(492,500)
Goodwill			£147,500

(b) **Disclosure**

Using the above figures

Investments	
Interests in associated undertakings	£597,500

3.3 Equity accounting in the consolidated profit and loss account

(a) **Calculation**

The group share of the following are brought in

(i) operating profit
(ii) exceptional items
(iii) interest receivable
(iv) interest payable
(v) taxation.

Amortisation of goodwill is charged against the group share of operating profit of associates, and must be separately disclosed.

Notional total turnover for the business (ie, group turnover plus the group share of associates' turnover) **may** be disclosed as a **memorandum** item in the profit and loss account. This disclosure enables users of the financial statements to appreciate the size of the business as a whole.

Example

Following on from the facts above, the consolidated profit and loss account of Eagle plc (before including any amounts for Hawk plc) and the profit and loss account of Hawk plc for the year ended 31 December 20X4 are as follows

	Eagle plc £'000	**Hawk plc** £'000
Turnover	11,000	4,000
Cost of sales	(6,500)	(3,000)
Gross profit	4,500	1,000
Distribution costs	(1,000)	(500)
Administrative expenses	(700)	(300)
Operating profit	2,800	200
Interest receivable	300	200
Interest payable	(100)	(100)
Profit on ordinary activities before taxation	3,000	300
Taxation	(1,200)	(60)
Profit on ordinary activities after taxation	1,800	240
Minority interests	(300)	–
Profit attributable to the group	1,500	240
Dividends proposed	(300)	(50)
Retained profit for the year	1,200	190
Retained profit b/f	6,300	950
Retained profit c/f	7,500	1,140

Prepare the consolidated profit and loss account for Eagle plc for the year ended 31 December 20X4.

(b) **Disclosure (and solution to example)**

	£'000	£'000
Turnover: group and share of associate	12,000	
Less: share of associate's turnover (25% × 4,000)	(1,000)	
Group turnover		11,000
Cost of sales		(6,500)
Gross profit		4,500
Distribution costs		(1,000)
Administrative expenses		(700)
Group operating profit		2,800
Share of operating profit in associates (25% × 200)		50

Interest receivable:		
Group	300	
Associates (25% × 200)	50	
		350
Interest payable		
Group	100	
Associates (25% × 100)	25	
		(125)
Profit on ordinary activities before taxation		3,075
Taxation		
Group	1,200	
Associates (25% × 60)	15	
		(1,215)
Profit on ordinary activities after taxation		1,860
Minority interests		(300)
Profit attributable to the group		1,560
Dividends		(300)
Retained profit for the year		1,260
Retained at 1 January 20X4 (W)		6,210
Retained at 31 December 20X4		7,470

WORKING

Eagle	6,300
Hawk (25% × (950 – 720))	58
Less: goodwill fully amortised (per previous example)	(148)
	6,210

3.4 Activity

What are the headings in the *CA 1985* group account formats for the balance sheet and the profit and loss account which are used for associated undertakings?

3.5 Activity solution

In the balance sheet under Fixed Asset Investments:

'Interests in associated undertakings'

In the profit and loss account after arriving at group operating profit:

'Income from interests in associated undertakings'.

3.6 Transactions between the group and the associate

Trading transactions and/or loans may be made between member companies of the group (ie, parent company and subsidiaries) and the associate. As the associate is not consolidated it follows that these transactions are *not* cancelled out. For example a loan made by the parent company to an associate will remain as a loan on the consolidated balance sheet (as an asset). The liability recorded in the associate's balance sheet will merely reduce the net assets (which are recorded as one figure - share of net assets - on the consolidated balance sheet).

(a) **Trading between group and associate**

An adjustment will only be required if there is unrealised profit at the balance sheet date ie, stocks exist as a result of the trading. FRS 9 requires an adjustment for the *group's* share of the unrealised profit. The elimination should be taken in the consolidated profit and loss against either the group or the associate according to which of them recorded the profit on the transaction. The adjustment in the balance sheet should be made against

(i) consolidated stock (if the unrealised profit is in respect of part of this stock) or
(ii) investment in associate (if the stock is in the associate).

(b) **Loans and inter company balances**

The table below states the position. Remember that the asset or liability recorded by the associate will automatically be reflected in the net asset calculation.

Treatment in the consolidated balance sheet

	Item		*Treatment*
(a)	Loans between associated undertakings and the group	(1)	these should be disclosed separately, but: (A) if long term, they may appear in the same B/S section as 'investment in associate' (B) otherwise they should appear as current assets or liabilities.
		(2)	loans to and from should not be netted off.
(b)	Debtors and creditors arising from trading transactions with associated undertakings	(1)	include under respective current assets or liabilities without netting off.
		(2)	disclose separately if material.

3.7 Applying the equity method - further points

Statement of total recognised gains and losses

The investor's share of the total recognised gains and losses of its associates should be included in the consolidated statement of total recognised gains and losses. If the amounts are material, they should be shown separately under each heading either in the statement or in a note to the statement.

General principles

(a) The consideration paid for the acquisition and the goodwill arising should be calculated using fair values.

(b) Investor and associate should apply the same accounting policies.

(c) The accounts of the associate should have the same financial year-end as those of the investor. If this is impracticable, earlier financial statements of the associate may be used, provided they are prepared for a financial year that ended not more than three months earlier.

(d) The date on which an investment becomes an associate is the date on which the investor begins to hold a participating interest and to exercise significant influence.

(e) The date on which an investment ceases to be an associate is the date on which the investor ceases to hold a participating interest and to exercise significant influence.

4 JOINT VENTURES

4.1 Introduction

FRS 9 sets out the accounting treatment for joint ventures in the consolidated financial statements.

The term 'joint venture' is used very widely in practice to cover all types of jointly controlled activity. Jointly controlled operations, assets and entities may all be described as joint ventures. FRS 9 defines 'joint venture' in a much narrower sense.

Definition A **joint venture** is an entity in which the reporting entity holds an interest on a long-term basis and is **jointly controlled** by the reporting entity and by one or more other venturers under a contractual arrangement.

Definition A reporting entity **jointly controls** a venture with one or more other entities if none of the entities alone can control that entity but all together can do so and decisions on financial and operating policy essential to the activities, economic performance and financial position of that venture require each venturer's consent.

Definition A **joint arrangement that is not an entity** is a contractual arrangement under which the participants engage in joint activities that do not create an entity because it would not be carrying on a trade or business of its own.

4.2 Distinguishing joint ventures from joint arrangements

For an investment to qualify as a joint venture, there must be:

(a) a separate **entity**;
(b) which carries on a **trade or business of its own**.

This means that the joint venture must have some independence to pursue its own commercial strategy and it must generally be able to buy and sell on the same terms as are available in the market.

FRS 9 provides further examples of indications that the arrangement is not carrying on a trade or business of its own:

(a) the participants derive their benefit from products or services taken in kind rather than by receiving a share in the results of trading; or

(b) each participant's share of the output or result of the joint activity is determined by its supply of key inputs to the process producing that output or result.

A cost or risk sharing means of carrying out a process in the participants' own trades or businesses (eg, a joint marketing or distribution network or a shared production facility) is not a joint venture.

A joint arrangement to carry out a single project is unlikely to meet the definition of a joint venture.

4.3 Activity

(a) A (a builder) and B (an estate agent) together buy a house which they let to tenants. A is responsible for the initial refurbishment and maintenance of the house and B finds the tenants and collects the rents. A and B each take an agreed share of the rental income from the house.

(b) A and B enter into an agreement to manufacture and sell a new product. They set up a company which carries out these activities. A and B each own 50% of the equity share capital of the company and are its only directors. They share equally in major policy decisions and are each entitled to 50% of the profits of the company.

Are these two joint activities joint ventures or joint arrangements?

4.4 Activity solution

(a) This is a joint arrangement that is not an entity because:

- no separate entity exists;
- the arrangement is a single project; and
- it appears to be simply a means of carrying out A and B's own businesses.

(b) This appears to be a joint venture because:

- there is a separate entity;
- the entity appears to be carrying out a business of its own; and
- the participants share in the profits of the business.

Conclusion A joint venture is an **entity** which is jointly controlled by the reporting entity and by one or more other venturers.

4.5 Accounting treatment

(a) **Joint arrangements that are not entities**

Participants in a joint arrangement that is not an entity should account for their own assets, liabilities and cash flows, measured according to the terms of the agreement governing the arrangement.

(b) **Joint ventures**

In the investor's **individual financial statements**, investments in joint ventures should be treated as fixed asset investments and shown either at cost, less any amounts written off, or at valuation.

In the **consolidated financial statements** joint ventures should be included using the gross equity method.

Definition The **gross equity method** is a form of equity method under which the investor's share of the aggregate gross assets and liabilities underlying the net amount included for the investment is shown on the face of the balance sheet and, in the profit and loss account, the investor's share of the investee's turnover is noted.

This means that the treatment is the same as for associates, but with additional disclosure:

– the investor's share of turnover is shown in the consolidated profit and loss account (but not as part of group turnover);

– the investor's share of the gross assets and liabilities are shown in the consolidated balance sheet (instead of the investor's share of the net assets).

(c) **Structures with the form but not the substance of a joint venture**

A structure has the form but not the substance of a joint venture when it is a separate entity in which the participants hold a long term interest and exercise joint management, but which operates as a means for each participant to carry on its own business, with each venturer able to identify and control its share of the assets, liabilities and cash flows of the venture.

In this situation, each entity should account directly for its part of the assets, liabilities and cash flows held within that structure. (This is very similar to proportional consolidation.)

Conclusion Joint ventures are included in the consolidated financial statements using the gross equity method.

4.6 Illustration

FRS 9 includes illustrative examples of ways of disclosing information about joint ventures. Example 1 from FRS 9 is shown below. Note that the example also includes associates.

CONSOLIDATED PROFIT AND LOSS ACCOUNT

	£m	£m
Turnover: group and share of joint ventures	320	
Less: share of joint ventures' turnover	(120)	
Group turnover		200
Cost of sales		(120)
Gross profit		80
Administrative expenses		(40)
Group operating profit		40
Share of operating profit in		
Joint ventures	30	
Associates	24	
		54
		94
Interest receivable (group)		6
Interest payable		
Group	(26)	
Joint ventures	(10)	
Associates	(12)	
		(48)
Profit on ordinary activities before tax		52
Tax on profit on ordinary activities*		(12)
Profit on ordinary activities after tax		40
Minority interests		(6)
Profit on ordinary activities after taxation and minority interest		34
Equity dividends		(10)
Retained profit for group and its share of associates and joint ventures		24

* Tax relates to the following:	Parent and subsidiaries	(5)
	Joint ventures	(5)
	Associates	(2)

CONSOLIDATED BALANCE SHEET

	£m	£m	£m
Fixed assets			
Tangible assets		480	
Investments			
Investments in joint ventures:			
Share of gross assets	130		
Share of gross liabilities	(80)		
		50	

Investments in associates	20	
		550
Current assets		
Stock	15	
Debtors	75	
Cash at bank and in hand	10	
	100	
Creditors (due within one year)	(50)	
Net current assets		50
Total assets less current liabilities		600
Creditors (due after more than one year)		(250)
Provisions for liabilities and charges		(10)
Equity minority interest		(40)
		300
Capital and reserves		
Called up share capital		50
Share premium account		150
Profit and loss account		100
Shareholders' funds (all equity)		300

5 DISCLOSURE REQUIREMENTS FOR ASSOCIATES AND JOINT VENTURES

5.1 All associates and joint ventures

(a) For each associate or joint venture included in the financial statements of the investing group, disclose the following:

  (i) name;

  (ii) proportion of the issued shares in each class held by the investing group;

  (iii) accounting period or date of the financial statements used if different from those of the investing group;

  (iv) an indication of the nature of its business.

(b) Disclose any notes relating to the financial statements of associates that are material to understanding the effect on the investor of its investments.

(c) Indicate the extent of any statutory, contractual or exchange control restrictions on the ability of an associate to distribute its reserves.

(d) Disclose the amounts owing and owed between the investor and its associates or joint ventures, analysed into amounts relating to loans and amounts relating to trading balances.

(e) Where an investor holding 20% or more of the voting rights of another entity does not treat it as an associate, a note should explain the reasons for this.

5.2 Detailed disclosures where associates and joint ventures are material to the investing group

One of the disadvantages of the equity method is that it only provides limited information about associates and joint ventures. In particular, only one figure is included in the balance sheet, representing the group share of the associates' net assets. It is possible for material liabilities to be hidden in this figure, enabling investors to use equity accounted entities as a form of off balance sheet finance.

For this reason, FRS 9 requires additional disclosures where size thresholds are exceeded. The thresholds are applied by comparing the investor's share for its associates or joint ventures of **any** of the following:

- gross assets
- gross liabilities
- turnover
- operating results (on a three year average)

with the corresponding amounts for the investor group (excluding associates and joint ventures).

(a) Where the **aggregate** of the investor's share in its associates or its joint ventures exceeds a **15% threshold** with respect to the investor group, a note should give the aggregate of the investor's share in its associates of the following:

- turnover (associates only; for joint ventures it must always be disclosed)
- fixed assets
- current assets
- liabilities due within one year
- liabilities due after one year or more.

(b) Where the investor's share in any **individual** associate or joint venture exceeds a **25% threshold** with respect to the investor group, a note should name that associate or joint venture and give its share of each of the following:

- turnover
- profit before tax
- taxation
- profit after tax
- fixed assets
- current assets
- liabilities due within one year
- liabilities due after one year or more.

5.3 Activity

You are provided with the following information about H plc and its associated undertaking, A Ltd for the year ended 30 June 20X8:

	H plc	*A Ltd*
	£'000	£'000
Turnover	110,000	60,000
Operating profit	30,000	16,000
Profit before tax	25,000	12,000
Taxation	10,000	4,000
Profit after tax	15,000	8,000
Fixed assets	250,000	160,000
Current assets	40,000	24,000
Creditors due within one year	45,000	24,000
Creditors due after more than one year	110,000	40,000

H plc holds 25% of the equity share capital of A Ltd.

Show the additional disclosures required in respect of A Ltd in the consolidated financial statements of the H plc group for the year ended 30 June 20X8.

5.4 Activity solution

Additional disclosures for associates

	£'000	£'000
Share of turnover of associates (25% × 60,000)		15,000
Share of assets		
Share of fixed assets (25% × 160,000)	40,000	
Share of current assets (25% × 24,000)	6,000	
		46,000
Share of liabilities		
Liabilities due within one year or less (25% × 24,000)	6,000	
Liabilities due after more than one year (25% × 40,000)	10,000	
		(16,000)
Share of net assets		30,000

WORKING

H plc's share of the total assets of the associate exceeds 15%. (Note that the disclosures have to be made if **any** of the thresholds are exceeded.)

Turnover $\frac{25\% \times 60,000}{110,000} =$ 14%

Operating profit $\frac{15\% \times 16,000}{30,000} =$ 13%

Total assets $\frac{25\% \times 184,000}{290,000} =$ 16%

Total liabilities $\frac{25\% \times 64,000}{155,000} =$ 10%

6 EVALUATION OF FRS 9

6.1 Advantages of the requirements

(a) The definitions of an associate and of significant influence are consistent with those in the Companies Act and ensure that the financial statements reflect the economic substance of the relationship.

(b) The extended disclosure requirements should reduce the scope for using associates as a form of 'off balance sheet finance'.

(c) The accounting and reporting of joint ventures is fully covered for the first time and the use of the gross equity method should provide useful information to users of the financial statements.

6.2 Criticisms of the requirements

(a) Many people believe that joint ventures are so commercially distinct from associates that they should be dealt with in a separate accounting standard. A separate standard would also have enabled the ASB to deal with jointly-controlled assets and operations and to explore the different shareholdings that might arise in a joint venture. (This would have been consistent with the position taken by the IASC.)

(b) The disclosure requirements might be very onerous in practice and will add to an already extensive list of additional disclosures introduced by recent FRSs.

6.3 Proportional consolidation

Some commentators believe that proportional consolidation should be used to account for all joint ventures. They argue that because joint control means a sharing of risks and rewards it gives a higher level of influence than mere significant influence. It is therefore appropriate to recognise the venturer's share of individual assets and liabilities. Proportional consolidation would give a better representation of the economic substance of the investment and would be consistent with international practice. It is argued that this would also be consistent with the requirements of FRS 5 (recognition of interests in assets).

The ASB has rejected proportional consolidation for joint ventures on the grounds that it would be inconsistent with the accounting treatment of both associates and subsidiaries. It argues that in most cases, the venturer controls an interest in the joint venture, rather than its share in individual assets and liabilities.

Proportional consolidation would also be inconsistent with the requirements of the Companies Act in most cases.

7 CHAPTER SUMMARY

Associated undertakings are included in the consolidated financial statements using the equity method. Joint ventures are included in the consolidated financial statements using the gross equity method. Proportional consolidation is not commonly used in the UK.

8 SELF TEST QUESTIONS

8.1 What is the definition of the equity method? (1.1)

8.2 What is the definition of the proportional consolidation method? (1.1)

8.3 What is the weakness of the use of the equity method for a subsidiary? (1.4)

8.4 What is a participating interest? (2.2)

8.5 What are the implications when 20% of another company is owned? (2.2)

8.6 What is the meaning of significant influence? (2.2)

8.7 How is trading between the group and the associate dealt with? (3.6)

8.8 What is the gross equity method? (4.5)

9 EXAMINATION TYPE QUESTION

9.1 Bold plc

Bold plc, the parent company of the Bold Group, acquired 25% of the ordinary shares of Face plc on 1 September 20X0 for £54,000. Face plc carried on business as a property investment company. The draft accounts as at 31 August 20X1 are as follows:

Profit and loss accounts for the year ended 31 August 20X1

	Bold Group £'000	*Face plc* £'000
Sales	175	200
Profit before tax	88	60
Taxation	22	20
	66	40

Profit on sale of property to Face plc	13	
	79	
Proposed dividends	61	-
	18	40

Balance sheets as at 31 August 20X1

	Bold Group	*Face plc*
Fixed assets	£'000	£'000
Tangible fixed assets	135	200
Investment in Face plc	54	
Current assets		
Stock	72	210
Debtors	105	50
Current liabilities		
Creditors	(95)	(20)
Overdraft	(14)	(100)
Net current assets	68	140
Total assets less current liabilities	257	340
Ordinary shares of £1 each	135	50
Reserves	122	90
10% loan	-	200
	257	340

On 1 September 20X0 Bold plc sold a property with a book value of £40,000 to Face plc at its market value of £60,000. Face plc obtained the funds to pay the £60,000 by raising a loan which is included in the 10% loan that appears in its balance sheet at 31 August 20X1.

Goodwill arising on acquisition is amortised through the profit and loss account over 5 years from the date of acquisition.

You are required:

(a) to prepare:

(i) The consolidated profit and loss account of the Bold group for the year ended 31 August 20X1 and a consolidated balance sheet as at that date, and

(ii) Relevant notes to comply with the requirements of FRS 9 *Associates and joint ventures*. **(8 marks)**

(b) to explain two defects of simple equity accounting and the remedies that you would propose to overcome these defects. Please illustrate your answer with the data from the Bold Group. **(4 marks)**

(c) if Face plc issued 30,000 ordinary shares, each of £1 value, to a third party on 1 September 20X1, for a cash consideration of £4 per share

(i) to explain any matters to be taken into consideration in finalising the 20X1 consolidated accounts; and

(ii) to calculate the carrying value of the investment in Face plc in the consolidated balance sheet at 31 August 20X2 and comment upon any related items. **(8 marks)**

(Total: 20 marks)

10 ANSWER TO EXAMINATION TYPE QUESTION

10.1 Bold plc

(Tutorial notes: For part (a) (i) eliminate only the group's share (25%) of the unrealised profit. Provide only two or three notes based on your workings for part (a) (i) when answering part (a) (ii).

For part (b) concentrate on the lack of information disclosed when using equity accounting when compared with full consolidation.

For part (c) consider the drop in percentage holding. For part (c) (i) consider this as a post balance sheet event and for part (c) (ii) consider the carrying value of the (now) trade investment.*)*

(a) (i) **Consolidated profit and loss account for year ended 31 August 20X1**

	£	£
Turnover		175,000
Group operating profit	88,000	
Share of operating profit of associate (including amortisation of goodwill £5,800) (£60,000 × 25% – 5,800)	9,200	
Profit on sale of property to associate (£13,000 - 5,000)	8,000	
Profit on ordinary activities before tax		105,200
Tax on profit on ordinary activities: group	22,000	
Share of taxation of associate (£20,000 × 25%)	5,000	
		27,000
Profit on ordinary activities after tax		78,200
Proposed dividends		61,000
Retained profit for the year		17,200

(Tutorial note: with only the group's share of net assets of Face plc being incorporated in the consolidated balance sheet it is only necessary to eliminate 25% of the profit made on the sale of the property ie 25% × (£60,000 – £40,000) = £5,000.*)*

Consolidated balance sheet as at 31 August 20X1

	£	£	£
Fixed assets			
Tangible			135,000
Investment in associated undertaking (W1)			53,200
			188,200

Current assets	Stock		72,000	
	Debtors		105,000	
			177,000	
Current liabilities	Creditors	95,000		
	Bank	14,000	109,000	
Net current assets				68,000
				256,200
Ordinary shares				135,000
Reserves (W3)				121,200
				256,200

WORKINGS

(W1) Goodwill on acquisition

	£	£
Cost of investment		54,000
Share of ordinary shares (25% × £50,000)	12,500	
Share of pre acq reserves (25% × £50,000)	12,500	
		25,000
		29,000
Amortisation (29,000 ÷ 5)		(5,800)
		23,200

(W2) Investment in associate

Share of net assets (25% × £140,000)	35,000
Elimination of share of unrealised profit	(5,000)
	30,000
Goodwill not yet amortised	23,200
	53,200

(W3) Reserves

Bold	122,000
Face (25% × £40,000)	10,000
Unrealised profit	(5,000)
Goodwill	(5,800)
	121,200

(ii) **Notes to the accounts**

Investment in associated undertaking

The group holds 25% of the ordinary shares of Face plc, a property investment company. The amounts shown in the consolidated profit and loss account and consolidated balance sheet can be expanded as follows:

	£'000
Share of turnover (200 × 25%)	50
Share of profit before tax (60 × 25%)	15

Share of taxation (20 × 25%)	(5)	
Share of profit after tax	10	
Share of assets		
Share of fixed assets (200 × 25%)	50	
Share of current assets (260 × 25%)	65	
	115	
Share of liabilities		
Share of liabilities due within one year (120 × 25%)	30	
Share of liabilities due after one year or more (200 × 25%)50		
	(80)	
Share of net assets at 31 August 20X1		35
Less: share of unrealised profit on sale of property within the group		(5)
		30
Goodwill		23
		53

(Tutorial note: Face plc clearly exceeds the '25% threshold' and therefore FRS 9 requires the additional disclosures shown above.*)*

(b) **Defect relating to equity accounting in the profit and loss account**

The results of the associate are incorporated without giving any indication as to whether or not the income reported will ever be received, by way of dividend, by the investing group. The group while having a degree of influence may not be able to guarantee the receipt of the reported profit, and in any case the associate may be in no position to make such a distribution.

For example, Face plc appears to have a serious liquidity problem with current liabilities in excess of double the company's debtors, and loans which are nearly double the equity investment. This level of gearing could result in serious problems if the associate were to suffer a reduction in the level of pre-interest profits. This problem could only be remedied by an extension of the disclosure requirements to cover details of the associate's liquidity position and gearing ratio.

FRS 9 requires disclosure where there are significant restrictions on the ability of an associate to distribute its reserves.

Defect relating to equity accounting in the balance sheet

The inclusion of only a single figure covering the group's share of net assets makes it very difficult to analyse the financial position of the associate. A considerable amount of the net assets may be represented by intangible fixed assets carried at a subjective valuation. In addition it is not possible to ascertain the make up of the tangible fixed assets, which in the case of Face plc total £200,000. In addition any liquidity or gearing problems are not apparent.

FRS 9 now requires additional disclosures where associates are material in the context of the group, but even these may not go far enough to provide a full picture of the financial position of the associate.

(c) (i) It may be necessary to include a note in the 20X1 accounts informing readers that the interest of the group in the associate has fallen from 25% to 15.625% $\left(\frac{£12,500}{£80,000}\right)$, and is therefore not automatically an associate. In fact with a single third party holding a 37.5% interest, it is unlikely that the group would have the level of significant influence for its investment in Face plc to be accounted for under the equity method as an associate. This event should probably be disclosed as a non-adjusting post balance sheet event in line with the requirements of SSAP 17. This should avoid misleading the users of the financial statements as to the investments held by the group.

(ii) The investment should be carried at the value attributed to the investment at the date it ceased to be considered an associate company. The investment in Face plc should be recorded at a valuation ie, 25% × £140,000 + 23,200 = £58,200. This valuation may be updated to 15.625% × (£140,000 + Cash from issue £120,000) + goodwill 23,200, £63,825 with the increase in valuation of £5,625 probably treated as an unrealised revaluation gain. This amount should be reviewed for impairment and written down to its recoverable amount if necessary.

18 OVERSEAS TRANSACTIONS

INTRODUCTION & LEARNING OBJECTIVES

Foreign currencies pose special accounting problems where accounts have been produced in a foreign currency and the results need to be incorporated within a UK sterling denominated set of accounts.

Examination questions on this area normally include both computational and discussion requirements.

For the discussion questions it is necessary to learn the circumstances in which the closing rate method or the temporal method is used.

The key to computational consolidation questions is to provide a clear working paper showing the translation rates used and the resultant sterling amounts. Once the sterling amounts have been obtained, most of the consolidation procedures are similar to a normal consolidation.

When you have studied this chapter you should be able to do the following:

- Discuss and apply the methods of foreign currency translation for both individual companies and groups.
- Demonstrate your knowledge of how to account for hedged investments.
- Show that you understand the accounting and disclosure requirements of *SSAP 20*.

1 SSAP 20: FOREIGN CURRENCY TRANSLATION

SSAP 20 identifies two sets of circumstances in which a business must consider how to deal with foreign currency amounts within its accounts: direct business transactions and operations conducted through a foreign entity.

1.1 Direct business transactions

Whenever a UK business enters into a contract where the consideration is expressed in a foreign currency, it will be necessary to translate that foreign currency amount at some stage into sterling for inclusion into its own accounts. Examples include

(i) imports of raw materials
(ii) exports of finished goods
(iii) importation of foreign-manufactured fixed assets
(iv) investments in foreign securities
(v) raising an overseas loan.

Translation may be necessary at more than one time. For example, the import of raw materials creates a foreign currency liability when the goods are supplied and for which a sterling value must be incorporated in the books. Where settlement is delayed due to normal credit terms, the actual sterling cost of settlement may differ from the liability initially recorded.

Similarly, the sterling value of a long-term foreign currency loan is likely to fluctuate from one period to another.

1.2 Operations conducted through a foreign entity

Companies frequently establish local subsidiaries in foreign countries through which to conduct their operations. These subsidiaries will maintain full accounts in the local currency and these accounts must clearly be translated into the currency of the parent before they can be consolidated.

This chapter deals firstly with the translation of direct business transactions (the individual company stage) and then with the translation of the accounts of foreign subsidiaries (the consolidated financial statements stage).

1.3 Foreign currency conversion and translation

Definition Foreign currency conversion is the process of physically exchanging one currency for another currency.

An individual converts currency when he buys, say, Spanish pesetas for sterling at the start of a holiday. If he has any money left at the end of the holiday, he reconverts the pesetas to sterling. If the exchange rate has changed in the meantime he will make a gain or loss on the transaction less the costs of commission and the buy/sell price spread.

A business will also convert currencies when it has to pay for an item which it has purchased which is denominated in another currency. For example a UK business may purchase goods from a French supplier and agree to pay X francs. When it comes to pay for the goods, it is likely to have to convert sterling into francs to pay for the goods.

From a business viewpoint however, the need to **translate** items denominated in a foreign currency is more important.

Definition Foreign currency translation is the statement of an item denominated in a foreign currency in terms of the domestic reporting currency.

1.4 The temporal and closing rate methods of translation

There are two exchange rates which can generally be used to translate any foreign currency balance. These are

(a) **The historic rate**

This is simply the exchange rate which applied at the date of the transaction.

(b) **The closing rate**

This is the rate of exchange ruling at the balance sheet date.

Thus, a fixed asset acquired for Fr 100,000 when the exchange rate was Fr 12 = £1 and now translated for inclusion in a balance sheet when the exchange rate has moved to Fr 10 = £1 could either be shown at

(a) Historic rate – £8,333 or
(b) Closing rate – £10,000

These two rates are used in the two **methods** as follows.

(a) **Closing rate method**

All items are translated at the closing rate.

(b) **Temporal method**

Transactions are initially recorded at the historic rate. If a monetary item denominated in a foreign currency exists at the balance sheet date, that item is retranslated to closing rate.

Under the temporal method, the retranslation of monetary items, such as debtors and creditors accords with the historic cost convention that monetary items are recorded at the latest estimate of amounts receivable or payable in cash.

It should be clear that selection of an appropriate translation rate will have a significant impact on balance sheet values and on reported profits. Where the historic rate is employed, the value of the asset is unchanging. However, if the closing rate is applied, the book value of the fixed asset above is increased by £1,667 and this must be reflected either in reported profits or as a movement in reserves.

2 THE REQUIREMENTS OF SSAP 20 AS THEY RELATE TO INDIVIDUAL COMPANIES

2.1 Basic principles

This stage concerns the translation of business transactions in an individual company.

It is quite likely that during an accounting period, a company (whether situated in the UK or abroad) will enter into transactions in a currency other than its own domestic (ie, functional) currency. The results of these transactions should be translated and recorded in the company's accounting records

(a) at the date the transaction occurred

(b) using the rate of exchange in operation on that date (or where appropriate, at the rate of exchange at which it is contracted to settle the transaction in the future).

No further translation will be required for non-monetary assets (eg, fixed assets) carried at historic costs. However, monetary items at the balance sheet date are retranslated at the closing rate of exchange with differences taken to profit and loss account. This would include debtors, creditors, bank balances and loans, where any of these amounts are expressed in a foreign currency.

2.2 Fixed assets

Once these assets have been translated at the historic rate and recorded they are carried in terms of the currency of the individual company.

Thus where a UK company purchases plant and machinery, for its own use in the UK, from an American supplier on 30 June 20X7 for $90,000 when the rate of exchange was £1 = $1.80, it will record the asset at £50,000 ($90,000 @ 1.80). No further translation will occur. All depreciation charged on this asset will be based on £50,000.

2.3 Debtors

Where goods are sold to overseas customers and payment is received in a currency other than the functional currency, the following transactions must be recorded

(a) the sale – at the rate of exchange applicable at the time of sale
(b) the receipt of cash – the actual proceeds.

Any exchange difference (the balance on the debtors' account) will be reported as part of the profit for the period from normal operations.

If on 7 May 20X6 a UK company sells goods to a German company for DM 48,000 when the rate of exchange was £1 = DM 3.2, the sale will be recorded:

	£	£
Dr Customer DM 48,000 @ 3.2	15,000	
Cr Sales		15,000

Assuming on 20 July 20X6 the customer remits a draft for DM 48,000 which realises £15,150

	£	£
Dr Bank	15,150	
Cr Customer		15,150

The credit balance of £150 on the debtor's account will represent a profit on exchange to be taken to profit and loss account as part of the operating profit for the year.

2.4 Example

Facts as in para 2.3 except that the company prepares accounts to 30 June annually. At the balance sheet date the rate of exchange was £1 = DM 3.15. What will be the movements on the debtors account?

2.5 Solution

Debtor's account

20X6		DM	£	20X6		DM	£
May 7	Sales a/c	48,000	15,000	Jun 30	Balance c/d (at 3.15)	48,000	15,238
June 30	P&L a/c- (profit on exchange)		238				
		48,000	15,238			48,000	15,238
Jul 1	Balance b/d	48,000	15,238	Jul 10	Bank a/c (proceeds)	48,000	15,150
				Jun 30	P&L a/c (loss on exchange)		88
		48,000	15,238			48,000	15,238

Note:

(a) As a monetary item, debtors are retranslated at the balance sheet date with the exchange difference taken to the profit and loss account

(b) average rates of exchange (say on a monthly basis) might be used in practice for translating the sales into the functional currency

(c) exchange differences would be transferred (as they were recognised) to a separate account, the balance on which would be transferred to profit and loss account at the end of the accounting period.

2.6 Creditors

The same principles as those set out for debtors apply to creditors.

2.7 Activity

A British company buys goods from a Swiss supplier for Sw Fr 8,700 when the rate of exchange was £1 = Sw Fr 3. The British company settled the amount due with a bankers draft for Sw Fr 8,700 when the rate of exchange was £1 = Sw Fr 2.8. Prepare the supplier's account.

2.8 Activity solution

The supplier's account would appear as follows

Supplier's account

	SwFr	£		*SwFr*	£
Bank account (remittance (2.8))	8,700	3,107	Purchases account (3)	8,700	2,900
			P&L a/c (loss on exchange)		207
	8,700	3,107		8,700	3,107

2.9 Loans

Where a company raises a loan abroad, denominated in a currency other than its own currency, the amount outstanding must be retranslated at the closing rate at each year end. Again, this is because a loan is a monetary item. Any difference on exchange must form part of the profit from normal operations.

A UK company takes out a 5 year loan of $1m from an American bank. The sterling proceeds amounted to £555,556 (when rate of exchange was £1 = $1.80). At the balance sheet date the rate had moved to £1 = $1.70.

The loan must be translated at this rate to £588,235. The loss on exchange of £(588,235 – 555,556) = £32,679 will be reported as part of profit from normal operations. Retranslation will occur at each balance sheet date.

2.10 Contracted rate of exchange

Where a transaction is to be settled at a contracted rate of exchange, that rate **should** be used.

A UK company purchased an item of plant from a German manufacturer for DM 100,000, when the rate was £1 = DM 3.18 but the contract specified settlement in three months at an exchange rate of £1 = DM 3.2. At the time of settlement, the actual exchange rate was £1 = DM 3.19.

The effect of the specified rate is to **freeze** the sterling cost of the plant ab initio. Accordingly, it will be debited in the accounts at the certain sterling cost of

DM 100,000 ÷ 3.2 = £31,250

2.11 Use of forward contracts

Where a trading transaction is covered by a related or matching forward contract, the rate of exchange specified in that contract **may** be used.

2.12 Example

A UK company sells goods to a US corporation on 30 June for $200,000. The contract provides for settlement on 30 September. The UK company sells $200,000 forward three months on 30 June.

Rates of exchange are

	Spot	*3 months forward*
30 June	1.75	1.78
30 September	1.72	

How will the sale and debtor be reflected?

2.13 Solution

By selling dollars forward, the UK company guarantees the ultimate sterling receipt, irrespective of exchange rate movements. Accordingly, these ultimate proceeds may be reflected immediately as a sale and as a debtor

$200,000 ÷ 1.78 = £112,360

In this case, no exchange differences will arise.

2.14 Individual companies that engage in foreign currency transactions

(a) **Summary of entries**

(i) **Transactions during accounting period**

These should be translated and recorded at the rate of exchange ruling at the date of the transaction. In practice, an average rate might be used.

(ii) **Monetary items at balance sheet date**

Where these items (debtors, creditors, bank balances, loans) are denominated in a foreign currency they should be translated and recorded at the closing rate (or, if appropriate, at the rate at which the transaction is contracted to be settled).

(iii) **Exchange differences**

Except to the extent that they relate to extraordinary items, all exchange differences should be reported as part of normal operating profit.

(b) **Classification of exchange differences**

(i) Gains or losses from trading transactions should normally be included under "other operating income or expense".

(ii) Gains or losses arising from financing arrangements should be disclosed separately as part of "other interest receivable (payable) and similar income (expense)".

2.15 The conflict between SSAP 20 and the Companies Act

All the exchange differences that we have calculated in this section are included in the profit and loss account and thus affect reported earnings. Consideration needs to be given to whether this effect is valid ie, are they 'proper' gains and losses which should be included in the profit and loss account? The general principle for inclusion of items in the profit and loss account is that gains should be realised (as in the SSAP 2 and Companies Act concept of realisation).

For transactions which have been **settled** in the accounting period, the inclusion of exchange gains and losses is valid as the gains/losses are already reflected in local currency cash flows. A settled transaction means the debtor, for example, has paid his debt or the business has paid a creditor.

Where a transaction has not been settled by the end of the accounting period we need to distinguish between short-term and long-term monetary items.

(a) A short-term trade debtor or creditor will be received or paid in cash shortly after the year end. The amount received or paid may be different from the rate of exchange ruling at the balance sheet date but, in most cases, not materially so. As the exchange difference is likely to be reflected in cash flows, the exchange gain/loss is validly reported as part of earnings.

(b) A long-term item, for example a foreign currency loan, is retranslated to closing rate at the end of each accounting period. This may result in reported gains in one period followed by a compensatory loss in the following accounting period as the exchange rates fluctuate. It is therefore uncertain as to whether a calculated gain or loss will eventually be reflected in cash flows.

SSAP 20 agrees that there is uncertainty but argues that exchange differences on long-term monetary items need to be reflected in the profit and loss account in accordance with the accruals concept. However in cases where there is doubt about the convertibility of the currency in question, exchange gains on long-term monetary items should be restricted ie, prudence overtakes the accruals concept.

2.16 Equity investment financed by foreign currency loan – hedging

It is not unusual for UK companies making overseas investments to raise the funds locally in an overseas currency. Such loans are known as **hedging loans** as they are designed to **hedge** against foreign currency movements since the sterling equivalent of both the equity investment and the overseas currency loans will move in the same direction – either both up or both down.

Were it not for special rules which cover **hedging** loans, the requirements of *SSAP 20* would apply unfairly and illogically where companies had financed equity investments by foreign currency loans.

Without them, the normal rules of *SSAP 20* would apply, with the following effect.

In the separate accounts of the investing company

(a) the loan as a monetary item would be retranslated at the closing rate of exchange and any resulting profit or loss would be taken to profit and loss account

(b) the investment in the foreign entity is a non-monetary item and would therefore be carried at the historic exchange rate with no subsequent exchange differences arising.

Assuming a weakening parent company functional currency, the deteriorating exchange rate will give

(a) an increased cost of repaying the foreign loan – charged to profit and loss account, and
(b) no increase in value for the fixed asset investment.

The economic reality is that the foreign loan matches the investment in the foreign entity. It will be repaid either out of the sale proceeds of the foreign investment or, more likely, out of cash flows – presumably dividends – from the investment. Logic therefore demands that the corresponding gains and losses should in some way be matched by offset and this is what *SSAP 20* permits.

SSAP 20 permits the investing company to treat the equity investment as a monetary item and translate the carrying amount (cost or value) at each balance sheet date at the closing rate of exchange. Differences arising are taken to reserves and the differences on translating the loan are taken to the same reserve for offset. The offset is subject to the following conditions

(a) in any accounting period exchange differences on the borrowings are offset only to the extent of differences on translating the investment (any excess must be dealt with in profit and loss account)

(b) the foreign currency borrowings should not exceed the total cash that the investments are expected to be able to generate (dividends plus sale value)

(c) the offset procedure should be applied consistently

(d) the loans need not be in the same currency as the investment

(e) the offset is available on any overseas equity investment (not merely subsidiary and associate relationships) financed by foreign borrowings.

2.17 Example

On 1 January 20X8 100% of a French subsidiary was acquired by H plc at a cost of FFr960,000 when the rate was FFr 6 = £1. Assume that the whole of the purchase price was borrowed from a Swiss bank when the rate was SF 4 = £1.

The following is the draft balance sheet at 31 December 20X8

	£'000		£'000
Shares in subsidiary		Share capital	1,800
(FFr 960,000 @ 6 = £1)	160	P&L a/c	1,200
Sundry net assets	3,000	Loan (160,000 × 4 = SF640,000)	160
	3,160		3,160

Rates at 31 December 20X8

£1 = 5 FFr = SF 3.2.

Show the carrying value of the investment, loan and any offset at 31 December 20X8.

2.18 Solution

			FFr(000)	*Rate*	£'000
(a)	Investment carrying value	– purchase	960	Cost	160
		– 31.12.X8	960	5	192
	Gain on restating carrying value				32
			SF(000)		
(b)	Loan – at borrowing date		640	4	160
	– at 31.12.X8		640	3.2	200
					(40)
(c)	Offset of 40,000 loss on loan				
	(i) Reserve movement (limited to gain on investment)				(32)
	(ii) Profit and loss account – excess				(8)
					(40)

Where offset has occurred additional disclosure is required

(a) the amount offset against reserves (of the differences on translating the loan), ie, £32,000 and
(b) the net amount charged or credited to profit and loss account ie, £8,000.

A specimen disclosure for H plc might be

Statement of total recognised gains and losses

	£'000	£'000
Profit for the financial year		X
Exchange gains for the year	32	
Offset of loss on hedging loans	(32)	
Net movement on exchange gains		X
Total gains and losses recognised since last annual report		X

Notes to the financial statements

(1) **Exchange differences on foreign currency borrowings**

	£'000
Loss on foreign currency borrowings	40
Offset in reserves	(32)
Charged to profit and loss account	8

(2) **Reserves**

	Profit and loss account	
	£'000	£'000
At beginning of year		X
Exchange gains for the year	32	
Offset of loss on hedging loans	(32)	
Net movement on exchange gains		X
At end of year		X

2.19 Activity

T Ltd sold a block booking of holidays in Spain to a German travel agent on 16 April 20X8 for 1,980,000 marks. An invoice was raised for this amount with sums payable by the travel agent to be:

30 August 980,000 marks
30 September 1,000,000 marks.

The amounts were paid on the due dates. T Ltd took out a forward cover contract to sell 980,000 marks on 30 August at DM 3.16 = £1 and 1,000,000 marks on 30 September at DM 3.17 = £1.

Relevant exchange rates for the year are as follows:

Date	*DM = £1*
16 April 20X8	3.12
30 August 20X8	2.96
30 September 20X8	3.24

Write up the sales and debtor account to record these transactions for the year ended 31 October 20X8.

2.20 Activity solution

A sale was made of holidays in April 20X8. Therefore at that date

Dr Debtors
Cr Sales

with 1,980,000 marks at forward exchange rates.

As T Ltd knows it can sell the marks at the forward rates, there is thus no exchange difference when the marks are received on the respective dates. The ledger accounts will therefore be as follows:

Sales

	£			£
		16.4.X8	$\frac{980,000}{3.16}$ Debtor	310,127
			$\frac{1,000,000}{3.17}$ Debtor	315,457

Debtor

	£			£
16.4.X8 Sales	310,127	30.8.X8	$\frac{980,000}{3.16}$ Cash	310,127
	315,457	30.9.X8	$\frac{1,000,000}{3.17}$ Cash	315,457
	625,584			625,584

2.21 The adequacy of the current regulations governing the treatment of foreign exchange losses

Under the hedging concept described (also known as the cover concept), losses on borrowings can go direct to reserves. There is a risk that the losses may not end up being covered from cash flows from the investment when the loan is repaid although SSAP 20 tries to set conditions which limit the likelihood of such an occurrence.

Under the CA85 the computation of a loss at the year end on a liability is a 'provision' and provisions, under company law, are realised losses (see the text dealing with distributable profits). As a consequence, the argument is that the loss should be recognised in the profit and loss account.

The arguments in support of SSAP 20 have been explained in the previous section. SSAP 20 is trying to record economic reality.

3 FOREIGN SUBSIDIARY UNDERTAKINGS

3.1 Introduction

Companies frequently establish local branches or subsidiaries in foreign countries through which to conduct their operations. These will maintain full accounts in the local currency and these must clearly be translated into the currency of the parent before they can be consolidated.

The translation method to be used depends on the relationship between parent and foreign entity.

(a) **Quasi-autonomous foreign entity**

Where the foreign entity is relatively independent of its parent, its transactions do not impinge directly on cash flows and profits of the parent. Accordingly, it is the **net investment** in the foreign entity which is of interest rather than the individual assets and liabilities. This net investment is translated at the **closing rate** of exchange and the resulting exchange difference dealt with in reserves.

(b) **Foreign entity as an extension of the parent**

Where the foreign entity is, in reality, the parent company operating abroad, foreign transactions will impinge directly on cash flows and profits of the parent. Accordingly, the foreign entity's transactions should be accounted for as if they were those of the parent by translation according to the **temporal method**.

3.2 When the net investment concept is appropriate

One of the general principles of SSAP 20 is the adoption of the closing rate/net investment method for the consolidation of foreign subsidiaries. Although this approach is widely supported, a small minority oppose it on the grounds that it displays an inconsistency in two areas. They consider that the net investment concept conflicts with the single entity approach which FRS 2 applies to consolidation procedures and that it is inappropriate to apply the closing rate to historical cost figures. SSAP 20 considers, however, that the principle is appropriate for the following reasons:

(a) the parent company's investment is normally in the net worth of a business operation rather than in its individual assets and liabilities;

(b) the method of translation ensures that the translated results and relationships do not differ significantly from those reported prior to translation;

(c) the method acknowledges the fact that operations which are conducted in currencies and in economic environments other than those of the parent are essentially different from the parent's own operations; and

(d) translation of the historical cost accounts at closing rates is merely a restatement of assets and liabilities for the purposes of consolidation and does not constitute a revaluation.

3.3 The circumstances where the temporal method of translation should be used

In **exceptional** circumstances, the subsidiary may be regarded as an extension of the trade of the parent company. This would apply where the cash flows of the subsidiary impact directly on the cash flows of the parent company. Examples of such situations are where

(i) the subsidiary acts as a selling agency, receiving stocks from the parent company, selling them locally and remitting the proceeds to the parent company, or

(ii) the subsidiary is a supplier of raw materials or components to the parent company, or

(iii) the subsidiary is located overseas for tax, exchange control or similar reasons to act as a means of raising finance for other companies in the group.

In such cases the historical **temporal** method should be used. This is the method you have seen at the individual company stage.

It is important to appreciate that identification of the relationship between parent and subsidiary will not always be clear cut. Many situations may require a balancing of criteria and the application of judgement. *SSAP 20* considers the following factors to be relevant

(i) the extent to which cash flows of the foreign entity impact directly on the parent
(ii) the extent to which functioning of the entity is directly dependent on the parent
(iii) the currency in which the majority of trading transactions are denominated
(iv) the major currency to which the operation is exposed in its financial structure.

It is important to appreciate that *SSAP 20* does not give a company the freedom to choose which method of translation should be used. It lays down the circumstances in which a particular method **must** be used.

3.4 The arguments for and against the temporal and closing rate methods of translation

The debate about the advantages and disadvantages of the two methods dates back to the time when many considered that a choice had to be made between one method or the other for all circumstances. SSAP 20 neatly defused this argument by putting forward the proposition that the two methods have different objectives and therefore both should be used. Which one is used in a particular situation depends on the individual circumstances as we have seen in the previous section.

The arguments for the temporal method reflect its objectives.

(a) It is compatible with the HC convention as non-monetary assets are stated at original cost and monetary assets and liabilities at their current worth.

(b) At the consolidation stage it uses the same rates as apply at the individual stage. Therefore it is closer to the normal concept of consolidation by assuming the group is one entity.

These arguments for the temporal method are arguments against the closing rate method.

The argument for the closing rate method also reflects its objective. Economic reality is reflected in the accounting treatment ie, the investment of the parent company is the net worth of its foreign subsidiary.

3.5 SSAP 20's requirements relating to the consolidation of foreign subsidiaries

(a) Choice of method

Closing rate or temporal depending on the circumstances.

(b) Treatment of exchange differences

If the temporal method is used, the treatment is the same as for differences at the individual company stage. If the closing rate method is used, the exchange differences are recorded as a movement in reserves ie, they bypass the profit and loss account for the period.

(c) Disclosure

Temporal method

Under this method gains and losses are part of normal profit. Thus no special disclosure is required. An amount of exchange differences that was unusual in its impact (compared with the normal level of exchange differences) may require disclosure, by way of note, as an **exceptional** item.

Closing rate method

The disclosure required under this method is

(i) the net amount of exchange differences on foreign currency borrowings (less deposits), and

(ii) the **net** movement on reserves arising from exchange differences.

4 CONSOLIDATED FINANCIAL STATEMENTS INCORPORATING A FOREIGN SUBSIDIARY

4.1 Closing rate method

(a) **Balance sheet**

All assets and liabilities are translated into the reporting currency at the closing rate. Where there is an intermediate foreign parent company the consolidation will be in two stages

(i) overseas consolidation – to the **reporting currency** of the overseas intermediate parent company

(ii) UK consolidation – to sterling.

(b) **Profit and loss account**

Amounts in the profit and loss account must be translated at either

(i) the **closing** rate for the period, or
(ii) an **average** rate for the accounting period.

Note:

(i) Advantages can be claimed for both methods of translating profits. The closing rate does maintain the relationships shown in the financial statements of the overseas enterprise.

(ii) The average rate better reflects the impact of cash flows throughout the period from the **group** viewpoint.

To be a true average it must reflect all factors involved, such as seasonal activity levels, wide fluctuations in the exchange rate etc. For many companies that prepare monthly/quarterly profit statements for the group the best estimate of the sterling annual profit will be the aggregate of those statements.

(c) **Exchange differences**

All exchange differences arising on consolidation should be accounted for as reserve movements.

4.2 Sources of exchange differences

Exchange differences arise because items are translated at different points in time at different rates of exchange.

It must be remembered that

Opening equity	+	Profit	=	Closing equity
(Opening net assets)	+	(Increase in net assets)	=	(Closing net assets)

(a) **Opening equity (= opening net assets)**

These will have been translated for the purpose of last year's accounts at last year's closing rate of exchange. For the purposes of the current year's accounts these items are translated at this year's closing rate of exchange since the opening net assets will be included within the closing net assets which are translated at the closing rate.

(b) **Profit for year (where average rate is used)**

The net assets generated by the profit must be translated at this year's closing rate (again within the closing net assets).

Thus the exchange difference will arise from the translation of

(i) **opening equity** – from last year's closing rate to this year's closing rate

(ii) **profit** – from the average rate to the closing rate (no difference arises where profit is translated at the closing rate).

4.3 Special points on consolidation

(a) **Goodwill on consolidation**

This must be computed using the principles set out in FRS 2 and FRS 10 by comparing

(i) the fair value of the cost of investment with
(ii) the fair value of net assets at acquisition.

For a foreign subsidiary, the net assets at acquisition are determined by translating the **share capital** and **pre-acquisition profits** at the **rate of exchange** at the **date of acquisition** of the shares in the subsidiary.

(b) **Minority interests**

(i) **Profit for the year**

The minority interests in the profit for the year will be their share of the sterling equivalent of the profit shown by the separate accounts of the subsidiary (whichever method of translation has been used).

(ii) **Net assets**

The minority interests for balance sheet purposes will be computed by reference to their interest in the net assets of the subsidiary translated at the closing rate at the balance sheet date. In effect the minority are credited (or debited) with their share of all exchange differences.

4.4 Example

The following draft financial statements are produced by a French subsidiary at 31 December

Balance sheets

	20X8	*20X9*		*20X8*	*20X9*
	Fr000	Fr000		Fr000	Fr000
Fixed assets	960	1,250	Share capital	750	750
Net current assets	720	1,080	Reserves	330	980
			Long-term loan	600	600
	1,680	2,330		1,680	2,330

Profit and loss account for 20X9

	Fr000
Profit on ordinary activities before taxation	1,050
Taxation	(400)
	650

Further information

(a) The loan was raised from a US bank in the sum of $165,000. There have been no repayments during the year.

(b) The UK parent company acquired a 100% interest on 1 January 20X8 at a cost of FFr960,000, when the subsidiary's reserves amounted to Fr120,000.

(c) The rates of exchange were

At	1 January	20X8	£1 = FFr6	
	31 December	20X8	£1 = FFr8	= $2.20
	31 December	20X9	£1 = FFr10	= $2.40
Average		20X8	£1 = FFr7.2	
Average		20X9	£1 = FFr9	

(d) Profits are translated at average rate.

4.5 Solution

(a) **Separate accounts of S Ltd**

The loan shown in the balance sheet at 31 December 20X8 is the dollar liability translated at the closing rate at that date (ie, FFr8 = $2.20).

At 31 December 20X9 this liability must be translated at the year end closing rate (ie, FFr10 = $2.40) = FFr687,500. The exchange loss of FFr87,500 must be charged against profit from normal operations.

The profit before tax will become FFr962,500 reducing the total retained profits to FFr892,500.

(b) **Consolidation**

The translation at 31 December 20X8 would have been as follows

	FFr000	*Rate*	£'000
Fixed assets	960	8	120
Net current assets	720	8	90
Long-term loan	(600)	8	(75)
	1,080		135

The net assets at acquisition would have been represented by share capital and reserves at that date. In order to compute the goodwill on consolidation, these net assets would have been translated at the rate of exchange at that date of acquisition (ie, £1 = FFr6)

	FFr000	*Rate*	£'000
Share capital	750	6	125
Pre-acquisition profits	120	6	20
	870		145
Cost of shares	960	6	160
Goodwill	90		15

The equity interest at 31 December 20X8 would have been translated as follows

	FFr000	*Rate*	£'000
Share capital	750	6	125.00
Reserves			
Pre-acquisition	120	6	20.00
Profit for year	210	7.2	29.17
	1,080	(average)	174.17
Exchange loss (balance)			(39.17)
Represented by net assets (ie, net investment)	1,080	8	135.00

The exchange difference relates to

		£'000	£'000
(i)	Equity interest at beginning of accounting period (FFr870,000)		
	At opening rate (£1 = FFr6)	145.00	
	At closing rate (£1 = FFr8)	108.75	(36.25)
(ii)	Profit for year (FFr210,000)		
	At average rate (£1 = FFr7.2)	29.17	
	At closing rate (£1 = FFr8)	26.25	(2.92)
			(39.17)

In the accounts to 31 December 20X8 (the first year of consolidation) this exchange difference of £39,170 would be taken to reserves. This does not imply a separate reserve. The loss is adjusted in the **statement of total recognised gains and losses** rather than directly to profit and loss account.

The translation at 31 December 20X9 would be as follows:

	FFr000	*Rate*	£'000
Fixed assets	1,250.0	10	125.00
Net current assets	1,080.0	10	108.00
Long-term loan (as adjusted)	(687.5)	10	(68.75)
Net investment 31.12.20X9	1,642.5		164.25

The equity interest must be analysed

	FFr000	*Rate*	£'000
Share capital	750.0	6	125.00
Reserves			
Pre-acquisition	120.0	6	20.00
Post-acquisition b/d (net of exchange loss (29.17 – 39.17))	210.0	actual	(10.00)
Profit for 20X9 (650 – 87.5)	562.5	9	62.50
Exchange loss (balance)	-	-	(33.25)
	1,642.5		164.25

The exchange loss for the current year can be reconciled as follows:

		£'000	£'000
(i)	Equity interest at beginning of accounting period (FFr1,080,000)		
	At opening rate (£1 = FFr8)	135.00	
	At closing rate (£1 = FFr10)	108.00	(27.00)
(ii)	Profit for year (FFr562,500)		
	At average rate (£1 = FFr9)	62.50	
	At closing rate (£1 = FFr10)	56.25	(6.25)
			(33.25)

4.6 Principles - closing rate method

(a) Separate accounts

Monetary items denominated in a foreign currency (ie, the dollar loan) must be recorded in the separate accounts at the closing rate at each balance sheet date.

(b) Goodwill on consolidation

In order to compute the goodwill, the share capital and pre-acquisition profits must always be translated at the rate ruling at the date of acquisition of the subsidiary.

(c) **Post-acquisition profits**

The sterling equivalent of the accumulated profit will be brought forward each year for incorporation in the current year's trial balance. No one exchange rate would be appropriate for translation purposes. The total includes past exchange differences.

(d) **Exchange differences**

(i) **Separate accounts stage**

Any difference arising at the separate accounts stage (of the subsidiary, or if appropriate, of the parent company) must be dealt with as part of the profit from normal operations.

(ii) **Consolidation stage**

All exchange differences arising on consolidation must be dealt with as reserve movements.

Statement of total recognised gains and losses

	£'000
Profit for the financial year	X
Currency translation differences on foreign currency net investment	X
Total gains and losses recognised since last annual report	X

Notes to the financial statements

(1) **Reserves**	*Profit and loss account* £'000
At beginning of year	X
Currency translation differences on foreign currency net investment	X
At end of year	X

4.7 Consolidation stage – temporal method

If the trade of the subsidiary is regarded as an extension of the trade of the parent company, the temporal method MUST be used. This means that the fixed assets must be translated at the rate ruling when the asset was acquired. For **consolidation** purposes this will be as follows

(a) **Owned at acquisition of shares by H plc** – at the rate ruling at that date (not the rate when the assets were acquired) – ie, cost to the group will be the fair value attributed at acquisition.

(b) **Acquired since acquisition** – at the rate when each asset was acquired.

Depreciation must be translated at the same rate as that applied to the relevant assets. Consequently the profit for the year will be translated

Profit before depreciation (strictly rate when transaction occurs) -	Average rate
Depreciation -	Asset rates

4.8 Example

Facts as in the example in para 4.4. The fixed assets may be reconciled as follows.

	FFr000
At 1.1.20X8	1,200.0
Depreciation 20X8 (20% × 1,200)	(240.0)
At 31.12.20X8	960.0
Additions (30.6.20X9 – £1 = FFr9)	662.5
Depreciation 20X9 (20% × (1,200 + 662.5))	(372.5)
At 31.12.20X9	1,250.0

Show the translation of the subsidiary's balance sheet into sterling

(a) at 31 December 20X8

(b) at 31 December 20X9.

4.9 Solution

(a) **Translation at 31.12.20X8**

	FFr000	*Rate*	£'000
Fixed assets	960	6	160
Net current assets	720	8	90
Loan	(600)	8	(75)
	1,080		175
Share capital	750.00	6	125.00
Reserves			
Pre-acquisition	120.00	6	20.00
Post-acquisition	210.00	(see below)	22.50
	1,080.00		167.50
Exchange (balance)			7.50
	1,080.00		175.00
Profit for year after depreciation	210.00		
Depreciation	240.00		
Profit before depreciation	450.00	7.2	62.50
Depreciation	(240.00)	6	(40.00)
Profit before taxation	210.00		22.50

Strictly there is no need to identify separately the exchange difference since it must be dealt with in arriving at the profit for the year from **normal** operations. Thus the profit for the year could be taken as the balancing figure in the translation process, ie, (£22,500 + £7,500) £30,000.

(b) **Translation at 31.12.20X9**

	Cost FFr000	*Depreciation* FFr000	FFr000	*Rate*	£'000
Fixed assets					
Deemed purchase 1.1.20X8	1,200.0	480.0	720.0	6	120.00
Acquired 30.6.20X9	662.5	132.5	530.0	9	58.89
	1,862.5	612.5	1,250.0		178.89

Net current assets	1,080.0	10	108.00
Loan	(687.5)	10	(68.75)
	1,642.5		218.14
Share capital	750.0	6	125.00
Reserves			
Pre-acquisition	120.0	6	20.00
Post-acquisition brought forward	210.0	actual	30.00
Profit for year	562.5	(balance)	43.14
	1,642.5		218.14

4.10 Hedging at the consolidated financial statements stage

You have already dealt with hedging in the individual company's financial statements. Remember

(a) without hedging – **loan** as a monetary item translated at closing rate of exchange and exchange difference taken to profit and loss account

– **investment** as a non-monetary item is recorded and left at the historic rate

(b) with hedging – both are retranslated and an offset (subject to certain limitations) achieved in reserves.

If this seems unfamiliar you should at this stage refer back to earlier in the chapter.

Where the **closing rate method** is used on consolidation hedging is also available. However, this works in a slightly different way

(a) cost of investment - this must, as you have seen, be translated at the historic rate, otherwise the calculation of goodwill will change each year

- if, therefore, this has been retranslated in the individual (holding) company's books, those entries must be reversed so that the cost of investment is ready, at its historic amount, for consolidation.

(b) loan - as for the individual company stage this is retranslated to the closing rate.

(c) offset - the offset is available between the exchange difference arising on the loan and that arising on the retranslation of the net investment in the subsidiary (ie, the exchange differences arising on consolidation).

The conditions which apply now are similar

(a) the investment must be one for which the **closing rate** method is applicable

(b) the differences on the borrowings are offset only to the extent of the differences on retranslating the investment

(c) the total borrowings do not exceed the cash flows that would be generated from the investment (ie, dividends due plus sale value)

(d) the treatment is consistently applied.

The *SSAP* makes it quite clear that the offset is available for all classes of investment

(a) subsidiaries – where the annual exchange difference (group share) is available for offset

(b) associates – same as subsidiaries

(c) other equity investments – **reproduce** the effect applied at separate accounts stage.

4.11 Example

Facts as in the example in para 2.17.

The subsidiary balance sheet at 31 December 20X8

	FFr000		FFr000
Sundry net assets	1,200	Share capital	500
		Profit – 1 January 20X8	300
		– for 20X8	400
	1,200		1,200

The group translates profit at the closing rate.

Show the offset for 20X8

4.12 Solution

	£'000
(a) **Loss on loan (para 2.18)**	40

(b) **Translation of net investment**

	FFr000		Rate	£'000
Sundry net assets	1,200		5	240.0
Share capital	500	Acquisition	6	83.3
Pre-acquisition profit	300	Acquisition	6	50.0
	800			133.3
Profit for 20X8	400	Closing	5	80.0
				213.3
Gain in translation (balance)				26.7
	1,200			240.0

Representing	FFr000		£'000
Opening net assets	800	@ 6	133.3
Restated		@ 5	160.0
			26.7

(c) **Offset**

The offset is now

	£'000
Loss on loan	(40.0)
Gain on translation	26.7
Charge to consolidated profit	(13.3)

(d) **Accounting adjustment**

Since at the separate accounts stage £8,000 was charged to profit the adjustment will be to charge consolidated profit and loss with the additional £5,300.

Note:

The difference can be identified as the goodwill on consolidation

	FFr000		*Rate*	£'000
Sundry net assets	1,200		5	240.0
Cost of shares	960			
Pre-acquisition capital	800			
Goodwill	160	at cost	6	26.7
Restated (as part of investment cost)			5	32.0
Gain				5.3

4.13 Disclosure of offset

Where offset has occurred additional disclosure arises

(a) the amount offset against reserves (of the differences on translating the loan), and
(b) the net amount charged or credited to profit and loss account.

Exempt companies (banks etc) need not disclose this.

This disclosure applies to both separate and consolidated financial statements.

A specimen disclosure based on the two examples in paras 2.17 and 4.11 might be

Statement of total recognised gains and losses

	H plc		*Group*	
	£'000	£'000	£'000	£'000
Profit for the financial year		X		X
Exchange gains for the year	32.0		26.7	
Offset of loss on hedging loans	(32.0)		(26.7)	
Net movement on exchange gains		X		X
Total gains and losses recognised since last annual report		X		X

Notes to the financial statements

(1) Exchange differences on foreign currency borrowings

	H plc	*Group*
	£'000	£'000
Loss on foreign currency borrowings	(40.0)	(40.0)
Offset in reserves	32.0	26.7
Charged to profit and loss account	(8.0)	(13.3)

(2) **Reserves**

	Profit and loss account			
	H plc		Group	
	£'000	£'000	£'000	£'000
At beginning of year		X		X
Exchange gains for the year	32.0		26.7	
Offset of loss on hedging loans	(32.0)		(26.7)	
Net movement on exchange gains		X		X
At end of year		X		X

4.14 Activity

R plc purchased equity shares in H Inc a US company for US$3,500,000 on 30 June 20X7 when the exchange rate was £1 = $1.50. This purchase was partially financed by means of a Swiss Franc loan of SFr 4,000,000 taken out on the same date at a rate of £1 = SFr 2.2.

R plc's year end is 31 March. Exchange rates at 31 March 20X8 were £1= $1.60 and £1 = SFr 2.4.

Calculate the exchange differences arising on the investment and loan at 31 March 20X8 and indicate how these will be dealt with in the financial statements to that date.

4.15 Activity solution

	£
Investment	
@ 30.6.X7	2,333,333
@ 31.3.X8	2,187,500
Loss on investment	(145,833)
Loan	
@ 30.6.X7	1,818,182
@ 31.3.X8	1,666,667
Gain on loan	151,515

£145,833 will be offset in reserves. The balance of £5,682 being the excess gain on the loan will be credited to profit and loss account.

4.16 The limitations and criticisms of SSAP 20

SSAP 20 attempts to portray a set of financial statements expressed in another currency in terms of the parent company's reporting currency. There is bound to be some loss of the quality and reliability of the information as a result. For example exchange differences arise in the translation process which do not represent changes in cash flows as there is no intention to convert all the assets in the foreign subsidiary into the parent company's reporting currency. An analogy is the translation of a novel from one language to another. Is not something lost in the translation process? This situation is not a specific criticism of SSAP 20 however. Any standard dealing with foreign currency translation has to try to express financial statements originally drawn up in one currency into another currency.

Specific criticisms of SSAP 20 include the following.

(a) Large exchange differences go direct to reserves under the closing rate method. Some commentators consider that all such gains and losses should go through the profit and loss account.

(b) Some treatments in the standard are optional, for example the cover concept. To aid comparison, it may be beneficial to remove the option.

(c) The guidance on the appropriate translation rates to use in hedge accounting and forward contracts is generally regarded as being insufficient and does not take account of the variety of (often) complex contracts that exist. The area has similarities to the complexities of capital instruments which are now regulated by FRS4. The ASB considers it needed to sort out capital instruments first. A standard on the measurement of instruments (which include forward contracts) is currently being developed.

(d) Transactions should be recorded at the rate ruling at the date the transaction occurred, but in some cases this date is difficult to establish. For example, it could be the order date, the date of invoice or the date on which the goods were received. SSAP 20 gives little guidance.

(e) Little guidance is given on the calculation and use of the average rate. SSAP 20 states that average rates can be used if these do not fluctuate significantly, but what period should be used to calculate average rates? Should the average rate be adjusted to take account of material transactions?

(f) SSAP 20 does not provide any guidance where there are two or more exchange rates for a particular currency.

(g) SSAP 20 makes a distinction between the translation of monetary and non-monetary items, but in practice some financial instruments may have characteristics of both.

(h) SSAP 20 does not address various issues relating to group accounts:

- Should the closing rate or the average rate be used when eliminating inter-group profits?
- How should cumulative exchange differences be treated when an investment in a foreign subsidiary is sold?
- Should the historic rate or the current rate be used to calculate goodwill on consolidation?

4.17 UITF Abstract 9

Where a foreign enterprise operates in a country in which a very high rate of inflation exists ('hyper-inflation') it may not be possible to present fairly in historical cost accounts the financial position of a foreign enterprise simply by a translation process. In such circumstances the local currency financial statements should be adjusted where possible to reflect current price levels before the translation process is undertaken.

UITF Abstract 9 *Accounting for operations in hyper-inflationary economies* was issued due to uncertainty as to when the adjustment above should be made.

The Task Force reached a consensus that adjustments are required where the distortions caused by hyper-inflation are such as to affect the true and fair view given by the group financial statements. In any event adjustments are required where the cumulative inflation rate over three years is approaching, or exceeds, 100% and the operations in the hyper-inflationary economies are material.

The following two methods of eliminating the distortions are consistent with SSAP 20 and therefore acceptable:

(a) as per SSAP 20 above, adjusting the overseas financial statements to reflect current price levels before the translation process is undertaken. This includes taking any gain or loss on the net monetary position through the profit and loss account;

(b) using a relatively stable currency as the functional currency (ie, the currency of measurement) for the relevant foreign operations. For example in certain businesses operating in Latin American territories the US dollar acts effectively as the functional currency for business operations. The functional currency would in effect be the 'local currency'.

If the transactions are not recorded in that stable currency, they must first be translated into that currency using the temporal method. The effect is that the movement between the original currency and the stable currency is used as proxy for the inflation index.

4.18 Example

On 1 January 20X1 Cinnamon plc set up a subsidiary, Anise Ltd, in a country which suffered from high rates of inflation. The currency of this country is measured in Tambala (T). On the same date Anise Ltd acquired freehold land for T400,000.

Relevant exchange rates are as follows:

1 January 20X1	T5 = £1
1 January 20X1	US$2.5 = £1
31 December 20X4	T25 = £1
31 December 20X4	US$ 1.75 = £1

The relevant price index was 100 at 1 January 20X1 and 550 at 31 December 20X4.

Show the value at which the freehold land would be included in the consolidated financial statements of Cinnamon plc at 31 December 20X4:

(a) using normal translation rules (the closing rate method)
(b) adjusting to reflect current price levels
(c) using US Dollars as a 'functional currency'.

4.19 Solution

(Tutorial note: the difference between the sterling value of the land at acquisition and at 31 December 20X4 illustrates the problems caused by hyperinflation. Hyperinflation gives rise to an exchange loss of £64,000.*)*

		T	**Rate**	**Inflation adjusted/US$**	**Rate**	£
	At 1 January 20X1	400,000			5	80,000
(a)	Closing rate	400,000			25	16,000
(b)	Current prices	400,000	550/100	2,200,000	25	88,000
(c)	US Dollars	400,000	2.5	160,000	1.75	91,429

4.20 UITF Abstract 19: Tax on gains and losses on foreign currency borrowings that hedge an investment in a foreign enterprise

Gains and losses on retranslation of foreign currency borrowings that hedge an investment in a foreign enterprise may now be taxable, following recent changes to UK tax legislation.

Exchange differences on foreign currency borrowings that have been used to provide a hedge against equity investments in foreign enterprises are taken to reserves and reported in the statement of total recognised gains and losses.

The UITF consensus is that tax charges or credits that are directly and solely attributable to such exchange differences should also be taken to reserves and reported in the statement of total recognised gains and losses.

The amount of tax charges and credits accounted for in this way should be disclosed.

5 TRANSLATION OF THE TRIAL BALANCE OF AN OVERSEAS BRANCH

5.1 Foreign associates and foreign branches

Exchange gains/losses arise in the same way with an investment in an associate as with a subsidiary - they simply represent different percentage stakes in the equity of another company. As the associate will be semi-independent, the closing rate/net investment method will be used to compute the sterling amount of net assets.

Foreign branches may be dealt with under the closing rate/net investment method, or the temporal method as appropriate. What is being said here is that although the branch is not a separate legal entity, the normal mechanics of the individual company stage may not be appropriate as, in accounting terms, the branch is a separate entity. SSAP 20 emphasises this by widening the normal meaning of a branch to include a *group* of assets and liabilities which are accounted for in foreign currencies.

The following are examples of situations where such a group of assets and liabilities should be accounted for under the closing rate/net investment method:

(a) a hotel in France financed by borrowings in French francs;

(b) a ship or aircraft purchased in US dollars - with an associated loan in US dollars - which earns revenue and incurs expenses in US dollars;

(c) a foreign currency insurance operation where the liabilities are substantially covered by the holding of foreign currency assets.

5.2 Example

A UK company has a branch in Bungholand, the unit of currency of which is the Bung. The branch's trial balance at 31 December 20X2 is as follows:

	Dr	*Cr*
	B	*B*
Fixtures and fittings:		
Bought 1 January	36,000	
Bought 1 July	26,000	
Stock - 1 January	15,000	
Goods from head office	9,680	
Purchases	87,120	
Debtors	9,216	
Bank	3,828	
Expenses	14,500	
Sales		120,886
Creditors		3,968
Head office account		76,490
	201,344	201,344

You are required to compute the amounts that would be used to produce the accounts of the company:

(a) using the closing rate method (translating profit and loss account items at an average rate),
(b) using the temporal method.

The following further information is given:

(i) All fixtures and fittings were bought during the current year:

B36,000 on 1 January when B40 = £1
B26,000 on 1 July when B52 = £1

(ii) Depreciation is provided at the rate of 10% pa on a time basis.

(iii) Closing rate of exchange = B64 = £1
Average rate of exchange = B52 = £1

(iv) Some stock was bought in the UK at £1 per article from head office. 186 articles had been received during the year.

(v) At 31 December 20X2 stock amounted to B44,286.

(vi) The balance on the branch account in head office books stood at £1,800 on 31 December, but goods were in transit amounting to £200 at cost price.

(vii) At 31 December the branch had accrued expenses of B500.

5.3 Solution to example

(a) **The closing rate method**

	Dr	*Cr*	*Rate of exchange*	*Dr*	*Cr*
	B	*B*	*B to £1*	£	£
Trial balance as presented					
Fixtures and fittings:					
Bought 1 January	36,000		64	563	
Bought 1 July	26,000		64	406	
Stock - 1 January	15,000		52	288	
Purchases	87,120		52	1,675	
Goods from head office	9,680		As goods to head office	186	
Debtors	9,216		64	144	
Bank	3,828		64	60	
Expenses	14,500		52	279	
Sales		120,886	52		2,325
Creditors		3,968	64		62
Head office account		76,490	As branch account		1,600
	201,344	201,344			
Adjustments					
Closing stock:					
Profit and loss account		44,286	52		852
Balance sheet	44,286		64	692	
Accruals:					
Profit and loss account	500		52	10	
Balance sheet		500	64		8
Depreciation - Fixtures bought 1 January:					
Profit and loss account	3,600		52	69	
Balance sheet		3,600	64		56
Depreciation - Fixtures bought 1 July:					
Profit and loss account	1,300		52	25	
Balance sheet		1,300	64		20
	251,030	251,030		4,397	4,923
Balance - difference on exchange				526	
				4,923	4,923

Notes:

(i) Adjustments to produce the final accounts for closing stock, accruals, prepayments, depreciation etc, are done in local currency before translation of the branch figures into sterling.

(ii) The sterling values for goods from head office and head office account are after eliminating items in transit.

(iii) All profit and loss account items have been translated at the average rate. The closing rate could equally have been used if the example had not specified otherwise.

Incorporation of translated sterling figures in head office accounts

The procedure now is essentially as for a sterling branch except that there is an additional profit or loss (the exchange difference) to be dealt with. In accounting terms the exchange difference is a profit/loss arising in the branch (ie, it is a figure on the branch's translated trial balance) and thus needs to be transferred into the head office.

(i) **Profit and loss account**

The following figures would be included for the branch:

	£	£
Sales		2,325
Opening stock	288	
Goods from head office	186	
Purchases	1,675	
	2,149	
Closing stock	852	
Cost of goods sold		1,297
Gross profit		1,028
Expenses	289	
Depreciation	94	
		383
Net profit from trading		645
Exchange loss		(526)
Total profit		119

(ii)

Branch account

	£	£		£
Balance b/d		1,800	Goods sent to branch account (Items in transit)	200
Reserves:			Balance c/d	1,719
Branch profit	645			
Exchange loss	(526)			
		119		
		1,919		1,919

(iii) **Balance sheet**

The head office balance sheet would substitute for the balance now shown on the branch, assets and liabilities at the sterling value shown in the translated branch trial balance:

	£
Fixed assets	893
Stock	692
Debtors	144
Bank	60
Creditors and accruals	(70)
	1,719

(b) **The temporal method**

	Dr B	*Cr* B	*Rate of exchange* B *to £1*	*Dr* £	*Cr* £
Trial balance as presented					
Fixtures and fittings:					
Bought 1 January	36,000		40	900	
Bought 1 July	26,000		52	500	
Stock - 1 January	15,000		40	375	
Purchases	87,120		52	1,675	
Goods from head office	9,680		As goods sent to branch account	186	
Debtors	9,216		64	144	
Bank	3,828		64	60	
Expenses	14,500		52	279	
Sales		120,886			2,325
Creditors		3,968	64		62
Head office account		76,490	As branch account		1,600
	201,344	201,344			
Adjustments					
Closing stock:					
Profit and loss account		44,286	64		692
Balance sheet	44,286		64	692	
Accruals:					
Profit and loss account	500		52	10	
Balance sheet		500	64		8
Depreciation - Fixtures bought 1 January:					
Profit and loss account	3,600		40	90	
Balance sheet		3,600	40		90
Depreciation - Fixtures bought 1 July:					
Profit and loss account	1,300		52	25	
Balance sheet		1,300	52		25
	251,030	251,030		4,936	4,802
Balance - difference on exchange					134
				4,936	4,936

Note: an alternative rate of exchange to use for trading account items (including opening and closing stock) would be the average rate. For example, the closing stock adjustment would be:

Credit trading account $\frac{44,286}{52}$ = £852

Debit balance sheet - either 852 or 692 (as above).

The rates used for stock in the trial balance and adjustments assume the stock was purchased on the balance sheet date.

Incorporation of translated sterling figures in head office accounts

(i) **Profit and loss account**

The following figures would be included for the branch:

	£	£
Sales		2,325
Opening stock	375	
Purchases	1,675	
Goods from head office	186	
	2,236	
Closing stock	692	
Cost of goods sold		1,544
Gross profit		781
Expenses	289	
Depreciation	115	
		404
Net profit from trading		377
Exchange profit/(loss)		134
Total profit		511

(ii)

Branch account

	£		£
Balance b/d	1,800	Goods sent to branch account (items in transit)	200
Reserves - branch total profit for year	511	Balance c/d	2,111
	2,311		2,311

The exchange profit is shown in the profit and loss account of the branch and in the profit and loss account of the combined business.

(iii) **Balance sheet**

The head office balance sheet would substitute for the balance now shown on the branch assets and liabilities at the sterling value shown in the translated branch trial balance:

	£
Fixed assets	1,285
Stock	692
Debtors	144
Bank	60
Creditors and accruals	(70)
	2,111

6 CHAPTER SUMMARY

SSAP 20 covers the individual company stage and the consolidated accounts stage. At the individual company stage the temporal method is used. At the consolidated accounts stage the temporal or closing rate methods may be used depending upon the circumstances,

Exchange differences are reported as part of operating profit under the temporal method and as part of the reserve movement under the closing rate method.

7 SELF TEST QUESTIONS

7.1 What are the two exchange rates which can generally be used to translate any foreign currency balance? (1.4)

7.2 How should monetary items denominated in a foreign currency at the balance sheet date be treated? (2.14)

7.3 How does *SSAP 20* allow an equity investment financed by a foreign currency loan to be accounted for by the investing company? (2.16)

7.4 What are the conditions for hedging to be permitted? (2.16)

7.5 In group accounts when must the temporal method be used? (3.3)

7.6 What are the disclosure requirements for exchange differences arising under the temporal method? (3.5)

7.7 How is goodwill arising on consolidation determined for a foreign subsidiary? (4.3)

7.8 How are exchange differences arising on consolidation dealt with under the closing rate method? (4.6)

7.9 Under the closing rate method on consolidation hedging is allowed but what is the offset available? (4.10)

7.10 Where foreign equity investments are the subject of a hedged loan what disclosures need to be made about exchange differences offset? (4.13)

8 EXAMINATION TYPE QUESTION

8.1 C & S

C Ltd acquired 75% of S BV on 1 January 20X7. The subsidiary is incorporated in a country whose currency is the Zoom. At 1 January 20X7 the net assets of S were Z156,000.

The following trial balances at 31 December 20X8 have been prepared:

	C	*S*
	£	Z
Fixed assets at cost	30,000	200,000
Stock at 31 Dec. 20X8	8,000	124,000
Investment in S	20,000	-
Cash	2,000	15,000
Expenses	18,000	120,000
Depreciation	3,000	32,000
Dividend paid	2,000	22,000
	83,000	513,000
Share capital	10,000	100,000
Profit and loss account at 31 Dec. 20X7	25,500	71,000
Trading income	30,000	190,000
Creditors	4,000	30,000

Dividend received	1,500	-
Depreciation provision	12,000	72,000
Long-term loan	-	50,000
	83,000	513,000

You are supplied with the following information:

(1) the fixed assets of S were all purchased on 1 October 20X6. A loan of Z50,000 was raised by S to assist with the purchase;

(2) C Ltd follows the closing rate method of currency translation per *SSAP 20* using the average rate to translate profit and loss items;

(3) the rates of exchange between sterling and the Zoom have been as follows:

30 Sep. 20X6	Z14.5 = £1
1 Jan. 20X7	Z14.0 = £1
1 Jan. 20X8	Z13.0 = £1
Average 20X8	Z12.0 = £1
31 Dec. 20X8	Z10.0 = £1

(4) Goodwill is amortised over 3 years from the date of acquisition.

In respect of the year ended 31 December 20X8, you are required to prepare, for the C Ltd group:

(a) a consolidated balance sheet;
(b) a consolidated profit and loss account; and
(c) a statement of the movement on group reserves.

Ignore tax and make calculations to the nearest £. **(24 marks)**

9 ANSWER TO EXAMINATION TYPE QUESTION

9.1 C & S

(a) **C Ltd – Consolidated balance sheet as at 31 December 20X8**

	£	£
Fixed assets:		
Intangible assets:		
Cost	11,643	
Amortisation	7,762	
		3,881
Tangible assets:		
Cost	50,000	
Depreciation	19,200	
		30,800
Current assets:		
Stocks	20,400	
Cash at bank and in hand	3,500	
	23,900	
Creditors: amounts falling due within one year	7,000	
Net current assets		16,900
Total assets less current liabilities		51,581

Creditors: amounts falling due after more than one year:	
Loan	(5,000)
Minority interests	(4,675)
	41,906
Capital and reserves:	
Called up share capital	10,000
Profit and loss account	31,906
	41,906

(b) **Consolidated profit and loss account for year ended 31 December 20X8**

	£
Profit on ordinary activities before taxation	8,285
Minority interests	791
	7,494
Dividend paid	2,000
Retained profit	5,494

(c) **Statement of reserves**

	£
Balance at 1 Jan. 20X8	23,127
Retained profit	5,494
Exchange adjustment	3,285
Balance at 31 Dec. 20X8	31,906

WORKINGS

(W1) **Translation of S balance sheet at 31 December 20X8**

	Z	*Rate*	£
Fixed assets:			
Cost	200,000	10	20,000
Depreciation	72,000	10	7,200
	128,000	10	12,800
Stock	124,000	10	12,400
Cash	15,000	10	1,500
	267,000		26,700
Ordinary share capital	100,000	14	7,143
Reserves (W2):			
Pre-acquisition	56,000	14	4,000
Post-acquisition	31,000	Bal	7,557
Creditors	30,000	10	3,000
Loan	50,000	10	5,000
	267,000		26,700

(W2) **Revenue reserves at 31 December 20X8**

	S	*C*
	Z	£
Revenue reserves at 31 Dec. 20X7	71,000	25,500
Trading income	190,000	30,000
Expenses	(120,000)	(18,000)
Depreciation	(32,000)	(3,000)
Dividend paid	(22,000)	(2,000)
	87,000	
Dividend received		1,500
		34,000

(W3) **Consolidation schedules**

Goodwill

	£	£
Cost of investment		20,000
Less: Share of net assets acquired		
Share capital	7,143	
Pre-acquisition reserves	4,000	
	11,143 (75%)	(8,357)
Goodwill		11,643
Amortisation (11,643 ÷ 3 × 2)		(7,762)
		3,881

Consolidated profit and loss account reserve

	£
C Ltd: (W2)	34,000
S BV: 75% × £7,557 (W1)	5,668
Less: Goodwill amortised	(7,762)
	31,906

Minority interest

	£
Share capital	7,143
Reserves: pre-acquisition	4,000
post-acquisition	7,557
	18,700
	(25%)
	4,675

(W4) **Profit and loss account translation**

	Z	*Rate*	£
Profit (after deducting sundry expenses)	70,000	12	5,833
Depreciation	32,000	12	2,667
	38,000		3,166

Dividends paid	22,000	Actual	2,000
Retained profit	16,000		1,166

Note: translation of dividend paid 100/75 × £1,500 = £2,000.

(W5) **Calculation of exchange difference**

(i) **Translation of opening balance sheet**

	Z	*Rate used last year*	£
Ordinary share capital	100,000	14	7,143
Reserves:			
Pre-acquisition	56,000	14	4,000
Post-acquisition (71,000 – 56,000)	15,000	Bal fig	2,011
	171,000		13,154
Net assets	171,000	13	13,154

(ii) **Sterling values**

	£
Sterling value of post-acquisition reserves at 1 Jan 20X8	2,011
Sterling value of post-acquisition reserves at 31 Dec 20X8	7,557
Increase	5,546
Sterling profit per profit and loss account	1,166
Gain on exchange	4,380

(W6) **Consolidated profit and loss account workings**

		£
(i)	Profit after expenses, depreciation and amortisation:	
	C (30,000 – 18,000 – 3,000 – 3,881)	5,119
	S	3,166
		8,285
(ii)	Minority interest 25% × 3,166	791
(iii)	Profit retained by subsidiary 75% × 1,166	875
(iv)	Profit retained by holding company (30,000 + 1,500 – 18,000 – 3,000 – 2,000)	8,500

(W7) **Reserves at 1 January 20X8**

	£	£
C		25,500
S:		
Translated post-acquisition reserves at beginning of year	2,011	

Group share 75% × 2,011	1,508
Less: goodwill amortised (11,643 ÷ 3)	(3,881)
	23,127

(W8) **Exchange difference**

	£
75% × 4,380	3,285

19 CASH FLOW STATEMENTS

INTRODUCTION & LEARNING OBJECTIVES

This chapter concentrates on the advanced computational aspects of preparing cash flow statements - groups and foreign currencies.

A revised version of FRS 1 was issued in October 1996. The mechanics of preparing a cash flow statement remain exactly the same, but there have been changes to the format of the cash flow statement and the standard headings under which cash flows are reported. The revised FRS also incorporates new definitions, of which the most important is the amended definition of cash.

FRS 9 has also introduced minor amendments to the format of the cash flow statement.

When you have studied this chapter you should be able to do the following:

- Prepare a consolidated cash flow statement.
- Prepare a consolidated cash flow statement involving a foreign subsidiary.

1 THE REQUIREMENTS OF FRS 1

1.1 Introduction

FRS 1: Cash flow statements was issued in 1991 and replaced *SSAP 10: Statements of source and application of funds*. It requires 'large' reporting entities to include a cash flow statement as part of their financial statements. A revised version of FRS 1 was issued in 1996.

1.2 Objective of cash flow statements

The objective of FRS 1 (revised) is to ensure that reporting entities falling within its scope:

(a) report their cash generation and cash absorption for a period by highlighting the significant components of cash flow in a way that facilitates comparison of the cash flow performance of different businesses; and

(b) provide information that assists in the assessment of their liquidity, solvency and financial adaptability.

Users of financial statements need information on the liquidity, viability and financial adaptability of entities. Deriving this information involves the user in making assessments of the future cash flows of the entity. Future cash flows are regarded (in financial management theory and increasingly in practice in large companies) as the prime determinant of the worth of a business.

To help to achieve the objective of cash flow reporting, the FRS requires that individual cash flows should be classified under certain standard headings according to the activity that gave rise to them. The standard headings required in a cash flow statement are:

(a) operating activities
(b) dividends from joint ventures and associates
(c) returns on investments and servicing of finance
(d) taxation
(e) capital expenditure and financial investment
(f) acquisitions and disposals

(g) equity dividends paid
(h) management of liquid resources
(i) financing.

The objective of the standard headings is to ensure that cash flows are reported in a form that highlights the significant components of cash flow and facilitates comparison of the cash flow performance of different businesses.

Cash flows relating to the management of liquid resources and financing can be combined under a single heading provided that the cash flows relating to each are shown separately and separate subtotals are given.

Each cash flow should be classified according to the substance of the transaction giving rise to it. The substance of a transaction determines the most appropriate standard heading under which to report cash flows that are not specified in the standard categories.

1.3 Cash flows and funds flows

The definition of cash is central to the preparation and interpretation of cash flow statements.

Definition **Cash** is cash in hand and deposits repayable on demand with any qualifying financial institution, less overdrafts from any qualifying financial institution repayable on demand. Deposits are repayable on demand if they can be withdrawn at any time without notice and without penalty or if a maturity or period of notice of not more than 24 hours or one working day has been agreed. Cash includes cash in hand and deposits denominated in foreign currencies.

Definition An **overdraft** is a borrowing facility repayable on demand that is used by drawing on a current account with a qualifying financial institution.

Definition A **qualifying financial institution** is an entity that as part of its business receives deposits or other repayable funds and grants credits for its own account.

Definition **Cash flow** is an increase or decrease in an amount of cash.

The bottom line in the cash flow statement is the **total cash flow** for the period, in other words, the total increase or decrease in the amount of cash.

The practical effect of these definitions is that the cash flow statement reports inflows and outflows of 'pure' cash. Short term deposits and loans are not included within the definitions.

1.4 Funds flow statements

The previous standard, SSAP 10 required the preparation of a **funds flow** statement.

Funds can be defined in different ways and/or different types of funds can be emphasised on a funds flow statement. They can be defined as:

- Cash, or
- Working capital, or
- Total finance.

The major difference between a funds flow statement and a cash flow statement is that non-cash items are represented on the funds flow statement. An inflow of funds can be a cash receipt but it can also be a non-cash receipt such as an issue of shares in exchange for non-cash assets.

Also, the accruals basis applies. Thus the purchase of a fixed asset on credit will represent an outflow of funds in the period even though the asset has not been paid for by the period end. The creditor will represent a source of funds (ie, no cash has as yet been spent and therefore the creditor is funding the expenditure on the fixed asset).

1.5 Illustration

The following illustration is included in FRS 1. It shows a cash flow statement for a single company. It illustrates the standard headings and examples of items within the standard headings.

The illustration includes the reconciliations and notes required by FRS 1. The reconciliations may be shown adjoining the cash flow statement or in the notes. If they adjoin the cash flow statement they should be clearly labelled and kept separate.

Note 1 gives the components of the net cash flows reported under each heading. These can be shown on the face of the cash flow statement or in the notes.

XYZ LTD

CASH FLOW STATEMENT FOR THE YEAR ENDED 31 DECEMBER 20X6

Reconciliation of operating profit to net cash inflow from operating activities

	£'000
Operating profit	6,022
Depreciation charge	899
Increase in stocks	(194)
Increase in debtors	(72)
Increase in creditors	234
Net cash inflow from operating activities	6,889

CASH FLOW STATEMENT

	£'000
Net cash inflow from operating activities	6,889
Returns on investments and servicing of finance (note 1)	2,999
Taxation	(2,922)
Capital expenditure (note 1)	(1,525)
	5,441
Equity dividends paid	(2,417)
	3,024
Management of liquid resources (note 1)	(450)
Financing (note 1)	57
Increase in cash	2,631

Reconciliation of net cash flow to movement in net debt (note 2)

Increase in cash in the period	2,631
Cash to repurchase debenture	149
Cash used to increase liquid resources	450
Change in net debt	3,230
Net debt at 1 January 20X6	(2,903)
Net funds at 31 December 20X6	327

Notes to Cash Flow Statement

(1) **Gross cash flows**

	£'000	£'000
Returns on investments and servicing of finance		
Interest received	3,011	
Interest paid	(12)	
		2,999
Capital expenditure		
Payments to acquire intangible fixed assets	(71)	
Payments to acquire tangible fixed assets	(1,496)	
Receipts from sales of tangible fixed assets	42	
		(1,525)
Management of liquid resources		
Purchase of treasury bills	(650)	
Sale of treasury bills	200	
		(450)
Financing		
Issue of ordinary share capital	211	
Repurchase of debenture loan	(149)	
Expenses paid in connection with share issues	(5)	
		57

(2) **Analysis of changes in net debt**

	At 1 Jan 20X6 £'000	*Cash flows* £'000	*Other changes* £'000	*At 31 Dec 20X6* £'000
Cash in hand, at bank	42	847		889
Overdrafts	(1,784)	1,784		
		2,631		
Debts due within 1 year	(149)	149	(230)	(230)
Debts due after 1 year	(1,262)		230	(1,032)
Current asset investments	250	450		700
Total	(2,903)	3,230	-	327

1.6 Net cash flow from operating activities

There are two main methods for reporting net cash flow from operating activities.

The **direct method** shows operating cash receipts and payments (including, in particular, cash receipts from customers, cash payments to suppliers and cash payments to and on behalf of employees), aggregating to the net cash flow from operating activities.

The **indirect method** starts with operating profit and adjusts it for non-cash charges and credits to reconcile it to the net cash flow from operating activities.

A comparison of the two methods is shown below. The methods differ only as regards the derivation of the item 'Net cash inflow from operating activities'. Subsequent inflows and outflows are the same.

Direct method		**Indirect method**	
	£'000		£'000
Cash received from customers	15,424	Operating profit	6,022
Cash payments to suppliers	(5,824)	Depreciation charges	899
Cash paid to and on behalf of employees	(2,200)	Increase in stocks	(194)
		Increase in debtors	(72)
Other cash payments	(511)	Increase in creditors	234
Net cash inflow from operating activities	6,889		6,889

1.7 The utility of the direct and indirect methods of presentation

The principal advantage of the direct method is that it shows operating cash receipts and payments. Knowledge of the specific sources of cash receipts and the purposes for which cash payments were made in past periods may be useful in assessing future cash flows. However, the ASB does not believe at present that in all cases the benefits to users of this information outweigh the costs to the reporting entity of providing it and, therefore, has not required the information to be given.

The principal advantage of the indirect method is that it highlights the differences between operating profit and net cash flow from operating activities. Many users of financial statements believe that such a reconciliation is essential to give an indication of the quality of the reporting entity's earnings. Some investors and creditors assess future cash flows by estimating future income and then allowing for accruals adjustments; thus information about past accruals adjustments may be useful to help estimate future adjustments.

Accordingly, the FRS requires the cash flow statement to show the **net** cash flow from operating activities, supplemented by a note reconciling this to the reporting entity's operating profit for the period. This reconciliation should not be given in the primary cash flow statement, in order to avoid confusing operating profit and the reconciling items with cash flows. The result is that reporting entities **must** give the information required by the indirect method.

The reference in the standard to a net or gross basis means that reporting entities **may** also give the information required by the direct method.

2 CLASSIFICATION OF CASH FLOWS

2.1 Returns on investments and servicing of finance

(a) Returns on investments and servicing of finance are receipts resulting from the ownership of an investment and payments to providers of finance, non-equity shareholders (eg, the holders of preference shares) and minority interests, excluding those items required to be classified under another heading.

(b) Cash inflows from returns on investments and servicing of finance include:

(i) interest received, including any related tax recovered;

(ii) dividends received, net of any tax credits (except dividends from any equity accounted entities).

(c) Cash outflows from returns on investments and servicing of finance include:

(i) interest paid (even if capitalised), including any tax deducted and paid to the relevant tax authority;

(ii) cash flows that are treated as finance costs under FRS 4 (this will include issue costs on debt and non-equity share capital);

(iii) the interest element of finance lease rental payments;

(iv) dividends paid on non-equity shares of the entity; and

(v) dividends paid to minority interests.

2.2 Taxation

The cash flows included under this heading are cash flows to or from the taxation authorities in respect of the reporting entity's revenue and capital profits. (In practice, this is normally the amnount paid for UK corporation tax.)

Value Added Tax (VAT) is **not** included under this heading. Cash flows should be shown net of any attributable VAT unless the tax is irrecoverable. The net movement on the VAT account should normally be allocated to cash flows from operating activities (ie, it is treated as a normal movement in working capital).

2.3 Capital expenditure and financial investment

(a) The cash flows included in 'capital expenditure and financial investment' are those related to the acquisition or disposal of any fixed asset other than one required to be classified under 'acquisitions and disposals' and any current asset investment not included in liquid resources. (Acquisitions and disposals and liquid resources are explained below).

If no cash flows relating to financial investment fall to be included under this heading the caption may be reduced to 'capital expenditure'.

(b) Cash inflows from capital expenditure and financial investment include:

(i) receipts from sales or disposals of property, plant or equipment; and

(ii) receipts from the repayment of the reporting entity's loans to other entities or sales of debt instruments of other entities other than receipts forming part of an acquisition or disposal or a movement in liquid resources.

(c) Cash outflows from capital expenditure and financial investment include:

(i) payments to acquire property, plant or equipment; and

(ii) loans made by the reporting entity and payments to acquire debt instruments of other entities other than payments forming part of an acquisition or disposal or a movement in liquid resources.

2.4 Acquisitions and disposals

(a) The cash flows included in 'acquisitions and disposals' are those related to the acquisition or disposal of any trade or business, or of an investment in an entity that is, or, as a result of the transaction, becomes or ceases to be either an associate, a joint venture, or a subsidiary undertaking.

(b) Cash inflows from acquisitions and disposals include:

(i) receipts from sales of investments in subsidiary undertakings, showing separately any balances of cash and overdrafts transferred as part of the sale;

(ii) receipts from sales of investments in associates or joint ventures; and

(iii) receipts from sales of trades or businesses.

(c) Cash outflows from acquisitions and disposals include:

(i) payments to acquire investments in subsidiary undertakings, showing separately any balances of cash and overdrafts acquired;

(ii) payments to acquire investments in associates and joint ventures; and

(iii) payments to acquire trades or businesses.

It follows that this caption does not normally appear in the cash flow statement of a single company. The exception would be if a company had acquired or disposed of an unincorporated business during the period.

Under the previous version of FRS 1, capital expenditure and acquisitions and disposals were reported together under the same caption, 'investing activities'.

Entities undertake investing activities in order to maintain the current level of operations and sometimes to expand the current level of operations. The cash flow statement does not distinguish between different types of investing activity, on the grounds that this is not feasible.

However, when the ASB revised FRS 1, it recognised that useful information would be provided by analysing investing activities into capital expenditure and acquisitions and disposals of investments. The notes to the FRS state that 'this distinction should not be interpreted as reflecting on the one hand maintenance expenditure and on the other expenditure for expansion because, depending on the circumstances, these may be included under either heading'.

2.5 Equity dividends paid

The cash outflows included in 'equity dividends paid' are dividends paid on the reporting entity's, or, in a group, the parent's equity shares.

This is another change introduced by the revised FRS. Previously, all dividends paid or received were reported under 'returns on investments and servicing of finance'.

Equity dividends paid are now reported separately from interest and other dividends paid to highlight the fact that payment of equity dividends is discretionary. In contrast, an entity has no discretion over the amount or the timing of interest payable and no discretion over the amount of non-equity dividends.

Equity and non-equity shares are defined in accordance with FRS 4 *Capital instruments*.

2.6 Management of liquid resources

(a) The 'management of liquid resources' section includes cash flows in respect of liquid resources as defined below.

Definition **Liquid resources** are current asset investments held in readily disposable stores of value. A readily disposable investment is one that:

(a) is disposable by the reporting entity without curtailing or disrupting its business;

and is either:

(b)(i) readily convertible into known amounts of cash at or close to its carrying amount; or

(b)(ii) traded in an active market.

This definition does not specify the type of investment that would be classed as a liquid resource. Instead it has been drafted in general terms, in order to emphasise the liquidity of the investment and its function as a readily disposable store of value. In practice, term deposits, government securities, loan stock, equities and derivatives might form part of an entity's liquid resources. Short term deposits would also fall within the definition. Because of the requirement that they should be readily convertible into known amounts of cash at or close to their carrying amount, deposits that are more than one year from maturity on acquisition would not normally be classed as liquid resources.

(b) Each entity should explain what it includes as liquid resources and any changes in its policy.

(c) Cash inflows in management of liquid resources include:

(i) withdrawals from short term deposits not qualifying as cash in so far as not netted (see below); and

(ii) inflows from disposal or redemption of any other investments held as liquid resources.

(d) Cash outflows in management of liquid resources include:

(i) payments into short term deposits not qualifying as cash in so far as not netted; and
(ii) outflows to acquire any other investments held as liquid resources.

(e) Cash inflows and outflows within the management of liquid resources may be netted against each other if they are due to short maturities and high turnover occurring from rollover or reissue (for example, short term deposits).

This section of the cash flow statement has been introduced by the revised version of FRS 1. It is designed to provide information about the way that entities manage their cash and similar assets. It distinguishes cash flows in relation to cash management from cash flows arising from other investment decisions (for example, the acquisition and disposal of fixed asset investments).

2.7 Financing

(a) Financing cash flows comprise receipts or repayments of principal from or to external providers of finance.

(b) Financing cash inflows include:

(i) receipts from issuing shares or other equity instruments; and

(ii) receipts from issuing debentures, loans, notes and bonds and from other long term and short term borrowings (other than overdrafts).

(c) Financing cash outflows include:

(i) repayments of amounts borrowed (other than overdrafts);
(ii) the capital element of finance lease payments;
(iii) payments to reacquire or redeem the entity's shares; and
(iv) payments of expenses or commissions on any issue of equity shares.

(d) The amounts of any financing cash flows received from or paid to equity accounted entities should be disclosed separately.

3 NET DEBT AND NON-CASH TRANSACTIONS

3.1 Reconciliation of movements in net debt

FRS 1 (revised) requires a note reconciling the movement of cash in the period with the movement in net debt. (An example of this reconciliation was illustrated earlier in the chapter.) This reconciliation can be given either adjoining the cash flow statement or in a note. If the reconciliation adjoins the cash flow statement, it should be clearly labelled and kept separate.

The objective of the reconciliation is to provide information that assists in the assessment of liquidity, solvency and financial adaptability.

Definition **Net debt** is the borrowings of the reporting entity (comprising debt as defined in FRS 4, together with related derivatives and obligations under finance leases) less cash and liquid resources. Where cash and liquid resources exceed the borrowings of the entity reference should be made to 'net funds' rather than to 'net debt'.

Non-equity shares of the entity are excluded from net debt because, although these have features that may be similar to those of borrowings, they are not actually liabilities of the entity. (This distinction between liabilities and non-equity shares is consistent with the requirements of FRS 4.)

The definition also excludes debtors and creditors because, while these are short term claims on and sources of finance to the entity, their main role is as part of the entity's trading activities. (Movements in debtors and creditors are dealt with as part of operating activities.)

The changes in net debt should be analysed from the opening to the closing component amounts showing separately, where material, changes resulting from:

(a) the cash flows of the entity;
(b) the acquisition or disposal of subsidiary undertakings;
(c) other non-cash changes; and
(d) the recognition of changes in market value and exchange rate movements.

Where several balance sheet amounts or parts thereof have to be combined to form the components of opening and closing net debt, sufficient detail should be shown to enable the cash and other components of net debt to be traced back to amounts shown under the equivalent captions in the balance sheet. This is done by means of a note analysing net debt.

3.2 Example

Extracts from the opening and closing balance sheets of a company show:

	31 Dec 20X8	*31 Dec 20X9*
	£'000	£'000
Current assets		
Investments - Government stock	118	74
Cash at bank	40	5
Creditors: amounts falling due within one year		
Loan	120	100
Overdraft	-	47
Creditors: amounts falling due after more than one year		
Loan	100	-

(a) The government stock consists of a number of holdings all of which were made with a view to disposal by the company within two months of acquisition.

(b) The loan was originally made in December 20X8 with repayments required of £20,000 every two months.

(c) The overdraft is repayable on demand.

Show the cash flow for the year ended 31 December 20X9, the reconciliation of net cash flow to movement in net debt and the note analysing movements in net debt.

3.3 Solution

	£'000
Decrease in cash for the year (40 – 5 + 47)	82

Reconciliation of net cash flow to movement in net debt (note)

Decrease in cash in the period	(82)
Cash outflow from decrease in debt	120
Cash inflow from sale of liquid resources (118 – 74)	(44)
Change in net debt	(6)
Net debt at 1 January 20X9	(62)
Net debt at 31 December 20X9	(68)

Analysis of changes in net debt

	At 1 Jan 20X9 £'000	*Cash flows* £'000	*Other changes* £'000	*At 31 Dec 20X9* £'000
Cash at bank	40	(35)		5
Overdrafts	-	(47)		(47)
		(82)		
Debts due within 1 year	(120)	120	(100)	(100)
Debts due after 1 year	(100)		100	-
Current asset investments	118	(44)		74
Total	(62)	(6)	-	(68)

3.4 Major non-cash transactions

Standard accounting practice

'Material transactions not resulting in movements of cash of the reporting entity should be disclosed in the notes to the cash flow statement if disclosure is necessary for an understanding of the underlying transactions.'

Consideration for transactions may be in a form other than cash. The purpose of a cash flow statement is to report cash flows and non-cash transactions should, therefore, not be reported in a cash flow statement. However, to obtain a full picture of the alterations in financial position caused by the transactions for the period, separate disclosure of material non-cash transactions is also necessary.

Examples of non cash transactions are:

(a) certain acquisitions and disposals of subsidiaries by a group;
(b) finance leases;
(c) certain changes in debt and equity.

3.5 HP and finance leases

Hire purchase and finance leases are accounted for by the lessee/purchaser capitalising the present value of the minimum lease payments. A liability and a corresponding asset are produced which do not reflect cash flows in the accounting period.

The cash flow statement records the cash flow, ie, the rentals paid. As each rental represents a payment of interest and capital FRS 1 requires a split between the two elements:

(a) the interest element shown under servicing of finance;
(b) the capital element shown under financing.

The interest element will already be computed as it is charged (and disclosed in the financial statements) in arriving at profit before taxation. Deducting the interest charge from rentals paid provides the capital paid in the year.

Note that the above paragraph assumes that rentals are paid frequently, eg, monthly, and there is thus effectively no/little difference between interest charged against profits for a twelve month period and interest within the rentals **paid** over a twelve month period. If the rental payment dates do not closely coincide with the end of an accounting period, it may be necessary to compute the interest element relating to rentals actually paid.

The non-cash flow elements of a finance lease may need to be disclosed:

(a) if the finance lease is of such significance that it is classified as a major non-cash transaction; and/or

(b) in the reconciliation of net cash flow to movement in net debt (as the finance lease liability may have been aggregated with, eg, bank loans on the balance sheet).

3.6 Example

A company entered into a number of finance leases during 20X1 and 20X2. There were no such leases in previous years.

Extracts from the accounts show:

Extracts from balance sheets

	31 Dec. 20X2	*31 Dec. 20X1*
	£'000	£'000
Fixed assets:		
Leased property under finance lease	5,710	4,000
Less: Accumulated depreciation	1,714	1,000
	3,996	3,000
Liabilities:		
Non-current obligations under finance leases	3,251	2,645
Current obligations under finance leases	1,315	1,150
	4,566	3,795

Notes to the accounts – Profit and loss account

Profit is stated after charging:

	£'000
Depreciation of owned assets	2,300
Depreciation of assets held under finance leases	714
Finance charges payable:	
Finance leases	856
Interest	1,325
Hire of plant and machinery – operating leases	360
Hire of other assets – operating leases	190

Produce extracts from the cash flow statement for 20X2 as far as information is available.

3.7 Solution

Extract from cash flow statement for year ended 31 December 20X2

	£'000
Returns on investments and servicing of finance:	
Interest element of finance lease rentals	(856)
Interest paid	(1,325)
Financing:	
Capital element of finance lease rentals (working)	(939)

WORKING

(Note: Grouping the current and non-current obligations together and deriving new finance leases from the increase in fixed asset cost allows the capital element of the rentals to be computed as a balancing figure.

Operating leases are treated like any other expense.*)*

Obligations under finance leases

	£'000		£'000
Capital element of rentals		Balance b/d	
paid in year	939	Current and non current	3,795
Balance c/d		New finance leases	
Current and non current	4,566	(from fixed asset increase)	1,710
	5,505		5,505

3.8 Exceptional items

Where cash flows relate to items that are classed as exceptional or extraordinary items in the profit and loss account the cash flows should be shown separately under the appropriate standard headings, according to the nature of each item. Disclosure of the nature of the cash flows should be given in a note to the cash flow statement.

These disclosures allow users of the financial statements to gain an understanding of the effect of the underlying transactions on the cash flows.

Re-organisation charges that are exceptional must be disclosed separately and explained.

Cash flows in respect of operating items relating to provisions are included in operating activities, even if the provision was not included in operating profit. Examples of such cash flows are redundancy payments falling under a provision for the termination of an operation or for a fundamental reorganisation or restructuring, also operating item cash flows provided for on an acquisition.

Exceptional cash flows

Where cash flows are exceptional because of their size or incidence but are not related to items that are treated as exceptional or extraordinary in the profit and loss account, sufficient disclosure should be given to explain their cause and nature.

For a cash flow to be exceptional on the grounds of its size alone, it must be exceptional in relation to cash flows of a similar nature. A large prepayment against a pension liability is an example of a possible exceptional cash flow unrelated to an exceptional or extraordinary item in the profit and loss account.

3.9 Further optional disclosure

FRS 1 suggests that the standard cash flow classifications could be subdivided further to give a fuller description of the activities of the reporting entity or to provide segmental information. One of the illustrative examples to the FRS shows a possible format for further optional disclosures based on the requirements of FRS 3.

Reconciliation of operating profit to net cash inflow from operating activities

	Continuing £'000	*Discontinued* £'000	*Total* £'000
Operating profit	18,829	(1,616)	17,213
Depreciation charges	3,108	380	3,488
Cash flow relating to previous year restructuring provision		(560)	(560)
Increase in stocks	(11,193)	(87)	(11,280)
Increase in debtors	(3,754)	(20)	(3,774)
Increase in creditors	9,672	913	10,585
Net cash inflow from continuing operating activities	16,662		
Net cash outflow in respect of discontinued activities		(990)	
Net cash inflow from operating activities			15,672

This illustration also includes an exceptional item (the cash flow relating to previous year restructuring provision).

4 APPLYING FRS 1 TO THE PREPARATION OF CONSOLIDATED CASH FLOWS

4.1 FRS 1 as it relates to consolidated cash flows

Where a company has subsidiaries, cash flow statements should be based on the group accounts, and the starting figure should therefore be the group operating net cash inflow.

Cash flows that are internal to the group should be eliminated in the preparation of a consolidated cash flow statement.

The standard has specific requirements in relation to minority interests, associates and acquisitions and disposals of subsidiaries. These are examined in the following sections.

4.2 Minority interests

Standard accounting practice

Dividends paid to minority interests are disclosed separately under 'returns on investments and servicing of finance'

4.3 Example

The following information has been extracted from consolidated financial statements of WG plc for the years ended 31 December:

	20X6 £'000	*20X5* £'000
Dividends payable to minority shareholders	100	160
Minority interest in group net assets	780	690
Minority interest in consolidated profit after taxation	120	230

What is the dividend paid to minority interests in the year 20X6?

4.4 Solution

Minority interests

	£'000		£'000
		Balance b/d dividends payable	160
Dividends paid (bal fig)	90	Balance b/d minority interest	690
Balance c/d dividends payable	100	Share of profits in year	120
Balance c/d minority interest	780		
	970		970

4.5 Associated undertakings

Associated undertakings reflect a cash flow in or out of the group to the extent that:

(a) dividends are paid or payable out of the profits of the associate;
(b) trading occurs between the group and associate; or
(c) further investment is made in the associate.

Associates are dealt with under the equity method of accounting and *FRS 1* uses this terminology.

Standard accounting practice

'The cash flows of any equity accounted entity should be included in the group cash flow statement only to the extent of the actual cash flows between the group and the entity concerned, for example dividends received in cash and loans made or repaid'.

Dividends

It is only dividends paid which represent a cash inflow. Proposed dividends represent an increase in group debtors (ie, the share of the dividend payable which is received by the investing company will not form part of the asset 'Investment in associate' but will be included in group debtors).

Thus, in reconciling group net cash inflow to group operating profit the balance sheet movement in debtors must exclude proposed dividends from the associate so that dividends received can be shown in the cash flow statement.

Dividends received from associates should be included as a separate item between operating activities and returns on investments and servicing of finance.

Trading between group and associate

Trading between the group and an associate will give rise to inter-company balances on the group balance sheet at the year end. The balances will be treated in the same way as any other trading debtors and creditors, ie, the balance sheet movement forms part of the reconciliation between group operating profit and group net cash inflow from operating activities.

It follows that when cash is paid/received in respect of inter-company balances the cash is included in the 'cash received from customers/cash payments to suppliers' section of the cash flow statement. It may, however, be appropriate to show the cash outflow/inflow separately from the group customers and suppliers.

Change in investment in associate

A change in investment in the associate can arise when:

(a) an additional shareholding is purchased or part of the shareholding is sold;
(b) loans are made to/from the associate or amounts previously loaned are repaid.

Provided cash consideration is involved, any change will be shown under the acquisitions and disposals section of the cash flow statement.

4.6 Example

The following information has been extracted from the consolidated financial statements of H plc for the year ended 31 December 20X1:

Group profit and loss account

	£'000	£'000
Operating profit		734
Share of profit of associated undertaking		122
Tax on profit on ordinary activities:		
UK corporation tax	(324)	
Share of tax of associated undertakings	(54)	
		(378)
Profit on ordinary activities after tax		478

Group balance sheet

	20X1 £'000	*20X0* £'000
Investments in associated undertakings		
Share of net assets	466	456
Loan to associate	380	300
Current assets		
Debtors	260	190

Included with group debtors are the following amounts:

Dividend receivable from associate	48	29
Current account with associate	40	70

Show the relevant figures to be included in the group cash flow statement for the year ended 31 December 20X1 and the amount at which debtors will be shown in the reconciliation of operating profit to net cash inflow.

4.7 Solution

Extracts from cash flow statement

	£'000	£'000
Reconciliation of operating profit to net cash inflow from operating activities		
Operating profit		734
Increase in debtors (W2)		(51)
Cash flow statement		
Dividend received from associate (W1)		39
Capital expenditure and financial investment:		
Loan to associated undertaking		(80)

WORKINGS

(W1) **Associate**

	£'000		£'000
Balance b/d		Share of tax	54
Share of net assets	456	Dividend received (bal fig)	39
Dividend receivable	29	Balance c/d	
Share of profits	122	Share of net assets	466
		Dividend receivable	48
	607		607

(***Tutorial note:***

An alternative approach to the above working is to construct initially a profit and loss account showing profit information relating to the associate:

	£'000
Share of profits	122
Share of tax	54
	68
Dividends from 20X1 profits (bal fig)	58
Increase in share of net assets (ie, share of retained profits 466 – 456)	10

Then adjust £58,000 by the opening and closing dividend receivable (29 + 58 – 48) £39,000.

(W2) **Increase in debtor**

	20X0 £'000	*20X1* £'000
Debtors per balance sheet	190	260
Less: Dividend receivable	(29)	(48)
	161	212
Increase	£51,000	

4.8 Acquisition of subsidiaries during the year

Standard accounting practice

(a) Where a subsidiary undertaking joins or leaves a group during a financial year the cash flows of the group should include the cash flows of the subsidiary undertaking concerned for the same period as that for which the group's profit and loss account includes the results of the subsidiary undertaking.

(b) A note to the cash flow statement should show a summary of the effects of acquisitions and disposals of subsidiary undertakings indicating how much of the consideration comprised cash.

(c) Material effects reported under each of the standard headings reflecting the cash flows of a subsidiary undertaking acquired or disposed of during the period should be disclosed, as far as practicable. This information could be given by dividing cash flows between continuing and discontinued operations and acquisitions.

(d) Payments to acquire subsidiaries and receipts from disposals of subsidiaries are reported under 'acquisitions and disposals'. Any balances of cash and overdrafts acquired or transferred should be shown separately.

4.9 Computational aspects of dealing with acquisitions and disposals

The substance of an acquisition of a subsidiary is that the group has purchased the assets of the subsidiary. However, in the cash flow statement we only wish to record the actual cash flow. Thus, for example, the additional fixed assets under the control of the group as a result of the acquisition will not be included under the heading 'capital expenditure'. Care needs to be taken when expenditure on fixed assets is derived as a balancing figure. Fixed assets of the subsidiary at acquisition must be included in the ledger account used to derive the balancing figure.

Similar care needs to be applied in relation to other assets and liabilities in the subsidiary at acquisition.

For example, the balance sheet movement in stock needs to be computed and shown as a reconciling item between operating profit and net cash inflow. Where there has been an acquisition the movement in stock can be analysed:

Beginning of year	*Part-way through year*	*End of year*
Group stock **excluding** subsidiary not yet acquired	Subsidiary acquired (£9,384 stock included in net assets acquired)	Group stock **including** subsidiary acquired in year
£53,019	Increase in stock	£74,666

Increase in stock = £74,666 – (53,019 + 9,384) = £12,263.

4.10 Activity

X plc acquired Y plc in the current accounting period. Extracts from the group accounts of X plc show:

	Last year £'000	*This year* £'000
NBV fixed assets	10,000	16,000

Depreciation charged in the group profit and loss account is £2,600,000, and the NBV of disposals is £600,000. The fair value of Y plc's fixed assets when Y plc was acquired by X plc is £4,800,000.

What was the expenditure on fixed assets during the current accounting period?

4.11 Activity solution

Fixed assets – NBV

	£'000		£'000
Balance b/d	10,000	Depreciation charge	2,600
In subsidiary at acquisition	4,800	Disposals	600
Additions (bal fig)	4,400	Balance c/d	16,000
	19,200		19,200

Conclusion Expenditure is £4,400,000

4.12 Partly-owned subsidiary acquired in current year

This is not as complicated as it sounds. The note to the cash flow statement summarising the net assets acquired and for what consideration will include an item 'minority interest'. The amount will be the minority interests' share of net assets of the subsidiary at the date of acquisition. It will have no direct bearing on the figures shown in the cash flow statement except where dividends paid to minority interests have to be computed as a balancing figure. In such an event the minority interests' share of net assets at acquisition will be a credit in the minority interest account constructed to derive dividends paid.

4.13 Disposal of subsidiary

A disposal is treated using the same principles as for an addition. To the extent that cash is received as consideration, this will be shown as a receipt under 'acquisitions and disposals'.

If any group assets or liabilities are being analysed to determine a cash inflow or outflow the book value of the subsidiary's assets/liabilities will need to form part of the analysis. For example tax liabilities in the subsidiary at the date of disposal will represent a debit in a taxation account being written up to determine tax paid.

Tax account

	£		£
Cash paid (bal fig)	X	Balance b/d: group (P + S) liability	X
Tax liability in subsidiary at date of disposal	X	Tax charge for year	X
Balance c/d: group (P) liability	X		
	X		X

The debit entry for the tax liability in the subsidiary is equivalent to the balance c/d at the end of the accounting period for the remaining part of the group liability.

4.14 Detailed example

Several years ago H plc acquired 80% of the ordinary share capital of S Ltd. It also acquired a 25% shareholding in A Ltd and the company is regarded as an associated company. On 1 January 20X8 H plc acquired the entire share capital of J Ltd. You are provided with the following information regarding the group accounts:

Consolidated profit and loss account for the year ended 31 December 20X8

Note		£	£
(1)	Group operating profit		3,976,300
	Share of operating profit of associate		59,000
(2)	Sale of freehold property		500,000
	Interest received		9,800
	Premium on redemption of preference shares		(15,000)
	Interest paid		(12,100)
	Profit before taxation		4,518,000
(3)	Taxation		2,247,160
	Profit after taxation		2,270,840
	Minority interest		41,664
	Profit attributable to members of the parent undertaking		2,229,176
	Dividends:		
	Interim (paid)	250,000	
	Final (proposed)	300,000	
			550,000
	Retained profit for year		1,679,176

Consolidated balance sheets (summarised)

Note		*31 Dec 20X7*	*31 Dec 20X8*
		£	£
(2)	Freehold property	8,276,718	9,744,658
(4)	Plant and machinery	2,673,400	3,955,400
	Goodwill on consolidation	66,500	192,500
(5)	Associated undertaking	80,750	98,570
	Stock	2,065,000	3,400,100
	Debtors	854,200	1,250,000
	Cash	21,100	136,750
		14,037,668	18,777,978
	Ordinary share capital (£1 shares)	3,000,000	4,200,000
(6)	Reserves	5,661,850	7,941,026
(7)	Preference shares	300,000	-
	Long-term loan	-	150,000
	Creditors	984,500	1,640,640
	Corporation tax	3,226,318	3,903,848
	Dividends	245,000	300,000
	Minority interest	620,000	642,464
		14,037,668	18,777,978

You are provided with the following additional information:

(1) **Operating profit**

Operating profit is arrived at after charging depreciation amounting to £558,000. Interest paid is after adjusting for an opening accrual of £600 and a closing accrual of £4,600.

(2) **Exceptional item**

This represents profit on sale of freehold property. The property was in the books at £940,000.

(3) **Taxation**

	£
Group companies	2,216,480
Associate	30,680
	2,247,160

(4) **Plant and machinery**

	Cost	*Agg. depn.*	*NBV*
	£	£	£
At 1 January 20X8	3,500,000	826,600	2,673,400
Additions:			
J Ltd	1,100,000	240,000	860,000
Others	980,000	-	980,000
Depreciation – charge for year		558,000	(558,000)
	5,580,000	1,624,600	3,955,400

(5) **Associate**

	At 31 December 20X7	At 31 December 20X8
	£	£
Cost	72,000	72,000
Accumulated profit	8,750	26,570
	80,750	98,570

Included within debtors are dividends receivable from associate: 31 December 20X7, £29,000; 31 December 20X8, Nil.

(6) **Reserves**

	Revenue	*Capital redemption*	*Share premium*	*Total*
	£	£	£	£
At 1 January 20X8	5,586,850	-	75,000	5,661,850
Retained profit	1,679,176	-	-	1,679,176
Issue of ordinary shares	-	-	600,000	600,000
Redemption of preference shares	(300,000)	300,000	-	-
At 31 December 20X8	6,966,026	300,000	675,000	7,941,026

(7) **Preference shares**

The preference shares were redeemed during the year at a premium of 5%. Ordinary shares were issued to finance the redemption.

(8) **Acquisition of J Ltd**

	£	£
Consideration:		
800,000 shares at £1.50		1,200,000
Cash		600,000
		1,800,000
Assets acquired:		
Plant and machinery	860,000	
Stock	836,500	
Debtors	449,300	
Creditors	(262,000)	
Cash	532,400	
Corporation tax	(742,200)	
		1,674,000
Goodwill		126,000

You are required to prepare a cash flow statement in a form suitable for publication. Ignore amortisation of goodwill.

4.15 Solution

Step 1 **Working capital movements**

	Start of year	Subsidiary	End of year	Movement
	£	£	£	£
Stock	2,065,000	836,500	3,400,100	498,600
Debtors	854,200	449,300	1,250,000	(24,500)
Dividend from associate	(29,000)		-	
Creditors	984,500	262,000	1,640,640	390,140
Interest accrual	(600)		(4,600)	

Step 2 **Associate**

As the dividends received from the associate have not been given, reconstruct the group's share of profits from the associate from available information:

	£
Profit	59,000
Tax	30,680
	28,320
Dividend (bal fig)	10,500
Retained profit	17,820
Dividend receivable b/d	29,000
Dividends out of current year's profit	10,500
Less: Dividend receivable c/d	-
Dividends paid	39,500

Step 3 **Minority interests**

Profits earned by subsidiaries are retained within the group, except to the extent that a dividend is paid to the minority shareholders.

Minority interest account

	£		£
Cash (bal fig)	19,200	Balance b/d	620,000
Balance c/d	642,464	Profit and loss	41,664
	661,664		661,664

It is assumed that there are no amounts in creditors relating to proposed dividends due to minority interests

Step 4 **Taxation**

Corporation tax account excluding associate

	£		£
Cash (bal fig)	2,281,150	Balance b/d	3,226,318
		Profit and loss (note 3)	2,216,480
		Corporation tax - balance on	
Balance c/d	3,903,848	J at acquisition	742,200
	6,184,998		6,184,998

The tax paid is normally arrived at as a balancing figure. As the subsidiary had a tax creditor at acquisition, the amount must be brought into the group corporation tax account because when the liability is paid, it will form part of group tax paid.

Step 5 **Property**

Property account – Cost

	£		£
Balance b/d	8,276,718	Disposals account (NBV)	940,000
Additions (bal fig)	2,407,940	Balance c/d	9,744,658
	10,684,658		10,684,658

Property disposals account

	£		£
Property at NBV	940,000	Cash proceeds	1,440,000
Profit on sale			
(exceptional item)	500,000		
	1,440,000		1,440,000

As the exceptional item relates to a disposal of a fixed asset, the sale proceeds are shown under capital expenditure.

Step 6 **Purchase of subsidiary**

Only the net cash effect of the purchase should be shown. Non-cash consideration is thus excluded and any cash in the subsidiary at acquisition effectively reduces the cash price paid. The opposite would apply if there were an overdraft in the subsidiary at acquisition.

	£
Cash paid	600,000
Cash in subsidiary	532,400
	67,600

Step 7 **Ordinary shares**

	NV £	*Premium* £
Increase in year	1,200,000	600,000
To purchase subsidiary	800,000	400,000
For cash	400,000	200,000

Step 8 Prepare cash flow statement

H plc
Consolidated cash flow statement for year ended 31 December 20X8

	£
Reconciliation of operating profit to net cash inflow from operating activities	
Operating profit	3,976,300
Depreciation charges	558,000
Increase in stocks	(498,600)
Decrease in debtors	24,500
Increase in creditors	390,140
Net cash inflow from operating activities	4,450,340

Cash flow statement

	£
Net cash inflow from operating activities	4,450,340
Dividends received from associate	39,500
Returns on investments and servicing of finance (Note 1)	(17,500)
Taxation: Corporation tax paid (W4)	(2,281,150)
Capital expenditure (Note 1)	(1,947,940)
Acquisitions and disposals (Note 1)	(67,600)
Equity dividends paid (245 + 250)	(495,000)
Cash outflow before financing	(319,350)
Financing (Note 1)	435,000
Increase in cash for the period	115,650

Reconciliation of net cash flow to movement in net debt (Note 2)

	£
Increase in cash for the period	115,650
Cash inflow from issue of long-term loan	(150,000)
Change in net debt	(34,350)
Net funds at 1 January 20X8	21,100
Net debt at 31 December 20X8	(13,250)

Notes to the cash flow statement

1 **Gross cash flows**	£	£
Returns on investments and servicing of finance:		
Interest received	9,800	
Interest paid (600 + 12,100 – 4,600)	(8,100)	
Dividends paid to minority interest	(19,200)	
		(17,500)
Capital expenditure:		
Payments to acquire tangible fixed assets (980,000 + 2,407,940)	(3,387,940)	
Receipts from sales of tangible fixed assets	1,440,000	
		(1,947,940)

Acquisitions and disposals:		
Cash consideration	(600,000)	
Cash in subsidiary at acquisition	532,400	
		(67,600)
Financing:		
Issue of ordinary share capital	600,000	
Issue of loan	150,000	
Redemption of preference shares (300 × 105%)	(315,000)	
		435,000

2 **Analysis of changes in net debt**

	At 1 January £	*Cash flows* £	*At 31 December* £
Cash at bank	21,100	115,650	136,750
Long-term loan	-	(150,000)	(150,000)
Total	21,100	(34,350)	(13,250)

3 **Major non-cash transactions**

Part of the consideration for the purchase of a subsidiary during the year comprised ordinary shares. The net assets acquired and form of consideration are shown below.

	£		£
Net assets acquired:		Discharged by:	
Fixed assets	860,000	Shares issued	1,200,000
Goodwill	126,000	Cash	600,000
Stock	836,500		
Debtors	449,300		
Creditors	(262,000)		
Taxation	(742,200)		
Cash	532,400		
	1,800,000		1,800,000

5 FOREIGN EXCHANGE GAINS AND LOSSES IN CASH FLOW STATEMENTS

5.1 Introduction

The treatment of foreign currencies is only mentioned in one paragraph of FRS 1, and deals with the treatment of foreign subsidiaries or associates.

Before considering group accounts, we will deal with the foreign currency transactions entered into directly by a company – the individual company stage per SSAP 20.

5.2 Individual company stage

Exchange differences arising at the individual company stage are in most instances reported as part of operating profit. If the foreign currency transaction has been settled in the year the cash flows will reflect the reporting currency cash receipt or payment and thus no problem arises. An unsettled foreign currency transaction will however give rise to an exchange difference for which there is no cash flow effect in the current year. Such exchange differences therefore need to be eliminated in computing net cash flows from operating activities.

Fortunately this will not require much work if the unsettled foreign currency transaction is in working capital. Adjusting profit by balance sheet movements in working capital will automatically adjust correctly for the non-cash flow exchange gains and losses.

5.3 Example

A company purchases raw materials for $200,000. These are translated into its books at £100,000. By the year end it has paid for half the goods (£48,000) and the remaining creditor is retranslated to closing rate at £45,000.

The purchase ledger control account shows

Purchase ledger control

	£		£
Cash	743,000	Balance b/d	300,000
Exchange gains		Purchases	910,000
On settled transaction			
(50,000 – 48,000)	2,000		
On unsettled transaction			
(50,000 – 45,000)	5,000		
Balance c/d			
Foreign currency creditor	45,000		
Other	415,000		
	£1,210,000		£1,210,000

Sales are for cash and amount to £1,003,000.

The company also has a US dollar loan which was recorded in last year's balance sheet at £235,000 and this year at £245,000.

Balance sheets

	Last year £	*This year* £
Fixed assets	-	-
Current assets		
Stock	300,000	300,000
Cash	335,000	595,000
Trade creditors	(300,000)	(460,000)
Loan	(235,000)	(245,000)
	£100,000	£190,000
Capital and reserves	£100,000	£190,000

Profit and loss account for the year

	£	£
Sales		1,003,000
Cost of sales		(910,000)
Operating profit before exchange differences		93,000
Exchange differences		
Trading	7,000	

Loan	(10,000)	
		(3,000)
Operating profit		90,000
Tax		-
Dividends		-
Retained for year		£90,000

Show the gross cash flows (ie, cash flows under the direct method) from operating activities and other elements of the cash flow statement for the year together with:

(a) reconciliation of operating profit to net cash inflow from operating activities
(b) reconciliation of net cash flow to movement in net debt/funds.

Ignore VAT.

5.4 Solution

Cash flow statement for the year

	£	£
Cash received from customers	1,003,000	
Cash payments to suppliers	743,000	
Net cash inflow from operations		260,000
Increase in cash		260,000

Reconciliation of operating profit to net cash inflow from operating activities

	£
Operating profit	90,000
Exchange loss on foreign currency loan	10,000
Increase in creditors	160,000
Net cash inflow from operations	£260,000

Reconciliation of net cash flow to movement in net funds (Note)

	£
Increase in cash for the period	260,000
Exchange difference	(10,000)
Change in net funds	250,000
Net funds at beginning of year (335 – 235)	100,000
Net funds at end of year (595 – 245)	350,000

5.5 Preparation of consolidated cash flow statements involving a foreign subsidiary

Standard accounting practice

(a) Where a portion of a reporting entity's business is undertaken by a foreign entity, the cash flows of that entity are to be included in the cash flow statement on the basis used for translating the results of those activities in the profit and loss account of the reporting entity.

(b) The same basis should be used in presenting the movements in stocks, debtors and creditors in the reconciliation between operating profit and cash from operating activities.

(c) Where intra-group cash flows are separately identifiable and the actual rate of exchange at which they took place is known, that rate, or an approximation thereto, may be used to translate the cash flows in order to ensure that they cancel on consolidation.

The key to the preparation of a group cash flow statement involving a foreign subsidiary is an understanding of the make up of the foreign exchange differences themselves. This make up will vary depending on whether the closing rate/net investment method or the temporal method is used for translating the results of the foreign enterprise.

None of the differences under either method reflects a cash inflow/outflow to the group however. The main concern therefore is to determine the real cash flows particularly if they have to be derived as balancing figures from the opening and closing balance sheets.

If cash balances are partly denominated in a foreign currency, the change in cash will be stated in the cash flow statement before the effect of foreign exchange rate changes. The reconciliation of net cash flow to movement in net debt and the note analysing changes in net debt will therefore show the effect of foreign exchange rate changes.

5.6 Temporal method

Using the temporal method, the exchange difference on translating the statements of the foreign enterprise will relate to the opening net monetary assets of that enterprise (ie, debtors, creditors, cash and loans). Under the temporal method all exchange differences pass through the profit and loss account.

5.7 Example - Temporal method

A gain of £100,000 was made on the translation of the financial statements of an 80% owned foreign subsidiary for the year ended 31 December 20X7. This gain is found to be made up as follows

	£
Gain on opening net monetary assets	
Debtors	80,000
Cash	70,000
Creditors	(50,000)
	£100,000

A loss of £40,000 was made on the parent company's foreign currency loan.

Consolidated financial statements are as follows

Balance sheets as at 31 December

	20X7	*20X6*
	£'000	£'000
Fixed assets	1,000	800
Stocks	600	400
Debtors	700	550
Cash	650	420
Creditors	(690)	(500)
Minority interest	(450)	(300)
Long-term loan	(200)	(160)
	1,610	1,210
Share capital	1,000	1,000
Consolidated revenue reserves	610	210
	1,610	1,210

There were no fixed asset disposals during the year.

Profit and loss account for the year ended 31 December 20X7

	£'000
Group profit before tax (after depreciation of £150,000)	2,900
Taxation	(800)
Group profit after tax	2,100
Minority interest	(300)
Profit attributable to members of parent undertaking	1,800
Dividend paid	(1,400)
Retained profit	400

Prepare a cash flow statement for the year ended 31 December 20X7.

5.8 Solution

Cash flow statement for the year ended 31 December 20X7

Reconciliation of operating profit to net cash inflow from operating activities

	Either £'000	*Or* £'000
Operating profit	2,900	2,900
Depreciation charges	150	150
Exchange differences on working capital £(80 – 50)	-	(30)
Exchange differences on loan and cash £(70 – 40)	(30)	(30)
Increase in stocks	(200)	(200)
Increase in debtors £(150 – 80)	(150)	(70)
Increase in creditors £(190 – 50)	190	140
Net cash inflow from operating activities	2,860	2,860

(Tutorial note: all exchange differences under the temporal method are included in operating profit. None represent a cash flow and thus should be adjusted for. For those items already appearing in the reconciliation statement - debtors and creditors - either the exchange differences are ignored thus allowing the full balance sheet movement to be recorded, or the exchange differences and the 'real' balance sheet movements are shown.*)*

	£'000
Cash flow statement	
Net cash inflow from operating activities	2,860
Returns on investments and servicing of finance	
Dividends paid to minority interests	(150)
Taxation	
Corporation tax paid	(800)
(no other information given in the example)	
Capital expenditure	
Purchase of fixed assets £(200 + 150)	(350)
Equity dividends paid	(1,400)
Net cash inflow before financing	160
Net cash inflow from financing	-
Increase in cash	160

Reconciliation of net cash flow to movement in net funds (Note)

	£'000
Increase in cash for the period	160
Exchange differences	30
Change in net funds	190
Net funds at 1 January 20X7	260
Net funds at 31 December 20X7	450

Note

Analysis of changes in net funds

	At 1 Jan 20X7 £'000	*Cash flows* £'000	*Exchange differences* £'000	*At 31 Dec 20X7* £'000
Cash	420	160	70	650
Long-term loan	(160)		(40)	(200)
Total	260	160	30	450

WORKING

Minority interest

	£'000		£'000
Dividend paid (bal fig)	150	Balance b/d	300
Balance c/d	450	P&L charge	300
	600		600

5.9 Closing rate/net investment method

Using the closing rate/net investment method, the exchange difference on translating the statements of the foreign enterprise will relate to the opening net assets of that enterprise (ie, fixed assets, stocks, debtors, cash, creditors and loans) and also to the difference between the average and the closing rates of exchange on translation of the profit and loss account, if an average rate has been used for translating the profit and loss account.

Under the closing rate/net investment method the group's share of the translation exchange differences will go directly to reserves. If there are foreign currency loans in the books of the parent company the exchange differences on the loan would normally pass through the profit and loss account, unless the parent company takes advantage of the 'cover' concept and offsets these exchange differences against the translation differences in the reserves.

Care needs to be taken in two areas

(a) **Analysis of fixed assets**

Fixed assets may require analysis in order to determine cash expenditure. Part of the movement in fixed assets may reflect an exchange gain/loss.

(b) **Analysis of minority interests**

If minority interests require analysis to determine dividend paid, it must be remembered that they have a share in the exchange gain/loss arising from the translation of the subsidiary's accounts.

5.10 Example

A gain of £160,000 was made on the translation of the financial statements of a 75% owned foreign subsidiary for the year ended 31 December 20X7. This gain is found to be made up as follows

	£
Gain on opening net assets	
Fixed assets	90,000
Stocks	30,000
Debtors	50,000
Creditors	(40,000)
Cash	30,000
	160,000

A loss of £70,000 was made on the parent company's foreign currency loan and this has been taken to consolidated reserves in accordance with the cover concept of SSAP 20.

Balance sheets as at 31 December

	20X7	*20X6*
	£'000	£'000
Fixed assets	2,100	1,700
Stocks	650	480
Debtors	990	800
Cash	500	160
Creditors	(870)	(820)
Minority interest	(520)	(370)
Long-term loan	(250)	(180)
	2,600	1,770
Share capital	1,000	1,000
Consolidated revenue reserves	1,600	770
	2,600	1,770

There were no fixed asset disposals during the year.

Profit and loss account for the year ended 31 December 20X7

	£'000
Group profit before tax (after depreciation of £220,000)	2,170
Taxation	(650)
Group profit after tax	1,520
Minority interests	(260)
Profit attributable to members of parent undertaking	1,260
Dividend paid	(480)
Retained profit	780

Prepare a cash flow statement for the year ended 31 December 20X7.

5.11 Solution

The first stage is to produce a statement of reserves so as to analyse the movements during the year.

Statement of reserves

	£'000
Reserves brought forward	770
Retained profit	780
Exchange gain £((160,000 × 75%) 120,000 – 70,000)	50
Reserves carried forward	1,600

Cash flow statement for the year ended 31 December 20X7

Reconciliation of operating profit to net cash inflow from operating activities

	£'000
Operating profit	2,170
Depreciation charges	220
Increase in stock £(170 – 30)	(140)
Increase in debtors £(190 – 50)	(140)
Increase in creditors £(50 – 40)	10
Net cash inflow from operating activities	2,120

(Tutorial note: since the group's share of all exchange differences goes straight to reserves, there are no foreign exchange adjustments.*)*

Cash flow statement	£'000
Net cash inflow from operating activities	2,120
Returns on investments and servicing of finance	
Dividends paid to minority interests (W1)	(150)
Taxation	
Corporation tax paid	(650)
(no other information supplied in the example)	
Capital expenditure	
Purchase of fixed assets (W2)	(530)
Equity dividends paid	(480)
Net cash inflow before financing	310
Net cash inflow from financing	-
Increase in cash £(340 – 30)	310

Reconciliation of net cash flow to movement in net debt (Note)

	£'000
Increase in cash for the period	310
Exchange differences	(40)
Change in net debt	270

	£'000
Net debt at 1 January 20X7	(20)
Net funds at 31 December 20X7	250

Note

Analysis of changes in net debt

	At 1 Jan 20X7	*Cash flows*	*Exchange differences*	*At 31 Dec 20X7*
	£'000	£'000	£'000	£'000
Cash	160	310	30	500
Long-term loan	(180)		(70)	(250)
Total	(20)	310	(40)	250

WORKINGS

(W1)

Minority interest

	£'000		£'000
Dividend paid (bal fig)	150	Balance b/d	370
Balance c/d	520	P&L charge	260
		Exchange gain (160 × 25%)	40
	670		670

(W2)

Fixed assets

	£'000		£'000
Balance b/d	1,700	Depreciation	220
Exchange gain	90		
Additions (bal fig)	530	Balance c/d	2,100
	2,320		2,320

6 EVALUATION OF FRS 1

6.1 Advantages of the cash flow statement

A cash flow statement can provide information which is not available from balance sheets and profit and loss accounts.

(a) It may assist users of financial statements in making judgements on the amount, timing and degree of certainty of future cash flows.

(b) It gives an indication of the relationship between profitability and cash generating ability, and thus of the quality of the profit earned.

(c) Analysts and other users of financial information often, formally or informally, develop models to assess and compare the present value of the future cash flow of entities. Historical cash flow information could be useful to check the accuracy of past assessments.

(d) A cash flow statement in conjunction with a balance sheet provides information on liquidity, viability and adaptability. The balance sheet is often used to obtain information on liquidity, but the information is incomplete for this purpose as the balance sheet is drawn up at a particular point in time.

(e) Cash flow cannot easily be manipulated and is not affected by judgement or by accounting policies.

6.2 Limitations of the cash flow statement

Cash flow statements should normally be used in conjunction with profit and loss accounts and balance sheets when making an assessment of future cash flows.

(a) Cash flow statements are based on historical information and therefore do not provide complete information for assessing future cash flows.

(b) There is some scope for manipulation of cash flows. For example, a business may delay paying creditors until after the year-end, or it may structure transactions so that the cash balance is favourably affected. It can be argued that cash management is an important aspect of stewardship and therefore desirable. However, more deliberate manipulation is possible (eg, assets may be sold and then immediately repurchased). Following the issue of FRS 5 *Reporting the substance of transactions* users of the financial statements will be alerted to the true nature of such arrangements.

(c) Cash flow is necessary for survival in the short term, but in order to survive in the long term a business must be profitable. It is often necessary to sacrifice cash flow in the short term in order to generate profits in the long term (eg, by investment in fixed assets). A huge cash balance is not a sign of good management if the cash could be invested elsewhere to generate profit.

Neither cash flow nor profit provide a complete picture of a company's performance when looked at in isolation.

6.3 Cash, liquid resources and net debt

The cash flow statement presents information about the components of cash flow (i.e. the increase or decrease in an entity's cash resulting from transactions during the accounting period). The definition of cash was stated at the beginning of the chapter.

Cash is very narrowly defined. It includes cash in hand, deposits repayable on demand and overdrafts. It does not include investments, however liquid or near maturity. The effect of this definition is that the bottom line of the cash flow statement shows the increase or decrease in 'pure' cash for the period.

In theory, there are alternatives to the strict cash approach. These are:

- use a wider definition of cash which includes some liquid resources; or
- change the focus of the statement from cash to movements in net funds or net debt.

(a) **A wider definition of cash**

Entities may borrow on a short term basis. Alternatively, they may invest cash in short term liquid investments. Many entities would argue that these activities form an important part of their cash management. For these entities, the distinction between pure cash, short term loans and liquid investments is artificial and means that the cash flow statement does not reflect the economic reality of their situation.

Under the original version of FRS 1, the cash flow statement showed the movement in cash and cash equivalents. Cash equivalents were defined as 'short term, highly liquid investments which are readily convertible into known amounts of cash without notice and which were within three months of maturity when acquired'.

This definition was widely criticised by commentators and by preparers of financial statements. In particular, the three-month limit was regarded as arbitrary. Deposits which in practice were used as part of treasury management had to be classified as investments, thus presenting a potentially misleading picture to users of the financial statements.

It would be difficult to draft a definition which did not depend on some kind of arbitrary limit. It would also be unacceptable to allow entities to determine their own basis for defining cash equivalents.

(b) **A focus on net funds or net debt**

One of the objectives of the cash flow statement is to provide information to assist users in assessing the liquidity, solvency and financial adaptability of an entity. Some commentators have argued that a cash flow statement cannot provide information about an entity's liquidity because it focuses only on changes in cash. Net debt is a widely used financial indicator and a statement which focused on net debt or net funds would provide more useful information.

6.4 Advantages of the strict cash approach

The ASB decided to use pure cash as the basis of the cash flows reported in the cash flow statement. However, it has also introduced a section for cash flows relating to the management of liquid resources. It believes that this approach has the following advantages:

(a) it avoids an arbitrary cut-off point in the definition of cash equivalents;

(b) it distinguishes cash flows arising from accumulating or using liquid resources from those for other investing activities; and

(c) it provides information about an entity's treasury activities that was not previously available to the extent that the instruments dealt in fell within the definition of cash equivalents.

The ASB believes that focusing on cash (rather than on a broader measure such as net debt):

(a) highlights the significant components of cash that make up a cash flow statement;

(b) shows as cash flow movements transactions that would not be captured by a broader measure such as net debt (eg, redemption of debentures for cash);

(c) facilitates comparison of the cash flow performances of different entities; and

(d) is in line with the international focus on cash (eg, with IAS 7).

6.5 Scope of FRS 1

FRS 1 applies to all financial statements intended to give a true and fair view of the financial position and profit or loss (or income and expenditure) except those of:

(a) subsidiary undertakings where 90 per cent or more of the voting rights are controlled within the group, provided that consolidated financial statements in which the subsidiary undertakings are included are publicly available.

(b) companies incorporated under companies legislation and entitled to the exemptions available in the legislation for small companies when filing accounts with the Registrar of Companies.

(c) entities that would have been in category (b) above if they were companies incorporated under companies legislation.

(d) mutual life assurance companies, pension funds, some open-ended investment funds and some building societies.

Regarding small enterprises, the ASB has issued a single financial reporting standard for smaller entities (FRSSE). This encourages, but does not require, small entities to prepare a cash flow statement.

FRS 1 exempts subsidiary undertakings where 90% or more of the voting rights in the subsidiary are controlled within its group. In this situation, it is likely that the liquidity, solvency and financial adaptability of the subsidiary will depend upon the group, rather than its own cash flows. Groups often have centralised cash management operations and cash balances can be moved around a group rapidly. For this reason, historical cash flow information of individual group companies does not always contribute to an assessment of future cash flows.

7 CHAPTER SUMMARY

FRS 1 has specific requirements in relation to minority interests, associates and acquisitions and disposals of subsidiaries. In all cases the emphasis is on determining the cash inflow or outflow in respect of such items.

Foreign exchange differences on the restatement of items denominated in a foreign currency do not represent cash flows in the accounting period and therefore need to be excluded from the cash flow statement. Whether a specific adjustment is required is dependent on the means by which a cash inflow or outflow is calculated.

8 SELF TEST QUESTIONS

8.1 What are the standard headings under which *FRS 1* requires cash flows to be classified? (1.2)

8.2 How does *FRS 1* define cash? (1.3)

8.3 What does the direct method of reporting net cash flows from operating activities show? (1.6)

8.4 How should minority interests be treated in a group cash flow statement? (4.2)

8.5 How does an associated undertaking reflect a cash flow into or out of a group? (4.5)

8.6 What are the cash flow effects of exchange differences dealt with at the individual company stage? (5.2)

8.7 What does FRS1 say regarding exchange differences at the consolidated stage? (5.5)

8.8 What two areas of identifying group cash flow may be a problem if the closing rate method has been used? (5.9)

9 EXAMINATION TYPE QUESTION

9.1 Orchard group

Orchard plc is a fruit packaging company operating in the United Kingdom. The company has an 80% interest in a foreign subsidiary that carries on business as a fruit producer. Consolidated accounts are prepared at 31 December each year. All sales are to wholesalers and are on 90 days credit.

A draft consolidated profit and loss account and balance sheet have been prepared for the year ended 31 December 20X0. The directors have requested the accountant to prepare forecast accounts for 20X1 on the assumption that there is to be major capital expenditure on the replacement of the packaging plant in the United Kingdom. Obsolete machinery which cost £690,000 with a book value at 31 December 20X0 of £345,000 is to be sold and new machinery is to be purchased.

The draft consolidated profit and loss accounts and balance sheets for the years ended 31 December 20X0 and 20X1 are as follows

Consolidated profit and loss accounts

		£'000	*20X0* £'000	£'000	*20X1* £'000
Sales			3,680		4,600
Cost of sales:	Material	1,840		2,300	
	Labour	690		805	
	Expenses	230		345	
			2,760		3,450
			920		1,150
Expenses		460		518	
Depreciation		115		161	
Loss of sale of plant		-		172	
			575		851
			345		299
Other income			55		55
Profit on ordinary activities before tax			400		354
Tax			140		105
Profit on ordinary activities after tax			260		249
Minority interest			45		42
Profit attributable to shareholders			215		207
Dividends			170		200
Profit retained for the financial year			45		7

Consolidated balance sheets

		£'000	*20X0* £'000	£'000	*20X1* £'000
Fixed assets					
Land and buildings			920		920
Plant	- at cost	1,150		1,610	
	- depreciation	690		506	
			460		1,104
Current assets					
Stock		403		576	
Investments		737		804	
Debtors		919		1,145	
Bank		58		(805)	
			2,117		1,720
Current liabilities					
Trade creditors		550		681	
Taxation		140		125	
			(690)		(806)
			2,807		2,938
Share capital			1,150		1,150
Consolidated reserves			1,207		1,264
Minority interest			300		344
Long-term loan			150		180
			2,807		2,938

The group uses the closing rate method for translating the financial statements of the foreign subsidiary and the accountant estimated that there would be a gain arising on translating the opening net investment made up as follows

	£
Plant	60,000
Stocks	20,000
Debtors	42,000
Cash	25,000
Creditors	(47,000)

An estimated loss of £30,000 made on the parent company's foreign currency loan has been charged against the consolidated reserves.

You are required:

(a) to prepare a cash flow statement for the Orchard group for the year ended 31 December 20X1 in accordance with FRS 1 (Revised), using the direct method.

(b) assuming that the profit and loss account has been translated using the average rate and that there is a translation gain of £10,000 arising from the difference between the average and the closing rates, to explain how the gain would be dealt with in the cash flow statement for the year ending 31 December 20X1 and its effect on the amounts that have been calculated under (a) above. **(18 marks)**

10 ANSWER TO EXAMINATION TYPE QUESTION

10.1 Orchard group

*(**Tutorial note:** a fairly straightforward question based on the presentation of the cash flow data in line with FRS 1. The only major problem is in dealing with the £100,000 and £30,000 exchange differences. Assume the amounts charged to the consolidated profit and loss account for labour and expenses are equal to the cash payments made during the period for such items.)*

(a) **Cash flow statement for the year ended 31 December 20X1**

	£'000	£'000
Operating activities		
Cash received from customers (W4)	4,416	
Cash paid to suppliers (W5)	(2,369)	
Expenses paid	(863)	
Cash paid to employees	(805)	
Net cash inflow from operating activities (Note 1)		379
Returns on investments and servicing of finance:		
Other income (assumed to be interest)	55	
Dividends paid to minority interests (W3)	(18)	
		37
Taxation:		
Corporation tax paid (W6)		(120)
Capital expenditure:		
Plant purchases (W1)	(1,090)	
Plant disposals (W2)	173	
		(917)
Equity dividends paid		(200)
Net cash outflow before use of liquid resources and financing		(821)

Management of liquid resources:	
Purchase of current asset investments (804 – 737)	(67)
Financing:	-
Decrease in cash in the period	(888)

Reconciliation of net cash flow to movement in net funds (Note 2)

Decrease in cash in the period	(888)
Cash outflow from purchase of current asset investments	67
Change in net funds resulting from cash flows	(821)
Exchange differences	(5)
Net funds at 1 January 20X1	645
Net debt at 31 December 20X1	(181)

Notes to the cash flow statement

(1) **Reconciliation of operating profit to net cash inflow from operating activities**

	£'000
Operating profit (354 – 55 + 172)	471
Depreciation charges	161
Increase in stocks (576 – 403 – 20)	(153)
Increase in debtors (1,145 – 919 – 42)	(184)
Increase in creditors (681 – 550 – 47)	84
Net cash inflow from operating activities	379

(2) **Analysis of changes in net funds**

	At 1 January 20X1	*Cash flows*	*Exchange differences*	*At 31 December 20X1*
	£'000	£'000	£'000	£'000
Cash at bank/bank overdraft	58	(888)	25	(805)
Long-term loan	(150)		(30)	(180)
Current asset investments	737	67		804
Total	645	(821)	(5)	(181)

(Tutorial note: an alternative is to show all £100,000 exchange differences in the movement in cash with the following balances operating in the statement:

	£'000
Cash received from customers	4,374
Cash paid to suppliers	(2,342)
Purchases of plant	(1,150)*)*

(b) The exchange gain has no effect on the actual cash flows for the period but it would be necessary to take account of the differences that arise from using an average rate in the profit and loss account and the closing rate in the balance sheet. The calculations based on the movements in certain accounts eg, debtors would have to be adjusted to reflect the exchange differences. It is possible to make a single adjustment of £10,000 as described in the tutorial note above instead of making adjustments to all calculations for the individual figures in the cash flow statements.

WORKINGS

			£'000	£'000
(W1)	Plant purchases	Opening balance	1,150	
		Exchange gain	60	
		Cost of disposals	(690)	
				520
		Closing balance		(1,610)
		Purchases (assume on cash basis)		1,090
(W2)	Plant sale proceeds	Book value of disposal (after dep'n)		345
		Loss on sale		(172)
		Proceeds		173
(W3)	Dividend to MI	Opening balance	300	
		Share of profits	42	
		Share of exchange gain	20	
				362
		Closing balance		(344)
		Dividends paid		18
(W4)	Cash received from customers			
		Debtors opening balance	919	
		Adjustment for exchange gain	42	
		Plus sales	4,600	
				5,561
		Debtors closing balance		(1,145)
		Cash received		4,416
(W5)	Cash paid to suppliers			
		Cost of sales	2,300	
		Opening stock balance	(403)	
		Adjustment for exchange gain	(20)	
		Closing stock	576	
		Purchases		2,453
		Creditors opening balance		550
		Adjustment for exchange loss		47
		Creditors closing balance		(681)
		Cash paid		2,369
(W6)	Taxation paid	Opening balance	140	
		Tax incurred	105	
				245
		Closing balance		(125)
		Tax paid		120

20 THE PREPARATION OF ADDITIONAL REPORTS

INTRODUCTION & LEARNING OBJECTIVES

This chapter considers the type of advice and reports a professional accountant in practice may be required to produce.

The two main types of advice relate to

(a) quoted companies and their relationship to the stock exchange and their investors
(b) share valuations.

This chapter concentrates on (a) above. Share valuations are dealt with in the next chapter.

The chapter starts by considering SSAP 25. This can (loosely) be termed a report but it is important to remember that SSAP 25 fits within the pure financial accounting reporting part of the syllabus. The other areas dealt with in this chapter relate to additional tasks the accountant may be called upon to perform.

When you have studied this chapter you should be able to do the following:

- Prepare a segmental report
- Prepare reports to (mainly) shareholders in a variety of situations.

1 SSAP 25: SEGMENTAL REPORTING

1.1 Introduction

Many enterprises carry on several classes of business or operate in several geographical areas, with different rates of profitability, different opportunities for growth and different degrees of risk. It is usually not possible for the reader of the financial statements of such enterprises to make judgements about the nature of different activities carried on by the enterprise or of their contribution to the overall financial results of the enterprise unless some segmental analysis of the financial statements is given. The purpose of segmental information is, therefore, to provide information to assist the readers of financial statements:

(a) to appreciate more thoroughly the results and financial position of the enterprise by permitting a better understanding of the enterprise's past performance and thus a better assessment of its future prospects; and

(b) to be aware of the impact that changes in significant components of a business may have on the business as a whole.

1.2 Determining reportable segments

The directors identify the **reportable segments** having regard to differences in:

(a) return on capital employed;
(b) risk;
(c) rate of growth;
(d) potential for future development for both classes of business and geographical areas.

All **significant** segments should be identified as reportable segments.

Definition A segment is significant if:

(a) its third party turnover is 10% or more of the total third party turnover; or

(b) its segment result is 10% or more of the combined result of all segments in profit, or in loss (whichever is greater, ie, do not net off profits and losses to a net profit figure of say £20,000 and use £2,000 as a significance test when total profits might be £5.02m and losses total £5.00m); or

(c) its net assets are 10% or more of the total net assets.

The directors should review the definitions annually and redefine when appropriate.

1.3 Classes of business

Definition A **class of business** is defined as a distinguishable component of an entity that provides a separate product or service or a separate group of related products or services.

To identify reportable classes of business, directors should consider the following factors:

(a) nature of products or services;
(b) nature of production processes;
(c) markets in which products or services are sold;
(d) the distribution channels for the products (eg, are the items sold by retail or mail order?);
(e) the manner in which the entity's activities are organised;
(f) any separate legislative framework relating to part of the business (eg, a bank or insurance company).

1.4 Geographical segments

Definition A **geographical segment** is a geographical area comprising an individual country or group of countries in which an entity operates or to which it supplies products or services.

The analysis should help the users to assess the extent to which the operations are subject to factors such as:

(a) expansionist or restrictive economic climates;
(b) stable or unstable political regimes;
(c) exchange control regulations;
(d) exchange rate fluctuations.

1.5 Requirements of SSAP 25 and the Companies Act in relation to segmental reporting

SSAP 25

If an entity has two or more classes of business or operates in two or more geographical segments it should:

(a) define its classes of business and geographical segments in its financial statements; and

(b) for each class of business and geographical segment, disclose;

(i) turnover, distinguishing

turnover derived from external customers; and
turnover derived from other segments;

(ii) result before tax, minority interests and extraordinary items;

(iii) net assets.

The standard distinguishes:

(a) **origin** of turnover – the geographical segment from which products or services are supplied;

(b) **destination** of turnover – the geographical segment to which products or services are supplied.

The geographical segmentation of turnover should be done by origin and also by destination where the latter is different.

Results should normally be given before interest unless the interest income or expense is central to the business when the result should be given after interest.

The net assets should normally be non-interest bearing unless the results are after interest in which case the interest bearing assets and liabilities should be included.

Segmental information should be presented on the basis of the consolidated financial statements.

Companies Act

Notes to the profit and loss account must show turnover broken down by classes of business and by geographical markets, having regard to the manner in which the company's activities are organised, in so far as these classes and markets differ substantially.

Classes or markets which do not differ substantially must be treated as one class or market. Immaterial amounts may be combined with those of another class or market.

This additional information on turnover may be omitted if disclosure would be seriously prejudicial to the company's interests. The fact that such information has not been disclosed must be stated in the notes.

1.6 Preparing segmental reports in accordance with current requirements

The illustrative example in SSAP 25 is a useful format to follow when preparing a statement.

Class of business	*Industry A*		*Industry B*		*Other*		*Group*	
	20X1	*20X0*	*20X1*	*20X0*	*20X1*	*20X0*	*20X1*	*20X0*
	£'000	£'000	£'000	£'000	£'000	£'000	£'000	£'000
Turnover								
Total sales	33,000	30,000	42,000	38,000	26,000	23,000	101,000	91,000
Inter-segment sales	(4,000)	-	-	-	(12,000)	(14,000)	(16,000)	(14,000)
Sales to third parties	29,000	30,000	42,000	38,000	14,000	9,000	85,000	77,000
Profit before taxation								
Segment profit	3,000	2,500	4,500	4,000	1,800	1,500	9,300	8,000
Common costs							300	300
Operating profit							9,000	7,700
Net interest							(400)	(500)
							8,600	7,200
Group share of the profits before taxation of associated undertakings	1,000	1,000	1,400	1,200	-	-	2,400	2,200
Group profit before taxation							11,000	9,400

Net assets								
Segment net assets	17,600	15,000	24,000	25,000	19,400	19,000	61,000	59,000
Unallocated assets							3,000	3,000
							64,000	62,000
Group share of net assets of associated undertakings	10,200	8,000	8,800	9,000	-	-	19,000	17,000
Total net assets							83,000	79,000

Common costs refer to costs where allocation between segments could mislead. Likewise, the segmental disclosure of net assets might include unallocated assets.

Geographical segments	*United Kingdom*		*North America*		*Far East*		*Other*		*Group*	
	20X1	*20X0*	*20X1*	*20X0*	*20X1*	*20X0*	*20X1*	*20X0*	*20X1*	*20X0*
	£'000	£'000	£'000	£'000	£'000	£'000	£'000	£'000	£'000	£'000
Turnover										
Turnover by destination										
Sales to third parties	34,000	31,000	16,000	14,500	25,000	23,000	10,000	8,500	85,000	77,000
Turnover by origin										
Total sales	38,000	34,000	29,000	27,500	23,000	23,000	12,000	10,500	102,000	95,000
Inter-segment sales	-	-	(8,000)	(9,000)	(9,000)	(9,000)	-	-	(17,000)	(18,000)
Sales to third parties	38,000	34,000	21,000	18,500	14,000	14,000	12,000	10,500	85,000	77,000

The following detailed points from the standard should also assist.

(a) **Associates**

The share of the results and net assets of associates should be shown separately by segment if the associate accounts for at least 20% of the total result or total net assets of the reporting entity.

This need not be shown where the information is unobtainable or where publication would be prejudicial to the business.

(b) **Reconciliation**

The total of the amounts disclosed by segment should agree with the total in the financial statements. If it does not, the reporting entity should provide a reconciliation between the two figures. Reconciling items should be properly identified and explained.

(c) **Comparatives**

Comparatives should be provided. If a change is made to the definitions of the segments or to the accounting policies that are adopted for reporting segmental information, the nature of the change should be disclosed.

(d) If the directors consider that disclosure of any information required by the standard would be seriously prejudicial to the interests of the reporting entity, the information need not be disclosed.

1.7 Areas in which SSAP 25 is too vague and flexible

SSAP 25 is a key accounting standard in assisting in the interpretation of a large enterprise and amplifies the disclosure provisions of the CA85. The ASC took a long time to issue a standard despite the clear need for further disclosures by investment analysts and other users, because of concerns by companies affected by the standard that they would be put at a competitive disadvantage by revealing such information.

Criticisms of the standard can be made as follows.

(a) The class and geographical segment split is decided by the directors. This, it is argued provides too much flexibility.

However it is difficult to envisage the incorporation of hard and fast rules in a standard. Each company is different and judgements have to be made under any system. Also the standard does give guidance regarding what constitutes a significant segment.

(b) The computation of return on capital employed (ROCE) is a key indicator of business performance as it measures how efficiently the company is managing to generate profits from the assets in the business. However ROCE may not be able to be validly computed for each segment under SSAP 25 as:

- common costs may or may not be included in the segment result (this is a decision of the directors)
- net assets may have an element of commonality across segments.

1.8 Activity

Innovations plc is preparing a segmental report to include with its financial accounts prepared for the year ended 30 June 20X9.

The relevant information given below is based on the consolidated figures of Innovations plc and its subsidiaries. Associate company information is not shown.

	20X9 £'000	*20X8* £'000
Sales to customers outside the group by the Fruit Growing Division	12,150	13,500
Sales to customers outside the group by the UK companies	27,000	24,300
Sales not derived from Fruit Growing, Canning or Bureau activities	2,700	1,350
Sales made to customers outside the group by the Canning Division	17,550	13,095
Assets used by the US companies	32,400	24,300
Assets not able to be allocated to Fruit Growing, Canning or Bureau activities	13,500	11,003
Assets used by Fruit Growing Division	33,750	32,400
Sales by the Canning Division to other group members	2,970	3,105
Assets used by the Bureau service	18,765	17,563
Assets used by the UK companies	43,200	40,500
Sales by the Fruit Growing Division to other group members	1,495	1,688
Sales not allocated to the UK, US or other areas	2,700	1,350
Sales made by group to other areas of the world	1,350	1,215
Expenses not allocated to UK, US or other areas	4,590	3,834
Sales to customers outside the group by US companies	6,750	5,130
Expenses not allocated to Fruit Growing, Canning or Bureau Service	5,130	4,104
Sales by US companies to group members	2,160	1,215
Sales to customers outside the group for Bureau Service	5,400	4,050
Sales made by UK companies to other group members	2,700	1,890
Assets used by Canning Division	40,500	33,750
Assets used by group in other areas	18,360	19,683
Assets not allocated to UK, US or other areas	12,555	10,233
Segmental net operating profit by industry		
Fruit Growing	2,565	3,375
Canning	4,725	3,600
Bureau	412	540
Consolidated segmental net operating profit by industry	7,695	6,750

Segmental net operating profit by geographical area		
UK	5,130	4,590
US	2,430	1,890
Other areas	270	405
Consolidated segmental net operating profit by geographical area	7,155	6,480

You are required: to draft an industry and geographical segmental report for inclusion in the annual report of Innovations plc to give the maximum information to the shareholders.

1.9 Activity solution

Draft geographical segmental report

Geographical segment	*UK*		*US*		*Other*		*Group*	
	20X9	*20X8*	*20X9*	*20X8*	*20X9*	*20X8*	*20X9*	*20X8*
	£'000	£'000	£'000	£'000	£'000	£'000	£'000	£'000
Turnover								
Total sales	29,700	26,190	8,910	6,345	1,350	1,215	39,960	33,750
Inter-segment sales	(2,700)	(1,890)	(2,160)	(1,215)	-	-	(4,860)	(3,105)
Unallocated sales	-	-	-	-	-	-	2,700	1,350
Sales to third parties	27,000	24,300	6,750	5,130	1,350	1,215	37,800	31,995
Profit before taxation								
Segment profit	5,130	4,590	2,430	1,890	270	405	7,830	6,885
Inter-segment profit							(675)	(405)
Common costs							(4,590)	(3,834)
Group share of profits before taxation							2,565	2,646
Net assets								
Segment net assets	43,200	40,500	32,400	24,300	18,360	19,683	93,960	84,483
Unallocated assets							12,555	10,233
Group share of net assets							106,515	94,716

Draft industry segmental report

Classes of business	*Fruit growing*		*Canning*		*Bureau*		*Group*	
	20X9	*20X8*	*20X9*	*20X8*	*20X9*	*20X8*	*20X9*	*20X8*
	£'000	£'000	£'000	£'000	£'000	£'000	£'000	£'000
Turnover								
Total sales	13,635	15,188	20,520	16,200	5,400	4,050	39,555	35,438
Inter-segment sales	(1,484)	(1,688)	(2,970)	(3,105)	-	-	(4,455)	(4,793)
Unallocated sales	-	-	-	-	-	-	2,700	1,350
Sales to third parties	12,150	13,500	17,550	13,095	5,400	4,050	37,800	31,995
Profit before taxation								
Segment profit	2,565	3,375	4,725	3,600	412	540	7,702	7,515
Inter-segment profit							(7)	(765)
Common costs							(5,130)	(4,104)
Group share of profits before taxation							2,565	2,646

Net assets								
Segment net assets	33,750	32,400	40,500	33,750	18,765	17,563	93,015	83,713
Unallocated assets							13,500	11,003
Group share of net assets							106,515	94,716

2 DISCUSSION PAPER: SEGMENTAL REPORTING

2.1 Introduction

The ASB believes that SSAP 25 is operating reasonably satisfactorily. However, in 1996 both the IASC and the FASB issued exposure drafts on this topic which have subsequently been issued as accounting standards. The ASB has issued a discussion paper *Segmental Reporting*, in order to seek views on these developments.

The Discussion Paper has identified three key issues:

(a) the basis for dividing the operations of an entity into segments

(b) the choice of information to be given segmentally

(c) the means by which amounts reported by segment are reconciled to the total amounts reported for that entity.

The ASB has now decided not to proceed with a revised version of SSAP 25 for the time being. However, the material in the Discussion Paper provides useful ideas as to how segmental disclosures might be improved in future.

2.2 The basis of segmentation: the IASC 'risks and returns' approach

Defining segments

The IASC proposed that segments should be identified by the different risks and returns an entity faces. This is broadly similar to the SSAP 25 approach. However, the IASC provided very much more detailed definitions. These would result in directors having far less scope to determine what constitutes a reportable segment than is currently allowed by SSAP 25.

Identifying segments

The IASC also introduced the concept of primary and secondary segments. Less information is required about secondary segments.

(a) If the enterprise's dominant risks and returns result from the products and services it produces, the primary format for reporting segment information should be business segments. If the enterprise's dominant risks and returns result from operating in different geographical areas, the primary format for reporting segment information will be geographical segments. Most enterprises are likely to use business segments as primary segments.

(b) The enterprise's system of internal reporting should normally be the basis of identifying reportable segments. If there is evidence that an enterprise's internally reported segments do not satisfy the definitions of business segments and geographical segments, the directors must determine the segments for the purposes of external reporting.

(c) A reportable segment is one which contributes 10% of the enterprise's revenue or profit or which has 10% or more of the enterprise's net assets. (This is very similar to the SSAP 25 requirement). However, the IASC proposals also state that once a segment has exceeded the

10% thresholds and becomes a reportable segment, it should continue to be a reportable segment in future periods, even if it falls below the 10% threshold subsequently.

2.3 The basis of segmentation: the FASB 'managerial' approach

The FASB proposed a 'managerial' approach, which bases both the segments reported and the information reported about them on the information used internally for decision making. This means that management define the reportable segments.

The FASB proposed that an identifiable segment (an 'operating segment') should be a component of an entity:

(a) that engages in business activities from which it earns revenues and incurs expenses;

(b) whose operating results are regularly reviewed by senior management to assess the performance of the individual segment and make decisions about resources to be allocated to the segment; and

(c) for which discrete financial information is available.

Arguments for the 'managerial approach' include the following:

(a) Segments based on an entity's internal structure are less subjective than those identified by the 'risks and returns' (ie, SSAP 25 and IASC) approach.

(b) It highlights the risks and opportunities that management believes are important.

(c) It provides information with predictive value because it enables users of the financial statements to see the entity through the eyes of management.

(d) The cost of providing the information is low (because it should already have been provided for management's use).

(e) It will produce segment information that is consistent with the way in which management discuss their business in other parts of the annual report (eg, in the Chairman's Statement and the OFR).

(f) Interim reporting of segmental information would be feasible.

Arguments against the 'managerial approach' include the following:

(a) Segments based on internal reporting structures are unlikely to be comparable between enterprises and may not be comparable from year to year for an individual entity.

(b) The information is likely to be commercially sensitive (because entities are organised strategically).

(c) Segmental information given other than by products or services or geographically may be more difficult to analyse using macroeconomic models.

(d) Using the managerial approach could lead to segments with different risks and returns being combined.

(e) Analysts define their area of expertise by industry segment, usually based on product or service. The SSAP 25 version of segmental reporting is more likely to reflect these.

(f) There is no standardised definition of segment result. This means information based on different levels of profit might be reported for different segments.

2.4 Evaluating the two approaches

The Discussion Paper suggests that the choice between the risks and returns approach and the managerial approach cannot be made on the basis of principle alone. This is because the results of applying the approaches in practice may differ from that expected.

The risks and returns approach provides information about the major sources of the different risks and opportunities that face an entity. The managerial approach provides information on the way an entity manages its business. The preferences of users depend on which they believe is the most important.

The choice between the two approaches may be influenced by the degree to which the amounts reported to management for the running of the business are consistent and comparable between segments and businesses.

Conclusion The Discussion Paper considers two alternative methods of defining segments: the 'risks and returns' approach (currently required by SSAP 25) and the 'managerial approach', which bases segments on information used internally for decision making.

2.5 Segmental disclosure

Both the IASC and the FASB proposed significant additional disclosures. These are summarised below:

	IASC		FASB
	Primary segment	**Secondary segment**	
Revenues from transactions with third parties	✓	✓	✓
Revenues from transactions with other segments	✓		✓
Basis of inter segment pricing	✓		✓
Segment result	✓		✓
Interest revenue	✓		✓
Interest expense	✓		✓
Research and development expense			✓
Depreciation/amortisation	✓		✓
Exceptional/unusual items	✓		✓
Share of income from joint ventures/associates	✓		✓
Taxation			✓
Extraordinary items	✓		✓
Non cash flow items (other than depreciation)	✓		✓
Total assets	✓	✓	✓
Total liabilities	✓		✓
Investments in associates/joint ventures	✓		✓
Capital expenditure	✓	✓	✓
Contingencies	✓		

In addition, the FASB proposed that the following information should be disclosed:

(a) factors that management considers most significant in determining operating segments;
(b) types of products and services from which each operating segment derives its revenues;
(c) where there are major customers (providing more than 10% of total turnover), the segment(s) affected.

Neither the IASC nor the FASB proposed any exemption from disclosing information on the grounds that it might be commercially sensitive (as is currently permitted by SSAP 25).

2.7 Reconciliation

Both the IASC and the FASB proposed that segmental disclosures should be reconciled with the totals in the financial statements of:

(a) third party turnover
(b) profit or loss
(c) total assets
(d) total liabilities.

3 REPORTS

The syllabus requires the preparation and presentation of reports for a variety of users and purposes.

3.1 The alternative user groups and their information needs

User groups have been defined in various documents including The Corporate Report issued by the ASC and the Statement of Principles by the ASB. The analysis should be well known to you from your previous studies. It should be remembered however that the analysis is framed in the context of those groups entitled to see the annual financial statements of a public company. We are more concerned in this chapter with the preparation of reports in specific situations. Due to this very little can be stated in general terms about user groups other than the fact that many of these additional reports are directed solely to one type of user eg, shareholders.

In giving advice in these reports you therefore need to remember the person(s) to whom the report is being directed and their requirements from the report.

4 PREPARING A REPORT OFFERING ADVICE AND GUIDANCE TO INVESTORS

4.1 Situations involving accountants' reports

The terms 'accountants' report' has a specialised meaning in the context of documentation issued by companies in certain situations.

Accountants' reports may be required in several different contexts; for example

(a) prospectuses of companies whose shares have not previously been listed (with which much of this section is concerned)

(b) acquisition circulars where listed companies have, during the year made material acquisitions involving, say, shares in unlisted companies

(c) take-over offer documents (see section 6).

This section will deal with the first of these situations. (The subject of *profit forecasts,* often met in the cases of (a) and (c) above, is dealt with in the next section).

4.2 What is a prospectus?

A prospectus is defined as *any prospectus, notice, circular, advertisement, or other invitation, offering to the public for subscription or purchase any shares in or debentures of a company (S744 CA 85).*

4.3 The contents of a prospectus

A typical prospectus of a limited company might include the following sections

(a) history and business
(b) management and employees
(c) proceeds of issue and working capital
(d) profits, prospectus and dividends
(e) directors
(f) accountants' report

(g) valuer's report
(h) statutory and general information
(i) profit forecasts
(j) procedures for application.

4.4 What considerations govern the form and content of a prospectus?

(a) **Legal requirements**

The Financial Services Act 1986 (FSA 1986) contains provisions governing the admission to listing on the Stock Exchange and offers of securities to the public.

The FSA 1986 provides a statutory framework giving authority to the Council of the Stock Exchange to issue rules governing the admission of securities to listing.

(b) **Stock Exchange requirements**

These are set out in The Listing Rules (referred to in this chapter as the Yellow Book) issued by the Stock Exchange.

4.5 Stock Exchange requirements - company not listed on the Stock Exchange

Say a company wishes to obtain a listing and make an issue of shares to the public. Where no part of its share capital is at present listed, requirements are stringent because little public information is available regarding the company.

The Stock Exchange requirements for the accountants' report are set out in the *Yellow Book*. The accountants' report should deal with the following matters for each of the *three* completed financial years prior to the issue of the prospectus.

(a) **Profit and loss account information**

Similar information to that shown in Format 1 of the CA85.

(b) **Balance sheet information**

Balance sheets of the company or group.

(c) **Cash flow statement**

Cash flow statements of the company or group.

(d) **Accounting policies**

Accounting policies regarding material or critical items.

(e) **Other relevant matters**

The report should also deal with any other matters which appear to be relevant for the purposes of the report.

(f) **Age of figures reported upon**

The latest financial period reported upon should normally end within six months of the date of the prospectus.

(g) **True and fair view**

The reporting accountant must give an opinion as to whether the financial information gives a true and fair view.

4.6 Statement of adjustments

After the investigating accountant has completed his financial investigation, he may decide that certain adjustments should be made to profit and asset figures which have been incorporated into previously audited accounts.

Why may adjustments be required? The answer is that they may be necessary to convey profit trends to the reader of the report. Such adjustments must be incorporated into a *statement of adjustments* as specified by the *Yellow Book.*

Although the statement does not form part of the accountant's report, it is referred to in that report and must be made available for inspection by members of the public so that they can see the relationship between figures referred to in the prospectus and the corresponding figures in audited accounts of the company. The statement should also give the reasons for the adjustments.

Where adjustments have been made, the reporting accountant is required to prepare a **statement of adjustments**, showing how the audited financial statements have been adjusted to arrive at the figures in his report. Although no particular format is required for the statement, it must be sufficiently detailed to reconcile the figures in the audited financial statements with those in the accountant's report.

Adjustments to previously reported figures should only be made

(i) to ensure that the financial information for all the years reported on is stated on a consistent basis; or

(ii) to ensure that the financial information is in all other respects properly comparable, for example by correcting any fundamental accounting errors in the financial statements of the periods reported on.

To enable the financial information to be stated on a consistent basis two different types of adjustment may be required

(i) Adjustments should be made to ensure that, wherever practicable, all the financial information in the report is stated on the basis of the current accounting policies.

However, although adjustments may be made in respect of accounting policies, adjustments should not normally be made to the company's accounting estimates, provided there were no fundamental errors. The effect of correcting an estimate in a later period should normally be reflected in the result of that period. The reporting accountant should consider whether separate disclosure in the profit and loss tabulations as an exceptional item is necessary. Consideration should also be given to any additional disclosure which may be necessary by way of notes.

(ii) If there has been a change in the group structure in the period reported on (for example, the acquisition or disposal of a subsidiary company or business, or a reorganisation of the group) it may sometimes be appropriate to make adjustments so that the effects of the change on the results of the group and its state of affairs do not distort the financial information.

The following list illustrates some of the types of adjustments which may be made with groups of companies.

(a) **Results and balance sheets**

It may be appropriate to prepare the financial information on the following basis

(i)	Acquisition by issue of share capital during the period reported upon.	Include the results of the acquired entity for the whole period.

(There may be difficulties in presenting the balance sheets whether merger or acquisition accounting principles have been applied. This may be due to differences in year ends or the inability to attribute fair values to periods prior to acquisition. Adjustment may not, therefore, be appropriate.)

(ii)	Acquisition subsequent to the period reported upon.	Present the financial information on the acquired entity as a separate section in the accountant's report.
(iii)	Acquisition for cash during the period reported upon.	Include the results of the acquired entity from the date of acquisition.

(Where acquisition accounting has been used, consideration should also be given to disclosing separately the results of the acquired business for the periods prior to acquisition.)

(iv)	Acquisition for a combination of cash and shares during the period reported upon.	Include the results of the acquired entity for the whole period.

(Consideration should be given to an adjustment for notional interest on the cash element of the purchase price for the period prior to the acquisition date.)

(v)	Disposal of a subsidiary or discontinuation of a material section of the business.	Show separately the results of that section of the business in the profit and loss table.
(vi)	Reorganisations prior to issue of shares to the public.	Where, for example, companies under common control but legally unconnected are formed into a legal group prior to issue or flotation, the accountant's report should be prepared on a combined basis and should explain fully the basis of preparation in the introductory paragraphs of the report.

(b) **Earnings per share**

Consequential adjustments may arise in calculating earnings per share for each period covered by the accountant's report. The principles in FRS 14 should be followed as far as practicable. If an acquisition has been made for shares the number of shares used in the calculation would normally be increased throughout the period covered by the accountant's report even if acquisition accounting was applied in the statutory financial statements. This would correspond to the increase in reported earnings reflecting the results of the acquired business.

5 PROSPECTIVE FINANCIAL INFORMATION

5.1 Introduction

Reports issued with 'prospective financial information' will involve one of three main areas

(a) an issue of shares
(b) mergers and acquisitions
(c) a report to a bank for a loan.

Prospective financial information can be defined as follows:

Definition Prospective financial information comprises information relating to one or more future dates or periods and to financial information relating to the whole or part of an expired period where the auditor has yet to report on the financial statements.

Prospective financial information therefore covers any situation where information concerning a company is issued in advance of audited accounts for a period by that company. This prospective financial information may be in the form of a formal profit forecast, or a cash flow statement, or it may simply be a written statement like 'profits are expected to increase next year'.

You should be aware of the different forms of prospective financial information.

(a) **A forecast**

Definition This is a statement of management's best estimates of future results.

It will be based on assumptions produced by management and indicates management's judgement on how they expect their company to perform in the future. The future here is normally only to the end of the current accounting period, except in rare cases as discussed later.

(b) **A projection**

Definition This may be either

(i) management's best estimate of future results, as in a forecast, but projection will be subject to more uncertainty than a forecast. The increased uncertainty will be caused by a lack of corroborative evidence due to such factors as

(1) how far ahead the future period is
(2) lack of a sufficient trading record
(3) volatility of the business
(4) especially uncertain business environment, and
(5) highly subjective assumptions; or

(ii) management's illustration of future results which is based on hypothetical assumptions which may or may not prevail, but the assumptions appear to be reasonable.

A projection therefore has a greater degree of uncertainty than a forecast. Examples are a statement of profits for the next two years in category (i), or for category (ii), the Channel Tunnel profit 'forecast' which looked 55 years into the future: the assumptions appeared reasonable, but were completely hypothetical!

Most companies will use a forecast where possible because of the greater degree of reliance that can be placed on it. A projection will normally be used either

(i) where the prospective financial information needs to be extended beyond the current accounting period, or

(ii) where a major new venture is being launched.

New companies must always use a projection because there is no partly expired accounting period to base a forecast on.

(c) **Statement of working capital requirement**

Definition This is a statement of management's estimates of the likely working capital requirement based on a cash flow statement.

(d) **A profit estimate**

Definition A profit estimate is the unaudited results for an expired period.

All of these types of prospective financial information will be accompanied by a *statement of assumptions* which gives the assumptions that have been used in preparing the statement. Assumptions can be either internal or external, and some may be hypothetical.

Internal assumptions are under the management's control (eg, amount of salaries paid), external assumptions are not under management's control (eg, the corporation tax rate), while hypothetical assumptions are usually reasonable assumptions, but are not verifiable due to (normally) the long time period to which they relate.

All material assumptions will be stated along with any forecast or projection; to be material an assumption must be able to have a significant or material effect on the outcome of the forecast or projection.

5.2 Responsibilities of management

The primary responsibility of management with respect to prospective financial information is to produce this information. Management's work on the prospective financial information may be summarised as

(a) to prepare the prospective financial information, including the making of all material assumptions that will affect it

(b) to provide written evidence of acceptance to the accountant of the information, which may be by letter or appropriately worded board minute. This will include a statement that the information presents the directors' best expectations of the forecast or projection. If the information includes a profit estimate then a statement indicating that this estimate is accurate to the best of the directors' knowledge and belief will also be required.

Without these written representations, the reporting accountant will not issue his report because he would not have collected all the normal evidence that he requires.

5.3 The reporting accountant

The company's auditor will normally be the reporting accountant, except in the situation where the company is applying to the Stock Exchange for a listing, in which case an independent accountant is required.

Where the prospective financial information is to be included in a prospectus, the reporting accountant may have to provide brokers and issuing houses with further reports, or 'comfort letters' on the financial information provided by their mutual client. Where these letters are required, the reporting accountant should contact the broker etc and agree the nature and extent of the report required.

5.4 Period covered by prospective financial information

The reporting accountant will need to ensure that the period covered by the prospective financial information is appropriate. This may be done by

(a) looking at the operating cycle of the company eg,

(i) a construction company may take the length of time to complete a relevant project as the reporting period, or

(ii) if a new product is being introduced a fairly short future time period could be appropriate, broken down into monthly or even weekly segments, or

(iii) a property company owning many properties under long term leases could take the length of the lease to be the appropriate reporting period

(b) alternatively, the purpose of the prospective financial information will determine the length of the reporting period. An obvious example here is a report for a bank to extend loan facilities. Here the period required by the bank would become the time period in the prospective financial information.

5.5 Work of the reporting accountant

The reporting accountant will need to perform his work in accordance with his professional standards. As a minimum his work will include the following

(a) **Management information system**

A review will be undertaken of the quality of any management information system and the experience of management themselves to ensure that any prospective financial information is reliable.

(b) **Accounting policies**

The accounting policies to be used in the prospective financial information must be reviewed for acceptability through comparison with the company's normal accounting policies, or to industry norms.

(c) **Key variables**

The accountant must ensure that management have identified the key variables that could affect the prospective financial information. This will be done by comparing his knowledge of the company and industry with the key variables already identified by management.

(d) **Assumptions**

Management will produce the assumptions, and convert them into the financial data in the prospective financial information. These assumptions must be checked by the accountant to confirm that they are reasonable, and in particular that

(i) the assumptions produced are appropriate and that no key assumptions have been omitted

(ii) key assumptions have been identified by checking how much the prospective financial information changes given changes in the assumptions (sensitivity analysis). The accountant will also ensure that management have considered the sensitivity of the assumptions in their work

(iii) there is sufficient support for the assumptions by

(1) agreement of assumptions to background information

(2) ensuring the consistency of assumptions with supporting information

(3) ensuring that they are consistent with each other

(4) checking that any audited financial information used to produce the assumptions is reliable

(5) ensuring they are realistic

(6) ensuring that they are appropriate to the business, and

(7) checking that any risks identified are compatible with the assumptions.

Internal assumptions should be well documented, but external assumptions need have far less documentation. Hypothetical assumptions will also require a review to ensure that they are reasonable. Evidence to support such assumptions is likely to be minimal, because they will normally relate to the long term future.

(e) **Profit estimates**

Prospective financial information can relate to expired, or partly expired accounting periods. The accountant must therefore ensure that any data taken from the accounting records has been correctly extracted. This will be ensured by

(i) reviewing the accounting system and any internal controls

(ii) applying analytical review techniques to the information extracted including ratio analysis, and comparison between the prospective financial information and management accounts for expected results and final accounts for expired accounting periods

(iii) enquiring of responsible personnel whether any problems were encountered in extracting the information

(iv) discussing with management any significant issues that arise from analytical review or other work

(v) checking consistency of the prospective financial information with the company's accounting policies

(vi) vouching supporting documentation for major transactions, and

(vii) reviewing in detail high risk areas.

(f) **Working capital**

The accountant must ensure that the working capital requirements of any forecast are correctly identified. Similarly, key assumptions in a working capital forecast should be adequately disclosed in the prospective financial information.

(g) **Borrowing facilities**

When the working capital requirement has been identified, the accountant must ensure that this requirement will be met from some source, be this a bank or perhaps a share issue. The facts regarding the sources of finance should also be agreed to the relevant assumptions in the prospective financial information.

(h) **Clerical accuracy of the forecast**

The accountant must ensure that the forecast is clerically accurate. The amount of work performed here will be determined by his assessment of the competence of the company's procedures.

5.6 Activity

What do you think are the differences in the accountant's work on a projection rather than a forecast?

5.7 Activity solution

The accountant's work on a projection is almost the same as the work required on a forecast. The only differences that should be taken account of are

(a) A projection may include hypothetical assumptions. If this is the case then the accountant will need to ensure that these assumptions are consistent with the purposes of the projection.

(b) The projection should be clearly stated to be a projection, perhaps with the words 'This projection does not constitute a forecast.....'

(c) The accountant's report will note the increased uncertainty which affect projections.

5.8 Work on cash flow and working capital requirements statements

The work of the reporting accountant on cash flows and working capital requirements will again be similar to the work required on a forecast or projection. The differences in the work for a cash flow or working capital report are as follows

(a) The accountant must check that the statement has been produced using the same assumptions as the corresponding forecast or projection, and that the additional assumptions required for the cash flow (eg, payment dates for debtors and creditors) are consistent with the initial assumptions, and have been correctly applied.

(b) The cash requirement of the business will be confirmed with the appropriate third party, that is the bank or other lending institution. If the lending requirements are not confirmed then this will be mentioned in the accountant's report.

(c) If a prospectus is issued, then the Stock Exchange will require the directors to produce a statement that the working capital of the company is sufficient to meet their present requirements. Although the directors will have to produce the cash flow forecasts so that they can make this statement, they will often ask the accountant to check their work and provide a 'comfort letter' on these statements.

5.9 Accountant's report on the prospective financial information

In *private* documents (eg, to a bank for loan finance) the accountant must report on whether anything has come to his attention that

(a) indicates that the assumptions do not provide a reasonable basis for management's forecast or projection, and

(b) that the prospective financial information has been properly compiled on the basis of the stated assumptions, and

(c) is presented on a basis consistent with the accounting policies normally adopted by the enterprise.

The accountant will not report on whether the results will be achieved, because he will not have the evidence to state this, the future is always uncertain.

Note that in *public* documents only the second and third statements will be given for the reasons highlighted above. This is because the Stock Exchange does not allow the publication of internal assumptions and the accountant cannot therefore give an opinion on assumptions that are not part of the document.

6 STOCK EXCHANGE CIRCULARS

6.1 Introduction

Shareholders in quoted companies usually receive interim accounts, containing summarised results for the first half of the year, plus the annual accounts after the end of the year. This section is concerned with the additional information which a shareholder may receive from the company. Examples include

(a) circulars giving details of material acquisitions and disposals
(b) circulars giving notification of proposed rights issues
(c) take-over offer documents
(d) circulars giving details of proposed changes in capital structure
(e) reminders to holders of convertible loan stock of the option to convert to ordinary shares.

Exam questions place you in the position of giving advice to the investor.

6.2 Acquisitions and realisations of assets by listed companies

During the year, a company may acquire or dispose of assets (eg, shareholdings) which are significant in relation to the group. Where such transactions are sufficiently material, the company must send a circular to its shareholders giving them the necessary information required by the *Yellow Book.*

For a transaction to be considered sufficiently material, one of the following four conditions must be satisfied

(a) value of assets acquired or disposed of amount to 25% or more of assets of the acquiring or disposing company

(b) pre-tax profits attributable to assets acquired or disposed of amount to 25% or more of assets of the acquiring or disposing company

(c) aggregate value of consideration given or received amounts to more than 25% of the assets of the acquiring or disposing company

(d) equity capital issued as consideration amounts to more than 25% of the equity capital previously in issue.

In such an event the *consent* of the shareholders to the proposed transaction is required.

The contents of the circular are as follows

(a) particulars of the assets being acquired or disposed of, including the name of any company or business, where this is relevant

(b) a description of the trade carried on

(c) the aggregate value of the consideration, explaining how this is being satisfied, including the terms of any arrangements for payment on a deferred basis

(d) in the case of a disposal, information concerning the effect on the realising company and, where appropriate, the use to which it is proposed to put the consideration

(e) in the case of a disposal for which shares and other securities are received in consideration, whether such securities are to be sold or retained

(f) the value of the assets being acquired or disposed of

(g) pre-tax profits attributable to the assets being acquired or disposed of

(h) the benefits which are expected to accrue to the company as a result of the transaction

(i) details of any service contracts of proposed directors of the company.

If the acquisition is an acquisition of an unlisted company which becomes a subsidiary as a result of the transaction, an *accountant's report* on the unlisted company is required. The accountant's report is similar to the report issued in connection with a prospectus for a company seeking a listing.

6.3 Exam questions

The type of questions you may expect in this area include

(a) Being presented with extracts from the circular and asked to explain the commercial reasons and financial accounts effects of the transaction. Your knowledge of merger and acquisition accounting will probably be of most relevance here.

(b) Being presented with financial accounts of an unlisted company and asked to discuss/compute figures for the accountant's report.

6.4 Rights issue circulars

If a listed company wishes to raise finance by means of an issue of shares, a rights issue involves less cost than an issue by prospectus. The rights issue gives each existing shareholder the right to subscribe cash for further shares in the company. If he does not wish to take up the rights issue, the shareholder may sell his rights for cash.

The following is an extract from the rights issue circular sent to the shareholders of Casket plc on 4 May 1990

Dear Shareholder

Introduction

Your directors yesterday announced a proposal to raise approximately £5.3 million, net of expenses, by way of a rights issue. The new ordinary shares will be offered at 15p per share, payable in full on acceptance, to shareholders on the register on 14 May 1990, on the basis of 1 new ordinary share for each ordinary share held. The issue has been underwritten by Renaissance. I am writing to you to explain why your board considers it desirable to raise additional finance in this way and to seek the necessary approvals.

Reasons for the rights issue

The interim report which is set out in Appendix I shows that in the six months to December 1989 the group suffered the effects of a high level of borrowings and the adverse impact of prevailing interest rates. Demand for many of the group's products was reduced by the poor retail climate which eroded margins, and the recent warm winters have led to a down-turn in the sales of quilted products, which represent a significant proportion of group turnover. In addition, the stock controls within the group were inadequate, resulting in unacceptably high levels of obsolete and slow-moving stock. The interim results include significant exceptional losses relating to the reduction of this stock.

During this time there were many changes in senior management personnel within the group, which reduced the effectiveness of any action taken to address these problems.

Following my appointment as Chief Executive in January 1990, it is now the group's strategy to

(a) Retain a vigorous textiles division whilst developing a spread of core businesses to reduce the group's dependence on the volatile textile sector. The businesses which are retained will be focused on specific market areas where the group has the potential to have a significant presence.

(b) Reduce bank indebtedness by the sale of non-core businesses and properties, introduce stock reduction programmes, and eliminate surplus production capacity and overheads.

The changes which have been implemented will take time to produce results and your board believes that an injection of new equity is required in order to reduce further the group's gearing, to increase its available working capital and, having strengthened its capital base, to enable it to take advantage of opportunities for acquisitions as they arise. No specific acquisitions are currently envisaged but your board intends to add to its existing activities as and when suitable acquisitions have been identified.

Details of the rights issues

(a) **Terms of the issue**

Subject, *inter alia,* to the passing of resolutions 1 and 2 set out in the Notice of extraordinary general meeting convened for 21 May 1990 at the end of this document, your board proposes to offer, by way of rights, to shareholders on the register at the close of business on 14 May 1990, 37,739,508 new ordinary shares of 10p each at 15p per share payable in full on acceptance on the basis of

1 new ordinary share for each ordinary share held

and so in proportion for any greater number of ordinary shares held on that date.

The new ordinary shares will, when fully paid, rank *pari passu* in all respects with the existing issued ordinary shares, save that they will not rank for any final dividend which may be declared, made or paid in respect of the financial period ended 31 March 1990.

Application has been made to the Council of the Stock Exchange for the new ordinary shares to be admitted to the Official List. It is expected that dealings in the new ordinary shares, in nil paid form, will commence on 22 May 1990.

(b) **Acceptance and payment**

It is expected that renounceable provisional allotment letters in respect of the new ordinary shares will be despatched by first class post on 21 May 1990 at the risk of the persons entitled thereto. The provisional allotment letters will contain full details regarding acceptance and payment and the procedure to be followed if you wish to dispose of all or part of your entitlement.

(c) **Underwriter**

The rights issue has been fully underwritten by Renaissance, whose registered office is at 10th Floor, Beaufort House, 15 St Botolph Street, London EC3A 7EE.

Extraordinary general meeting

There is set out at the end of this document a notice convening an extraordinary general meeting for 11.00am on 21 May 1990. The present authorised but unissued share capital of Casket is insufficient to permit implementation of the rights issue. Accordingly, a resolution will be proposed (a) to increase the authorised ordinary share capital from £5,000,000 to £10,000,000 by the creation of 50,000,000 new ordinary shares in order to implement the rights issue and leave a margin of authorised but unissued ordinary share capital and (b) to authorise your directors to allot the increased ordinary share capital. A resolution will also be proposed at this meeting to approve the underwriting arrangements with the underwriter.

Yours sincerely

J Smith
Chief Executive

6.5 Exam questions

The most likely area to be tested is a general discussion required on the commercial reasons for the rights issue ie, why the company is raising funds. The reasons should be stated in the documentation.

In addition you may be required to show the detailed financial effects to a shareholder ie,

(a) the amount of cash to be paid

(b) when the new shares rank for dividend

(c) explain the options not set out in the documentation

  (i) sale of the rights (if a price is quoted on the Stock Market)
  (ii) sale of part of his shares cum rights in order to finance the balance of the rights issue and thus not lose out on the 'bonus' element.

6.6 Take-over offer documents

As stated earlier in this section, a listed company needs to circularise its shareholders when it acquires a subsidiary which is of a significant size (25%) in relation to the existing group and the consent of the shareholders is required prior to the event.

In addition, where a listed company (A) wishes to take over another listed company (B), A plc (or its agent) will need to issue a *takeover offer document* to the shareholders of company B. A is in many cases making a share-for-share offer, and it therefore needs to inform the B company shareholders of the benefits of accepting the offer. Often the same circular will be sent to the shareholders of A plc, as the contents will satisfy their information needs as laid down in the *Yellow Book.*

The example below is an extract from a recommended offer by Schroders (acting on behalf of Williams Holdings) to the shareholders of Yale & Valor plc. The term 'recommended offer' means that the board of Yale & Valor plc are in agreement with the bid and its terms.

The important extract is the statement of the financial effects of the offer. It is a simple statement and is typical of the manner in which the advantages of accepting the offer are computed. In particular, note the dates at which the market values of the shareholdings are taken. The market value of the Williams shares is taken at the latest practical date prior to the issue of the document, as this gives the best indication to the Yale & Valor shareholders of the value of the new shares at the latest date before rumour relating to a possible offer caused an upward movement in the share price, as this gives the best indication to the Yale & Valor shareholders of the value of their shares if the bid does not go through.

Extract from Offer Document

2. THE OFFER

On behalf of Williams, we hereby offer to acquire, on the terms and subject to the conditions set out or referred to in this document and in the Form of Acceptance, all the Yale and Valor Ordinary Shares on the following basis:

For every 4 Yale and Valor Ordinary Shares 5 New Williams Ordinary Shares

and so in proportion for any other number of Yale and Valor Ordinary Shares.

Yale and Valor will, upon the Offer becoming or being declared unconditional in all respects pay a special second interim dividend of 12.65p net per Yale and Valor Ordinary Share in respect of the year ending 31 March 1991. This compares with a final dividend of 6.15p net per Yale and Valor Ordinary Share in respect of the year ended 31 March 1990. This dividend will be payable to Yale and Valor Shareholders on the register at the close of business on the date on which the Offer becomes or is declared unconditional in all respects and to other persons who become holders of Yale and Valor Ordinary Shares as a result of the exercise of options under the Yale and Valor Share Option Schemes while the Offer remains open for acceptance. It will be paid within 21 days of the date on which the Offer becomes or is declared wholly unconditional or, in the case of Yale and Valor Ordinary Shares arising on the exercise of options as referred to above, within 21 days after the date of issue of such shares if this is later.

The New Williams Ordinary Shares to be issued pursuant to the Offer will rank pari passu in all respects with existing Williams Ordinary Shares, except that they will not rank for the final dividend in respect of the year ended 31 December 1990; the Directors of Williams have stated that they expect to recommend a final dividend of 7.25p net.

Fractions of New Williams Ordinary Shares will not be allotted or issued to accepting Yale and Valor Shareholders. Fractional entitlements to New Williams Ordinary Shares will be aggregated and sold in the market and the net proceeds of sale distributed pro rata to the Yale and Valor Shareholders entitled to them. However, individual entitlement to amounts of less than £2.50 will not be paid to Yale and Valor Shareholders but will be retained for the benefit of the Enlarged Group.

3. FINANCIAL EFFECTS OF ACCEPTANCE OF THE OFFER

The following table shows, for illustrative purposes only, the effect on capital value and income for accepting Yale and Valor Shareholders upon the Offer becoming or being declared unconditional in all respects, on the basis set out below:

(a) **Capital value**

Value of the Offer per Yale and Valor Ordinary Share(1)	288.8p
Market quotation of each Yale and Valor Ordinary Share(2)	175.5p
A premium of	113.3p
This represents an increase of(3)	**64.5%**

(b) **Income**

Gross dividend income on five New Williams Ordinary Shares(4)	78.3p
Gross dividend income on four Yale and Valor Ordinary Shares(5)	53.6p
An increase of	24.7p
This represents an increase of	**46.1%**

Notes:

(1) The value of the Offer is based on the middle market quotation of Williams Ordinary Shares of 231p as derived from The Stock Exchange Daily Official List for 6 February 1991 (being the latest practicable date prior to the posting of this document).

(2) The market quotation of Yale and Valor Ordinary Shares is based on their middle market quotation as derived from The Stock Exchange Daily Official List for 28 January 1991 (being the day before rumour relating to a possible offer for Yale and Valor caused an upward movement in the share price).

(3) Based on the middle market quotation of a Yale and Valor Ordinary Share of 199.5p as derived from the Stock Exchange Daily Official List for 29 January 1991 (the day before the announcement by Yale and Valor that it was in discussions which might lead to an offer), the Offer would represent an increase in capital value of 44.7 per cent.

(4) The gross dividend income on New Williams Ordinary Shares is based on the aggregate of the final dividend of 7.0p net for each Williams Ordinary Share paid in respect of the year ended 31 December 1989 and the interim dividend of 4.75p net per Williams Ordinary Share paid in respect of the year ended 31 December 1990 together with associated tax credits of 25/75ths of the net dividends paid.

(5) The gross dividend income on Yale and Valor Ordinary Shares is based on the aggregate of the final dividend of 6.15p net per Yale and Valor Ordinary Share in respect of the year ended 31 March 1990 and the interim dividend of 3.9p net per Yale and Valor Ordinary Share paid in respect of the current financial year, together with associated tax credits of 25/75ths of the net dividends paid.

Save as stated in notes (4) and (5) no account has been taken on any liability for taxation or the treatment of fractions of shares in assessing the financial effects of acceptance of the Offer.

6.7 Exam questions

A typical exam question presents extracts from the offer without the section showing the financial effects of the offer. You are then required to show the financial effects. There is no set format but clearly the illustrative example is a useful format to follow.

6.8 Activity

Hood plc had carried on business since 20X1 as the manufacturer of ceramic products used in the electronic industry. At 31 March 20X7 the company was considering undertaking a major capital investment programme which would start in 20X8 to support its current success in building up sales volume in Europe.

The following information is available based on the consolidated profit and loss accounts of the Hood Group for the five years ended 31 March 20X7

Year ended 31 March	*20X3*	*20X4*	*20X5*	*20X6*	*20X7 (draft)*
	£'000	£'000	£'000	£'000	£'000
Turnover	9,712	12,382	15,331	18,492	26,894
Profit after tax	446	580	1,544	1,860	2,500
Dividends per share:					
Ordinary shares (p)	4.7	5.7	6.2	7.0	8.5

Cloak plc is a company that operates in the same industry as Hood plc with strong sales in the UK and USA. The directors of Cloak plc have become aware of Hood's success in penetrating the European market and considered that a merger of the two companies made sound commercial sense. They have indicated that they were considering an offer of two Cloak plc shares for each Hood plc share or a cash alternative of 550p per share.

The following information is available concerning the Cloak Group

Year ended 31 March	*20X3*	*20X4*	*20X5*	*20X6*	*20X7*
Turnover (£m)	300	350	425	495	550
Dividends per share:					
Ordinary shares (p)	4.8	4.8	4.8	5.2	6.5

Price data

The share price of an ordinary share in Cloak plc was 300p on 31 March 20X7.

The finance director of Hood plc has advised his board that based on his analysis of stock market companies, in his estimation the value of a Hood plc share would be 500p if the company's shares were themselves to be quoted on the stock market.

The FT Actuaries fixed interest average gross redemption yield for 25 year high coupon gilts on 31 March 20X7 was 6.5%.

Calculate the financial effects on the holder of 100 ordinary shares in Hood plc of accepting shares or cash from Cloak plc ignoring UK taxation of capital gains. Assume tax credits are available at $^{10}/_{90}$ of the net dividends paid.

6.9 Activity solution

Accepting shares

		£
Capital	Current position, 100 shares × 500p	500
	After accepting share offer, 100 shares × 2 × 300p	600
	Increase in capital value	100
	(Ignoring other price changes)	
Income	Current position, 100 shares × 8.5p × $^{100}/_{90}$	9.44
	(Using 20X7 as typical future dividend)	
	After accepting share offer, 200 shares × 6.5p × $^{100}/_{90}$	14.44
	Increase in gross income	5.00

Capital would increase by 20% and income by over 50%.

Accepting cash

		£
Capital	Current position	500
	Cash	550
	Increase in capital	50
Income	Current position (see above)	9.44
	Cash invested in 'gilts' £550 × 6.5%	35.75
	Increase in income	26.31

Capital would increase by only 10%, but income would increase by nearly four times.

7 OTHER REPORTS

7.1 Introduction

Other reports specifically included in the syllabus are to

(a) lenders to assist in decisions relating to company loan obligations
(b) employees.

7.2 Preparing a report offering advice and guidance to lenders

Information of particular relevance to lenders is covered in various places in this text

(a) Use of prospective financial information

Reporting on forecast profits and cash flow is covered in an earlier section of this chapter. It should be appreciated that this approaches the problem from a 'legalistic' point of view ie, ensuring that the report is only checking the accuracy of the data in relation to the assumptions.

(b) Interpretation of historical financial information

Refer to later chapters covering failure prediction, analysis of cash flow statements and calculation of solvency ratios, both short and long term.

(c) Appointment of receiver and manager or dissolving the company

See later chapter.

7.3 Preparing a report offering advice and guidance to employees

The most common preparation of reports for employees is the production of simplified annual reports that are issued by (mainly) large companies to their employees. These are similar in content to the 'summary financial statements' which listed companies are now allowed to send to their shareholders by the CA89. In addition to the statutory requirements, these will often include 'results at a glance' or 'highlights' statements which give key figures of performance in the accounting period. The figures will often be presented in graphical form such as bar or pie charts.

The following points need to considered if an examination question is set on other reports:

(a) **Profit sharing scheme**

A profit sharing scheme is likely to be set up to comply with the conditions of a profit sharing scheme under the tax legislation. Under such schemes, the share of profits paid to employees are deductible as wage costs for corporation tax but are tax free to the employees. Clearly in such a situation, the accountant will be suggesting a scheme which falls within the legislation. Such questions are unlikely to be set in the FRE examination but you will need to use your knowledge of such schemes from the Tax Planning syllabus.

A scheme may however be set up outside the framework of the tax legislation. There are quite strict limits on the amounts payable under such schemes and the employer company may wish its employees (or a certain class of its employees) to participate in a much more significant way in the profits of the company. Your main task is likely to be the production of expected profit shares to a number of employees under a range of profit estimates. Past profits may be used to estimate the range of profits arising in the future.

The scheme may involve the gift of shares or share options to selected employees. Such schemes are a means of sharing profits in that the shares will have an entitlement to dividends rather than an immediate distribution of profits as a wage cost. In practice, tax considerations will weigh heavily as to the precise form of the scheme.

(b) **Pay negotiations**

An accountant is only likely to be involved in this area if he is employed by a trade union or other employee organisation. Matters that he may need to cover include:

- analysis of current pay and monetary worth of benefits
- comparison with other employer companies in same industry and other sectors

- effect of claims on employer showing expected benefits (eg, increased productivity, increased turnover) as well as expected costs

- recommendations on possible success of scheme and suggestions of alternative points to raise during the negotiation process.

(c) **Redundancies**

The same accountant employed in (b) above may also have the task of advising on redundancies. Most accountants are more likely to be involved in this area in devising a redundancy scheme for the employer. Clearly, it is essential to remember in an exam question to whom the report is being written.

The range of situations you may be presented with is wide. For example the impetus for a report may be the desire to save jobs and thus the scheme proposed by the employer needs to be examined with a view to fighting off redundancies by countering the employer's claims regarding the state of the market or suggesting productivity gains that may be achieved. Alternatively the employees may have accepted the inevitability of the redundancies and are asking for advice as to the amount of redundancy pay being offered under a voluntary redundancy scheme.

8 INTERIM REPORTS

8.1 Introduction

Interim reports are required by the London Stock Exchange as a condition of listing. They play an important role as a progress report in the continuing reporting process of the operating, financing and investing activities of a business.

Apart from the London Stock Exchange requirements, there has been little guidance for preparers of UK interim reports.

In September 1997 the ASB issued a Statement *Interim Reports*. Like the Statement on Operating and Financial Review it is intended to be a statement of best practice and its adoption is voluntary.

One of the recommendations of the Committee on the Financial Aspects of Corporate Governance (the Cadbury Committee) was that the ASB and the London Stock Exchange should clarify the accounting principles to be adopted by companies when preparing their interim reports. It also recommended that balance sheet information should be included with the interim report. The Statement has been developed in response to these recommendations.

8.2 Approaches

There are two possible approaches to the preparation of interim reports:

(a) the 'discrete' approach, which treats the interim period as a distinct accounting period and therefore applies the same accounting principles as are applied at the year-end; and

(b) the 'integral' approach, which treats the interim period as part of the larger financial reporting period, meaning that revenues and expenses are recognised as a proportion of estimated annual amounts.

The ASB has adopted the 'discrete' approach. The only exception to this is taxation, which can only be determined at the end of the financial year.

8.3 Main recommendations

(a) Interim reports should be drawn up using the same measurement and recognition bases and accounting policies as are used in the preparation of annual financial statements.

(b) The interim period's tax charges should be based on an estimate of the annual effective tax rate, applied to the interim period's results.

(c) Interim reports should contain the following items:

- Management commentary (an explanation of significant events and trends since the previous annual financial statements)
- Summarised profit and loss account (including segmental analysis and disclosure of discontinued operations and acquisitions). Basic earnings per share should be derived from the results for the interim period and calculated and disclosed in the same manner as at the year end
- Statement of total recognised gains and losses, where relevant
- Summarised balance sheet (based on similar classifications to those used in the annual financial statements)
- Summarised cash flow statement (including reconciliation of operating profit to net operating cash flow and reconciliation of cash flow to the movement in net debt).

(d) Companies are encouraged to make their interim reports available within 60 days of the period end (the Stock Exchange Listing Rules require publication within four months of the end of the period to which they relate).

8.4 Evaluation of the recommendations

Although the recommendations are not mandatory, they are expected to generally improve the standard of interim reporting. In particular, companies are encouraged to present balance sheet and cash flow information and a statement of total recognised gains and losses. (In the past, some companies did not provide this information.)

The recommendations have other advantages:

(a) Most companies will prepare interim statements using the discrete approach and comparability of information between entities should be improved. Previously, some companies have taken the discrete approach and some have taken the integral approach.

(b) Use of the discrete approach should mean that companies will be unable to hide the impact of seasonal trends on their results. Assets and liabilities at the interim period end will have the same meaning as at the year end.

However, the recommendations have been criticised on the following grounds:

(a) Some commentators believe that the recommendations in the Statement should be compulsory, rather than simply a statement of best practice.

(b) Many preparers of interim reports dislike the discrete approach. They argue that the integral approach provides more useful information because it uses the interim results to predict and explain the full year's results. It enables users to assess trends.

9 PRELIMINARY ANNOUNCEMENTS

9.1 Introduction

The London Stock Exchange requires quoted companies to notify the Exchange of their preliminary statement of annual results immediately after Board approval. The preliminary announcement is the first external communication by companies of their financial performance and position for the year. However, there has been very little guidance on their content.

The ASB has issued a Statement on Preliminary Announcements. Like the Statement on Interim Reports, the Statement on Preliminary Announcements is intended to be a non-mandatory guide to best practice.

9.2 Main recommendations

(a) **Content**

The content should be similar to that recommended for interim reports, i.e.:

(i) a narrative commentary
(ii) a summarised profit and loss account
(iii) a statement of total recognised gains and losses
(iv) a summarised balance sheet
(v) a summarised cash flow statement.

As well as the results for the full year, data for the final interim period (ie, the second half-year) should be separately presented and commented upon.

(b) **Timeliness**

Companies are encouraged to issue their preliminary announcement within 60 days of the year end.

(c) **Reliability**

Information given should be reliable and consistent with the 'yet to be published' audited financial statements. It should therefore be based on material upon which the audit is substantially complete.

The recommendation that the second half-year's results should be presented in addition to results for the full year may prove controversial. The reasoning behind this is that the market tends to react more quickly to previously unreported information about the second half-year (the period not covered by the interim report). However, many preparers of accounts may believe that the usefulness of the second half-year's results does not outweigh the additional cost of presenting the extra information unless it is particularly relevant (eg, where the business is highly seasonal).

10 YEAR END FINANCIAL REPORTS: IMPROVING COMMUNICATION

10.1 Reasons for reviewing present practice

The financial statements that listed companies prepare each year for their shareholders have become much longer and more complex in recent years. Recent changes in financial reporting requirements are widely acknowledged to have improved the quality of information provided. However, there is evidence that much of the more detailed information now required to be disclosed is aimed at and understood only by institutional investors and other expert users. There are two potential disadvantages of this:

(a) the cost of preparing and distributing annual financial statements may exceed the benefit to shareholders;

(b) the majority of shareholders, who have less time and expertise, are worse off than before because the information that is of interest and importance to them is lost in the detail.

Listed companies are permitted to send summary financial statements to shareholders who choose to receive them instead of the full financial statements, but in practice many companies do not do so.

The ASB has responded to these concerns by issuing a Discussion Paper: *Year-end financial reports: Improving communication.* The Paper reviews the ways in which financial statements of listed companies could be simplified for private shareholders. It also considers the implications of the growing importance of the Internet, although it does not make any firm proposals.

The publication of the Discussion Paper coincides with a review of company law by the Department of Trade and Industry (DTI). One of the issues that this review is considering is possible changes to reporting requirements.

10.2 Is there a need for change?

It has been suggested that the problem of information overload could be addressed without changing the reporting framework:

(a) Good referencing within the financial statements and possibly colour coding different sections might enable private shareholders who have a serious interest in the performance of a company to identify the information of interest to them. However, there is evidence that many shareholders read only a small proportion of the full financial statements and would prefer a shorter document. In addition, it is not necessarily easy to highlight key financial information of general interest within the full financial statements. If key disclosures are placed together they are out of context within the full financial statements and if they are colour coded shareholders still have to read through the full financial statements in order to find them.

(b) Unnecessary disclosures could be eliminated from the full financial statements; this would benefit professional users, as well as private shareholders. Research has been undertaken to identify required disclosures that were not used in the decisions made by financial analysts. As a result of this, the ASB has concluded that there was very limited scope for reducing the content of the full financial statements.

(c) Summary financial statements may already be sent to shareholders who prefer them to the full financial statements. However, many listed companies choose not to prepare them partly because of the additional cost and partly because it was felt that it was unwise to reduce the information provided to shareholders in a post-Cadbury climate where fuller disclosure is being emphasised. There is also evidence that in practice summary financial statements are not as user friendly as legislation intended.

10.3 Possible solutions

As a result of the problems outlined above, the ASB considered ways in which the process of producing summary financial statements might be made attractive to companies.

(a) The law could be reframed so that summary financial statements become the main reports sent to shareholders. This would have the advantage of overcoming concern that shareholders might be deprived of information. Although it would not in itself reduce costs, the role of the full financial statements would probably change, so that they became either 'plain paper' or electronic documents. This would be in tune with current developments, such as the growth of reporting via the Internet.

(b) A single two-part document could be prepared, instead of two stand-alone documents. The first part would contain the summary financial statements and would be sent to all shareholders. The second would contain the additional information required to make up the full financial statements and would be available only on request. This alternative would reduce both costs and administrative problems associated with preparing two separate documents, but also has disadvantages:

- The notes to the financial statements might not be easy to allocate to either one of the two parts. Some would have to be split between the two, making the financial statements less comprehensible.

- It could be especially difficult to divide the operating and financial review between the two parts. Therefore the whole of the operating and financial review would be included in the summary financial statements, obscuring the information of particular interest to private shareholders.

10.4 Main proposals

The ASB proposes that:

(a) the law should be reframed so that summary financial statements become the main report for shareholders. All listed companies would prepare them.

(b) the full audited financial statements should continue to be produced for those who request them and for filing purposes. They could become less important as promotional documents and in time might evolve into 'plain paper' formats.

(c) summary financial statements should be required by legislation to contain at least the financial information recommended by the Statement of best practice on preliminary announcements (discussed above) together with details of directors remuneration.

The advantages of basing the requirements and recommendations for summary financial statements on those for preliminary announcements would be that:

(a) the preliminary announcement is carefully designed to provide a focused summary of the key aspects of the company's financial performance for the period. Although it is prepared for institutional investors, its succinct format could be an ideal basis for the summary financial statements.

(b) costs and administrative efforts would be minimised if the contents of the two reports were similar.

(c) because only a very basic financial content would be prescribed, companies would retain the flexibility to adapt the summary financial statements to best reflect their widely varying circumstances and the needs of their particular shareholders.

The Discussion Paper also proposes that companies legislation should also be amended to permit (but not require) companies to offer their shareholders the option of receiving a simplified financial review instead of summary financial statements. This would comprise a few pages of narrative highlighting key financial measures and explaining them in a readily understandable manner.

If these proposals meet with support, the ASB will submit proposals for changes in legislation to the Department of Trade and Industry (DTI). The proposals will be developed into a non-mandatory Statement of best practice.

10.5 The impact of the Internet on financial reporting

Introduction

The Internet has several implications for financial reporting:

(a) on-line trading is relatively cheap and this means that the number of private investors is growing;

(b) information about companies and other organisations is being accessed by an increasing number of people, many of whom are private investors; and

(c) the technology itself allows information to be presented in innovative ways.

The DTI is at present considering whether to allow companies to communicate with their shareholders via the Internet if their shareholders so wish. It is likely that in the near future annual reports, interim reports and preliminary announcements will be published on the company's Website as well as, or instead of being distributed to shareholders in printed form. Most large companies already place their annual report on their Website. The ASB believes that entities should also be encouraged to post preliminary announcements and other financial information given to analysts and institutional investors on their Websites. This means that there should be more equality between investors in terms of the information that is available.

New possibilities

At present, most companies simply post the printed annual report and accounts. There are other possibilities:

- 'Hyperlinks' enable users to jump from one area of the financial statements to other areas where the same topic is discussed. This means that users can easily find the information that they need. Use of hyperlinks could help to overcome 'information overload' without removing detailed disclosures that are useful to analysts.

- Some companies already post financial statements on spreadsheets that can be downloaded and merged with those of other companies. This enables comparisons to be made. In future, companies may be able to place a database of audited financial information on the Internet from which users could prepare their own reports, presented in a way that best meets their particular needs.

Another possibility not highlighted by the ASB is that companies may report to shareholders at much more frequent intervals, so that much less emphasis is placed on the traditional annual report. Some commentators (although not all) believe that eventually companies will report in 'real time' so that annual financial statements will become obsolete.

Increased risks

The ASB believes that users will benefit from financial reporting on the Internet, but in its Discussion Paper *Year end financial reports* it also draws attention to the potential risks:

(a) There is an increased risk that information will be inaccurate. Even if electronic financial statements are checked when they are first published, in the absence of adequate controls they might be selectively updated subsequently.

(b) It may be unclear which information is regulated (prepared in accordance with statutory or other requirements) and which is unregulated. Because information can be placed on a Website very easily it is likely that companies will supplement their standardised reports to shareholders with further information, for example, alternative presentations or additional analyses. Users might be misled into thinking that information is regulated when it is not.

(c) Information that is inconsistent with the audited financial statements might be given. Users have no guarantee that unregulated information is consistent with standard financial reports sent to shareholders.

10.6 Responses to the proposals

Although the Discussion Paper has been broadly welcomed, it has been criticised for concentrating on conventional reporting channels. Commentators have pointed out that it does not fully address the possibilities of the Internet, nor does it consider developments such as environmental and social reporting.

11 CHAPTER SUMMARY

SSAP 25 requires listed companies to analyse their operations into geographical and business segments.

The preparation of a report must address the needs of the users of the report and attempt to give clear recommendations.

Reports to shareholders need to be framed within the framework of any regulations governing the issue of financial information eg, is it a prospectus? Other reports to shareholders as to their financial position need to be presented with a straightforward explanation of their income and or capital gain.

12 SELF TEST QUESTIONS

12.1 What is the definition of a class of business? (1.3)

12.2 What is the definition of a geographical segment? (1.4)

12.3 What are the CA85 disclosure requirements regarding the analysis of turnover? (1.5)

12.4 What is a prospectus? (4.2)

12.5 What are the stock exchange requirements for listed companies called? (4.4)

12.6 Who prepares the statement of adjustments? (4.6)

12.7 How should the disposal of a subsidiary be dealt in with a statement of adjustments? (4.6)

12.8 What is the definition of prospective financial information? (5.1)

12.9 What is a profit estimate? (5.1)

12.10 To whom is a take-over offer document sent? (6.6)

13 EXAMINATION TYPE QUESTION

13.1 Betee group

You are required by using the information relating to the Betee group and Baubles plc set out below:

(a) to prepare a brief report to the holder of shares in Baubles plc on the comparative performance of the two groups on the assumption that you are employed as an accountant with the Betee group. **(14 marks)**

(b) to calculate the financial effects of accepting the offer for a holder of 100 Baubles shares. **(10 marks)**

(c) to explain what further information you would require in order to be able to give the holder of Baubles shares independent advice on whether or not to accept the offer. **(6 marks)**

(Total: 30 marks)

Assume income tax at 25% and tax credits at $^{10}/_{90}$ of net dividends.

The Betee group has been considering making a takeover bid for Baubles plc, a company whose share price performance has underperformed the FT Actuaries Industrial Index for the past five years. The following information is available

(i) graph of share price performance

(ii) consolidated profit and loss accounts of the Betee group and of Baubles plc for the six years ending 31 December 20X10

(iii) consolidated balance sheets of the Betee group and of Baubles plc as at 31 December 20X10

(iv) the offer to acquire all of the Baubles shares.

(i) **Graph of share price performance**

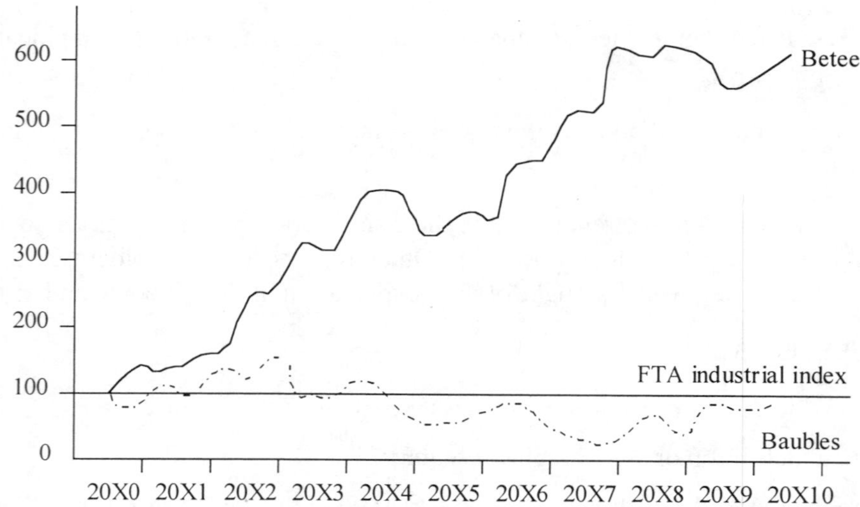

(ii) **Consolidated profit and loss accounts**

The consolidated profit and loss accounts of the Betee group for the six financial years to 31 December 20X10 are set out below

	20X10	*20X9*	*20X8*	*20X7*	*20X6*	*20X5*
	£'000	£'000	£'000	£'000	£'000	£'000
Sales turnover	7,000.0	6,000.0	3,500.0	1,300.0	1,200.0	900.0
Earnings for the year	456.1	339.7	198.3	120.1	99.9	75.3
Earnings per share	24.0p	18.0p	13.0p	9.0p	8.0p	7.0p
Dividends per share	9.0p	6.0p	4.0p	3.0p	3.0p	2.0p

The consolidated profit and loss accounts of Baubles plc for the six financial years to 31 December 20X10 are set out below

	20X10	*20X9*	*20X8*	*20X7*	*20X6*	*20X5*
	£'000	£'000	£'000	£'000	£'000	£'000
Sales turnover	2,283.0	2,185.0	1,990.0	1,800.0	1,700.0	2,000.0
Licence fees	17.0	15.0	10.0	-	-	-
Total turnover	2,300.0	2,200.0	2,000.0	1,800.0	1,700.0	2,000.0
Earnings for the year	56.9	70.0	40.6	7.2	(11.1)	57.6
Earnings per share	15.0p	22.0p	13.0p	2.0p	(4.0p)	24p
Dividends per share	13.0p	12.0p	11.0p	10.0p	10.0p	12.0p

(iii) **Consolidated balance sheets as at 31 December 20X10**

	Betee group	*Baubles plc*
	£'000	£'000
Capital employed		
Fixed assets		
Tangible	1,782.3	1,852.8
Intangible - patents	20.0	450.0

Current assets	3,600.2	1,273.5
Creditors due within one year	(2,322.4)	(821.6)
Net current assets	1,277.8	451.9
Total assets less current liabilities	3,080.1	2,754.7
Creditors due after more than one year	(946.4)	(392.2)
Provisions for liabilities and charges	(211.2)	(314.2)
	1,922.5	2,048.3
Financed by		
Shareholders' funds	1,777.2	1,745.9
Minority interests	145.3	302.4
	1,922.5	2,048.3

(iv) **The offer to acquire all of the Baubles shares**

Betee plc offered to acquire all of the Baubles shares on the following terms

For every 100 Baubles shares

45 new Betee ordinary shares, and
£135 nominal of Betee convertible stock, and
£270 in cash.

The following additional information was available

(i) The middle market quotation for a Betee share was 280p.
(ii) The middle market quotation for a Baubles share was 497p.
(iii) The Betee convertible stock was valued at £95 per cent.

The Betee convertible stock was to carry interest at the rate of 9.0% pa payable half yearly in June and December and was to be convertible into Betee ordinary shares during the month of July in any of the years from 20X15 to 20X30 at the rate of one Betee ordinary share for every 350p nominal of Betee convertible stock. The first interest payment on the Betee convertible stock was to be made on 30 June 20X11 and was to be in respect of the period from the date of first issue of any of the Betee convertible stock to 30 June 20X11, both dates inclusive. All outstanding Betee convertible stock will be redeemed at par on 31 December 20X30.

(iv) Ordinary shares in Betee are expected to receive a net dividend of 11.25p per share in 20X11.

(v) The return on long dated government bonds is 7% gross.

(vi) Ordinary shares in Baubles are expected to receive a net dividend of 13.5p per share in 20X11.

14 ANSWER TO EXAMINATION TYPE QUESTION

14.1 Betee group

(Tutorial notes:

(1) Remember that your answer to part (a) should be in report format, and that it is addressed to a shareholder of one company but prepared by the accountant of the other company. Your answer should therefore concentrate on the relatively favourable aspects of the performance of the company employing the accountant.

(2) Calculations for part (b) should cover both capital and earnings effect of the offer.

(3) General accounting knowledge should allow you to develop a relevant answer for part (c).*)*

(a) **REPORT**

To: A shareholder of Baubles plc

From: AN Accountant, Betee group

Date: X-X-20XX

Subject: **Relative performance of Baubles plc and the Betee group**

During the six year period 20X5 to 20X10 the turnover of Baubles plc has been variable and has grown by only 15% over this period from £2,000,000 in 20X5 to £2,300,000 in 20X10. By comparison the turnover of the Betee group has grown rapidly, as can be seen from the following analysis

	Turnover £'000	*Annual percentage increase*	*Percentage of base year: 20X5*
20X5	900	-	100.0
20X6	1,200	33.3	133.3
20X7	1,300	8.3	144.4
20X8	3,500	169.2	388.9
20X9	6,000	71.4	666.7
20X10	7,000	16.7	777.8

The Betee group has been able to generate an increasing level of profitability from this expanding activity. The earnings per share in 20X10 was nearly 3.5 times that which was achieved in 20X5 and, in particular, growth in the past two years has averaged over 30%. In contrast, the earnings per share of Baubles plc has been very variable, being negative in 20X6 and for the most recent year declined by nearly 32% from the previous year's figure. Clearly the consistent increase of turnover and earnings of the Betee group compares very favourably with the performances achieved by Baubles plc.

The directors of Baubles plc have attempted to maintain a reasonably consistent dividend per share even though the earnings have been variable. Compare this with the constantly increasing level of dividend for the shareholders of the Betee group. In addition, the dividend payouts of Baubles plc have not always been covered by the earnings achieved during that period eg, a loss in 20X6 clearly does not cover the 10.0p dividend per share payout. For the Betee group dividend cover has usually been around 3 times, although the cover in the most recent year, 20X10, was only 2.67 times. Based on these figures it can be concluded that the ability of the Betee group to cover its dividends is better than that of Baubles plc. This point should be remembered when considering the forecast net dividend of 13.5p of Baubles plc.

As a result of these past performances the Betee group is currently reporting returns on shareholders' capital in excess of 22%. The return attributable to the shareholders' funds of Baubles plc for the same period, 20X10, was only 2.4%. Similar levels of funds are generating very different levels of return.

This should give you some insight into the relative performance of the Betee group and Baubles plc. If you require any further details or a clarification of any of the points made in this report, do not hesitate to contact me.

(b) **Capital financial effects on 100 shares of Baubles plc**

	£	£
Current market value of offer		
Betee ordinary shares 45 × 280p	126.00	

Betee convertible stock $135 \times \frac{£95}{£100}$	128.25	
Cash	270.00	
		524.25
Current market value of 100 shares in Baubles plc 100 × 497p		497.00
Gain		£27.25

Gain would be reduced by £20.25 if convertible stock converted to ordinary shares.

Income financial effects on 100 shares of Baubles plc

Income on offer	£	£
Gross dividend on 45 Betee shares 45 × 11.25p × $^{100}/_{90}$	5.63	
Interest on convertible stock £135 × 9%	12.15	
Interest on cash investments in government bonds £270 × 7%	18.90	
		36.68
Current gross dividend of 100 shares in Baubles plc 100 × 13.5p × $^{100}/_{90}$		15.00
Gain		£21.68

If the convertible stock were converted, gross dividend would be $\frac{£135}{£3.50} \times 11.25p \times {}^{100}/_{90} = £4.82$. Gain would be reduced by £7.33.

In all cases there are clearly capital and income gains to be made by a holder of Baubles shares under this offer.

(c) Before giving advice on whether or not to accept the offer, additional information required would probably include the following

(i) the relevance of past performance to attainable future performance

(ii) detailed analysis of the net assets of the two groups, including a trend analysis of the past few years; details of capital expenditure budgets may prove to be useful

(iii) the effect on the management and organisation of Betee group of the acquisition of Baubles plc

(iv) details of the patents held by Baubles plc

(v) an assessment of the usefulness of the relatively low gearing of Baubles plc to the Betee group

(vi) the effect that such an acquisition may have on the customers and suppliers of Baubles plc and the Betee group.

21 SHARE VALUATION

INTRODUCTION & LEARNING OBJECTIVES

This chapter considers the type of advice and reports a professional accountant in practice may be required to produce.

The two main types of advice relate to

(a) quoted companies and their relationship to the stock exchange and their investors
(b) share valuations.

The emphasis in this chapter is on the methods used in practice to value shares. The more sophisticated methods in financial management theory such as DCF and CAPM tend to be used to assist financial analysts in the valuation of quoted shares. In the context of an unquoted company, there is generally insufficient information to use these methods.

Share valuations will often be set in the examination within the context of the preparation of a report and thus the principles of report writing explained in the previous chapter apply in this chapter as well.

You should find that your knowledge already gained or yet to be gained for the Financial Strategy paper is complementary to this area of the FRE syllabus.

When you have studied this chapter you should be able to do the following:

- Calculate a range of values for shares in an unquoted company.
- Prepare reports to prospective buyers/sellers.

1 ASSESSING THE VALUATION OF SHARES IN UNQUOTED COMPANIES

1.1 Introduction

Unquoted companies may be required to be valued for various reasons. The two main reasons in the context of this syllabus are

(a) for a balance sheet valuation for a company which has a minority shareholding in an unquoted company (ie, a trade investment)

(b) for determining a value of a company being acquired by another company.

In the second situation, the final value is negotiated between the acquirer and the acquiree. The share valuation is an opening reference point in the negotiations.

1.2 Calculating a range of acceptable values for shares in an unquoted company

Shareholdings may be valued in essentially two different ways - either asset based value or income based value. Each of these may be further subdivided

Asset based	-	book value
	-	replacement cost/deprival value
	-	break up value.
Income based	-	dividend yield
	-	PE ratio
	-	NPV of future earnings.

Additionally methods based on a mixture of 'assets' and 'income' may be used.

Although from a theoretical point of view, the only sustainable valuation model is that based on the Net Present Value of future earnings, this model is generally impossible to apply because of the practical difficulties associated with estimating future earning streams, choosing an appropriate discount rate, etc. Accordingly in practice the other methods are more widely used, and may in any event be considered as surrogates for the one theoretically sound method.

Each method is generally considered appropriate to certain sets of circumstances. However, it is common that several valuations of the shares are computed using different bases, and an 'average' of these will form the basis of the figure for final negotiation between the interested parties.

1.3 Dividend yield

The gross dividend yield is defined as

$$\frac{\text{Total annual dividend (gross)}}{\text{Share price}} \times 100\%$$

Note that it is the gross dividend, inclusive of tax credit (where this applies), that is taken into account in computing the gross dividend yield. This is done in order to ease comparison by investors with yields on other securities which are subject to income tax on the whole amount of the income (eg, quoted loan stock).

Thus, for unquoted companies the formula is turned around to give

$$\text{Share value} = \frac{\text{Total annual dividend}}{\text{Suitable dividend yield}}$$

There are then two elements to determine: the total annual dividend to be paid by the private company and what is a 'suitable dividend yield'.

It is essential to compare like with like and consequently it is the current annual dividend which is taken into account irrespective of any growth prospects, etc.

The dividend yield to be applied is chosen by looking at the dividend yield which may be obtained in 'similar' quoted companies.

Any value so found is then normally adjusted downwards, by between 20% and 40% to take into account the non-marketability of the shares in the private company being valued. Alternatively the suitable dividend yield is uplifted with the same end result.

1.4 Activity

You are required to place a value on a 2% holding of shares in Claygro Ltd, a privately owned company manufacturing flowerpots.

You establish the following additional information

Issued share capital: 100,000 £1.00 shares

Current dividend (gross): 4p per share

Quoted companies involved in the manufacture of flowerpots generally have a gross dividend yield of 4%.

1.5 Activity solution

Basic value	=	$\frac{\text{Dividend}}{\text{Dividend yield}}$	
	=	$\frac{4\text{p}}{4\%}$	= £1.00
Less: Discount for non-marketability – say 25%			(0.25)
Value per share			£0.75

∴ value of 2,000 shares is estimated to be £1,500.

This figure might well form a reasonable basis for valuing a small holding of shares, where the owner has little or no influence over the affairs of the company, and is or will be simply the passive recipient of dividends.

1.6 Level of future dividends

The simple formula above considers only the current year's dividend. For a fair comparison the expected rate of growth of dividends of the private and public companies should be similar. Whilst these figures themselves are rarely available a comparison of 'dividend cover' (earnings after tax available to pay dividends ÷ net dividend paid) between the companies may be readily computed, and this may indicate whether a similar level of funds are being retained within the business to finance future growth.

An additional problem with private companies is that typically the shareholders are the same as management and therefore profits may be paid out as salaries, or high pension contributions rather than dividends. This can mean that dividends are often held at an artificially low level in shareholder managed companies compared with what might reasonably be expected by a provider of risk capital.

1.7 Dividend yield to apply

Dividend yields to be applied are those prevailing for quoted companies in the same industrial sector. However, there are a number of reasons why these may need to be adjusted before being used to value the shares

(a) quoted companies are often more diversified in their activities than private companies; consequently it may be difficult to find a quoted company with a similar range of activities

(b) quoted companies are often bigger than private companies; because of the generally accepted benefits which size brings, a higher dividend yield should be sought from a smaller, but otherwise comparable company

(c) levels of gearing may differ between companies and hence affect the dividend yield

(d) other specific factors may need to be taken into account

(e) although a small shareholding is being valued it may hold particular importance to either or both parties (eg, a 2% shareholding being acquired by a 49% shareholder); in such cases the purchaser may be prepared to pay far more than would be indicated by a valuation based on dividend yield.

1.8 Earnings yield or PE ratio

As with dividend yield the PE ratio is turned around to value shares in unquoted companies

Value per share = EPS × a suitable PE ratio

Again, any value thence computed is then normally reduced to take into account the non marketability of the shares.

The earnings yield is the reciprocal of the PE ratio. Thus if given a suitable earnings yield, the formula becomes

$$\text{Value per share} = \frac{\text{EPS}}{\text{Yield \%}}$$

The basic choice for a suitable PE ratio will be that of a quoted company of comparable size in the same industry; and the same difficulties apply as when a suitable dividend yield is sought.

In addition there is a tendency for dividends to be more stable than earnings, consequently since share prices are broadly based on expected future earnings a PE ratio - based on a single year's reported earnings, may be very different for companies in the same sector.

For example, a high PE ratio may indicate

(a) growth stock

the share price is high because continuous high rates of growth of earnings are expected from the stock

(b) no growth stock

the PE ratio is based on the last reported earnings, which perhaps were exceptionally low yet the share price is based on future earnings which are expected to revert to a 'normal' relatively stable level

(c) take-over bid

the share price has risen pending a takeover bid

(d) high security share

shares in property companies typically have low income yields but the shares are still worth buying because of the prospects of capital growth and the high level of security.

Similarly a low PE ratio may indicate

(a) losses expected

future profits are expected to fall from their most recent levels eg, in cyclical industries

(b) share price low

as noted previously share prices may be extremely volatile - special factors, such as a strike at a manufacturing plant of a particular company may depress the share price and hence the PE ratio.

Consequently the main difficulty in trying to apply the model is finding a similar company, with similar growth projects - which again may perhaps be estimated by considering dividend cover, and hence the level of retained profits.

A further difficulty is that the reported earnings are based on historical cost accounts which in general makes a nonsense of trying to compare two companies.

In spite of these serious shortcomings the PE ratio is regarded as an important measure by investment analysts etc, and cannot therefore be disregarded. As a broad brush measure, and as long as exceptional items are identified and treated as such, it may be used to value shares.

It is generally considered to be appropriate where the size of the shareholding is sufficient to influence dividend policy - and therefore the shareholder is more concerned with the underlying level of earnings, rather than just dividends.

1.9 Activity

You are given the following information regarding Accrington Ltd, an unquoted company

(a) Issued ordinary share capital is 400,000 25p shares.

(b) Extract from profit and loss account for the year ended 31 July 20X4

	£	£
Profit before taxation		220,000
Less: Corporation tax		80,000
Profit after taxation		140,000
Less: Preference dividend	20,000	
Ordinary dividend	36,000	
		56,000
Retained profit for the year		£84,000

(c) The PE ratio applicable to a similar type of business (suitable for an unquoted company) is 12.5.

Value 200,000 shares in Accrington Ltd on an earnings yield basis.

1.10 Activity solution

Valuation of 200,000 shares

$$= 200{,}000 \times \text{PE ratio} \times \text{EPS}$$

$$= 200{,}000 \times 12.5 \times £\,\frac{(140{,}000 - 20{,}000)}{400{,}000}$$

$$= £750{,}000$$

1.11 Asset based measures

Asset based measures are generally considered appropriate as a 'check' on the PE basis when shareholdings greater than 50% are being valued. Such shareholdings give the holder the right to control the acquisition and disposal of the underlying assets, therefore, if there are assets not needed for generation of income the controlling shareholder may cause these to be realised to generate cash.

As described above there are several possible asset based measures which could be used

(a) Book value - this will normally be a meaningless figure as it will be based on historical costs

(b) Replacement cost/deprival value - this should provide a measure of the maximum amount that any purchaser should pay for the whole business, since it represents the total cost of forming the business from scratch. However, a major element of any business as a going concern is likely to be the 'goodwill'. Since this can only be defined as 'income based value of business, less value of tangible assets' it may be seen that there is no real way of applying a pure 'asset based value' to a business - it is always necessary to consider an 'income based value' as well.

(c) Break up value - the break up value of the assets in the business will often be considerably lower than any other computed value. It normally represents the minimum price which should be accepted for the sale of a business as a going concern, since if the income based valuations give figures lower than the break up value it is apparent that the owner would be better off by ceasing to trade and selling off all the assets piecemeal.

However, when a break up is considered in this way it must be remembered to include such items as redundancy costs, liquidator's expenses, etc, which may have a significant effect on the final position.

In spite of these difficulties an asset value per share, based on deprival value, perhaps excluding goodwill, often provides a useful comparison with valuations based on capitalisation of income streams.

1.12 Activity

The following is an abridged version of the balance sheet of Grasmere Contractors Ltd, as at 30 April year 4

	£
Fixed assets (net book value)	450,000
Net current assets	100,000
	£550,000

	£
Represented by	
£1 ordinary shares	200,000
Reserves	250,000
6% Debentures year 19 (Repayable at 102)	100,000
	£550,000

You ascertain that

(a) market value of goodwill (not recorded in the books) is £50,000
(b) current market value of freehold property exceeds book value by £30,000
(c) all assets, other than property, are estimated to be realisable at their book value.

Value an 80% holding of ordinary shares on an assets basis.

1.13 Activity solution

Calculation of value of 200,000 shares on an assets basis, as at 30 April year 4

	£	£
Fixed assets per balance sheet		450,000
Add: Unrecorded goodwill	50,000	
Undervalued freehold property	30,000	
		80,000
Adjusted value of fixed assets		530,000
Net current assets		100,000
Net assets		630,000
Less: Payable to debenture holders on redemption		102,000
		£528,000
Valuation of 80% holding = $\frac{80}{100}$ × £528,000		£422,400

Note: the debentures have been taken at redemption cost in Year 19. State this is some years distant, a fairer valuation might be produced by calculating the net present value, based on market rates of interest, of the future interest payments and redemption cost.

1.14 Other methods of valuation

(a) Berliner method

This attempts to take into account both the asset value of a company and its earnings potential. Two values of the company are obtained

(i) based on capitalising expected future profits at an acceptable rate of return
(ii) based on the going concern value of the company's net tangible assets.

The value placed is then calculated as $\frac{(\text{i})+(\text{ii})}{2}$ ie, the mean of the two values.

This is a compromise which has no particular theoretical support but it may produce an acceptable purchase figure.

(b) Dual capitalisation method

This is similar to the Berliner method, but it recognises the two different types of asset - tangible and intangible; the latter, such as goodwill, are often risky investments.

The method used is to determine acceptable yields for both types of asset. Tangible assets are then valued and application of the yield determined for such assets gives a figure representing return on tangible assets. This is deducted from the profits figure to arrive at profit attributable to intangible assets, which is capitalised at the appropriate rate and added to the tangible assets value previously calculated to produce an overall company value.

Example

Flynch Ltd has estimated maintainable profits of £1,400 pa. Its net tangible assets are valued at £10,000 and the required rate of return on such assets is 10%. On intangible assets the required rate of return is 16%.

What is the value of Flynch Ltd under the dual capitalisation method?

	£
Estimated maintainable profits	1,400
Estimated return from tangible assets at 10% = £10,000 × 10%	1,000
Return attributable to intangible assets	£400
Capitalised value of intangible assets @ 16% = £400 ÷ 16%	£2,500
Total value of Flynch Ltd = Value of tangible assets + Value of intangible assets = £(10,000 + 2,500)	£12,500

1.15 Summary of valuation methods

Method	*Dividend yield*	*Earnings yield*	*Assets basis*
Share value	$\frac{\text{Dividend (gross)} \times 100}{\text{Dividend yield \% (gross)}}$	Earnings × PE ratio	Net asset value
Required information	(1) Future dividends (2) Dividend yield expected	(1) Future earnings (2) PE ratio expected	Asset & liability valuations

Method	*Dividend yield*	*Earnings yield*	*Assets basis*
Advantages	(1) Cash paid out is the key figure (2) Objective	Independent of management's dividend policy	Useful check on other methods
Problems	(1) Forecasting dividends (2) Deciding on dividend yield (3) Management's dividend policy	(1) Forecasting earnings (2) Deciding on PE ratio (3) Subjectivity of earnings (4) Effect of inflation on earnings	(1) Assigning values to individual assets (2) Limited applicability
Suitable for	(1) Quoted companies (2) Small shareholdings (up to approx 20%) in companies with stable dividend policies	(1) Quoted companies (2) Shareholdings in private companies of a size which enables the holder to influence dividend policy (eg, 20% → 100% holding)	(1) Going concern basis - as a check on earnings yield method. (2) Asset-stripping - useful information if assets are valued at disposal value

2 ADVISING A PROSPECTIVE BUYER/SELLER ON A SHARE VALUATION

2.1 Example

You are asked to value a 60% holding in Shade Ltd for the purposes of share transfer. The company manufactures high quality children's toys, and is well known in this field.

The management of the company is regarded as satisfactory, having passed from the hands of the original founding family (a senior member of which is selling his shares) into the hands of professional management. The continuity of management is, at present, well organised.

Profit and dividend record (approximate figures)

Year to 31 Jan	*Turnover*	*Pre-tax profit*	*Dividend*	
	£'000	£'000	%	£
20X4	900	150	5	7,500
20X5	1,000	165	10	15,000
20X6	1,200	210	12	18,000

Net asset position, per balance sheet at 31 January 20X6

	£'000	£'000	£'000
Fixed assets			
Freehold land and buildings, at cost			430
Plant and machinery, at cost less depreciation			60
			490
Current assets			
Stock		200	
Debtors		350	
		550	
Current liabilities			
Creditors	165		
Taxation	50		

Dividends	18		
Overdraft	50		
		283	
			267
			757
8% debenture 20X9			50
			707

(1) A note to the accounts indicates that the freeholds have this year been revalued, on an existing use basis, at £600,000.

(2) Share capital at 31 January 20X6 consists of 150,000 £1 ordinary shares.

(3) Assume corporation tax at 30%.

You ascertain the following data from the Financial Times

	(Net) dividend yield %	*PE ratio*
500 share index	6.2	9.7
Consumer goods (non-durable)	6.7	10.0
Toys and games	8.1	6.6

Indicate how you would value

(a) The 60% holding.
(b) A 5% holding.

Note: since there can never be a perfect solution, what follows are the suggested steps that would be worked through.

2.2 60% holding

(a) The normal bases of valuing a holding of this size are by reference to assets and to earnings. Assuming the purchaser wished to continue the business of the company, the earnings basis is more relevant.

(b) The assets basis should include the revaluations of the property, less, arguably, taxation. Being prudent, the full liability of 30% on a chargeable gain should be allowed for.

	£'000	£'000
Net assets, per balance sheet		707
Revaluation of freeholds (600 – 430)	170	
Less: 30% thereof	51	
		119
		826

Value per share £826,000 ÷ 150,000 = £5.51 per share

(c) The earnings basis requires the PE, which would have applied to the shares had they been quoted, to be determined and applied to the likely future earnings per share. The PE for a similar quoted company is 6.6; a similar unquoted company would operate on a lower PE of, say, 4.5. (Remember, however, that PE ratios of companies quoted on the Stock Exchange relate to dealings in relatively small parcels of shares, so a higher PE than 4.5 may be more appropriate.)

Earnings per share must be calculated from past figures. There seems little point in averaging past years, since they reveal an increasing trend. The figure of EPS required is that for future years - the past is merely a guide to the future. In the circumstances, the results of the most recent year (to 31 January 20X6) appear to be the best to use as a guide to the future.

	£
Pre-tax profit	210,000
Less: Corporation tax at 30%	63,000
Earnings	£147,000

Earnings per share = $\frac{£147,000}{150,000}$ = 98 pence

Value per share 4.5 × 98 pence = £4.41 per share

(d) Other factors which can be extracted from the information given

Current ratio	$\frac{550}{283} = 1.94$	Satisfactory
Liquid ratio	$\frac{350}{283} = 1.24$	Satisfactory, if debtors are all recoverable and overdraft limit not yet reached

(e) The range of prices indicated for this majority holding is approximately £4 to £6 per share. The higher end of the range reflects the high asset backing, and perhaps a continuation of the profit trend upwards. The assets, however, are unlikely to be realised, so that a more prudent valuation would be towards the lower end of the scale.

2.3 5% holding

(a) The normal basis of valuing a holding of this size is by reference to dividends.

(b) High asset backing, favourable ratios and trend of profits, all discussed above, are factors which would again influence the valuation.

(c) Dividend cover is important when valuing shares on a dividend basis. An impressive level of distributions may be marred, and be unlikely to continue, if there is low cover. Earnings were taken as £147,000, and the most recent dividend is £18,000, indicating what would be regarded as very good cover of 8.2.

(d) The yield obtainable on similar quoted securities is 8.1%. It is normal to uplift this by 25% to 40% to compensate for the unmarketability of unquoted securities. One must also allow, at this stage, for the impressive factors referred to above - dividend cover, profits trend and asset backing. Accordingly, the lower uplift (25% × 8.1%) may be appropriate, producing a yield of 10%.

(e) The dividend yield valuation would thus be

$$\frac{100}{10} \times 12 \text{ pence} = \underline{120 \text{ pence per share}}$$

This is considerably lower than the value per share of the majority holding - and this is always so when valuing unquoted shares.

3 RELATED MATTERS

3.1 The impact on profit reporting and balance sheet of share valuations

As we have seen the available methods of valuation are based on dividends, earnings and assets. If a company has purchased an investment in another company and negotiated the price paid in line with one of these methods, the profits reported subsequent to the acquisition should reflect the method of valuation.

Thus the purchase of a small minority holding will have been negotiated on a dividend yield basis. In the profit and loss account of the investing company, it will be appropriate to record the dividends received and if the investing company prepares group accounts there will be no change to the balance sheet statement of the investment or the amount of income recorded in the profit and loss account.

If a larger percentage of the share capital has been acquired, the investing company will have negotiated a price based on the earnings potential of the investee company. In the individual accounts of the investing company, the different method of arriving at a value will not affect reported profits however. Only dividends will be accounted for rather than a share of profits as only dividends will be realised profits in the context of the individual company. In the group accounts however the share of profits accounted for either under the equity method or the consolidation method will reflect the earnings basis of valuation.

3.2 The impact of recent legislation allowing companies to purchase their own shares

In 1981, company law was changed to allow any type or share to be redeemed or purchased by the company which issued the shares. For private companies, the redemption or purchase can exceed the amount of distributable profits in the company ie, a repayment out of capital can be made. These provisions are examined in more detail in the next chapter and you will have come across the provisions earlier in your studies.

As a consequence an investment in an unquoted company has been made more attractive as the opportunities for effectively selling the investment have been increased. Situations where the provisions are of a particular advantage include the following.

(a) In a family business, a shareholder who has worked for the company and wishes to retire can effectively sell his shares to other members of the family. As the company buys back his shares the interest of the remaining shareholders is automatically increased without them having to find funds themselves to buy out the 'retiring' shareholder.

(b) Venture capitalists are more ready to accept an equity stake in the company rather than have debt. In the venture capital agreement, provisions can be included requiring repayment to the venturer in X years time. The advantage to the company is that it is not burdened with interest payments in the financing period.

(c) Employee share schemes become more attractive to employees as the provisions provide an exit route for the sale of shares without the need for the company to go public.

4 CHAPTER SUMMARY

A share price can be negotiated on a dividend yield basis or an earnings basis depending upon the amount being valued. The assets basis is normally used as a secondary check on the earnings basis.

Expected dividend yields and PE ratios are normally based on 'comparable quoted companies'.

5 SELF TEST QUESTIONS

5.1 Why is the NPV model not often used in practice? (1.2)

5.2 Why might the dividend yield of a comparable company need to be adjusted? (1.7)

5.3 How is the earnings yield calculated from the PE ratio? (1.8)

5.4 A low PE ratio indicates what? (1.8)

5.5 What are alternative asset based share valuation methods? (1.11)

5.6 What is the Berliner method? (1.14)

6 EXAMINATION TYPE QUESTION

6.1 R Johnson

R Johnson inherited 810,000 £1 ordinary shares in Johnson Products Ltd on the death of his uncle in 20X5. His uncle had been the founder of the company and managing director until his death. The remainder of the issued shares were held in small lots by employees and friends with no one holding more than 4%.

R Johnson is planning to emigrate and is considering disposing of his shareholding. He has had approaches from three parties who are

(i) **A competitor - Sonar Products Ltd**

Sonar Products Ltd considers that Johnson Products Ltd would complement its own business and it is interested in acquiring all of the 810,000 shares. Sonar Products Ltd currently achieves a post-tax return of 12.5% on capital employed.

(ii) **Senior employees**

Twenty employees are interested in making a management buy-out with each acquiring 40,500 shares from R Johnson. They have obtained financial backing, in principle, from the company's bankers.

(iii) **A financial conglomerate - Divest plc**

Divest plc is a company that has extensive experience of acquiring control of a company and breaking it up to show a profit on the transaction. Its policy is to seek a return of 20% from such an exercise.

The company has prepared draft accounts for the year ended 30 April 20X9.

The following information is available

(1) **Past earnings and distributions**

Year ended 30 April	*Profit/(loss) after tax*	*Gross dividends declared*
	£	%
20X5	79,400	6
20X6	(27,600)	-
20X7	56,500	4
20X8	88,300	5
20X9	97,200	6

(2) **Balance sheet of Johnson Products Ltd as at 30 April 20X9**

	£	£
Fixed assets		
Land at cost		376,000
Premises at cost	724,000	
Aggregate depreciation	216,000	
		508,000
Equipment at cost	649,000	

Aggregate depreciation	353,000	
		296,000
Current assets		
Stock	141,000	
Debtors	278,000	
Cash at bank	70,000	
	489,000	
Current liabilities		
Creditors	(335,000)	
Net current assets		154,000
Non current liabilities		(158,000)
		£1,176,000
Represented by		
Share capital and reserves		
Ordinary shares of £1 each		1,080,000
Profit and loss account balance		96,000
		£1,176,000

(3) **Information on the nearest comparable listed companies in the same industry**

Company	*Profit after tax for 20X9* £	*Retention* %	*Gross dividend yield* %
Eastron plc	280,000	25	15.0
Westron plc	168,000	16	10.5
Northron plc	243,000	20	13.4

Profit after tax in each of the companies has been growing by approximately 8% per annum for the past five years.

(4) **Net realisable values**

The following is an estimate of the net realisable values of Johnson Products Ltd's assets as at 30 April 20X9

	£
Land	480,000
Premises	630,000
Equipment	150,000
Debtors	168,000
Stock	98,000

You are required:

(a) as accountant for R Johnson advise him of the amount that could be offered for his shareholding with a reasonable chance of being acceptable to the seller, based on the information given in the question, by each of the following

(i) Sonar Products Ltd **(6 marks)**
(ii) the twenty employees **(6 marks)**
(iii) Divest plc. **(6 marks)**

(b) As accountant for Sonar Products Ltd estimate the maximum amount that could be offered by Sonar Products Ltd for the shares held by R Johnson. **(4 marks)**

(c) As accountant for Sonar Products Ltd state the principal matters you would consider in determining the future maintainable earnings of Johnson Products Ltd and explain their relevance. **(8 marks)**

(Total: 30 marks)

7 ANSWER TO EXAMINATION TYPE QUESTION

7.1 R Johnson

(Tutorial notes:

(1) For part (a) look at the position from the point of view of the respective buyers, even though you are the accountant adviser to the seller.

(2) Base your answer to part (b) on the returns currently achieved by Sonar Products Ltd.

(3) For part (c), while listing the principal matters, do not forget to explain the relevance of each to the circumstances of **this** question.*)*

(a) (i) Sonar Products Ltd would achieve a controlling interest in Johnson Products Ltd by this acquisition. This would enable the company to determine the level of payout based on the earnings achieved. Earnings, and not dividends, would therefore be the relevant income measure on which to base a valuation. In the computations below all of the past five years have been taken as relevant, including the loss-making year 20X6, but the latter years have been given more relevance by using a weighting factor. (If the early years are not considered to represent feasible future earnings levels, they should be ignored.)

Year	*Earnings* £'000	*Weighting factor*	*Weighted earnings* £'000
20X5	79.4	1	79.4
20X6	(27.6)	1	(27.6)
20X7	56.5	2	113.0
20X8	88.3	2	176.6
20X9	97.2	3	291.6
		9	633.0

Weighted average earnings = £70,000 (round thousands).

To calculate a value these earnings need to be expressed as a percentage return. Using the details concerning the nearest comparable listed companies in the same industry, the following average return can be computed.

If earnings are not retained, they are assumed to be distributed by way of dividend. Therefore, if for Eastron plc 25% is retained, then 75% must be distributed - the dividend yield of 15% therefore represents 75% of the earnings yield, which must have been 20%.

Applying the same argument to Westron plc and Northron plc

Westron plc $\frac{10.5\%}{100\% - 16\%} = 12.5\%$

Northron plc $\frac{13.4\%}{100\% - 20\%} = 16.75\%$

The simple average of these three earnings yields = 16.42%. To allow for a marketability reassessment let the earnings return be (say) 18%. This gives a valuation of

$$\frac{£70,000}{18\%} = £389,000$$

This is the value of the whole company. R Johnson has a 75% holding which on this basis is valued at £290,000.

(ii) With each manager holding only a minority shareholding and probably looking on dividends as a form of periodic return, it is probably more realistic to consider the valuation from a dividend yield point of view rather than from an earnings yield point of view.

The simple average of the three comparable companies dividend yield is 13%. Allowing for lack of marketability of Johnson Products Ltd's shares, a rounded figure of 15% could be used. Reviewing the five previous years' gross dividends, a dividend of 5p would not appear to be unrealistic. This gives a valuation of

$$\frac{5p}{15\%} \times 810,000 \text{ shares} = £270,000$$

(iii) With 'asset stripping' appearing to be the objective of Divest plc, neither the earnings nor dividend yield based valuations are applicable. Any valuation should be based on the net realisable values of Johnson Products Ltd. This asset based valuation would be as follows

	£'000
Land	480
Premises	630
Equipment	150
Debtors	168
Stock	98
Cash at bank	70
	1,596
To pay creditors	(493)
	1,103
To minority interest shareholders (25%)	276
Value to Divest plc (75%)	827

The amount that Divest plc would pay would be dependent on the return the company would expect on the acquisition at a piecemeal sale. A return of 25% would set the price at $\frac{£827,000}{1.25} = £661,000$.

(b) The current post-tax return of 12.5% would need to be at least maintained. If the company accepts that the 20X9 profit of Johnson Products Ltd can be maintained, then Sonar Products plc may consider a price of $\frac{97,200}{12.5\%} = £777,600$ as the absolute maximum value of a 100% shareholding. A 75% interest would therefore be valued at £583,200.

Any valuation based on average earnings or an increased risk adjusted rate of return would obviously reduce this maximum.

(c) The future maintainable earnings of Johnson Products Ltd would be dependent on many variables but the important matters to consider would include

(i) economic predictions of the industrial sector in which Johnson Products Ltd exists; this could include assessment of the 'size' of the sector and the proportion of that market in that sector that is likely to be held by Johnson Products Ltd.

(ii) the level of profitability that the company can achieve in the market share it can expect to hold; this would include an assessment of past performance and its relevance to future performance, and a comparison of the trend of Johnson Products Ltd's performance over years 20X5 to 20X9 with that of other companies in the industrial sector

(iii) any changes in the strategic development of the company - possible changes to product mix, manufacturing method, market distribution and financial arrangements would need to be considered.

(iv) the likelihood or otherwise of Johnson Products Ltd maintaining its past management team and organisational structure - are future changes likely to affect future levels of performance and profitability?

(v) the budgets and forecasts produced by management would also be of interest together with variance reports for past periods, so that an assessment of the accuracy of management's plans could be made.

(vi) any changes to the financial structure of the company, with particular reference to changes in the level of interest-bearing loans.

Finally, the earnings will be based on the accounting policies adopted by the company. If any of the policies are to change, efforts should be made to revise the past earnings figures to bring them into line with those that would have been produced had the new policies been adopted at that time.

22 CHANGES IN ORGANISATIONAL STRUCTURE

INTRODUCTION & LEARNING OBJECTIVES

This chapter covers the various ways in which a company can change its organisation and its financial structure by changes in capital and long term liabilities. Most of the law and the subsequent accounting entries will already be known by you. It is however important for the FRE examination to understand the commercial context in which these changes occur. You may well have to comment on the advisability or otherwise of the reorganisation.

When you have studied this chapter you should be able to do the following:

- Consider and implement schemes to reorganise the capital of companies.
- Account for and explain reconstruction schemes.

1 REGULATIONS RELATING TO CAPITAL REDUCTIONS AND REORGANISATIONS

1.1 Capital reorganisations

Capital may need to be reorganised in profitable companies and companies which are in financial difficulties. In this section we examine the legal provisions which allow a company to reduce its capital without prejudicing the rights of creditors. Much of the detail of the law exists to ensure that creditors' rights are not affected.

1.2 Capital reduction scheme: S135 CA85

In such a scheme there will be a corresponding reduction in authorised capital. S135 CA85 specifies three possible modes of reduction

(a) Cancellation wholly or in part of liability on issued shares not fully paid up.

Consider a simple example of an issued capital of 50 £1 shares, 50p paid. The unpaid sum of 50p on each share could be cancelled; this would reduce the authorised and issued capital by £25, leaving 50 shares of 50p fully paid as the reduced issued capital; the resources of capital available to pay the company's debts are thereby reduced.

(b) Cancellation of some part of the paid up value of the issued shares which is lost or unrepresented by available assets eg, if a company has an authorised issued and fully paid capital of £100 in £1 shares, it could cancel, say, 50p per share and reduce its authorised issued and fully paid capital to £50 in 100 issued shares of 50p. The £50 so cancelled would permit a corresponding reduction in, for example, a debit balance on profit and loss account in the balance sheet.

(c) Repayment to members of some part of the paid up value of their shares which is in excess of the wants of the company eg, taking the same initial situation as in (b) above, the company might repay to members 50p per share in cash and so reduce its capital to £50 in 100 shares of 50p. In this case the asset side of the balance sheet would be reduced by £50 in cash paid out to members.

In cases (a) and (c), where the effect is to reduce the actual or potential fund available to meet the company's debts, the creditors would have grounds for objection, and accordingly they are given a right to object.

A procedure is laid down by Ss135-138 CA85 as follows

(a) the company must have power in its articles (eg, Art 46 Table A) to reduce its capital. If necessary the article must be altered to this effect before proceeding to stage (b) below, but the alteration may be made at a prior stage of the same meeting.

(b) The company must pass a special resolution setting out the terms of the reduction.

(c) It then applies to the court by petition for an order confirming the reduction.

(d) The court is then required to consider the position of creditors of the company in cases (a) and (c) of the preceding paragraph, and may do so in any other case; but has a general discretion as to what should be done.

(e) If the court is satisfied it may make a court order confirming the reduction on such conditions and terms as it thinks fit.

(f) A copy of the order and of a minute approved by the court setting out the reduced share capital is delivered to the Registrar of Companies, who registers it. The reduction then takes effect and the Registrar issues a certificate.

When the application is made to the court at stage (c) above, an affidavit will be made by one of the directors setting out all the circumstances and reason and submitting a statement of assets and liabilities. If possible the position of creditors will be safeguarded in advance by producing, for example, a bank guarantee that all creditors will be paid in full. It is only creditors to whom debts are owing at the time who must be considered (and also landlords to whom the company has future obligations to pay rent under existing leases). If the creditors are not afforded safeguards in this way the court may order that an advertisement be published inviting creditors to appear; it may later refuse to approve the reduction until creditors have consented or been paid off.

1.3 Power of a company to issue redeemable shares: Ss159 & 160 CA85

Prior to the CA81 a limited company could issue and later redeem redeemable preference shares. The CA81 gave greater flexibility, as redeemable shares need no longer be preference shares.

The restrictions on the issue and redemption of redeemable shares are

(a) the issue of redeemable shares must be authorised by the company's articles

(b) redeemable shares can only be issued when there are other issued shares which are not redeemable

(c) shares cannot be redeemed unless they are fully paid

(d) redemption may be made only out of profits otherwise available for appropriation or out of the proceeds of a fresh issue of shares made for the purposes of the redemption, or a combination of both methods.

Where shares are redeemed wholly or partly out of profits available for appropriation, an amount equal to the excess of the nominal value of the shares redeemed over the proceeds of any fresh issue of shares must be transferred to a capital redemption reserve. This reserve may only be used to make a bonus issue of shares.

The capital redemption reserve does not have to replace any premium payable on redemption. Except as detailed below, any premium on redemption must be provided out of distributable profits.

Where the shares to be redeemed were issued at a premium and a fresh issue of shares is made for the purposes of the redemption, any premium payable on redemption may be charged against the share premium account. The premium so charged cannot exceed the lower of

(a) the premium received on the issue of the shares now being redeemed, or

(b) the current balance of the share premium account, including any premium on the new share issue.

The premium on any redeemable preference shares issued before S160 CA85 came into effect may be charged against share premium account up to the balance on that account.

1.4 Purchase by a company of its own shares: S162 CA85

Any limited company may, if authorised to do so by its articles, purchase its own shares (including redeemable shares), subject to the same conditions as apply to the redemption of redeemable shares, except that the terms and manner of purchase need not be determined by the articles.

The procedure prescribed for the purchase of shares varies according to whether or not the purchase takes place through a recognised stock exchange.

(a) **An off-market purchase**

An off-market purchase must be in pursuance of an interim contract of purchase, approved in advance by a special resolution of the company. The contract, or a memorandum thereof, must have been available for inspection by members for 15 days before the meeting and at the meeting at which it is approved.

(b) **Market purchase**

A company cannot purchase its shares on a recognised stock exchange unless the purchase has been authorised by an ordinary resolution of the company. Such resolutions must specify the maximum number of shares that may be purchased, the maximum and minimum prices to be paid and the date the authority expires.

For both types of purchase there are detailed requirements for notice to the registrar and disclosure in the directors' report.

1.5 Redemption or purchase out of capital: S171 CA85

In addition to (1.3) and (1.4) above a private company may, if authorised by its articles, redeem or purchase its shares out of capital. However, this is only to the extent that the purchase or redemption price exceeds available distributable profits and the proceeds of a new share issue.

The Act refers to the permissible capital payment (PCP).

Definition This is the amount by which the purchase or redemption cost exceeds the amount of distributable profits plus the proceeds of any new share issue.

The difference between the PCP and the nominal value of the shares redeemed is dealt with as follows

(a) if the total of PCP plus proceeds of share issue is less than the nominal value of the shares redeemed, the difference is transferred to capital redemption reserve

(b) if the total of PCP plus proceeds of share issue is more than the nominal value of the shares redeemed, the excess may be used to reduce any of the following

(A) capital redemption reserve
(B) share premium account
(C) fully paid share capital
(D) revaluation reserve.

There are in addition elaborate safeguards both for members and for creditors

(a) the purchase or redemption must be authorised by special resolution (with voting restrictions on intending vendors)

(b) directors must make a statutory declaration specifying the amount of the payments and stating that in their opinion the company could pay all existing debts, after the capital payment, and will be able to pay its debts throughout the ensuing year.

(c) the directors' report must be supported by the auditor stating that he has enquired into the company's affairs and considered that the amount specified in the declaration conforms to the requirements and that the opinion expressed by the directors is not unreasonable

(d) the special resolution authorising payment must be passed within a week of the directors' statutory declaration, and the payment itself should be made not earlier than five nor later than seven weeks after the date of the resolution

(e) details of the transaction must be published in the London Gazette and a national newspaper and a copy of the directors' statutory declaration, with the auditors' report attached, must be delivered to the Registrar of Companies.

(f) a member of the company or creditor has five weeks from the date of the resolution to apply to the court to set aside the resolution

(g) if the company is wound up within one year of making the payment and is unable to pay its debts the payment may be recovered earlier from the person who sold or redeemed the shares or the directors signing the statutory declaration.

2 THE REORGANISATION OF CAPITAL - ACCOUNTING TREATMENT

2.1 Introduction

Section 1 has summarised the legal provisions for reorganising capital. Examples of the accounting implications are shown in this section.

2.2 Capital reduction

Open a capital reduction account. This will show all the asset write-offs on the debit side, and the reduction in share capital on the credit. The entries made will be as follows

(a) Amounts written off assets

Dr Capital reduction account
Cr Asset accounts (including debit balance on P&L account)

(b) Reduction in share capital

Dr Share capital account
Cr Capital reduction account

(c) Normally the asset reductions will equal the reductions in share capital; however, any remaining credit balance on the capital reduction account would be transferred to a capital reserve.

2.3 Example

Decline Ltd balance sheet as at 31 December 20X8

	£	£
Net assets		
Building	105,000	
Plant	65,000	
Goodwill	60,000	
		230,000
Current assets	20,000	

Less: Current liabilities	70,000	
		(50,000)
		£180,000
Capital employed		
Ordinary shares of £1		150,000
Preference shares of £1		100,000
Share premium		50,000
Revenue reserves		(120,000)
		£180,000

The shareholders of Decline Ltd have agreed to, and the court has confirmed, a capital reduction scheme under S135 as follows

(1) each ordinary share is to be redesignated as a share of 50p
(2) each preference share is to be redesignated as a share of 25p
(3) each preference shareholder is to receive ordinary shares on a 1:1 basis
(4) goodwill and the debit balance on revenue reserves is to be written off
(5) the share premium account will be used to reduce capital
(6) the building has been revalued at £140,000.

You are required:

(a) to show the necessary journal entries to effect the capital reduction.
(b) to prepare the balance sheet after the reduction.

2.4 Solution

Tutorial note: if a question asks for journal entries, then show in normal form

(i) debit entry before credit entry
(ii) narrative for each entry
(iii) rule between each entry.

Date	*Ref*		*Dr* £	*Cr* £
31.12.20X8	1	Ordinary shares of £1 each	150,000	
		Ordinary shares of 50p each		75,000
		Capital reduction account		75,000
		Redesignation of issued ordinary share capital as 50p shares and transferring excess nominal value to capital reduction account		
	2	Preference shares of £1 each	100,000	
		Preference shares of 25p each		25,000
		Capital reduction account		75,000
		Redesignation of issued preference share capital as 25p shares and transferring excess nominal value to capital reduction account		
	3	Capital reduction account	50,000	
		Ordinary shares of 50p each		50,000
		Issue of 100,000 50p ordinary shares to preference shareholders		

		Dr	Cr
4	Capital reduction account	180,000	
	Goodwill		60,000
	Revenue reserves		120,000
	Writing off goodwill and debit balance on revenue reserves.		
5	Share premium account	50,000	
	Capital reduction account		50,000
	Utilisation of share premium account in the capital reduction		
6	Building	35,000	
	Capital reduction account		35,000
	Revaluation of building, per revaluation report dated		

(b) **Preparation of balance sheet**

This should be straightforward. The only unusual item may be the treatment of any balance on the capital reduction account.

Decline Ltd
Balance sheet as at 1 January 20X9

	£
Net assets	
Building	140,000
Plant	65,000
	205,000
Net current liabilities	(50,000)
	£155,000
Capital employed	
Ordinary shares of 50p	125,000
Preference shares of 25p	25,000
Capital reserve (see working)	5,000
	£155,000

WORKINGS

Capital reduction account

Jnl		£	*Jnl*		£
3	OSC	50,000	1	OSC	75,000
4	Write off of goodwill and debit P&L a/c balance	180,000	2	PSC	75,000
	Balance to capital reserve	5,000	5	Share premium	50,000
			6	Building revaluation	35,000
		£235,000			£235,000

2.5 Achieving a capital reduction by a purchase of own shares

Companies can effectively reduce their capital by making use the redemption/purchase provisions of company law. The legal provisions have already been explained and this section provides some examples. The purchase of shares provisions are particularly useful to plcs as they can go onto the stock market and purchase their own shares. When these shares are subsequently cancelled by the company, it has reduced its capital in a cost effective way.

For private companies the redemption/purchase provisions could be particularly useful to companies with a small number of shareholders where one of them dies, retires or leaves the service of the company. The other shareholders may be unable or unwilling to purchase his shares themselves, but can arrange for the company to do so.

2.6 Example

A plc purchases 5,000 of its shares on the stock market for £30,000 as it does not have suitable opportunities for investment of surplus funds and it regards its share price as being relatively low at the present time.

The shares were originally issued at a premium of 50p per share.

The summarised balance sheet of A plc before the purchase is

	A plc
	£
Net assets	£100,000
Ordinary shares of £1	20,000
Share premium	10,000
Revaluation reserve	15,000
Profit and loss account	55,000
	£100,000

What is the balance sheet of A plc after the purchase?

2.7 Solution

The balance sheet becomes

	£
Net assets £(100 – 30(cash))	£70,000
Ordinary shares £(20 – 5)	15,000
Share premium	10,000
Revaluation reserve	15,000
Capital redemption reserve	5,000 (W1)
Profit and loss account	25,000 (W2)
	£70,000

WORKINGS

(W1) **Transfer to CRR**

	£
NV of shares redeemed	5,000
Less: Proceeds of fresh issue of shares	Nil
	5,000

(W2) **Profit and loss account**

	£
Original balance	55,000
Less: Premium on redemption	(25,000)
To CRR	(5,000)
	£25,000

(***Tutorial note:*** the premium on redemption must come from distributable profits as there is no fresh issue of shares.)

The reason for these legal provisions is to protect the right of creditors. Capital can be returned to shareholders provided that the fund of assets available to pay creditors (the creditors' buffer) is not reduced as a result of the redemption/purchase of shares.

Proof

	Before purchase of shares	*After purchase of shares*
	£	£
Net assets	100,000	70,000
Less: Reduction of assets if maximum dividend paid to shareholders (balance on profit and loss account)	55,000	25,000
Creditors' buffer	£45,000	£45,000

Despite the return of capital the creditors' buffer remains the same amount because the legal provisions reduce the amount of distributable profits.

2.8 Redemption out of capital

Only private companies may redeem shares out of capital and even then the redemption will be firstly out of distributable profits and a fresh issue of shares. Therefore the first step is to consider whether a payment has or has not been made out of capital.

Example

Wessex Ltd issued 20,000 £1 ordinary shares and 6,000 £1 redeemable A ordinary shares several years ago at par. The A ordinary shares are now to be redeemed at a total of £7,000. Distributable reserves amount to £5,400. There is to be no new share issue.

Is the payment out of capital?

	£
Total redemption cost	7,000
Distributable profits	5,400
PCP	£1,600

As the redemption cost is greater than the available distributable profits, the redemption is partly out of capital.

The journal entries are

		Dr	*Cr*
		£	£
(1)	A ordinary share capital	6,000	
	Distributable profits	1,000	
	Bank		7,000
	Being redemption of A ordinary shares at a premium totalling £1,000.		
(2)	Distributable profits	4,400	
	Capital redemption reserve		4,400

Being transfer to capital redemption reserve of excess of nominal value of shares over permissible capital payment.

Share capital and non-distributable reserves consist of

	Before redemption	*After redemption*
	£	£
Ordinary shares	20,000	20,000
A ordinary shares	6,000	
Capital redemption reserve		4,400
	£26,000	£24,400

The £1,600 reduction is the amount of the PCP.

Journal entry 2 can alternatively be calculated by reference to the PCP. The company law provisions (dealt with earlier) state that if the total of the PCP plus proceeds of a share issue is less than the nominal value of the shares redeemed, the difference is transferred to capital redemption reserve ie,

	£
Nominal value of shares redeemed	6,000
PCP	1,600
CRR	£4,400

The main point to grasp with the payment out of capital provisions is that although a payment out of capital is allowed, the redemption must, to the extent that they are available, come out of *the proceeds of a fresh issue of shares made to finance the redemption and distributable profits.*

2.9 Activity

A plc in paragraph 2.6 above redeems 25% of its ordinary shares for £30,000. It finances the redemption by issuing £30,000 10% Preference shares.

The shares were originally issued at a premium of 50p per share.

What is the balance sheet of A plc after the purchase?

2.10 Activity solution

The balance sheet becomes

	£
Net assets £(100 + 30 – 30)	100,000
Ordinary shares £(20 – 5)	15,000
Preference shares	30,000
Share premium	7,500 (W2)
Revaluation reserve	15,000
Profit and loss account	32,500 (W3)
	100,000

WORKINGS

		£	£
(W1)	**Transfer to CRR**		
	NV of shares redeemed		5,000
	Less: Proceeds of fresh issue of shares		30,000
	∴ No transfer to CRR		

(W2) **Share premium account**

Original balance		10,000
Less: Lowest of		
Actual premium on redemption	25,000	
Original premium on shares now being redeemed 5,000 × 50p	2,500	
Current balance on share premium account	10,000	
		(2,500)
		£7,500

(Tutorial note: the premium offset against share premium is effectively the lowest of three figures

(a) the actual premium on redemption ie, if there is no premium on redemption then there can be no offset!

(b) the original premium on issue

(c) the balance on share premium ie, a negative balance on share premium account is not allowed.*)*

(W3) **Profit and loss account**

	£
Original balance	55,000
Less: Premium on redemption to the extent not set off against share premium £(25,000 – 2,500)	(22,500)
	£32,500

As fresh capital of £30,000 has replaced old capital of £30,000 the creditors' buffer should be maintained without any transfers to CRR.

In this case the creditors' buffer actually increases as most of the premium on redemption reduces distributable profits even though new capital has come in to replace the old.

3 CAPITAL REDUCTION USING SEC 110 OF THE INSOLVENCY ACT 1986

3.1 Introduction

The previous section on the reorganisation of capital covered changes which are limited in scope. In particular, capital reduction schemes under S135 CA85 cannot compromise the rights of creditors of the company, nor can a new company be formed out of the old.

There are other sections of the Companies Act and the Insolvency Act 1986 which allow a more drastic reorganisation of a company's affairs to take place. However, as these sections do allow a more fundamental change there are a number of provisions to safeguard the interests of dissentient shareholders and creditors.

3.2 Sale of assets for shares by a company in voluntary liquidation: Ss110 &111 IA86

This procedure might apply if a company wished to reconstruct and to make a fresh start by transferring its whole business to a new company whose shares would, of course, go to the members of the old company. It can also be used in either the merger of the undertakings of two companies or a division between two companies of a single company's undertaking. Finally, if company B wishes to acquire company A's undertaking but does not wish to make an offer for company A's shares (eg, because company A has a complicated tax situation) it can acquire the undertaking in exchange for its shares if both sides are agreed.

The main points are as follows

(a) the company must be in, or about to go into, voluntary winding up

(b) with the sanction of a special resolution of the transferor company the liquidator may sell all or part of its business or property in exchange for shares of the transferee company for distribution to the members of the transferor company, but

(c) any member of the company who did not vote for the special resolution may, by giving notice in writing to the liquidator within seven days, require him either

  (i) to abandon the sale, or
  (ii) to purchase for cash the objector's interest in the company at a price to be agreed or determined by arbitration

(d) if an order is made within a year for winding up the company by or under the supervision of the court, the special resolution is not valid unless sanctioned by the court.

3.3 Schemes of arrangement: S425 CA85

The main points of schemes of arrangement effected under S425 CA85 are

(a) They can apply to any type of compromise or arrangement with either creditors or members of a company eg, such a scheme can effect some reduction or change of their existing rights in or against the company or transfer those rights to another company which issues shares or assumes liabilities as consideration for the cancellation of existing rights against the first company. The procedure is useful both in complex merger situations and in capital reconstruction.

(b) Application is made to the court by the company or liquidator or by any member or creditor. With the application is submitted the proposed scheme, and also an explanatory memorandum which must be issued with the scheme when it is circulated to those concerned: S426 CA85.

(c) If the court is satisfied that the documents submitted are in order and that the scheme is not *ultra vires* or an endeavour to use S425 in an improper way (eg, as a reduction of capital for which S135 procedure should apply) it will order that a meeting or meetings be held of members or creditors or of separate classes (if there is a possible conflict of interests). As the scheme is to be voted on at these meetings the court will not require detailed evidence of its merits at this point, but it will usually prescribe that a substantial quorum of members or creditors shall be present at the meetings.

(d) If the scheme is approved at the meeting or meetings by a majority representing at least three quarters in value of those who attend and vote at each meeting, the outcome is reported back to the court.

(e) The court will then listen to any minority objections but will sanction the scheme unless it considers that the requirements of majority vote and quorum have not been satisfied or that grounds exist on which the court in its discretion should withhold approval. Such grounds could be that the scheme is not proposed in good faith or is unfair to those who voted against it because the majority in favour were seeking to secure advantages to themselves as members of another class. However, most schemes, if approved at the meetings ordered by the court, are likely to be sanctioned by the courts without query.

(f) A copy of the order is delivered to the Registrar of Companies and the scheme then takes effect without further action being required.

3.4 A comparison

As compared with *schemes of arrangement under S425 CA85, S110 IA86* has the advantage that no application need be made to the court. Its main disadvantage is the right given under (c) above to a dissentient minority to enforce the buying out of their interest for cash instead of shares and the necessity of putting the company into liquidation as a preliminary step. In addition, creditors must be paid off in full.

The advantages of S425 are its flexibility and the need to secure approval of only a three-quarter majority (in value) of those voting at the meetings ordered by the court.

Its disadvantage is the expense of preparing elaborate documents (usually printed) and of making two applications to the court. It is uneconomic unless substantial amounts or values are involved.

4 PREPARING FINANCIAL STATEMENTS IN ACCORDANCE WITH A GIVEN SCHEME

4.1 Calculating and allocating the purchase consideration

A capital reduction or reorganisation is normally recommended when a company is in financial difficulties and it must 'clean up' its balance sheet before new capital is subscribed.

In most cases the company is ailing: losses have been incurred with the result that capital and long-term liabilities are out of line with the current value of the company's assets and their earning potential. New capital is normally desperately required to regenerate the business, but this will not be forthcoming without a restructuring of the existing capital and liabilities.

The general procedure to follow would be

(a) write off fictitious assets and the debit balance on profit and loss account; revalue assets to determine their current value to the business

(b) determine whether the company can continue to trade without further finance or, if further finance is required, determine the amount required, in what form (shares, loan stock) and from which persons it is obtainable (typically existing shareholders)

(c) given the size of the write-off required in (a) above and the amount of further finance required, determine a reasonable manner in spreading the write off (the capital loss) between the various parties that have financed the company (shareholders and creditors).

The alternative is the liquidation of the company. How sums are distributed to the various interested parties in such an event is covered in a later chapter. What needs to be shown to the shareholders and other interested parties is that they should be better off accepting the scheme rather than allowing the company to go into liquidation.

4.2 Normal features of a scheme

(a) The main burden of the losses should be borne primarily by the ordinary shareholders, as they are last in line in repayment of capital on a winding up. In many cases, the capital loss is so great that they would receive nothing upon a liquidation of the company. They must, however, be left with some remaining stake in the company if further finance is required from them.

(b) Preference shares normally, though not necessarily, give the holders a preferential right to repayment of capital on a winding up. Thus, the loss to be borne by them should be less than the loss borne by ordinary shareholders. They may agree to forgo arrears of preference dividends in anticipation that the scheme will lead to a resumption of their dividends. However, if they are expected to suffer some reduction in the nominal value of their capital, they may require an increase in the rate of their dividend or a share in the equity. The share in the equity will give them a stake in future profits if profits are made.

(c) Creditors, including debenture and loan stock holders, may agree to a reduction in their claims against the company if they anticipate that full repayment would not be received on a liquidation or they wish to protect (as far as trade creditors are concerned) a company which will continue to be a customer to them. Like preference shareholders, an incentive may be given in the form of a small stake in the equity of the company.

4.3 Accounting entries

Major reconstructions will involve the use of the procedures in Ss425-427 rather than S135, as the rights of creditors will normally be affected. From an accounting viewpoint it is important to remember that a S425 scheme will not be approved by the court if it conflicts with any particular statutory provision. The most important statutory provision in an accounting context is S130 CA85 - the issue of shares at a premium. Where shares are issued as part of a S425 scheme for cash or *otherwise* (eg, in satisfaction of an existing liability) then a share premium account must be created to the extent that the cash or the agreed value of the liability extinguished exceeds the nominal value of the shares issued.

4.4 Example

The Shires Property Construction Co Ltd found itself in financial difficulty. The following is a trial balance at 31 December 20X9 extracted from the books of the company

	£
Land	156,000
Building (net)	27,246
Equipment (net)	10,754
Goodwill	60,000
Investment in shares, quoted	27,000
Stock and work-in-progress	120,247
Debtors	70,692
Profit and loss account	39,821
	£511,760
Ordinary shares of £1 each	200,000
5% Cumulative preference shares of £1 each	70,000
8% Debenture 20X12	80,000
Interest payable on debenture	12,800
Trade creditors	96,247
Loans from directors	16,000
Bank overdraft	36,713
	£511,760

The authorised share capital is 200,000 ordinary shares of £1 each and 100,000 5% cumulative preference shares of £1 each.

During a meeting of shareholders and directors, it was decided to carry out a scheme of internal reconstruction. The following scheme has been agreed

(1) Each ordinary share is to be redesignated as a share of 25p.

(2) The existing 70,000 preference shares are to be exchanged for a new issue of 35,000 8% cumulative preference shares of £1 each and 140,000 ordinary shares of 25p each.

(3) The ordinary shareholders are to accept a reduction in the nominal value of their shares from £1 to 25p, and subscribe for a new issue on the basis of 1 for 1 at a price of 30p per share.

(4) The debenture holders are to accept 20,000 ordinary shares of 25p each in lieu of the interest payable. It is agreed that the value of the interest liability is equivalent to the nominal value of the shares issued. The interest rate is to be increased to 9.5%. A further £9,000 of this 9.5% debenture is to be issued and taken up by the existing holders at £90 per £100.

(5) £6,000 of directors loan is to be cancelled. The balance is to be settled by issue of 10,000 ordinary shares of 25p each.

(6) Goodwill and the profit and loss account balance are to be written off.

(7) The investment in shares is to be sold at the current market price of £60,000.

(8) The bank overdraft is to be repaid.

(9) £46,000 is to be paid to trade creditors now and the balance at quarterly intervals.

(10) 10% of the debtors are to be written off.

(11) The remaining assets were professionally valued and should be included in the books and accounts as follows

	£
Land	90,000
Building	80,000
Equipment	10,000
Stock and work-in-progress	50,000

(12) It is expected that, due to changed conditions and new management, operating profits will be earned at the rate of £50,000 pa after depreciation but before interest and tax. Due to losses brought forward and capital allowances it is unlikely that any tax liability will arise until 20X12.

You are required:

(a) to show the necessary journal entries including cash, to effect the reconstruction scheme

(b) to prepare the balance sheet of the company immediately after the reconstruction

(c) to show how the anticipated operating profits will be divided amongst the interested parties before and after the reconstruction. (Ignore the debit balance on profit and loss in determining whether any dividends are payable).

(d) to comment on the capital structure of the company subsequent to reconstruction.

4.5 Solution

The Shires Property Construction Co Ltd

(a) **Journal entries**

		Dr	*Cr*
		£	£
(1)	Ordinary shares of £1 each	200,000	
	Ordinary shares of 25p each		50,000
	Reconstruction account		150,000

Redesignation of issued ordinary share capital as 25p shares (formerly £1 shares) and transferring excess nominal value to reconstruction account.

		Dr	*Cr*
(2)	5% Cumulative preference shares of £1 each	70,000	
	8% Cumulative preference shares of £1 each		35,000
	Ordinary shares of 25p each		35,000

Exchange of 5% preference shares for 8% preference shares and 25p ordinary shares.

			Dr	Cr
(3)	Cash		60,000	
	Ordinary shares of 25p each - 200,000			50,000
	Share premium account 5p - 200,000			10,000
	Issue of 200,000 25p ordinary shares at a premium of 5p to present ordinary shareholders.			
(4)	(a)	Interest payable on debentures	12,800	
		Ordinary shares of 25p each - 20,000		5,000
		Reconstruction account - difference		7,800
		Capitalisation of unpaid debenture interest		
	(b)	8% Debentures 20X12	80,000	
		9.5% Debentures 20X12		80,000
		Increase in interest rate on 20X12 Debentures to 9.5%		
	(c)	Cash	8,100	
		Reconstruction account	900	
		9.5% Debenture 20X12		9,000
		Issue of £9,000 debentures at a discount of 10% (Note The £900 could have been debited to share premium account).		
(5)	Loans from directors		16,000	
	Ordinary shares of 25p each - 10,000			2,500
	Share premium			7,500
	Reconstruction account (amount of loans cancelled)			6,000
	Capitalisation and writing off of directors' loans			
(6)	Reconstruction account		99,821	
	Goodwill			60,000
	Profit and loss account			39,821
	Writing off of goodwill and debit balance on profit and loss account.			
(7)	Cash		60,000	
	Investment in shares quoted			27,000
	Reconstruction account			33,000
	Sales of shares at a profit of £33,000.			
(8)	No journal entry required.			
(9)	Trade creditors		46,000	
	Cash			46,000
(10)	Reconstruction account		7,069	
	Debtors			7,069
	Writing off of bad debts.			
(11)	Land			66,000
	Building		52,754	
	Equipment			754
	Stock and work-in-progress			70,247
	Reconstruction account		84,247	
	Revaluation of fixed assets.		£137,001	£137,001

(b)

The Shires Property Construction Co Ltd
Balance sheet at 1 January 20X10 (after reconstruction)

	£	£
Fixed assets		
Land at valuation		90,000
Building at valuation		80,000
Equipment at valuation		10,000
		180,000
Current assets		
Stock	50,000	
Debtors	63,623	
Cash	45,387	
	159,010	
Creditors: amounts falling due within one year		
Trade creditors	50,247	
Net current assets		108,763
Total assets less current liabilities		288,763
Creditors: amounts falling due beyond one year		
9.5% Debenture 20X12		89,000
		£199,763
Called up share capital		
Issued ordinary shares of 25p each		142,500
Issued 8% cumulative preference shares of £1 each		35,000
Share premium account		17,500
Capital reconstruction account		4,763
		£199,763

(c) **Division of pre-tax profit**

Interested parties before reconstruction			*After reconstruction*	
		£	£	£
Debenture holders				
Gross interest	(W2)	6,400		8,455
5,000 Ords	(W4)	-		1,360
		6,400		9,815
Preference shareholders				
Dividend	(W3)	3,500	2,800	
35,000 Ords	(W4)	-	9,516	
				12,316
Directors	(W4)			680
Ordinary shareholders				
Balance	(W4)	40,100		27,189
		£50,000		£50,000

(d) **Comments on the capital structure**

$$\text{Gearing is } \frac{£35,000 + £89,000}{£288,763} = 43\%$$

Whether gearing is viewed as high or not depends upon the current economic climate. It will however reduce when the large debenture is paid off in 20X12. Indeed, dividends on ordinary shares will have to be very restrained if cash is to be available to redeem the debentures. Alternatively, debenture holders might agree to exchange them for ordinary shares.

The shareholders' funds cover the cost of the fixed assets. The capital structure is reasonably satisfactory.

The debenture holders have done very well. Their interest has been increased by 1% but the redemption date has not been changed. The 10% capital gain over a period of less than three years is another advantage.

WORKINGS

(W1) **Trial balance after reconstruction**

	Dr	*Cr*
	£	£
Land	90,000	
Building	80,000	
Equipment	10,000	
Stock	50,000	
Debtors	63,623	
Cash	45,387	
Ordinary shares of 25p		142,500
8% Cumulative preference shares of £1		35,000
9.5% Debenture 20X12		89,000
Trade creditors		50,247
Share premium account		17,500
Reconstruction account		4,763
	£339,010	£339,010

(W2) Debenture interest gross

Before 8% × £80,000 = £6,400
After 9.5% × £89,000 = £8,455

This does, of course, include interest on capitalised interest.

(W3) Preference dividends

Before 5% × £70,000 = £3,500
After 8% × £35,000 = £2,800

(W4) The balance of the profits of £50,000 belongs to the ordinary shareholders

	£	£		£	£
Before		50,000	After		50,000
Less: Debenture interest	6,400			8,455	
Preference div	3,500			2,800	
		9,900			11,255
Available for ordinary shareholders		£40,100			£38,745

After	*Shares*
Issued share capital	
Debenture holders	20,000
Preference shareholders	140,000
Directors' shares	10,000
Other shareholders	400,000
	570,000

Profits available to pay dividends

		£
Debenture holders	20,000/570,000 × £38,745	1,360
Preference shareholders	140,000/570,000 × £38,745	9,516
Directors	10,000/570,000 × £38,745	680
Others	400,000/570,000 × £38,745	27,189
		£38,745

5 AMALGAMATIONS AND ABSORPTIONS

5.1 Definitions

The terms 'amalgamations' and 'absorptions' which are referred to in the syllabus have largely been supplanted by the terms 'mergers' and 'take-overs' respectively. Some commentators distinguish between the terms 'amalgamations' and 'mergers' by restricting the use of amalgamation to the purchase of assets by a new company and the liquidation of the old companies. Whatever name is given to these transactions, the end result is that there is a **business combination.** Two former separate entities form one legal grouping.

In accounting terms it is important to distinguish clearly the different methods that may be used to bring limited companies together. Two criteria provide four methods of combination

(a) asset purchase or share purchase ie, a deal with the company taken over to its shareholders direct

(b) whether a new company is formed or not.

Using these criteria the following possibilities emerge

TAKEOVER No new company formed	Asset purchase 'A1'	Share purchase 'A2'
MERGER New company formed	Asset purchase 'B1'	Share purchase 'B2'

The mechanics of each situation can be represented diagrammatically as follows.

5.2 A takeover - no new company formed

(A1) *Asset purchase*

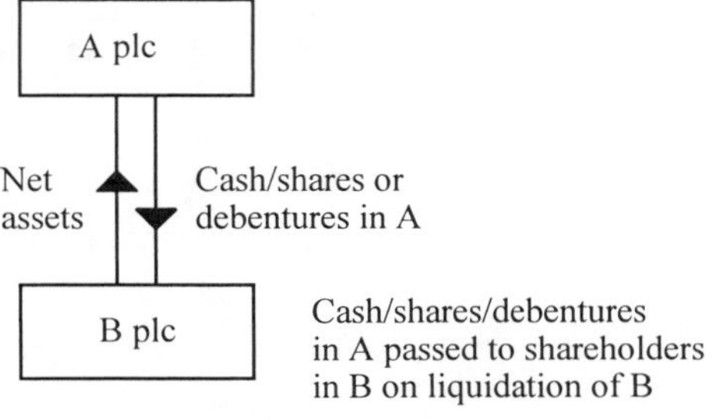

In this situation company A deals directly with company B buying specific assets in return for cash and/or an issue of shares or debentures. If B sells all its assets it will be forced into liquidation, whereupon the purchase consideration will be distributed to its shareholders, who may thereby become members of A. Accounting for an asset sale and liquidation will be required in B's books.

(A2) *Share purchase*

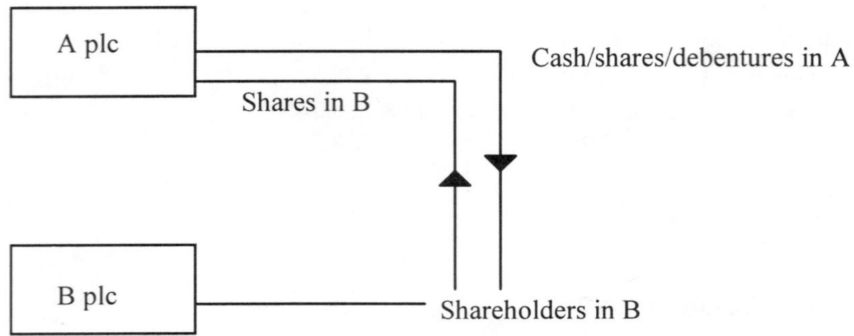

Here A makes an offer to B's shareholders to buy up their shares in return for cash and/or shares or debentures in A. No entry is necessary in the books of B plc, as it is merely the identity of the shareholders that has changed. B retains its operating identity and becomes a subsidiary of A. Group accounts must be prepared for A plc.

5.3 Merger - new company formed

(B1) *Asset purchase*

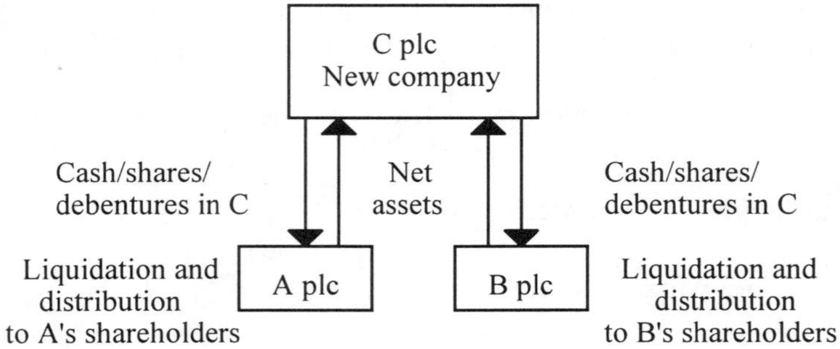

In this situation A and B sell their assets to a new company in return for cash, shares or debentures which, on liquidation, are distributed to their shareholders. Accounting for an asset sale and liquidation will be required in the books of A and B. The balance sheet of the newly formed company will appear as follows

C plc - Balance sheet after amalgamation

	£
Fixed assets of A and B, specified	x
Current assets of A and B, specified	x
Current liabilities of A and B, specified	(x)
Debentures	(x)
	xx
Share capital	x
Share premium	x
	xx

It should be noted that on amalgamation C has no revenue reserves, although the former balance sheets of A and B are likely to have contained distributable profits. Basically C has made an issue of shares (probably at a premium) and debentures in return for A and B's net assets, some of which were previously distributable, being represented by revenue reserves. The effect of the amalgamation is therefore to replace these reserves by share capital and debentures, so 'freezing' the distributable profits. It is not until C, itself, has traded profitably that it can create revenue reserves.

(B2) *Share purchase*

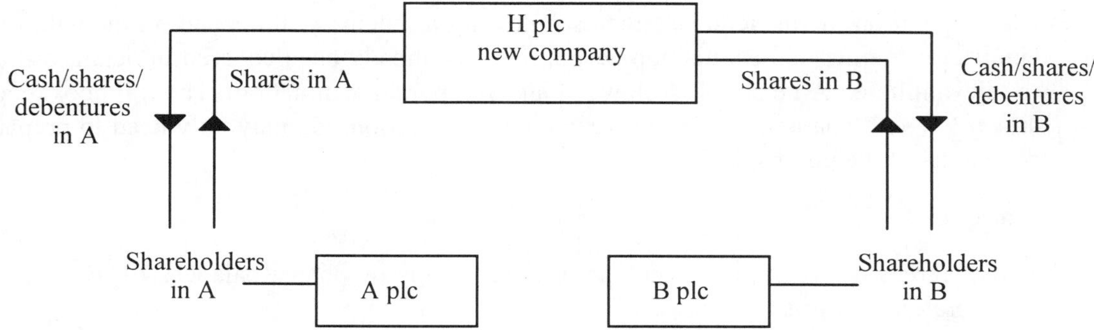

Here H buys up the shares of A and B in return for cash or an issue of its own shares or debentures. A and B retain their trading identities and become subsidiaries of H plc. No accounting entries are therefore needed in their books. H becomes a holding or parent company, holding investments in A and B, receiving dividends from them, and making its own distributions to its own shareholders. H's balance sheet after the merger would appear as follows

H plc - Balance sheet

	£
Investment in A, at cost	x
Investment in B, at cost	x
	xx
Share capital	x
Share premium/merger reserve	x
	xx

Consolidated accounts of the H plc group would be required.

5.4 Calculating and allocating the purchase consideration

If the shares (or assets) of B plc are paid for in cash by A plc, either A plc must have enough spare cash to hand (unlikely unless B plc is very small in relation to A plc), or it must be able to raise the money by borrowing or the issuing of further shares.

However, one of the attractions of acquisitions as a means of expansion is that they may be self-financing. Instead of paying for the shares of B plc in cash, it will normally be possible to do so with shares and debentures of A plc. Thus A plc owns the additional assets of B plc without having had to go to the market for further capital.

This raises the problem of the *mixture* of cash, debentures and shares that A plc should offer to the shareholders of B plc. A number of factors will influence the decision

(a) the amount of liquid funds readily available (if A plc has surplus cash it may wish to utilise it)

(b) the marketability of the shares/debentures in A plc; if A plc has a stock exchange quotation, the shareholders of B plc will be happy to accept shares, especially if B plc's own shares are unquoted - see below

(c) the relative cost to A plc of shares as opposed to debentures (see Financial Strategy text)

(d) the capital structure A plc wants to end up with

(e) what the shareholders of B plc will accept; in evaluating the offer, the shareholders of B plc will be particularly concerned with (b) above.

5.5 The financial statements of companies after carrying out a scheme of amalgamation

The preparation of financial statements following a scheme will depend on the nature of the scheme. The use of merger and acquisition accounting has already been covered in detail in this text and may be relevant here. An example follows of an asset purchase situation. The full bookkeeping entries are shown for both companies but in an examination question you may only need to prepare the financial statements of the purchaser.

5.6 Example

A plc agrees to acquire the net assets, excluding the bank balance, of B plc. The purchase consideration comprises

	£
50,000 £1 ordinary shares issued at a premium of 10p	55,000
£30,000 8% debentures issued at 90	27,000
Cash	18,000
	£100,000

When computing the consideration the directors of A plc valued B's land and buildings at £40,000, the stock at £15,000 and the debtors at book value subject to 3% doubtful debt provision.

After the sale B plc is liquidated. The preference shares are redeemed at a premium of 5%, and the shares and debentures in A plc together with the remaining cash are distributed to the ordinary shareholders of B plc.

The balance sheet of B plc prior to the acquisition appears as follows

B plc - balance sheet

	Cost £	*Dep'n* £	£
Fixed assets			
Freehold land and buildings	24,000		24,000
Plant and machinery	32,000	10,000	22,000
	56,000	10,000	46,000
Current assets			
Stock	19,000		
Debtors	20,000		
Bank	5,000		
		44,000	
Current liabilities			
Trade creditors		14,000	
			30,000
			£76,000
Share capital and reserves			
£1 ordinary shares		30,000	
£1 6% preference shares		20,000	
Share premium account		10,000	
Revenue reserves		16,000	
			£76,000

You are required:

(a) to show the opening entries in the books of A plc, and

(b) to show the closing entries in the books of B plc.

5.7 Solution

(a) **A plc - opening entries**

B plc - vendor's personal account

	£		£
Liabilities acquired		Assets taken over at agreed values	
Trade creditors	14,000	Freehold land and buildings	40,000
Doubtful debt provision		Plant and machinery	22,000
3% × £20,000	600	Stock	15,000
Purchase consideration		Debtors	20,000
Ordinary share capital	50,000	Debenture discount	3,000
Share premium account	5,000	Goodwill (bal fig)	17,600
8% debentures	30,000		
Cash	18,000		
	£117,600		£117,600

The effect of acquiring the net assets can best be seen by constructing A's balance sheet which, assuming that it had no other assets or liabilities, would appear as follows

	£	£	£
Fixed assets			
Goodwill (will be amortised over its useful economic life in accordance with FRS 10)			17,600
Freehold land and buildings at cost			40,000
Plant and machinery, at cost			22,000
			79,600
Current assets			
Stock		15,000	
Debtors	20,000		
Less: Doubtful debt provision	600		
		19,400	
		34,400	
Less: Creditors - amounts falling due within 12 months			
Trade creditors	14,000		
Bank overdraft	18,000		
		32,000	
			2,400
Total assets less current liabilities			82,000
Creditors - amounts falling due beyond 12 months			
8% debentures			30,000
			£52,000
Share capital and reserves			
Ordinary shares of £1			50,000
Share premium account		5,000	
Less: Debenture discount written off		3,000	
			2,000
			£52,000

(b) **B plc - closing entries**

(Numbers refer to sequences of journal entries.)

Realisation account

	£		£
Assets sold, transferred at book values		Liabilities taken over	
(1) Freehold land and buildings	24,000	(2) Trade creditors	14,000
(1) Plant and machinery	22,000	(3) A plc purchaser's account - monetary value of purchase consideration	100,000
(1) Stock	19,000		
(1) Debtors	20,000		
(5) Sundry members' account - profit on sale (bal fig)	29,000		
	£114,000		£114,000

A plc - purchaser's personal account

	£		£
(3) Realisation account - monetary value of purchase consideration	100,000	Discharge of purchase consideration - sundry members' account	
		(8) Ordinary shares at issue price	55,000
		(8) Debentures at issue price	27,000
		(8) Cash account	18,000
	£100,000		£100,000

6% Preference share account

	£		£
(7) Cash - redemption	21,000	Balance b/d	20,000
		(6) Sundry members' account - 5% redemption premium	1,000
	£21,000		£21,000

Sundry members' account

	£		£
(6) Preference shares account - redemption premium	1,000	(4) Ordinary share capital account	30,000
A plc Purchaser's account		(4) Share premium account	10,000
(9) Ordinary shares in A plc	55,000	(4) Revenue reserves account	16,000
(9) Debentures in A	27,000		
(9) Cash	2,000		56,000
		Ordinary shareholders' funds	
		(5) Realisation account - profit on sale	29,000
	£85,000		£85,000

Cash account

	£		£
Balance b/d	5,000	(7) Preference shares account - redemption	21,000
(8) A plc purchaser's account	18,000	(9) Sundry members' account (bal fig)	2,000
	£23,000		£23,000

Note: when answering questions like this you must bear in mind which set of books is being written up. As far as the buying company is concerned goodwill is the surplus of the purchase consideration over the value placed on the net tangible assets. From the seller's point of view the profit on sale is the difference between the purchase consideration and the book value of the assets sold.

6 THE ADVANTAGES OF BUSINESS COMBINATIONS

6.1 Why a company may prefer to be acquired or to merge

Most acquisitions are by mutual agreement; so most small companies being acquired must welcome such a move. There are a number of possible reasons

(a) personal reasons - for example to retire, for security, because of the problem of inheritance tax

(b) business reasons - an expanding small company may find that it reaches a size where it is impossible to stop growth, but funds or management expertise are lacking

(c) technical factors - increasing sophistication presents a problem for the smaller company, for example

(i) prohibitive cost of research and development
(ii) inability to employ specialised expertise
(iii) inability to offer a complete range of services or products to customers.

6.2 Why a company may wish to acquire another

There are the following possible reasons

(a) for the purposes of asset-stripping - in this type of operation, a company is acquired for the purpose not of running it as a going concern, but of breaking it up into components and selling them off

(b) horizontal integration - so as to acquire greater market dominance by acquiring other companies serving the same market

(c) vertical integration - to secure supplies and/or markets by acquiring either suppliers, or customers

(d) creation of a conglomerate - to diversify into completely unrelated areas of business

(e) international integration - to avoid having to start from scratch in a new country

(f) to obtain economies of scale

(g) to acquire management expertise.

This list is only indicative of the type of factors that may be involved. Taken in total they are sometimes referred to as *synergy* ie, the value of the group companies is greater than the sum of the individual companies.

6.3 Disadvantages of acquisitions and mergers

It should not be supposed that all the advantages are automatically in favour of mergers and acquisitions. In many cases they do not produce the results expected.

Some of the disadvantages may be as follows

(a) personal reasons - many small businesses much prefer to carry on as they are than to be swallowed up into a larger organisation

(b) 'woolly thinking' - many acquisitions and mergers are made without proper evaluation of the likely benefits

(c) failure to properly follow through a merger to gain the benefit of size.

7 CHAPTER SUMMARY

There are various provisions of company law which can be used to reduce the share capital of a company. For companies in financial difficulties, a capital reduction scheme can be used under S135 if the rights of creditors are not involved or S425 if they are. S110 IA can also be used.

Other companies may also wish to consider the use of the provisions allowing the purchase or redemption of share capital out of profits (all companies) or out of capital (private companies).

8 SELF TEST QUESTIONS

8.1 What are the three possible modes of reduction envisaged by S135? (1.2)

8.2 How can a company purchase its own shares? (1.4)

8.3 What is a PCP? (1.5)

8.4 What is the creditors' buffer? (2.7)

8.5 What does S110 IA86 permit? (3.2)

8.6 Who has to agree to a S425 scheme? (3.3)

8.7 Who should bear most loss in a reconstruction scheme? (4.2)

9 EXAMINATION TYPE QUESTION

9.1 Contemplation Ltd

Contemplation Ltd is a company that carries on business as film processors. For the past few years it has been making losses due to the low price competition.

The company's balance sheet as at 30 June 20X8 was as follows

	£'000
Fixed assets	3,600
Net current assets	3,775
	7,375
Share capital	
Ordinary shares of £1 each fully paid	10,000
8% cumulative preference shares of £1 each, fully paid	2,500
Reserves	
Profit and loss balance	(8,625)
Debentures	
11% debentures redeemable 20X15	3,500
	7,375

The company has changed its marketing strategy and is now aiming at the specialist portrait print market. It is expected that the company will earn annual profits after tax of £1,500,000 for the next five years - the figure is before an interest charge. Corporation tax is assumed to be at a rate of 35%.

The directors are proposing to reconstruct the company and have produced the following proposal for discussion

(a) to cancel the existing ordinary shares

(b) the 11% debentures are to be redeemed and the debenture holders issued in exchange with

(i) £3,000,000 14% redeemable debentures 20X35, and
(ii) 2,000,000 ordinary shares of 25p each, fully paid up

(c) the 8% cumulative preference shareholders to be issued with 2,000,000 ordinary shares of 25p each, fully paid up, in payment of the four years' arrears of preference dividend

(d) the existing ordinary shareholders will be issued with 3,500,000 ordinary shares of 25p each, fully paid up

In the event of a liquidation, it is estimated that the net realisable value of the assets would be £3,100,000 for the fixed assets and £3,500,000 for the net current assets.

You are required:

(a) to prepare a balance sheet as at 1 July 20X8 after the reconstruction has been effected and describe the legal process required. **(6 marks)**

(b) to prepare computations to show the effect of the proposed reconstruction scheme on each of the debenture holders, preference shareholders and ordinary shareholders. **(8 marks)**

(c) to write a brief report to advise a shareholder who owns 10% of the issued ordinary share capital on whether to agree to the reconstruction as proposed. The shareholder has informed you that he feels the proposals are unfair. **(8 marks)**
(Total: 22 marks)

10 ANSWER TO EXAMINATION TYPE QUESTION

10.1 Contemplation Ltd

(Tutorial note:

(1) A time-consuming question, with each part of the question probably taking longer than expected.

(2) Make sure that you have sufficient workings to show how your reconstructed balance sheet was computed and put at least three points for the legal process.

(3) Note that part (b) requires computations only. Do not add narrative where it is not required.

(4) Part (c) requires a report. Be careful not to repeat yourself and make sure that the report is clearly relevant to the recipient.*)*

(a) **Balance sheet as at 1 July 20X8**

	£'000
Fixed assets	3,600
Net current assets	3,775
14% debentures 20X35	(3,000)
	4,375

Capital and reserves	
7,500,000 25p ordinary shares	1,875
8% cumulative £1 preference shares	2,500
	4,375

The legal process would involve

(i) ensuring that the capital reduction is within S135 Companies Act 1985

(ii) ordering a meeting of creditors and/or members if required by the court under Ss425 and 426 Companies Act 1985; this will be essential where the reconstruction involves arrangements with creditors and/or members

(iii) obtaining a 75% majority of the creditors and/or members voting, to agree to the arrangement and obtaining a sanction from the court so that it becomes binding on all the creditors and members of the class involved, and also the company

(iv) filing a copy of the reconstruction scheme with the Registrar of Companies.

WORKINGS

The proposed scheme would be accounted for using the following journals (references are to paragraphs in the question)

		Dr £'000	*Cr* £'000
(a)	£1 ordinary shares	10,000	
	Capital reconstruction account		10,000
(b)	11% debentures	3,500	
	14% debentures		3,000
	25p ordinary shares		500
(c)	Capital reconstruction account	500	
	25p ordinary shares		500
(d)	Capital reconstruction account	875	
	25p ordinary shares		875
In addition			
	Capital reconstruction account	8,625	
	Profit and loss account		8,625

Reconstruction account

	£'000		£'000
25p Ordinary shares	500	£1 Ordinary shares	10,000
25p Ordinary shares	875		
Profit and loss	8,625		
	10,000		10,000

(b) **Debenture holders**

	£
Without reconstruction	
Interest 11% × £3,500,000	385,000
Less: Tax @ 35%	134,750
Reduction of after tax profit	£250,250

With reconstruction

Interest 14% × £3,000,000	420,000
Less: Tax @ 35%	147,000
Reduction of after tax profit	£273,000

Therefore, £(1,500,000 – 273,000) = £1,227,000 is available for shareholders. (8% × £2,500,000) = £200,000 goes to preference shareholders, leaving £1,027,000 to the ordinary shareholders.

Old debenture holders portion $= \frac{2{,}000{,}000 \text{ shares}}{7{,}500{,}000 \text{ shares}} \times £1{,}027{,}000$

= £273,867

Total share of after tax profit = £(273,000 + 273,867)

= £546,867

Preference shareholders

Without reconstruction With the current profit and loss account deficit no dividend is possible in the near future.

With reconstruction

	£
Preference dividend	200,000
Share of balance	
$\frac{2{,}000{,}000 \text{ shares}}{7{,}500{,}000 \text{ shares}} \times £1{,}027{,}000$	273,867
	£473,867

Ordinary shareholders

Without reconstruction Nil for the near future.

With reconstruction $\frac{3{,}500{,}000 \text{ shares}}{7{,}500{,}000 \text{ shares}} \times £1{,}027{,}000$

£479,266

(c) **REPORT**

To: A shareholder

From: AN Accountant

Date: X-X-20XX

Subject: **Company reconstruction of Contemplation Ltd**

As a current ordinary shareholder you are being asked to participate in a capital reconstruction which the management considers necessary for the survival of the business. From our previous correspondence I note that you feel that the proposals are unfair. It is necessary for you to consider the following

(i) In the event of the liquidation of the company the net realisable value of £6,600,000 would first be used to clear the £3,500,000 debentures, secondly to pay the cumulative preference dividend of £800,000, with the final balance of £2,300,000 being paid to the preference shareholders. These shareholders would therefore be 'losing' £200,000 and the ordinary shareholders would receive nil.

(ii) The ordinary shareholders are not being asked for finance and you will therefore not be putting any additional funds at risk.

(iii) There is a 'good' chance that in the future your investment will give a return. At present no such return, in the form of dividends or capital, is likely.

(iv) The current ordinary shareholders have 100% control of the company; after the scheme they will only have a 46.7% holding and therefore relinquish control. This may be seen as unfair and a reduction in the number of new ordinary shares given to the preference shareholders could be made to 1,500,000, thus leaving the ordinary shareholders with a more equitable 50% stake.

If you require any advice on the above information, please do not hesitate to contact me.

23 RECONSTRUCTIONS, MERGERS AND TAKEOVERS

INTRODUCTION & LEARNING OBJECTIVES

The FRE syllabus requires an understanding of the *major* features of mergers, takeovers and dissolution. There is a heavy emphasis on law rather than on accounting in this area. It is to be expected that these areas will be tested as one part of a larger question or perhaps a question with a smaller number of marks.

When you have studied this chapter you should be able to do the following:

- Explain the major features of administrative receivership and liquidation.
- Explain the major features of the regulatory background to mergers and take-overs.

1 WINDING UP

1.1 Means of dissolving a company

Winding up, or liquidation, is concerned with bringing the business and existence of the company to an end, although dissolution, as such, follows the completion of winding up. It is the company law equivalent of bankruptcy in the case of sole traders and partners, although the parallels are by no means precise. There are several reasons why winding up may be sought eg, the company may simply wish to cease trading, a minority shareholder may resort to winding up as a remedy against the majority, or a creditor, secured or unsecured, may wish to protect his position, to ensure that the company does not disable itself from repaying him.

In the last case, a debenture holder may be better advised to utilise his power to appoint an administrative receiver rather than to bring down the company (see later). A creditor may wish to apply for an administration order instead (see later) in which case, the company cannot be wound up while the administration order is in effect.

A company is a creation of the law. It can only be dissolved and its name removed from the register of companies when the proper legal procedure has been completed. Generally a company cannot be dissolved until its assets have been realised and then applied in payment of its debts (in due order) and any surplus distributed among its members according to their entitlement to participate in a return of capital. That is the process of liquidation or winding up.

1.2 Choice of method

Liquidation begins either by court order *(compulsory liquidation)* or by the members of the company passing a resolution to wind up *(voluntary liquidation).* Voluntary liquidation is of two types (members' and creditors' VWU). The choice of method of dissolution may be shown in diagrammatic form as follows:

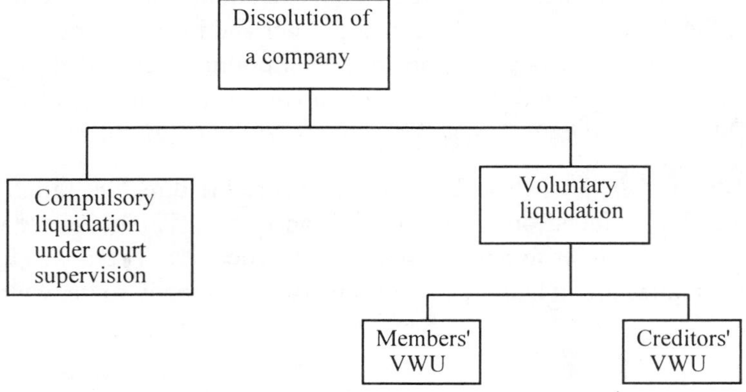

2 COMPULSORY WINDING UP

2.1 Commencement by petition

A *petition* is presented by the court eg, the Chancery Division of the High Court.

2.2 Grounds - general

S122(1) IA86 states a number of grounds on which a company may be wound up by the court. Of these grounds only two are of any real significance

(a) the company is unable to pay its debts
(b) the court is of the opinion that it is just and equitable that the company should be wound up.

2.3 Company is unable to pay its debts

A company is deemed to be unable to pay its debts if any one of three circumstances is shown to exist:

(a) the petitioner has delivered to the company at its registered office a written demand for payment of a debt owing to him of at least £750 and within the ensuing three weeks the company has neither paid the debt nor given security for its payment

(b) judgement has been obtained against the company for debt and execution ie, the attempt to obtain payment out of the company's assets remains unsatisfied

(c) the court is satisfied after taking account of contingent and prospective as well as immediate liabilities that the company is unable to pay its debts.

In practice the court applies the same minimum of £750 in cases (b) and (c) as is prescribed in case (a). Where the petition is based on an unsatisfied demand for payment the court will not make an order if the company denies liability and appears to have a reasonable defence to the claim.

2.4 The just and equitable ground

The *just and equitable ground* is a flexible concept to which new and unprecedented additions may be made in suitable cases.

Examples are

(a) That a state of *deadlock* exists in the management of the company; *Re Yenidje Tobacco Co (1916)*. This situation is most likely to occur when the company has a small number of directors who are also the majority shareholders.

(b) Where the company is like a small partnership based on mutual trust and confidence and that trust and confidence is broken, the court might consider it just and equitable to wind the company up.

In *Ebrahimi v Westbourne Galleries (1973)* a partnership was converted to a private company with the understanding that both partners would act as directors. One of the partners introduced his son into the business. The articles provided that shares could not be transferred without consent of the directors. The one original partner and his son removed Mr Ebrahimi as a director. (They had the voting power to do so.) Mr Ebrahimi petitioned for the company to be wound up. *Held:* Order granted because the company was formed on the basis of shared management and Mr Ebrahimi could not sell his shares without consent of the directors.

(c) The situation in *Loch v John Blackwood Ltd (1924)* where the directors failed to hold general meetings, recommend a dividend or lay and deliver accounts. The objective was to keep the shareholders in the dark in order to acquire their shares cheaply. There was a justifiable lack of confidence in the management and the court ordered the company to be wound up.

(d) Possibly if the directors and majority shareholders deliberately break the City Code on takeovers and mergers: *Re St Piran (1981).*

2.5 Who may petition?

A petition may be presented by the company, the directors (as a group), a creditor or a contributory.

The term contributory includes every person liable to contribute to the assets of the company in the event of its being wound up. It includes the present members and certain past members of the company. It has been held that a holder of fully paid up shares is a contributory and entitled to present a petition (even though he will not, in fact, be liable to contribute anything).

In addition, the Official Receiver may present a petition where the company is already in voluntary liquidation, and the interests of the creditors or contributories are not adequately protected. The Department of Trade may petition as the result of an investigation when such course is expedient in the public interest.

2.6 Procedure

A compulsory liquidation is commenced by presenting a petition which sets out the grounds on which the petitioner seeks to obtain an order of the court winding up the company. When the court issues the petition a court hearing date will be given. The petitioner must be able to prove at the court hearing that the grounds set out in his petition are true and convince the court that a winding up order should be made.

The petitioner will have to serve a copy of the petition on the company. He must also advertise the petition, to enable other interested parties to be aware that he is seeking a winding up order and to attend the hearing if they so wish. As the advertisement of a petition to wind a company up could damage its reputation the rules provide that he cannot advertise the petition for seven days after he has served it on the company. This is to enable the company to apply to have the petition struck out if there are in fact no grounds on which the court could grant an order. The advertisement must also be at least seven days before the date of the court hearing to give those persons who wish to attend the hearing sufficient notice to be able to attend.

2.7 Effect of an order for compulsory liquidation

If an order is made it is retrospective in effect to the date on which the petition was presented which becomes the *date of commencement* of liquidation (unless the company has already gone into voluntary liquidation at an earlier date).

The Official Receiver becomes provisional liquidator and remains in office until someone else is appointed liquidator.

Among the legal consequences of an order for compulsory winding up are

(a) the company must cease business except as necessary to wind up

(b) the directors' powers are assumed by the liquidator

(c) all floating charges crystallise

(d) all invoices, letters, orders, must show the company is being wound up

(e) the effective dismissal of the directors and employees.

(f) The Official Receiver *may require* officers of the company (present or within the previous year) or any persons employed by the company (present or within the previous year) to submit to him a *statement of affairs* within twenty-one days of the date of receipt of notice requiring the statement to be supplied. Anyone who fails without reasonable excuse to comply is liable to a fine. The Official Receiver may release anyone from the duty or extend the period for compliance.

The statement must be in the prescribed form, verified by affidavit of the person making it, and include:

(i) details of the company's assets, debts and liabilities
(ii) names and addresses of the creditors
(iii) details of securities held by creditors and
(iv) any other information required by the rules.

(g) The Official Receiver *may* summon meetings of the members and creditors to choose a liquidator. He must decide whether or not to do this within twelve weeks of the making of the winding up order and if he decides not to he must notify the court, the members and creditors. One-quarter in value of the creditors may require him to call a meeting.

(i) If meetings are called the creditors and members may nominate a person to be liquidator and if different people are nominated the creditors' nominee will generally take office. The liquidator must be a *qualified insolvency practitioner.*

The liquidator is under a duty to ensure that the assets of the company are realised and distributed to the creditors and any balance to the persons entitled under the company's articles. He must provide such information and assistance as the Official Receiver may reasonably require. This includes the production of bank papers and other records.

(ii) The meetings of creditors and contributories may also establish a 'liquidation committee' to act with the liquidator.

(h) At the conclusion of the liquidation the liquidator must call a meeting and report.

2.8 Activity

Write down the main stages in a compulsory liquidation.

2.9 Activity solution

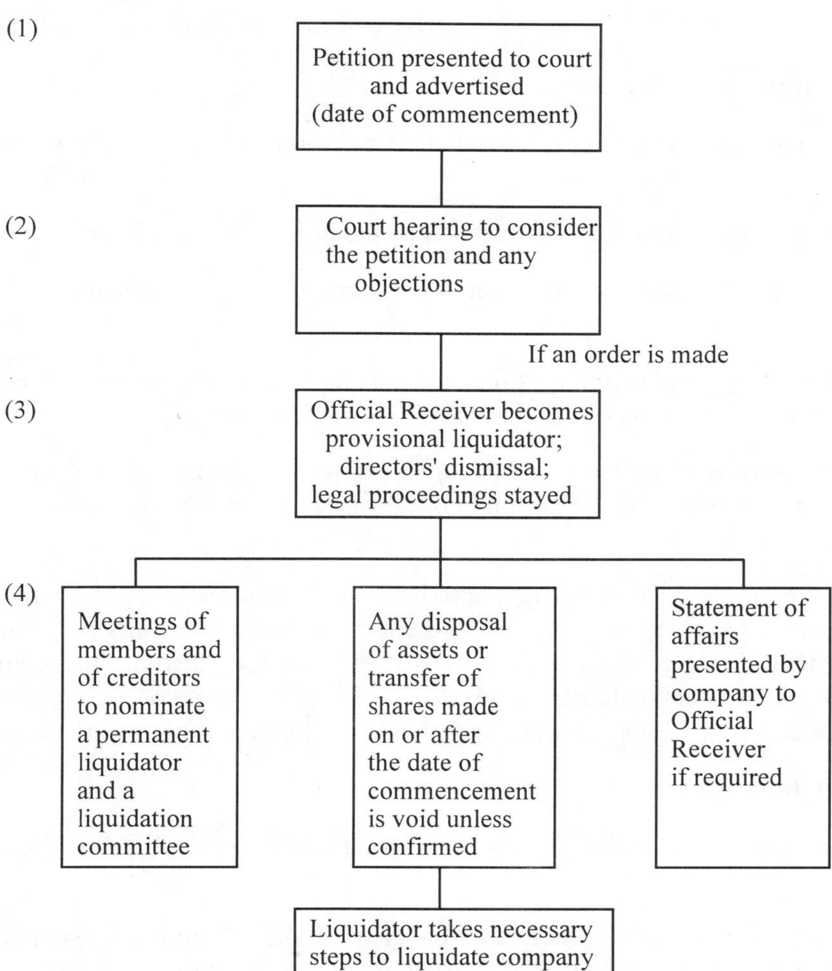

3 VOLUNTARY WINDING UP

3.1 Initiation

A voluntary liquidation is effected and has its commencement from the passing in general meeting of the company of a resolution for voluntary winding up.

3.2 The declaration of solvency

The choice between a *members' voluntary winding up* in which the creditors take no part since they may expect to be paid their debts in full, and a *creditors' voluntary winding up,* which is effectively controlled by the creditors, depends on whether or not the directors are prepared to assume the responsibility of making a *statutory declaration of solvency,* the main conditions of which are

(a) the directors (or a majority of them if their number exceeds two) must declare that having made full enquiry (a statement of assets and liabilities is attached) they are of the opinion that the company will be able to pay its debts in full within a specified period not exceeding twelve months

(b) the declaration must be made not more than five weeks before the date of the resolution to wind up or on that date but before the passing of that resolution and shall be delivered to the Registrar of Companies before the expiry of the period of fifteen days immediately following the date on which the resolution for winding up is made

(c) if the debts are not in fact paid in full within the specified period the directors who make the declaration are deemed to have made it without reasonable grounds until they prove that they did have such grounds. If they cannot justify themselves they are guilty of a criminal offence.

3.3 Members' voluntary liquidation

If the directors *do* make a statutory declaration the liquidation will proceed as a *members' voluntary liquidation*

(a) the meeting of members appoints a qualified insolvency practitioner as liquidator

(b) all directors' powers cease except as sanctioned by the company in general meeting or the liquidator

(c) the liquidator must call a general meeting of the company at the end of the first year and each succeeding year and give an account of his conduct of the winding up

(d) when the company's affairs have been wound up the liquidator must call a final general meeting of the company and give an account of how the company's property has been distributed

(e) if in a members' voluntary liquidation the liquidator believes that the company is unable to pay its debts he must call a creditors' meeting and present a statement of affairs describing the company's assets, liabilities, etc. As from the date of the creditors' meeting the liquidation proceeds as if it were a creditors' voluntary liquidation. This solves some of the problems of a company going into members' voluntary winding-up and later turning out to be insolvent.

3.4 Creditors' voluntary liquidation

If the directors do *not* make a statutory declaration the liquidation proceeds as a *creditors' voluntary liquidation*

(a) A creditors' meeting must be held within fourteen days of the winding up resolution. A statement of affairs, verified by affidavit by at least some of the directors, must be laid before the creditors' meeting over which one of the directors must preside. Notice of the meeting must be sent to all creditors at least seven days before the meeting and notice must be published in the London Gazette.

(b) The members may have appointed a liquidator at the meeting which decided to wind up the company. If so, he is entitled to act until the creditors' meeting, but with limited powers. Except in emergency (eg, in respect of perishable goods) he cannot exercise most of his powers without the court's consent.

The creditors may nominate the liquidator and if this person is different from the person selected by the members the creditors' nominee becomes liquidator.

The liquidator must be a qualified insolvency practitioner.

A liquidator may be removed either by the general meeting or by the creditors' meeting. However, special rules apply if the liquidator was appointed by the court.

(c) The creditors may, if they think fit, appoint a 'liquidation committee' of not more than five people. The members may also appoint five people to act as members of the committee.

The purpose of the liquidation committee is to have a body which represents both members and creditors to keep a check on the liquidator and to which the liquidator can turn for guidance.

(d) On appointment of a liquidator the directors' powers cease except so far as the liquidation committee (or the creditors if there is no committee) sanction.

(e) The liquidator must call separate meetings of both members *and* creditors every year (compare to members' voluntary liquidation where only members' meetings called).

(f) The liquidator must also call meetings of members and creditors when the company's affairs are fully wound up and send accounts to the Registrar.

3.5 Activity

Summaries the stages in the commencement of a members' VWU and a creditors' VWU.

3.6 Activity solution

Members' VWU

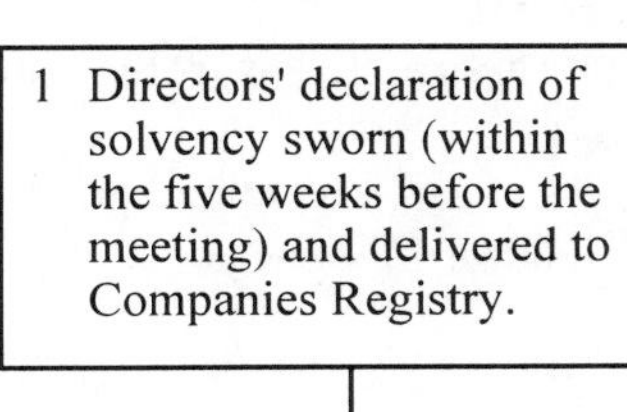

2 General meeting of members to:
(a) resolve to wind up
(b) appoint a liquidator

Creditors' VWU

1 General meeting of members to:
(a) resolve to wind up
(b) nominate a liquidator
(c) appoint members (up to five) for liquidation committee

2 Creditors' meeting to:
(a) appoint a liquidator
(b) appoint creditors (up to five) for liquidation committee
(c) consider directors' financial statement

4 THE LIQUIDATOR AND THE LIQUIDATION

4.1 Control and realisation of assets

The liquidator is under a duty to take control of the company's assets, including its business undertaking if it is still trading, and to convert those assets into money with which to pay the liquidation expenses, discharge the company's debts and, if any surplus then remains, to distribute it to members in accordance with their entitlement.

4.2 Disclaimer of assets

Some assets eg, a lease of empty premises or an unprofitable contract, may be a burden rather than a benefit to the company in liquidation. The liquidator may therefore disclaim 'onerous' property.

4.3 Application of assets

The assets of the company are applied in a certain order. This order is summarised on a **statement of affairs** which is examined in more detail in a later chapter.

5 THE ALTERNATIVE TO WINDING UP - ADMINISTRATION ORDERS

5.1 When used

Administration orders are a newer procedure to enable an attempt to be made to rescue a company in financial difficulty by placing its affairs in the hands of an administrator. While the order is in force, the leave of the court is needed before any winding-up proceedings can be taken or any process, charge, hire-purchase or other agreement can be enforced. Thus, the idea is that the granting of an administration order will 'buy time' for the company and give a procedure similar to that of receivership used by secured creditors (see next section) to secure the company in financial difficulties.

5.2 Application for orders

An application may be made to court for an order by petition presented by the company, the directors, or a creditor (or creditors). Notice of the petition must be given to any persons entitled to appoint an administrative receiver (see next section).

Once the petition has been presented

(a) *No* resolution may be passed to wind up the company

(b) A moratorium is imposed on the company's debts until such time as the court decides to make the order or dismiss the petition. This means that creditors may not

  (i) take any steps to enforce any security over the company's property

  (ii) repossess goods under a hire-purchase agreement, leasing agreement, retention of title or conditional sale agreement

  (iii) commence legal proceedings or levy executions or distress.

  However, these actions may be taken with the court's permission.

5.3 Making the order

The court must dismiss the petition and may not make an order if an administrative receiver has been appointed, unless it is satisfied that the persons on whose behalf the receiver was appointed have consented to the making of the order.

In addition, before making such an order, the court must be convinced that the order would be likely to achieve one or more of

(a) the survival of the whole or part of the company as a going concern
(b) a scheme of arrangement under S425 CA85 or
(c) a more advantageous realisation of assets than a winding-up would bring.

5.4 Consequences of administration order

If the court makes an order

(a) Every invoice, order or letter issued must contain the administrator's name and a statement that the company is being managed by him.

(b) Any petition for winding up the company is dismissed.

(c) Any administrative receiver must vacate office. In addition, any receiver must also vacate office if the administrator requires him to do so.

  Thus, the holders of a floating charge may feel less protected by an administration order than by appointing their own administrative receiver. However, there are other reasons why they may prefer an administration order, in particular the wide powers of an administrator.

(d) A qualified insolvency practitioner is appointed to administer the affairs of the company. The administrator is given the same wide powers as an administrative receiver to manage the business and property of the company, including the power to bring and defend legal proceedings, sell assets, borrow money, insure and appoint agents. In case of difficulty the administrator may apply to the court for directions.

5.5 Carrying out the order

(a) The administrator must require a statement of affairs from officers (current and past), employees or independent contractors (current or in the past year).

(b) The administrator must, within three months of the order, send a statement of his proposals to the Registrar, creditors and members.

(c) A copy of the proposal must be presented to a meeting of creditors at which they shall decide whether to approve them. They may only make modifications to the proposals with the administrator's consent.

(d) The administrator must report the results of the meeting to the Registrar and to the court. If the meeting did not approve the proposals the court may dismiss the order or make such provisions as it thinks fit.

If the proposals are approved the administrator must carry out the proposals as stated. If he wishes to make any 'substantial' revisions he must call a further meeting of creditors and obtain their approval.

5.6 Discharge and the administrator

The administrator may apply to the court for discharge at any time. He must make such an application when it appears that the purpose of the order has been achieved or is incapable of being achieved.

6 ADMINISTRATIVE RECEIVERSHIP

6.1 Debenture holders' remedies

A debenture holder is in a contractual relationship with the company. The terms of the contract, and obligations thereunder, are fixed when the debenture is issued and are not variable subsequently, except on normal contractual principles (unlike the articles of association between the members). Therefore the debenture holder is entitled to seek a remedy for action taken by the company in breach of contract.

An important question is whether the debenture is unsecured or secured. If it is unsecured any action to enforce payment of principal or interest is limited to an action for debt or steps are taken to have the company wound up ie, the normal remedies of an unsecured creditor.

If, however, the debenture is secured the debenture holder has the normal rights of an unsecured creditor and in addition he may enforce his security in the following ways.

(a) If his debenture is (as is normal) issued under the common seal of the company he has a statutory power to sell the property or to appoint a receiver of its income in specified circumstances of default.

(b) He can resort to any *express power given by the debenture* to be exercised on the occurrence of any one of the specified happenings or defaults of the company. Typical instances of events on which the power is exercisable are default in payment of principal or interest; commencement of winding up; appointment of a receiver (by another secured creditor); ceasing to carry on business; breach of various restrictions imposed by the debenture such as a substantial disposal of assets without the debenture holder's consent.

(c) He can in the last resort *apply to the court* for an order for:

(i) sale
(ii) delivery of possession
(iii) foreclosure or
(iv) appointment of a receiver of the property subject to the charge.

The court will order sale or appoint a receiver only in three cases ie, when principal or interest is in arrears, when the company has gone into liquidation and when the security is *in jeopardy*. The last of these situations is generally established by showing that other creditors are about to seize assets in execution of a judgement for debt or are about to petition for a compulsory winding up or by showing that the company has or is about to cease to carry on its business or to transfer its assets to its shareholders or some other person.

Since a forced sale of assets is often an uncompromising means of realising the security, the secured creditor is most likely to appoint (or apply to the court to appoint) a receiver (who is usually an accountant specialising in insolvency). The receiver may be able to restore the financial position of the company and discharge the secured debt, by sale or otherwise. If he is unable to do so his receivership may be a preliminary to the company going into liquidation.

6.2 Appointment of a receiver/administrative receiver

A receiver is appointed to get in the assets charged (if any - there usually will be), to collect income due on them, to realise the assets and to pay the proceeds to the debenture holders in reduction of what is owed to them. If something has happened to destroy or reduce the value of the security (eg, a factory has burned down) or if there is no security, the debenture holders, or trustees for debenture stockholders, may petition for a winding up (so may a receiver). But this is a drastic remedy and it will generally be preferable for the company to carry on business but for the receiver to be appointed as a *receiver and manager* so that he has the additional power of carrying on the company's business.

The receiver may be appointed as receiver of *part only* of the company's property or only of the *income* or part of the income arising from the property. He is then called a *receiver.* An example of this would be a receiver appointed under a fixed charge on a factory owned by the company. If the receiver is appointed under a floating charge over *the whole,* or *substantially the whole,* of the company's property he is called an *'administrative receiver'.*

The court may also appoint a receiver/administrative receiver. If the company is being wound up by the court, the court may appoint the Official Receiver to act.

The appointment is a sign that the company is or may be in financial difficulty. Accordingly every invoice, order or business letter of the company must state that a receiver has been appointed. The appointment causes any floating charge to crystallise unless this has already occurred.

6.3 Position of receiver (other than administrative receiver) and effect of appointment

(a) **Control of assets/position of directors**

On taking up his appointment the receiver assumes control of the assets subject to the charge. The powers of the directors with regard to those assets are in suspense so long as the receiver is in control. The restoration of the company's financial position may require a variety of drastic measures.

(b) **Application to court for directions**

A receiver appointed by the court will be an officer of the court and will act according to the court's directions. A receiver appointed by the debenture holders will act according to their instructions. However, if he has doubts as to any particular matter he may apply to the court for directions.

(c) **Liability on contracts**

If the company is carrying on its business at the time of his appointment the receiver is likely to find that a number of substantial contracts are in course of performance eg, the employment of staff, the purchase of materials, the sale of finished goods. The appointment in no way terminates the *existing contracts.* He has no personal liability on these contracts since he did not make them.

If appointed by the court, employees are dismissed. However, if he is appointed by debenture holders as agent for the company it will not automatically terminate the employment contracts. S37 IA86 provides that the receiver will be personally liable on any contract of employment adopted by him. However, S37 IA86 provides that he will not be taken to have adopted a contract of employment within the first fourteen days after his appointment. Thus, it would appear that he is given fourteen days to decide whether to adopt them or not.

The receiver may also have to make *new contracts* in order to carry on the business. On such contracts he is personally liable but has a right of indemnity out of the company's assets.

In principle, the receiver has power to break the existing contracts. But if such actions would injure the company's goodwill (as well as expose it - as it must - to liability for breach of contract) the receiver, whether appointed in or out of court, should apply to the court for approval of his proposed action. The court would not sanction permanent damage to the company's long-term future merely to secure some immediate advantage to its creditors. But, on the other hand, it would not compel a receiver to go on with existing contracts if he had to assume personal liability for new loans raised to finance them.

(d) **Accounts to be delivered to Registrar**

The receiver appointed under a debenture must deliver accounts showing receipts and payments to the Registrar of Companies within thirteen months of his appointment and thereafter at six-monthly intervals while he acts and within one month of the date he ceases to act.

6.4 Position of administrative receiver

(a) **Control of assets/position of directors**

Basically the position is the same as for a receiver, except that, as the administrative receiver assumes control over the whole or substantially the whole of the company's undertakings, the whole of the directors' powers are suspended.

(b) **Application to court for direction**

Basically the same as for receivers.

(c) **Liability on contracts**

Basically the same as for receivers. The IA86 also specifically provides that the administrative receiver is deemed to be the agent of the company unless and until it goes into liquidation. Thus, the company will also be liable on the contract.

(d) **Accounts delivered to Registrar**

There is a corresponding duty to deliver accounts as imposed on receivers.

(e) **Information to be given by administrative receiver**

When the administrative receiver is appointed he must give notice to the company forthwith and to the creditors within twenty-eight days.

(f) **Statement of affairs**

The administrative receiver must require any or all officers, employees (current or within the previous year) or persons who took part in forming the company within the previous year to submit a statement of affairs showing details including

(i) the company's assets, debts and liabilities and
(ii) the creditors' names and addresses and securities held by them.

(g) **Report by administrative receiver**

Within three months of his appointment the administrative receiver must send a report to the Registrar of Companies and to all secured creditors setting out details of

(i) events leading to his appointment
(ii) disposals or proposed disposals of company property by him
(iii) carrying on or proposed carrying on of the company's business by him
(iv) principal and interest payable to the debenture holders who appointed him
(v) the amount, if any, likely to be available to pay other creditors.

In addition, he must call a meeting of all unsecured creditors unless the court allows him to dispense with the meeting. If the meeting is called it may establish a creditors' committee to maintain contact with the administrative receiver and obtain information from him on a regular basis.

If the company is in or goes into liquidation the administrative receiver must also send a copy of his report to the liquidator.

(h) **General powers of administrative receiver**

The powers conferred on the administrative receiver by the debenture are deemed to include the following, so far as they are not inconsistent with the provisions of the debenture

(i) take possession of and realise company property

(ii) sell or dispose of company property

(iii) borrow money and give securities over company property

(iv) bring/defend legal proceedings or refer matters to arbitration

(v) insure the business and property

(vi) appoint agents

(vii) carry on the business

(viii) use the company seal, execute deeds, bills of exchange etc, in the company's name

(ix) make payments

(x) grant or accept surrender of leases or take a lease

(xi) establish subsidiaries, transfer business or property to a subsidiary, make any arrangements or compromise on behalf of the company

(xii) call up any uncalled capital

(xiii) claim in any bankruptcy, insolvency etc

(xiv) present or defend a petition to wind up the company

(xv) change the registered office, and

(xvi) anything incidental to the above.

(i) **Power to dispose of charged property**

In addition to the above powers, the administrative receiver has specific power to dispose of any company asset which is subject to a charge other than the one under which he is appointed as if it were not subject to a charge. To do so he must apply to the court for leave which will be granted if the court is satisfied that the sale is likely to promote a more advantageous sale of the asset and the proceeds will be used to pay the sums secured by the charge.

(j) **Vacation of office**

The administrative receiver may resign or be removed by court order. He cannot be removed by the debenture holders. On vacation of office he must notify the Registrar of Companies.

6.5 Payments by the receiver/administrative receiver

There is a set order of priority in which the receiver should apply the moneys which he can raise. In brief

(a) he must first pay the *expenses* of his operations (including his own remuneration) and the fees etc, due to the debenture holders' trustee and the expenses (if any) of the court proceedings leading to his appointment

(b) if the security for the debentures is a floating charge only, the receiver must next discharge the debts owing by the company to its *preferential creditors*

(c) he may then repay the *debenture debt and interest* thereon.

7 REGULATION OF TAKEOVERS AND MERGERS

7.1 City Code on take-overs and mergers

The acquisition of quoted companies is circumscribed by the City Code on Takeovers and Mergers ('the City Code'), which is the responsibility of the Panel on Takeovers and Mergers. This code does not have the force of law, but it is enforced by the various City regulatory authorities, including the Stock Exchange, and specifically by the Panel on Takeovers and Mergers (the 'Takeover Panel'). Its basic principle is that of equity between one shareholder and another, and it sets out rules for the conduct of such acquisitions.

Examples of regulations are

(a) **3% disclosure**

A would-be bidder, together with related parties, can build up a stake of 3% without any obligations to disclose this to the target company. Over 3% the stake must be disclosed to the target company under the statutory rules for disclosure of substantial interests, thus giving warning to the management of a possible bid.

(b) **Compulsory offer if shareholding exceeds 30%**

A bidder must make an offer conditional on a minimum acceptance of 50% and no Competition Commission reference and no European Commission reference, if his shareholding exceeds 30%.

(***Tutorial note***: The Competition Commission has replaced the Monopolies and Mergers Commission - see below.)

(c) **Offer period**

The offer period starts when an announcement is made of a proposed or possible offer.

This date is significant in determining the value of the offer to shareholders. If the offeror has purchased shares in the offeree company within three months prior to the commencement of the offer period, the offer to shareholders must not be on less favourable terms.

(d) **'Unconditional as to acceptances'**

When an offer receives acceptances from shareholders, the offer and acceptance are conditional upon

- a minimum percentage of share capital being acquired by the offeror
- a time period within which the shareholder can withdraw his acceptance.

The term 'unconditional as to acceptances' means that the offeror has obtained the minimum percentage and declares that accepting shareholders can no longer withdraw their acceptance.

If a would-be bidder decides to make an offer, the City Code is specific about the information it must contain. Furthermore, it cannot be withdrawn without the Takeover Panel's consent, unless it lapses or certain conditions are not met. Two conditions are common to most offers

(a) no reference to the Competition Commission

(b) acceptances in excess of 50% and, at the option of the bidder, 90% of the shareholding is received.

If acceptances exceed 90%, the offer can in general be enforced compulsorily for 100% of the shares (see minorities below).

7.2 Competition Commission

Under the provisions of the *Fair Trading Act 1973,* where any proposed merger means

(a) a quarter or more of any category of goods or services in the UK are controlled by the resultant company, or

(b) the value of assets to be taken over exceeds £70m

it may be referred by the Director General of Fair Trading to the Commission. The Commission must report on the merger within six months, stating whether or not it is in the public interest. If it is not, the Department of Trade may make it illegal.

7.3 The Competition Act 1998

The Competition Act 1998 came into force on 1 March 2000. It reforms and strengthens UK competition law in line with new European rules. With effect from 1 April 1999 the Competition Commission has taken on the previous functions of the Monopolies and Mergers Commission. Fines for companies that operate anti-competitive agreements can be up to 10% of the company's turnover in the year of infringment ie, very large amounts for a large company.

7.4 EC regulations

EC regulations are similar to Competition Commission regulations in the UK but set in an EC context.

If an offer gives rise to a *concentration* (ie, a potential monopoly) within the EC the European Commission may initiate proceedings. This can result in considerable delay.

7.5 The ways in which the rights of the minority are protected

Generally speaking, company law in the UK is not primarily concerned with changes in the ownership of companies, and therefore with acquisition by share transfer. However, there is one important exception, and that is the provisions (Ss428-430 CA85) that enable

(a) the acquiring company, once it has obtained 90% in value of the shares concerned within four months of making the offer, compulsorily to acquire the other 10% on the same terms (subject to a right of appeal to the court by the dissenting minority), and

(b) the dissenting minority, once the acquiring company obtains 90% in value of the shares concerned, to require that company to buy their shares on the same terms.

7.6 The obligations on directors during takeover bids

The obligations on directors during a take-over are set by the procedures in the City Code. As we saw above, the City Code requires certain actions to be performed by the offeror company prior to and during a bid, and the company's actions are, of course performed by the directors.

In addition there are obligations on the offeree company directors. Clearly the directors in the target company have a large element of self interest in the outcome of the bid. If it is successful they may lose their jobs or the independence which they formerly experienced. Examples of obligations include the following.

(a) The directors in the offeree company must allow the shareholders to decide about the offer being made.

(b) They must communicate with their shareholders to recommend or not recommend the offer, giving full information to support their recommendation.

(c) They are encouraged to seek independent advice eg, from a merchant bank.

8 CHAPTER SUMMARY

A liquidation may be one of three types, one compulsory and two voluntary. Each method has specified grounds for the winding up to commence and set procedures to follow.

Administration orders are an alternative to winding up to allow the company time to sort out its affairs.

Persons with fixed or floating charges on the assets of a company will have the power to appoint a receiver to help to ensure payments of debts.

9 SELF TEST QUESTIONS

9.1 What are the three methods of winding up a company? (1.2)

9.2 What are the two main grounds for compulsory winding up? (2.2)

9.3 Who may petition for compulsory winding up? (2.5)

9.4 What is the significance of a statutory declaration of solvency? (3.2)

9.5 What is a new alternative procedure to winding up? (5.1)

9.6 What is the difference between a receiver and an administrative receiver? (6.2)

9.7 What does the report of the administrative receiver contain? (6.4)

9.8 What is the order of priority of payments made by a receiver? (6.5)

9.9 What monopolies may be referred by the Director General of Fair Trading? (7.2)

9.10 What obligations are imposed on offeree company directors during a take-over bid? (7.6)

10 EXAMINATION TYPE QUESTIONS

10.1 Winding up procedures

Where directors feel that a company ought to be wound up what procedure must be followed to carry this out? **(10 marks)**

10.2 Duties of an administrative receiver

Explain the position and duties of an administrative receiver appointed by the trustees for the debenture holders under a power in the trust deed. In what ways would his position and duties be changed if he were a liquidator in a creditors' voluntary liquidation? **(10 marks)**

11 ANSWERS TO EXAMINATION TYPE QUESTIONS

11.1 Winding up procedures

There are two methods of winding up a company

(a) compulsory winding up by the court; and
(b) voluntary winding up.

Compulsory winding up

S122 IA86 outlines a number of situations under which the court may wind up a company.

A petition for winding up may be presented by the company (but more usually comes from a creditor). If made by the company it will obviously be the directors who make the presentation.

The court is not forced to make an order but if it does, it will appoint a liquidator and once he has finished will make an order dissolving the company.

The directors will be disinclined to use a compulsory winding up because it is expensive and lengthy.

Voluntary winding up

There are two types:

(a) **Members' voluntary winding up**

(i) The directors must sign a statutory declaration saying the company will be able to meet its debts as they fall due.

(ii) The company must pass a special resolution. A meeting will have to be called.

(iii) The company in general meeting will appoint a liquidator.

(b) **Creditors' voluntary winding up**

(i) Extraordinary general meeting and extraordinary resolution

With a creditors' voluntary winding up the company's directors must call an extraordinary general meeting in which an extraordinary resolution needs to be passed to sanction winding up on grounds that the company cannot continue its business because of its liabilities.

(ii) Creditors' meeting

(1) A company must call a creditors' meeting within fourteen days of the resolution.

(2) Notice must be sent by post to creditors. It must also be placed in the London Gazette.

(iii) At the creditors' meeting the directors must produce

(1) a full statement of the company's affairs
(2) a list of creditors.

(iv) A liquidation committee may be appointed comprising

(1) five persons appointed by creditors at a meeting
(2) five members as well.

Creditors can veto company appointees.

The liquidation committee has three purposes:

(1) to assist the liquidator as a representative body
(2) to keep an eye on him
(3) to exercise certain powers (eg, paying off a certain class) thus removing the need to call a full meeting every time a decision is made.

(v) Appointment of liquidator

Creditors and members can nominate a liquidator; but the creditors' choice prevails.

11.2 Duties of an administrative receiver

An administrative receiver is a receiver appointed under a floating charge over the whole or substantially the whole of the company's property. He may be appointed by the court or by the debenture holders or by a trustee for the debenture holders under a power contained in the debenture or trust deed. He will be appointed to protect the interests of the debenture holders in circumstances where their loan is not being repaid or their security is in jeopardy.

Position

The administrative receiver's purpose is to ensure that the debenture holders are paid. His position depends on the terms of the debenture and provisions contained in the IA86.

The administrative receiver is not personally liable on existing contracts of the company. An administrative receiver is deemed to be the agent of the company unless and until it goes into liquidation. He is personally liable on any contract entered into by him and on contracts of employment adopted by him. Thus both he and the company will be liable on such contracts. However, the section also provides that nothing he does or does not do within fourteen days of his appointment can be regarded as adopting contracts of employment. Thus he is given fourteen days to decide whether to adopt the employment contracts or not.

An administrative receiver is entitled to an indemnity in respect of contractual liabilities provided he had authority to enter into the contracts.

Duties

The receiver's duty is to take possession of the property of the company subject to the charge and realise it for the benefit of the debenture holders.

He must give notice of his appointment to the company forthwith and to the creditors within twenty eight days.

Every invoice, order and letter must contain a statement that he has been appointed.

He must require a statement of affairs showing details including the company's assets, debts and liabilities and the creditors' names, addresses and securities held by them. The statement may be prepared by any relevant officer or employee.

Within three months of his appointment, unless the court allows an extension of time, he must make a report to the Registrar and all secured and unsecured creditors setting out details of the events leading to his appointment, disposals of company property by him, the amount due to the debenture holders and the amount available to pay other creditors.

He must ensure that he applies assets which come into his hands according to the rights of the persons concerned. He must take account of the rights of mortgagees and suppliers with effective reservations of title. He must pay claims accordingly to statutory preferential creditors. Failure to do so renders the receiver liable to the preferential creditors.

Once his duties have been discharged he resigns and sends notice to the Registrar.

Liquidator

A liquidator is the person who is appointed to carry out the winding up of a company. In a creditors' voluntary liquidation he is appointed by the creditors and members. If the person selected by the members is different from the person selected by the creditors, the creditors' nominee becomes liquidator.

Position

The liquidator's purpose is to wind up the company. His position depends almost entirely on provisions in IA86 and the rules made under that Act.

The liquidator acts as an agent of the company. He is not personally liable on existing contracts of the company, nor on contracts which he enters into on behalf of the company.

Duties

A liquidator's duty is towards the creditors to ensure fair distribution on the winding up of the company.

He must call separate meetings of both members and creditors every year and when the company's affairs are fully wound up.

He must within fourteen days of his appointment publish in the Gazette and deliver to the Registrar a notice of his appointment.

Similarities of administrative receiver and liquidator

Both must be qualified insolvency practitioners.

Both may be liable for breach of duty and neither may make a secret profit from their position and may be ordered by the court to repay or restore property to the company.

24 FINANCIAL ANALYSIS - RATIO ANALYSIS

INTRODUCTION & LEARNING OBJECTIVES

This and the next three chapters consider the exam question or part of an exam question requiring an analysis of financial and related information. Much of this chapter should be a revision to you of ratios. There is little that is new compared to your previous studies in the type of ratios to compute. What the examiner does expect is a higher level of awareness as to the significance of the ratios computed.

When you have studied this chapter you should be able to do the following:

- Understand the background to the use of financial analysis
- Compute ratios and understand their meaning
- Appreciate the use of financial analysis in a variety of situations.

1 SOURCES OF INFORMATION FOR THE PURPOSE OF COMPARISONS

1.1 The demand for financial analysis and the sources of information

The demand for financial analysis comes from user groups interested in the performance and financial position of a business. The main user groups are:

- Management
- Existing and potential shareholders
- Agents for shareholders; investment analysts
- Lenders.

The sources of information for these user groups varies as not all have the same access to information.

External users have access to published accounts and interim statements. Commentaries on these statements can be found in the financial press and a useful compendium of all press comment is to be found in McCarthy cards. For the individual shareholder, McCarthy's is expensive but many public libraries include the service in their business reference department.

Records of financial data in a standard format for all companies are available in two main references - Moody's and Extel. Once again these are expensive to the non-professional analyst but are available in public libraries.

Internal users ie, management have access to any information from the data collected by the company but how good this information is depends on the quality of the management information system. In practice, management is often basing decisions on inadequate information due to a poor management information system.

Data on competitors can be available to management if the business participates in an inter-firm comparison scheme.

All types of users also need information about the industry in which the company operates and the economy in general. If the industry is in a recessionary period, this will fundamentally affect the analysis for a particular company within the industry. The main sources of information are Government statistics and market research organisations.

1.2 The role of accounting theory

Accounting theory should provide a framework for consistently applied standards to the data produced by entities. However there are many difficulties in comparing entities in practice. For example:

(a) Businesses may operate in different sectors of the market. One business aims at the 'quality' end of the market and has low volume and high margins whilst another concentrates on the supply of basic versions of the product or service.

(b) Many entities operate in a number of markets (ie they have different degrees of diversification) and thus comparison is difficult on the relatively limited amount of segmental data supplied.

(c) There may be valid differences in accounting policies.

1.3 The social and political considerations affecting corporate regulation and reporting

There are many reasons why corporate regulation and reporting is at a certain level. Disclosure of information may be required as a result of a combination of the following influences

- Country being member of political/social/economic grouping eg, EU
- Employee rights legislation
- Environmental concerns
- Financial scandals (can result in tightening of regulatory supervision).

An understanding of the reason why a particular regulation exists can help in determining the relative importance of that information to the financial analysis of the business.

1.4 The problems that multi-national companies face

The problems of multi-national companies have been addressed in an earlier chapter. In summary the problems include the following.

(a) Accounting standards and accounting policies can vary significantly between countries. This means that financial statements may have to be restated to comply with local practice. There is a general tendency for accounting standards to become more prescriptive with the result that particular accounting treatments which are required in some countries may not be allowed in others. For example, there are some significant differences between UK reporting practice and US GAAP:

  (i) SSAP 15 requires the use of the partial provision method for deferred tax; US GAAP requires full provision.

  (ii) Revaluation of fixed assets is not allowed under US GAAP; while it is increasingly encouraged in the UK.

  (iii) SSAP 24 and US GAAP require different treatments of pension costs and different methods for valuing pension scheme assets.

(b) A country may require additional information about the group and not just information on the transactions directly entered into by the subsidiary. For example, internal transfer prices are set by the group and may materially affect the level of declared profit in a particular country. The country therefore needs to know about possible losses of revenue.

(c) Local tax legislation may impose commercial restrictions on operations.

(d) A group listed on more than one stock exchange will need to comply with different rules.

1.5 The role the Stock Exchange plays in the operation of the efficient market hypothesis

The EMH should be well known to you from financial management. It provides a theoretical view of the extent to which share prices reflect publicly available and/or inside information.

If the Stock Exchange is 'efficient', all publicly available information is reflected in the share price. Transaction costs do not deter the buying/selling of stocks and the market should not be dominated by a few people/institutions.

As a result share prices should reflect the economic performance of the company, the business in which it operates and the economy in general. Creative accounting should not influence the share price as the market sees through such practices. It also means that 'fundamental analysis' (ie, examining and analysing accounting and other information) cannot identify profitable opportunities.

1.6 The nature of insider information

Definition Insider information is information which if available to the stock market, would affect the share price.

As a consequence the stock market needs to place restrictions on those possessing such information (eg, directors) from using such information to their personal advantage.

1.7 Stock Exchange regulations and their effectiveness to prevent insider dealing

There are statutory and Stock Exchange provisions relating to insider dealing. Examples of the regulations include the following.

(a) A director cannot deal in shares in the two months before interim and final results.

(b) Details of 'significant transactions' (eg, major acquisitions of businesses), and preliminary results must be notified to the Stock Exchange. As a consequence the information then becomes public knowledge.

Insider dealing is a criminal offence with a seven years maximum imprisonment and/or a fine. In addition, inspectors of companies may be appointed.

1.8 The other regulations relating to membership of the Stock Exchange

A most important condition for listing is acceptance of the *continuing obligations* which will apply following admission. These obligations form the basis of the relationship between an issuer and the Stock Exchange, governing the disclosure of information necessary to protect investors and maintain an orderly market.

Examples of the continuing obligations:

(a) **Annual report**

The company must include in its annual report and accounts about twenty specific items including, for example:

(i) the name of the principal country in which each subsidiary operates - where the number of subsidiaries is large, particulars with regard to those of less importance can be omitted;

(ii) a statement as at the end of the financial year, showing the interests of each director in the capital of any member of the group, together with any options in respect of such capital, distinguishing between beneficial or non-beneficial interests: the statement should include by way of note any change in those interests or options occurring between the end of the financial year and a date not more than one month prior to the date of the notice of meeting or, if there has been no such change, disclosure of that fact.

(b) **Historical summaries**

The chairman of the Stock Exchange wrote to all listed companies in 1964 recommending that they should include a ten-year historical summary in their annual financial statements.

In practice, because the historical summary is additional voluntary information, many listed companies now give only a five-year historical summary.

(c) **Half-yearly reports and preliminary profits statements for the full year**

As soon as possible after the draft accounts, even though subject to final audit, have been agreed with the auditors as the basis for completing the annual report, those accounts, adjusted to reflect any dividend decision, should be approved, in view of their price sensitive nature, as the basis of a preliminary profits statement. The completion of the annual report and accounts would then proceed after the announcement.

A company must prepare a half-yearly report on the group's activities and profit or loss during the first six months of each financial year. The half-yearly report must be either sent to the holders of listed securities or inserted as a paid advertisement in two national daily newspapers not later than four months after the end of the period to which it relates.

2 INTER TEMPORAL ANALYSIS

2.1 Horizontal analysis

The most straightforward method of analysing financial statements is to simply compare the current year with the previous year and to note and rationalise any significant changes. This is often performed in analytical review procedures before proceeding to any detailed audit work. It is known as 'horizontal analysis', but its formal title is hardly important as it amounts to the application of basic common sense. It is a form of 'inter temporal' analysis ie, a comparison between accounting periods.

The line by line comparison must be performed whilst also considering

(a) the change in turnover, and
(b) the relevance of anything else you may know about the company.

In practice an analyst will find any other information in the directors' report, in the chairman's report or in press cuttings about the company or the industry in which it operates.

In an examination question, this other information is usually found in the opening lines of the question, where you will be told

(a) what the company does, and
(b) why you are being asked to interpret the accounts.

Further information is then usually provided in the notes following on from the numerical information.

You must ensure that your answer makes best use of this additional information. In a good answer all of the points will be referred to and used to rationalise the observed trends.

The change in turnover underpins the analysis. Assuming a 30% increase in turnover, we might predict a 30% increase in everything else in the profit and loss account. Balance sheet changes, for example in stocks and debtors, may be rationalised in the same way. The following sections are intended to prompt some ideas for the profit and loss account.

2.2 Gross profit

If gross profit has not increased in line with turnover, you need to establish why not. Is the discrepancy due to

(a) increased 'purchase' costs; if so are the costs under the company's control (ie, does the company manufacture the goods sold)?

(b) stock write offs (likely where the company operates in a volatile market place, such as fashion retail), or

(c) other costs being allocated to cost of sales - for example, research and development expenditure.

The other information in the question should provide some clues.

2.3 Operating profit

By the time you have reached operating profit there are many more factors to consider. If you are provided with a breakdown of expenses you can use this for further line by line comparisons. Bear in mind that

(a) some costs are fixed or semi-fixed (for example property costs) and therefore not expected to change in line with turnover

(b) other costs are variable (for example, packing and distribution, and commission).

2.4 The likely causes of changes in profitability identified by calculating its component parts

Also remember that in arriving at operating profit various items which affect the analysis may have been included, for example

(a) exceptional items
(b) depreciation and profits or losses on disposal of fixed assets
(c) research and development (if not already dealt with)
(d) advertising expenditure
(e) staff costs which may have risen in line with inflation
(f) pension costs including any surpluses or deficiencies (dealt with according to SSAP 24)
(g) amortisation of intangibles (including goodwill)
(h) directors' emoluments, and
(i) government grants received.

The list above is not intended to be comprehensive, but it may serve as a source of ideas and it should prompt your own thoughts.

2.5 Profit before tax

In moving from operating profit to profit before tax, certain items appear

(a) unusual items required to be disclosed by FRS 3,
(b) investment income, and
(c) interest payable.

It is unlikely that any of these will move in line with turnover. However, a simple year on year comparison may highlight other changes, such as

(a) changes in holdings of investments
(b) leasing charges, and
(c) increased borrowings.

These figures may tie in with the balance sheet. Check them against

(a) the investments held (both fixed and current), and
(b) the level of borrowings (particularly the bank overdraft).

2.6 Profit after tax

It is useful to compute the 'rate' of tax by comparing the tax charge to the profits before tax. The rate should be fairly constant from year to year. The company's policy for providing deferred tax may also be relevant.

2.7 Dividends

Dividends should be compared to the previous year. Even when profit for the year has declined, a fall in dividends for a plc is an extremely worrying sign. Major companies usually try to avoid this where at all possible.

2.8 Trend analysis

Extending the horizontal analysis over a number of years provides *trends.* To see more clearly the trend, the figure in the first year of the series is given a value of 100. Subsequent years figures are related to this base.

2.9 Example

Trend analysis: Mack plc

	20X0	*20X1*	*20X2*	*20X3*	*20X4*
Turnover (£m)	629.8	688.0	770.5	951.9	1,156.5
Index (20X0 base = 100)	100.0	109.2	122.3	151.1	183.6
Trading profit (£m)	44.8	48.0	55.9	72.6	93.8
Index (20X0 base = 100)	100.0	107.1	124.7	162.0	209.4

If inflation is taken account of, the figures or the indices could be restated. If in the above example the average RPI for each of the years was:

	20X0	*20X1*	*20X2*	*20X3*	*20X4*
RPI	130	136	146	140	160

The figures could be converted into 20X4 £m.

	20X0	*20X1*	*20X2*	*20X3*	*20X4*
Turnover (20X4 £m)	775.1	809.4	844.4	1,087.9	1,156.5
Trading profit (20X4 £m)	55.1	56.5	61.3	83.0	93.8

The working is:

$$\text{Figure} \times \frac{\text{RPI 20X4}}{\text{RPI for year figure taken from}}$$

Or the index could be adjusted.

	20X0	*20X1*	*20X2*	*20X3*	*20X4*
Turnover index	100.0	109.2	122.3	151.1	183.6
Adjusted for inflation	100.0	104.4	108.9	140.3	149.2

The working is:

$$\text{Index for the year} \times \frac{\text{Index for base year}}{\text{Index for the year}}$$

The problems of changing price levels are further examined in the next chapter.

In the examination you are unlikely to be required to compute trends owing to the time involved but you may be asked to interpret them.

3 DEFINITION, VARIATIONS IN DEFINITION AND CALCULATION OF IMPORTANT RATIOS

3.1 Introduction

Ratio analysis is a more sophisticated technique for analysing financial statements. It is the next step after the so-called horizontal analysis. (Ratios can also be shown in trends).

In general, ratio analysis should only be used in answering exam questions where the question specifically calls for use of ratios.

For example the question might state 'using the principal analytical ratios'. In this case the following should be calculated

(a) return on capital employed
(b) profit margin (usually net profit to sales)
(c) current or quick ratio, and
(d) gearing ratio.

Very often the question gives no indication of which ratios to calculate, in which case you must make a choice.

3.2 The aspects of financial performance that each ratio is intended to assess

The variety of ratios that could be calculated is vast; so it is important to restrict the calculations by being selective. The ratios chosen should be the key ones relevant to the requirements of the question. These may be further limited by the available information (ie, there may be some you are simply unable to calculate). This point is considered further below.

Ratios can be classified into three main groups, these are summarised in the table below.

Type	Reflects	Examples
Profitability	Performance of company and its managers including the efficiency of asset usage	ROCE GP% Stock turnover Debtors and creditors days
Financial	Financial structure and stability of the company	Gearing Current and liquidity ratios
Investment	Relationship of the number of ordinary shares and their price to the profits, dividends and assets of the company	EPS P/E ratio Dividend yield Dividend cover Net assets per share

The managers of the company are likely to be concerned about all aspects of the company and therefore may want to know about all of the key ratios in each category.

Shareholders or potential investors are concerned primarily with the investment ratios though certain financial stability and profitability measures are also likely to be of interest (for example gearing and ROCE).

Creditors are most likely to be concerned about financial stability, though a bank, acting as a major source of finance, will usually also look at profitability.

3.3 Commenting on the ratio

Ratios are meaningless on their own, thus most of the marks in an exam question will be available for sensible, well explained and accurate comments on key ratios.

If you doubt that you have anything to say the following points should serve as a useful checklist

(a) what does the ratio literally mean?
(b) what does a change in the ratio mean?
(c) what is the norm?
(d) what are the limitations of the ratio?

3.4 The acceptable range of values that a healthy company should achieve for those ratios

There is little that can be stated in general terms about the acceptable range of values. Profitability rates will vary between industry sectors and within industries for many reasons. The financial structure of a business can also vary considerably and yet the business operates 'healthily'. An oft quoted norm for the current ratio is 2 and the quick ratio is 1 but a supermarket for example with no credit customers and strong influence on its suppliers will have ratios far lower than this. In general the most meaningful analysis of ratios in terms of their acceptability is how well a business does in relation to its competitors.

3.5 Further information required

Any analyst in practice will be limited in the analysis he can perform by the amount of information available. He is unlikely to have access to all the facts which are available to a company's management.

Similarly, an auditor carrying out analytical review perhaps at the planning stage of the audit is likely to come up with a long list of further information he needs, or questions he would like to ask.

In the examination the information which can be provided about a company in any one question will be limited. Part (a) of such a question could well ask you to interpret the available information, perhaps in the context of an auditor planning the audit. Part (b) could easily ask you to state what further information you require.

4 PROFITABILITY RATIOS

4.1 Return on capital employed (ROCE)

The absolute figure of profit earned is not, in itself, significant since the size of the business earning that profit may vary enormously. It is significant to consider the size of the profit figure relative to the size of the business, size being expressed in terms of the quantity of capital employed by that business.

The return on capital employed is the ratio which measures this relationship. It is a key *business objective,* and is thus the key ratio in assessing financial achievement. It reflects the *earning power* of the business operations.

The ratio in simple form is

$$\frac{\text{Profit}}{\text{Capital employed}} \times 100\%$$

ROCE is also known as the primary ratio because it is often the most important measure of profitability.

The ratio shows how efficiently a business is using its resources. If the return is very low, the business may be better off realising its assets and investing the proceeds in a high interest account! (This may sound extreme, but should be considered particularly for a small, unprofitable business with valuable assets such as freehold property). Furthermore a low return can easily become a loss if the business suffers a downturn.

Once calculated, ROCE should be compared with

(a) *previous years' figures* - provided there have been no changes in accounting policies unless suitable adjustments have been made to facilitate comparison (note, however that the effect of not replacing fixed assets is that their value will decrease and ROCE will increase)

(b) *company's target ROCE* - where the company's management has determined a target return as part of its budget procedure, consistent failure by a part of the business to meet the target may make it a target for disposal

(c) *the cost of borrowings* - if the cost of borrowing is say 10% and ROCE 7%, then further borrowings will reduce EPS unless the extra money can be used in areas where the ROCE is higher than the cost of borrowings

(d) *other companies in same industry* - care is required in interpretation, since there may be

(i) different accounting policies eg, research and development expenditure, stock valuation and depreciation

(ii) different ages of plant - where assets are written down to low book values the ROCE will appear high

(iii) leased assets which may not appear in the balance sheet at all. (SSAP 21 requires assets held under finance leases to be on the balance sheet but not those held under operating leases).

4.2 The problem of defining profit and net assets

Note that any upwards revaluation of fixed assets causes a reduction in ROCE by

(a) increasing the capital employed, and
(b) decreasing profits, by a higher depreciation charge.

Return on capital employed can be calculated in a number of different ways.

One version is the return on shareholders' equity which is more relevant for existing or prospective shareholders than management.

$$\text{Return on equity} = \frac{\text{Profit after interest after preference dividend}}{\text{Ordinary share capital + reserves}}$$

Profit may be before or after tax. After tax is a more accurate reflection of profits (management should seek to minimise tax) however as you will know deferred tax provisions are likely to be subjective so profit before tax may be more objective.

The other commonly used ROCE is

$$\text{Overall return} = \frac{\text{Operating profit}}{\text{Share capital + reserves + all borrowings}}$$

This is used by managers assessing performance.

Further points

(a) Treatment of associates and investments

Where the profit excludes investment income, the balance sheet carrying amounts for associates and investments should be deducted from the capital employed.

This gives an accurate measure of trading performance. If associates and investments are not deducted, the overall profit figure should include income from investments and associates.

(b) Large cash balances are not contributing to profits and some analysts therefore deduct them from capital employed (to compare operating profits with operating assets). However it is usually acceptable not to make this adjustment as ROCE is a performance measure and management have decided to operate with that large balance.

4.3 Gross profit percentage

$$\frac{\text{Gross profit}}{\text{Turnover}} \times 100\%$$

This is the margin that the company makes on its sales.

It is expected to remain reasonably constant. Since the ratio consists of a small number of components, a change may be traced to a change in

(a) selling prices - normally deliberate though sometimes unavoidable for example, because of increased competition

(b) sales mix - often deliberate

(c) purchase cost - including carriage or discounts

(d) production cost - materials, labour or production overheads

(e) stock - errors in counting, valuing or cut-off; stock shortages.

Inter-company comparison of margins can be very useful but it is especially important to look at businesses within the same sector. For example food retailing is able to support low margins because of the high volume of sales. A manufacturing industry would usually have higher margins.

Low margins usually suggest poor performance but may be due to expansion costs (launching a new product) or trying to increase market share. Lower margins than usual suggest scope for improvement.

Above average margins are usually a sign of good management although unusually high margins may make the competition keen to join in and enjoy the 'rich pickings'.

A trading profit margin is

$$\frac{\text{Trading profit}}{\text{Turnover}} \text{(before interest, investment income and tax)}$$

This is affected by more factors than the gross profit margin but it is equally useful and if the company does not disclose a cost of sales (perhaps using format 2) it may be used on its own in lieu of the GP%.

One of the many factors affecting the trading profit margin is depreciation, which is open to considerable subjective judgement. Inter-company comparisons should be made after suitable adjustments to align accounting policies.

4.4 Stock turnover

$$\frac{\text{Cost of sales}}{\text{Stocks}}$$

This yields a multiple expressed as, say, 10 times per annum. If format 2 is used, then simply compare turnover and stocks, though bear in mind that this is also affected by the margin achieved by the company.

An alternative is to express this as so many days stock

$$\frac{\text{Stocks}}{\text{Cost of sales}} \times 365 \text{ days}$$

Sometimes an average (based on the average stock) is calculated which has a smoothing effect but may dampen the effect of a major change in the period.

An increasing number of days (or a diminishing multiple) implies that stock is turning over less quickly. This is usually regarded as a bad sign

(a) it may reflect lack of demand for the goods
(b) it may reflect poor stock control, with its associated costs such as storage and insurance
(c) it may ultimately lead to stock obsolescence and related write offs.

However, it may not necessarily be bad where

(a) management are buying stock in larger quantities to take advantage of trade discounts

(b) management have increased stock levels to avoid stockouts, and

(c) the increase is slight and due to distortion of the ratio caused by comparing a year end stock figure with cost of sales for the year and that year has been one of increasing growth.

Stock turnover ratios vary enormously with the nature of the business. For example, a fishmonger would have a stock turnover period of 1-2 days, whereas a building contractor may have a stock turnover period of 200 days. Manufacturing companies may have a stock turnover ratio of 60-100 days; this period is likely to increase as the goods made become larger and more complex.

For large and complex items (for example rolling stock or aircraft) there may be sharp fluctuations in stock turnover according to whether delivery took place just before or just after the year end.

A manufacturer should take into consideration

(a) reliability of suppliers; if the supplier is unreliable it is prudent to hold more raw materials, and

(b) demand; if demand is erratic it is prudent to hold more finished goods.

4.5 Debtors turnover

$$\frac{\text{Trade debtors}}{\text{Turnover}} \times 100\%$$

This can be expressed as a percentage as above or as a number of days

$$\frac{\text{Trade debtors}}{\text{Turnover}} \times 365 \text{ days}$$

The trade debtors used may be a year end figure or the average for the year. Where an average is used to calculate a number of days the ratio is the average number of days' credit taken by customers.

For cash based businesses like supermarkets, debtors days is unlikely to exceed 1 as there are no true credit sales.

For other businesses the result should be compared with the stated credit policy. A period of 30 days or 'at the end of the month following delivery' are common credit terms.

Increasing debtors days is usually a bad sign as it suggests lack of proper credit control. However, it may be due to

(a) a deliberate policy to extend the stated credit period to attract more trade, and
(b) one major new customer being allowed different terms.

Falling debtors days is usually a good sign, though it could indicate that the company is suffering a cash shortage.

The debtors days ratio can be distorted by

(a) using year end figures which do not represent average debtors

(b) debt factoring which results in very low debtors, and

(c) other credit finance agreements such as hire purchase, where there is insufficient analysis of turnover (HP debtors should be shown separately) to calculate proper ratios.

4.6 Creditors days

This is usually expressed as

$$\frac{\text{Trade creditors}}{\text{Purchases}} \times 365 \text{ days}$$

and represents the credit period taken by the company from its suppliers. An average of trade creditors may also be used.

Where purchases are not known, cost of sales is used, or failing that, sales.

The ratio is always compared to previous years. Once again there are two main contrasting points

(a) a long credit period may be good as it represents a source of free finance, or

(b) a long credit period may indicate that the company is unable to pay more quickly because of liquidity problems.

Note that if the credit period is long

(a) the company may develop a poor reputation as a slow payer and may not be able to find new suppliers

(b) existing suppliers may decide to discontinue supplies, and

(c) the company may be losing out on worthwhile cash discounts.

5 THE LIQUIDITY POSITION OF COMPANIES

5.1 Calculation and explanation of importance of a company's cash cycle

The investment made in working capital is largely a function of sales and, therefore, it is useful to consider the problem in terms of a firm's (**cash operating**) cycle.

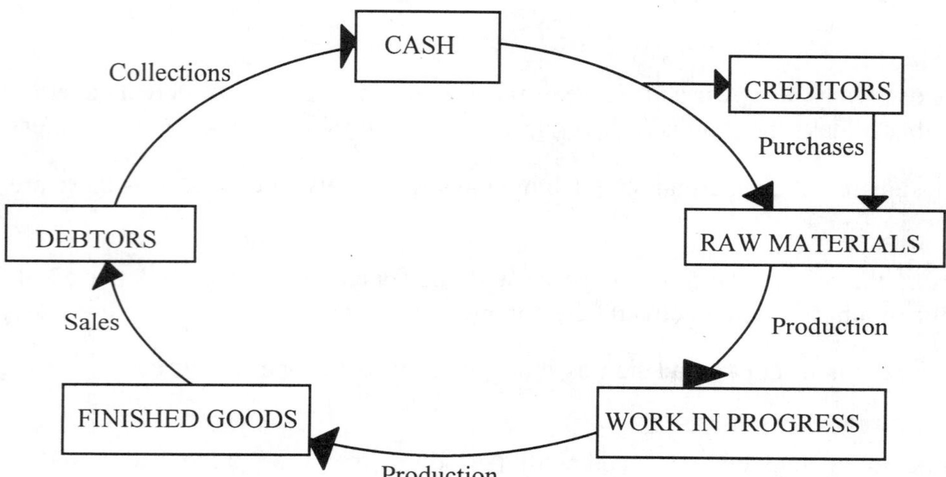

The cycle reflects a firm's investment in working capital as it moves through the production process towards sales. The investment in working capital gradually increases, firstly being only in raw materials, but then in labour and overhead as production progresses. This investment must be maintained throughout the production process, the finished goods holding period and up to the final collection of cash from trade debtors. Note that the net investment can be reduced by taking trade credit from suppliers.

The faster a firm can 'push' items around the operating cycle the lower its investment in working capital will be. However, too little investment in working capital can lose sales since customers will generally prefer to buy from suppliers who are prepared to extend trade credit, and if items are not held in stock when required by customers, sales may be lost.

With some fairly basic financial information it is possible to measure the length of the working capital cycle for a given firm.

5.2 Activity

Extracts from the profit and loss account for the year and the balance sheet as at the end of the year for a company show:

	£
Sales	250,000
Cost of goods sold	210,000
Purchases	140,000
Debtors	31,250
Creditors	21,000
Stock	92,500

Note: assume all sales and purchases are on credit terms.

Calculate the working capital cycle.

5.3 Activity solution

(1) Creditors

Average payment collection period

$= \left(365 \times \frac{\text{Creditors}}{\text{Purchases}}\right)$ $\quad 365 \times \frac{21}{140} =$ $\quad$ (55 days)

(2) Debtors:

Average collection period

$= \left(365 \times \frac{\text{Debtors}}{\text{Sales}}\right)$ $\quad 365 \times \frac{31.25}{250} =$ $\quad$ 46 days

(3) Stock turnover:

$= 365 \times \frac{\text{Stock}}{\text{Cost of goods sold}}$ $\quad 365 \times \frac{92.5}{210}$ $\quad$ 161 days

Length of working capital cycle $\quad$ 152 days

5.4 Ratios

Two ratios are used to measure a business's ability to meet its own short-term liabilities; these are

(a) current or working capital ratio

$$\frac{\text{Current assets}}{\text{Current liabilities}}$$

(b) liquidity, acid test or quick assets ratio

$$\frac{\text{Current assets - stock}}{\text{Current liabilities}}$$

It is not usually appropriate to calculate both ratios when answering a time pressured exam question as trends in the ratios are likely to be similar.

As a general rule calculate only the current ratio unless the company has slow moving stocks (for example in the construction industry) in which case calculate the quick ratio instead.

5.5 Current ratio

The current ratio measures the adequacy of current assets to meet its short term liabilities. It reflects whether the company is in a position to meet its liabilities as they fall due.

Traditionally a current ratio of 2 or higher was regarded as appropriate for most businesses to maintain creditworthiness, however more recently a figure of 1.5 is regarded as the norm.

A higher figure should be regarded with suspicion as it may be due to

(a) high levels of stocks and debtors (check working capital management ratios), or

(b) high cash levels which could be put to better use (for example by investing in fixed assets).

The current ratio should be looked at in the light of what is normal for the business. For example, supermarkets tend to have low current ratios because

(a) there are no trade debtors, and

(b) there is usually very tight cash control as there will be considerable investment in developing new sites and improving existing sites.

It is also worth considering

(a) availability of further finance, for example is the overdraft at the limit? - very often this information is highly relevant but not disclosed in the accounts

(b) seasonal nature of the business - one way of doing this is to compare the interest charges in the profit and loss account with the overdraft and other loans in the balance sheet; if the interest rate appears abnormally high this is probably because the company has had higher levels of borrowings during the year

(c) long term liabilities and when they fall due and how will they be financed, and

(d) nature of the stocks - as stated above where stocks are slow moving, the quick ratio probably provides a better indicator of short term liquidity.

5.6 Quick ratio

This is also known as the acid test ratio because by eliminating stocks from current assets it provides the acid test of whether the company has sufficient resources (debtors and cash) to settle its liabilities. Norms for the quick ratio range from 1 to 0.7.

Like the current ratio it is relevant to consider the nature of the business (again supermarkets have very low quick ratios).

Sometimes the quick ratio is calculated on the basis of a six week time frame (ie, the quick assets are those which will turn into cash in six weeks; quick liabilities are those which fall due for payment within six weeks). This basis would usually include the following in quick assets

(a) bank, cash and short term investments, and
(b) trade debtors

thus excluding prepayment and stocks.

Quick liabilities would usually include

(a) bank overdraft which is usually repayable on demand
(b) trade creditors, tax and social security, and
(c) proposed dividends.

Corporation tax may be excluded.

When interpreting the quick ratio, care should be taken over the status of the bank overdraft. A company with a low quick ratio may actually have no problem in paying its creditors if sufficient overall overdraft facilities are available.

Both the current and quick ratio may be distorted by window dressing; for example, if the current ratio is 1.4 and trade creditors are paid just before the year end out of positive cash balances, the ratios improve as shown below

	Before	*Payment of £400 trade creditors*	*After*
Current assets	£1,400	-£400	£1,000
Current liabilities	£1,000	-£400	£600
Current ratio	1.4		1.7

5.7 The component cause of changes in liquidity

'Financial balance' is the balance between the various forms of available finance relative to the requirements of the business.

A business must have a *sufficient level of long-term capital* to finance its long-term investment in fixed assets. Part of the investment in current assets would also be financed by relatively permanent capital with the balance being provided by trade credit and other short-term borrowings. Any expansion in activity will normally require a broadening of the long-term capital base, without which 'overtrading' may develop.

Suitability of finance is also a key factor. A permanent expansion of a company's activities should not be financed by temporary, short-term borrowings. A short-term increase in activity such as the 'January sales' in a retail trading company could ideally be financed by overdraft.

A major addition to fixed assets such as the construction of a new factory would not normally be financed on a long-term basis by overdraft. It might be found, however, that the expenditure was temporarily financed by short-term loans until construction was completed, when the overdraft would be 'funded' by a long-term borrowing secured on the completed building.

5.8 The importance of maintaining a healthy liquid position

Overtrading arises where a company expands its turnover fairly rapidly without securing additional long-term capital adequate for its needs. The symptoms of overtrading are

(i) stocks increasing, possibly more than proportionately to sales
(ii) debtors increasing, possibly more than proportionately to sales
(iii) cash and liquid assets declining at a fairly alarming rate, and
(iv) creditors increasing rapidly.

The above symptoms simply imply that the company has expanded without giving proper thought to the necessity to expand its capital base. It has consequently continued to rely on its creditors and probably its bank overdraft to provide the additional finance required. It will reach a stage where creditors will withhold further supplies and bankers will refuse to honour further cheques until borrowings are reduced. The problem is that borrowings cannot be reduced until sales revenue is earned, which in turn cannot be achieved until production is completed, which in turn is dependent upon materials being available and wages paid. Overall result - deadlock and rapid financial collapse!

5.9 Corrective action where weaknesses are identified

This is a particularly difficult stage for any small to medium company. They have reached a stage in their life when conventional creditor and overdraft facilities are being stretched to the maximum, but they are probably too small to manage a flotation. In many cases, by proper planning, the company can arrange fixed term loan funding from the bank rather than relying exclusively on overdraft finance.

6 LONG-TERM FINANCIAL STABILITY

6.1 Gearing

'Gearing' is the relationship between a company's equity capital (also known as residual return capital) and reserves and its fixed return capital.

A company is *highly geared* if it has a substantial proportion of its capital in the form of preference shares or debentures or loan stock.

A company is said to have *low gearing* if only a small proportion of its capital is in the form of preference shares, debentures or loan stock.

A company financed entirely by equity shares has *no gearing.*

6.2 The implications of high or low gearing

The importance of gearing can be illustrated by an example as follows

Example

Two companies, A plc and B plc, both have capital of £10,000. A plc has it all in the form of equity shares of £1 each, B plc has 5,000 £1 equity shares and £5,000 of 10% debentures.

Both companies earn profits of £5,000 in year 1 and £2,000 in year 2. Tax is assumed at 35% and the dividend paid is 10p per share.

The position will be as follows

	A plc	*B plc*
	£	£
Shares	10,000	5,000
Debentures	-	5,000
	£10,000	£10,000

	A plc		*B plc*	
	Year 1	*Year 2*	*Year 1*	*Year 2*
	£	£	£	£
Profit before tax and debenture interest	5,000	2,000	5,000	2,000
Debenture interest	-	-	500	500
			4,500	1,500
Taxation (35%)	1,750	700	1,575	525
Earnings	3,250	1,300	2,925	975
Dividend (10%)	1,000	1,000	500	500
Retained profits	£2,250	300	£2,425	475
Earnings per share	32.5p	13p	58.5p	19.5p

The effects of gearing can be seen to be as follows

(a) debenture interest is an allowable deduction *before taxation,* whereas dividends are paid out of profits *after taxation;* company B has consistently higher retained profits than Company A.

(b) earnings of a highly geared company are more sensitive to profit changes; this is shown by the following table

Company	*A plc*	*B plc*
Change in profit before interest and taxation	-60%	-60%
Change in earnings	-60%	$-66\frac{2}{3}\%$

The reason for the fluctuation is obviously the element of debenture interest which must be paid regardless of profit level.

This more than proportionate change in earnings is important in relation to the share price of the companies. Many investors value their shares by applying a multiple (known as the P/E ratio) to the earnings per share. Applying a multiple of say 10 to the EPS disclosed above would indicate share valuations as follows

Company	*A plc*		*B plc*	
Year	1	2	1	2
Share price	£3.25	£1.30	£5.85	£1.95

Thus the price of a highly geared company will often be more volatile than a company with only a small amount of gearing.

Not all companies are suitable for a highly geared structure. A company must have two fundamental characteristics if it is to use gearing successfully. These are as follows

(a) **Relatively stable profits**

Debenture interest must be paid whether or not profits are earned. A company with erratic profits may have insufficient funds in a bad year with which to pay debenture interest. This would result in the appointment of a receiver and possibly the liquidation of the company.

(b) **Suitable assets for security**

Most issues of loan capital are secured on some or all of the company's assets which must be suitable for the purpose. A company with most of its capital invested in fast depreciating assets or stocks subject to rapid changes in demand and price would not be suitable for high gearing.

The classic examples of companies which are suited to high gearing are those in property investment and the hotel/leisure services industry. These companies generally enjoy relatively stable profits and have assets which are highly suitable for charging. Note that nonetheless these are industries that could be described as cyclical.

Companies not suited to high gearing would include those in the extractive industries and high-tech industries where constant changes occur. These companies could experience erratic profits and would generally have inadequate assets to pledge as security.

6.3 Methods of computation

There are two methods commonly used for expressing gearing

(a) the debt/equity ratio, calculated by taking

$$\frac{\text{Loans} + \text{redeemable preference share capital}}{\text{Ordinary share capital} + \text{reserves} + \text{minority interest}}$$

This is more sensitive than (b).

(b) the percentage of capital employed represented by borrowings

$$\frac{\text{Loans} + \text{redeemable preference share capital}}{\text{Total capital}}$$

where total capital is loans, redeemable preference share capital, ordinary share capital, reserves and minority interests.

Advanced aspects of computing the gearing ratio are dealt with below.

6.4 Ways in which the application of GAAP affects the gearing of an individual company

GAAP affects the gearing of an individual company because the variation in accounting policies affects the amount at which debt and equity are stated. An accounting standard of particular relevance here is FRS 4 which attempts to restrict the past ability of companies to classify debt as equity and to state debt at lower than its repayable amount (see later chapter). Other GAAP which affect gearing include the following.

(a) Treatment of development expenditure under SSAP 13 may result in the creation of an intangible asset. Alternatively, development expenditure may be written off as it is incurred.

(b) Revaluation of assets changes the value of equity but revaluation may not be undertaken by all companies.

(c) Non-recording of assets as they fall within the definition of operating leases. A company may have engineered a lease to ensure that it does fall within the operating lease definition rather than the finance lease definition.

6.5 The difficulty in assessing the gearing of a group

Earlier in the text we have seen the following possibilities

(a) Acquisition accounting - where an investment meets the definition of a subsidiary
(b) Merger accounting - as above but where certain other conditions are also fulfilled
(c) Equity accounting - where an investment meets the definition of an associate
(d) Proportional consolidation - permitted for non-corporate joint ventures (likely to be very rare following FRS 9)
(e) Non-consolidation of a subsidiary.

The following activity which is overly simplistic illustrates the effect each of these policies has on the gearing ratio and ROCE.

6.6 Activity

H Ltd, which has a number of 100% subsidiaries, acquired on 30 June 20X1 50% of the shares in S Ltd for £85,000. Balance sheets are as follows

	H Ltd Group	*S Ltd*	
	31 December 20X1	*30 June 20X1*	*31 December 20X1*
	£	£	£
Fixed assets	150,000	120,000	135,000
Net current assets	50,000	50,000	45,000
Long term debt	(20,000)	(40,000)	(40,000)
	£180,000	£130,000	£140,000
Share capital - £1 Ords	100,000	100,000	100,000
Profit and loss	80,000	30,000	40,000
	£180,000	£130,000	£140,000

The H Ltd Group made a profit after interest for 20X1 of £30,000, S Ltd a profit of £20,000. Consolidated balance sheets are to be prepared on the following bases of dealing with S Ltd:

(a) acquisition accounting
(b) merger accounting
(c) equity accounting
(d) proportional consolidation
(e) non-consolidation (ie, leave S Ltd in fixed assets at cost).

ROCE and gearing ratios should also be calculated. Ignore the fact that (b) could not be used with only a 50% holding and that (d) could not be used for a corporate body. Assume that goodwill has an indefinite useful economic life.

6.7 Activity solution

	(a) Acquisition accounting	*(b) Merger accounting*	*(c) Equity accounting*	*(d) Proportional consolidation*	*(e) Non consolidation*
	£	£	£	£	£
Fixed assets (150 – 85 + 135 + 20)	220,000	200,000	155,000	152,500	150,000
Net current assets	95,000	95,000	50,000	72,500	50,000
Long term debt	(60,000)	(60,000)	(20,000)	(40,000)	(20,000)
	£255,000	£235,000	£185,000	£185,000	£180,000
Share capital - £1 Ords	100,000	100,000	100,000	100,000	100,000
Profit and loss	85,000	65,000	85,000	85,000	80,000
	185,000	165,000	185,000	185,000	180,000
Minority interest	70,000	70,000	-	-	-
	£255,000	£235,000	£185,000	£185,000	£180,000

$$\text{ROCE} = \frac{\text{Profit}}{\text{Equity capital employed}}$$

	(a)	(b)	(c)	(d)	(e)
	$\frac{30+5}{255}$	$\frac{30+10}{235}$	$\frac{30+10}{185}$		$\frac{30}{180}$
	= 13.7%	= 17.0%	= 21.6%	= 21.6%	= 16.7%
Gearing = $\frac{\text{Debt}}{\text{Equity}}$	$\frac{60}{255}$	$\frac{60}{235}$	$\frac{20}{185}$	$\frac{40}{185}$	$\frac{20}{180}$
(Treating minority as equity)	= 23.5%	= 25.5%	= 10.8%	= 21.6%	= 11.1%

WORKINGS

		£
(W1)	**Goodwill**	
	Cost	85,000
	Share of net assets (50% × 130,000)	(65,000)
		£20,000
	Reserves	
	H Ltd	80,000
	S Ltd 50% (40,000 – 30,000)	5,000
		£85,000

(W2) **Difference on consolidation**

Cost	85,000
Share of share capital (50% × £100,000)	(50,000)
	£35,000

Reserves

H Ltd	80,000
S Ltd 50% × £40,000	20,000
Difference on consolidation	(35,000)
	£65,000

(W3) **Fixed assets**

H Ltd less cost of investment	65,000
S Ltd - share of net assets 50% × £140,000	70,000
Goodwill	20,000
	£155,000

6.8 Commentary

Clearly this simplistic example cannot bring out every relevant point. The main point is to realise just how different the ratios can be. A company concerned about ROCE in the above situation may well prefer to insist that it only has significant influence over S Ltd and not control. Prior to the CA89 and its extensive definitions of subsidiaries many companies successfully managed to keep subsidiaries off their balance sheet ie, not consolidated.

7 USE OF FINANCIAL ANALYSIS FOR AUDIT REVIEW

7.1 Introduction

This section reviews the various uses which can be made of financial analysis for audit purposes and any one of these could be the focus of attention in an examination question. There are no new ratios to learn; it is a case of slanting the analysis so that the objectives of the analysis can be achieved.

7.2 Review of financial statements

The auditor needs to carry out a review of the financial statements such as is sufficient, in conjunction with the conclusions drawn from the other audit evidence obtained, to give him a reasonable basis for his opinion on the financial statements. In broad terms, the auditor has performed his detailed checks and needs to consider what further evidence is required to conclude whether a true and fair view is shown by the financial statements.

A number of the review tasks involve analysis of the financial information and are summarised below. Most of these areas are touched on elsewhere in this text or in your earlier studies.

	Review task	**Regulations or guidance available**
(a)	Confirm acceptability of accounting policies	CA85 Accounting standards Exposure Drafts Industry practice Accounting standards in force in other countries, covering areas not yet covered by UK

(b)	Confirm compliance with disclosure requirements	CA85 Accounting standards Stock Exchange requirements
(c)	Review credibility	SAS 470 'Overall review of financial statements'
(d)	Going concern review	SAS 130 'The going concern basis in financial statements'
(e)	Post balance sheet audit review of contingencies	SSAP 17 and FRS 12 SAS 150 'Subsequent events'
(f)	Review of the directors' report to ensure consistency with financial statements, and general review of other financial information issued with financial statements	SAS 160 'Other information in documents containing audited financial statements'
(g)	Review of preceding financial statements and corresponding figures	SAS 450 'Opening balances and comparatives'
(h)	Review of related party transactions with directors	CA85 FRS 8 SAS 460 'Related parties'

7.3 Assessing going concern

The techniques of corporate failure prediction are particularly relevant here and are covered in a later chapter. The pointers to going concern problems which can be concentrated on in the analysis of financial statements include the following:

(a) Rapidly increasing costs which cannot be matched by increasing sales prices.

(b) Shortages of supplies.

(c) Adverse movements in exchange rates.

(d) Business failures amongst customers or suppliers.

(e) Loan repayments falling due in the near future.

(f) Higher gearing (fixed interest borrowing becoming a larger proportion of long-term finance).

(g) Long-term assets financed by short-term borrowing.

(h) Nearness to present borrowing limits with no sign of a reduction in borrowing requirements.

(i) Small companies financed by loans from directors. If these rank *pari passu* with other creditors they should be treated as current liabilities.

7.4 Cut off errors

Cut off refers to sales, purchases and stocks being accounted for in the correct accounting period. An analysis of working capital ratios including debtor collection, creditor payment and stock turnover may reveal changes at the year end compared to during the accounting period. These changes may result from different levels of activity but may also indicate manipulation of invoice dates etc.

7.5 Profit forecasts

This is not an audit function. A reporting accountant may be involved in work on a forecast and this has been examined in an earlier chapter. The main duty of the reporting accountant is to confirm the financial data has been correctly prepared from the assumptions rather than the correctness of the forecast itself and therefore the projection of past results to the future is of little direct relevance to the accountant. Financial analysis will however be relevant to the accountant within the organisation preparing the forecast in terms of extrapolating trends.

7.6 Audit risk

Definition Audit risk is the risk that an auditor fails to qualify his report when there is a material misstatement in the financial statements.

Preliminary analysis of a client each year enables an initial risk assessment to be made. This would involve a broad analytical review. Key ratios can be calculated from budget data for the current year and compared with the previous year. Significant and unexpected changes can thus be identified and examined further. Depending on the explanations given for the changes, the analysis helps to identify the risk areas of the audit.

8 RATIOS RELEVANT TO POTENTIAL INVESTORS

8.1 Earnings per share (EPS)

The calculation of EPS was covered earlier.

The EPS is used primarily as a measure of profitability thus an increasing EPS is seen as a good sign. The EPS is also used to calculate the price earnings ratio which is dealt with below.

8.2 The relationship between the market price of a share and its EPS

The price earnings ratio is the most widely referred to stock market ratio, also commonly described as an earnings multiple. It is calculated as the 'purchase of a number of years' earnings' but it represents the market's consensus of the future prospects of that share. The higher the P/E ratio, the faster the growth the market is expecting in the company's future EPS. Correspondingly, the lower the P/E ratio the lower the expected future growth.

Another aspect of interpreting it, is that a published EPS exists for a year and therefore the P/E ratio given in a newspaper is generally based on an increasingly out of date EPS. To give an extreme but simple example

X plc

For the year ended 31 December 20X6 EPS = 10p

- Overall market P/E ratio = 10
- P/E ratio for X plc = 20 (because market expects above average growth)
- Market price at 30 April 20X7 (date of publication of previous year's accounts) = £2
- During the year X plc does even better than expected and by 29 April 20X8 the share price is up to £3, therefore giving a P/E ratio of 30 (based on EPS for year ended 31 December 20X6)
- Year ended 31 December 20X7 EPS = 15p, announced on 30 April 20X8. This is in line with expectations so share price is unchanged and P/E ratio drops again to 20 (£3/15p).

8.3 Dividend yield gross

This is the percentage of the (gross) dividend to the market price. The dividends are grossed up to show the amount including tax credit (at the rate of $^{10}/_{90}$ of the net amount).

8.4 Dividend cover

This is the relationship between available profits and the ordinary dividends payable out of those profits, reflecting how sustainable the dividend level is likely to be in the future. The *Financial Times* adjusts profits to exclude exceptional profits and losses.

9 CHAPTER SUMMARY

There is a demand for financial analysis from a variety of users. Analysis may be inter-temporal and use ratios to clearly show the relationship between components of the financial statements.

10 SELF TEST QUESTIONS

10.1 What are McCarthy cards? (1.1)

10.2 What is the significance of EMH to financial analysis? (1.5)

10.3 What is insider information? (1.6)

10.4 What is horizontal analysis? (2.1)

10.5 What is trend analysis? (2.8)

10.6 How does an associate company affect the calculation of ROCE? (4.2)

10.7 What is overtrading? (5.8)

10.8 What are two methods of computing balance sheet gearing? (6.3)

11 EXAMINATION TYPE QUESTIONS

11.1 Figureitout plc

(1) Capital and reserves as at 31 December 20X8

	£
£1 ordinary shares	2,000,000
5% £1 preference shares	1,000,000
Share premium account	1,000,000
Profit and loss account	4,000,000
	£8,000,000

(2) Ordinary share price as at 31 December 20X8 = £3.50

(3) Sales (including £1,500,000 VAT) = £12,000,000

(4) Figureitout plc has no long-term liabilities

(5) Dividend yield (net) = 5%

(6) Dividend cover (net basis) = 1.4

(7) Debtors' turnover (based on year-end debtors and gross sales) = 4

(8) Fixed assets: net current assets ratio = 4

(9) Current ratio = 1.32

(10) Quick ratio = 0.92

(11) Stock turnover (based on year-end stock) = 3

(12) Profit before tax as a percentage of sales = 10%.

You are required to prepare a balance sheet as at 31 December 20X8 and a profit and loss account for the year then ended for Figureitout plc. **(18 marks)**

11.2 The Bureau Ltd

The Bureau Ltd is a company that is being incorporated to organise and manage a computer bureau operation. The directors are considering whether to finance the company by equity or by equity and loan.

They estimate that the company will require £5,000,000 and that the rate of return on capital employed, calculated on the basis of profit before interest and tax to capital employed, could range from 10% to 20% as follows

(1) a return on capital employed of 20% if the company is able to obtain a contract with the government for processing monthly statistics, or

(2) a return on capital employed of 15% if it is able to obtain a contract with a major commercial organisation for routine processing of the weekly payroll, or

(3) a return on capital employed of 10% if it is only able to obtain a series of small contracts.

You are required:

(a) to calculate the earnings per share on the basis of the three possible rates of return on capital employed assuming that

  (i) the company is financed wholly by equity of £1 ordinary shares (assume corporation tax at 30%)

  (ii) the company is financed half by ordinary shares of £1 each issued at par and half by 10% loan stock (assume corporation tax at 30%). **(5 marks)**

(b) to explain how the shareholders of The Bureau Ltd would be advantaged or disadvantaged by introducing a 50% gearing. **(5 marks)**

(Total: 10 marks)

12 ANSWERS TO EXAMINATION TYPE QUESTIONS

12.1 Figureitout plc

Figureitout plc
Balance sheet as at 31 December 20X8

	£	£
Fixed assets (W4)		6,400,000
Current assets		
Stocks (bal fig)	2,000,000	
Debtors (W3)	3,000,000	
Cash (W6)	1,600,000	
	6,600,000	
Creditors: amounts falling due within one year (W5)	(5,000,000)	
Net current assets (W4)		1,600,000
		£8,000,000
Capital and reserves		
Called up share capital		3,000,000
Share premium account		1,000,000
Profit and loss account		4,000,000
		£8,000,000

Profit and loss account for the year ended 31 December 20X8

	£
Turnover	10,500,000
Cost of sales (W7)	6,000,000
Gross profit	4,500,000
Expenses (bal fig)	3,450,000
Profit before tax (10% × 10,500,000)	1,050,000
Taxation (bal fig)	510,000
Profit after tax (W2)	540,000
Preference dividend (W2)	50,000
Ordinary dividend (W1)	350,000
Retained profit	140,000
Reserves b/d (bal fig)	3,860,000
Reserves c/d	£4,000,000

WORKINGS

(W1) **Dividend yield of 5%**

Dividend = 350p × 5%
= 17.5p
= 17.5p × 2,000,000
= £350,000

(W2) **Dividend cover of 1.4**

Profit after tax less preference dividend = £350,000 × 1.4
= £490,000

Preference dividend = £1,000,000 × 5%
= £50,000

Profit after tax = £540,000

(W3) **Debtors' turnover of 4**

Ratio $= \frac{\text{Sales}}{\text{Debtors}}$

Year-end debtors $= \frac{£12{,}000{,}000}{4}$

= £3,000,000

(W4) **Fixed assets: net current assets ratio = 4**

Fixed assets plus net current assets = £8,000,000 (from capital and reserves)

		£
Fixed assets	4	?
Net current assets	1	?
	5	£8,000,000

Fixed assets $= £8{,}000{,}000 \times \frac{4}{5}$
= £6,400,000

Net current assets $= £8{,}000{,}000 \times \frac{1}{5}$
= £1,600,000

(W5) **Current ratio of 1.32**

		£
Current assets	1.32	?
Current liabilities	(1.00)	?
	0.32	£1,600,000

Current assets $= £1{,}600{,}000 \times \dfrac{1.32}{0.32}$

$= £6{,}600{,}000$

Current liabilities $= £1{,}600{,}000 \times \dfrac{1}{0.32}$

$= £5{,}000{,}000$

(W6) **Quick ratio of 0.92**

Debtors and cash = £5,000,000 × 0.92
= £4,600,000

Cash = £4,600,000 – £3,000,000
= £1,600,000

(W7) **Stock turnover of 3**

Stock ratio $= \dfrac{\text{Cost of sales}}{\text{Stock}}$

Cost of sales = £2,000,000 × 3
= £6,000,000

12.2 The Bureau Ltd

(a) (i) Rate of return

	20%	*15%*	*10%*
	£'000	£'000	£'000
Profit	1,000	750	500
Tax	300	225	150
	700	525	350
Earnings per share	14p	10.5p	7p

(ii)

Profit before interest and tax	1,000	750	500
Interest	250	250	250
Profit after interest	750	500	250
Tax (30%)	225	150	75
	525	350	175
Earnings per share	21p	14p	7p

(b) In general terms, if the return on capital employed (ROCE) is less than the cost of borrowing, then earnings per share will be lower if the company is geared. If the ROCE is higher than interest rates then earnings per share will be higher. The advantage or disadvantage to the shareholders therefore relates to the expected ROCE and expected interest rates. In the examples given the earnings per share with gearing is always greater than or equal to the earnings per share with no gearing.

There are, however, other factors to take into account

(i) risk and uncertainty in relation to expected ROCE

(ii) gearing allows a larger capital investment than may be available using shareholders' capital

(iii) an initial high gearing may lead to funding problems if it is found that the investment required has been underestimated.

25 FINANCIAL ANALYSIS - ADDITIONAL STATEMENTS

INTRODUCTION & LEARNING OBJECTIVES

This chapter considers the interpretation of financial statements which take into account changing price levels. Examination questions have been quite common in this area.

Other topics covered are the use of cash flow information and the usefulness of information that is supplied to the user of accounts alongside the accounts.

When you have studied this chapter you should be able to do the following:

- Calculate and interpret ratios based on current cost and current purchasing power accounting.
- Examine the usefulness of cash flow information.
- Appreciate the usefulness of other sources of information.

1 RATIOS BASED ON CURRENT COST AND CURRENT PURCHASING POWER ACCOUNTS

1.1 Ratios based on CPP accounts

CPP removes the effects of different values of a currency. As a result the financial information should be comparable over time. Earlier in the text we examined the mechanics of CPP accounting applied to HC accounts. In fact, there is no reason why similar adjustments cannot be made to current cost accounts.

In this section we consider the calculation of ratios based on CPP accounts prepared from HC accounting data.

The same type of ratios can be computed for CPP accounts as HC accounts in terms of method. We need to be aware however of why there are different results in the ratios computed which in turn can assist us in the interpretation of the effect inflation is having on the particular business being examined.

In the three key areas of profitability, gearing and the relationship of profitability to capital employed, CPP accounts will tend to show lower profitability, lower ROCE and lower gearing.

Profitability rates will tend to be lower because of the effect of uplifting the HC depreciation charge to current price levels. How significant the reduction depends on the age of the assets and the relative amounts invested in depreciable fixed assets. A company with a high investment in fixed assets with many old assets will probably have a large reduction in profitability. This type of company will also have a large lowering of its ROCE due not only to the reduction in the numerator compared to the HC accounts but also the increase in capital employed arising from the restatement of old fixed assets to current price levels.

Gearing will also fall because debt is a monetary item and therefore is already stated at the current year end CPP units whilst equity includes the uplift to the fixed assets.

1.2 Examining a company's financial performance based on current value accounts

As we have seen earlier in the text, there are several versions of CC accounts. In the pure CC accounts with physical capital defined as non-monetary assets, there will be two additional charges against operating profit in respect of depreciation and stock.

Profitability margins will be reduced due to these charges; the extent of the reduction being a function of the amount of the capital of the business invested in physical capital and the age of the fixed assets. The same reasoning as stated for CPP accounts applies here. If the specific price changes have been more than general price changes then the effect will be greater on the CC accounts than the CPP accounts and vice versa.

Similarly ROCE and gearing will be lower for the similar reasons as stated for CPP accounts. Once again monetary items are not adjusted as they are already stated at current value.

If the CC accounts produced include adjustments to profits for monetary working capital and/or gearing then the effect of these adjustments is quite easy to interpret. The MWCA is a direct computation of the cost or benefit to the business of its monetary working capital in the accounting period. The gearing adjustment shows the benefit to the shareholders of using third party funds.

1.3 The quality and value, to alternative users, of current value financial statements

CC information emphasises the perspective of the business as a separate entity rather than reporting changes in wealth of the owners of the business. Therefore it can be argued that it is more relevant to the needs of management as users than others. Part of their functions is to protect the long-term existence of the business and CCA provides information as to the additional charges required to maintain the physical capacity of the business.

However it can also be argued that management use other, internal, information to maintain the long-term capacity of the business to trade. Therefore CC published accounts are only of real use to other users. Shareholders can use CC information to broadly judge the effect of rising input prices on the business.

It should also be appreciated however that CC information suffers the same deficiency as HC information insofar as trends are being examined. Financial information stated at CC in the financial statements four years ago is stated at current value **at that date** ie, four years ago. Therefore a comparison of data from previous years' accounts cannot be made to the current year without knowing the price changes that have occurred over the period. This weakness is examined in a later chapter when we examine the distortion inflation causes to trend analysis.

1.4 Example

The controversy continues as to the best method (or best combination of methods) of accounting for changing price levels.

You are required:

(a) from the data given below, to compute six significant accounting ratios for the group for each of the three alternative accounting paradigms (historical cost, current purchasing power, and current cost);

(b) to comment briefly on the position indicated by each of the three sets of ratios computed in (a) above.

(c) to give your opinion as to the usefulness for the user of financial statements of each of the three alternative sets of figures.

Uptodate plc and its subsidiaries
Accounts for the year ended 31 December 20X5 (simplified)

		Historical cost	Current purchasing power	Current cost
		£'000	£'000	£'000
Consolidated profit and loss account				
Turnover		10,000	10,300	10,000
Cost of sales		(7,000)	(7,145)	(7,000)
Gross profit		3,000	3,155	3,000
Overheads		(2,000)	(2,200)	(2,000)
Depreciation adjustment		-	-	(100)
Cost of sales adjustment		-	-	(46)
Monetary working capital adjustment		-	-	(39)
		1,000	955	815
Income from interest in associated undertaking		100	95	90
Interest:	On bank overdrafts	(40)	(42)	(40)
	On debenture loans	(225)	(232)	(225)
	Gearing adjustment	-	-	35
	Gain on net monetary liabilities	-	30	-
Profit on ordinary activities before taxation		835	806	675
Tax on ordinary activities		(350)	(350)	(350)
Profit on ordinary activities after taxation		485	456	325
Minority interests		(50)	(49)	(40)
Attributable to shareholders in Uptodate plc		435	407	285
Extraordinary profit (after taxation)		100	104	100
Profit for the financial year		535	511	385
Dividends		(350)	(357)	(350)
Retained earnings for the financial year		185	154	35

		Historical cost	Current purchasing power	Current cost
		£'000	£'000	£'000
Consolidated balance sheet				
Fixed assets:	Property, plant and equipment - gross	5,000	6,500	7,900
	Depreciation	(2,175)	(3,110)	(3,945)
		2,825	3,390	3,955
	Interest in associated undertakings	600	690	750
		3,425	4,080	4,705
Current assets:	Stocks	1,000	1,012	1,010
	Debtors	1,500	1,500	1,500
	Bank and cash balances	1,100	1,100	1,100
		3,600	3,612	3,610

Current liabilities:	Bank overdrafts	(200)	(200)	(200)
	Creditors	(900)	(900)	(900)
	Corporation tax	(325)	(325)	(325)
	Proposed dividend	(200)	(200)	(200)
		(1,625)	(1,625)	(1,625)
Net current assets		1,975	1,987	1,985
Net assets less current liabilities		5,400	6,067	6,690
Debenture loans		(1,500)	(1,500)	(1,500)
Deferred tax		(200)	(200)	(200)
		3,700	4,367	4,990
Share capital and reserves:	Paid up capital:			
	Preference	500		500
	Ordinary	2,000		2,000
		2,500		2,500
Reserves:	Share premium account	250		250
	Current cost reserve	-		1,180
	Profit and loss account	450		290
	Group's proportion of post-acquisition reserves of associates	200		350
		900		2,070
Equity of shareholders of Uptodate plc		3,400	3,967	4,570
Minority interests		300	400	420
		3,700	4,367	4,990

Notes

(1) Consolidation is effected throughout by the acquisition method.

(2) Associates are accounted for by the equity method.

(3) Uptodate plc's share capital consists of 10% cumulative preference shares of £1 each, and of ordinary shares of 25p each.

(4) The group's debentures carry an average interest rate of 15% pa.

(5) No securities have been issued, redeemed or purchased during the year.

(6) The general price level (as measured by the Index of Retail Prices) rose during 20X5 by 6%. During the same year the average prices of physical fixed assets rose by 10%, and those of stocks by 5%.

(7) In the current purchasing power balance sheet above, shareholders' equity is not analysed as such analysis is inappropriate to this method of accounting.

1.5 Solution

(a) **Six significant accounting ratios for three alternative accounting paradigms**

		Historical cost	*Current purchasing power*	*Current cost*
(1)	Gross profit/ Turnover	3,000 × 100%/ 10,000 = 30.0%	3,155 × 100%/ 10,300 = 30.6%	(3,000 – 46) × 100%/10,000 = 29.5%
(2)	Trading profit/ Turnover	1,000 × 100%/ 10,000 = 10.0%	955 × 100%/ 10,300 = 9.3%	815 × 100%/ 10,000 = 8.2%
(3)	Current assets/ Current liabilities	3,600/1,625 = 2.2	3,612/1,625 = 2.2	3,610/1,625 = 2.2
(4)	Proprietary ratio (Shareholders' funds/ Net assets)	3,400/5,400 = 0.6	3,967/6,067 = 0.7	4,570/6,690 = 0.7
(5)	Return on capital employed (pre-tax)	(835 + 225) × 100% pa/5,400 = 19.6% pa	(806 + 232) × 100% pa/6,067 = 17.1% pa	(675 + 225) × 100% pa/6,690 = 13.5% pa
(6)	Return on equity funds (post-tax)	(535 - 50) × 100% pa/2,900 = 16.7% pa	(511 - 52) × 100% pa/ (3,967 - 500) = 13.2% pa	(385 - 50) × 100% pa/4,070 = 8.2% pa

Note: the above six ratios appear the most significant of the many that it is possible to compute from the given figures.

(b) **Comments on the position shown by the three sets of ratios**

(i) **Historical cost**

Both the gross profit and the trading profit (before interest and tax) show very satisfactory percentages on turnover (30% and 10% respectively), suggesting a high degree of expertise in the commercial management of the group. In the balance sheet, the financial structure appears very sound, with a current assets ratio comfortably in excess of 2 and a proprietary ratio of 0.6. Comparison of the year's results with capital employed shows a very satisfactory return of 19.6% pa before tax - almost twice the percentage of trading profit to turnover, since the latter (£10m) is almost twice the net operating assets (£5.4m), and this ratio is about optimal for a commercial undertaking. The return on equity funds after tax is nearly as great, at 16.7% pa - an effect of the high gearing ratio, which in a year of poor results might cause a disastrous fall in the return on equity funds.

(ii) **Current purchasing power**

With a rate of inflation at 6% pa the deviations between the HC and CPP ratios are not large. The first four ratios shown above are little different, as they rest predominantly on cash flows, and on monetary items in the balance sheet. Only the rates of return, on capital employed and on equity funds, are materially reduced as compared with historical cost. That fact arises from the doubly deflationary effect of a reduction in the numerator (profit) through disproportionate increases in depreciation charged on older fixed assets, coupled with an enlargement of the denominator (capital) by upward revaluation of non-monetary assets. If the HC balance sheet had had a recent revaluation the differences between the two conventions would have been even less.

It should be pointed out that it is only the ratios that can be properly compared as between the two paradigms. The actual numbers cannot be compared, as they are in different units of measure - the HC numbers in actual pounds, and the CPP numbers in units of purchasing power as at the end of 20X5.

(iii) **Current cost**

In relation to HC, the system of current cost accounting has a sharper effect on the 'results' and 'return' ratios (numbers 1, 2, 5 and 6) than the CPP system. Because the prices of physical fixed assets have risen faster than the general price level, the depreciation adjustment is larger than the corresponding adjustment in the CPP profit and loss account, while the cost of sales adjustment is not offset by any rise in the amount of turnover. There is a partial reduction in the burden of these charges, through the gearing adjustment; but this has its counterpart in the CPP figures, in the shape of the gain on net monetary liabilities.

The effect of these differences is that, as compared with HC, the CC return on capital employed is only about two-thirds as high, and the return on equity funds only half as high, through this deflation of the profit figures and the upward revaluation of the non-monetary assets, as reflected in the current cost reserve.

(c) (i) **Historical cost**

Historical cost accounts are useful mainly because users feel that they understand the figures. Although they may recognise that inflationary forces make the accounts less useful, HC information is considered better than any attempt that has yet been made at alternative systems. It is also useful for stewardship purposes eg, the balance sheet correctly records the assets and liabilities of the business.

For decision-making HC accounts have little to commend them in an era of changing prices. Their limitations include:

(1) Reported results may be distorted as a result of the matching of current revenues with costs incurred at an earlier date. The full distribution of profits calculated on that basis may result in the distribution of sums needed to maintain capital. A distribution which appears well covered when measured against historical cost profit may appear much less well covered when compared with a measurement of profit that takes account of changing prices.

(2) The amounts reported in a balance sheet in respect of assets may not be realistic, up-to-date measures of the resources employed in the business.

(3) As a result of (1) and (2), calculations to measure return on capital employed may be misleading.

(4) Because holding gains or losses attributable to price level changes are not identified, management's effectiveness in achieving operating results may be concealed.

(5) There is no recognition of the loss that arises through holding assets of fixed monetary value and the gain that arises through holding liabilities of fixed monetary value.

(6) A misleading impression of the trend of performance over time may be given because no account is taken of changes in the real value of money, unless it is expressed in units of constant purchasing power.

An impressive list of limitations.

(ii) **Current purchasing power**

CPP is felt by many to be of limited use because it only has regard to general price changes and does not deal with the specific price changes affecting a company. Knowledge of specific price changes is necessary for decision-making purposes.

Some aspects of CPP accounting are of use; in particular the adjustment of financial information for earlier years to a common price basis gives a far better impression of trends of performance over time than either HC or CCA.

(iii) **Current cost**

CCA has had a hard time trying to become established, so far without success. Its main limitations tend to be on the profit statement. Many are far from clear as to the significance and meaning of some of the current cost operating adjustments.

Most people, however, would view the CCA balance sheet as providing useful information. It gives a current valuation of each of the assets of the business and it is against the current worth of the assets of the business that the profitability of the business should be judged.

2 INTERPRETATION OF CASH FLOW DATA

2.1 Interpretation of a company's cash flow statement

Points to watch for within the various headings in the cash flow statement include

(a) **Cash generation from trading operations**

The figure should be compared to the operating profit. The reconciliation of operating profit to net cash flow from operating activities is useful in this regard. Overtrading may be indicated by

(i) high profits and low cash generation
(ii) large increases in stock, debtors and creditors.

(b) **Dividend and interest payouts**

These can be compared to cash generated from trading operations to see whether the normal operations can sustain such payments. In most years they should.

(c) **Capital expenditure and acquisitions and disposals**

The nature and scale of a company's investment in fixed assets is clearly shown. Remember however that a group may have increased significantly in size through 'paper' transactions (eg, share for share issues) which will not be reflected on the statement.

(d) **Financing**

The subtotal 'cash inflow/outflow before use of liquid resources and financing' indicates the financing required unless existing cash is available. The changes in financing (in pure cash terms) are clearly shown. The reconciliation of cash flow to movement in net debt and the note analysing net debt link the inflows/outflows with the balance sheet movement. As with acquisitions and disposals there may be significant non-cash flow changes in the capital structure of the business.

Gearing can be considered at this point.

(e) **Cash flow**

The statement clearly shows the end result in cash terms of the company's operations in the year. Do not overstate the importance of this figure alone however. A decrease in cash in the year may be for very sound reasons (eg, there was surplus cash last year) or may be mainly the result of timing (eg, a new loan was raised just after the end of the accounting period).

2.2 The value of cash flow information

A cash flow statement can provide information which is not available from balance sheets and profit and loss accounts.

However, a historical cash flow statement does not provide complete information for assessing future cash flows. Cash flow statements should normally be used in conjunction with profit and loss accounts and balance sheets when making an assessment of future cash flows. The accruals accounting basis used in preparing profit and loss accounts and balance sheets provides relevant information for projections.

Some cash flows result from transactions that took place in an earlier accounting period and some cash flows are expected to result in further cash flows in a future period.

To help in determining the future cash position other areas of the published accounts should be considered as illustrated below.

2.3 Cash requirements

There are four areas to consider when identifying whether or not the company has sufficient cash.

(a) **Repayment of existing loans**

All loans to be repaid in the next couple of years should be considered including any convertible loans if the conversion rights are unlikely to be exercised.

(b) **Increase in working capital**

If the business is expanding (making more sales) working capital will also need to increase. The extra cash needed to finance the expansion can easily be calculated by comparing working capital to sales.

$$\frac{\text{Stocks} + \text{debtors} - \text{creditors}}{\text{Turnover}} \times 100\%$$

Suppose this is 20% and turnover is currently £5m, a 10% increase in turnover requires finance of £0.1m (£5m × 10% × 20%) to increase the working capital.

(c) **Capital expenditure requirements**

The notes to the financial statements should disclose capital expenditure contracted for.

It is necessary to consider if the company will have sufficient cash to meet this capital expenditure.

(d) **Other commitments**

(i) **Contingent liabilities**

Most contingent liabilities do not crystallise, but if the liabilities are very high their crystallisation can cause real problems for the company. Some analysts compare the contingent liabilities with ordinary shareholders' funds to assess the materiality of those commitments. In particular any sharp increases in the amounts involved should act as a warning.

(ii) **Leasing commitments**

If these are material, they should be carefully monitored in relation to the cash available. The accounts should disclose both finance lease commitments (for new leases where repayments have not commenced) and also operating lease commitments.

3 THE REQUIREMENTS OF SSAP 17

3.1 SSAP 17 - post balance sheet events

Post balance sheet events fall into two categories: adjusting events and non-adjusting events.

Definition **Post balance sheet events** are those events, both favourable and unfavourable, which occur between the balance sheet date and the date on which the financial statements are approved by the board of directors.

Definition **The date on which the financial statements are approved by the board of directors** is the date the board of directors formally approves a set of documents as the financial statements. In respect of unincorporated enterprises, the date of approval is the corresponding date. In respect of group accounts, the date of approval is the date when the group accounts are formally approved by the board of directors of the holding company.

Definition **Adjusting events** are post balance sheet events which provide additional evidence of conditions existing at the balance sheet date. They include events which because of statutory or conventional requirements are reflected in financial statements.

Definition **Non-adjusting events** are post balance sheet events which concern conditions which did not exist at the balance sheet date.

3.2 Adjusting events

These events provide additional evidence on conditions existing at the balance sheet date. For example, bad debts arising one or two months after the balance sheet date may help to quantify the bad debt provision as at the balance sheet date. Adjusting events may, therefore, affect the amount at which items are stated in the balance sheet.

Examples include:

(a) Provisions for stock and bad debts.

(b) Amounts received or receivable in respect of insurance claims which were being negotiated at the balance sheet date.

(c) Certain special items occurring after the balance sheet date which, for various reasons, are reflected in the current year's financial statements:

(i) Proposed dividends.
(ii) Appropriations to reserve.
(iii) Effects of changes in taxation.
(iv) Dividends receivable from subsidiary companies.

3.3 Non-adjusting events

These are events arising after the balance sheet date but which, unlike those events above, do **not** concern conditions existing at the balance sheet date. Such events will not, therefore, have any effect on items in the balance sheet or profit and loss account. However, in order to prevent the financial statements from presenting a misleading position, some form of additional disclosure is required if the events are material, say by way of memorandum note or pro forma consolidated balance sheet indicating what effect the events would have had on the year end balance sheet.

Examples of non-adjusting events include:

(a) The issue of new share or loan capital.

(b) Major changes in the composition of the company (for example, acquisitions of new businesses).

(c) Financial consequences of losses of fixed assets or stock as a result of fires or floods.

3.4 Explanation and examples of window dressing

'Window dressing' refers to the practice of entering into certain transactions before the year end and reversing those transactions after the year end. Thus no real transaction has occurred (ie, no substance, only legal form) but the balance sheet reflects the transaction (as it primarily records the legal form of assets and liabilities). The hoped-for effect is to improve the appearance of the balance sheet.

SSAP 17 requires a **disclosure** of such transactions if they are material. They are **not**, however, adjusting events.

Example

UK plc is concerned that it has over-lent to customers in the year to 31 December 20X8 and that its liquid assets to total assets ratio is too low. It thus arranges a loan of £40 million from another company in December. The loan is repaid in January.

	(a)	*(b)*
	£m	£m
Liquid assets	10	50
Investments:		
Advances to customers	200	200
Fixed assets	20	20
Less: Creditors – amounts falling due within one year	(10)	(50)
Total assets less current liabilities	220	220
$\frac{\text{Liquid assets}}{\text{Total assets less current liabilities}}$	$\frac{10}{220} \times 100$	$\frac{50}{220} \times 100$
	= 5%	= 23%

(a) refers to the balance sheet if the transaction had not been entered into; (b) shows the actual balance sheet at the year end. Clearly (b) looks better if an accepted measure of security/solvency is a 'liquidity' ratio such as calculated above.

3.5 Standard accounting practice – SSAP 17

SSAP 17 – Accounting for post balance sheet events requires that:

'Financial statements should be prepared on the basis of conditions existing at the balance sheet date.

A material post balance sheet event requires changes in the amounts to be included in financial statements where:

(a) it is an adjusting event; or

(b) it indicates that application of the going concern concept to the whole or a material part of the company is not appropriate.

A material post balance sheet event should be disclosed where:

(a) it is a non-adjusting event of such materiality that its non-disclosure would affect the ability of the users of financial statements to reach a proper understanding of the financial position; or

(b) it is the reversal or maturity after the year-end of a transaction entered into before the year-end, the substance of which was primarily to alter the appearance of the company's balance sheet.

In respect of each post balance sheet event which is required to be disclosed the following information should be stated by way of notes in financial statements:

(a) the nature of the event; and

(b) an estimate of the financial effect, or a statement that it is not practicable to make such an estimate.

The estimate of the financial effect should be disclosed before taking account of taxation, and the taxation implications should be explained where necessary for a proper understanding of the financial position.

The date on which the financial statements are approved by the board of directors should be disclosed in the financial statements.'

Paras 21-26 SSAP 17

3.6 Activity

How would the following be dealt with?

When drafting the final accounts, a company's accountant includes a figure of £2,000 as the net realisable value of damaged items of stock.

The cost of these items was £3,000, and the normal selling price would be £4,000. Between the balance sheet date and the approval of the accounts the items are sold for £3,100.

3.7 Activity solution

The valuation in the accounts should be adjusted to £3,000, ie, cost, since net realisable value has, in the event, turned out to be greater than cost. This is an adjusting post balance sheet event.

3.8 CA85

Para 6 Sch 7 CA85 requires the directors' report to contain:

(a) particulars of any important events affecting the company or any of its subsidiaries which have occurred since the end of that year;

(b) an indication of likely future developments in the business of the company and of its subsidiaries.

4 FURTHER INFORMATION OBTAINED FROM THE FINANCIAL STATEMENTS

4.1 Report of the directors

The company's annual report and accounts must include a Directors' Report. The information to be disclosed is set out in *Sch 7 CA85*. A checklist of the requirements is given here.

Checklist of requirements

(a)	Principal activities	Give the principal activities of the company or group together with any changes in those activities during the financial year.
(b)	Business review	A fair review of the activities of the company or group during the year and the position at the end of it.
(c)	Post balance sheet events	Important events affecting the company or group which have occurred since the end of the year.
(d)	Future developments	An indication of likely future developments in the business.
(e)	Research and development	An indication of the activities of the company or group in the field of research and development.
(f)	Dividend	The amount which the directors recommend to be paid as dividends.
(g)	Asset values	Significant differences between the balance sheet value and market value of freehold or leasehold interests in land.
(h)	Directors	The names of those who were directors of the company at any time during the financial year.
(i)	Interests of directors	For each director who holds office at the end of the year disclose the following: (a) number of shares held; (b) amount of debentures held; (c) options for shares or debentures (Nil figures should be given if no interest exists.) The information should be given for the following dates: (i) At the beginning of the financial year or on the date of appointment if appointed during the year; and (ii) At the end of the financial year.
(j)	Purchase of own shares	Where a company purchases its own shares, or acquires its own shares by forfeiture or in any other manner, there must be disclosure of: (a) the number; (b) the nominal value; (c) the consideration paid; (d) the reasons for their purchase; and (e) the percentage of called-up share capital which they represent.
(k)	Disabled employees	If the average number of the company's UK employees exceeds 250, a statement of its policy: (a) for giving full and fair consideration to applications for employment by the company made by disabled persons, having regard to their particular aptitudes and abilities;

(b) for continuing the employment of, and for arranging appropriate training for, employees of the company who have become disabled persons during the period when they were employed by the company; and

(c) otherwise for the training, career development and promotion of disabled persons employed by the company.

(l) Employee involvement

If the average number of the company's UK employees exceeds 250, a statement of its policy for:

(a) providing employees systematically with information on matters of concern to them as employees;

(b) consulting employees or their representatives on a regular basis so that the views of employees can be taken into account in making decisions which are likely to affect their interests;

(c) encouraging the involvement of employees in the company's performance through an employees' share scheme or by some other means;

(d) achieving a common awareness on the part of all employees of the financial and economic factors affecting the performance of the company.

(m) Donations

Disclose the total of political and charitable donations if the total is in excess of £200. The total must be split between those for charitable purposes and those for political purposes.

In respect of political donations only, disclose for each donation of more than £200:

(a) the name of the party or organisation concerned; and
(b) the amount given.

(n) Payment of creditors

If the company is a public company or a 'large' company within a group of which the parent is a public company, for the financial year immediately following that covered by the report the company must state:

(a) whether it follows any code or standard on payment practice, and if so, the name of the code or standard and the place where information about this can be obtained;

(b) whether it is the company's policy to settle the terms of payment with suppliers when agreeing the terms of each transaction, to ensure that suppliers are made aware of the terms of payment and to abide by the terms of payment; or

(c) where the company's policy is not covered by either of the above, details of its policy.

If the company's policy is different for different suppliers or classes of suppliers, the report must identify the suppliers or classes of suppliers to which the different policies apply.

(o) Approval — The board of directors must approve the directors' report and authorise either a director or the company secretary to sign the directors' report on behalf of the board.

Comments on report of the directors

(a) The items listed above are the minimum required to meet the requirements of *CA85* (as amended by a Statutory Instrument issued in February 1996). It is common practice for other matters to be disclosed in the directors' report although not required by law (eg, the reappointment of auditors at the next annual general meeting).

(b) There are further disclosure requirements which apply to special category companies such as banks and insurance companies. There are further disclosure requirements under Stock Exchange regulations.

(c) There is no particular order of these matters which must be followed to meet legal requirements.

4.2 The Chairman's report

The Chairman's report is not required by law or any other regulation but is a common feature of published accounts of listed companies. It normally gives a general review of the operations of the business and its importance has increased over the years, so much so that the principles of disclosure in many Chairman's statements have been incorporated in the ASB's guidance on the publication of an **Operating and Financial Review.**

4.3 Operating and financial review

The ASB issued a Statement in July 1993 recommending that an Operating and Financial Review (OFR) should be included in the annual reports of large companies.

The purpose of an OFR is to give the directors of a company the opportunity to discuss and explain, in a structured and comprehensive way, some of the main factors underlying the company's financial statements, and thus to help users to understand more fully the business and environment in which the company operates.

The ASB recognises that many listed companies' annual reports already include detailed discussion of operations and financing, often in the Chairman's Report. The OFR provides general guidelines to indicate what should be covered in such a review to ensure that it is balanced and complete.

The main characteristics of the OFR are that it should

(a) be fair, in the sense of being a balanced and objective statement of both good and bad news

(b) focus on matters of significance

(c) be presented in the way most likely to be helpful to the user of the annual report in gaining an understanding of the financial circumstances of the business.

The OFR covers two main areas

(a) The *operating* section of the review would normally include a discussion of the results for the period, indicating the main factors and influences that may have an impact on the future, and a discussion of the ways in which the business is investing to meet future needs and challenges.

(b) The *financial* review would cover such aspects as the capital structure of the business; the treasury policies adopted; cash flow and current liquidity; borrowing requirements and future needs; and any restrictions on the transfer of funds held overseas.

It is for boards of directors to decide how best the information should be presented within a company's annual report; it is not part of the Statement that a particular format should be followed. The ASB believes however that it is important that the OFR should clearly be seen to be the responsibility of the board of directors as a whole.

The ASB takes the view that much of the material to be included in the OFR is not suitable for inclusion in notes to accounts, and should therefore not be made a requirement of an accounting standard. The Statement on Operating and Financial Review is therefore not mandatory but sets out a generally accepted view on what should be regarded as best practice in this area.

4.4 Directors' share options

The amount of share options granted to directors, especially of the recently privatised utilities, has become controversial in recent years. The UITF has issued Abstract 10 to try to standardise what should be disclosed in this area.

UITF Abstract 10: Disclosure of directors' share options

The issue

It is generally agreed that the granting of share options to directors is a benefit to be included in the aggregate of directors' remuneration to be disclosed, but no agreement exists as to how to place a meaningful money value on options. The Cadbury Report has led to companies providing more information about options in issue, but again different companies have presented the information in different ways.

Principal requirements

Unfortunately the UITF has concluded that it is not presently practicable for it to specify an appropriate valuation method for options as a benefit in kind. Instead it is recommended that for all companies information concerning the option prices applicable to individual directors, together with market price information at the year-end and at the date of exercise, should be disclosed.

4.5 UITF Abstract 20: Year 2000 issues: accounting and disclosures

The issue

Many businesses need to adapt their computer software so that it can cope with dates in the next century. This Abstract addresses the accounting for external and internal costs of modifying existing computer equipment to achieve year 2000 compliance.

There are two main accounting issues:

(i) Should the costs of year 2000 compliance be capitalised (treated as part of fixed assets) or should they be written off as expenses as they are incurred?

(ii) Should provisions be made for estimated future costs?

UITF Consensus

Costs incurred in rendering existing software year 2000 compliant should be written off to the profit and loss account except in those cases where:

(i) the entity already has an accounting policy of capitalising software costs; and

(ii) the expenditure clearly represents an enhancement of the software, rather than merely maintaining its service potential.

In some cases these costs may need to be treated as exceptional items in accordance with FRS 3 *Reporting financial performance*.

Entities should disclose significant commitments at the balance sheet date in respect of year 2000 software costs (whether these are to be treated as capital or revenue). Following the issue of FRS 12 *Provisions, contingent liabilities and contingent assets* provisions can no longer be made unless the entity has an obligation to transfer economic benefits; an intention to incur expenditure is not sufficient.

The following disclosures should be made:

(i) the risks and uncertainties associated with the year 2000 problem (or a statement that they have not been addressed);

(ii) the entity's general plans to address the year 2000 issues relating to its business and operations;

(iii) whether the total estimated costs of these plans, including amounts to be spent in future periods, have been quantified, and, where applicable, an indication of the total costs likely to be incurred.

These disclosures may either be made in the Directors' Report or in the Operating and Financial Review.

4.6 UITF Abstract 21: Accounting issues arising from the proposed introduction of the euro

This Abstract addresses the accounting for external and internal costs of the changeover to the euro (the single European currency).

(a) Costs of making the necessary modifications to assets to deal with the euro should be written off to the profit and loss account unless:

  (i) the entity already has an accounting policy to capitalise assets of the relevant type; or

  (ii) the expenditure clearly results in enhancement of an asset, rather than merely maintaining its service potential.

(b) Other costs associated with the introduction of the euro should be written off to the profit and loss account.

(c) Expenditure incurred in preparing for the changeover to the euro and regarded as exceptional should be disclosed in accordance with FRS 3.

(d) Particulars of commitments at the balance sheet date in respect of costs to be incurred should be disclosed where they are regarded as relevant to assessing the entity's state of affairs.

(e) Cumulative foreign exchange translation differences recognised in the statement of total recognised gains and losses in accordance with SSAP 20 should remain in reserves after the introduction of the euro. They should not be reported in the profit and loss account.

4.7 UITF Abstract 22: Acquisition of a Lloyd's business

FRS 7 *Fair values in acquisition accounting* requires that profits earned before the date of acquisition must not be reported as post-acquisition profits.

Lloyd's businesses adopt a three year basis of accounting, under which their accounts are kept open for at least three years. The UITF Consensus is that estimated pre-acquisition profits should be reflected in the fair values of the acquired assets of Lloyd's businesses, even if the accounts are not yet closed for the periods before the acquisition.

5 THE NATURE AND VALUE OF INFORMATION FROM OTHER INTERNAL REPORTS

This section considers the usefulness of other reports that a company may issue regularly or occasionally.

5.1 Value added statements

The ASC in **The Corporate Report** issued in 1975 recommended that companies issue value added statements as part of the annual report. As a consequence there was a brief flurry of activity but currently there are few companies publishing such a statement. The ASB has not expressed any interest in such a statement.

A value added statement shows the amounts of 'value' added to raw materials and services by the various parties interested in the business and how the interested parties share in the resultant added value. A value added statement is merely the re-analysis of a published profit and loss account with the addition of certain detailed information drawn from the cost of sales.

The example below shows how a group value added statement is constructed from the group's published profit and loss account and its trading account.

Example

Group trading account

	£
Sales	23,397
Cost of sales	
Raw materials	12,523
Rent	400
Wages	6,215
Rates	200
Depreciation	1,197
	20,535
Group gross profit	2,862

Group published profit and loss account

	£
Group gross profit	2,862
Investment income	225
	3,087
Interest payable	196
	2,891
Corporation tax	1,430
	1,461
Minority interest	300
	1,161
Dividends	348
Group retained profit	813

Group value added statement

Funds available	£	£
Sales		23,397
Less: Bought-in materials and services		12,923
Value added		10,474
Add: Investment income		225
Total funds available for allocation		10,699
Applied in the following way		
To employees:		
Wages, pensions and other benefits		6,215

To governments:		
Corporate taxes	1,430	
Rates	200	
		1,630
To providers of capital:		
Interest on loans	196	
Dividend to minority shareholders (say)	248	
Dividends to parent company Ltd shareholders	348	
		792
Retained by the company and its subsidiaries:		
To pay for capital expenditure to replace existing assets, to expand working capital and for growth:		
Depreciation	1,197	
Retained earnings 813 + (300 – 248)	865	
		2,062
Total allocation of funds		10,699

5.2 Comments on presentation

(a) **Value added**

Value added has no precise definition, but is normally shown as being turnover (excluding VAT) less materials and services purchased. Value added, therefore, constitutes wealth which has been created by the combined efforts of capital (shareholders and loan stock holders), management and employees.

(b) **Non-trading credits**

Various methods are used to cope with income which arises outside a group's trading income.

Some companies set off the income against bought-in materials while others reduce one of the applications of value added. Perhaps the most sensible way is the treatment in the Example above.

Sundry income is added to value added to show total funds available for allocation.

(c) **Non-trading credits - associated undertaking**

Associates cause an additional problem in that the amount of profits dealt with in the consolidated profit and loss account in relation to an associated company normally exceeds the income (ie, dividends) coming into the group from the associate. The easiest way is to deal with the dividends received only on the same basis as sundry income.

(d) **Depreciation**

It is conventional to show the depreciation profit and loss account charge as a retention by the group under the general description 'to pay for capital expenditure and to replace existing assets'.

Many would argue that it would be more appropriate to include depreciation as part of bought-in materials and services and thus deduct in *arriving* at value added rather than as application of value added. Certainly, in an historical cost system of accounting, depreciation is only a method of spreading the cost of an input consumed in the trading operations over several accounting periods. There is no justification for presenting depreciation in a way that implies more than this.

(e) **Minority interests**

Many companies show the minority interests' share in profits as an application of value added in the providers of capital section. A more sensible treatment is to split the minorities' share in profit in the same way as the group profit attributable to the members of the trading company is split ie, between dividends paid or payable and retained profits. Thus, in the Example the minority interest per the profit and loss account of £300 has been split:

Dividends paid and payable	£248 - Providers of capital
Retained profits	£52

5.3 Employee reports

There are two types of 'employee' reports:

(a) A report about the employees in a business (an employment report)
(b) A report to employees describing the current performance of the business.

The first was recommended by the Corporate Report and, as a consequence of this and the EC 4th Directive, some information is required to be included in published accounts ie,

Costs of

(1) Wages and salaries;
(2) Social security costs;
(3) Other pension costs.

In all cases the notes must show the average number of employees during the year, wherever located, and the average number of employees in categories selected by the directors having regard to the manner in which the company's activities are organised (such as by class of business or geographical location).

In addition information on disabled employees and employee involvement are included in the Directors' Report (see above).

There has been relatively little demand for more information from users.

Reports to employees are quite common in listed companies however. These may be similar to the summary financial statements that may be sent to shareholders but may have less figures and more graphical information showing data analysed by pie charts for example. Employee reports are unlikely to have any information which is not already included in other reports.

5.4 Prospectuses and profit statements

The role of the accountant in the preparation of such reports was covered in an earlier chapter. The main point to remember is the cautious view taken by company law of the advisability of directors making quantitative or narrative statements about the future. The future is uncertain and therefore statements cannot be relied upon unless the future is in fact only a few months to the end of the current accounting period.

The forecasts are dependent on the assumptions made and thus they need to be closely examined by the user to see whether they are in accord with his judgement of future circumstances.

6 INFORMATION FROM NATIONAL AND INTERNATIONAL EXTERNAL SOURCES

6.1 Stockbrokers' circulars

Stockbrokers issue statements to their clients giving their opinions of the current worth of a company relative to its share price and or the relative worth of the company compared to its competitors. Recommendations such as 'buy', 'sell' or 'hold' will be made.

Stockbrokers make their money by the commission obtained on share transactions and the issue of a circular stimulates interest in buying or selling.

The circular will be based on audited and unaudited information. The broker may have spoken to key personnel in the company and been on a visit (often along with other brokers) to the company. The broker has therefore had more access to information than the normal shareholder and therefore his recommendation may be useful to the shareholder. In addition, the broker has the time to study the available information on the company in detail, which is something which many shareholders do not have the time to do.

6.2 Credit rating agencies

Credit rating agencies exist to provide companies with information about the financial standing of other companies. Large listed companies are given credit ratings which are generally made available. These ratings affect the cost of finance of the companies concerned eg, a 'triple A' rating means the company is regarded as very sound and thus the interest costs on any loan finance it raises is reduced as a result.

Agencies also run specific checks on companies following a request from other companies such as banks. Major purchasers such as local authorities will also check out the solvency of its suppliers.

6.3 Press comment

The financial pages of all newspapers contain comment on listed companies with the most extensive coverage being in the Financial Times. The commentaries can be on the published accounts and interim statements that shareholders receive but more importantly, they will initially be based on the preliminary results sent by the company to the Stock Exchange. They therefore precede the financial information sent directly to the shareholders.

In addition the press will summarise the views of the various stockbroker firms employing analysts who specialise in researching the particular company and industry sector and thus a wide view can be obtained on the 'market opinion' of the company.

7 INTRA AND INTER-FIRM COMPARISONS

7.1 Introduction

Comparisons in financial and non-financial terms may usefully be made

(a) between different organisations providing similar outputs
(b) within an organisation between different departments/divisions.

Comparisons between different organisations give rise to problems of obtaining information about competitor firms. This can be resolved if use is made of an *interfirm comparison* scheme. In the public sector, some of the problems have been resolved by government requiring public sector organisations to present performance indicators in their annual report (ie, a report including accounts which is available to the public).

7.2 Interfirm comparison schemes

In order to provide the basis of comparison referred to above, schemes of interfirm comparisons have been set up in a number of industries. The general principle of such schemes is that particular firms supply data to an independent collator. In order to ensure comparability, data must be presented on a uniform basis.

Data on other companies is collated and made available to participants in an anonymous form (firms are identifiable by a number only). This last point is important, since companies do not normally wish their close rivals to be provided with detailed financial information about their operations. Individual companies may then compare their ratios with those typical of the industry, so as to establish which areas of operations appear to be operating below par and may be improved - since firms are identified by a number, the results can be represented so that Firm No 1 has the highest return on capital, Firm No 2 the next highest, and so on. Management will know their own firm and its position and will study the report to see the detailed reasons from its high or low placing.

Companies taking part in an IFC scheme usually do so under the auspices and guidance of a Trade Association, or of the Centre for Inter-Firm Comparisons (CIFC) which was set up by the British Institute of Management and the British Productivity Council in 1959.

For an IFC scheme to be successful:

(a) Participants must be assured that the information they supply will be treated confidentially.
(b) The participants must all belong to a similar industry.
(c) Uniform accounting must be used.

Uniform costing may be defined as 'the use by several undertakings of the same costing systems' ie, the same basic costing methods and superimposed principles and techniques. The main factors requiring a uniform approach are:

(a) bases for overhead apportionment and absorption methods;
(b) depreciation treatment;
(c) classification of costs;
(d) accounting periods.

7.3 Advantages and disadvantages

Advantages of IFC schemes are:

(a) Areas of inefficiency in relation to competitors are revealed.

(b) The ratios are so selected by the trade association that management's attention is focused on the vital areas of the business.

(c) The expertise of the trade association is available to participators.

(d) Management is motivated by the competition with other companies.

(e) Cost of subscription is low.

Disadvantages of IFC schemes are:

(a) There is no guarantee that truly uniform information has been submitted.
(b) Participants are anonymous.
(c) A company has to submit its own figures.

7.4 Example of interfirm comparison

Some ratios for a company, AB Ltd, which is a light engineering company are shown below.

	Management ratios		*Unit*	*Industry*	*AB Ltd*
(a)	Operating profit	1st quartile		15.1	
	Operating capital	median	%	27.0	14.1
		3rd quartile		37.2	

	Ratio		Unit	Industry	Company
(b)	Operating profit / Sales	1st quartile		6.0	
		median	%	9.3	5.2
		3rd quartile		41.6	
(c)	Marketing cost / Sales	1st quartile		6.2	
		median	%	8.6	9.4
		3rd quartile		10.9	
(d)	Sales / Finished goods stock	1st quartile		15.2	
		median	times	20.7	54.6
		3rd quartile		35.9	
(e)	Debtors / Average daily sales	1st quartile		30.2	
		median	days	33.5	42.8
		3rd quartile		35.4	
(f)	Sales / Number of salesmen	1st quartile		170,000	
		median	£	195,000	152,000
		3rd quartile		215,000	

7.5 Interdepartmental comparisons

An organisation needs to be able to monitor the performance of the various parts of its business. Examples are:

(a) stores
(b) different factories
(c) products.

Departments can be usefully split between *cost centres* and *profit centres* and you have covered these in detail in your cost and management accounting studies. It is useful to recall the measurement problems that can exist in such comparisons.

7.6 Problems of measurement

(a) **Lack of 'goal congruence'**

The lack of 'goal congruence' refers to the problem of a manager of part of a business making a decision which enhances the performance of his department but only at the expense of another department and therefore does not benefit the organisation as a whole.

(b) **Transfer pricing**

Profit centres may also do work for each other giving rise to the problems of determining the price charged between the departments. Some profit centres may have no external sales as they provide a service to other parts of the business but a price needs to be established so that it can make 'sales' to the other parts of the business.

(c) **Using contribution rather than profits**

The central problem in using contribution not profits to measure performance, is that no department has an obligation to make pricing decisions, for example, which will result in the fixed costs of the organisation being covered.

A possible solution is to design a performance report which shows the split of costs between controllable and non-controllable costs, but the danger is that the managers may still mainly have regard to the contribution rather than ultimate profit.

8 CHAPTER SUMMARY

Ratios based on financial statements which take into account changing price levels can be computed in a similar way to any other ratios. The extent to which these ratios differ from the HC accounts ratios is a measure of the extent to which the organisation is affected by changing price levels.

Cash flow information provides further useful information for the purpose of analysing the performance and financial solvency of a business but needs to be used in conjunction with the accruals found in the profit and loss account and balance sheet.

Other information in the financial statements and accompanying statements are useful in giving a more rounded view of the organisation.

9 SELF TEST QUESTIONS

9.1 What is the advantage of CPP data over HC and CC data? (1.1)

9.2 What primarily affects the profit margin in CC accounts compared to HC accounts? (1.2)

9.3 From what perspective does CCA concentrate? (1.3)

9.4 How can overtrading be seen in a cash flow statement? (2.1)

9.5 What do notes to the accounts indicate in respect of capital expenditure requirements in the future? (2.3)

9.6 What is the definition of a post balance sheet event? (3.1)

9.7 Are there any required contents of an operating and financial review? (4.3)

9.8 Who are the 'interested parties' in a value added statement? (5.1)

9.9 What is an employee report? (5.3)

9.10 What is a 'AAA' rating? (6.2)

10 EXAMINATION TYPE QUESTION

10.1 SR plc

You are the management accountant of SR plc. PQ plc is a competitor in the same industry and it has been operating for twenty years.

Summaries of PQ plc's profit and loss accounts and balance sheets for the previous three years are given below:

Summarised profit and loss accounts for year ended 31 December

	20X7	*20X8*	*20X9*
	£m	£m	£m
Turnover	840	981	913
Cost of sales	554	645	590
Gross profit	286	336	323
Selling, distribution and administration expenses	186	214	219
Profit before interest	100	122	104
Interest	6	15	19
Profit on ordinary activities before taxation	94	107	85
Taxation	45	52	45
Profit on ordinary activities after taxation	49	55	40
Dividends	24	24	24
Retained profit for year	25	31	16

Summarised balance sheets at 31 December

	20X7	*20X8*	*20X9*
	£m	£m	£m
Fixed assets:			
Intangible assets	36	40	48
Tangible assets at net book value	176	206	216
	212	246	264
Current assets:			
Stocks	237	303	294
Debtors	105	141	160
Bank	52	58	52
	606	748	770
Creditors – Amounts falling due within one year:			
Trade creditors	53	75	75
Other creditors	80	105	111
	133	180	186
Creditors – Amounts falling due after more than one year:			
Long-term loans	74	138	138
	207	318	324
Shareholders' interests:			
Ordinary share capital	100	100	100
Retained profits	299	330	346
	606	748	770

You may assume that the index of retail prices has remained constant between 20X7 and 20X9.

You are required to write a report to the finance director of SR plc

(a) analysing the performance of PQ plc and showing any calculations in an appendix to this report; **(20 marks)**

(b) summarising *five* areas which require further investigation, including reference to other pieces of information which would complement your analysis of the performance of PQ plc. **(10 marks)**

(Total: 30 marks)

11 ANSWER TO EXAMINATION TYPE QUESTION

11.1 SR plc

(***Tutorial notes:***

(1) Do the calculations for your ratio analysis first, pointing out that the details would be appended to the report.

(2) Group your ratios to discuss operating profitability, solvency and long term capital structure.

(3) Ensure your comments are consistent with the ratios calculated and the data given in the question.

(4) For part (b) look for the dramatic changes that have taken place during the past three years and also consider the other types of statement that may help your analysis. Remember the level of detail that is available in the notes to published accounts.)

(a) **Workings re ratios**

These would be included as an appendix to the report to the finance director:

	20X7	*20X8*	*20X9*
Operating ratios			
ROCE			
$\left(\dfrac{\text{Profit before tax}}{\text{Capital + reserves}}\right)$	$\dfrac{94}{399} \times 100 = 23.6\%$	24.9%	19.1%
Gross profit/sales	$\dfrac{286}{840} \times 100 = 34.0\%$	34.3%	35.4%
Net profit/sales (before tax)	$\dfrac{94}{840} \times 100 = 11.2\%$	10.9%	9.3%
Asset turnover			
(Fixed + current)	$\dfrac{840}{606} = 1.4$ times	1.3 times	1.2 times
Solvency ratios			
Current ratio	394 : 133 = 3.0 : 1	2.8 : 1	2.7 : 1
Liquidity ratio	157 : 133 = 1.2 : 1	1.1 : 1	1.1 : 1
Debtors collection period	$\dfrac{105}{840} \times 365 = 46$ days	52 days	64 days
(based on total sales and closing debtors)			
Stock turnover period	$\dfrac{237}{554} \times 365 = 156$ days	171 days	182 days
(based on cost of sales and closing stock)			
Other ratios			
Interest cover	$\dfrac{100}{6} = 16.7$ times	8.1 times	5.5 times
Gearing	$\dfrac{74}{74 + 399} = 15.6\%$	24.3%	23.6%
Percentage change in sales from prior year	–	17%	– 7%

REPORT

To: Finance director

From: Management accountant

Date: X-X-20XX

Subject: **Performance of PQ plc for the three year period 20X7 to 20X9**

The level of turnover of PQ plc has fluctuated but has increased by nearly 9% from 20X7 to 20X9. However, this increased level of activity has not resulted in an increase in the profitability performance of the company. While the gross profit percentage has remained fairly constant, with a slight increase in 20X9, the net profit per £ of sales has dropped by 2%. This fall in relative profit levels is reflected in the substantial decline in the return, before tax, achieved by PQ plc on the equity funds available. Despite this, the dividend paid has remained constant over the three year period.

The company does not appear to have a short term liquidity problem. Debtors and bank balances can more than cover the short term creditors of the company but the company may be having credit control problems because the length of time it takes to collect outstanding debts has, on average, grown by twelve days. This is a drain on finance that could be more profitably used to buy working assets. The number of days of stock has also increased although the actual level of stocks dropped in 20X9. This may indicate problems of stock control or co-ordination between stock levels and activity levels.

Interest cover has dropped dramatically and while not appearing to be significant now may prove to be a problem in the future, particularly if loans are to be used to finance any further expansion. This was clearly the case in 20X8 when loans of £64m were raised. No expansion of equity share capital has occurred in the three year period.

This brief analysis is based on the summarised financial statements of PQ plc plus the ratio analysis appended to this report. Below is a short list of some of the areas where a more detailed level of analysis and investigation may prove useful.

(b) **Areas requiring further investigation**

(i) **Fluctuations in activity:** Was the increase in 20X8 a 'one-off' or was it indicative of the level of activity that PQ plc would normally be operating at. A review of the market position of PQ plc may prove to be helpful.

(ii) **Interest charges:** Why the increase in interest charges in 20X9 with no new loans. An analysis of “other creditors” may reveal items that bear interest, eg bank overdrafts.

(iii) **Analysis of costs:** A re-analysis of costs, perhaps in some form of value added statement may be a useful aid to forecasting the level of profitability achievable by PQ plc.

(iv) **“Aged” analysis of debtors:** With substantial amounts now owing an analysis of the debtors by age may reveal any underlying credit control problem.

(v) **Analysis of intangible assets:** The analysis of this group of assets, as will be shown in the notes to the balance sheet, will give a useful insight into the research and development, company acquisition (goodwill) etc, activities of PQ plc.

26 CORPORATE FAILURE PREDICTION

INTRODUCTION & LEARNING OBJECTIVES

This is a brief chapter covering one aspect of ratio analysis which has been the subject of much work by academics and has found some practical application. The advantage to a bank for example in being able to use ratios to predict corporate failure, is worth a lot of money as bad debts can be reduced as a result.

This chapter summarises the major 'going concern' models that have been developed.

When you have studied this chapter you should be able to do the following:

- Explain the use of multi-variate analysis to predict corporate failure.
- Advise and critically comment on the information provided in a statement of affairs.

1 CORPORATE FAILURE

1.1 The importance of corporate failure prediction

A number of entities are interested in knowing whether a company will fail before it does fail. For example:

(a) Banks need to monitor loans to customers and whether additional finance should be provided.
(b) Auditors need to assess the going concern status of a client.
(c) Industrial companies need to monitor the credit worthiness of customers.
(d) The company itself needs to assess whether it is in danger.

1.2 The major causes of insolvency

Insolvency arises from the inability to pay debts when they fall due. There are a number of causes why this can happen.

(a) Overtrading which results in insufficient working capital.

(b) Large investments in assets which cannot be realised due to changed market conditions. For example a property company which invests in property using substantial debt finance. The price of property falls and interest costs go up.

(c) High gearing in expectation of growth which does not happen.

(d) Loss of major customer(s) including material bad debts.

(e) Company does not respond to changing market conditions.

2 THE USE OF MULTI-VARIATE ANALYSIS TO PREDICT CORPORATE FAILURE

2.1 Going concern models

A number of models have been developed to use key ratios to determine whether a company has prospective financial difficulties and may be in danger of going bust. Most models calculate a 'score' for the company, which is then compared to a 'pass mark'. If the score is above the pass mark the company is considered safe.

The original model was developed by the American Professor Altman in 1968 and is known as the Z-score. The Z-score equation consists of five ratios and each ratio is given a weighting. The ratios and weightings were derived from an empirical study of American companies and were the ratios and weightings that best discriminated between failed and successful companies.

2.2 Altman's Z-score

$$Z = 1.2X_1 + 1.4X_2 + 3.3X_3 + 0.6X_4 + 1.0X_5$$

where $X_1 = \dfrac{\text{Working capital}}{\text{Total assets}}$

$X_2 = \dfrac{\text{Retained earnings}}{\text{Total assets}}$

$X_3 = \dfrac{\text{Profit before interest and tax}}{\text{Total assets}}$

$X_4 = \dfrac{\text{Market capitalisation}}{\text{Book value of debts}}$

$X_5 = \dfrac{\text{Sales}}{\text{Total assets}}$

The pass mark for the Z-score is 3.0. Above that level companies should be safe (for two or three years anyway!). A score below 1.8 indicates potential problems.

2.3 Taffler

Variations of the Z-score have been developed for the analysis of UK companies. The best known was developed by Professor Taffler, originally in 1977 but subsequently amended. In the UK based model the first stage was to compute more than 80 ratios from the accounts of large samples of failed and solvent companies. Then using, among other things, a statistical technique known as stepwise linear discriminant analysis, the solvency model was derived by determining the best sub-set of ratios which, when taken together and appropriately weighted, distinguished optimally between the two samples.

If a Z-score model is correctly developed its component ratios typically reflect certain key dimensions of corporate solvency and performance, such as profitability, working capital adequacy, financial risk and liquidity.

Different combinations of ratios and coefficients are required for companies operating in different sectors, although the underlying principles are the same.

The model for quoted UK industrial corporates is:

$$z = 0.53x_1 + 0.13x_2 + 0.18x_3 + 0.16x_4$$

where $x_1 = \dfrac{\text{Profit before tax}}{\text{Current liabilities}}$

$x_2 = \dfrac{\text{Current assets}}{\text{Total liabilities}}$

$x_3 = \dfrac{\text{Current liabilities}}{\text{Total assets}}$

x_4 = No credit interval

x_1 measures profitability, x_2 working capital position, x_3 financial risk and x_4 liquidity.

The no credit interval is:

$$\frac{\text{Immediate assets} - \text{Current liabilities}}{\text{Operating costs} - \text{Depreciation}}$$

A negative score means the company has a financial profile similar to previously failed businesses.

2.4 Criticisms of Z-scores

Criticisms have included:

(a) **Lack of commonality of definition**

There may be different classification of similar items between companies. This is a weakness of all comparative analysis of companies.

(b) **Retrospective information is used**

Ideally prospective estimates are required if the score is to be really useful in predicting failure. Published information is quite old by the time of its publication, particularly for companies in financial difficulty.

(c) **No underlying theory**

Little attempt is made to formulate an underlying logic to the models. It therefore suffers from the weaknesses of all 'black boxes' in that although it may seem to work, there is no evidence that it will continue to work particularly if accounting policies change.

(d) **Little success in predicting time scale of failure**

To be a useful prediction tool, Z-score analysis needs to estimate the time scale within which corrective actions must be taken in order to avoid corporate failure. Altman made particular claims about the length of warning but this has been subject to considerable criticism.

Conclusion Despite these criticisms Z-score analysis is widely used by:

(a) banks which use the system for credit risk management and monitoring customer portfolios;

(b) local authorities to monitor supplier risk;

(c) industrial companies to monitor credit worthiness and occasionally to assess competitors;

(d) auditing firms to help in the analytical review and going concern review of audit clients;

(e) investment institutions to compare stock market risk with fundamental risk.

Provided that the models are used as an additional analytical resource by a skilled financial analyst, they serve a useful purpose.

2.5 Argenti's failure model

Argenti developed a failure model only partly based on financial information. It was developed from a wide review of actual cases and discussions with bankers, businessmen and receivers. It lacks the robustness of Z-scores as it has no precise definitions.

The model is summarised below. Points are either fully given or a nil is scored.

The main rules of interpretation are:

(a) Less than 25 total: company not in danger of failing.

(b) More than 25 total: company may fail within five years. The higher the mark, the fewer the years.

(c) More than 10 for defects: management sufficiently defective to warn observer they may make a fatal mistake.

(d) More than 15 for mistakes (and less than 10 for defects): a (competent) management is running the company at some risk. It is probably aware of this.

Argenti's model

		Points score
Defects		
Management:		
autocratic chief executive		8
chief executive is also chairman		4
unbalanced skill and knowledge on board		2
passive board		2
weak finance director		2
lack of professional managers below the board		1
Accounting systems:		
budgetary control		3
cash flow plans		3
costing systems		3
Response to change:		
products, processes, markets, employee practices etc		15
	Total possible	43
	(Danger mark	10)
Mistakes		
Over-trading:		
expanding faster than cash (funding)		15
Gearing:		
bank overdraft (loans) imprudently high		15
Big project:		
project failure jeopardising company		15
	Total possible	45
	(Danger mark	15)
Symptoms		
Financial:		
deteriorating ratios or Z-scores		4
Creative accounting:		
signs of window dressing		4
Non-financial signs:		
declining quality, morale, market share etc		3
Terminal signs:		
writs, rumours, resignations		1
	Total possible	12
	Overall total possible	100
	(Danger mark	25)

3 STATEMENTS OF AFFAIRS PRODUCED UNDER THE INSOLVENCY ACT 1986

3.1 Preparation of statement

In a winding up the directors have the responsibility for the preparation of a statement of affairs which is delivered to the liquidator in a compulsory liquidation or laid before creditors in a voluntary winding up.

The liquidator has a duty to sell the assets and apply them to pay expenses, debts and finally the entitlement of shareholders.

We must therefore first examine the law which states the order in which assets are applied.

3.2 Application of assets

The assets of the company are applied in the following order

(a) Three categories of creditor may have a priority claim to be paid out of *particular assets* ie,

   (i) a secured creditor
   (ii) a judgement creditor and
   (iii) a landlord who has distrained for rent.

(b) Costs of winding up

(c) Preferential creditors

(d) Creditors having floating charges

(e) Ordinary unsecured creditors

(f) Deferred debts

(g) Distribution of any remaining assets to members according to their rights under the articles.

3.3 Secured and judgement creditors and landlords

(a) A *secured creditor* may sell his security and pay himself out of the proceeds. If there is a surplus he must hand it over to the liquidator. Alternatively a secured creditor may wait for the liquidator to redeem his security by paying the debt. There are a number of subsidiary rules. If the security proves to be insufficient the secured creditor may claim for the balance of his debt as an unsecured creditor.

(b) In a compulsory winding up a *judgement creditor* or a *landlord* who has distrained for rent is likely to lose his priority claim to assets seized unless execution or distress is completed before the commencement of the winding up. He may then claim as an ordinary creditor for his debt.

(c) If execution has begun of a judgement debt of more than £250 the sheriff must retain the proceeds of sale (less his expenses) for fourteen days. If during that time notice is served on him of the presentation of a petition or of the calling of a meeting to commence a voluntary liquidation he must retain the money and, if liquidation does commence, hand it over to the liquidator.

3.4 Preferential debts

Preferential debts are unsecured debts which must be paid in priority to other unsecured debts. Broadly they fall into two categories

(a) taxes and other sums due to public authorities and

(b) wages and other money sums due to employees.

In both cases there are limits on the amounts due to these creditors which are preferential.

Preferential debts are

(a) *VAT* falling due within the six months before the relevant date.

(b) *income tax* deducted under *PAYE* rules within the twelve months up to the relevant date from salaries and wages of employees,

(c) other *tax liabilities* of certain specified kinds and also employer's *social security contributions* due within the twelve months up to the relevant date

(d) amounts owing as contributions to an occupational or state pension scheme

(e) *wages and salaries* of employees due in respect of the four months ended on the relevant date up to a maximum of £800 in any one case. A director or company secretary as such does not fall into this category. But if he is also an employee he may be a preferential creditor for his salary (within the above limits).

(f) *accrued holiday remuneration* of an employee due on termination of his employment before or at the relevant date.

The *relevant date* in a *compulsory winding up* is the date of appointment of a provisional liquidator (usually the date of the court order for winding up but the court may appoint a provisional liquidator while proceedings are still in progress). In a *voluntary winding up* the relevant date is that on which the resolution to wind up is passed.

The primary significance of a claim being a preferential debt is that it carries a priority right of payment ie, preferential debts must be paid in full before any unsecured debts are paid at all. If assets are insufficient for payment in full preferential debts participate *pro rata* to their amount in the available assets.

In two cases preferential debts may be paid out of assets to which other creditors have a prior claim (as against unsecured creditors generally).

These cases are:

(a) if there is a *floating charge* and the company's assets not subject to the charge are insufficient to pay preferential debts, the liquidator must resort to the assets subject to the charge to pay those debts

(b) if in a compulsory winding up a *landlord* has *distrained within three months* before the winding up order is made preferential debts are a first charge on the goods seized or on the proceeds of selling them. But the landlord is subrogated to the rights of preferential creditors to whom he makes payment (for the amount so paid).

3.5 Ordinary unsecured creditors

Ordinary debts include among others any sums owing for taxes or wages which are not preferential or exceed the limit of preference. Ordinary debts rank equally by value for participation in assets remaining after preferential debts have been paid in full.

3.6 Deferred debts and distributions to members

Debts owing to members of the company as members (but not as loan creditors for money lent) are *deferred debts* which are paid only after ordinary debts have been paid in full but before share capital is repaid. The important case here is dividends declared but unpaid at the commencement of winding up.

Once the deferred debts have been paid the members' capital is returned in accordance with the terms of the articles.

3.7 Activity

A winding-up order has been made against Exe plc following the presentation of a petition by Vee plc, a creditor, for £10,000. An investigation of the affairs of Exe plc reveals the following creditors:

	£'000
Wye Insurance plc - loan secured by a fixed charge on freehold property	300
Zed Finance plc - loan secured by a floating charge on the undertaking of Exe plc	200
Customs and Excise - VAT	50
Inland Revenue - PAYE deductions	30
Dee Bank plc - amount advanced to pay wages	25
Unsecured creditors (including Vee plc)	150

You are required to compare the position of Wye Insurance plc, Zed Finance plc and Vee plc.

3.8 Activity solution

Wye Insurance plc has first claim on the freehold property charged with its secured loan after the costs of the winding-up have been paid. The security would be void as against the liquidator and administrator only if it had not been registered.

If the proceeds were less than £300,000 Wye Insurance would be an unsecured creditor for the balance. It would be paid any balance after Zed Finance plc (holders of a floating charge), and would be treated equally with Vee plc and the other unsecured creditors.

Zed Finance plc, as holders of a floating charge, rank after:

(a) Wye Insurance plc (fixed charge); and

(b) preferred creditors (Customs and Excise for the last six months' VAT; Inland Revenue for the last twelve months' PAYE; Dee Bank plc, who are subrogated to the rights of employees as preferred creditors for four months' wages up to a maximum of £800 per employee).

Zed Finance plc will rank before ordinary unsecured creditors, who must wait until Zed has satisfied itself from the proceeds of Exe plc's undertaking.

Zed's floating charge would, however, be void if it was not registered. If Zed's charge was void, Zed would still rank as an unsecured creditor equally with Vee plc.

Vee plc is an unsecured creditor. It comes at the end of the list of creditors given in the question, ranking equally with other unsecured creditors. Vee plc obtains no advantages from having presented the petition. It should be noted that Vee will not rank equally with Dee Bank plc, who at first impression seems also to be an ordinary creditor. As Dee Bank advanced money to pay wages, it will be subrogated to the rights of the employees whose wages were paid, and so become a preferred creditor.

Summary

Provided there are no irregularities, Wye Insurance plc will be paid first from the proceeds of the freehold property; Zed Finance will be paid after the preferred creditors; Vee plc will rank equally with other unsecured creditors. The unsecured creditors will include Wye Insurance for any part of its debt which could not be met from the proceeds of the freehold.

3.9 Calculating the proceeds interested parties would receive if a company is liquidated

The statement of affairs can be prepared in an informal way when a reconstruction of a business is being contemplated. Where a company is in financial difficulties, it will need to raise further funds from the shareholders. Part of the persuasion process of selling the scheme to the shareholders (and thus requiring them to part with some more money) is to show the poor position as to any entitlements to capital if they fail to support the scheme and the company is then liquidated.

The statement of affairs is actually produced on standard forms and requires some narrative information about the creditors of the company and the type of security held. The main schedule however is a straightforward listing of the net book values of the assets of the company and an estimate of their realisable value, from which the liabilities of the company are deducted in the order that they should be paid.

An example is shown below.

3.10 Example

Approximate statement of affairs as at 4 November 20X8

	Net book value	*Estimated to realise*
	£	£
Assets subject to fixed charge		
(Any Bank plc)		
Leasehold property	34,000	20,000
Book debts	6,750	3,000
	40,750	23,000
Less fixed charge		40,000
Deficiency as regards fixed charge (see below)		17,000
Assets subject to floating charge		
(Any Bank plc)		
Equipment	10,000	2,000
Furniture and fittings	15,000	1,000
Motor vehicles	24,000	16,000
Work in progress	34,000	Uncertain
Cash at bank	1,295	1,295
	84,295	20,295
Liabilities		
Preferential creditors		
PAYE and NI contributions		5,600
VAT		10,500
Employees' claims		3,400
		19,500
Estimated surplus as regards preferential creditors		795
Less floating charge (see above)		17,000
Estimated deficiency as regards floating charge		16,205
Unsecured creditors		
Employees' claims	4,500	
HP and lease creditors	8,000	
Trade and expense creditors (as per Schedule)	14,200	
		26,700

Estimated deficiency as regards creditors	42,905
Issued share capital	1,000
Estimated total deficiency as regards contributories subject to costs and realisation	43,905

Note: this statement has been prepared from the books and records of the company and from information supplied by the Directors. It must be read in conjunction with a verbal report to be presented to a Meeting of the Creditors to be held on..........................

4 CHAPTER SUMMARY

A number of corporate failure prediction models have been developed which allow ratios to be calculated and prescribed weights so that a score is obtained.

A statement of affairs is relevant for determining the proceeds interested parties would receive on a liquidation.

5 SELF TEST QUESTIONS

5.1 Why are auditors interested in corporate failure prediction? (1.1)

5.2 What can cause insolvency? (1.2)

5.3 What is the name of the main failure prediction model developed for UK companies? (2.3)

5.4 What is the no credit interval? (2.3)

5.5 What is the Argenti failure model? (2.5)

5.6 How much wages and salaries constitute preferential debts? (3.4)

6 EXAMINATION TYPE QUESTION

6.1 Provincial Motor Spares Ltd

The trial balance of Provincial Motor Spares Ltd as at 31 December 20X3

	Dr £'000	*Cr* £'000
Ordinary shares of £1 each		3,600
10% cumulative preference shares of £1 each		1,000
General reserve		1,820
Profit and loss account at 1 January 20X3		2,250
8% Debentures		500
Profit for 20X3		3,780
Debenture redemption reserve		290
Creditors		4,130
Tax payable on 1 January 20X4		700
Deferred taxation on 1 January 20X3		1,655
Investment income		14
Premises	7,200	
Equipment	3,800	
Investments	251	
Stock	6,580	
Debtors	1,480	
Bank	428	
	19,739	19,739

(a) Profits accrue evenly throughout the year.

(b) Provision is to be made for

(i) tax of £1,900,000 on the profits of the current year, payable in 20X5
(ii) the preference dividend
(iii) the proposed ordinary dividend of 10%.

(c) A transfer of £170,000 is to be made to the general reserve.

(d) Sales for the year totalled £21,000,000 of which £1,000,000 was value added tax.

One of the directors had recently read an article on methods of predicting company failure. One of the methods combined five variables and calculated a Z score by multiplying each variable by a discriminant coefficient.

The five variables (labelled X_1, X_2, X_3, X_4, X_5) were as follows

X_1	=	net working capital/total assets	(%)
X_2	=	retained earnings/total assets	(%)
X_3	=	earnings before interest and taxes/total assets	(%)
X_4	=	market value of equity/book value of total debt securities	(%)
X_5	=	sales/total assets	(times)

The Z score was calculated using the following formula

$$Z \text{ score} = 0.012\ X_1 + 0.014\ X_2 + 0.033\ X_3 + 0.006\ X_4 + 0.999\ X_5$$

The score was interpreted on the basis that all companies with a score less than 1.81 were likely to become bankrupt; all companies with a score greater than 2.99 were unlikely to become bankrupt; companies with scores between 1.81 and 2.99 were likely to consist of companies that may become bankrupt.

The market value of equity is calculated using a PE ratio of 5:1 applied to earnings before tax and investment income, but after debenture interest.

You are required:

(a) to briefly explain the possible reasons for selecting each of the five variables that have been included in the formula given above. **(5 marks)**

(b) to calculate the Z score for Provincial Motor Spares Ltd using the formula provided. **(9 marks)**

(c) to briefly give your own views, with supporting calculation, of the company's liquidity and suggest what further reports you would advise the company to prepare. **(11 marks)**

(Total: 25 marks)

7 ANSWER TO EXAMINATION TYPE QUESTION

7.1 Provincial Motor Spares Ltd

(a) $X_1 = \dfrac{\text{Net working capital}}{\text{Total assets}}$

Firms with heavier fixed assets proportions are less liquid and more likely to go into liquidation. Companies with negative working capital will be given lower Z scores and traditional analysis would point to liquidation as such companies have low current ratios also.

$$X_2 = \frac{\text{Retained earnings}}{\text{Total assets}}$$

Total assets are financed by debt or equity. Short or long-term borrowings increase the risk of failure to survive through not being able to service debt. Lower geared companies are a lesser risk and should be given a better chance of survival. Companies that can demonstrate high finance by equity particularly through retention of earnings rather than cash calls are even more likely to survive.

$$X_3 = \frac{\text{Earnings before interest and taxes}}{\text{Total assets}}$$

This measures (ROCE) return on capital employed. Firms are unlikely to go into liquidation if they earn a good ROCE, as further finance would be made available if there were liquidity problems. Those with low or negative X_3s, will strain their liquidity and struggle to renew finance sources.

$$X_4 = \frac{\text{Market value of equity}}{\text{Book value of total debt}}$$

This ratio will be lowest for those heavily dependent on debt to finance total assets. Highly geared companies are known to be more prone to forced liquidation.

$$X_5 = \frac{\text{Sales}}{\text{Total assets}}$$

To get a good ROCE (see X_3) companies must get high asset turnovers. Companies that do not work their assets intensively will fail.

(b) **Z score**

0.012	X_1	=	$\frac{3,198}{19,739}$ $\frac{(W1)}{(W2)}$ × 100%	=	0.012 × 16.2	= 0.19
0.014	X_2	=	$\frac{5,504}{19,739}$ (W3) × 100%	=	0.014 × 27.88	= 0.39
0.033	X_3	=	$\frac{3,820}{19,739}$ (W4) × 100%	=	0.033 × 19.35	= 0.64
0.006	X_4	=	$\frac{18,900}{1,500}$ (W5) × 100%	=	0.006 × 1,260	= 7.56
0.999	X_5	=	$\frac{20,000}{19,739}$ (W6) × 100%	=	0.999 × 1.013	= 1.01
Total Z score						9.79

(c) Current ratio $= \frac{\text{Current assets}}{\text{Current liabilities}} = \frac{8,488}{5,290} = 1.6$

This is less than the 'ideal' of 2

Quick assets (acid) ratio $= \frac{\text{Current assets} - \text{stock}}{\text{Current liabilities}} = \frac{8,488 - 6,580}{5,290} = 0.36$ which is very much less than the 'ideal' of 1.

The above suggests the company could be at risk of being forced into liquidation. However, the Z score suggests that the company is safe for the time being.

Such summary statistics give only a general picture and do not take account of variation between industries or the availability of future finance. A cash budget month by month would be the most valuable extra information

WORKING

(1) **Net working capital**

	£'000	£'000
Stock		6,580
Debtors		1,480
Bank		428
Current assets		8,488
Current tax	700	
Creditors	4,130	
Dividends - pref	100	
Dividends - ord	360	
Current liabilities		5,290
Working capital		3,198

(2) **Total assets**

	£'000
Premises	7,200
Equipment	3,800
Investments	251
Current assets (W1)	8,488
	19,739

(3) **Retained profits**

	£'000
Profits for 20X3	3,780
Investment income	14
Profit before tax	3,794
Tax	1,900
Profit after tax	1,894
Dividends	460
	1,434
Retained profit - 1 January	2,250
General reserves b/f	1,820
	5,504

(4) **Earnings before interest and tax**

	£'000
Profit for 20X3	3,780
Interest 8% × £500	40
	3,820

(5) **Market value of equity**

£3,780,000 × 5 = £18,900,000

(6) **Turnover**

	£'000
Sales	21,000
VAT	1,000
Turnover	20,000

27 LIMITATIONS OF RATIO ANALYSIS

INTRODUCTION & LEARNING OBJECTIVES

Throughout the chapters dealing with financial analysis, we have been concerned with the correct interpretation of ratios which means that the weaknesses of the underlying data have been stressed. We reinforce that message in this chapter and also consider two areas which may give rise to problems - inflation and related parties.

When you have studied this chapter you should be able to do the following:

- Explain the impact and distortion inflation can cause to trend analysis.
- Discuss the implications of related parties.

1 ASSESSING THE IMPACT OF PRICE LEVEL CHANGES ON THE ANALYSIS

1.1 The impact and distortion inflation causes to trend analysis

A significant weakness of HC accounting is the misleading impression of the trend of a company's performance over a period of time as no account is taken of changes in the real value of money. Current cost valuations do not remedy this defect as the valuations reflect prices ruling at a balance sheet date and previous years' accounts only reflect valuations at previous years' prices.

Published accounts give comparative information in two main areas

(a) The corresponding amounts for items shown in the balance sheet, profit and loss account and notes. Such amounts are required by *Companies Act 1985* for virtually all items disclosed in the accounts.

(b) Any historical summary provided. Such summaries, which often taken the form of five or ten year summaries, are not required by law, but have nevertheless become a common feature in the annual reports of listed companies. Historical summaries will usually be disclosed as information supplemental to the financial statements.

1.2 Methods of overcoming lack of comparability

(a) **The use of ratios**

The following ratios are comparable from one year to another

(i) current cost operating profit/net operating assets
(ii) current cost earnings/equity interest
(iii) total gains/total assets
(iv) total gains/equity interest
(v) operating assets/equity interest
(vi) net borrowings/equity interest.

These ratios can provide useful information, but such information is inevitably limited.

(b) **Restatement of comparative information in terms of a constant unit of measurement**

Amounts expressed in pounds sterling of different dates can be restated in units of constant purchasing power by using a general price index. The form of the calculation is thus similar to the adjustment made to shareholders funds in 'real terms accounting'.

1.3 The ASC Handbook

The ASC Handbook on Changing Prices recommends that *historical* summaries of *current cost* information should be restated in units of constant purchasing power. The Handbook suggests it is desirable that *corresponding* amounts in the main accounts are also restated but it puts forward the points made by some commentators that

(a) when corresponding amounts in the main accounts are restated annually into units of constant purchasing power it is necessary to disclose two sets of corresponding amounts (being the amounts before and after restatement) in order to comply with the *Companies Act 1985;* this could be confusing to some users of the accounts, and

(b) the distortion of the figures will often not be very significant as changes in the value of the pound over only one year are involved.

The Handbook does not recommend that *historical cost* information is restated in units of current purchasing power.

The objective of restating amounts in units of constant purchasing power is to eliminate the distortion of inter-year comparisons caused by the effects of changing prices. As this restatement will not reflect the effect of changing prices on the company's performance during the period or on its position at the end of the period, it is not a complete system of accounting for the effects of changing prices.

Nevertheless, historical cost information restated in units of constant purchasing power is sometimes mistakenly thought or taken to be a proper system of accounting for the effects of changing prices. In order to prevent such misunderstanding occurring it will usually be appropriate to restate only historical cost figures which will be the same under the current cost convention, such as turnover and dividends per ordinary share.

1.4 The role of accounting theory

Current cost balance sheet information is based on current costs at the balance sheet date. Consequently only prior year balance sheets will need to be restated.

Current cost profit and loss account information is based on average current costs during the accounting period. This means that to be strictly comparable with the balance sheet information, profit and loss account information will need to be restated into pounds of the balance sheet date. Whether it is worthwhile restating the profit and loss account information into year-end pounds rather than average pounds will depend upon the comparisons to be made and the rate of general inflation involved.

The restated figures can be calculated in two ways; by reference to the movement in the average RPI for each year (the average method) or by reference to the movement in the RPI from one year-end to the next (the year-end method). The average method is the more appropriate method for restating profit and loss account information. The year-end method is more appropriate for the restatement of balance sheet information and is consistent with the objective of restating previously reported figures in pounds of the balance sheet date. Either method is acceptable as long as it is applied consistently.

In the following illustration the average RPI for each year has been used. Thus the 20X2 turnover figure has been calculated as

$$\frac{\text{Index for current year}}{\text{Index for year data taken from}} \times \text{Data}$$

$$\frac{373.1}{320.4} \times 29{,}314 = 34{,}136 \text{ (20X5 £m)}$$

1.5 Illustration

PLC historical summary

As reported			**£ million**		
	20X1	*20X2*	*20X3*	*20X4*	***20X5***
Turnover	25,737	29,314	32,381	37,933	**40,986**
Current cost operating profit	2,460	2,930	3,289	3,901	**4,438**
Earnings per ordinary share	63.9p	39.4p	47.5p	76.8p	**87.4p**
Dividends per ordinary share	20.25p	20.25p	24.0p	30.0p	**34.0p**
Net assets at current cost	32,564	38,799	47,021	52,564	**56,163**
Adjusted for the average UK retail price index of	295.0	320.4	335.1	351.8	**373.1**
			£ million		
Turnover	32,551	34,136	36,053	40,230	**40,986**
Current cost operating profit	3,111	3,412	3,662	4,137	**4,438**
Earnings per ordinary share	80.8p	45.9p	52.9p	81.4p	**87.4p**
Dividends per ordinary share	25.61p	23.58p	26.72p	31.82p	**34.0p**
Net assets at current cost	41,185	45,181	52,353	55,747	**56,163**

2 EVALUATING INTERNAL CONSISTENCY OF INFORMATION

2.1 Assessing informational weaknesses/limitations of statements and analyses

We have seen the use of ratio analysis as the main means of analysing the performance of an entity. In this section we examine the limitations of the financial data which is used for the ratios. Clearly, if the data has weaknesses then the ratios will suffer from the same weaknesses. You must be prepared in commenting upon the significance of ratios to examine the subjectivity which may be present in the underlying statements.

2.2 The arbitrary nature of profit

Unless ratios are calculated in a uniform manner, from uniform data, comparisons can be very misleading.

The consistency concept in SSAP 2 provides some uniformity within the same organisation over time but does not, in itself narrow the differences between organisations.

Below are some examples of areas of subjectivity of accounting standards.

(a) **FRS 14**

The main problem with the effect of the extraordinary/exceptional classification has been removed by FRS 3. However EPS can still be manipulated by changes in capital structure during the year and the time lag between the actual effect on earnings of such changes and the point at which they are dealt with in the EPS calculation.

For example a purchase of own shares during the year will reduce pro rata the weighted average number of shares. This is done because the outflow of cash will lead to reduced earnings. However, there is likely to be a delay in the reduction of earnings (perhaps until next year) and in the short term EPS may appear to increase. Obviously a share issue at full market price during the year would have the opposite effect.

(b) **SSAP 4**

Only the deferred credit method is allowable under the *Companies Act 1985*. Since this method releases the grant to profit and loss account in line with depreciation on the asset concerned it suffers from the same limitations as FRS 15 (see below).

(c) **FRS 15**

The choice of depreciation method is left with the directors of a company provided it achieves the objectives of FRS 15. This involves an assessment of the useful economic life and the pattern of wearing out over that life (ie, whether a straight line or reducing balance charge would be most appropriate). Because of this choice there is scope for manipulation.

Many companies do not charge depreciation on freehold properties on the grounds that high ongoing maintenance and refurbishment costs mean that estimated residual value is always kept at greater than cost and that the asset's life effectively becomes infinite. FRS 15 discourages, but does not absolutely prohibit, this practice (although the requirement to carry out impairment reviews should mean that there is less danger that the value of fixed assets will be overstated).

In addition a change of method or useful economic life, neither of which are dealt with as a prior period adjustment, can be used to adjust profits. For a change of method the effect on *current period* profits has to be disclosed where material, but such a change can increase profits for many years to come.

(d) **FRS 12**

Although there are now strict conditions for recognising provisions, preparers of accounts must still decide whether a transfer of economic benefits is 'probable' or 'remote'.

(e) **SSAP 21**

The main scope for manipulation here is with the misuse of the so-called '90% test'. Companies have used this to keep leased assets and their corresponding liabilities off the balance sheet and so improve ratios such as gearing.

(f) **SSAP 24**

Although the detail of an actuary's work is beyond this syllabus you are aware that there are different valuation methods. So two different actuaries at identical companies may value the pension fund differently. One company may end up with a surplus to account for, another perhaps a deficit.

There are also different possible means of spreading a surplus. We considered primarily the straight line method. This divides the surplus by the average remaining service lives (an estimate in itself) to give a level capital amount per annum. Interest could be added to the unamortised balance each year to give a total charge. The total amount spread will be greater than the original surplus because of this interest element. There are other methods which could lead to very different figures in the profit and loss account.

(g) **SSAP 25**

Applying only to listed companies, this standard increased significantly the amount of information that has to be disclosed. The more information is disaggregated, the more useful it is for interpretation or analytical review purposes.

However, there is scope for manipulation. The 'common costs' and 'unallocated assets' can hide a multitude of sins. It is up to the directors to decide what constitutes a reportable segment, and they may decide that a particular loss making division does not, until it is combined with one that makes greater profits.

(h) **FRS 11**

To determine whether a fixed asset has suffered an impairment in value, it is normally necessary to calculate its value in use. This calculation is based on cash flow forecasts which by their nature can only be subjective.

2.3 The impact that seasonal trading can have on calculated ratios

The accounting periods covered by the financial statements may not reflect representative financial positions.

Many businesses produce accounts to a date on which there is relatively low amount of trading activity. Retail organisations often have an end of February accounting date (after the peak pre-Christmas trading and the January sales). As a result the items on a balance sheet are not representative of the items throughout the accounting period.

Consider stock levels in a retail organisation. They may vary as shown in the graph below

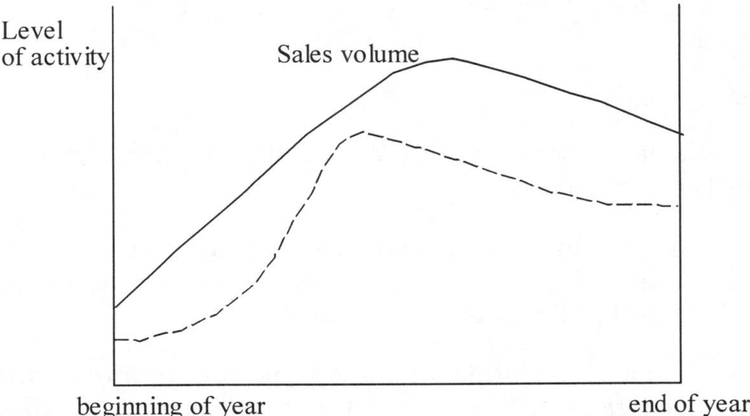

Adding opening and closing stock and dividing by two, will not produce a fair average.

3 BACKGROUND TO THE ORGANISATION

3.1 Introduction

Further problems of excessively relying on ratios include the following.

(a) The earning power of a business may well be affected by factors which are not reflected in the financial statements. Thus, these do not necessarily represent a complete picture of a business, but only a collection of those parts which can be translated into money terms (eg, the size of the order book is normally ignored in financial statements).

(b) Ratios must not be used as the sole test of efficiency. Concentration on ratios may inhibit the incentive to grow and expand, to the detriment of the long-term interests of the company.

(c) A few simple ratios do not provide an automatic means of running a company. Business problems usually involve complex patterns which cannot be solved solely by the use of ratios.

In this section we consider a range of other factors which should be considered in the analysis of an organisation. There is a tendency particularly among accountants to overemphasise the analysis of available financial data provided in the annual report. Other aspects may however be far more important in understanding the present and expected future position of a company.

3.2 Future trends affecting the organisation (national and international)

In two sister exams to the FRE exam, Financial Strategy and Management and Strategy, emphasis is placed in the strategic planning process of understanding the environment within which the organisation is operating.

Thus factors such as the current and prospective economic environment and the strengths and weaknesses of competitors need to be analysed in order to establish a strategic plan and achieve set targets.

The management structure of the organisation also needs to be analysed in order to see whether it is compatible with the aims of the organisation.

As these matters are dealt with in detail in the other subjects they are not covered here but it is important to include such matters in FRE exam questions. For example, you may be given a situation of a company which has currently a small market share with competitors dominating the market. The company is considering raising finance in order to expand. You are provided with detailed historical financial accounts in the question.

Clearly it is relevant in your answer to consider strategic issues such as expected growth of the overall market, strengths of existing competitors and how the company is to establish a 'competitive advantage' in such a situation.

3.3 Non-financial indicators

Definition A non-financial indicator is based wholly or partly on information not contained in the financial or cost accounts.

Accounting has been successful because it is the only model of an organisation which can express inputs and outputs in the same units of measurement ie, money. As a result the information systems of organisations are usually dominated by the accounting system.

However, this has led to a simplistic use of the accounting measurements when setting targets and measuring the organisation's performance. The pursuit of short-term profit which often results can be detrimental to an organisation's operations, particularly when these profit measurements are so easily manipulated.

3.4 Examples of non-financial indicators

These include

(a) production statistics (eg, average time spent on a process); these are often referred to as *costing* ratios and have been developed by management accountants over the years

(b) sales and marketing statistics (eg, percentage of enquiries converted to orders)

(c) quality statistics (eg, percentage of units needing rework).

It should be appreciated that a non-financial indicator may be partly based on financial information. Costs or sales may be measured against a non-monetary item eg,

(a) **Employees**

Computation of sales per employee, profit per employee, average wages.

(b) **Space**

Profit or contribution or sales per unit of 'space' eg, floor space for a retail department.

(c) **Salesmen**

Profit or contribution or sales per call made by a salesman.

3.5 Advantages of non-financial indicators

The advantages of non-financial indicators over accounting statistics include the following

(a) they are easy to calculate

(b) they are more directly comparable with results of previous periods (eg, they do not suffer from inflation)

(c) they are more easily understood by non-financial managers

(d) they are less likely to be manipulated.

The disadvantage to the external analyst of a business is the lack of non-financial information available in the annual report. They are often therefore of more use to a person within the business.

3.6 Value for money

Value for money (VFM) is assessed by reference to the 3 Es. The 3 Es stand for economy, effectiveness and efficiency. The terms were first widely used in the public sector as bases for assessing VFM.

(a) 'Economy' is a measure of inputs to achieve a certain service
(b) 'Effectiveness' is a measure of outputs ie, services and facilities
(c) 'Efficiency' is the optimum of economy and effectiveness ie, the measure of outputs over inputs.

The Chartered Institute of Public Finance and Accountancy (CIPFA) defines economy, effectiveness and efficiency in the context of a local authority

Economy

The terms and conditions under which the authority acquires human and material resources. An economical operation acquires resources of the appropriate quality and provides a service to the appropriate standard at the lowest cost.

Effectiveness

This is the extent to which a programme achieves its established goals or other intended effects.

Efficiency

This is the relationship between goods or services produced and resources used to produce them. An efficient operation produces the maximum output for any given set of resource inputs; or, it has minimum inputs for any given quantity and quality of services provided.

The terms economy, effectiveness and efficiency are the fundamental pre-requisites of achieving VFM. Their importance has grown in the public sector, so much so that external auditors of local authorities are now charged with the responsibility of ensuring that bodies have made adequate arrangements for securing economy, effectiveness and efficiency in the use of public funds.

The terms are increasingly used in the private sector.

3.7 Quality

There is an increasing awareness in the private sector of establishing and maintaining the quality of products and services. Quality needs to be considered in a number of ways

(a) attention is given to building quality into products at the design stage rather than waiting to the end of the production process

(b) large companies in particular are working closely with their suppliers to ensure that high quality components and raw materials are received

(c) checks are made and product quality problems are resolved at each stage of the production process; therefore there is not a build up of low quality products at the end of the production process.

Traditionally there has been a tendency for performance measures to over-emphasise the quantity of output at the expense of quality. This is often the situation where only financial indicators are used. A concentration on costs and revenues in performance reports often results in an exclusive focus on cost control (as management can more easily influence the level of costs rather than the level of sales).

Raw materials, for example, may therefore be purchased at the lowest cost which results in a purchasing manager being shown as a good manager in the performance report. No report is however made on the relative poor quality of the materials he may have purchased. The poor quality of the raw material may result in the business losing more money, due to faulty goods produced as a consequence, than it has saved by purchasing the raw materials more cheaply.

British Rail have in the past provided indicators of quality in their Annual Report

Quality of service - Inter City

Punctuality	*Objective*	*Performance*	
		1989/90	*1990/91*
Trains arriving on time or within ten minutes	90%	84.2%	85%
Cancellations: (% of services to run)	at least 99.5%	98%	97.8%
Train enquiry bureaux:	95% of calls to be answered in thirty seconds	79.8%	78.7%
Ticket offices	Maximum queuing time		
	three minutes off peak	95%	95%
	five minutes peak	91%	91%
Carriage cleaning			
Interior daily clean	100%	98%	98%
Exterior daily wash	95%	95%	95%
Heavy interior (every twenty-eight days)	95%	91%	90%

These quality indicators were for part of British Rail's business, Inter City. It has only met one of its objectives, which may be considered a poor performance. However, consideration needs to be given as to the reasonableness of the objectives set. They may have been set as a target to attain within say five years and what therefore would be important is the comparison of performance between 1990/91 and 1989/90.

Also some of the objectives can only be failed. For example if the maximum queuing time objective is three minutes off peak and the actual results are

98 test occasions - maximum 2 minutes waiting
2 test occasions - 3 minutes and 5 seconds waiting

the performance percentage is 98%.

4 RELATED PARTY TRANSACTIONS

4.1 The distortion that related party transactions can cause to financial statements

A related party relationship can affect the financial position and operating results of an enterprise in a number of ways:

(a) transactions may be entered into with a related party which may not have occurred if the relationship did not exist, eg, a company may sell a large proportion of its production to its parent company, where it might not have found an alternative customer if the parent company had not purchased the goods;

(b) transactions may be entered into with a related party on terms different from those with an unrelated party, eg, the terms under which a subsidiary leases equipment to another subsidiary of a common parent may be imposed by the common parent and might vary significantly from one lease to another because of circumstances entirely unrelated to market prices for similar leases; indeed, the terms may be such that no financial consideration passes between the parties;

(c) transactions with third parties may be affected by the existence of the relationship, eg, two enterprises in the same line of business may be controlled by a common party that has the ability to increase the volume of business done by each.

4.2 Companies Act and Stock Exchange requirements concerning related party transactions

The Companies Act provisions dealing with related parties are mainly concerned with directors and persons connected to directors (which can include companies).

If a company has a 'significant contract' with one of its directors, there is a need for disclosure if the director has a 'material interest'. 'Material' is decided by the other directors (or the auditor if they cannot decide).

Loans to a director from a company are illegal except for sums up to £5,000 or if they are funds for business expenditure (there needs to be prior approval by members).

The Stock Exchange has numerous provisions relating to transactions between a company and its directors or substantial shareholders. They are referred to as Class 4 parties. Basically a circular to shareholders is required if, for example, there is an acquisition or disposal of assets between the company and a class 4 party.

The requirements of the Stock Exchange are extensive and can be argued to be effective in reducing the amount of related party transactions that occur. However they only apply to listed companies and the ASB (as did the ASC) consider that an accounting standard is necessary.

4.3 Requirements of FRS 8

FRS 8 *Related party disclosures* was issued in October 1995. It requires that financial statements disclose:

(a) information on related party transactions; and

(b) the name of the party controlling the reporting entity and, if different, that of the ultimate controlling party, whether or not any transactions between the reporting entity and those parties have taken place.

4.4 Related parties

FRS 8 contains a very detailed definition of **related parties**, of which the most important part is the first.

Definition

(a) Two or more parties are related parties when at any time during the financial period:

(i) one party has direct or indirect control of the other party; or

(ii) the parties are subject to common control from the same source; or

(iii) one party has influence over the financial and operating policies of the other party to an extent that that other party might be inhibited from pursuing at all times its own separate interests; or

(iv) the parties, in entering a transaction, are subject to influence from the same source to such an extent that one of the parties to the transaction has subordinated its own separate interests.

(b) For the avoidance of doubt, the following are related parties of the reporting entity:

(i) its ultimate and intermediate parent undertakings, subsidiary undertakings, and fellow subsidiary undertakings;

(ii) its associates and joint ventures;

(iii) the investor or venturer in respect of which the reporting entity is an associate or a joint venture;

(iv) directors of the reporting entity and the directors of its ultimate and intermediate parent undertakings; and

(v) pension funds for the benefit of employees of the reporting entity or of any entity that is a related party of the reporting entity.

(c) The following are presumed to be related parties of the reporting entity unless it can be demonstrated that neither party has influenced the financial and operating policies of the other in such a way as to inhibit the pursuit of separate interests:

(i) the key management of the reporting entity and the key management of its parent undertaking or undertakings;

(ii) a person owning or able to exercise control over 20 per cent or more of the voting rights of the reporting entity, whether directly or through nominees;

(iii) each person acting in concert in such a way as to be able to exercise control or influence over the reporting entity; and

(iv) an entity managing or managed by the reporting entity under a management contract.

(d) Additionally, because of their relationship with certain parties that are, or are presumed to be, related parties of the reporting entity, the following are also presumed to be related parties of the reporting entity:

(i) members of the close family of any individual falling under parties mentioned in (a) - (c) above; and

(ii) partnerships, companies, trusts or other entities in which any individual or member of the close family in (a) - (c) above has a controlling interest.

The definition concludes by stating that this list is not intended to be exhaustive.

Definition A **related party transaction** is the transfer of assets or liabilities or the performance of services by, to or for a related party irrespective of whether a price is charged.

4.5 Control and influence

The terms **control** and **influence** are central to the definition of related parties. In establishing whether or not a related party relationship exists, it is often necessary to consider **common control** and **common influence**.

The definition of control is very similar to that found in FRS 2:

Definition **Control** is the ability to direct the financial and operating policies of an entity with a view to gaining economic benefit from its activities.

Two subsidiaries of the same parent company would obviously be under common control and would therefore be related parties. Common control would also exist where both parties are subject to control from boards having a controlling nucleus of directors in common.

Example

The directors of A Ltd are X, Y and Z. The directors of B Ltd are W, X and Y. A Ltd and B Ltd are related parties.

Influence is not defined. The explanation to the FRS states that while control brings with it the ability to cause the controlled party to subordinate its separate interests, the exercise of influence has a less certain outcome.

The FRS gives some examples of situations where there may be **common influence** but where a related party relationship does **not** necessarily exist:

(a) two entities are both associated companies of the same investor;

(b) one party is subject to control and another party is subject to influence from the same source (for example, if A has a subsidiary B and an associate C, that situation in itself would not make B and C related parties); and

(c) two entities have a director in common.

In order for there to be a related party relationship in these and similar situations, one or both parties must have **subordinated their own separate interests in entering into a transaction**.

4.6 Types of transactions

Transactions between related parties are a normal feature of business. FRS 8 gives some examples.

(a) purchases or sales of goods (finished or unfinished);
(b) purchases or sales of property and other assets;
(c) rendering or receiving of services, eg, accounting, management, engineering or legal services;
(d) agency arrangements;
(e) leasing arrangements, eg, allowing the use of an asset, whether for a rental or not;
(f) transfer of research and development;
(g) licence agreements;
(h) finance (including loans and equity contributions in cash or in kind);
(i) guarantees or collaterals;
(j) management contracts.

Note that disclosure is required of **all material** related party transactions.

Definition Transactions are material when their disclosure might reasonably be expected to influence decisions made by the users of general purpose financial statements.

4.7 Disclosures

(a) **Disclosure of control**

Where the reporting entity is controlled by another party, there should be disclosure of the related party relationship and, if different, that of the ultimate controlling party. If either of these is not known, that fact should be disclosed.

These disclosures must be made whether or not any transactions have taken place between the controlling parties and the reporting entity.

(b) **Disclosure of transactions and balances**

Financial statements should disclose material transactions undertaken with a related party by the reporting entity. Disclosure should be made irrespective of whether a price is charged. The disclosure should include:

(i) the names of the transacting related parties;

(ii) a description of the relationship between the parties;

(iii) a description of the transactions;

(iv) the amounts involved;

(v) any other elements of the transactions necessary for an understanding of the financial statements;

(vi) the amounts due to or from related parties at the balance sheet date and provisions for doubtful debts due from such parties at that date; and

(vii) amounts written off in the period in respect of debts due to or from related parties.

Transactions with related parties may be disclosed on an aggregated basis (aggregation of similar transactions by type of related party) unless disclosure of an individual transaction, or connected transactions, is necessary for an understanding of the impact of the transactions on the financial statements of the reporting entity or is required by law.

4.8 Exemptions

Certain transactions do not have to be disclosed:

(a) Intra-group items that have been eliminated on consolidation:

(i) in the consolidated financial statements;

(ii) in the parent's own financial statements, where these are presented with the consolidated financial statements; and

(iii) in the financial statements of subsidiaries, provided that at least 90% of their voting rights are controlled within the group and provided that the consolidated financial statements have been published.

(b) Pension contributions paid to a pension fund.

(c) Emoluments in respect of services as an employee of the reporting entity.

Note that the existence of the **relationship** would still have to be disclosed.

Relationships and transactions with the following do not have to be disclosed:

(a) providers of finance;
(b) utility companies;
(c) government departments and their sponsored bodies; and
(d) customers, suppliers, franchisers, distributors and general agents with whom the entity transacts a significant volume of business.

4.9 Evaluation of FRS 8

There are two main ways in which it is possible to deal with transactions between related parties:

(a) Adjust the financial statements to reflect the transaction as if it had occurred with an independent third party and record the transaction at the corresponding arm's length price. However, as a study by the Accountants International Study Group states, 'it often is impossible to establish what would have been the terms of any non-arm's length transaction had it been bargained on an arm's length basis, because no comparable transactions may have taken place and, in any event, the transaction might never have taken place at all if it had been bargained using different values'.

(b) As a result of the above difficulty, accounting standards internationally have concentrated on the disclosure of related party transactions and relationships.

ED 46 which was the ASC version of a proposed standard in this area, proposed that only **abnormal** transactions be disclosed. FRS does not draw this distinction since, in its view, when transactions with related parties are material in aggregate, they are of interest whether or not made at arm's length. This view coincides with current international treatment.

4.10 Identifying related parties

In order to identify related parties it is necessary to apply the definition in FRS 8. There are many situations in which it is obvious that a related party relationship exists. For example, a subsidiary is clearly a related party of a parent.

In more complicated situations it may be necessary to consider whether the parties are included in the list in parts (b) to (d) of the definition **and** to consider the basic principle of control and influence. What actually happens within a relationship in practice is often important.

Example

X plc is an 80% owned subsidiary of T plc. Its directors are A, B, C and D. Which of the following are related parties of X plc?

(a) V Ltd, which is not part of the T plc group, but of which A is a director
(b) Y, who owns 20% of the shares in X plc
(c) K, the financial controller of X plc (who is not a director)
(d) M, the common law wife of the chairman of B plc, a company in the T plc group.

Solution

(a) V Ltd and X plc are subject to common influence from A, but V Ltd is not a related party unless one or both companies have **subordinated their own separate interests** in entering into a transaction. (This assumes that A is the only director to serve on both boards; if there were a common nucleus of directors, a related party relationship would almost certainly exist.)

(b) Y is almost certainly not a related party. According to the definition Y is presumed to be a related party, but the existence of a parent company means that Y is unlikely to be able to exert influence over X plc in practice.

(c) K may be a related party, despite the fact that he or she is not a director. A financial controller would probably come within the definition of **key management** (ie, 'those persons in senior positions having authority or responsibility for directing or controlling the major activities and resources of the reporting entity'). The issue would be decided by the extent to which K is able to control or influence the policies of the company in practice.

(d) M may be a related party. B plc and X plc are under common control and M falls within the definition of close family of a related party of B plc. (**Close family** means 'those family members, or members of the same household, who may be expected to influence, or be influenced by, that person in their dealings with the reporting entity.') M is not a related party if it can be demonstrated that she has not influenced the policies of X plc in such a way as to inhibit the pursuit of separate interests.

5 CHAPTER SUMMARY

Certain ratios do not distort despite changing price levels but more information is available if price adjusted data is disclosed.

Strategic issues need to be considered to properly examine the current performance of an entity.

Related parties potentially distort the transactions entered into by an entity and FRS 8 requires disclosure of all material related party transactions.

6 SELF TEST QUESTIONS

6.1 Where do published accounts provide comparative information? (1.1)

6.2 What are the two ways in which the lack of comparability can be overcome? (1.2)

6.3 Why does the Handbook not recommend that HC information is restated in units of CPP? (1.3)

6.4 Should year end or average rates be used to adjust data? (1.4)

6.5 What is a non-financial indicator? (3.3)

6.6 What are three ways in which the quality of goods and services provided can be considered? (3.7)

6.7 What is a related party? (4.4)

6.8 Why does FRS 8 suggest disclosures rather than adjustments to the financial statements? (4.9)

7 EXAMINATION TYPE QUESTION

7.1 Five year record

The five year financial record of a company as presented in the published accounts prepared on the historical cost basis is shown below

	Year ended 31 December				
	20X10	*20X9*	*20X8*	*20X7*	*20X6*
	£m	£m	£m	£m	£m
Capital employed					
Capital and reserves	600	455	372	317	261
Loans	149	29	34	33	35
	749	484	406	350	296
Fixed assets	734	417	278	239	208
Net current assets					
Stock	9	14	24	22	24
Net monetary assets	6	53	104	89	64
	749	484	406	350	296

Profit after taxation	169	89	57	69	49

Current cost data has been computed as follows

	Year ended 31 December				
	20X10	*20X9*	*20X8*	*20X7*	*20X6*
	£m	£m	£m	£m	£m
Fixed assets	764	460	326	297	268
Stock	10	15	25	24	26
Current cost profit after taxation	152	78	44	54	37

The indices which represent the price changes appropriate to the particular assets held by the company and the general price index over the years were

	Year ended 31 December				
	20X10	*20X9*	*20X8*	*20X7*	*20X6*
Beginning of year					
General prices	188	168	146	117	100
Fixed assets	165	144	121	120	100
Stocks, other current assets and current liabilities	180	160	140	120	100
Average during year					
General prices	197	182	157	135	108
Fixed assets	172	154	133	116	105
Stocks, other current assets and current liabilities	190	170	150	130	110
End of year					
General prices	204	188	168	146	117
Fixed assets	180	165	144	121	110
Stocks, other current assets and current liabilities	200	180	160	140	120

You are required:

(a) to present a revised five year financial record which reflects the application of inflation accounting principles insofar as the data provided permits, explaining any calculations you make. **(14 marks)**

(b) to comment on three significant differences between this new record and the original data. **(6 marks)**

(Total: 20 marks)

8 ANSWER TO EXAMINATION TYPE QUESTION

8.1 Five year record

(a) **Five year financial record**

	Year ended 31 December (current cost data restated to 20X10 £m)				
	20X10	*20X9*	*20X8*	*20X7*	*20X6*
	£m	£m	£m	£m	£m
Profit after taxation	152	85	53	75	64
Fixed assets	764	499	396	415	467
Working capital	16	74	157	158	157
	780	573	553	573	624
Loans	149	31	41	46	61

Capital and reserves (bal fig)	631	542	512	527	563

Method of computation

All figures for years prior to 20X10 have been uplifted by movement in the general price index between the relevant year-end and 31 December 20X10.

The calculation is

$$\text{Item} \times \frac{\text{Index at 31 December 20X10}}{\text{Index at date at which it appears in balance sheet}}$$

(Tutorial note: both historical cost data and current cost data suffer from the same defect; they fail to adjust for the changing purchasing power of the unit of currency used to record data.

The solution shows a meaningful way in which comparisons of financial data can be made. It is a two-stage process

(1) HC data ⟶ CC data

(2) CC data uplifted to current purchasing power units.

Stage (1) is necessary so that the price distortions of assets being purchased at different dates are eliminated at each balance sheet date.*)*

(b) The five year financial record of the company in historical cost and current cost terms seems to show two major pieces of information

(i) the company had experienced a steady growth in its profits and a steady growth in the size of the business as indicated by the fixed asset trend

(ii) there was a great expansion in capacity in the year ended 20X10 with additional loans of £120m and a very large reduction in net monetary assets; in fact, the size of the reduction in net monetary assets from the year ended 31 December 20X8 to the year ended 31 December 20X10 would seem to indicate that the amount in net monetary assets up to 20X8 was largely surplus cash rather than necessary working capital.

The restatement of the financial data to a common unit of currency has produced some significant differences from the historical cost and current cost data but those differences relate to point (i) above rather than point (ii). They still show the very real additional investment made by the company in 20X10 in its fixed assets.

Three significant differences are

(1) **Profit after taxation**

Profits did not increase in real terms from 20X6 to 20X8 but it remains clear that profits made in 20X10 are very impressive when compared with those of previous years.

(2) **Fixed assets**

Investment in fixed assets in fact declined over the period of 20X6 to 20X8 with the real amount of investment in fixed assets only being returned to in 20X9.

(3) **Financing of the business**

The real investment by third parties in the business declined quite markedly in the period 20X6 to 20X9, presumably due to the high level of net monetary assets in this period. The view that the amount of net monetary assets in those years represented surplus cash is reinforced by the inflation adjusted data as that data in the years 20X6 to 20X8 shows the constant level of working capital which would explain the real decline in the loans. The historical cost data (and by implication the current cost data as it does not 'revalue' monetary items) in this same period gives the impression that, although the amount of net monetary assets was increasing, no attempt was made to reduce the borrowings outstanding.

The uplift of a company's historical cost data and preferably its current cost data to current year-end money values does show clearly whether the company has satisfied the most critical test of its performance ie, has it maintained the real level of sales, profit, dividend and investment in assets over time?

28 FINANCIAL INSTRUMENTS

INTRODUCTION & LEARNING OBJECTIVES

Capital instruments and financial instruments have become increasingly important in recent years. Companies use increasingly sophisticated and complex instruments in order to finance their activities. This can cause many problems for preparers and users of financial statements.

FRS 4 *Capital instruments* is concerned with the way in which complex capital instruments are treated and disclosed in financial statements. More recently, the ASB has turned its attention to derivatives and has issued a Discussion Paper *Derivatives and other financial instruments* and FRS 13 *Derivatives and other financial instruments: disclosures.*

When you have studied this chapter you should be able to do the following:

- Understand and apply the requirements of FRS 4.
- Understand the problems of accounting for derivatives.
- Understand and apply the requirements of FRS 13.

---

1 FRS 4: CAPITAL INSTRUMENTS

1.1 Introduction

Definition A capital instrument is any type of share, loan stock or other instrument issued as a means of raising finance.

FRS 4 was issued in December 1993 to consider the accounting for capital instruments due to the increase in recent years of often complex forms of issues designed, in part, to allow companies to show an issue as equity rather than debt and also to avoid charging the profit and loss account with interest until the accounting period in which the issue was redeemed. Companies were therefore manipulating their gearing ratio either from the balance sheet or the profit and loss account perspective.

1.2 Objectives of standard

FRS 4 considers the following areas:

(a) the circumstances in which capital instruments should be reported as debt - that is, amongst liabilities - and as shares.

(b) the methods by which the amounts representing such instruments and transactions in respect of them, such as payments of interest and the costs of issuing them, should be stated in the accounts.

(c) disclosure requirements.

1.3 The classification of capital instruments

It is sometimes suggested that examples of instruments which seem not to be easy to classify as liabilities or as shares require either the abandonment of the distinction or the introduction of a new category into the balance sheet. FRS 4 does not propose this course should be taken. It is required instead that the distinction between shares and debt be maintained, and that guidance is given for accounting for capital instruments within these categories. In the case of group accounts, minority interests represent a third category.

Extract from FRS 4 (para 24)

Capital instruments should be classified as liabilities if they contain an obligation to transfer economic benefits (including a contingent obligation to transfer economic benefits). Capital instruments that do not contain an obligation to transfer economic benefits should be reported within shareholders' funds.

The FRS is thus following the definition of a liability in the Statement of Principles.

1.4 Effect of legal status of shares

The above classification is not used to determine the accounting for a company's shares. Shares have a distinct legal status reflected in the limitations imposed by companies legislation on the circumstances in which payments may be made in respect of them. It is also impossible to classify shares as liabilities within the constraints of the statutory formats for the balance sheet.

Although there are practical and legal difficulties in classifying shares as liabilities, another distinction - that between equity and non-equity shares - is practicable.

1.5 Summary of classification

The principal distinctions envisaged by the FRS may be summarised as follows

Item	*Analysed between*	
Shareholders' funds	Equity interests	Non-equity interests
Minority interests in subsidiaries	Equity interests in subsidiaries	Non-equity interests in subsidiaries
Liabilities	Convertible liabilities	Non-convertible liabilities

For example

(a) Although convertible debt may be settled by the issue of shares, the company remains liable to repay it until such time as the holder elects to convert. It is therefore required that

Convertible debt should be reported within liabilities, but in order that the reader can assess the prospective cash flows relating to the instrument, the amount attributable to convertible debt should be stated separately from that of other liabilities.

(b) The law requires that shares are reported separately from liabilities, but some kinds of shares have features which resemble debt in some respects. It is therefore required that

Shareholders' funds should be analysed between the amount attributable to equity interests and the amount attributable to non-equity interests. Non-equity shares are essentially defined in terms of the amounts of dividends or participation in a winding up or payment in respect of redemption being independent of the companys' assets or profits, or of a requirement that they be redeemed.

(c) Outside interests in shares in subsidiaries are normally reported as minority interests in subsidiaries. Since such shares, like those issued by the company itself, may either be equity or non-equity, it is also required that

The amount of minority interests shown in the balance sheet should be analysed between the aggregate amount attributable to equity interests and amounts attributable to non-equity interests.

1.6 Accounting for capital instruments

There are two main issues

(a) the amount at which the instrument is recorded in the balance sheet (the carrying amount)
(b) the calculation of the finance costs and their allocation between accounting periods.

(a) and (b) are to a large extent interdependent. The first step is to calculate the initial carrying amount. This will be the fair value of the consideration less issue costs. Fair value is not defined and thus general principles should be used.

1.7 Accounting for issue costs

The previous practice for the costs of issuing capital instruments was diverse. It is now required that

The direct costs incurred in connection with the issue of capital instruments should be deducted from the proceeds of the issue.

The effect of this requirement is that, where material costs are incurred in the issue of debt, the amount at which the debt is initially stated will be less than it would otherwise be.

In the case of an issue of equity shares, the requirement is consistent with the provisions of the *Companies Act* that the costs of issue be taken to the share premium account. Where there is no share premium account, the cost of issuing shares should be taken directly to reserves. The issue costs will be reported in the statement of total recognised gains and losses.

1.8 Accounting for finance costs

Once the initial carrying amount has been determined the capital instrument will be stated at that amount on the balance sheet. If the instrument is *equity* shares this amount will not change in subsequent accounting periods. For other instruments the carrying amount may well change because of the allocation of finance costs.

The finance cost is defined as the difference between the net proceeds of an instrument and the total amount of the payments that the issuer may be required to make in respect of the instrument.

The finance costs for liabilities and non-equity shares should be allocated to periods at a constant rate based on the carrying amount (ie, the same requirement as in SSAP 21 for lessees accounting for their obligations under finance leases).

The carrying amount of instruments (other than equity shares) thus becomes

> the net proceeds plus finance charges recognised in the accounts less payments made.

1.9 Example

Debt is issued for £1,000. The debt is redeemable at £1,250. The term of the debt is five years and carries interest of 5.9%.

The debt would initially be recognised at £1,000. The finance cost of the debt is the difference between the payments required by the debt which total £1,545 ((5 × £59) + £1,250) and the proceeds of £1,000, that is £545. In order to allocate these costs over the term of the debt at a constant rate on the carrying amount they must be allocated at the rate of 10%. The movements on the carrying amount of the debt over its term would be as follows:

Year	*Balance at beginning of year*	*Finance cost for year (10%)*	*Cash paid during year*	*Balance at end of year*
	£	£	£	£
1	1,000	100	(59)	1,041
2	1,041	104	(59)	1,086
3	1,086	109	(59)	1,136
4	1,136	113	(59)	1,190
5	1,190	119	(1,250 + 59)	-

1.10 Other matters

(a) **Repurchase of debt**

Gains and losses arising on the repurchase or early settlement of debt should be recognised in the profit and loss account in the period during which the repurchase or early settlement is made.

(b) **The maturity of debt**

An analysis of the maturity of debt should be presented showing amounts falling due:

(i) in one year or less, or on demand;
(ii) in more than one year but not more than two years;
(iii) in more than two years but not more than five years; and
(iv) in more than five years.

The maturity of debt should be determined by reference to the earliest date on which the lender can require repayment.

(c) **Scrip dividends**

Where shares are issued (or proposed to be issued) as an alternative to cash dividends, the value of such shares should be deemed to be the amount receivable if the alternative of cash had been chosen. Where the number of shareholders who will elect to receive the shares is uncertain, the whole amount should be treated as a liability to pay cash dividends.

(d) **Equity shares and warrants**

The net proceeds from the issue of equity shares and warrants for equity shares should be credited direct to shareholders' funds. The amount attributed to equity shares or warrants should not be subsequently adjusted to reflect changes in the value of the shares or warrants.

When a warrant is exercised, the amount previously recognised in respect of the warrant should be included in the net proceeds of the shares issued.

When a warrant lapses unexercised, the amount previously recognised in respect of the warrant should be reported in the statement of total recognised gains and losses.

1.11 Disclosures

Additional disclosures

(a) **Disclosures relating to shares**

An analysis should be given of the total amount of non-equity interests in shareholders' funds relating to each class of non-equity shares and series of warrants for non-equity shares.

A brief summary of the rights of each class of shares should be given. This should include the following:

(i) the rights to dividends;

(ii) the dates at which the shares are redeemable and the amounts payable in respect of redemption;

(iii) their priority and the amounts receivable on a winding up;

(iv) their voting rights.

This information will usually make clear why a class of share has been classified as equity or non-equity, but, if necessary, additional information should be given to explain the classification.

The aggregate dividends for each class of share should be disclosed including the total amount in respect of each of: dividends on equity shares; participating dividends; and other dividends on non-equity shares.

(b) **Disclosures relating to debt**

In respect of convertible debt, details of the dates of redemption and the amount payable on redemption should be disclosed. The number and class of shares into which the debt may be converted and the dates at or periods within which the conversion may take place should be stated. It should also be stated whether conversion is at the option of the issuer or at that of the holder.

A brief description should be given of the legal nature of any instrument included in debt where it is different from that normally associated with debt, for example where the debt is subordinated or where the obligation to repay is conditional.

Gains and losses arising on the repurchase or early settlement of debt should be disclosed in the profit and loss account as separate items within or adjacent to 'interest payable and similar charges'.

1.12 Instruments with issuer call options

Different practices arose to account for issuer call options in accordance with FRS 4, so the UITF issued Abstract 11 on this topic.

UITF Abstract 11: Capital instruments: issuer call options

The issue

The terms of a capital instrument may include an issuer call option ie, a right of the issuer (but not the investor) to redeem the instrument early, usually on the payment of a premium. The question arises as to how to account for an instrument that includes an issuer call option following FRS 4.

Principal requirements

Issuers of capital instruments should not have to account for possible payments that they are not obliged to make, and may very well elect not to make. Payment of a premium on exercise of an issuer call option is a cost that stems directly from the decision to exercise the option and should therefore be reported in the period in which exercise takes place.

The payment required on exercise of such an option does not form part of the finance costs which have to be spread over the instrument's term in accordance with FRS 4.

2 APPLICATION NOTES

2.1 Introduction

Application notes specify how some of the requirements of FRS 4 are to be applied to transactions that have certain features. However, the notes are not an exhaustive guide to all the requirements that may be relevant and should therefore be read in conjunction with the FRS itself.

Capital instruments may have a combination of features and accordingly more than one note may be relevant to a single capital instrument.

2.2 Auction Market Preferred Shares ('AMPS')

Features

(a) AMPS are preference shares that are entitled to dividends determined in accordance with an auction process in which a panel of investors participates, the shares being transferred at a fixed price to the investor who will accept the lowest dividend. If the auction process fails - for example because no bids are received - the shares remain in the ownership of the former holder and the dividend is increased to a rate, known as the default rate, that is calculated in accordance with a prescribed formula.

(b) Analysis and required accounting

As AMPS are shares, dividends cannot be paid in respect of them except out of distributable profits, nor can they be redeemed unless the redemption is financed out of distributable profits or by a fresh issue of shares. Because they are redeemable at a fixed amount, and because the dividend rights are limited, AMPS constitute non-equity shares.

In accordance with the requirements of the FRS, AMPS should be reported within shareholders' funds as non-equity shares and included in the amount attributable to non-equity shares. The finance cost for each period should be the dividend rights accruing in respect of the period.

2.3 Convertible capital bonds

(a) Features

Convertible capital bonds are debt instruments on which interest is paid periodically, typically issued by a special purpose subsidiary incorporated outside the UK. Prior to maturity they may be exchanged for shares of the subsidiary which, at the option of the bondholder, are either immediately redeemed or immediately exchanged for ordinary shares of the parent. The bonds and payments in respect of the shares of the subsidiary are guaranteed by the parent. The parent has the right to issue convertible redeemable preference shares of its own in substitution for the bonds should it wish to do so.

(b) Analysis and required accounting

From the standpoint of the subsidiary, convertible capital bonds are clearly debt since the obligation to pay interest is an obligation to transfer economic benefits. In addition, FRS 4 requires that conversion of debt should not be anticipated. In the subsidiary's financial statements the bonds should therefore be accounted for as debt.

From the standpoint of the group they are also liabilities. Even though the parent has the option to issue convertible preference shares in substitution for the bonds, the requirements of FRS 4 again entail that such conversion should not be anticipated.

Since the liabilities are convertible, the amount attributable to convertible capital bonds should be included in the amount of convertible debt, which should be stated separately from other liabilities.

2.4 Convertible debt with a premium put option

(a) Features

Convertible debt with a premium put option contains an option for the holder to demand redemption (either at the maturity of the debt or at some earlier date) for an amount that is in excess of the amount originally received for the debt. At the time the debt is issued, it is uncertain whether the debt will be converted before the redemption option may be exercised, and hence whether the premium on redemption will be paid.

(b) Analysis and required accounting

The premium put option provides a higher guaranteed return to the holder of the debt than would be received on identical debt without such a put option. Often this higher return corresponds to that which the holder would have expected to receive on non-convertible debt. The holder's decision as to whether to exercise the option will depend on the relative values of the shares to which he would be entitled on conversion and the cash receivable, including the premium, on exercise of the option.

The term of convertible debt with a premium put option should be considered to end on the earliest date at which the holder has the option to require redemption. The premium payable on exercise of the premium put option falls to be included in the calculation of the finance costs for the debt.

On conversion the proceeds of the shares issued should be deemed to be the carrying amount of the debt, including accrued premium, immediately prior to conversion.

2.5 Convertible debt with enhanced interest

(a) Features

As an alternative to the premium put structure discussed above, convertible debt may contain an undertaking that the interest will be increased at a date in the future. At the time the debt is issued, it is uncertain whether the debt will be converted before the enhanced interest is payable.

(b) Analysis and required accounting

The enhanced rate of interest increases the guaranteed return to the holder. Often this higher return corresponds to that which the holder would have expected to receive on non-convertible debt. The holders' decision as to whether to convert the debt will take into account the interest forgone by such a decision.

The interest for the full term of the convertible debt should be taken into account in the allocation of finance costs, which should be allocated at a constant rate.

2.6 Illustration

Convertible debt is issued on 1 January 2000 for £1,000 and is redeemable at the same amount on 31 December 2014. It carries interest of £59 a year (a nominal rate of 5.9 per cent) for the first five years, after which the rate rises to £141 a year (a nominal rate of 14.1 per cent).

In order to comply with FRS 4 the finance costs should be allocated to accounting periods at the rate of 10 per cent a year. The movements on the carrying amount over the term of the debt would be as follows:

Year ending	*Balance at beginning of year* £	*Finance costs for year (10%)* £	*Cash paid during year* £	*Balance at end of year* £
31.12.2000	1,000	100	(59)	1,041
31.12.2001	1,041	104	(59)	1,086
31.12.2002	1,086	109	(59)	1,136
31.12.2003	1,136	113	(59)	1,190
31.12.2004	1,190	119	(59)	1,250
31.12.2005	1,250	125	(141)	1,234
31.12.2006	1,234	124	(141)	1,217
31.12.2007	1,217	122	(141)	1,198
31.12.2008	1,198	120	(141)	1,177
31.12.2009	1,177	118	(141)	1,154
31.12.2010	1,154	116	(141)	1,129
31.12.2011	1,129	113	(141)	1,101
31.12.2012	1,101	110	(141)	1,070
31.12.2013	1,070	107	(141)	1,036
31.12.2014	1,036	105*	(141 + 1,000)	-

* Increased by £1 rounding difference

2.7 Debt issued with warrants

(a) Features

Debt is sometimes issued with warrants. The issue is often made for the par value of the debt and the debt will be redeemed at the same amount. The warrants and the debt are capable of being transferred separately.

(b) Analysis and required accounting

The proceeds of the issue should be allocated between the debt and the warrants. As a result, the amount of the proceeds deemed to relate to the debt will be less than par value.

2.8 Deep discount bonds

Deep discount bonds are bonds that carry a low nominal rate of interest and accordingly are issued at a discount to the value at which they will be redeemed. In the extreme case where no interest at all is payable they are sometimes referred to as zero coupon bonds.

An example of this has been shown in the previous section.

2.9 Income bonds

(a) Features

The distinctive feature of income bonds is that interest is payable only in the event that the issuer has sufficient reported profits (after allowing for interest on other kinds of debt) to make the payment. If profits are insufficient the issuer is not in default and no additional rights accrue to the holder of the bond, although interest payments may be cumulative. Income bonds must be redeemed by the issuer at a fixed amount on a specific date.

(b) Analysis and required accounting

The requirement to redeem the bonds is an obligation to transfer economic benefits. The bonds must therefore be accounted for as a liability.

2.10 Index linked loans

(a) Features

Sometimes loan agreements do not state a specific amount for the payments; instead they include a formula to be used for their calculation. For example, in the case of floating rate loans, the amount of periodic payments of interest will be calculated by reference to a base rate - eg, LIBOR + 2 per cent.

Another example is that of index linked loans which may be redeemable at the principal amount multiplied by an index.

(b) Analysis and required accounting

FRS 4 requires that finance costs contingent on uncertain events such as changes in an index should be adjusted to reflect those events only once they have occurred. The effect is that the initial carrying amount will take no account of those events but the carrying amount at each subsequent balance sheet date will be recalculated to take account of the changes occurring in that reporting period. The resulting change in carrying amount is accounted for as an increase or decrease in finance costs for the period.

2.11 Illustration

A loan of £1,250 is issued on 1 January 2000 on which interest of 4 per cent (£50) is paid annually and the principal amount is repayable based on an index. The balance at the end of each year is found by multiplying the original principal amount by the index at the end of the year: the change in the amount is treated as additional finance costs.

Year ending	*Balance at beginning of year* £	*Finance costs for year (10%)* £	*Cash paid during year* £	*Balance at end of year* £	*Index at end of year*
31.12.2000	1,250	125	(50)	1,325	106
31.12.2001	1,325	100	(50)	1,375	110
31.12.2002	1,375	75	(50)	1,400	112
31.12.2003	1,400	150	(50)	1,500	120
31.12.2004	1,500	175	(1,625 + 50)	-	130

2.12 Perpetual debt

(a) Features

Perpetual debt is debt in respect of which the issuer has neither the right nor the obligation to repay the principal amount of the debt. Usually, interest is paid at a constant rate, or at a fixed margin over a benchmark rate such as LIBOR.

(b) Analysis and required accounting

Sometimes it is suggested that as the principal amount will never be repaid there is no need for the balance sheet to reflect a liability in respect of the debt. However, the obligation to pay interest is an obligation to transfer economic benefits and hence the instrument is a liability. As there are no repayments of principal the burden of this liability never diminishes.

The FRS is based on the principle that debt should be accounted for having regard to all the payments required by the debt, irrespective of their legal description, in the determination of the appropriate finance charge and capital repayment for each accounting period. In the case of perpetual debt where interest is paid at a constant rate, or at a fixed margin over a benchmark, the correct finance charge will be equal to the coupon payable for each period. Hence no part of the repayments will reduce the carrying amount and the debt will always be shown at the amount of net proceeds.

3 THE PROBLEMS OF ACCOUNTING FOR DERIVATIVES AND OTHER FINANCIAL INSTRUMENTS

3.1 Derivatives

Definition A **derivative** is a financial instrument that derives its value from that of an underlying asset, price, rate or index.

Examples of derivatives include the following:

(a) **Forward contracts**

Derivatives that oblige the holder to buy or sell a defined amount of a specific underlying asset at a specified future date. For example, under a forward contract for foreign currency, the holder might contract to exchange £100,000 for $150,000 on 25 October.

(b) **Forward rate agreements**

Two parties agree the interest rate to be paid on a notional deposit with a specified maturity at an agreed future date. At the agreed future date, the seller pays the buyer if rates have risen above the contracted rate and, conversely, the buyer pays the seller if rates have fallen. The payment is the difference between the market rate and the contracted rate multiplied by the notional principal amount.

(c) **Futures contracts**

Derivatives that oblige the holder to buy or sell a standard quantity of a specific underlying item at a specified future date. Futures contracts are very similar to forward contracts, the distinction being that futures contracts have standardised terms and are traded on a financial exchange whereas the terms of a forward contract are tailored to meet the needs of the transacting parties and forward contracts are not traded on a financial exchange.

(d) **Swaps**

Two parties agree to exchange periodic payments at specified intervals over a specified time period. For example, in an interest rate swap, the parties may agree to exchange fixed and floating interest payments calculated by reference to a notional principal amount (eg, to swap 8% for LIBOR on a notional principal of £100 million at six monthly intervals for a period of five years). In a currency swap, the parties agree to exchange interest payments on principal amounts in different currencies and, sometimes, also to exchange the principal amounts themselves either at the date the swap is entered into and/or its maturity.

(e) **Options**

These give the holder the right, but not the obligation, to buy or sell a specific underlying asset on or before a specified future date.

3.2 The need for an accounting standard

Large companies are making increasing use of derivatives to finance their activities. Derivatives can be easily acquired, often for little or no cost, but their values can change very rapidly, exposing companies to the risk of large profits or losses. Because many derivatives have no cost, they might not appear in the balance sheet, even if they represent substantial assets or liabilities of the company. Gains and losses are normally not recorded until cash is exchanged. Gains and losses can be easily realised, often simply by making a telephone call, and this enables management to choose when to report gains and losses on realisation.

Derivatives can rapidly transform the position, performance and risk profile of a company, but this is not usually apparent from the financial statements and there may be little or no disclosure of the risks arising from using derivatives.

3.3 Risks associated with financial instruments

Because the value of derivatives depends on movements in underlying items, if an entity uses derivatives, it is exposed to risk.

Definition **Risk** is uncertainty as to the amount of benefits. The term includes both potential for gain and exposure to loss (FRS 5).

Entities may use derivatives in order to manage risk.

Example

On 1 January 20X9 a UK company buys goods from a French company. This results in a liability for FF8 million which must be settled on 31 March 20X9. The exchange rate on 1 January is FF8 = £1. The company takes out a forward exchange contract to buy FF8 million for £1 million on 31 March 20X9. This is at the exchange rate ruling at 1 January (ie, FF8 = £1).

At 31 March the exchange rate is actually FF8.5 = £1. If the UK company had not taken out the forward exchange contract it would have made an exchange gain of £58,824 (1,000,000 – 941,176). By taking out the forward exchange contract it has given up the chance to make this gain, but has also protected itself against the possibility of making a loss. In other words, it has used the forward exchange contract to eliminate exchange rate risk.

However, in recent years there have been several cases in which companies have failed as a result of using derivatives, sometimes as a result of speculating on price, exchange or interest rate changes.

An Appendix to FRS 13 describes the types of risks associated with financial instruments. The two most familiar of these are credit risk and liquidity risk.

Definition **Credit risk** is the possibility that a loss may occur from the failure of another party to perform according to the terms of a contract.

Credit risk can be assessed from the nature of an entity's business and the numerical disclosures of gross debtors and provisions.

Definition **Liquidity risk** (or funding risk) is the risk that an entity will encounter difficulty in realising assets or otherwise raising funds to meet commitments associated with financial instruments.

Liquidity risk can be deduced from the current and quick ratios and from the disclosure of the terms and conditions of borrowing.

Two other important types of risk are associated with financial instruments - cash flow risk and market price risk.

Definition **Cash flow risk** is the risk that future cash flows generated by a monetary financial instrument will fluctuate in amount.

Definition **Market price risk** is the possibility that future changes in market prices may change the value, or the burden, of a financial instrument.

The main components of market price risk likely to affect most entities are:

(a) **Interest rate risk** - the risk that the value of a financial instrument will fluctuate because of changes in market interest rates.

(b) **Currency risk** - the risk that the value of a financial instrument will fluctuate because of changes in foreign exchange rates.

(c) **Other market price risk** - the risk that the value of a financial instrument will fluctuate as a result of changes in market prices caused by factors other than interest rates or currencies. This category includes risks stemming from commodity prices and share prices.

The relationship between cash flow risk and market price risk can have a significant effect on the risk profile of the entity. Transactions to reduce one of these risks may have the effect of increasing the other risk.

3.4 Activity

An entity has two interest bearing investments. One of the investments earns interest at a fixed rate of 8% per annum. The rate of interest earned on the other is 1% above base rate.

The base rate rises to 10%. What happens to:

(a) the market price of the two investments
(b) the cash flow of the entity?

3.5 Activity solution

Fixed rate investment: the market price will probably fall, so that the entity may make a loss when it sells the investment, but the amount of interest and therefore cash received stays the same. In other words, there is market price risk, but no immediate cash flow risk.

Floating rate investment: the market price is likely to stay about the same, but the interest and cash receivable increases. This investment exposes the entity to cash flow risk, but not to significant market price risk.

From this example we can see that the choice of which risk the management seeks to reduce will have an important bearing on the entity's financial position, financial results and cash flows. However, users of the financial statements have had very little information about an entity's exposure to these risks.

3.6 The ASB's approach to the financial instruments problem

The ASB is tackling this problem in two stages. It has issued FRS 13, which requires detailed disclosures that will enable users of the financial statements to assess the risks that the entity has assumed in connection with financial instruments. It is also looking at the issues surrounding the measurement of financial instruments. As the issue of an FRS on the measurement of derivatives will probably involve far reaching changes to present practice, the ASB wishes to allow ample time for preparers, users and auditors of accounts to debate the issues. It may be several years before a new standard is issued.

4 FRS 13: DERIVATIVES AND OTHER FINANCIAL INSTRUMENTS: DISCLOSURES

4.1 Objectives

FRS 13 was issued in order to ensure that reporting entities disclose information that enables users to assess:

(a) the risk profile of the entity for each of the main financial risks arising in connection with financial instruments; and

(b) the significance of such instruments and contracts to the entity's financial position, performance and cash flows.

4.2 Definitions

Definition A **financial instrument** is any contract that gives rise to both a financial asset of one entity and a financial liability or equity instrument of another entity.

Definition A **derivative financial instrument** is a financial instrument that derives its value from the price or rate of some underlying item, such as interest rates, exchange rates and stock market and other indices.

Derivative financial instruments include futures, options, forward contracts, interest rate and currency swaps, interest rate caps, collars and floors, forward interest rate agreements, and commitments to purchase shares or bonds.

Underlying items include equities, bonds, interest rates, exchange rates and stock market and other indices.

4.3 Scope of FRS 13

(a) **Entities**

FRS 13 applies to public and listed companies.

(b) **Instruments to be dealt with in the disclosures**

FRS 13 applies to **all financial instruments** (except those specifically excluded), not just to derivatives. Financial instruments give rise to both a financial asset of one entity and a financial liability or equity instrument of another entity.

Definition A **financial asset** is any asset that is:

(a) cash;

(b) a contractual right to receive cash or another financial asset from another entity;

(c) a contractual right to exchange financial instruments with another entity under conditions that are potentially favourable; or

(d) an equity instrument of another entity.

Definition A **financial liability** is any liability that is a contractual obligation:

(a) to deliver cash or another financial asset to another entity; or

(b) to exchange financial instruments with another entity under conditions that are potentially unfavourable.

The following items are **excluded** from the disclosures:

(a) interests in subsidiary, quasi-subsidiary and associated undertakings, partnerships and joint ventures (unless held exclusively with a view to subsequent resale)

(b) employers' obligations to employees under employee share option and employee share schemes

(c) pension and similar assets and liabilities

(d) rights and obligations under operating leases

(e) equity shares and options and warrants relating to equity shares issued by the reporting entity.

(c) **Short term debtors and creditors**

Either all or none of short term debtors and creditors should be excluded from the disclosures. Although technically short term debtors and creditors fall within the definition of financial instruments, the focus of FRS 13 is on financial instruments that are complex or have a significant impact on the risk profile of the entity. Therefore they do not have to be included in the disclosures, but the FRS acknowledges that some entities may wish to include them. An explanation of how these items have been dealt with should be provided.

(d) **Non-equity shares**

Non-equity shares should be dealt with in the disclosures in the same way as financial liabilities, but should be disclosed separately.

4.4 Activity

Which of the following items are financial instruments?

(a) debentures to be settled in cash
(b) plant and equipment
(c) goodwill
(d) warrants or options to subscribe for shares of the issuing entity
(e) a forward contract that will be settled in another financial instrument
(f) prepayments for goods or services
(g) stocks
(h) a forward contract that will be settled by the delivery of goods

4.5 Activity solution

Items (a), (d) and (e) are financial instruments.

4.6 Narrative disclosures

(a) An explanation should be provided of the role that financial instruments have had during the period in creating or changing the risks the entity faces in its activities. This should include:

- an explanation of the objectives and policies for holding or issuing financial instruments and similar contracts; and

- the strategies for achieving those objectives (in both cases as agreed by the directors) that have been followed during the period

(b) If these disclosures reflect a significant change from the explanations provided for the previous accounting period, this should be disclosed and the reasons for the change explained.

(c) If the directors agreed, before the date of approval of the financial statements, to make a significant change to the role that financial instruments will have in creating or changing the risks of the entity, that change should be explained.

(d) An explanation should be provided of how the period end numerical disclosures shown in the financial statements reflect the objectives, policies and strategies disclosed.

These disclosures should be given in the financial statements or in some other statement available with the financial statements, eg, the operating and financial review.

4.7 Numerical disclosures

(a) **Interest rate risk**

Analyse the aggregate carrying amount of financial liabilities, by principal currency, between liabilities:

- at fixed interest rates
- at floating interest rates
- on which no interest is paid.

(b) **Currency risk**

Provide an analysis of the net amount of monetary assets and liabilities at the balance sheet date, showing the amount denominated in each currency, analysed by reference to the functional currencies of the operations involved.

(c) **Liquidity**

Present a maturity profile of the carrying amount of financial liabilities, showing amounts falling due:

- in one year or less, or on demand
- in more than one year but not more than two years
- in more than two years but not more than five years
- in more than five years.

Determine the maturity profile by reference to the earliest date on which payment can be required or on which the liability falls due.

Analyse material undrawn committed borrowing facilities, showing amounts expiring:

- in one year or less;
- in more than one year but not more than two years; and
- in more than two years.

(d) **Fair values**

Group the financial assets and financial liabilities (whether recognised or unrecognised) into appropriate categories and for each category disclose either:

- the aggregate fair value at the balance sheet date together with the aggregate carrying amount; or

- the aggregate fair value of items with a positive fair value and, separately, the aggregate fair value of items with a negative fair value, in both cases as at the balance sheet date and in each case accompanied by the relevant aggregate carrying amount.

Disclose the methods and any significant assumptions used in determining fair value.

Fair values need not be disclosed if it is not practicable to estimate them with sufficient reliability. The following should be provided instead:

- a description of the item and its carrying amount

- the reasons why it is not practicable to estimate fair value with sufficient reliability

- information about the principal characteristics of the underlying financial asset or liability that is pertinent to estimating its fair value.

(e) **Other disclosure requirements**

These concern:

- financial assets and financial liabilities held or issued for trading
- financial liabilities and financial assets used as hedges
- commodity contracts.

You are unlikely to be examined on the detail of these, but you should be aware that entities are required to disclose gains and losses on these items that have not been recognised in the profit and loss account for the year.

Entities are also encouraged, but not required, to provide numerical disclosures that show the magnitude of market price risk arising over the period for all financial instruments.

4.8 Illustrations

FRS 13 contains an illustration of the disclosures that many companies will need to make in order to comply with the FRS. This is intended for guidance only and is reproduced below.

Narrative disclosures

[*For the purposes of this illustration, it has been assumed that the narrative disclosures are provided in the operating and financial review. As such, the notes to the financial statements will need to contain a cross-reference to the disclosures below. This cross-reference is not shown in this illustration.*

It is envisaged that the discussion set out below will usually be preceded by a general discussion of, inter alia, the entity's activities, structure and financing. This discussion will typically consider the financial risk profile of the entity as a whole as a prelude to the narrative disclosures required by the FRS.]

The Group's financial instruments, other than derivatives, comprise borrowings, some cash and liquid resources, and various items, such as trade debtors, trade creditors etc, that arise directly from its operations. The main purpose of these financial instruments is to raise finance for the Group's operations.

The Group also enters into derivatives transactions (principally interest rate swaps and forward foreign currency contracts). The purpose of such transactions is to manage the interest rate and currency risks arising from the Group's operations and its sources of finance.

It is, and has been throughout the period under review, the Group's policy that no trading in financial instruments should be undertaken.

The main risks arising from the Group's financial instruments are interest rate risk, liquidity risk and foreign currency risk. The Board reviews and agrees policies for managing each of these risks and they are summarised below. These policies have remained unchanged since the beginning of 20X0.

Interest rate risk

The Group finances its operations through a mixture of retained profits and bank borrowings. The Group borrows in the desired currencies at both fixed and floating rates of interest and then uses interest rate swaps to generate the desired interest profile and to manage the Group's exposure to interest rate fluctuations. The Group's policy is to keep between 50 per cent and 65 per cent of its borrowings at fixed rates of interest. At the year-end, 62 per cent of the Group's borrowings were at fixed rates after taking account of interest rate swaps.

Liquidity risk

As regards liquidity, the Group's policy has throughout the year been that, to ensure continuity of funding, at least 50 per cent of its borrowings should mature in more than five years. At the year-end, 57 per cent of the Group's borrowings were due to mature in more than five years.

Short-term flexibility is achieved by overdraft facilities.

Foreign currency risk

The Group has one significant overseas subsidiary – Foreign – which operates in the USA and whose revenues and expenses are denominated exclusively in US dollars. In order to protect the Group's sterling balance sheet from the movements in the US dollar/sterling exchange rate, the Group finances its net investment in this subsidiary by means of US dollar borrowings.

About one-third of the sales of the Group's UK businesses are to customers in continental Europe. These sales are priced in sterling but invoiced in the currencies of the customers involved. The Group's policy is to eliminate all currency exposures on sales at the time of sale through forward currency contracts. All the other sales of the UK businesses are denominated in sterling.

Numerical information (Notes to the accounts)

[*Although not shown in this illustration, an explanation of the material accounting policies adopted in accounting for financial instruments will need to be provided. The Group would also need to explain that it has taken advantage of the exemption available for short-term debtors and creditors.*

The accounting period dealt with in this illustration is the 12 months to 31 December 20X1. Although corresponding amounts are not shown in the illustration, they will need to be provided except in respect of the first accounting period in which the FRS comes into effect.]

Interest rate risk profile of financial assets and financial liabilities

Financial assets

The Group has no financial assets, other than short-term debtors and an immaterial amount of cash at bank.

Financial liabilities

After taking into account the various interest rate swaps and forward foreign currency contracts entered into by the Group, the interest rate profile of the Group's financial liabilities at 31 December 20X1 was:

Currency	Total £ million	Floating rate financial liabilities £ million	Fixed rate financial liabilities £ million	Financial liabilities on which no interest is paid £ million
Sterling	415	150	250	15
US dollar	200	80	120	–
Total	615	230	370	15

	Fixed rate financial liabilities		Financial liabilities on which no interest is paid
Currency	**Weighted average interest rate** **%**	**Weighted average period for which rate is fixed** **Years**	**Weighted average period until maturity** **Years**
Sterling	10	5	1.4
US dollar	7	8	–
Total	–	6	1.4

The floating rate financial liabilities comprise:

- sterling denominated bank borrowings and overdrafts that bear interest at rates based on the six-month LIBOR, and
- US dollar denominated bank borrowings that bear interest at rates based on the US Prime rate.

Currency exposures

As at 31 December 20X1, after taking into account the effects of forward foreign exchange contracts the Group had no currency exposures.

Maturity of financial liabilities

The maturity profile of the Group's financial liabilities at 31 December 20X1 was as follows:

	£m
In one year or less, or on demand	200
In more than one year but not more than two years	15
In more than two years but not more than five years	60
In more than five years	340
	615

Borrowing facilities

The Group has various undrawn committed borrowing facilities. The facilities available at 31 December 20X1 in respect of which all conditions precedent had been met were as follows:

	£m
Expiring in one year or less	40
Expiring in more than one year but not more than two years	7
Expiring in more than two years	3
	50

Fair values of financial assets and financial liabilities

Set out below is a comparison by category of book values and fair values of the Group's financial assets and liabilities as at 31 December 20X1.

	Book value £ million	Fair value £ million
Primary financial instruments held or issued to finance the Group's operations:		
Short-term financial liabilities and current portion of long-term borrowings	(215)	(223)
Long-term borrowings	(400)	(370)
Financial assets	7	8
Derivative financial instruments held to manage the interest rate and currency profile:		
Interest rate swaps	–	15
Forward foreign currency contracts	–	(5)

The fair values of the interest rate swaps, forward foreign currency contracts and sterling denominated long-term fixed rate debt with a carrying amount of £250 million have been determined by reference to prices available from the markets on which the instruments involved are traded. All the other fair values shown above have been calculated by discounting cash flows at prevailing interest rates.

Gains and losses on hedges

The Group enters into forward foreign currency contracts to eliminate the currency exposures that arise on sales denominated in foreign currencies immediately those sales are transacted. It also uses interest rate swaps to manage its interest rate profile. Changes in the fair value of instruments used as hedges are not recognised in the financial statements until the hedged position matures. An analysis of these unrecognised gains and losses is as follows:

	Gains £ million	Losses £ million	Total net gains/(losses) £ million
Unrecognised gains and losses on hedges at 1.1.X1	**9**	**12**	**(3)**
Gains and losses arising in previous years that were recognised in 20X1	8	9	1
Gains and losses arising before 1.1.X1 that were not recognised in 20X1	**1**	**3**	**(2)**
Gains and losses arising in 20X1 that were not recognised in 20X1	18	6	12
Unrecognised gains and losses on hedges at 31.12.X1	**19**	**9**	**10**

Of which:			
Gains and losses expected to be recognised in 20X2	12	6	6
Gains and losses expected to be recognised in 20X3 or later	7	3	4

Market price risk

The Group's exposure to market price risk comprises interest rate and currency risk exposures. It monitors these exposures primarily through a process known as sensitivity analysis. This involves estimating the effect on profit before tax over various periods of a range of possible changes in interest rates and exchange rates. The sensitivity analysis model used for this purpose makes no assumptions about any interrelationships between such rates or about the way in which such changes may affect the economies involved. As a consequence, figures derived from the Group's sensitivity analysis model should be used in conjunction with other information about the Group's risk profile.

The Group's policy towards currency risk is to eliminate all exposures that will impact on reported profit as soon as they arise. This is reflected in the sensitivity analysis, which estimates that five and ten percentage point increases in the value of sterling against all other currencies would have had minimal impact on profit before tax.

On the other hand, the Group's policy is to accept a degree of interest rate risk as long as the effects of various changes in rates remain within certain prescribed ranges. On the basis of the Group's analysis, it is estimated that a rise of one percentage point in all interest rates would have reduced 20X1 profit before tax by approximately 1.5 per cent and that a three percentage point increase would have reduced such profits by 4.2 per cent. This is well within the ranges that the Group regards as acceptable.

Conclusion FRS 13 requires public and listed companies to make narrative and numerical disclosures of information about their financial instruments. They must provide an explanation of the ways in which financial instruments have created or changed the risks the company faces during the period.

4.9 Effect of FRS 13

Most commentators accept the need for greater disclosure regarding derivatives and for this reason FRS 13 will probably prove relatively non-controversial. Although it could be argued that the additional disclosures would contribute still further to an 'information overload', most commentators believe that the extra cost is justified.

The disclosures have the further advantage that gathering and preparing the information will provide preparers of the accounts with useful experience of the problems involved in accounting for derivatives. This will enable interested parties to participate in the debate over the next stage of the ASB's proposals.

5 DISCUSSION PAPER: DERIVATIVES AND OTHER FINANCIAL INSTRUMENTS

5.1 Introduction

In July 1996 the ASB issued a Discussion Paper: *Derivatives and other financial instruments*. The Discussion Paper deals with both disclosure and measurement issues; the disclosure proposals have since been developed into FRS 13.

As we have seen, the use of derivatives poses problems for preparers and users of financial statements because:

- Many derivatives, such as futures and forward contracts, do not have a meaningful 'cost' that can be recognised in the financial statements.

- Gains and losses are normally not recorded until cash is exchanged, despite the fact that potential gains and losses often occur almost immediately. Under current accounting principles, gains and losses cannot be included in the profit and loss account before they are realised. Although SSAP 20 provides some guidance on forward exchange contracts used for trading (the forward exchange rate may be used to translate assets and liabilities into sterling) there is no guidance in any accounting standard on when to recognise gains and losses on other forms of derivative, especially where these are used for speculation, rather than for trading purposes.

The Discussion Paper attempts to address these problems.

The Paper's proposals would apply to listed and similar public interest companies only.

5.2 Measurement

The main proposal is that all financial instruments should be measured at **current value.**

Current value would be used for all derivatives, for holdings of shares or debt instruments of other entities and for the entity's own borrowings. The entity's own equity shares would continue to be measured at historic cost. All gains and losses would be recognised as they occur.

5.3 Evaluation of the main proposal

Arguments for using current value

The ASB believes that historical cost is no longer viable for financial instruments because:

(a) it does not report the actual transactions entered into

(b) unrealised gains and losses are not reported

(c) it does not actively reflect the management of risk

(d) it gives rise to a need for hedge accounting (which would be greatly reduced if all financial instruments were measured at current value)

(e) it results in a lack of comparability in that identical instruments that were acquired at different times may be recorded at different amounts.

Current value has other advantages:

(a) it provides relevant, up to date information about performance and stewardship

(b) current value information has predictive value

(c) it is increasingly used for internal management information

(d) it reflects the readily realisable nature of financial instruments (they are very similar to actual cash)

(e) it is practical, because many financial instruments are traded in an active market (and can therefore be easily valued).

Arguments against current value

(a) Assets and liabilities would be measured on different bases, because assets are likely to be non-financial and measured on the cost basis, while most liabilities are likely to be financial instruments

(b) it might result in volatile profits

(c) it reflects opportunity costs for transactions that may not be undertaken, rather than actual costs, and gains which may never be realised

(d) it may be impractical (some instruments may be difficult to value)

(e) it would result in far-reaching changes to accounting practice.

The ASB considered several 'halfway house' approaches, under which some instruments would be measured at current value and others at cost. It concluded that the anomalies that would result from such halfway houses are such as to rule them out, even as an interim solution.

5.4 Reporting gains and losses arising on financial instruments

In theory, there are several ways in which such gains and losses could be reported.

(a) **All gains and losses could be reported in the profit and loss account**

Arguments for:

- All gains and losses represent the performance of management who are responsible for the decision to buy or sell instruments.
- If all changes in value are taken to the profit and loss account the scope for manipulation of profit is reduced.

Arguments against:

- Gains and losses on financial instruments have different characteristics from trading profits and losses. If gains and losses on financial instruments were reported outside the profit and loss account this would emphasise their different nature.
- If unrealised gains and losses on fixed rate debt were reported in the profit and loss account this would imply that fixed rate debt carried risk (because its value changes as interest rates move) and that floating rate debt is risk free. This might mislead users.

(b) **Report certain gains in the profit and loss account and others in the statement of total recognised gains and losses (STRGL)**

Arguments for:

- Different types of gains and losses would be reported separately. For example, gains and losses on long term instruments could be reported in the STRGL and those on short term investments in the profit and loss account. This would highlight their different natures.
- The profit and loss account would be protected from volatility.

The main argument against this approach is that there would be problems in drawing a distinction between those gains and losses to be reported in the profit and loss account and those to be reported in the STRGL. The need to draw up principles for distinguishing the two has resulted in the ASB's separate project on reporting financial performance (discussed in an earlier chapter).

(c) **Defer changes in value in a balance sheet caption and transfer them to the profit and loss account in a future period**

Gains and losses could be 'recycled' to the profit and loss account once they were realised or gradually over the term of the instrument. This approach has the advantage of avoiding volatility in the profit and loss account. There would also be little change to present practice.

Arguments against:

- Gains and losses would not be reported in the period in which they occurred. This would provide opportunities for manipulation of the earnings figure.
- The amounts recorded in the balance sheet would be meaningless as the deferred debits and credits are not assets and liabilities. Losses would give rise to assets and gains to liabilities. Gains and losses could be shown as part of shareholders' funds, but this would effectively amount to reserve accounting and is difficult to justify.

(d) **Report some gains and losses in the STRGL and recycle them to the profit and loss account in a future period**

This is a similar method to (c) above and again, items could be recycled when they are realised or over the life of the instrument. The main advantage is that all gains and losses would be recorded in the period in which they occur.

Arguments against:

- Reported figures can be meaningless as an item can be reported in two performance statements at different times For example, if a loss on an instrument is initially reported in the STRGL and is recycled to the profit and loss account in a later period, the STRGL will then include a gain relating to an instrument on which only losses have arisen in a previous period. This effect is difficult to explain.
- The STRGL becomes a 'holding tank' for gains and losses that have not yet been reported in the profit and loss account. This is contrary to the way in which the statement is used for other items.
- The approach is inconsistent with FRS 3 *Reporting financial performance*. FRS 3 requires that a gain arising on the revaluation of a fixed asset that is initially recorded in the STRGL should not be reported again in the profit and loss account when the gain is realised.

The Discussion Paper recommends the second approach described above. It proposes that changes in the value of:

(a) fixed rate borrowings;

(b) related derivatives used to manage the interest basis of borrowings (eg, an interest rate swap that serves to 'convert' a borrowing from fixed rate to floating); and

(c) borrowings and derivatives that hedge a net investment in an overseas operation (this would be consistent with the requirements of SSAP 20)

would be reported in the statement of total recognised gains and losses.

All other changes in value, whether realised or unrealised, would be recognised in the profit and loss account.

These proposals are likely to be modified in the light of the ASB's project on reporting financial performance. This proposes that the profit and loss account and statement of total recognised gains and losses should be amalgamated into one single performance statement.

5.5 Future developments

Since the Discussion Paper was originally published the ASB has combined with eight other international standard setters and the IASC in a joint working group (JWG) to develop a common approach to accounting for financial instruments.

The JWG's working premise is that:

- all financial instruments will be carried at fair value; and
- all gains and losses arising from changes in those fair values will be recognised immediately in the profit and loss account.

The JWG is due to publish its proposals in mid 2000. These are likely to form the basis of the FRED on the measurement of financial instruments that will eventually be issued by the ASB. The US standard setting body, the Financial Accounting Standards Board (FASB) is also considering the problem of measurement and its conclusions are expected to influence the work of the JWG and the ASB.

6 CHAPTER SUMMARY

FRS 4 gives prescriptive conditions for the split between debt and equity and deals with the accounting entries for capital instruments. There are many types of capital instruments as the application notes demonstrate. The nature of liabilities should be understood and accounted for accordingly.

The use of derivatives is increasing, but this leads to many problems. FRS 13 and the ASB Discussion Paper *Derivatives and other financial instruments* set out proposals for the disclosure and measurement of derivatives.

7 SELF TEST QUESTIONS

7.1 When should capital instruments be classified as liabilities? (1.3)

7.2 Should convertible debt be recorded as equity or a liability? (1.5)

7.3 How should finance costs for liabilities and non-equity shares be treated in the financial statements? (1.8)

7.4 What are the principal requirements of UITF Abstract 11? (1.12)

7.5 What is an income bond? (2.9)

7.6 What is a derivative? (3.1)

7.7 What is a financial instrument? (4.2)

7.8 How should derivatives be measured in the financial statements, according to the proposals in the ASB's Discussion Paper? (5.2)

8 EXAMINATION TYPE QUESTION

8.1 Stone plc

On 1 October 20X4, Stone plc issued 50,000 debentures, with a par value of £100 each, to investors at £55 each. The debentures are redeemable at par on 30 September 20X9 and have a coupon rate of 2%, which was significantly below the market rate of interest for such debentures issued at par. In accounting for these debentures to date, Stone plc has simply accounted for the cash flows involved.

Profit and loss accounts for the years ended 30 September 20X7 and 20X8 are as follows.

	Years ended 30 September	
	20X8	*20X7*
	(Draft)	*(Published)*
	£'000	£'000
Turnover	6,700	6,300
Cost of sales	(3,025)	(2,900)
Gross profit	3,675	3,400
Overheads	(600)	(550)
Interest payable - debenture	(100)	(100)
- other	(275)	(250)
Profit for financial year	2,700	2,500
Retained profit brought forward	4,300	1,800
Retained profit carried forward	7,000	4,300

Extracts from the balance sheet are as follows.

Share capital	2,250	2,250
Share premium	550	550
Profit and loss account	7,000	4,300
	9,800	7,100
Debentures	2,750	2,750
	12,550	9,850

You are required to detail an alternative set of entries in the books of Stone plc for the issue of the debentures and subsequently to comply with FRS 4. Draw up a revised profit and loss account for the year ended 30 September 20X8 and balance sheet - together with comparatives - taking account of this alternative accounting treatment. **(15 marks)**

Ignore taxation. The implicit rate of interest for the cash flows relating to the debentures is 15.62%; make calculations to the nearest £'000.

9 ANSWER TO EXAMINATION TYPE QUESTION

9.1 Stone plc

Profit and loss accounts

	Years ended 30 September			
		20X8		*20X7*
	£'000	£'000	£'000	£'000
Turnover		6,700		6,300
Cost of sales		(3,025)		(2,900)
Gross profit		3,675		(3,400)
Overheads		(600)		(550)
Interest payable - debenture (W2)		(609)		(541)
- other		(275)		(250)
Profit for the financial year		2,191		2,059

Retained profit brought forward				
As originally reported	4,300		1,800	
Prior period adjustment (W3)	(1,152)		(711)	
As restated		3,148		1,089
Retained profit carried forward		5,339		3,148

Balance sheets

Share capital	2,250	2,250
Share premium	550	550
Profit and loss account	5,339	3,148
	8,139	5,948
Debentures	4,411	3,902
	12,550	9,850

WORKINGS

(W1) Finance costs

	£'000
Redemption £50,000 × £100	5,000
Interest £100,000 × 5	500
	5,500
Net proceeds of issue	2,750
Total finance costs	2,750

(W2) Movements in carrying amount of debt

Period ended 30 September	*Balance at beginning of year* £'000	*Finance costs pa @ 15.62%* £'000	*Cash paid* £'000
20X5	2,750	430	(100)
20X6	3,080	481	(100)
20X7	3,461	541	(100)
20X8	3,902	609	(100)
20X9	4,411	689	(5,100)
Total		2,750	(5,500)

(W3) Retained profits brought forward

	20X8 £'000	*20X7* £'000
Additional charges required		
20X5	330	330
20X6	381	381
20X7	441	
	1,152	711

29 CURRENT ISSUES AND CONTROVERSIES

INTRODUCTION & LEARNING OBJECTIVES

This chapter considers a number of issues of importance to auditors and preparers of financial statements, which are currently being discussed by the profession.

When you have studied this chapter you should be able to do the following:

- Discuss whether smaller entities should be exempted from the detailed requirements of accounting standards.
- Discuss the legal liability of auditors.
- Appreciate developments in ethical issues.
- Discuss international issues affecting auditing.
- Discuss other current issues and controversies relating to auditors.

1 THE FINANCIAL REPORTING STANDARD FOR SMALLER ENTITIES (FRSSE)

1.1 Introduction to the small companies debate

The number and complexity of accounting standards is increasing. Within the profession there is currently a debate as to whether accounting standards place an unnecessary burden on small companies. One view is that accounting standards should apply to all financial statements which are intended to show a true and fair view. Another view is that small companies should be exempted from the requirements of certain standards. A third view is that there should be a completely different set of accounting standards for small companies.

The debate centres on the definition of 'small companies'. The current definition is contained within the Companies Acts and is based on size. But is a small company simply a smaller version of a large company or is it fundamentally different in nature? The requirements of financial reporting standards are mainly designed to satisfy the information needs of external investors. Some commentators argue that small company financial statements are used by a very different and limited range of people (normally the owners of the business, the Inland Revenue and the bank). The recognition and measurement criteria used by large companies may not be appropriate.

1.2 The traditional position

Small companies are already exempt from certain requirements of the Companies Act and of accounting standards.

(a) **The Companies Act**

- Companies which meet the definition of 'small' or 'medium sized' contained in the Act may file abbreviated accounts with the Registrar of Companies. Abbreviated accounts for 'small' companies consist of a simplified balance sheet and limited notes.

- 'Small' companies may circulate simplified accounts to shareholders.

- 'Small' and 'medium sized' companies are not required to state whether they have complied with accounting standards.

- 'Small' and 'medium sized' groups are exempt from preparing group accounts.

(b) **Accounting standards**

- A company which meets the Companies Act definition of a 'small' company is exempt from the requirement to prepare a cash flow statement under FRS 1.
- Companies which fall below the criteria multiplied by ten for defining a 'medium sized' company are exempt from making certain disclosures required by SSAP 13 *Accounting for research and development* and SSAP 25 *Segmental reporting*.

1.3 Recent developments

In 1994 a CCAB working party was set up to consider the application of accounting standards to smaller entities.

In November 1994 it issued a report which proposed that only SSAPs 4, 9, 13, 17 and 18 and UITF Abstract 7 should continue to apply to small companies.

In December 1995 the working party issued a consultative paper, which proposed that small companies should be allowed to follow one single accounting standard specifically designed to meet their needs. This standard, known as the *Financial Reporting Standard for Smaller Entities* (FRSSE), was issued in November 1997 and subsequently updated in December 1998 and December 1999.

1.4 Contents of the FRSSE

Scope

The FRSSE may be applied by all entities that are small companies or groups as defined by companies legislation, or which would qualify if they had been incorporated as companies.

Entities falling within this scope may either produce their financial statements as normal following FRSs, SSAPs, UITF Abstracts etc, or may choose to produce simplified statements in compliance with the FRSSE.

Accounting requirements

The FRSSE lists the extant SSAPs, FRSs and UITF Abstracts, and specifies the simplifications that it believes are appropriate in respect of each requirement. The controversial areas are as follows:

(a) should a summary cash flow statement be required in financial statements drawn up under the FRSSE? FRS 1 exempts small companies from having to prepare cash flow statements, but some commentators have argued that management of cash is particularly important in smaller companies. The FRSSE believes that in many small companies with straightforward transactions, a cash flow statement would add little to what is already apparent from the balance sheet and profit and loss account, so there is no requirement for a cash flow statement in the FRSSE.

(b) should the FRSSE be capable of application to small groups? Small groups are not required by law to prepare consolidated accounts, but may do so voluntarily. In practice few small groups do prepare consolidated accounts, so the FRSSE does not go into detail about simplifications that could be made in this area, but simply states that all accounting standards that are relevant to group situations should be applied where the FRSSE is being applied to consolidated statements.

1.5 Conclusion

There is growing support in the profession for the general principle that the reporting requirements should be reduced for small companies, on a cost-benefit argument, but there is still some discussion about the precise nature of the relaxations from accounting standards that should be permitted.

2 THE LEGAL LIABILITY OF AUDITORS

2.1 Liability in contract

The company has a contract with the auditor and hence can sue the auditor for breach of contract if there is suspected negligence. Since the company rarely sues, the more important liability of the auditor is that to third parties in tort, which is discussed below.

Note that the shareholders do not have a contract with the auditor so shareholders cannot sue in contract (an important decision in the Caparo v Touche Ross case).

The auditor may also be liable to others who have relied on the financial statements upon which he expressed an opinion.

2.2 Duty of care of the auditor

When carrying out his duties the auditor must exercise care and skill. The degree of care and skill to be shown, in particular in relation to the depth of his investigation and the types of check to be made, is shown by judicial decision.

In general, the auditor must exercise a reasonable degree of care and skill. As stated in Re London and General Bank (No 2) (1895)

'It is the duty of an auditor to bring to bear on the work he has to perform that skill, care and caution which a reasonably careful and cautious auditor would use. What is reasonable skill, care and caution must depend on the particular circumstances of each case. An auditor ... is not bound to do more than exercise reasonable care and skill in making enquiries. He is not an insurer; he does not guarantee that the books do correctly show the true position of the company's affairs; he must be honest ie, he must not certify what he does not believe to be true, and he must take reasonable care and skill before he believes that what he certifies is true.'

The meaning of reasonable in this respect has been expanded and clarified by later decided cases. It should, however, be appreciated that decisions in older cases will tend to under-state rather than over-state the degree of care and skill required, since what is regarded as reasonable by the courts will necessarily be affected by current standards of auditing practice.

In the absence of suspicious circumstances, an auditor would not be liable for failing to uncover fraud and falsities which were not discoverable by the exercise of normal skill and care - Re City Equitable Fire Insurance (1925). Similarly, in the absence of suspicious circumstances, the auditor is entitled to accept the word of a responsible company official. But once an auditor's suspicions have been aroused there is a duty to probe the matter to the bottom. (Re Kingston Cotton Mill Co (1896)).

2.3 Liability in tort

A third party (ie, a person who has no contractual relationship with the auditor) may sue the auditor in the tort of negligence for damages.

In the tort of negligence, the plaintiff (ie, the third party) must prove that

(a) the defendant (ie, the auditor) owes a duty of care, and

(b) the defendant has breached the appropriate standard of care (ie, has been negligent), and

(c) the plaintiff has suffered loss resulting from the defendant's breach.

To whom a person making a negligent mis-statement causing economic loss owes a duty of care has been the subject of litigation, viz Hedley Byrne v Heller (1963) and JEB Fasteners v Marks Bloom (1980-2), albeit in this case it was obiter dicta.

The principles were established in Hedley Byrne v Heller. A duty of care exists where there is a special relationship between the parties ie, where the auditors knew, or ought to have known, that the audited accounts would be made available to, and would be relied on by, a particular person (or class of person).

For example, suppose that X, a director of a company, said to the auditors: I am going to show the audited accounts to Mr John Brown and members of my Yacht Club as they are thinking of buying shares in the company.

The auditors would then owe a duty of care to Mr John Brown because they knew that he, a particular person, would rely on the accounts. Similarly the auditors would owe a duty of care to the members of the Yacht Club because the auditors knew that they, a particular class of persons would rely on the accounts.

The essence of Hedley Byrne is that the third parties must have been identified in some way to the auditors.

If, to continue the example, the directors, without telling or warning the auditors, showed the accounts to a prospective take-over bidder, then under Hedley Byrne there would appear to be no duty of care.

The principles of JEB Fasteners v Marks Bloom

At first instance, and obiter dicta, it was stated that a duty of care will exist where the defendant auditors

(i) knew or reasonably should have foreseen at the time that the accounts were audited that a person might rely on those accounts for the particular purpose, and

(ii) that in all the circumstances it would be reasonable for such reliance to be placed on those accounts for that particular purpose.

The question that therefore arises is the possible liability of an auditor to a member of the general public who reads the accounts and then buys shares in the company in reliance on those accounts. Does the auditor owe a duty of care to such an unknown person? It is likely that it would be held that an auditor should reasonably foresee that a member of the public might read the accounts since they are available for public inspection at Companies House. But whether it is reasonable for a member of the public to rely on the accounts in making an investment decision would depend on all the surrounding circumstances; for example, the length of time which has elapsed between preparation and auditing the accounts and reliance by the third party upon them.

One case in particular is indicative of the current trend towards limiting the circumstances in which a duty of care is owed. In 1990 the House of Lords gave its decision on the following case

Caparo Industries v Dickman and Touche Ross & Co

Fidelity plc was taken over by Caparo Industries. Fidelity's accounts had been audited by Touche Ross. Caparo alleged that the accounts overstated the profits of Fidelity plc and that its purchases of shares and take-over bid were all made in reliance on the audited accounts.

Held by the House of Lords, that a duty of care was not owed to potential investors in, or take-over bidders for, the company having regard to

(a) the lack of proximity between auditor and potential investor and

(b) the fact that it would not be just and reasonable to impose a duty on the auditor to such investors.

In the above case, the House of Lords identified the auditor's functions as being

(a) to protect the company itself from errors and wrongdoing

(b) to provide shareholders with information such that they can scrutinise the conduct of a company's affairs and remove or reward those responsible.

The auditor does not exist to aid investment decisions.

Since the Caparo case there have been no fundamental changes to the legal position with respect to auditors' liability. However, one case, Morgan Crucible Co plc v Hill Samuel & Co Ltd and others (1990) has established that duty of care may be owed to take-over bidders in some circumstances. In the court of appeal it was held that directors, auditors and financial advisers of a company which is the subject of a contested take-over bid can owe a duty to identified bidders to take reasonable care with regard to financial statements on which the bidders could foreseeably rely when deciding whether or not to make or increase their offer.

This does not contradict or amend the Caparo decision. However, it makes clear that accountants may owe a duty when producing financial information for the purposes of a take-over bid. The case is distinguished from Caparo because the financial information was additional to a Companies Act audit report.

Conclusion

To sum up, an auditor does not owe a duty of care to potential take-over bidders when auditing company accounts.

However, an auditor who produces other or additional information in the context of a contested take-over bid may owe a duty to the identified bidders not to mislead them.

3 CURRENT ETHICAL ISSUES

3.1 Corporate governance - the Cadbury Report

The Cadbury Committee was set up in 1991 by the FRC, the Stock Exchange and the accountancy profession to examine the reporting and control functions of boards of directors and the role of auditors and shareholders. Its full title was "The Committee on the Financial Aspects of Corporate Governance", chaired by Sir Adrian Cadbury. In the wake of a number of large company disasters a better title might have been "The Committee on How to Stop Fraud".

The draft report entitled "The Financial Aspects of Corporate Governance" was issued in May 1992. The final report followed in December. It contains two main areas of recommendation relevant to auditors which are briefly summarised below.

3.2 The annual audit

Two central issues were considered with regard to this vital part of corporate governance.

(a) How to ensure that a professional and objective relationship exists between auditors and management.

It was concluded that this would be helped by

(i) The ASB's development of more effective accounting standards
(ii) The formation of audit committees (see below)
(iii) Full disclosure of fees paid to auditors for non-audit work
(iv) Periodic change of audit partner

(b) How to increase the effectiveness and value of the audit.

The report contains a *recommendation* that reporting practice is extended in the areas of internal control and going concern. It also *recommends* that the Companies Act be amended to allow auditors the freedom to report a 'reasonable suspicion of fraud' without breaking their fiduciary duty to a client company.

3.3 Code of best practice for company directors

The Cadbury code is applicable to the boards of all listed companies in the UK from June 1993 and has been incorporated into the Stock Exchange's Combined Code on corporate governance. Annual reports now have to carry a statement of compliance. Non-compliance has to be explained.

Broadly the Cadbury code covers

- membership of the board with effective division of responsibility (combination of executive and non-executive directors)
- independence of the board (no financial connection with the company except fees and shareholdings)
- remuneration committees to be established and service contracts over three years approved by shareholders
- reporting and disclosure (including disclosure of directors' emoluments and reporting on internal control systems)
- establishment of audit committees (with at least three non-executive directors, at least two being independent).

3.4 Audit committees

In the US over 80% of large companies have audit committees and the Securities and Exchange Commission has made them compulsory for all companies listed on the New York Stock Exchange.

An audit committee can be defined as a committee of directors, usually without executive responsibility, or top-ranking managers, which considers both the external and internal auditors' plans and activity with a specific brief to review internal control arrangements.

(a) **Objectives and advantages**

Three main objectives are usually associated with audit committees.

(i) Increasing public confidence in the credibility and objectivity of published financial information (including unaudited interim statements).

(ii) Assisting directors (particularly non-executive directors) in meeting their responsibilities in respect of financial reporting.

(iii) Strengthening the independent position of a company's external auditor by providing an additional channel of communication.

In addition

(iv) They may improve the quality of management accounting; being better placed to criticise internal functions.

(v) They should lead to better communication between the directors, external auditors and management.

(b) **Disadvantages**

Audit committees may lead to

(i) fear that their purpose is to catch management out
(ii) non-executive directors being over-burdened with detail
(iii) a 'two-tier' board of directors.

Finally, there is undoubtedly additional cost in terms of, at the least, time involved.

(c) **The functions of an audit committee**

These could include the following:

(i) Review of a company's internal control procedures.

(ii) Review of the internal audit function - the audit committee providing an independent reporting channel.

(iii) Review of the company's current accounting policies and possible changes resulting from the introduction of new accounting standards.

(iv) Review of regular management information (for example, monthly management accounts.)

(v) Review of the annual financial statements presented to shareholders.

(vi) Review of the results of the external auditors' examination to ensure that the auditors have performed an effective, efficient and independent audit.

(vii) Procedures for reviewing published interim (preliminary) statements, draft prospectus, profit forecast, etc.

(viii) Receiving and dealing with external auditors' criticisms of management, and ensuring that recommendations of internal auditors have been implemented.

(ix) Recommending nomination and remuneration of the external auditors.

3.5 Going concern and financial reporting

The Cadbury Committee recommended that directors should state in their report and accounts that the business is a going concern. In November 1994 the Cadbury Committee issued a paper *Going concern and financial reporting* to give guidance to help directors in complying with this recommendation.

3.6 Going concern

The paper explains the significance of going concern in relation to the financial statements. It refers to the requirements of the Companies Act 1985 and of SSAP 2. It also discusses the term 'foreseeable future', making the following points:

(a) The foreseeable future depends on the specific circumstances at a point in time, including the nature of the company's business, its associated risks and external influences.

(b) Any judgement made, whilst reasonable at the time, can be valid only at that time and can be overturned by subsequent events.

(c) In assessing going concern, directors should take account of all information of which they are aware at the time. It is not possible to specify a minimum period to which they should pay particular attention in assessing going concern. Where the period considered has been limited, for example, to a period of less than one year from the date of approval of the financial statements, additional disclosure may be necessary in order to explain the assumptions that underlie the adoption of the going concern basis.

3.7 Procedures

The paper describes the procedures that an explicit statement may entail. The procedures are described in broad terms, with more detailed suggestions in an Appendix.

Directors are best placed to know which factors are likely to be of greater significance in relation to their company. These factors will vary by industry and from company to company within a particular industry. Major areas in which procedures are likely to be appropriate are:

(a) forecasts and budgets
(b) borrowing requirements
(c) liability management
(d) contingent liabilities
(e) products and markets
(f) financial risk management
(g) financial adaptability.

The directors should consider the range of potential outcomes and their probability in order to determine the likely commercial outcome.

If the directors become aware of factors that cast doubt on the ability of the company to continue in operational existence, then they will need to carry out more detailed investigations. Such work will provide evidence in support of their statement on going concern and additional disclosure in their statement may be appropriate.

3.8 Disclosure by directors

Directors should include their statement on going concern in the Operating and Financial Review (OFR), if they include an OFR in their accounts.

There are three possibilities:

(a) **Going concern presumption appropriate**

The directors should make a basic statement to that effect.

(b) **Going concern basis used despite doubts on going concern presumption**

The directors should explain the circumstances so as to identify the factors which give rise to the problems (including any external factors outside their control which may affect the outcome) and an explanation of how they intend to deal with the problem so as to resolve it.

(c) **Going concern basis not appropriate**

The directors should state that, in their opinion, the company is no longer a going concern. They should consider taking legal advice on the wording of the statement.

Where the company is not a going concern, the company is not necessarily insolvent. The directors should consider whether the company is or may become insolvent. Section 214 of the Insolvency Act states that an action for wrongful trading may be brought against a director if at some time before the commencement of the winding up of the company he knew or ought to have concluded that there was no reasonable prospect that the company would avoid going into insolvent liquidation.

3.9 Internal control and financial reporting

The Cadbury Committee required that directors of listed companies should report on the effectiveness of the company's system of internal control. This requirement was deferred pending the issue of guidance. A Working Group of the Cadbury Committee issued a paper *Internal Control and Financial Reporting* in December 1994, to provide this guidance.

3.10 Directors' statement

The directors' report on internal control should contain as a minimum:

(a) an acknowledgement by the directors that they are responsible for the company's system of internal financial control;

(b) an explanation that such a system can provide only reasonable and not absolute assurance against material misstatement or loss;

(c) a description of the key procedures that the directors have established, and which are designed to provide effective internal financial control; and

(d) confirmation that the directors (or a board committee) have reviewed the effectiveness of the system of internal financial control.

Directors may also wish to state their opinion on the effectiveness of the system of internal financial control.

Where weaknesses in internal financial control have resulted in material losses, contingencies or uncertainties that require disclosure in the financial statements or in the auditors' report, the directors should either describe what corrective action has been taken or is intended to be taken, or explain why no changes are considered necessary.

3.11 Internal financial control effectiveness

The APB issued a discussion paper entitled *Internal financial control effectiveness* in April 1995. The objective of the paper was to promote further debate about the auditor's responsibility to report on a client's internal controls, and to seek to prevent bad practice and the development of new expectation gaps.

Among the issues discussed were:

- how the 'effectiveness' of controls should be assessed
- whether auditors should report on the control system itself or on the directors' review of the system
- to what degree the reporting on internal controls would expand the scope of the audit, and
- the implications on the auditor's liability.

3.12 The Greenbury Report: directors' remuneration

Early in 1995 the CBI set up a committee to draw up guidelines on directors' remuneration. The committee was headed by Sir Richard Greenbury. This move was a response to increasing public concern that financial statements did not adequately reflect management remuneration. The committee included members from the Institute of Directors, the National Association of Pension Funds and the Stock Exchange.

The committee reported in September 1995. The report set out a code of best practice in determining and accounting for directors' remuneration. The detailed provisions were prepared with large companies mainly in mind, but the Committee stated that the principles apply equally to small companies.

All listed companies registered in the UK must comply with the Code from 31 October 1995. They must include a statement about their compliance in the annual reports to shareholders or in the annual report of the remuneration committee. Any areas of non-compliance should be explained and justified.

The Code of Practice is summarised below.

3.13 The remuneration committee

(a) Boards of Directors should set up remuneration committees to determine the company's policy on remuneration for each of the executive directors. These should consist exclusively of non-executive directors with no personal financial interest other than as shareholders in the matters to be decided.

(b) The chairman of the remuneration committee should account directly to the shareholders for the decisions their committees reach.

(c) The members of the remuneration committee should be listed each year in the committee's report to shareholders.

(d) The Chairman of the committee should attend the Annual General Meeting to answer shareholders' questions about directors' remuneration.

3.14 Disclosure and approval provisions

(a) The remuneration committee should make a report each year to the shareholders on behalf of the Board. The report should form part of, or be annexed to, the company's Annual Report and Accounts. It should be the main vehicle through which the company accounts to shareholders for directors' remuneration.

(b) The report should set out the company's policy on executive directors' remuneration, including levels, comparator groups of companies, individual components, performance criteria and measurement, pension provision, contracts of service and compensation commitments on early termination.

(c) The report should state that the committee has given full consideration to the best practice provisions set out in the Code in forming its remuneration policy.

(d) The report should include:

- full details of all elements in the remuneration package of each individual director by name (eg, basic salary, benefits in kind, annual bonuses and long term incentive schemes)
- information on share options (in accordance with UITF Abstract 10)
- pension entitlements earned by each individual director during the year.

(e) The amounts stated for each director under (d) above should be subject to audit.

(f) Any service contracts which provide for, or imply, notice periods in excess of one year should be disclosed and the reasons for the longer notice periods explained.

(g) Shareholdings and other relevant business interests and activities of the directors should continue to be disclosed as required in the Companies Act 1985 and the Stock Exchange Listing Rules.

(h) Shareholders should be invited to approve all new long term incentive schemes (eg, share option schemes) in which directors will participate and which potentially commit shareholders' funds over more than one year or dilute the equity.

3.15 Remuneration policy

The Code sets out broad principles which the remuneration committee should follow when determining directors' remuneration. It also considers service contracts and compensation. Remuneration committees must provide the packages needed to attract, retain and motivate directors of the quality required but should avoid paying more than is necessary for this purpose.

3.16 The Hampel Report

In January 1998 another report on corporate governance was issued, this time from a committee under the chairmanship of Sir Ronnie Hampel. While both the Cadbury and Greenbury reports concentrated on preventing abuses, the Hampel report 'is concerned with the positive contribution which good corporate governance can make'. Throughout, it aims to restrict the regulatory burden facing companies and substitute broad principles where practicable.

Each company's circumstances are different. A 'one-size-fits-all' approach to corporate governance issues is rejected. Instead, each listed company must include in the annual report a narrative explaining how the broad principles of corporate governance have been applied.

The general message of Hampel is that a board must not approach the various corporate governance requirements in a compliance mentality: the so-called 'tick-box' approach. Good corporate governance is not achieved by satisfying a checklist. Directors must comply with the substance as well as the letter of all best practice pronouncements.

3.17 Recommendations of the Hampel Report

Companies

- should include a narrative in the annual report explaining how they have applied the broad principles.
- should explain their governance policies, justifying any departures from best practice.

Directors

- the majority of non-executive directors should be independent. The annual report should identify which of the non-executive directors are independent.
- the roles of chairman and chief executive should normally be separate. A board must justify any decision to combine these roles in one person.
- whether or not the roles of chairman and chief executive are combined, a senior independent non-executive director should be identified in the annual report as an alternative point of contact for shareholders.
- names and biographical details should be disclosed for directors seeking re-election.

Directors' remuneration

- It is acceptable for non-executive directors to have some of their remuneration in shares.
- Boards should aim to reduce directors' contract periods to one year or less, but it is recognised that this cannot be achieved immediately.

3.18 Subsequent developments

After publishing its report, the Hampel Committee drew up a single Code of Best Practice, incorporating the Cadbury, Greenbury and Hampel recommendations, and submitted this to the Stock Exchange, recommending that it should be incorporated into the Listing Rules, after consultation on the details.

The Hampel Report should therefore be the last of the ad hoc committees set up to deal with particular issues of corporate governance. In future, minor changes to the principles and code should be dealt with by the Stock Exchange, while the Financial Reporting Council (FRC) should also keep the topic under review.

The UK goverment's response to the Hampel report was lukewarm, with Margaret Beckett, then the President of the Board of Trade, announcing a major review of the Companies Acts on the very day that the Hampel report was launched.

3.19 The Combined Code

The 'supercode' envisaged by Hampel, incorporating the recommendations of Cadbury, Greenbury and Hampel, and endorsed by the Stock Exchange, was issued in June 1998. The 'Principles of good governance and Code of best practice' is known as the 'Combined Code', and listed companies must disclose how they have applied the principles and complied with the code, in their annual report, for accounting periods ending on or after 31 December 1998.

3.20 Conclusion

The Combined Code has replaced the Cadbury and Greenbury Codes and the recommendations of the Hampel report. The aim is to avoid a 'checklist' approach to corporate governance. Listed companies must now explain how (not just whether) they have applied the broad principles.

But the rules may change again if the UK government is serious about its review of company law. This may require new rules on corporate governance affecting all companies, rather than the Combined Code which only affects listed companies.

4 INTERNATIONAL ISSUES AFFECTING AUDITING

4.1 EC and European Directives

The European Community (EC) issues Directives, some of which (such as those on company law) have an impact on audit practice. For example, the 8th Company Law Directive was the Directive which resulted in the RSB system being introduced in the UK by the CA89.

More recently, the EC has proposed a voluntary Community environmental auditing scheme. This aims to improve the impact that a company has on the environment. Environmental auditing is covered below.

4.2 International auditing bodies

The International Federation of Accountants (IFAC) has about 140 member bodies from about 100 separate countries. One of its committees, the International Auditing Practices Committee (IAPC) publishes International Standards on Auditing (ISAs). The APB tries to ensure that its own national standards embrace the principles contained in the relevant ISAs.

In the EC, the FEE (Fédération des Experts Comptables Européens) attempts to co-ordinate the activities of European accountancy bodies, but does not publish standards.

4.3 Environmental audit

Definition An audit which determines the degree of compliance with emission and pollution standards.

This type of audit is slowly increasing in importance due to the concern of the public, and hence governments with the effects that organisations, particularly industrial, can have on the environment.

The method of audit is straightforward. Predetermined targets are established either voluntarily by the organisation or set by government and actual outcomes are compared to the targets.

4.4 Eco-audit scheme

The EC has adopted a scheme for the establishment of a voluntary Community environmental auditing scheme - the **eco-audit scheme.** It is aimed at companies carrying on industrial activities.

A company would, under the scheme, have an environmental audit on each of its sites at regular intervals and set up a framework for acting on the audit findings. A statement would be prepared on the results of the audit which would be available for public inspection. The statement could be carried out by internal staff but would need to be validated by authorised environmental auditors.

4.5 Impact on annual reports

A recent report has been produced which suggests that companies should act in a number of areas to respond to the growing importance of 'green issues'.

The annual report should contain details of:

- the company's environmental policy and objectives
- the impact of the business on the environment
- the extent to which the company complies with external requirements
- identity of director with environmental responsibility.

External auditors need to be aware of contingent liabilities that may require disclosure because of the consequences of damage caused to the environment. The auditor may view many of these liabilities as too remote to be included within the financial statements under the FRS 12 criteria. Therefore it may be appropriate to have additional environmental reports.

5 OTHER CURRENT ISSUES AFFECTING AUDITING

5.1 Audit expectations

There has been considerable discussion in recent years on the role of the auditor, and the 'Expectation Gap'.

In general terms this can be described as the gap that exists between what the public, especially users of financial statements, believe auditors do (or ought to do) and what the auditors actually do. Such a gap usually surfaces on the unexpected failure of a company.

Various elements of this gap have been identified

(a) **A standards gap**

Where the public perceive Auditing Standards as different from what they actually are.

(b) **A performance gap**

Where auditors perform below existing standards.

(c) **A liability gap**

Where the public does not know to whom an auditor is legally responsible. This has arisen particularly after the Caparo decision.

5.2 Potential ways of closing the gap

(a) **Understanding financial statements and the audit report**

False or unrealistic expectations in users of financial statements are frequent. They may not appreciate the conventions on which accounts are prepared, the inevitable degree of estimation and judgement involved or the test nature of audit work.

Communication with these users to improve their understanding could be improved. The most significant work on this area has been the Statement of Auditing Standards (SAS) to 'expand' the old form of audit report.

(b) **Fraud**

When questioned, a high proportion of the public believes the auditor has a responsibility to detect fraud of all kinds, or that he should actively search for fraud. However, deep-seated fraud with wide collusion may be virtually impossible to identify, given the limitations of audit techniques. The auditor may not reasonably be expected to have discovered a particular fraud in particular circumstances.

Once again, the profession should attempt to explain these limitations to the users of accounts, so that they are aware our responsibility is to have only a 'reasonable expectation' of detecting material fraud.

Alternatively the auditor could be required to limit the opportunity for fraud in the first place. A requirement could be set for companies and their auditors to review the effectiveness of controls to prevent serious fraud, and to report serious deficiencies.

(c) **Control of the auditing profession**

The Companies Act 1985 now requires the Professional bodies to implement a regime of practice quality control inspection, the intention being to reassure the public.

Audit failures are sometimes due to poor performance. Education (keeping up to date) should remedy this. Legal action and disciplinary proceedings serve as a warning.

5.3 Money laundering

Recent money laundering regulations are an example of an area where the auditor's liability has been recently extended.

Definition Money laundering is the process of disguising criminal proceeds so that they appear to come from a legitimate source.

Criminal activities such as drug trafficking produce huge amounts of cash (around $500 bn pa internationally), which needs to be laundered into legitimate-looking money which does not arouse the suspicions of the authorities. Since London is one of the world's major financial centres, it inevitably attracts its share of money laundering attempts.

Under the Money Laundering Regulations 1994 auditors must report suspected cases of money laundering to the authorities, and accountants have new duties with regard to verifying clients' identities, keeping records and training staff. Any individual convicted of assisting a money launderer can be imprisoned for up to 14 years.

This is one further example of 'whistle blowing' duties imposed by statute on the auditor which increasingly lift the veil of client confidentiality. Auditors who hope that their increasing responsibilities will be matched by higher fees are likely to be disappointed.

5.4 The audit agenda

The Audit Agenda was published by the APB as a Discussion Paper in December 1994. The paper sets out a framework for the future development of auditing and is based on responses to the 1992 discussion paper *The Future Development of Auditing*. The key proposals of the paper are set out below.

In February 1996 the APB published a further paper entitled *The Audit Agenda - Next Steps*. This paper sets out steps that the APB intends to take in order to implement, or encourage others to implement, the proposals in *The Audit Agenda* in the light of comments received. *Next Steps* follows the same structure as *The Audit Agenda* and its contents are summarised below each key proposal.

5.5 The future role of auditors and scope of audit

(a) The scope of audits for listed companies and major economic entities should be differentiated from that for unlisted, owner managed businesses.

The APB will consult with the Stock Exchange and others to establish a differential scope of audit assurances required for listed companies, whilst maintaining the quality of the core audit service (providing an opinion on the financial statements).

(b) The scope of listed company audits should be extended to include:

- assurance to shareholders on the consistency of all textual information accompanying the financial statements with the view portrayed by the financial statements;
- the provision of reports to the board and audit committee on governance issues;
- the provision of reports to shareholders as to whether governance statements published by directors are in accordance with the Code of Best Practice and are an appropriate reflection of the necessary compliance.

The APB will consider the need for additional guidance to auditors of listed companies to strengthen the application of SAS 160 *Other information in documents containing audited financial statements.* It also proposes to address the degree to which financial information issued by a listed company other than the annual report is subject to scrutiny by its auditors. In particular, the APB intends to consider and discuss with the Stock Exchange the extent of the auditors' involvement in interim statements and preliminary announcements.

The APB will discuss the issue of reporting on corporate governance with the Stock Exchange and the Committee on Corporate Governance in the light of the debate on corporate governance and the auditors' role. It will also review the operation of SAS 300 *Accounting and internal control systems and audit risk assessments* and SAS 610 *Reports to directors or management* in the context of listed companies.

The APB will keep under review the extent to which reports on governance issues are of value to shareholders of listed companies and the action needed by auditors to provide such reports. It will also review the guidance given in the Bulletin *Disclosures relating to corporate governance* in the light of amendment to the Stock Exchange's Listing Rules and will issue revised guidance if necessary.

(c) The APB will develop guidance on the application of auditing standards to the audit of owner managed businesses.

(d) The ASB should develop Financial Reporting Standards for reporting on risks and sensitivity by directors to support their statements on going concern.

(e) In relation to fraud:

- a revised Statement of Auditing Standards has been issued (SAS 110);
- auditors of listed companies should report to boards and audit committees observations as to the appropriateness and adequacy of systems intended to minimise the risk of fraud;
- the accountancy bodies should review the education and training process to develop auditors' understanding of behavioural and forensic issues and undertake seminars discussing experience and means of detecting fraud;
- boards should commission periodic forensic audits;
- the statutory framework relating to penalties for directors and staff deceiving auditors should be reviewed.

The APB regards the issue of fraud as a primary priority.

(f) The APB will undertake research jointly with the ASB into developing a framework for reporting and giving assurance to secondary and tertiary stakeholders (eg, lenders, employees and potential investors).

5.6 Objectivity

(a) Audit opinions should be signed by the responsible partner identifying his or her name as well as that of the audit firm.

The APB will issue proposals to amend SAS 600 *Auditors reports on financial statements* to give effect to this proposal.

(b) The APB will develop standards and guidance on the qualities required of a partner responsible for an audit and on the process for signing reports and reporting to directors.

(c) The partner responsible for the audit of a listed company should not have overall responsibility for the marketing of non-audit services to that company.

(d) Audit committees of listed companies should have specific responsibility, as a proxy for shareholders, for the appointment and removal of auditors and the approval of non-audit services by the audit firm.

The APB intends to discuss with the Stock Exchange whether requirements for the involvement of independent directors in these issues can be incorporated in the Listing Rules.

(e) The Chairman of the audit committee should report to primary stakeholders (ie, shareholders) on matters relating to the appointment and remuneration of auditors, both in writing and orally in general meeting.

The APB will discuss with The Stock Exchange ways in which such reports can be encouraged, including proposals for the introduction of requirements for appointment of auditors into the Listing Rules.

(f) The APB will develop guidance for non-executive directors who act as members of an audit committee.

(g) The APB will continue its dialogue with others on the need for a further institutional framework to support the objectivity of the total governance process, including the role of external audit and of audit committees comprising non-executive directors.

5.7 Litigation

The APB will seek to encourage that the extended scope of the audit in relation to listed companies and private reporting to directors on governance issues can be contracted with restriction of liability and falls outside s310 of the Companies Act 1985.

5.8 Other developments and research

(a) The APB will commission a review of total quality management techniques to ensure quality of the audit process at effective cost.

(b) The recognised qualifying professional bodies should undertake a review of the syllabus for pre and post-qualifying education and training to meet the requirements of the future audit agenda.

(c) The APB will commission a programme of research to underpin future changes in auditing to monitor the effect of implementing new auditing standards and to generate a greater understanding of ideas not yet fully accepted or developed but which the APB considers to have potential in the longer term as a means of meeting user expectations.

5.9 The audit of small businesses

Following *The audit agenda's* discussion of the applicability of auditing standards to owner managed businesses, the APB published a Practice Note *The audit of small businesses* in July 1997. This points out that most businesses in the UK are small, so that most audits are carried out on small businesses. The Note discusses the special considerations in the audit of small businesses and provides a commentary on each of the SASs, giving additional guidance on their applicability to small businesses where appropriate.

Although many small companies are now exempted from having to conduct an annual statutory audit, they may still choose to have an audit to secure the very real advantages that the audit can deliver.

6 AUDITING THEORY

6.1 Introduction

The objective of auditing theory is to give a theoretical structure to the work of auditing. If this is not possible, the auditor is simply a person who does a list of jobs. If he does these badly he will be sued for negligence. An understanding of the theory of auditing should reduce this risk.

6.2 Postulates of auditing

Postulates are assumptions that do not lend themselves to direct verification. Once postulates are accepted, propositions can be deduced from them. They provide a framework for developing and testing theory. If the postulates are consistent and sufficient and if the inferences drawn from them follow the rules of logic and reason, the results should be consistent and satisfactory.

6.3 Tentative postulates of auditing theory

(a) Financial statements and financial data are verifiable.

(b) There is no necessary conflict of interest between the auditor and the management of the enterprise under audit.

(c) The financial statements and other information submitted for verification are free from collusive and other unusual irregularities. Collusion means, in this context, staff working together in secret for dishonest purposes.

(d) The existence of a satisfactory system of internal control eliminates the probability of irregularities.

(e) Consistent application of generally accepted principles of accounting results in the fair presentation of the financial position and the results of operations.

(f) In the absence of clear evidence to the contrary, what was held true in the past for the enterprise under examination will hold true in the future.

(g) When examining financial data for the purpose of expressing an independent opinion thereon, the auditor acts exclusively in the capacity of an auditor.

(h) The professional status of the independent auditor imposes corresponding professional obligations.

6.4 Discussion of the postulates

Each postulate is considered further.

(a) Financial data is verifiable. Unless financial data is verifiable, auditing is impossible.

(b) No necessary conflict of interest between auditor and management. This can be considered further in an examination of the agency relationships between the various parties involved.

(c) Freedom from collusion and otherwise unusual irregularities. If it is assumed that the data under examination does include irregularities resulting from extensive collusion between staff it would be necessary to design a very extensive audit programme. Indeed, there is some question whether any type of examination could be designed that would give even a reasonable assurance of discovering all such irregularities.

On the other hand if an irregularity brought about by collusion was so apparent that the auditor should have discovered it through the application of reasonable tests, he would not be excused if his examination failed to disclose it. The degree of care required of auditors must be further explored before this and similar questions can be settled; thus, this postulate leads directly to the concept of due audit care.

(d) Internal control eliminates the probability of irregularities. It should be noted that the term probability rather than possibility is used. It is doubtful whether the possibility of irregularities can ever be eliminated, although of course the likelihood can be reduced. Irregularities are still possible under good internal control, but they are no longer probable. On the other hand, if the internal control is not satisfactory, then errors and irregularities must be considered something more than merely possible.

(e) Generally accepted principles of accounting and fair presentation. To judge the fairness of financial statement presentation, auditors must have some form of standards. Auditing borrows from accounting the latter's generally accepted principles and uses them as a standard for judging the propriety of the financial data submitted for examination.

(f) That which was held true in the past will hold true in the future. Unless the auditor can assume that what has held true in the past will hold true in the future for the enterprise under examination, barring any clear indications to the contrary, he has no basis for accepting or rejecting management's statements about the valuation of such assets as debtors and stock in trade, the economic usefulness of fixed assets, or the adequacy of internal control. This is the 'continuity' or 'going concern' concept of accounting (SSAP 2).

(g) An auditor acts exclusively as an auditor. Although an independent accountant may serve his clients in a considerable variety of ways, once he has commenced an audit examination he must act exclusively in the role of an auditor while performing the examination. Additional services such as accountancy, consultancy and taxation must be regarded as of secondary importance and if they interfere in any way with the appropriate discharge of the auditor's duties, they must be considered as damaging to the disinterested nature of his audit. It follows from this postulate that anything that tends to infringe upon independence must be viewed with serious concern.

(h) Professional status imposes corresponding obligations. Auditors have long claimed professional status, and with increasing public recognition of this status they have accepted more and more professional obligations. The auditing standards adopted by the profession reflect the acceptance of such obligations.

6.5 Imported theories

The term 'imported theories' means theories which have been developed in other academic disciplines which have been introduced into auditing theory as they may be of some relevance in understanding the audit process. Two areas of relevance are agency theory and the efficient market hypothesis (EMH). You will have met these elsewhere in your studies.

7 INTERIM REPORTS

In September 1997, the ASB issued a Statement *Interim Reports*. Like the Statement on Operating and Financial Review, it is intended to be a statement of best practice and its adoption is voluntary. The content of the statement was covered in chapter 20 of this book, and you should refer back to that chapter to refresh your memory as to its main recommendations.

8 INDEPENDENCE AND THE BUSINESS APPROACH TO AUDIT RISK

8.1 Introduction

You will already be familiar with the principle that the objectivity of a member of the ACCA must be beyond question if he is to report as auditor. That objectivity can only be assured if the member **is,** and is **seen to be** independent.

The ACCA's 'Qualification and Audit Regulations', which came into force in 1991, set out the main areas of risk as far as integrity, objectivity and independence are concerned.

8.2 Integrity, objectivity and independence - areas of risk

(a) **Undue dependence on an audit client**

It is recognised that a dependence on income from a particular client may impair objectivity. A firm which derives most of its income from one client for instance might find it difficult to make a stand on a particular issue as the loss of that client (either through the auditor's removal or his resignation) would have a disastrous effect on the firm's financial position.

It is therefore recommended that recurring fees paid by one client or group of connected clients should not exceed 15% of the gross practice income (this requirement is relaxed for those years when a practice is being established or wound down).

However, where the public interest is involved (for example in the case of listed and other public interest companies) the appropriate figure should be 10% of the gross practice income.

(b) **Family and other personal relationships**

Problems may arise where:

(i) a practice or anyone closely connected with it has a mutual business interest with a client, or with an officer or employee of a client;

(ii) an officer or employee is closely connected with a partner or member of staff.

The following persons would normally be regarded as being closely connected with a *person:*

(i) spouse;
(ii) minor children (including stepchildren);
(iii) a company in which he has a $\geq$ 20% interest.

The following persons should normally be regarded as being closely connected with a *practice*:

(i) a partner or, in the case of a corporate practice, a director or shareholder;
(ii) a person closely connected with (i) above;
(iii) an employee of the practice.

These categories are not exhaustive. For example, persons not related in any way by blood or marriage, may nevertheless enjoy a friendship closer than any blood relationship. The auditor must always bear in mind the need to maintain not merely independence but also the manifest appearance of independence.

The threat to independence may be less where a partner or senior member of staff is not personally engaged on the audit in question, where his or her office is distant from the reporting office and where effective safeguards are in place in the internal procedures of the practice. Such safeguards might include rotation of the engagement partner and/or of senior members of staff. Similarly, a connection with a junior member of staff of the practice is less likely to be a threat than a connection with a senior member of staff or partner.

A member should not personally take part in the conduct of the audit of a company if he or she has, during the period upon which the report is to be made, or at any time in the two years prior to the first day thereof been an officer (other than auditor) or employee of that company.

(c) **Beneficial interests in shares and other investments**

A practice should ensure that it does not have as an audit client a company in which a partner or anyone closely connected with a partner has a beneficial interest, nor should it employ on the audit a member of staff if that member of staff, or a person closely connected with him has a beneficial interest.

(d) **Loans**

Again, independence may be threatened.

A practice or anyone closely connected with it should not, either directly or indirectly, or by way of a trust or other intermediary:

(i) make a loan to or guarantee borrowings by an audit client;
(ii) accept a loan from such a client; or
(iii) have borrowings or other obligations guaranteed by such a client.

(e) **Goods and services: hospitality**

Objectivity may be threatened or appear to be threatened by acceptance of goods, services or hospitality from an audit client.

(f) **Provision of other services to audit clients**

There is no objection in principle to this but care must be taken not to perform management functions or to make management decisions.

Accountancy work, however, should not be performed for a public company except in relation to assistance of a routine clerical nature or in emergency situations. Such assistance might include, for example, work on the finalisation of statutory accounts, including consolidations and tax provisions. The scale and nature of such work should be regularly reviewed.

(g) **Actual or threatened litigation**

Objectivity may be threatened (or appear to be) where there is actual or threatened litigation between an auditor and his client. The adversarial position would call into question the auditor's ability to report fairly and impartially on the company's accounts. In an action, under the circumstances, management may be unwilling to disclose relevant information to the auditor.

8.3 Audit risk

While mindful of the fact that independence must be preserved, the auditor must also determine an acceptable level of audit risk. Ultimately, this is the risk that he gives an incorrect audit opinion. It is calculated by the determination of inherent risk, control risk and detection risk, as defined in SAS 300 *Audit risk assessment.*

Although not mentioned in SAS 300 it is worthwhile mentioning also 'business risk' - the risk that the auditor will suffer loss or injury to his or her professional practice as a result of an actual audit failure. Even if a court subsequently holds the auditor not liable for negligence or incompetence, the associated poor publicity can cause damage to the auditor's business.

The auditor must maintain the highest degree of independence while accepting an appropriately low level of audit risk. It can be argued that if not adequately independent of a client, he will not be in a position accurately to determine audit risk, as his judgement may be clouded. Lack of independence can cause an unacceptably high level of risk.

9 CHAPTER SUMMARY

The Financial Reporting Standard for Smaller Entities (FRSSE) considers that small companies should be excused from the detailed requirements of accounting standards, but that their financial statements will still be able to present a true and fair view. The legal liability of auditors currently centres around the decision in the Caparo case. The Cadbury report and Greenbury report tried to improve standards of corporate governance and ethical behaviour in the UK; the recommendations of these reports have now been incorporated into the Stock Exchange's Combined Code.

10 SELF TEST QUESTIONS

10.1 What entities fall within the scope of the FRSSE? (1.4)

10.2 Does the FRSSE require a summarised cash flow statement? (1.4)

10.3 Under which tort may a third party sue an auditor for damages? (2.3)

10.4 Summarise the facts in the Caparo decision. (2.3)

10.5 What is an audit committee? (3.4)

10.6 What was the purpose of the Greenbury Report? (3.11)

10.7 Identify three elements of the expectations gap. (5.1)

11 EXAMINATION TYPE QUESTION

11.1 Millers Villas Ltd

Millers Villas Ltd operate five holiday centres on freehold sites in the British Isles. The company's financial statements for the year ended 31 May 20X3 disclose total turnover for the year of £3,800,000 and net profit before taxation of £420,000. The following matters have arisen from your audit work on these financial statements.

(a) Cost of brochures and advertising relating to the 20X3 summer season of £132,000 have been carried forward in the balance sheet as a prepayment.

(b) Bar stocks at one site were not physically counted on 31 May 20X3 but were estimated by the bar manager at £7,000 based on the previous physical stocktaking at 30 April 20X3 which disclosed a value of £6,400 and sales during the month of May which amounted to £11,000. The subsequent physical stocktaking took place on 30 June 20X3. Using the estimated value on 31 May 20X3, a review of the trading results from the months of May and June disclosed a gross profit percentage of 60% and 39% respectively, compared with an average of 46% for the other months of the year.

(c) The manager of each camp is responsible for paying casual labour taken on during the six peak holiday weeks in the summer and for shorter periods at other times of the year. These payments are made in cash and amount to approximately £40,000 per centre for the year, but no receipts or vouchers are available apart from the weekly lists of payments signed by each manager. However, all necessary PAYE and Social Security requirements have been complied with in respect of such payments.

(d) Provisions for liabilities and charges include a provision for future maintenance of £200,000 representing one third of the estimated cost of totally renovating all camp buildings. During March each year one third of the properties on each site is fully renovated.

You are required:

(a) to comment on the further considerations required of each of the above matters in order to conclude the audit and **(14 marks)**

(b) to indicate the possible effects on the audit report. **(6 marks)**
(Total: 20 marks)

12 ANSWER TO EXAMINATION TYPE QUESTION

12.1 Millers Villas Ltd

(a) **Cost of brochures and advertising**

(i) **Accruals concept**

The auditor should ascertain whether advance booking receipts are deferred until the time the holiday-maker actually takes the holiday or credited to the profit and loss account on a cash basis.

If the company adopts the former policy, then the carrying forward of brochure costs and advertising to match the associated revenue would be appropriate and acceptable as it represents a material expense.

It could, however, be argued that there is no real **future** benefit expected in the post year end period as the primary objective of printing brochures and advertising is to encourage advance bookings. If the brochures were printed before the end of May 20X3 to achieve this objective, both advance booking receipts and related brochure costs could justifiably be accounted for as they arise.

(ii) **Consistency**

The auditor should also consider whether the above policy has been consistently applied. If the carrying forward of brochure costs represents a change in policy the auditor will hence be concerned with the appropriateness of the new policy **and** its current treatment and disclosure in compliance with SSAP 2 and FRS 3 (prior period adjustment).

Effect on audit report

The auditor would have to consider the need to qualify his report on the grounds of disagreement (material but not fundamental) if he is dissatisfied with:

(i) the policy itself, and/or

(ii) implementation and disclosure of the policy (particularly if it represents a change in policy where an FRS 3 prior period adjustment would be required).

(b) **Bar stock at one site**

Points to be considered

(i) This is not a material problem in terms of forming an audit opinion since the unexplained difference in contribution is only £1,500. However this could become a risk area if allowed to go unchecked.

The auditor would compare the average of 46% with the gross profit margin at other sites (this margin sounds reasonable for the type of business). He would also compare the estimated stock figure with the results of physical stocktakings at other dates (eg, April and June of 20X3 and of April, May and June of 20X2) making necessary adjustments for changes in turnover levels.

(ii) Internal control implications.

The auditor would wish to identify whether this control breakdown is an isolated departure - the implication is that bar stocks were counted satisfactorily on 31 May at the other four centres.

He would consider reporting the control problem to management in his weakness letter.

Effect on audit report

This minor control breakdown would not, in isolation, warrant an audit report qualification.

(c) **Casual labour**

Points to be considered in respect of each camp

(i) The auditor would familiarise himself with the PAYE/Social Security regulations and test that the individual payments per the weekly lists are within the thresholds permitted by the authorities for sanctioning payments by cash and any non-deduction of income tax and national insurance contributions. Any correspondence from the authorities querying payments should be reviewed.

(ii) As no statutory records are maintained in respect of the casual workers there is the possibility that dummy names have been entered on the weekly lists. It may be possible and advisable to carry out a test circularisation of the names on the lists - assuming addresses are available - to confirm existence. Non-replies would have to be followed up carefully and tactfully with the respective managers.

(iii) The adequacy of the accounting records must be determined to ensure, for example, that the cash payments can be reconciled to the weekly lists. This will depend on whether these disbursements are made by formal withdrawal from petty cash and are hence identifiable in the petty cash book (or equivalent) or, less satisfactorily, made out of cash takings before such takings are recorded and subsequently banked.

(iv) Analytical review procedures should be applied comparing one centre with another and with previous periods. The review would be particularly concerned with total cash receipts, gross profit percentages, total casual labour costs and the relationship between casual labour costs and cash receipts for each centre.

Effect on audit report

If, as a result of his investigations, the auditor is unable to substantiate the casual payments for any or all centres he will have to consider qualifying his report on the grounds of uncertainty as he has not obtained all the information and explanations he considers necessary (ie, a limitation in the scope of his audit).

Furthermore he should report that he has been unable to satisfy himself that proper accounting records, in respect of casual payments, have been kept in accordance with S221 Companies Act 1985.

(d) **Provision for future maintenance**

Points to be considered

(i) **Past experience**

The auditor should ascertain whether this is a new accounting policy. If not, the provision last year and the actual costs of renovation incurred in the current year, against which the provision brought forward was presumably released, should be determined. The amount transferred to and from the provision should be disallowed for tax purposes.

(ii) **Classification**

Depending on the policy chosen, the provision should be correctly classified under the heading 'provisions for liabilities and charges'.

The auditor must carefully consider whether this amount qualifies as a provision under FRS 12 ie, whether an obligation to transfer economic benefits exists at the balance sheet date. If a contract has been signed for the renovation work, then it is possible that such an obligation does exist. If no contract exists, and there is only an intention to renovate rather than an obligation, then no provision exists at the balance sheet date.

The auditor should determine the audit evidence available to confirm provision of £200,000. This will include discussions with management and formal representations. If possible, documentary evidence of external estimates of costs of renovation should be obtained, and a review made of past provisions compared with actual costs incurred.

Effect on audit report

If a valid provision exists, it must be disclosed per the Companies Act 1985 under the heading 'provisions for liabilities and charges'. It should be shown separately as the provision is material when assessing the company's state of affairs. Such disclosure may be made either on the face of the balance sheet or in the notes to the financial statements. Assuming that the auditor is satisfied with the disclosure and the validity of the provision there will be no requirement for a qualification.

APPENDIX: AUDITING STANDARDS AND GUIDELINES

This appendix contains the Auditing Standards and Guidelines which have already been examined at earlier stages of the examinations (Paper 6 **Audit Framework** and Paper 10 **Accounting and Audit Practice**). These documents remain examinable at Paper 13 and you should already be familiar with all the principles that they contain, however we reproduce here the key elements as they relate to today's reporting environment.

1 SAS 010: The scope and authority of APB pronouncements

(a) **SASs**

(i) **Scope**

Within each SAS bold type indicates an actual Auditing Standard. Auditors are expected to comply with these in the conduct of any audit. Other material included is designed to assist in interpretation and application.

(ii) **Authority**

Where a member fails to comply with SASs an enquiry is liable to follow and disciplinary or regulatory action may result. The latter could include the withdrawal of registration as the SASs represent the rules and practices which the ACCA as an RSB has as to technical standards of audit.

(iii) **Development**

Exposure drafts and other consultative documents will first be issued for public comment. A SAS can only be issued with the approval of at least three quarters of the voting members of the APB.

(iv) **International Standards on Auditing (ISAs)**

In formulating SASs regard will be taken of ISAs. Each SAS will explain how it relates to its equivalent ISA. In most cases compliance with a SAS will ensure compliance with the relevant ISA. If the requirements differ the SAS should be followed.

(b) **Practice Notes (PNs) and Bulletins**

PNs and Bulletins are persuasive rather than prescriptive. They have a similar status to the explanatory material in SASs.

2 SAS 011: The auditor's code

The auditor's code sets out the fundamental principles which the APB expects auditors to follow. Nine principles of independent auditing are identified: accountability, integrity, objectivity and independence, competence, rigour, judgement, clear communication, association (ie, auditors should allow their reports to be included in documents only if they are not conflicting), and providing value.

3 SAS 100: Objective and general principles governing an audit of financial statements

Auditing standards

100.1 The auditor is required to:

(a) obtain sufficient appropriate evidence in accordance with SASs to determine if the financial statements are free of material misstatement and are prepared in accordance with relevant legislation and Accounting Standards;

(b) issue a report containing a clear expression of his opinion.

100.2 Auditors are required to comply with all ethical guidance issued by their relevant professional body.

4 SAS 110: Fraud and error

Auditing standards

110.1 Auditors should plan and perform their audit procedures and evaluate and report the results thereof, recognising that fraud or error may materially affect the financial statements.

110.2 When planning the audit the auditors should assess the risk that fraud or error may cause the financial statements to contain material misstatements.

110.3 Based on their risk assessment the auditors should design audit procedures so as to have a reasonable expectation of detecting misstatements arising from fraud and error which are material to the financial statements.

5 SAS 120: Consideration of law and regulations

Auditing standards

120.1 Auditors should plan and perform their audit procedures, and evaluate and report on the results thereof, recognising that non compliance by the entity with law or regulations may materially affect the financial statements.

120.2 The auditors should obtain sufficient appropriate audit evidence about compliance with those laws and regulations which relate directly to the preparation of, or the inclusion or disclosure of specific items in, the financial statements.

120.3 The auditors should perform procedures to help identify instances of non compliance with those laws and regulations which provide a legal framework within which the entity conducts its business.

120.4 When carrying out their procedures for the purpose of forming an opinion on the financial statements, the auditors should in addition be alert for instances of possible or actual non compliance with law or regulations which might affect the financial statements.

120.5 When the auditors become aware of information concerning a possible instance of non compliance with law or regulations, they should obtain an understanding of the nature of the act and the circumstances in which it has occurred, and sufficient other information to evaluate the possible effect on the financial statements.

120.6 When the auditors believe there may be non compliance with law or regulations, they should document their findings and, subject to any requirement to report them direct to a third party, discuss them with the appropriate level of management.

120.7 The auditors should consider the implications of suspected or actual non compliance with law or regulations in relation to other aspects of the audit, particularly the reliability of management representations.

Reporting non-compliance

(a) **To management**

120.8 The auditors should, as soon as practicable, either

(a) communicate with management, the board of directors or the audit committee; or

(b) obtain evidence that they are appropriately informed, regarding any suspected non compliance with law or regulations that comes to the auditors' attention.

120.9 If, in the auditor's judgement, the non compliance with law or regulations is material or is believed to be intentional, the auditors should communicate the finding without delay.

(b) **To shareholders**

120.10 Where the auditors conclude that the non-compliance leads to a fundamental uncertainty in the financial statements, they should include an explanatory paragraph referring to the matter in their report.

120.11 Where the auditors conclude that a suspected instance of non compliance with law or regulation has a material effect on the financial statements and they disagree with the accounting treatment or with the extent, or the lack, of any disclosure in the financial statements of the instance or of its consequences they should issue an adverse or qualified opinion. If the auditors are unable to determine whether non compliance with law or regulations has occurred because of limitation in the scope of their work, they should issue a disclaimer or a qualified opinion.

(c) **To third parties**

The SAS gives guidance to auditors on the circumstances in which to report to third parties who have a proper interest in receiving such information. In addition, auditors of financial institutions subject to statutory regulation, who are required to report certain information direct to the relevant regulator, have separate responsibilities. Guidance on these responsibilities is given in SAS 620 **The auditors' right and duty to report to regulators in the financial sector** and the associated Practice Notes.

6 SAS 130: The going concern basis in financial statements

SAS 130 has introduced two main areas of change from previous best practice.

(a) **More thorough assessment of the going concern basis**

The previous guideline only required the auditor to perform additional procedures if he became aware that the going concern basis may not be valid ie, there were specific procedures to test this presumption.

By contrast, SAS 130 requires auditors to perform procedures specifically designed to identify indications that the going concern basis may not be valid. Only if these specific procedures and the auditor's other work do not reveal such indications can the auditor conclude that the going concern basis is appropriate. The change is designed to reduce the possibility of auditors not detecting going concern problems.

(b) **Fuller disclosures and effect on audit report**

(i) **Inherent uncertainty**

It is considered that previous guidance has not been conducive to the full disclosure of uncertainties regarding a company's ability to continue as a going concern.

Under SAS 130, if an inherent uncertainty exists which could affect this ability the auditors should consider whether disclosure of the matters giving rise to the uncertainty is adequate to give a true and fair view.

(1) **Adequate disclosure**

The auditors should draw attention to the matters in their report. This is consistent with the treatment of significant inherent uncertainties as outlined in the SAS on the audit report.

(2) **Inadequate disclosure**

An 'except for' or 'adverse' qualification should be given in respect of the inadequate disclosure.

(ii) **Disagreement**

If the auditors disagree with the presumption that the company is a going concern they should give an 'adverse' opinion and provide in their report such additional information as they consider necessary and are able to provide.

(iii) **Limitation in scope**

A total disclaimer should be issued in this rare circumstance.

(iv) **Financial statements prepared on a non-going concern basis**

If considered appropriate, and the financial statements contain the necessary disclosures, the auditors should not qualify but should draw attention to the basis of preparation and the notes concerning this basis.

7 SAS 140: Engagement letters

The guidance notes accompanying SAS 140 state that the SAS is intended for audit engagements and notes that auditors often prepare separate letters for services such as tax and accounting. The notes specifically state that an engagement for the provision of 'investment business' advice would ordinarily require a separate letter.

Auditing standards

140.1 The auditors and the client should agree on the terms of the engagement, which should be recorded in writing.

140.2 Auditors should agree the terms of their engagement with new clients in writing. Thereafter auditors should regularly review the terms of engagement and if appropriate agree any updating in writing.

140.3 Auditors who, before the completion of the audit, are requested to change the engagement to one which provides a different level of assurance, should consider the appropriateness of so doing. If auditors consider that it is appropriate to change the terms of engagement, they should obtain written agreement to the revised terms.

140.4 Auditors should ensure that the engagement letter documents and confirms their acceptance of the appointment, and includes a summary of the responsibilities of the directors and of the auditors, the scope of the engagement and the form of any reports.

8 SAS 150: Subsequent events

SAS 150 gives mandatory guidance in the area of post balance sheet events.

Definition A subsequent event is an event between the end of the accounting period and the date when the financial statements are laid before the members.

It is thus a longer period than the post balance sheet event period of SSAP 17.

SAS 150 considers the subsequent events period which is divided into three periods:

(a) up to the date of the audit report
(b) after the date of the audit report but before the financial statements are issued
(c) after the financial statements are issued but before they are laid before the members.

Auditing standards

General

150.1 Auditors should consider the effect of subsequent events on the financial statements and on their report.

Responsibilities to the date of the audit report

150.2 Auditors should perform procedures designed to obtain sufficient appropriate audit evidence that all material subsequent events up to the date of their report which require adjustment of, or disclosure in, the financial statements have been identified and properly reflected therein.

SSAP 17 contains the mandatory accounting guidance in this area.

Responsibilities after the date of the audit report, but before the financial statements are issued

150.3 When, after the date of their report but before the financial statements are issued, auditors became aware of subsequent events which may materially affect the financial statements, they should establish whether the financial statements need amendment, should discuss the matter with the directors and should consider the implications for their report, taking additional action as appropriate.

Responsibility after the financial statements have been issued, but before their laying before the members

150.4 In such circumstances the auditors should consider whether the financial statements need amendment, should discuss the matter with the directors, and should consider the implications for their report, taking additional action as appropriate.

9 SAS 160: Other information in documents containing audited financial statements

The auditor has very limited statutory responsibilities in respect of other financial information issued with audited financial statements. Nevertheless, it should be reviewed by the auditor as, where there is a material inconsistency with the audited financial statements or an item which is misleading in some other respect, the credibility of the audited financial statements may be undermined. A revised version of SAS 160 was issued in October 1999.

Auditing standards

160.1 Auditors should read other information in documents containing audited financial statements. If as a result they become aware of any apparent misstatements therein, or identify any material inconsistencies with the audited financial statements, they should seek to resolve them.

160.2 If auditors identify an inconsistency between the financial statements and the other information, or a misstatement within the other information, they should consider whether an amendment is required to the financial statements or to the other information and should seek to resolve the matter through discussion with the directors.

160.3 If, after discussion with the directors, the auditors conclude that the financial statements require amendment and no such amendment is made, they should consider the implications for their report. If, after discussion with the directors, the auditors conclude that the other information requires amendment and no such amendment is made, they should consider appropriate action.

10 SAS 200: Planning

The overall plan should describe in broad terms the scope and conduct of the audit, involving such matters as:

- knowledge of the client;
- risk and materiality;
- nature, timing and extent of procedures;
- co-ordination, direction, supervision and review;
- other matters including going concern, special conditions, special terms of engagement and the need for reports.

Auditing standards

200.1 Auditors should plan the audit work so as to perform the audit in an effective manner.

200.2 Auditors should develop and document an overall audit plan describing the expected scope and conduct of the audit.

200.3 Auditors should develop and document the nature, timing and extent of planned audit procedures required to implement the overall audit plan.

200.4 The audit work planned should be reviewed and, if necessary, revised during the course of the audit.

11 SAS 210: Knowledge of the business

The content of this SAS makes previous good practice mandatory. It deals with the knowledge of the business both prior to accepting appointment and following acceptance.

Auditing standards

210.1 Auditors should have or obtain a knowledge of the business of the entity to be audited sufficient to enable them to identify and understand the events, transactions and practices that may have a significant effect on the financial statements or the audit thereof.

210.2 The audit engagement partner should ensure that the audit team obtains such knowledge of the business of the entity being audited as may reasonably be expected to be sufficient to enable it to carry out the audit work effectively.

Prior to acceptance of an engagement, the auditors should obtain a preliminary knowledge of the industry and of the ownership, management and operations of the entity to be audited, sufficient to enable them to consider their ability and willingness to undertake the audit.

Following acceptance of an engagement, the auditors should obtain further and more detailed knowledge and information sufficient to enable them to plan the audit and develop an effective audit approach.

In succeeding periods, the auditors should consider the information gathered previously and should perform procedures designed to identify significant changes that have taken place since the last audit.

12 SAS 220: Materiality and the audit

Materiality is defined in the APB Glossary of terms as follows:

Definition Materiality is an expression of the relative significance or importance of a particular matter in the context of financial statements as a whole. A matter is material if its omission or misstatement would reasonably influence the decisions of an addressee of the auditors' report.

220.1 Auditors are required to consider materiality and its relationship with audit risk when conducting an audit.

Auditors should plan and perform the audit to be able to provide reasonable assurance that the financial statements are free of material misstatement. The assessment of what is material is a matter of professional judgement. The amount (quantity) and nature (quality) of misstatements need to be considered.

The possibility of small errors should be considered cumulatively.

As regards qualitative aspects, these are concerned with inadequate descriptions or information contained within the financial statements.

Materiality should be considered at both the overall financial statements level and in relation to an individual account balance.

Materiality and audit work

220.2 Auditors are required to consider materiality when determining the nature, timing and extent of audit procedures.

If factors are identified which result in the revision of their preliminary materiality assessment the auditors should consider the implications for their audit approach and, if necessary, modify the nature, timing and extent of planned audit procedures.

220.3 In evaluating whether the financial statements give a true and fair view, auditors should assess the materiality of the aggregate of uncorrected misstatements.

13 SAS 230: Working papers

SAS 230 contains extensive guidance in relation to the content of working papers and the retention of notes on queries arising from review (which can be discarded once the relevant matter has been cleared). Working papers should show the detailed reasoning on matters of judgement.

Auditing standards

230.1 Auditors should document in their working papers matters which are important in supporting their report.

230.2 Working papers should record the auditors' planning, the nature, timing and extent of the audit procedures performed, and the conclusions drawn from the audit evidence obtained.

230.3 Auditors should record in their working papers their reasoning on all significant matters which require the exercise of judgement, and their conclusions thereon.

230.4 Auditors should adopt appropriate procedures for maintaining the confidentiality and safe custody of their working papers.

14 SAS 240: Quality control for audit work

SAS 240 contains guidance on maintaining quality control over audit work generally. A draft replacement to the original SAS 240 was issued in January 2000 containing a broader scope than the original SAS.

240.1 Quality control policies and procedures should be implemented both at the level of the audit firm and on individual audits.

Quality control for the firm

240.2 A firm is required to:

1. establish and monitor quality control policies and procedures designed to ensure that all audits are conducted in accordance with SASs;

2. communicate these policies and procedures to all personnel in an appropriate manner.

Individual audit

For the individual audit the requirements are as follows:

240.3 The audit engagement partner should apply quality control procedures appropriate to the particular audit which ensure compliance with SASs.

240.4 Any work delegated to assistants should be directed, supervised and reviewed in a manner which provides reasonable assurance that such work is performed competently.

15 SAS 300: Accounting and internal control systems and audit risk assessments

Total audit risk is determined by three individual factors:

(a) **Inherent risk**

Definition The risk that a material error may arise from the nature of the business.

This risk will be affected by such items as how much the company is subject to market forces, the cash situation of the company, the trading history of the company, and the nature and incidence of unusual transactions.

(b) **Control risk**

Definition The risk that a material error will be neither prevented nor detected by the internal control system of the business.

This risk will be affected by such factors as the internal control system at the company and the integrity of the staff operating the system and the extent of supervisory controls.

(c) **Detection risk**

Definition The risk that any remaining material error (ie, material error not detected from the analysis of inherent risk, or material error not identified by the internal control system), is not detected by the auditor's own tests.

These three risks multiplied together give total audit risk.

Thus:

$$AR = IR \times CR \times DR$$

The wording and order of the individual standards within the SAS illustrate very well the procedures for assessing audit risk. They are as follows:

300.1 Auditors should obtain an understanding of the accounting and internal control systems sufficient to plan the audit and develop an effective audit approach. Auditors should use professional judgement to assess the components of audit risk and to design audit procedures to ensure it is reduced to an acceptably low level.

300.2 In developing their audit approach and detailed procedures, auditors should assess inherent risk in relation to financial statement assertions about material account balances and classes of transactions, taking account of factors relevant both to the entity as a whole and to the specific assertions.

300.3 In planning the audit, auditors should obtain and document an understanding of the accounting system and control environment sufficient to determine their audit approach.

300.4 If auditors, after obtaining an understanding of the accounting system and control environment, expect to be able to rely on their assessment of control risk to reduce the extent of their substantive procedures, they should make a preliminary assessment of control risk for material financial statement assertions, and should plan and perform tests of control to support that assessment.

300.5 If intending to rely on tests of control performed in advance of the period end, auditors should obtain sufficient appropriate audit evidence as to the nature and extent of any changes in design or operation of the entity's accounting and internal control systems within the accounting period since such procedures were performed.

300.6 Having undertaking tests of control, auditors should evaluate whether the preliminary assessment of control risk is supported.

300.7 Auditors should consider the assessed levels of inherent and control risk in determining the nature, timing and extent of substantive procedures required to reduce audit risk to an acceptable level.

300.8 Regardless of the assessed levels of inherent and control risks, auditors should perform some substantive procedures for financial statement assertions of material account balances and transaction classes.

16 SAS 400: Audit evidence

The APB Glossary of terms defines audit evidence as follows:

Definition Audit evidence is the information auditors obtain in arriving at the conclusions on which their report is based. Audit evidence comprises source documents and accounting records underlying the financial statement assertions and corroborative information from other sources.

Financial statement assertions are the representations of the directors that are embodied in the financial statements.

The APB has issued SAS 400 to give guidance on the quantity and quality of evidence that auditors must collect before expressing their opinion.

Auditing standards

400.1 Auditors should obtain sufficient appropriate audit evidence to be able to draw reasonable conclusions on which to base the audit opinion.

400.2 In seeking to obtain audit evidence from tests of control, auditors should consider the sufficiency and appropriateness of the audit evidence to support the assessed level of control risk.

400.3 In seeking to obtain audit evidence from substantive procedures, auditors should consider the extent to which that evidence together with any evidence from tests of controls supports the relevant financial statement assertions.

17 SAS 410: Analytical procedures

The APB Glossary of terms defines analytical procedures as follows:

Definition Analytical procedures are the analysis of relationships:

(a) between items of financial data, or between items of financial and non-financial data, deriving from the same period; or

(b) between comparable financial information deriving from different periods,

to identify consistencies and predicted patterns or significant fluctuations and unexpected relationships, and the results of investigations thereof.

SAS 410 **Analytical procedures** gives examples of comparisons that may usefully be made:

(a) comparing financial information with:

  (i) comparable information for prior periods;
  (ii) anticipated results of the entity, from budgets or forecasts;
  (iii) predictive estimates prepared by the auditors;
  (iv) similar industry information.

(b) values of appropriate accounting ratios.

The SAS lays down best practice for these techniques.

Auditing standards

410.1 Auditors should apply analytical procedures at the planning and overall review stages of the audit.

410.2 Auditors should apply analytical procedures at the planning stage to assist in understanding the entity's business, in identifying areas of potential audit risk and in planning the nature, timing and extent of other audit procedures.

410.3 When completing the audit, auditors should apply analytical procedures in forming an overall conclusion as to whether the financial statements as a whole are consistent with their knowledge of the entity's business.

410.4 When significant fluctuations or unexpected relationships are identified that are inconsistent with other relevant information or that deviate from predicted patterns, auditors should investigate and obtain adequate explanations and appropriate corroborative evidence.

18 SAS 420: Audit of accounting estimates

Definition An accounting estimate is an approximation of the amount of an item in the absence of a precise means of measurement.

Examples are depreciation and other provisions, the reduction of stock to NRV and the doubtful debt provisions against debtors.

The risk of a material misstatement in this area is greater than others because of uncertainties regarding the outcome of events.

In addition, evidence supporting accounting estimates is generally more persuasive than conclusive and therefore auditor judgement is important.

Auditing standards

420.1 Auditors should obtain sufficient appropriate audit evidence regarding accounting estimates.

420.2 Auditors should obtain sufficient appropriate audit evidence as to whether an accounting estimate is:

(a) reasonable in the circumstances; and

(b) appropriately disclosed (when required).

420.3 Auditors should adopt one or a combination of the following approaches in the audit of an accounting estimate:

(a) review and test the process used by management or the directors to develop the estimate;

(b) use an independent estimate for comparison with that prepared by management or the directors;

(c) review subsequent events.

420.4 Auditors should make a final assessment of the reasonableness of the accounting estimate based on their knowledge of the business and whether the estimate is consistent with other audit evidence obtained during the audit.

19 SAS 430: Audit sampling

Definition Audit sampling is defined as the application of a compliance or substantive test to less than 100% of the items within an account balance, class of transactions or other population, as representative of that population, to enable the auditor to obtain and evaluate evidence of some characteristic of that population and to assist in forming a conclusion concerning that characteristic.

Sampling is normally appropriate for areas in which there are a large number of similar transactions. In such areas eg, credit sales for the period, it is not cost effective to test all transactions. Even if the costs were ignored, full testing would not necessarily achieve the specified audit objectives for that area eg, full testing on sales invoices for example would not verify that all sales are recorded (ie, it may not demonstrate completeness).

The use of sampling allied to properly thought out objectives and properly constructed tests allows more valid conclusions to be reached than the (now outdated) traditional system of testing as 'many transactions as possible' in the time available.

Auditing standards

430.1 When using either statistical or non-statistical sampling, auditors should design and select an audit sample, perform audit procedures thereon, and evaluate sample results so as to obtain appropriate audit evidence.

430.2 When designing the size and structure of an audit sample, auditors should consider the specific audit objectives, the nature of the population from which they wish to sample, and the sampling and selection methods.

430.3 When determining sample sizes, auditors should consider sampling risk, the amount of error that would be acceptable and the extent to which they expect to find errors.

Definition Sampling risk arises from the possibility that the auditors' conclusion, based on a sample, may be different from the conclusion that would be reached if the entire population were subjected to the same audit procedure.

430.4 Auditors should select sample items in such a way that the sample can be expected to be representative of the population in respect of the characteristics being tested.

430.5 Having carried out, on each sample item, those audit procedures which are appropriate to the particular audit objective, auditors should

(a) analyse any errors detected in the sample; and

(b) draw inferences for the population as a whole.

20 SAS 440: Management representations

Representations by management are one source of audit evidence. They may be an important part of audit evidence in the audit of companies of all sizes. SAS 440 **Management representations** lays down rules on the procedures to adopt in collecting and using such evidence.

The advice given is important because there are certain dangers in relying too heavily upon representations by management, for example:

(a) The representations may not be properly recorded in the working papers.

(b) The representations may be misunderstood by the auditor. This is particularly likely if they are given by word of mouth rather than in a written form.

(c) The representations may be biased. It is therefore important for the auditor to get independent corroborative evidence whenever he can.

SAS 440's auditing standards set down best practice to be adopted.

Auditing standards

440.1 Auditors should obtain written confirmation of appropriate representations from management before their report is issued.

440.2 Auditors should obtain evidence that the directors acknowledge their collective responsibility for the preparation of the financial statements and have approved the financial statements.

440.3 Auditors should obtain written confirmation of representations from management on matters material to the financial statements when those representations are critical to obtaining sufficient appropriate audit evidence.

440.4 If a representation appears to be contradicted by other audit evidence, the auditors should investigate the circumstances to resolve the matter and consider whether it casts doubt on the reliability of other representations.

440.5 If management refuses to provide written confirmation of a representation that the auditors consider necessary, the auditors should consider the implications of this scope limitation for their report.

21 SAS 450: Opening balances and comparatives

Auditing standards

450.1 Auditors should obtain sufficient appropriate audit evidence that amounts derived from the preceding period's financial statements are free from material misstatements and are appropriately incorporated in the financial statements for the current period.

450.2 Auditors should obtain sufficient appropriate audit evidence that:

(a) opening balances have been appropriately brought forward;

(b) opening balances do not contain errors or misstatements which materially affect the current period's financial statements; and

(c) appropriate accounting policies are consistently applied or changes in accounting policies have been properly accounted for and adequately disclosed.

In the event that the auditors are unable to obtain such audit evidence, they need to consider the implications for their report.

450.3 Auditors should obtain sufficient appropriate audit evidence that:

(a) the accounting policies used for the comparatives are consistent with those of the current period and appropriate adjustments and disclosures have been made where this is not the case;

(b) the comparatives agree with the amounts and other disclosures presented in the preceding period and are free from errors in the context of the financial statements of the current period; and

(c) where comparatives have been adjusted as required by relevant legislation and accounting standards, appropriate disclosures have been made.

In the event that the auditors are unable to obtain such audit evidence, they need to consider the implications for their report.

22 SAS 460: Related parties

The APB issued SAS 460: **Related parties**, in November 1995 shortly after FRS 8 was issued. The implications of related party transactions for the auditor are explained below.

(a) **General objectives**

The overriding objective of the audit is to express an opinion, backed up by sufficient audit evidence, as to whether or not financial statements present a true and fair view. As part of this process the auditor should endeavour to establish

(i) the existence of related parties
(ii) the nature and volume of transactions with those related parties
(iii) whether those transactions have been fairly presented in the financial statements.

(b) **Establishing the existence of related parties**

In the course of his audit work, the auditor will normally be aware of the existence of certain related parties. He will, however, need to make specific enquiries to be reasonably assured that all major related parties have been discovered. He may adopt some of the following procedures

(i) make other members of his audit team aware of the importance of related parties and be on the watch and report the discovery of such parties

(ii) ascertain whether the company has any established system for identifying related parties and reporting transactions with them to management, together with a review of the results of the system

(iii) a review of the board minutes to establish whether directors have disclosed their interests in contracts in pursuance of S317 CA85

(iv) a review of any statements giving 'conflict of interest' details which directors may be required to deposit with the company and which should be regularly reviewed by the board

(v) a review of the directors' other directorships and of the list of shareholders contained in the statutory books

(vi) a review of previous years' audit files or consultation with previous auditors

(vii) a review of services or goods provided 'free-of-charge' either by or to the client company

(viii) a review of invoices and correspondence relating to professional fees, particularly relating to the purchase or sale of significant assets and interests in land and property

(ix) a review of confirmations from third parties received during the audit, particularly regarding loans payable and receivable.

(c) **Establishing the nature and volume of related party transactions**

The prime requirement here is for the auditor to understand the nature and functioning of his client's business. He will not wish to expend too much effort dealing with immaterial items.

He should, however, pay particular attention to

(i) transactions involving the borrowing or lending of sums either being interest free or at rates appreciably below market rates, or where repayment terms have not been specified

(ii) non-monetary transactions involving perhaps the exchange of assets without a valid identification of a fair value should be fully investigated

(iii) unusual transactions should be considered individually, particularly those which have taken place near the end of the accounting year and which may indicate an attempt to manipulate the financial statements for the year

(iv) it will normally be sufficient to test a small sample of related party transactions which occur within the normal course of business; such tests may be covered as part of other audit procedures

(v) transactions outside the normal course of business should be examined individually; independent evidence such as agreements with third party documentation should be obtained to support any management representations and the auditor should examine minutes of board meetings to ensure that board approval has been obtained.

Reporting on the effects of related party transactions

(a) **To the directors of the company**

It should be noted that if the auditor believes that the board as a whole are unaware of related party transactions (eg, approval of a transaction was not discovered in the board minutes) the auditor should formally notify the board of such transactions.

He should also obtain, as part of the letter of representation, a statement that no related party transactions, other than those already disclosed to him, have taken place.

(b) **To the members of the company**

If related party transactions have taken place within the normal course of business and the disclosure of them in the financial statements is fair, the auditor will be able to give an unqualified opinion. He may consider the transactions to be so significant to the understanding of the financial statements that specific reference to the matter should be made as an emphasis of matter paragraph. This might apply for instance where a subsidiary makes all its sales to its holding company.

If inadequate disclosure is made, the audit report will need to be qualified if the transactions involved are material to the adequate appreciation of the financial statements.

If related party transactions have taken place, full details of the transactions should be disclosed, including

(i) the relationship of the parties
(ii) the nature of the transactions
(iii) the amounts involved
(iv) the terms of settlement.

If such disclosure is not made, or the accounting treatment adopted does not conform to the commercial substance of the transaction, the auditor may need to qualify his report.

In addition the auditor must ensure that the financial statements comply with the disclosure requirements of the CA85 or any other relevant statutory obligation.

23 SAS 470: Overall review of financial statements

An overall review of the financial statements based on the auditor's knowledge of the business of the enterprise is not of itself a sufficient basis for the expression of an audit opinion on those statements. However, it provides valuable support for the conclusions arrived at as a result of the other audit work. In addition apparent inconsistencies could indicate areas in which material errors, omissions or irregularities may have occurred which have not been disclosed by other auditing procedures.

Auditing standards

470.1 Auditors should carry out such a review of the financial statements as is sufficient in conjunction with the conclusions drawn from the other audit evidence obtained, to give them a reasonable basis for their opinion on the financial statements.

470.2 Auditors should consider whether:

(a) the information presented is in accordance with statutory requirements

(b) the accounting policies employed are in accordance with accounting standards, properly disclosed, consistently applied and appropriate to the entity.

470.3 Auditors should consider whether:

(a) the financial statements as a whole and the assertions contained therein are consistent with their knowledge of the entity's business and with the results of other audit procedures

(b) the manner of disclosure is fair.

24 SAS 480: Service organisations

SAS 480 was issued in January 1999 to provide guidance to auditors on audits of entities that use service organisations to undertake activities on its behalf (eg, maintenance of investments, or information processing).

Auditing standards

480.1 Auditors should identify whether a reporting entity uses service organisations and assess the effect of any such use on the procedures necessary to obtain sufficient appropriate audit evidence to determine with reasonable assurance whether the user entity's financial statements are free of material misstatement.

480.2 In planning the audit, user entity auditors should determine whether activities undertaken by service organisations are relevant to the audit.

480.3 User entity auditors should obtain and document an understanding of:

(a) the contractual terms which apply to relevant activities undertaken by service organisations; and

(b) the way that the user entity monitors those activities so as to ensure that it meets its fiduciary and other legal responsibilities.

480.4 User entity auditors should determine the effect of relevant activities on their assessment of inherent risk and the user entity's control environment.

480.5 If a service organisation maintains all or part of a user entity's accounting records, user entity auditors should assess whether the arrangements affect their reporting responsibilities in relation to accounting records arising from law or regulations.

480.6 Based on their understanding of the aspects of the user entity's accounting system and control environment relating to relevant activities, user entity auditors should:

(a) assess whether sufficient appropriate audit evidence concerning the relevant financial statement assertions is available from records held at the user entity; and if not,

(b) determine effective procedures to obtain evidence necessary for the audit, either by direct access to records kept by service organisations or through information obtained from the service organisations or their auditors.

480.7 When using a report issued by the service organisation auditors, the user entity's auditors should consider the scope of the work performed and assess whether the report is sufficient and appropriate for its intended use.

480.8 If user entity auditors conclude that evidence from records held by a service organisation is necessary in order to form an opinion on the user entity's financial statements and they are unable to obtain such evidence, they should

(a) include a description of the factors leading to the lack of evidence in the basis of opinion section of their report; and

(b) qualify their opinion or issue a disclaimer of opinion on the financial statements.

25 SAS 500: Considering the work of internal audit

Internal auditors are established by the management of a company to benefit the organisation by reviewing and reporting on the accounting and internal control systems. SAS 500 gives guidance on how external auditors can tailor their work most effectively where an internal audit department exists.

Auditing standards

The external auditor is required to:

500.1 Consider the activities of the internal auditors

500.2 Obtain a sufficient understanding of internal audit to assist in planning an effective audit

500.3 Perform a preliminary assessment of internal audit during planning

500.4 Evaluate and confirm the adequacy of internal audit work if it is used to reduce the extent of other audit procedures.

26 SAS 510: The relationship between principal auditors and other auditors

This SAS sets out standards for principal auditors and other auditors regarding the use by the principal auditor of the other auditor's work. It extends the scope of the guidance beyond that set out in the previous guideline to circumstances other than involving group financial statements. Thus it covers for example, a situation where an auditor may use the services of an affiliated firm to audit a branch of a company. The affiliated firm is used because of their geographical closeness to the branch.

Auditing standards

510.1 When using the work of other auditors, principal auditors should determine how that work will affect their audit.

510.2 Auditors should consider if their own participation is sufficient to enable them to act as principal auditors.

510.3 Consider the professional competence of the other auditors at the planning stage.

510.4 Obtain satisfactory evidence that the work of the other auditors is adequate.

510.5 Consider the significant findings of the other auditors.

510.6 There is a requirement for other auditors to co-operate with and actively assist the principal auditors.

27 SAS 520: Using the work of an expert

An auditor has a general knowledge of business, but he cannot be expected to have a detailed knowledge in all disciplines. During the course of an audit, therefore, the auditor may need to consider audit evidence from specialists in arriving at an audit opinion.

Auditing standards

The auditor is required to:

520.1 Obtain sufficient appropriate evidence that the expert's work is adequate for the purposes of the audit

520.2 Assess the objectivity and competence of the expert

520.3 Assess the scope of the expert's work

520.4 Assess the appropriateness of the expert's work as audit evidence.

28 SAS 600: Auditors' reports on financial statements

SAS 600 *Auditors' reports on financial statements* replaced the old Auditing Standard *The Audit Report*.

Reasons for change

Auditors cannot 'guarantee' or 'certify' that financial statements are correct, they can only express *opinions* on the two matters required by statute ie,

(a) Truth and fairness
(b) Proper preparation in accordance with CA85.

The previous 'short-form' report did not set out the respective responsibilities of directors and auditors and it was felt that clarification of the issue on the face of the audit report might help dispel public confusion (and criticism) in relation to the precise extent of auditors' responsibilities in particular. The standard unqualified report is therefore now worded as follows.

AUDITORS' REPORT TO THE SHAREHOLDERS OF XYZ PLC

We have audited the financial statements on pages.... to.... which have been prepared under the historical cost convention (as modified by the revaluation of certain fixed assets) and the accounting policies set out on page....

Respective responsibilities of directors and auditors

As described on page.... the company's directors are responsible for the preparation of financial statements. It is our responsibility to form an independent opinion, based on our audit, on those statements and to report our opinion to you.

Basis of opinion

We conducted our audit in accordance with Auditing Standards issued by the Auditing Practices Board. An audit includes examination, on a test basis, of evidence relevant to the amounts and disclosures in the financial statements. It also includes an assessment of the significant estimates and judgements made by the directors in the preparation of the financial statements, and of whether the accounting policies are appropriate to the company's circumstances, consistently applied and adequately disclosed.

We planned and performed our audit so as to obtain all the information and explanations which we considered necessary in order to provide us with sufficient evidence to give reasonable assurance that the financial statements are free from material misstatement, whether caused by fraud or other irregularity or error. In forming our opinion we also evaluated the overall adequacy of the presentation of information in the financial statements.

Opinion

In our opinion the financial statements give a true and fair view of the state of the company's affairs as at 31 December 20… and of its profit (loss) for the year then ended and have been properly prepared in accordance with the Companies Act 1985.

Registered auditors *Address*
Date

The nature and types of audit qualifications

All qualifications arise from either disagreements or uncertainties.

The qualification 'grid' is a useful summary of the decisions to be made in drafting a qualified audit report.

		Material	*Fundamental*
(a)	**Uncertainty**		
	ie, Scope limitations - inability to carry out audit procedures (perhaps because of a lack of accounting records or information and explanations from officers)	'Except for'	'Unable to form an opinion' = Disclaimer of opinion
(b)	**Disagreement** (i) Inappropriate accounting policies (ii) Re facts or amounts (eg, failure to provide for a bad debt)	'Except for'	'Do not give a true and fair view' = Adverse opinion

(iii) Re manner or extent of disclosure of facts or amounts

(iv) Re compliance with legislation or other requirements

29 SAS 601: Imposed limitation of audit scope

SAS 601 was issued in March 1999 to provide guidance to auditors on whether to accept or to continue with an audit engagement in circumstances where a limitation of audit scope is imposed.

Auditing standards

601.1 If the auditors are aware, before accepting an audit engagement, that the directors of the entity, or those who appoint its auditors, will impose a limitation on the scope of their work which they consider likely to result in the need to issue a disclaimer of opinion on the financial statements, they should not accept that engagement, unless required to do so by statute.

601.2 If the auditors become aware, after accepting an audit engagement, that the directors of the entity, or those who appointed them as its auditors, have imposed a limitation on the scope of their work which they consider likely to result in the need to issue a disclaimer of opinion on the financial statements, they should request the removal of the limitation. If the limitation is not removed, they should consider resigning from the audit engagement.

30 SAS 610: Reports to directors or management

SAS 610 contains guidance on how management letters should be sent to directors, including any audit committee, or to management.

Auditing standards

610.1 Auditors should consider the matters which have come to their attention during the audit and whether they should be included in a report to directors or management.

610.2 When material weaknesses in the accounting and internal control systems are identified during the audit, auditors should report them in writing to the directors, the audit committee or an appropriate level of management on a timely basis.

31 SAS 620: The auditors' right and duty to report to regulators in the financial sector

SAS 620 offers guidance on the circumstances when the auditors of a financial institution subject to statutory regulation are required to report direct to a regulator information which comes to their attention in the course of their audit work.

Each of the Banking Act 1987, the Financial Services Act 1986, the Building Societies Act 1986, the Insurance Companies Act 1986 and the Friendly Societies Act 1992 contains provisions for auditors to report to regulators in specific circumstances (eg, a suspicion of serious fraud).

An auditor of a financial institution should be sure that he knows the relevant provisions of the Act under which his audit client is operating.

32 Statement of standards for reporting accountants: Audit exemption reports

There have been a number of attempts over the last decade to relax the statutory audit requirement for small companies. Regulations in this area first came into force in August 1994; these can be summarised as follows:

(a) A company is totally exempt if:

(i) it qualifies as a small company under CA 85;
(ii) its turnover is not more than £90,000; and
(iii) its balance sheet total is not more than £1.4m.

(b) A company is exempt from the audit requirement but must have an accountant's report if:

(i) it qualifies as a small company under CA 85;
(ii) its turnover is more than £90,000 but not more than £350,000; and
(iii) its balance sheet total is not more than £1.4m.

(c) The above exemptions do not apply to public companies, banks, insurers, those authorised under the Financial Services Act, parent companies or subsidiaries.

(d) A company is not exempt if members holding 10% or more of its shares demand an audit at least one month before the end of the financial year.

(e) Where a company takes advantage of the exemption its directors must make a statement on the balance sheet acknowledging their responsibility for keeping proper accounting records and for preparing accounts that give a true and fair view and comply with the Companies Act.

However a statutory instrument in 1997 amended these requirements so that, with effect from April 1997, the turnover limit in (a) (ii) above is raised for non-charitable companies from £90,000 to £350,000. The effect of this is that companies with a turnover of £350,000 or less are now generally exempt from audit; the previous requirement for an accountant's report for those companies with turnover between £90,000 and £350,000 is repealed.

The ASB had issued guidance to reporting accountants in a Statement of standards for reporting accountants *Audit exemption reports* in October 1994. This guidance is now less important since the statutory requirement for the preparation of such a report has been removed.

33 Statements of Investment Circular Reporting Standards (SIRs)

The APB has published two SIRs:

- SIR 100 Investment Circulars and Reporting Accountants
- SIR 200 Accountants' Reports on Historical Financial Information in Investment Circulars

Investment circulars are the documents such as prospectuses that provide potential investors with the information they need to make an informed investment decision. The Stock Exchange Listing Rules require certain tasks to be carried out by reporting accountants; SIRs ensure that these tasks can be carried out efficiently and properly.

34 Auditing guideline 308: Guidance for internal auditors

In contrast to SAS 500 **Considering the work of internal audit**, which looks at how the external auditor places reliance on the internal audit function in a company, Auditing Guideline 308 **Guidance for internal auditors** gives guidance to internal auditors about how they should structure their work to make it effective. The aim of the Guideline is to give positive assistance to internal auditors.

The Guideline considers eight areas that are essential for the internal audit department to be effective. Many of these areas, and the explanations of procedures within them could equally apply to external auditors, which is not surprising given that the internal and external auditors' work is similar in many ways.

35 Auditing guideline 405: Attendance at stocktaking

The overall purpose of the auditor's attendance is to assess the effectiveness of the client's stocktaking procedures. There are three aspects of the auditor's duties, covering the times before, during and after the stocktaking.

Before the stocktaking

The auditor should carry out the following:

(a) review prior year's working papers;

(b) familiarise himself with the nature, volume and location of stocks;

(c) consider controlling and recording procedures over stock;

(d) identify problem areas in relation to the system of internal control;

(e) decide whether reliance can be placed on internal auditors;

(f) if stock held by third parties is material, or the third party is insufficiently independent or reliable, then arrange a stocktake attendance at the third party's premises;

(g) otherwise, arrange third party confirmation;

(h) if the nature of the stocks is specialised then he will need to arrange expert help or to review the client's own arrangements.

(i) examine the client's stocktaking instructions: if found to be inadequate, the matter should be discussed with the client with a view to improving them prior to the stocktake.

During the stocktaking

The main task is to ensure that the client's staff are carrying out their duties effectively. The auditor should:

(a) Make two-way test counts from factory floor to stock sheets, and from stock sheets to factory floor.

(b) Make notes of items counted, damaged stock, instances where the stocktaking procedures are not being followed.

(c) Examine and test control over the stock sheets. The client should keep a stock sheet register.

(d) Examine cut-off procedures (see below).

(e) Pay particular attention to goods held on behalf of third parties (for example, goods on consignment).

(f) Reach a conclusion as to whether or not the stocktaking was satisfactory, and hence provides reliable evidence supporting the final stock figure.

After the stocktaking

The auditor should check cut-off details, review the final stock sheets and follow up test counts and queries. He should also ensure that any continuous stock records have been adjusted or reconciled to the physical count and all differences investigated.

Accountants' report 498
Accounting for investments 88
Accruals 26, 27
Acquisition of subsidiaries 350
Actuarial method to allocate finance charges 216
Adjusting events 624
Administration orders 577
Administrative receivership 579, 580
Amalgamations and absorptions 559
Amortisation 102
Application of assets on liquidation 577
ASB 2
ASC Handbook – Accounting for the effects of changing prices 308, 656
Assets 18
Associate 397
Associated undertaking 396, 397
Audit Agenda - Next Steps 711
Audit committees 703
Audit of small businesses 714
Auditing theory 714

Barriers to international harmonisation 36
Berliner method 532
Business combination 380, 559

Caparo Industries 701
Capital grants 86
Capital instrument 672
Capital reduction scheme 542
Changes of parent company interest 350
City code on take-overs and mergers 583
Closing rate method 416
Combined Code 709
Comparability 16
Compulsory winding up 572
Conceptual framework 9, 46
Consistency 16, 26, 28
Consolidated profit and loss account 411
Constructive obligation 201
Contingent asset 200
Contingent liability 200
Contingently issuable shares 265
Control 14
Convertibles 261
Corporate failure 642
Corporation tax 131
Cost 54
Creative accounting 198
Creditors' voluntary liquidation 576
Current cost accounting 293
Current purchasing power accounting 289
Current tax 131

Dangling debit 97
Declaration of solvency 575
Defined benefit schemes 169
Defined contribution schemes 169
Demerger 365
Depreciable amount 65
Depreciation 65
Deprival value 76
Derivatives and other financial instruments 691
Derivatives 681
Development expenditure 107
Diluted earnings per share 261
Direct method 453
Directors' Report 626
Disabled employees 627
Discontinued activities 242, 255
Discounting in financial reporting 32
Discussion Paper: Year-end financial reports: Improving communication 517
Discussion Paper: Business Combinations 380
Discussion Paper: Reporting Financial performance: Proposals for change 232, 250
Disposal of subsidiaries 350, 354
Duty of care 700

Earnings per share 610
Earnings 256
Eco-audit scheme 709
Elements of financial statements 18
EMH 590
Employee share schemes 263
Environmental audit 709
Equity accounting 398, 413
Estimation techniques 29
EU Directives 7
Exceptional items 244, 254
Exclusion of subsidiary undertakings from consolidation 329
Exemptions from preparing group accounts 328
Extraordinary items 247

Fair value in the context of acquisition accounting 381
Fair value 94
FASB Conceptual Framework Project 46
Finance costs 56
Financial asset 684
Financial instruments 681, 684
Financial liability 684
Financial Reporting Standard for Smaller Entities (FRSSE) 698
Forecast 502
Foreign currency conversion 416
Foreign currency translation 416
Foreign subsidiary undertakings 424
Forward contracts 419
FRC 3
FRED 19 156
FRED 20 181
FRED 21 26
FRS 1 450
FRS 4 672
FRS 5 190
FRS 6 371

FRS 7 382
FRS 8 663
FRS 9 413
FRS 10 101
FRS 11 74
FRS 12 199
FRS 13 683
FRS 15 53
FRS 16 132
FRS 240
Full provision for deferred tax 152
Fundamental accounting concepts 27
Funded pensions 170
Future operating losses 204

'G4 + 1' group 37
Gearing 604
Geographical segment 490
Going concern 26, 27
Goode report 180
Gross equity method 404

Harmonisation 35
Hedging at the consolidated financial statements stage 433
Hedging 421
Horizontal analysis 592

IASC 8, 36
Identifiable assets and liabilities 94
Impairment reviews 103
Impairment 74
Income generating units 78
Independence 716
Indirect method 453
Inherent goodwill 94
Initial measurement of fixed assets 53
Insider information 591
Intangibles 99
Inter temporal analysis 592
Interim reports 515, 716
International auditing bodies 709
International Federation of Accountants (IFAC) 37
International harmonisation 35
International issues affecting auditing 709
Internet 519
Investments 87

Joint arrangement that is not an entity 403
Joint ventures 403
Just and equitable grounds 572

Legal obligation 200
Liabilities 18, 200
Liability gap 710
Liquid resources 456
Liquidity position of companies 600

Materiality 16
Mccarthy cards 589
Members' voluntary liquidation 576
Mixed groups. 335
Money laundering 711
Monopolies and Mergers Commission 584
Moody's and Extel 589

Negative goodwill 98
Net cash flow from operating activities 453
Net debt 458
Net realisable value 76, 77
Nil provision 152
Non-adjusting events 624
Non-financial indicators 660
Non-purchased goodwill 94

Objective of financial statements 12
Onerous contracts 204
Operating and financial review 629
Options 263
Organisation for Economic Co-operation and Development (OECD) 37
Ownership interest 19

Partial provision 152
Participating interest 321
Participating interest 397
Pensions Act 1995 180
Performance gap 710
Postulates of auditing 714
Potential ordinary share 261
Preferential debts 646
Presentation of financial information 22
Prior period adjustments 247
Private Finance Initiative 197
Profitability ratios 596
Projection - financial information 502
Prospective financial information 501
Prospectus 498
Provision 200
Prudence 15, 26, 28
Purchase by a company of its own shares: S162 544
Purchased goodwill 94

Qualitative characteristics of financial information14
Quality 661

Receiver and manager 580
Recognition of items in financial statements 19
Reconciliation statements 41
Reconciliation of movements in shareholders' funds 249
Recoverable amount 76
Recycling 253
Redeemable shares 543
Redemption or purchase out of capital: S171 CA85 544

Reimbursement 203
Related parties 663
Reliability 15
Renewals accounting 69
Report of the directors 626
Reportable segments 489
Reporting entity 13
Reports 498
Residual value 65
Restructuring 204
Return on capital employed (ROCE) 596
Revaluation deficits 277
Revaluation 59
Revenue grants 86
Rights issue circulars 508
Rights 259
Risk 682, 718

Sale of assets for shares by a company in voluntary liquidation 551
Sale and leaseback 227
Schemes of arrangement 552
Separate write off reserve 97
Significant influence 397
SSAP 2 26
SSAP 4: Accounting for government grants 85
SSAP 5 130
SSAP 13: Research and development 107
SSAP 17 624
SSAP 19: Investment properties 71
SSAP 25: Segmental reporting 489
Standards gap 710
Statement of adjustments 499
Statement of Principles - The Way Ahead 11
Statement of Principles 10, 312
Statement of total recognised gains and losses 248
Statements of affairs 646
Statements of Recommended Practice (SORPS) 31
Stock exchange circulars 506
Stock Exchange requirements 499
Stock Exchange 2
Subsequent expenditure 58

Tax credit 134
Temporal method 416
Termination of leases 229
Tort 700
Trend analysis 593
True and fair 11

UITF - Abstract 4 7
UITF Abstract 5 88
UITF Abstract 7 74
UITF Abstract 9 437
UITF Abstract 10 630
UITF Abstract 11 676
UITF Abstract 17 208
UITF Abstract 18 179
UITF Abstract 19 438
UITF Abstract 20 630
UITF Abstract 21 631
UITF Abstract 22 631
UITF Abstract 23 70
UITF 5, 7, 232, 247
Understandability 16
Unfranked investment income (UFII) 131
Unfunded pensions 170
United Nations (UN) 37
Useful economic life 65

Valuation of fixed assets 59
Value added statements 631
Value for money 661
Value in use 76, 77
Value to the business 76
Vertical groups 335
Voluntary winding up 575

Withholding tax 133

FOULKS LYNCH
4 The Griffin Centre
Staines Road
Feltham
Middlesex, TW14 0HS
United Kingdom

HOTLINES: Telephone: +44 (0) 20 8831 9990
Fax: +44 (0) 20 8831 9991
E-mail: info@foulkslynch.com

For information and online ordering, please visit our website at :

www.foulkslynch.com

PRODUCT RANGE

We have been the **official publisher for ACCA** since 1995. Our publications cover all exam modules for both ACCA current syllabus and the new syllabus starting in December 2001.

Our ACCA product range consists of:

Textbooks	£18.95 - £23.95	Tracks Audio Tapes	£10.95
Revision Series	£10.95	Distance Learning Courses	£85
Lynchpins	£5.95		

NEW ONLINE PRODUCT! – TO BE LAUNCHED 2001

OTHER PUBLICATIONS FROM FOULKS LYNCH

We publish a wide range of study materials in the accountancy field and specialize in texts for the following professional qualifications :

- **Chartered Institute of Management Accountants (CIMA)**
- **Association of Accounting Technicians (AAT)**
- **Association of International Accountants (AIA)**
- **Certified Accounting Technician (CAT)**

FOR FURTHER INFORMATION ON OUR PUBLICATIONS:

I would like information on publications for: ACCA ☐ CAT ☐ CIMA ☐ AAT ☐ AIA ☐

Please keep me updated on new publications : ☐ By E-mail ☐ By Post ☐

Your name .... Your email address:..

Your address: ....

....

....

....

Prices are correct at time of going to press and are subject to change
SOURCE CODE : ACCA/TEXT/JUN00